Developing Cybersecurity Programs and Policies

Omar Santos

Developing Cybersecurity Programs and Policies

ISBN-13: 978-0-7897-5940-5

ISBN-10: 0-7897-5940-3

Library of Congress Control Number: 2018942730

13 2022

Trademarks

All terms mentioned in this book that are known to be trademarks or service marks have been appropriately capitalized. Pearson IT Certification cannot attest to the accuracy of this information. Use of a term in this book should not be regarded as affecting the validity of any trademark or service mark.

Warning and Disclaimer

Every effort has been made to make this book as complete and as accurate as possible, but no warranty or fitness is implied. The information provided is on an "as is" basis. The author and the publisher shall have neither liability nor responsibility to any person or entity with respect to any loss or damages arising from the information contained in this book.

Special Sales

For information about buying this title in bulk quantities, or for special sales opportunities (which may include electronic versions; custom cover designs; and content particular to your business, training goals, marketing focus, or branding interests), please contact our corporate sales department at corpsales@pearsoned.com or (800) 382-3419.

For government sales inquiries, please contact governmentsales@pearsoned.com.

For questions about sales outside the U.S., please contact intlcs@pearson.com.

Editor-in-Chief
Mark Taub

Product Line Manager
Brett Bartow

Executive Editor
Mary Beth Ray

Development Editor
Christopher Cleveland

Managing Editor
Sandra Schroeder

Senior Project Editor
Tonya Simpson

Copy Editor
Barbara Hacha

Indexer
Erika Millen

Proofreader
Larry Sulky

Technical Editors
Sari Greene
Klee Michaelis

Publishing Coordinator
Vanessa Evans

Cover Designer
Chuti Prasertsith

Compositor
codemantra

Contents at a Glance

Table of Contents

About the Author

Omar Santos is a principal engineer in the Cisco Product Security Incident Response Team (PSIRT) within the Cisco Security Research and Operations. He mentors and leads engineers and incident managers during the investigation and resolution of security vulnerabilities in all Cisco products, including cloud services. Omar has been working with information technology and cybersecurity since the mid-1990s. Omar has designed, implemented, and supported numerous secure networks for Fortune 100 and 500 companies and the U.S. government. Prior to his current role, he was a technical leader within the World-Wide Security Practice and the Cisco Technical Assistance Center (TAC), where he taught, led, and mentored many engineers within both organizations.

Omar is an active member of the security community, where he leads several industrywide initiatives and standard bodies. His active role helps businesses, academic institutions, state and local law enforcement agencies, and other participants that are dedicated to increasing the security of the critical infrastructure.

Omar often delivers technical presentations at many conferences and to Cisco customers and partners. He is the author of dozens of books and video courses. You can follow Omar on any of the following:

Personal website: omarsantos.io

Twitter: @santosomar

LinkedIn: https://www.linkedin.com/in/santosomar

Dedication

I would like to dedicate this book to my lovely wife, Jeannette, and my two beautiful children, Hannah and Derek, who have inspired and supported me throughout the development of this book.

I also dedicate this book to my father, Jose, and to the memory of my mother, Generosa. Without their knowledge, wisdom, and guidance, I would not have the goals that I strive to achieve today.

Acknowledgments

This manuscript is a result of concerted efforts of various individuals—without their help, this book would have not been a reality. I would like to thank the technical reviewers Sari Green and Klee Michaelis for their significant contributions and expert guidance.

I would also like to express my gratitude to Chris Cleveland, development editor, and Mary Beth Ray, executive editor, for their help and continuous support during the development of this book.

We Want to Hear from You!

As the reader of this book, *you* are our most important critic and commentator. We value your opinion and want to know what we're doing right, what we could do better, what areas you'd like to see us publish in, and any other words of wisdom you're willing to pass our way.

We welcome your comments. You can email or write to let us know what you did or didn't like about this book—as well as what we can do to make our books better.

Please note that we cannot help you with technical problems related to the topic of this book.

When you write, please be sure to include this book's title and author as well as your name and email address. We will carefully review your comments and share them with the author and editors who worked on the book.

Email: feedback@pearsonitcertification.com

Reader Services

Register your copy of *Developing Cybersecurity Programs and Policies* at www.pearsonitcertification.com for convenient access to downloads, updates, and corrections as they become available. To start the registration process, go to www.pearsonitcertification.com/register and log in or create an account*. Enter the product ISBN 9780789759405 and click Submit. When the process is complete, you will find any available bonus content under Registered Products.

*Be sure to check the box that you would like to hear from us to receive exclusive discounts on future editions of this product.

Introduction

The number of cyber attacks continues to rise. Demand for safe and secure data and other concerns mean that companies need professionals to keep their information safe. Cybersecurity risk includes not only the risk of a data breach, but also the risk of the entire organization being undermined via business activities that rely on digitization and accessibility. As a result, learning how to develop an adequate cybersecurity program is crucial for any organization. Cybersecurity can no longer be something that you delegate to the information technology (IT) team. Everyone needs to be involved, including the Board of Directors.

This book focuses on industry-leading practices and standards, such as the International Organization for Standardization (ISO) standards and the National Institute of Standards and Technology (NIST) Cybersecurity Framework and Special Publications. This book provides detailed guidance on how to effectively develop a cybersecurity program within your organization. This book is intended for anyone who is preparing for a leadership position in business, government, academia, financial services, or health-care. Mastering the material presented in this book is a must for any cybersecurity professional.

This book starts by providing an overview of cybersecurity policy and governance, and how to create cybersecurity policies and develop a cybersecurity framework. It then provides details about governance, risk management, asset management, and data loss prevention. You will learn how to incorporate human resource, physical, and environmental security as important elements of your cybersecurity program. This book also teaches you best practices in communications and operations security, access control management, and information systems acquisition, development, and maintenance. You will learn principles of cybersecurity incident response and how to develop an incident response plan. Organizations across the globe have to be aware of new cybersecurity regulations and how they affect their business in order to remain compliant. Compliance is especially crucial because the punishments for noncompliance typically include large fines. Three chapters in this book cover regulatory compliance for financial institutions and health-care institutions and provide detailed insights about the Payment Card Industry Data Security Standard (PCI DSS). The last chapter provides an overview of the NIST Cybersecurity Framework, and Appendix A provides comprehensive lists of resources covered throughout the book. Anyone—from cybersecurity engineers to incident managers, auditors, and executives—can benefit from the material covered in this book.

Chapter 1

Understanding Cybersecurity Policy and Governance

Chapter Objectives

After reading this chapter and completing the exercises, you should be able to do the following:

- Describe the significance of cybersecurity policies.
- Evaluate the role policy plays in corporate culture and civil society.
- Articulate the objective of cybersecurity-related policies.
- Identify the different characteristics of successful cybersecurity policies.
- Define the life cycle of a cybersecurity policy.

We live in an interconnected world where both individual and collective actions have the potential to result in inspiring goodness or tragic harm. The objective of cybersecurity is to protect each of us, our economy, our critical infrastructure, and our country from the harm that can result from inadvertent or intentional misuse, compromise, or destruction of information and information systems.

The United States Department of Homeland Security defines several critical infrastructure sectors, as illustrated in Figure 1-1.

The United States Department of Homeland Security describes the services provided by critical infrastructure sectors as "the backbone of our nation's economy, security, and health. We know it as the power we use in our homes, the water we drink, the transportation that moves us, the stores we shop in, and the communication systems we rely on to stay in touch with friends and family. Overall, there are 16 critical infrastructure sectors that compose the assets, systems, and networks, whether physical or virtual, so vital to the United States that their incapacitation or destruction would have a debilitating effect on security, national economic security, national public health or safety, or any combination thereof."[1]

FIGURE 1-1   United States Critical Infrastructure Sectors

FYI: National Security

Presidential Policy Directive 7 — Protecting Critical Infrastructure (2003) established a national policy that required federal departments and agencies to identify and prioritize United States critical infrastructure and key resources and to protect them from physical and cyber terrorist attacks. The directive acknowledged that it is not possible to protect or eliminate the vulnerability of all critical infrastructure and key resources throughout the country, but that strategic improvements in security can make it more difficult for attacks to succeed and can lessen the impact of attacks that may occur. In addition to strategic security enhancements, tactical security improvements can be rapidly implemented to deter, mitigate, or neutralize potential attacks.

Ten years later, in 2013, *Presidential Policy Directive 21—Critical Infrastructure Security and Resilience* broadened the effort to strengthen and maintain secure, functioning, and resilient critical infrastructure by recognizing that this endeavor is a shared responsibility among the federal, state, local, tribal, and territorial entities, as well as public and private owners and operators of critical infrastructure.

Then, four years later, in 2017, Presidential Executive Order on Strengthening the Cybersecurity of Federal Networks and Critical Infrastructure was implemented by President Trump. It is worth highlighting that large policy changes with wide-ranging effects have been implemented through executive orders, although most do not affect all government sectors. In the case of cybersecurity, however, this executive order requires that all federal agencies adopt the Framework for Improving Critical Infrastructure Cybersecurity, developed by the National Institute of Standards and Technology (NIST). The framework was developed by experts with input from the private sector, as well as the public, and is described as "a common language for understanding, managing, and expressing cybersecurity risk both internally and externally."

Policy is the seminal tool used to protect both our critical infrastructure and our individual liberties. The role of policy is to provide direction and structure. Policies are the foundation of companies' operations, a society's rule of law, or a government's posture in the world. Without policies, we would live in a state of chaos and uncertainty. The impact of a policy can be positive or negative. The hallmark of a positive policy is one that supports our endeavors, responds to a changing environment, and potentially creates a better world.

In this chapter, we explore policies from a historical perspective, talk about how humankind has been affected, and learn how societies have evolved using policies to establish order and protect people and resources. We apply these concepts to cybersecurity principles and policies. Then we discuss in detail the seven characteristics of an effective cybersecurity policy. We acknowledge the influence of government regulation on the development and adoption of cybersecurity policies and practices. Last, we will tour the policy life cycle.

Information Security vs. Cybersecurity Policies

Many individuals confuse traditional information security with cybersecurity. In the past, information security programs and policies were designed to protect the confidentiality, integrity, and availability of data within the confinement of an organization. Unfortunately, this is no longer sufficient. Organizations are rarely self-contained, and the price of interconnectivity is exposure to attack. Every organization, regardless of size or geographic location, is a potential target. Cybersecurity is the process of protecting information by preventing, detecting, and responding to attacks.

Cybersecurity programs and policies recognize that organizations must be vigilant, resilient, and ready to protect and defend every ingress and egress connection as well as organizational data wherever it is stored, transmitted, or processed. Cybersecurity programs and policies expand and build upon traditional information security programs, but also include the following:

- Cyber risk management and oversight
- Threat intelligence and information sharing
- Third-party organization, software, and hardware dependency management
- Incident response and resiliency

Looking at Policy Through the Ages

Sometimes an idea seems more credible if we begin with an understanding that it has been around for a long time and has withstood the test of time. Since the beginning of social structure, people have sought to form order out of perceived chaos and to find ways to sustain ideas that benefit the advancement and improvement of a social structure. The best way we have found yet is in recognizing common problems and finding ways to avoid causing or experiencing them in our future endeavors. Policies, laws, codes of justice, and other such documents came into existence almost as soon as alphabets and the written word allowed them. This does not mean that before the written word there were no policies or laws. It does mean that we have no reference to spoken policy known as "oral law," so we will confine our discussion to written documents we know existed and still exist.

We are going to look back through time at some examples of written policies that had and still have a profound effect on societies across the globe, including our own. We are not going to concern ourselves with the function of these documents. Rather, we begin by noting the basic commonality we can see in why and how they were created to serve a larger social order. Some are called laws, some codes, and some canons, but what they all have in common is that they were created out of a perceived need to guide human behavior in foreseeable circumstances, and even to guide human behavior when circumstances could not be or were not foreseeable. Equal to the goal of policy to sustain order and protection is the absolute requirement that our policy be changeable in response to dynamic conditions.

Policy in Ancient Times

Let's start by going back in time over 3,300 years. Examples of written policy are still in existence, such as the Torah and other religious and historical documentation. For those of the Jewish faith, the Torah is the Five Books of Moses. Christians refer to the Torah as the Old Testament of the Bible. The Torah can be divided into three categories—moral, ceremonial, and civil. If we put aside the religious aspects of this work, we can examine the Torah's importance from a social perspective and its lasting impact on the entire world. The Torah articulated a codified social order. It contains rules for living as a member of a social structure. The rules were and are intended to provide guidance for behavior, the choices people make, and their interaction with each other and society as a whole. Some of the business-related rules of the Torah include the following:

- Not to use false weights and measures
- Not to charge excessive interest
- To be honest in all dealings
- To pay wages promptly
- To fulfill promises to others

What is worth recognizing is the longevity and overall impact of these "examples of policies." The Torah has persisted for thousands of years, even driving cultures throughout time. These benefits of "a set of policies" are not theoretical, but are real for a very long period of time.

The United States Constitution as a Policy Revolution

Let's look at a document you may be a little more familiar with: the Constitution of the United States of America. The Constitution is a collection of articles and amendments that provide a framework for the American government and define citizens' rights. The articles themselves are very broad principles that recognize that the world will change. This is where the amendments play their role as additions to the original document. Through time, these amendments have extended rights to more and more Americans and have allowed for circumstances our founders could not have foreseen. The founders wisely built in to the framework of the document a process for changing it while still adhering to its fundamental tenets. Although it takes great effort to amend the Constitution, the process begins with an idea, informed by people's experience, when they see a need for change. We learn some valuable lessons from the Constitution—most important is that our policies need to be dynamic enough to adjust to changing environments.

The Constitution and the Torah were created from distinct environments, but they both had a similar goal: to serve as rules as well as to guide our behavior and the behavior of those in power. Though our cybersecurity policies may not be used for such lofty purposes as the Constitution and the Torah, the need for guidance, direction, and roles remains the same.

Policy Today

We began this chapter with broad examples of the impact of policy throughout history. Let's begin to focus on the organizations for which we will be writing our cybersecurity policies—namely, profit, nonprofit, and not-for-profit businesses, government agencies, and institutions. The same circumstances that led us to create policies for social culture exist for our corporate culture as well.

Guiding Principles

Corporate culture can be defined as the shared attitudes, values, goals, and practices that characterize a company, corporation, or institution. *Guiding principles* set the tone for a corporate culture. Guiding principles synthesize the fundamental philosophy or beliefs of an organization and reflect the kind of company that an organization seeks to be.

Not all guiding principles, and hence corporate cultures, are good. In fact, there are companies for whom greed, exploitation, and contempt are unspoken-yet-powerful guiding principles. You may recall the deadly April 24, 2013, garment factory collapse in Bangladesh, where 804 people were confirmed dead and more than 2,500 injured.[2] This is a very sad example of a situation in which the lives of many were knowingly put at risk for the sake of making money.

Culture can be shaped both informally and formally. For instance, cultures can be shaped informally by how individuals are treated within an organization. It can also be shaped formally by written policies. An organization may have a policy that could allow and value employee input, but the actual organization may never provide an opportunity for employees to provide any input. In this case, you may have a great policy, but if it is not endorsed and enacted, it is useless.

Corporate Culture

Corporate cultures are often classified by how corporations treat their employees and their customers. The three classifications are negative, neutral, and positive, as illustrated in Figure 1-2.

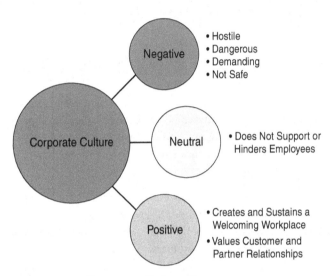

FIGURE 1-2   Corporate Culture Types

A negative classification is indicative of a hostile, dangerous, or demeaning environment. Workers do not feel comfortable and may not be safe; customers are not valued and may even be cheated. A neutral classification means that the business neither supports nor hinders its employees; customers generally get what they pay for. A positive classification is awarded to businesses that strive to create and sustain a welcoming workplace, truly value the customer relationship, partner with their suppliers, and are responsible members of their community.

Let's consider a tale of two companies. Both companies experience a data breach that exposes customer information; both companies call in experts to help determine what happened. In both cases, the investigators determine that the data-protection safeguards were inadequate and that employees were not properly monitoring the systems. The difference between these two companies is how they respond to and learn from the incident, as illustrated in Figure 1-3.

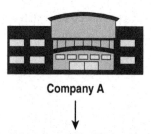

Company A

Quick to respond by blaming the department management, firing key employees, and looking for ways to avoid legally required customer notification.

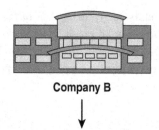

Company B

Leadership shares the report with the department, solicits internal and external feedback on how to improve, researches new controls, methodically implements enhancements, and informs customers in a timely manner so they can take steps to protect themselves.

FIGURE 1-3   Corporate Culture Types

As shown in Figure 1-3, Company A is quick to respond by blaming the department management, firing key employees, and looking for ways to avoid legally required customer notification. Company B leadership shares the report with the department, solicits internal and external feedback on how to improve, researches new controls, methodically implements enhancements, and informs customers in a timely manner so they can take steps to protect themselves.

A positive corporate culture that focuses on protecting internal and customer information, solicits input, engages in proactive education, and allocates resources appropriately makes a strong statement that employees and customers are valued. In these organizations, policy is viewed as an investment and a competitive differentiator for attracting quality employees and customers.

In Practice

The Philosophy of Honoring the Public Trust

Each of us willingly shares a great deal of personal information with organizations that provide us service, and we have an expectation of privacy. Online, we post pictures, profiles, messages, and much more. We disclose and discuss our physical, emotional, mental, and familial issues with health professionals. We provide confidential financial information to accountants, bankers, financial advisors, and tax preparers. The government requires that we provide myriad data throughout our life, beginning with birth certificates and ending with death certificates. On occasion, we may find ourselves in situations where we must confide in an attorney or clergy. In each of these situations, we expect the information we provide will be protected from unauthorized disclosure, not be intentionally altered, and used only for its intended purpose. We also expect that the systems used to provide the service will be available. The philosophy of honoring the public trust instructs us to be careful stewards of the information with which we have been entrusted. It is one of the main objectives of organizations that truly care about those they serve. As you plan your career, consider your potential role in honoring the public trust.

Cybersecurity Policy

The role of policy is to codify guiding principles, shape behavior, provide guidance to those who are tasked with making present and future decisions, and serve as an implementation roadmap. A *cybersecurity policy* is a directive that defines how the organization is going to protect its information assets and information systems, ensure compliance with legal and regulatory requirements, and maintain an environment that supports the guiding principles.

The objective of a cybersecurity policy and corresponding program is to protect the organization, its employees, its customers, and its vendors and partners from harm resulting from intentional or accidental damage, misuse, or disclosure of information, as well as to protect the integrity of the information and ensure the availability of information systems.

FYI: Cyber What?

The word "cyber" is nothing new. Since the early 1990s, the prefix "cyber"[3] is defined as involving computers or computer networks. Affixed to the terms *crime*, *terrorism*, and *warfare*, cyber means that computer resources or computer networks such as the Internet are used to commit the action.

Richard Clarke, former cybersecurity adviser to Presidents Bill Clinton and George W. Bush, commented that "the difference between cybercrime, cyber-espionage, and cyber-war is a couple of keystrokes. The same technique that gets you in to steal money, patented blueprint information, or chemical formulas is the same technique that a nation-state would use to get in and destroy things."

What Are Assets?

Information is data with context or meaning. An asset is a resource with value. As a series of digits, the string 123456789 has no discernible value. However, if those same numbers represented a social security number (123-45-6789) or a bank account number (12-3456789), they would have both meaning and value. *Information asset* is the term applied to the information that an organization uses to conduct its business. Examples include customer data, employee records, financial documents, business plans, intellectual property, IT information, reputation, and brand. Information assets may be protected by law or regulation (for example, patient medical history), considered internally confidential (for example, employee reviews and compensation plans), or even publicly available (for example, website content). Information assets are generally stored in digital or print format; however, it is possible to extend our definition to institutional knowledge.

In most cases, organizations establish cybersecurity policies following the principles of defense-in-depth. If you are a cybersecurity expert, or even an amateur, you probably already know that when you deploy a firewall or an intrusion prevention system (IPS) or install antivirus or advanced malware protection on your machine, you cannot assume you are now safe and secure. A layered and cross-boundary "defense-in-depth" strategy is what is required to protect network and corporate assets. The primary benefit of a defense-in-depth strategy is that even if a single control (such as a firewall or IPS) fails, other controls can still protect your environment and assets. The concept of defense-in-depth is illustrated in Figure 1-4.

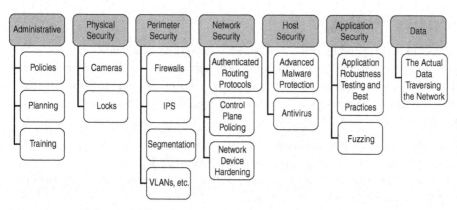

FIGURE 1-4   Defense-in-Depth

The following are the layers illustrated in Figure 1-4 (starting from the left):

- Administrative (nontechnical) activities, such as appropriate security policies and procedures, risk management, and end-user and staff training.

- Physical security, including cameras, physical access control (such as badge readers, retina scanners, and fingerprint scanners), and locks.

- Perimeter security, including firewalls, IDS/IPS devices, network segmentation, and VLANs.

- Network security best practices, such as routing protocol authentication, control plane policing (CoPP), network device hardening, and so on.

- Host security solutions, such as advanced malware protection (AMP) for endpoints, antiviruses, and so on.

- Application security best practices, such as application robustness testing, fuzzing, defenses against cross-site scripting (XSS), cross-site request forgery (CSRF) attacks, SQL injection attacks, and so on.

- The actual data traversing the network. You can employ encryption at rest and in transit to protect data.

Each layer of security introduces complexity and latency while requiring that someone manage it. The more people are involved, even in administration, the more attack vectors you create, and the more you distract your people from possibly more important tasks. Employ multiple layers, but avoid duplication—and use common sense.

Globally, governments and private organizations are moving beyond the question of whether to use cloud computing. Instead they are focusing on how to become more secure and effective when adopting the cloud. Cloud computing represents a drastic change when compared to traditional computing. The cloud enables organizations of any size to do more and faster. The cloud is unleashing a whole new generation of transformation, delivering big data analytics and empowering the Internet of Things; however, understanding how to make the right policy, operational, and procurement decisions can be difficult. This is especially true with cloud adoption, because it has the potential to alter the paradigm of how business is done and who owns the task of creating and enforcing such policies.

In addition, it can also bring confusion about appropriate legislative frameworks, and specific security requirements of different data assets risk slowing government adoption. Whether an organization uses public cloud services by default or as a failover option, the private sector and governments must be confident that, if a crisis does unfold, the integrity, confidentiality, and availability of their data and essential services will remain intact. Each cloud provider will have its own policies, and each customer (organization buying cloud services) will also have its own policies. Nowadays, this paradigm needs to be taken into consideration when you are building your cybersecurity program and policies.

Successful Policy Characteristics

Successful policies establish what must be done and why it must be done, but not how to do it. Good policy has the following seven characteristics:

- **Endorsed:** The policy has the support of management.
- **Relevant:** The policy is applicable to the organization.
- **Realistic:** The policy make sense.
- **Attainable:** The policy can be successfully implemented.
- **Adaptable:** The policy can accommodate change.
- **Enforceable:** The policy is statutory.
- **Inclusive:** The policy scope includes all relevant parties.

Taken together, the characteristics can be thought of as a policy pie, with each slice being equally important, as illustrated in Figure 1-5.

Endorsed

We have all heard the saying "Actions speak louder than words." For a cybersecurity policy to be successful, leadership must not only believe in the policy, they must also act accordingly by demonstrating an active commitment to the policy by serving as role models. This requires visible participation and action, ongoing communication and championing, investment, and prioritization.

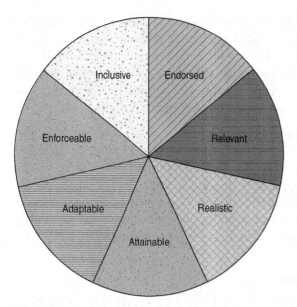

FIGURE 1-5   The Policy Pie

Consider this situation: Company A and Company B both decide to purchase mobile phones for management and sales personnel. By policy, both organizations require strong, complex email passwords. At both organizations, IT implements the same complex password policy on the mobile phone that is used to log in to their webmail application. Company A's CEO is having trouble using the mobile phone, and he demands that IT reconfigure his phone so he doesn't have to use a password. He states that he is "too important to have to spend the extra time typing in a password, and besides none of his peers have to do so." Company B's CEO participates in rollout training, encourages employees to choose strong passwords to protect customer and internal information, and demonstrates to his peers the enhanced security, including a wipe feature after five bad password attempts.

Nothing will doom a policy quicker than having management ignore or, worse, disobey or circumvent it. Conversely, visible leadership and encouragement are two of the strongest motivators known to humankind.

Policies can also pertain to personal or customer data management, security vulnerability policies, and others.

Let's look at one of the biggest breaches of recent history, the Equifax breach. On September 2017, Equifax was breached, leaving millions of personal records exposed to attackers. The exposed data was mostly of customers in the United States of America. On the other hand, Equifax has personal data management policies that extend to other countries, such as the United Kingdom. This policy can be found at: http://www.equifax.com/international/uk/documents/Equifax_Personal_Data_Management_Policy.pdf.

As stated in that document, there are many regulations that enforce organizations such as Equifax to publicly document these policies and specify what they do to protect customer data:

> "While this is not an exhaustive list, the following regulations (as amended from time to time) are directly applicable to how Equifax manages personal data as a credit reference agency:
>
> (a) Data Protection Act 1998
>
> (b) Consumer Credit (Credit Reference Agency) Regulations 2000
>
> (c) Data Protection (Subject Access) (Fees and Miscellaneous Provisions) Regulations 2000
>
> (d) Consumer Credit Act 1974
>
> (e) The Consumer Credit (EU Directive) Regulations 2010
>
> (f) The Representation of the People (England and Wales) Regulations 2001"

Relevant

Strategically, the cybersecurity policy must support the guiding principles and goals of the organization. Tactically, it must be relevant to those who must comply. Introducing a policy to a group of people who find nothing recognizable in relation to their everyday experience is a recipe for disaster.

Consider this situation: Company A's CIO attends a seminar on the importance of physical access security. At the seminar, they distribute a "sample" policy template. Two of the policy requirements are that exterior doors remain locked at all times and that every visitor be credentialed. This may sound reasonable, until you consider that most Company A locations are small offices that require public accessibility. When the policy is distributed, the employees immediately recognize that the CIO does not have a clue about how they operate.

Policy writing is a thoughtful process that must take into account the environment. If policies are not relevant, they will be ignored or, worse, dismissed as unnecessary, and management will be perceived as being out of touch.

Realistic

Think back to your childhood to a time you were forced to follow a rule you did not think made any sense. The most famous defense most of us were given by our parents in response to our protests was, "Because I said so!" We can all remember how frustrated we became whenever we heard that statement, and how it seemed unjust. We may also remember our desire to deliberately disobey our parents—to rebel against this perceived tyranny. In very much the same way, policies will be rejected if they are not realistic. Policies must reflect the reality of the environment in which they will be implemented.

Consider this situation: Company A discovers that users are writing down their passwords on sticky notes and putting the sticky notes on the underside of their keyboard. This discovery is of concern because multiple users share the same workstation. In response, management decides to implement a policy that prohibits employees from writing down their passwords. Turns out that each employee uses at least six different applications, and each requires a separate login. What's more, on average, the passwords change every 90 days. One can imagine how this policy might be received. More than likely, users will decide that getting their work done is more important than obeying this policy and will continue to write down their passwords, or perhaps they will decide to use the same password for every application. To change this behavior will take more than publishing a policy prohibiting it; leadership needs to understand why employees were writing down their passwords, make employees aware of the dangers of writing down their passwords, and most importantly provide alternative strategies or aids to remember the passwords.

If you engage constituents in policy development, acknowledge challenges, provide appropriate training, and consistently enforce policies, employees will be more likely to accept and follow the policies.

Attainable

Policies should be attainable and should not require impossible tasks and requirements for the organizations and its stakeholders. If you assume that the objective of a policy is to advance the organization's guiding principles, you can also assume that a positive outcome is desired. A policy should never set up constituents for failure; rather, it should provide a clear path for success.

Consider this situation: To contain costs and enhance tracking, Company A's management adopted a procurement policy that purchase orders must be sent electronically to suppliers. They set a goal of 80% electronic fulfillment by the end of the first year and announced that regional offices that do not meet this goal will forfeit their annual bonus. In keeping with existing cybersecurity policy, all electronic documents sent externally that include proprietary company information must be sent using the secure file transfer application. The problem is that procurement personnel despise the secure file transfer application because it is slow and difficult to use. Most frustrating of all, it is frequently offline. That leaves them three choices: depend on an unstable system (not a good idea), email the purchase order (in violation of policy), or continue mailing paper-based purchase orders (and lose their bonus).

It is important to seek advice and input from key people in every job role to which the policies apply. If unattainable outcomes are expected, people are set up to fail. This will have a profound effect on morale and will ultimately affect productivity. Know what is possible.

Adaptable

To thrive and grow, businesses must be open to changes in the market and be willing to take measured risks. A static set-in-stone cybersecurity policy is detrimental to innovation. Innovators are hesitant to talk with security, compliance, or risk departments for fear that their ideas will immediately be discounted as contrary to policy or regulatory requirement. "Going around" security is understood as the way to get things done. The unfortunate result is the introduction of products or services that may put the organization at risk.

Consider this situation: Company A and Company B are in a race to get their mobile app to market. Company A's programming manager instructs her team to keep the development process secret and not to involve any other departments, including security and compliance. She has 100% faith in her team and knows that without distractions they can beat Company B to market. Company B's programming manager takes a different tack. She demands that security requirements be defined early in the software development cycle. In doing so, her team identifies a policy roadblock. They have determined that they need to develop custom code for the mobile app, but the policy requires that "standard programming languages be used." Working together with the security officer, the programming manager establishes a process to document and test the code in such a way that it meets the intent of the policy. Management agrees to grant an exception and to review the policy in light of new development methodologies.

Company A does get to market first. However, its product is vulnerable to exploit, puts its customers at risk, and ultimately gets bad press. Instead of moving on to the next project, the development team will need to spend time rewriting code and issuing security updates. Company B gets to market a few months later. It launches a functional, stable, and secure app.

An adaptable cybersecurity policy recognizes that cybersecurity is not a static, point-in-time endeavor but rather an ongoing process designed to support the organizational mission. The cybersecurity program should be designed in such a way that participants are encouraged to challenge conventional wisdom, reassess the current policy requirements, and explore new options without losing sight of the fundamental objective. Organizations that are committed to secure products and services often discover it to be a sales enabler and competitive differentiator.

Enforceable

Enforceable means that administrative, physical, or technical controls can be put in place to support the policy, that compliance can be measured, and, if necessary, appropriate sanctions applied.

Consider this scenario: Company A and Company B both have a policy stating that Internet access is restricted to business use only. Company A does not have any controls in place to restrict access; instead, the company leaves it up to the user to determine "business use." Company B implements web-filtering software that restricts access by site category and reviews the filtering log daily. In conjunction with implementing the policy, Company B conducts a training session explaining and demonstrating the rationale for the policy with an emphasis on disrupting the malware delivery channel.

A workstation at Company A is infected with malware. It is determined that the malware came from a website that the workstation user accessed. Company A's management decides to fire the user for "browsing" the Web. The user files a protest claiming that the company has no proof that it wasn't business use, that there was no clear understanding of what "business use" meant, and besides, everyone (including his manager) is always surfing the Web without consequence.

A user at Company B suspects something is wrong when multiple windows start opening while he is at a "business use" website. He immediately reports the suspicious activity. His workstation is immediately quarantined and examined for malware. Company B's management investigates the incident. The logs substantiate the user's claim that the access was inadvertent. The user is publicly thanked for reporting the incident.

If a rule is broken and there is no consequence, then the rule is essentially meaningless. However, there must be a fair way to determine if a policy was violated, which includes evaluating the organizational support of the policy. Sanctions should be clearly defined and commensurate with the associated risk. A clear and consistent process should be in place so that all similar violations are treated in the same manner.

You should also develop reports and metrics that can be evaluated on an ongoing basis to determine if your policy is effective, who is abiding and conforming, who is violating it, and why it is being violated. Is it hindering productivity? Is it too hard to understand or follow?

Inclusive

It is important to include external parties in our policy thought process. It used to be that organizations had to be concerned about information and systems housed only within their walls. That is no longer the case. Data (and the systems that store, transmit, and process it) are now widely and globally distributed. For example, an organization can put information in a public cloud (such as Amazon Web Services (AWS), Microsoft Azure, Google Cloud, and so on) and may also have outsourcers that can also handle sensitive information. For example, in Figure 1-6, Company A is supported by an outsourcing company that provides technical assistance services (call center) to its customers. In addition, it uses cloud services from a cloud provider.

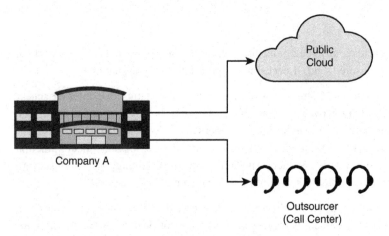

FIGURE 1-6 Outsourcing and Cloud Services

Organizations that choose to put information in or use systems in "the cloud" may face the additional challenge of having to assess and evaluate vendor controls across distributed systems in multiple locations. The reach of the Internet has facilitated worldwide commerce, which means that policies may have to consider an international audience of customers, business partners, and employees. The trend toward outsourcing and subcontracting requires that policies be designed in such a way as to incorporate third parties. Cybersecurity policies must also consider external threats such as unauthorized access, vulnerability exploits, intellectual property theft, denial of service attacks, and hacktivism done in the name of cybercrime, terrorism, and warfare.

A cybersecurity policy must take into account the factors illustrated in Figure 1-7.

**Cybersecurity Policies Need
to Take Into Consideration:**

| Organizational Objectives | International Law | The Cultural Norms of Its Employees, Business Partners, Suppliers, and Customers | Environmental Impact and Global Cyber Threats |

FIGURE 1-7 Cybersecurity Policy Considerations

If the cybersecurity policy is not written in a way that is easy to understand, it can also become useless. In some cases, policies are very difficult to understand. If they are not clear and easy to understand, they will not be followed by employees and other stakeholders. A good cybersecurity policy is one that can positively affect the organization, its shareholders, employees, and customers, as well as the global community.

What Is the Role of Government?

In the previous section, we peeked into the world of Company A and Company B and found them to be very different in their approach to cybersecurity. In the real world, this is problematic. Cybersecurity is complex, and weaknesses in one organization can directly affect another. At times, government intervention is required to protect its critical infrastructure and its citizens. Intervention with the purpose of either restraining or causing a specific set of uniform actions is known as *regulation*. *Legislation* is another term meaning statutory law. These laws are enacted by a *legislature* (part of the governing body of a country, state, province, or even towns). Legislation can also mean the process of making the law. Legislation and regulation are two terms that often confuse people that are not well-versed in law terminologies.

Regulations can be used to describe two underlying items:

■ A process of monitoring and enforcing legislation

■ A document or set of documents containing rules that are part of specific laws or government policies

Law is one of the most complicated subjects and has various different terms and words that often mean different things in different contexts. Legislation and regulation should not be confused; they are completely different from each other.

In the 1990s, two major federal legislations were introduced with the objective of protecting personal financial and medical records:

- The Gramm-Leach-Bliley Act (GLBA), also known as the Financial Modernization Act of 1999, Safeguards Rule

- The Health Insurance Portability and Accountability Act of 1996 (HIPAA)

Gramm-Leach-Bliley Act (GLBA)

On November 12, 1999, President Clinton signed the GLB Act (GLBA) into law. The purpose of the act was to reform and modernize the banking industry by eliminating existing barriers between banking and commerce. The act permitted banks to engage in a broad range of activities, including insurance and securities brokering, with new affiliated entities. Lawmakers were concerned that these activities would lead to an aggregation of customer financial information and significantly increase the risk of identity theft and fraud. Section 501B of the legislation, which went into effect May 23, 2003, required that companies that offer consumers financial products or services, such as loans, financial or investment advice, or insurance[4], ensure the security and confidentiality of customer records and information, protect against any anticipated threats or hazards to the security or integrity of such records, and protect against unauthorized access to or use of such records or information that could result in substantial harm or inconvenience to any customer. GLBA requires financial institutions and other covered entities to develop and adhere to a cybersecurity policy that protects customer information and assigns responsibility for the adherence to the Board of Directors. Enforcement of GLBA was assigned to federal oversight agencies, including the following organizations:

- Federal Deposit Insurance Corporation (FDIC)

- Federal Reserve

- Office of the Comptroller of the Currency (OCC)

- National Credit Union Agency (NCUA)

- Federal Trade Commission (FTC)

> **Note**
>
> In Chapter 13, "Regulatory Compliance for Financial Institutions," we examine the regulations applicable to the financial sector, with a focus on the cybersecurity interagency guidelines establishing cybersecurity standards, the FTC Safeguards Act, Financial Institution Letters (FILs), and applicable supplements.

Health Insurance Portability and Accountability Act of 1996 (HIPAA)

Likewise, the HIPAA Security Rule established a national standard to protect individuals' electronic personal health information (known as ePHI) that is created, received, used, or maintained by a covered entity, which includes health-care providers and business associates. The Security Rule requires appropriate administrative, physical, and technical safeguards to ensure the confidentiality, integrity, and security of electronic protected health information. Covered entities are required to publish comprehensive cybersecurity policies that communicate in detail how information is protected. The legislation, while mandatory, did not include a stringent enforcement process. However, in 2012, one of the provisions of the Health Information Technology for Economic and Clinical Health Act (HITECH) assigned audit and enforcement responsibility to the Department of Health and Human Services Office of Civil Rights (HHS-OCR) and gave state attorneys general the power to file suit over HIPAA violations in their jurisdiction.

Note

In Chapter 14, "Regulatory Compliance for the Health-Care Sector," we examine the components of the original HIPAA Security Rule and the subsequent HITECH Act and the Omnibus Rule. We discuss the policies, procedures, and practices that entities need to implement to be HIPAA-compliant.

In Practice

Protecting Your Student Record

The privacy of your student record is governed by a federal law known as FERPA, which stands for the Family Educational Rights and Privacy Act of 1974. The law states that an educational institution must establish a written institutional policy to protect confidentiality of student education records and that students must be notified of their rights under the legislation. Privacy highlights of the policy include the requirement that schools must have written permission from the parent or eligible students (age 18 and older) in order to release any information from a student's education record. Schools may disclose, without consent, "directory" information, such as a student's name, address, telephone number, date and place of birth, honors and awards, and dates of attendance. However, schools must tell parents and eligible students about directory information and allow parents and eligible students a reasonable amount of time to request that the school not disclose directory information about them.

States, Provinces, and Local Governments as Leaders

Local governments (states, provinces or even towns) can lead the way in a nation or region. For example, historically the United States Congress failed repeatedly to establish a comprehensive national security standard for the protection of digital nonpublic personally identifiable information (NPPI), including notification of breach or compromise requirements. In the absence of federal legislation, states have taken on the responsibility. On July 1, 2003, California became the first state to enact consumer cybersecurity notification legislation. SB 1386: California Security Breach Information Act requires a business or state agency to notify any California resident whose unencrypted personal information was acquired, or reasonably believed to have been acquired, by an unauthorized person.

The law defines personal information as: "any information that identifies, relates to, describes, or is capable of being associated with, a particular individual, including, but not limited to, his or her name, signature, social security number, physical characteristics or description, address, telephone number, passport number, driver's license or state identification card number, insurance policy number, education, employment, employment history, bank account number, credit card number, debit card number, or any other financial information, medical information, or health insurance information."

Subsequently, 48 states, the District of Columbia, Guam, Puerto Rico, and the Virgin Islands have enacted legislation requiring private or governmental entities to notify individuals of security breaches of information involving personally identifiable information.

> **Note**
>
> In Chapter 11, "Cybersecurity Incident Response," we discuss the importance of incident response capability and how to comply with the myriad of state data-breach notification laws.

Another example is when Massachusetts became the first state in the United States to require the protection of personally identifiable information of Massachusetts residents. 201 CMR 17: Standards for the Protection of Personal Information of Residents of the Commonwealth establishes minimum standards to be met in connection with the safeguarding of personal information contained in both paper and electronic records and mandates a broad set of safeguards, including security policies, encryption, access control, authentication, risk assessment, security monitoring, and training. Personal information is defined as a Massachusetts resident's first name and last name, or first initial and last name, in combination with any one or more of the following: social security number, driver's license number or state-issued identification card number, financial account number, or credit or debit card number. The provisions of this regulation apply to all persons who own or license personal information about a resident of the Commonwealth of Massachusetts.

The New York State Department of Financial Services (DFS) has become increasingly concerned about the number of cybersecurity incidents affecting financial services organizations. The NY DFS was also concerned with the potential risks posed to the industry at large (this includes multinational companies that could provide financial services in the United States). In late 2016, NY DFS proposed new requirements relating to cybersecurity for all DFS-regulated entities. On February 16, 2017, the finalized NY DFS cybersecurity requirements (23 NYCRR 500) were posted to the New York State Register. The NYCRR is published at the following link:

http://www.dfs.ny.gov/legal/regulations/adoptions/dfsrf500txt.pdf

Financial services organizations will be required to prepare and submit to the superintendent a Certification of Compliance with the NY DFS Cybersecurity Regulations annually.

Regulatory compliance is a powerful driver for many organizations. There are industry sectors that recognize the inherent operational, civic, and reputational benefit of implementing applicable controls and safeguards. Two of the federal regulations mentioned earlier in this chapter—GLBA and HIPAA— were the result of industry and government collaboration. The passage of these regulations forever altered the cybersecurity landscape.

Additional Federal Banking Regulations

In recent years, three federal banking regulators issued an advance notice of proposed rulemaking for new cybersecurity regulations for large financial institutions:

- The Federal Reserve Bank (FRB)
- The Office of the Comptroller of the Currency (OCC)
- The Federal Deposit Insurance Corporation (FDIC)

What is a large financial institution? These are institutions with consolidated assets of $50 billion and critical financial infrastructure. This framework was intended to result in rules to address the type of serious "cyber incident or failure" that could "impact the safety and soundness" of not just the financial institution that is the victim of a cyberattack, but the soundness of the financial system and markets overall. After these initial attempts, the FRB has archived and documented all regulation-related letters and policies at the following website:

https://www.federalreserve.gov/supervisionreg/srletters/srletters.htm

You will learn more about federal and state regulatory requirements and their relationship to cybersecurity policies and practices in Chapters 13, 14, and 15.

Government Cybersecurity Regulations in Other Countries

These types of regulations are not only in the United States. There are several regulatory bodies in other countries, especially in Europe. The following are the major regulation entities within the European Union (EU):

- **European Union Agency for Network and Information Security (ENISA):** An agency initially organized by the Regulation (EC) No 460/2004 of the European Parliament and of the Council of 10 March 2004 for the purpose of raising network and information security (NIS), awareness for all inter-network operations within the EU. Currently, ENISA currently runs under Regulation (EU) No 526/2013, which has replaced the original regulation in 2013. Their website includes all the recent information about policies, regulations, and other cybersecurity-related information: https://www.enisa.europa.eu.[5]

- **Directive on Security of Network and Information Systems (the NIS Directive):** The European Parliament set into policy this directive, created to maintain an overall higher level of cybersecurity in the EU.

- **EU General Data Protection Regulation (GDPR):** Created to maintain a single standard for data protection among all member states in the EU.

The Challenges of Global Policies

One of the world's greatest global governance challenges is to establish shared responsibility for the most intractable problems we are trying to solve around the globe. This new global environment presents several challenges for governance.

The steadily growing complexity of public policy issues makes a global policy on any topic basically impossible to attain, specifically related to cybersecurity. Decision makers in states and international organizations are having to tackle more and more issues that cut across areas of bureaucratic or disciplinary expertise and whose complexity has yet to be fully understood.

Another challenge involves legitimacy and accountability. The traditional closed-shop of intergovernmental diplomacy cannot fulfill the aspirations of citizens and transnationally organized advocacy groups who strive for greater participation in and accountability of transnational policymaking.

Cybersecurity Policy Life Cycle

Regardless of whether a policy is based on guiding principles or regulatory requirements, its success depends in large part upon how the organization approaches the tasks of policy development, publication, adoption, and review. Collectively, this process is referred to as the *policy life cycle*, as illustrated in Figure 1-8.

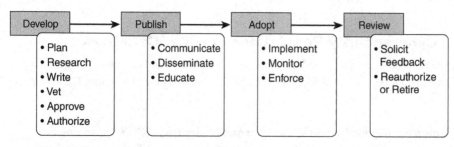

FIGURE 1-8   Cybersecurity Policy Life Cycle

The activities in the cybersecurity policy life cycle described in Figure 1-8 will be similar among different organizations. On the other hand, the mechanics will differ depending on the organization (corporate vs. governmental) and also depending on specific regulations.

The responsibilities associated with the policy life cycle process are distributed throughout an organization as outlined in Table 1-1. Organizations that understand the life cycle and take a structured approach will have a much better chance of success. The objective of this section is to introduce you to the components that make up the policy life cycle. Throughout the text, we examine the process as it relates to specific cybersecurity policies.

TABLE 1-1   Cybersecurity Policy Life Cycle Responsibilities

Position	Develop	Publish	Adopt	Review
Board of Directors and/or Executive Management	Communicate guiding principles. Authorize policy.	Champion the policy.	Lead by example.	Reauthorize or approve retirement.
Operational Management	Plan, research, write, vet, and review.	Communicate, disseminate, and educate.	Implement, evaluate, monitor, and enforce.	Provide feedback and make recommendations.
Compliance Officer	Plan, research, contribute, and review.	Communicate, disseminate, and educate.	Evaluate.	Provide feedback and make recommendations.
Auditor			Monitor.	

Policy Development

Even before setting pen to paper, considerable thought and effort need to be put into developing a policy. After the policy is written, it still needs to go through an extensive review and approval process. There are six key tasks in the development phase: planning, researching, writing, vetting, approving, and authorizing.

- The seminal *planning* task should identify the need for and context of the policy. Policies should never be developed for their own sake. There should always be a reason. Policies may be needed to support business objectives, contractual obligations, or regulatory requirements. The context could vary from the entire organization to a specific subset of users. In Chapters 4 through 12, we identify the reasons for specific policies.

- Policies should support and be in agreement with relevant laws, obligations, and customs. The *research* task focuses on defining operational, legal, regulatory, or contractual requirements and aligning the policy with the aforementioned. This objective may sound simple, but in reality is extremely complex. Some regulations and contracts have very specific requirements, whereas others are extraordinarily vague. Even worse, they may contradict each other.

  For example, federal regulation requires financial institutions to notify consumers if their account information has been compromised. The notification is required to include details about the breach; however, Massachusetts Law 201 CMR 17:00: Standards for the Protection of Personal Information of Residents of the Commonwealth specifically restricts the same details from being included in the notification. You can imagine the difficult in trying to comply with opposing requirements. Throughout this text, we will align policies with legal requirements and contractual obligations.

- To be effective, policies must be written for their intended audience. Language is powerful and is arguably one of the most important factors in gaining acceptance and, ultimately, successful implementation. The *writing* task requires that the audience be identified and understood. In Chapter 2, "Cybersecurity Policy Organization, Format, and Styles," we explore the impact of the plain writing movement on policy development.

- Policies require scrutiny. The *vetting* task requires the authors to consult with internal and external experts, including legal counsel, human resources, compliance, cybersecurity and technology professionals, auditors, and regulators.

- Because cybersecurity policies affect an entire organization, they are inherently cross-departmental. The *approval* task requires that the authors build consensus and support. All affected departments should have the opportunity to contribute to, review, and, if necessary, challenge the policy before it is authorized. Within each department, key people should be identified, sought out, and included in the process. Involving them will contribute to the inclusiveness of the policy and, more importantly, may provide the incentive for them to champion the policy.

- The authorization task requires that executive management or an equivalent authoritative body agree to the policy. Generally, the authority has oversight responsibilities and can be held legally liable. Both GLBA and HIPAA require written cybersecurity policies that are Board-approved and subject to at least annual review. Boards of Directors are often composed of experienced, albeit nontechnical, business people from a spectrum of industry sectors. It is helpful to know who the Board members are, and their level of understanding, so that policies are presented in a meaningful way.

Policy Publication

After you have the "green light" from the authority, it is time to publish and introduce the policy to the organization as a whole. This introduction requires careful planning and execution because it sets the stage for how well the policy will be accepted and followed. There are three key tasks in the publication phase: communication, dissemination, and education.

1. The objective of the *communication* task is to deliver the message that the policy or policies are important to the organization. To accomplish this task, visible leadership is required. There are two distinct types of leaders in the world: those who see leadership as a responsibility and those who see it as a privilege.

   Leaders who see their role as a responsibility adhere to all the same rules they ask others to follow. "Do as I do" is an effective leadership style, especially in relation to cybersecurity. Security is not always convenient, and it is crucial for leadership to participate in the cybersecurity program by adhering to its policies and setting the example.

   Leaders who see their role as a privilege have a powerful negative impact: "Do as I say, not as I do." This leadership style will do more to undermine a cybersecurity program than any other single force. As soon as people learn that leadership is not subject to the same rules and restrictions, policy compliance and acceptance will begin to erode.

Invariably, the organizations in which leadership sets the example by accepting and complying with their own policies have fewer cybersecurity-related incidents. When incidents do occur, they are far less likely to cause substantial damage. When the leadership sets a tone of compliance, the rest of the organization feels better about following the rules, and they are more active in participating.

When a policy is not consistently adopted throughout the organization, it is considered to be inherently flawed. Failure to comply is a point of weakness that can be exploited. In Chapter 4, "Governance and Risk Management," we examine the relationship between governance and security.

2. Disseminating the policy simply means making it available. Although the task seems obvious, it is mind-boggling how many organizations store their policies in locations that make them, at best, difficult to locate and, at worst, totally inaccessible. Policies should be widely distributed and available to their intended audience. This does not mean that all policies should be available to everyone, because there may be times when certain policies contain confidential information that should be made available only on a restricted or need-to-know basis. Regardless, policies should be easy to find for those who are authorized to view them.

3. Companywide training and education build culture. When people share experiences, they are drawn together; they can reinforce one another's understanding of the subject matter and therefore support whatever initiative the training was intended to introduce. Introducing cybersecurity policies should be thought of as a teaching opportunity with the goal of raising awareness and giving each person a tangible connection to the policy objective. Initial education should be coupled with ongoing awareness programs designed to reinforce the importance of policy-driven security practices.

Multiple factors contribute to an individual's decision to comply with a rule, policy, or law, including the chance of being caught, the reward for taking the risk, and the consequences. Organizations can influence individual decision making by creating direct links between individual actions, policy, and success. Creating a *culture of compliance* means that all participants not only recognize and understand the purpose of a policy, they also actively look for ways to champion the policy. Championing a policy means being willing to demonstrate visible leadership and to encourage and educate others. Creating a culture of cybersecurity policy compliance requires an ongoing investment in training and education, measurements, and feedback.

> **Note**
>
> In Chapter 6, "Human Resources Security," we examine the National Institute of Standards and Technology (NIST) Security Awareness, Training, and Education (SETA) model.

Policy Adoption

The policy has been announced and the reasons communicated. Now the hard work of adoption starts. Successful adoption begins with an announcement and progresses through implementation, performance evaluation, and process improvement, with the ultimate goal being normative integration. For our purposes, ***normative integration*** means that the policy and corresponding implementation is expected behavior—all others being deviant. There are three key tasks in the adoption phase: implementation, monitoring, and enforcement:

1. *Implementation* is the busiest and most challenging task of all. The starting point is ensuring that everyone involved understands the intent of the policy as well as how it is to be applied. Decisions may need to be made regarding the purchase and configuration of supporting administrative, physical, and technical controls. Capital investments may need to be budgeted for. A project plan may need to be developed and resources assigned. Management and affected personnel need to be kept informed. Situations where implementation is not possible need to be managed, including a process for granting either temporary or permanent exceptions.

2. Post-implementation, compliance and policy effectiveness need to be *monitored* and reported. Mechanisms to monitor compliance range from application-generated metrics to manual audits, surveys, and interviews, as well as violation and incident reports.

3. Unless there is an approved exception, policies must be *enforced* consistently and uniformly. The same is true of violation consequences. If a policy is enforced only for certain circumstances and people, or if enforcement depends on which supervisor or manager is in charge, eventually there will be adverse consequences. When there is talk within an organization that different standards for enforcement exist, the organization is open to many cultural problems, the most severe of which involve discrimination lawsuits. The organization should analyze why infractions against a policy occur. This may highlight gaps in the policy that may need to be adjusted.

Policy Review

Change is inherent in every organization. Policies must support the guiding principles, organizational goals, and forward-facing initiatives. They must also be harmonized with regulatory requirements and contractual obligations. The two key tasks in the review phase are soliciting feedback and reauthorizing or retiring policies:

1. Continuing acceptance of cybersecurity policies hinges on making sure the policies keep up with significant changes in the organization or the technology infrastructure. Policies should be reviewed annually. Similar to the development phase, feedback should be *solicited* from internal and external sources.

2. Policies that are outdated should be refreshed. Policies that are no longer applicable should be retired. Both tasks are important to the overall perception of the importance and applicability of organizational directives. The outcome of the annual review should either be policy *reauthorization* or policy *retirement*. The final determination belongs with the Board of Directors or equivalent body.

Summary

In this chapter, we discussed the various roles policies play, and have played, in many forms of social structures—from entire cultures to corporations. You learned that policies are not new in the world. When its religious intent is laid aside, the Torah reads like any other secular code of law or policy. The people of that time were in desperate need of guidance in their everyday existence to bring order to their society. You learned that policies give us a way to address common foreseeable situations and guide us to make decisions when faced with them. Similar to the circumstances that brought forth the Torah 3,000 years ago, our country found itself in need of a definite structure to bring to life the ideals of our founders and make sure those ideals remained intact. The U.S. Constitution was written to fulfill that purpose and serves as an excellent example of a strong, flexible, and resilient policy document.

We applied our knowledge of historical policy to the present day, examining the role of corporate culture, specifically as it applies to cybersecurity policy. Be it societal, government, or corporate, policy codifies guiding principles, shapes behavior, provides guidance to those who are tasked with making present and future decisions, and serves as an implementation roadmap. Because not all organizations are motivated to do the right thing, and because weaknesses in one organization can directly affect another, there are times when government intervention is required. We considered the role of government policy—specifically the influence of groundbreaking federal and state legislation related to the protection of NPPI in the public and privacy sectors.

The objective of a cybersecurity policy is to protect the organization, its employees, its customers, and also its vendors and partners from harm resulting from intentional or accidental damage, misuse, or disclosure of information, as well as to protect the integrity of the information and ensure the availability of information systems. We examined in depth the seven common characteristics of a successful cybersecurity policy as well as the policy life cycle. The seven common characteristics are endorsed, relevant, realistic, attainable, adaptable, enforceable, and inclusive. The policy life cycle spans four phases: develop, publish, adopt, and review. Policies need champions. Championing a policy means being willing to demonstrate visible leadership and to encourage and educate others with the objective of creating a culture of compliance, where participants not only recognize and understand the purpose of a policy, they also actively look for ways to promote it. The ultimate goal is normative integration, meaning that the policy and corresponding implementation is the expected behavior, all others being deviant.

Throughout the text, we build on these fundamental concepts. In Chapter 2, you learn the discrete components of a policy and companion documents, as well as the technique of plain writing.

Test Your Skills

MULTIPLE CHOICE QUESTIONS

1. Which of the following items are defined by policies?

   A. Rules

   B. Expectations

   C. Patterns of behavior

   D. All of the above

2. Without policy, human beings would live in a state of _____.

   A. chaos

   B. bliss

   C. harmony

   D. laziness

3. A guiding principle is best described as which of the following?

   A. A financial target

   B. A fundamental philosophy or belief

   C. A regulatory requirement

   D. A person in charge

4. Which of the following best describes corporate culture?

   A. Shared attitudes, values, and goals

   B. Multiculturalism

   C. A requirement to all act the same

   D. A religion

5. The responsibilities associated with the policy life cycle process are distributed throughout an organization. During the "develop" phase of the cybersecurity policy life cycle, the board of directors and/or executive management are responsible for which of the following?

   A. Communicating guiding principles and authorizing the policy

   B. Separating religion from policy

   C. Monitoring and evaluating any policies

   D. Auditing the policy

6. Which of the following best describes the role of policy?

    A. To codify guiding principles

    B. To shape behavior

    C. To serve as a roadmap

    D. All of the above

7. A cybersecurity policy is a directive that defines which of the following?

    A. How employees should do their jobs

    B. How to pass an annual audit

    C. How an organization protects information assets and systems against cyber attacks and nonmalicious incidents

    D. How much security insurance a company should have

8. Which of the following is not an example of an information asset?

    A. Customer financial records

    B. Marketing plan

    C. Patient medical history

    D. Building graffiti

9. What are the seven characteristics of a successful policy?

    A. Endorsed, relevant, realistic, cost-effective, adaptable, enforceable, inclusive

    B. Endorsed, relevant, realistic, attainable, adaptable, enforceable, inclusive

    C. Endorsed, relevant, realistic, technical, adaptable, enforceable, inclusive

    D. Endorsed, relevant, realistic, legal, adaptable, enforceable, inclusive

10. A policy that has been endorsed has the support of which of the following?

    A. Customers

    B. Creditors

    C. The union

    D. Management

11. Who should always be exempt from policy requirements?

    A. Employees

    B. Executives

    C. No one

    D. Salespeople

12. "Attainable" means that the policy _____.

    A. can be successfully implemented

    B. is expensive

    C. only applies to suppliers

    D. must be modified annually

13. Which of the following statements is always true?

    A. Policies stifle innovation.

    B. Policies make innovation more expensive.

    C. Policies should be adaptable.

    D. Effective policies never change.

14. If a cybersecurity policy is violated and there is no consequence, the policy is considered to be which of the following?

    A. Meaningless

    B. Inclusive

    C. Legal

    D. Expired

15. Who must approve the retirement of a policy?

    A. A compliance officer

    B. An auditor

    C. Executive management or the board of directors

    D. Legal counsel

16. Which of the following sectors is not considered part of the "critical infrastructure"?

    A. Public health

    B. Commerce

    C. Banking

    D. Museums and arts

17. Which term best describes government intervention with the purpose of causing a specific set of actions?

    A. Deregulation

    B. Politics

    C. Regulation

    D. Amendments

18. The objectives of GLBA and HIPAA, respectively, are to protect _____.

    A. financial and medical records

    B. financial and credit card records

    C. medical and student records

    D. judicial and medical records

19. Which of the following states was the first to enact consumer breach notification?

    A. Kentucky

    B. Colorado

    C. Connecticut

    D. California

20. Which of the following terms best describes the process of developing, publishing, adopting, and reviewing a policy?

    A. Policy two-step

    B. Policy aging

    C. Policy retirement

    D. Policy life cycle

21. Who should be involved in the process of developing cybersecurity policies?

    A. Only upper-management-level executives

    B. Only part-time employees

    C. Personnel throughout the company

    D. Only outside, third-party consultants

22. Which of the following does *not* happen in the policy development phase?

    A. Planning

    B. Enforcement

    C. Authorization

    D. Approval

23. Which of the following occurs in the policy publication phase?

    A. Communication

    B. Policy dissemination

    C. Education

    D. All of the above

24. How often should policies be reviewed?

    A. Never

    B. Only when there is a significant change

    C. Annually

    D. At least annually, or sooner if there is a significant change

25. Normative integration is the goal of the adoption phase. This means _____.

    A. There are no exceptions to the policy

    B. The policy passes the stress test

    C. The policy becomes expected behavior, all others being deviant

    D. The policy costs little to implement

EXERCISES

EXERCISE 1.1: **Understanding Guiding Principles**

1. Reread the section "Guiding Principles" in this chapter to understand why guiding principles are crucial for any organization. Guiding principles describe the organization's beliefs and philosophy pertaining to quality assurance and performance improvement.

2. Research online for different examples of public references to organizational guiding principles and compare them. Describe the similarities and differences among them.

EXERCISE 1.2: **Identifying Corporate Culture**

1. Identify a shared attitude, value, goal, or practice that characterizes the culture of your school or workplace.

2. Describe how you first became aware of the campus or workplace culture.

EXERCISE 1.3: **Understanding the Impact of Policy**

1. Either at school or workplace, identify a policy that in some way affects you. For example, examine a grading policy or an attendance policy.

2. Describe how the policy benefits (or hurts) you.

3. Describe how the policy is enforced.

EXERCISE 1.4: **Understanding Critical Infrastructure**

1. Explain what is meant by "critical infrastructure."

2. What concept was introduced in Presidential Executive Order on Strengthening the Cybersecurity of Federal Networks and Critical Infrastructure, and why is this important?

3. Research online and describe how the United States' definition of "critical infrastructure" compares to what other countries consider their critical infrastructure. Include any references.

EXERCISE 1.5: **Understanding Cyber Threats**

1. What is the difference between cybercrime, cyber-espionage, and cyber-warfare?

2. What are the similarities?

3. Are cyber threats escalating or diminishing?

PROJECTS

PROJECT 1.1: Honoring the Public Trust

1. Banks and credit unions are entrusted with personal financial information. By visiting financial institution websites, find an example of a policy or practice that relates to protecting customer information or privacy.

2. Hospitals are entrusted with personal health information. By visiting hospital websites, find an example of a policy or practice that relates to protecting patient information or privacy.

3. In what ways are the policies or practices of banks similar to those of hospitals? How are they different?

4. Do either the bank policies or the hospital policies reference applicable regulatory requirements (for example, GLBA or HIPAA)?

PROJECT 1.2: Understanding Government Regulations

The United States Affordable Care Act requires all citizens and lawful residents to have health insurance or pay a penalty. This requirement is a government policy.

1. A policy should be endorsed, relevant, realistic, attainable, adaptable, enforceable, and inclusive. Choose four of these characteristics and apply it to the health insurance require-ment. Explain whether the policy meets the criteria.

2. Policies must be championed. Find an example of a person or group who championed this requirement. Explain how they communicated their support.

PROJECT 1.3: Developing Communication and Training Skills

You have been tasked with introducing a new security policy to your campus. The new policy requires that all students and employees wear identification badges with their name and picture and that guests be given visitor badges.

1. Explain why an institution would adopt this type of policy.

2. Develop a strategy to communicate this policy campuswide.

3. Design a five-minute training session introducing the new policy. Your session must include participant contribution and a five-question, post-session quiz to determine whether the training was effective.

Case Study

The Tale of Two Credit Unions

Best Credit Union members really love doing business with the credit union. The staff is friendly, the service is top-notch, and the entire team is always pitching in to help the community. The credit union's commitment to honoring the public trust is evident in its dedication to security best practices. New employees are introduced to the cybersecurity policy during orientation. Everyone participates in annual information security training.

The credit union across town, OK Credit Union, doesn't have the same reputation. When you walk in the branch, it is sometimes hard to get a teller's attention. Calling is not much better, because you may find yourself on hold for a long time. Even worse, it is not unusual to overhear an OK Credit Union employee talking about a member in public. OK Credit Union does not have a cyber-security policy. It has never conducted any information security or privacy training.

Best Credit Union wants to expand its presence in the community, so it acquires OK Credit Union. Each institution will operate under its own name. The management team at Best Credit Union will manage both institutions.

You are the Information Security Officer at Best Credit Union. You are responsible for managing the process of developing, publishing, and adopting a cybersecurity policy specifically for OK Credit Union. The CEO has asked you to write up an action plan and present it at the upcoming management meeting.

Your action plan should include the following:

- What you see as the biggest obstacle or challenge to accomplishing this task.
- Which other personnel at Best Credit Union should be involved in this project and why.
- Who at OK Credit Union should be invited to participate in the process and why.
- How you are going to build support for the process and ultimately for the policy.
- What happens if OK Credit Union employees start grumbling about "change."
- What happens if OK Credit Union employees do not or will not comply with the new information security policy.

References

1. "What Is Critical Infrastructure?" official website of the Department of Homeland Security, accessed 04/2018, https://www.dhs.gov/what-critical-infrastructure.

2. "Bangladesh Building Collapse Death Toll over 800," BBC News Asia, accessed 04/2018, www.bbc.co.uk/news/world-asia-22450419.

3. "Cyber," Merriam-Webster Online, accessed 04/2018, https://www.merriam-webster.com/dictionary/cyber.

4. "Gramm-Leach-Bliley Act," Federal Trade Commission, Bureau of Consumer Protection Business Center, accessed 04/2018, https://www.ftc.gov/tips-advice/business-center/privacy-and-security/gramm-leach-bliley-act.

5. "The European Union Agency for Network and Information Security (ENISA)", accessed on 04/2018, https://www.enisa.europa.eu.

Regulations and Directives Cited

"Presidential Executive Order on Strengthening the Cybersecurity of Federal Networks and Critical Infrastructure," official website of the White House, accessed 05/2018, https://www.whitehouse.gov/presidential-actions/presidential-executive-order-strengthening-cybersecurity-federal-networks-critical-infrastructure/.

"Presidential Policy Directive—Critical Infrastructure Security and Resilience," official website of the White House, accessed 05/2018, https://obamawhitehouse.archives.gov/the-press-office/2013/02/12/presidential-policy-directive-critical-infrastructure-security-and-resil.

"Homeland Security Presidential Directive 7: Critical Infrastructure Identification, Prioritization, and Protection," official website of the Department of Homeland Security, accessed 05/2018, https://www.dhs.gov/homeland-security-presidential-directive-7.

"Interagency Guidelines Establishing Information Security Standards," accessed 05/2018, https://www.federalreserve.gov/bankinforeg/interagencyguidelines.htm.

"The Security Rule (HIPAA)," official website of the Department of Health and Human Services, accessed 05/2018, https://www.hhs.gov/hipaa/for-professionals/security/index.html.

"State of California SB 1386: California Security Breach Information Act," University of California San Francisco, accessed 05/2018, https://it.ucsf.edu/policies/california-senate-bill-1386-sb1386.

"201 CMR 17.00: Standards for the Protection of Personal Information of Residents of the Commonwealth," official website of the Office of Consumer Affairs & Business Regulation (OCABR), accessed 05/2018, www.mass.gov/ocabr/docs/idtheft/201cmr1700reg.pdf.

"Family Educational Rights and Privacy Act (FERPA)," official website of the U.S. Department of Education, accessed 05/2018, https://www2.ed.gov/policy/gen/guid/fpco/ferpa/index.html.

"Directive on Security of Network and Information Systems," accessed 05/2018, https://ec.europa.eu/digital-single-market/en/network-and-information-security-nis-directive.

"EU General Data Protection Regulation (GDPR)", accessed 05/2018, https://www.eugdpr.org.

Other References

Krause, Micki, CISSP, and Harold F. Tipton, CISSP. 2004. *Information Security Management Handbook, Fifth Edition*. Boca Raton, Florida: CRC Press, Auerbach Publications.

Chapter | **2**

Cybersecurity Policy Organization, Format, and Styles

Chapter Objectives

After reading this chapter and completing the exercises, you will be able to do the following:

- Explain the differences between a policy, a standard, a procedure, a guideline, and a plan.
- Know how to use "plain language when creating and updating your cybersecurity policy."
- Identify the different policy elements.
- Include the proper information in each element of a policy.

In Chapter 1, "Understanding Cybersecurity Policy and Governance," you learned that policies have played a significant role in helping us form and sustain our social, governmental, and corporate organizations. In this chapter, we begin by examining the hierarchy and purpose of guiding principles, policy, standards, procedures, and guidelines, as well as adjunct plans and programs. Returning to our focus on policies, we examine the standard components and composition of a policy document. You will learn that even a well-constructed policy is useless if it doesn't deliver the intended message. The end result of complex, ambiguous, or bloated policy is, at best, noncompliance. At worst, it leads to negative consequences, because such policies may not be followed or understood. In this chapter, you will be introduced to "plain language," which means using the simplest, most straightforward way to express an idea. Plain-language documents are easy to read, understand, and act on. By the end of the chapter, you will have the skills to construct policy and companion documents. This chapter focuses on cybersecurity policies in the private sector and not policies created by governments of any country or state.

Policy Hierarchy

As you learned in Chapter 1, a policy is a mandatory governance statement that presents management's position. A well-written policy clearly defines guiding principles, provides guidance to those who must make present and future decisions, and serves as an implementation roadmap. Policies are important, but alone they are limited in what they can accomplish. Policies need supporting documents to give them context and meaningful application. Standards, baselines, guidelines, and procedures each play a significant role in ensuring implementation of the governance objective. The relationship between the documents is known as the ***policy hierarchy***. In a hierarchy, with the exception of the topmost object, each object is subordinate to the one above it. In a policy hierarchy, the topmost objective is the guiding principles, as illustrated in Figure 2-1.

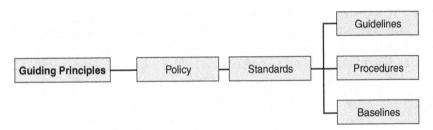

FIGURE 2-1   Policy Hierarchy

Cybersecurity policies should reflect the guiding principles and organizational objectives. This is why it is very important to communicate clear and well-understood organizational objectives within an organization. Standards are a set of rules and mandatory actions that provide support to a policy. Guidelines, procedures, and baselines provide support to standards. Let's take a closer look at each of these concepts.

Standards

Standards serve as specifications for the implementation of policy and dictate mandatory requirements. For example, our password policy might state the following:

1. All users must have a unique user ID and password that conforms to the company password standard.

2. Users must not share their password with anyone regardless of title or position.

3. If a password is suspected to be compromised, it must be reported immediately to the help desk, and a new password must be requested.

The password standard would then dictate the required password characteristics, such as the following:

- Minimum of eight upper- and lowercase alphanumeric characters

- Must include at least one special character (such as *, &, $, #, !, or @)

■ Must not include the user's name, the company name, or office location

■ Must not include repeating characters (for example, 111)

Another example of a standard is a common configuration of infrastructure devices such as routers and switches. Organizations may have dozens, hundreds, or even thousands of routers and switches, and they may have a "standard" way of configuring authentication, authorization, and accounting (AAA) for administrative sessions. They may use TACACS+ or RADIUS as the authentication standard mechanism for all routers and switches within the organization.

As you can see, the policy represents expectations that are not necessarily subject to changes in technology, processes, or management. The standard, however, is very specific to the infrastructure.

Standards are determined by management, and unlike policies, they are not subject to Board of Directors authorization. Standards can be changed by management as long as they conform to the intent of the policy. A difficult task of writing a successful standard for a cybersecurity program is achieving consensus by all stakeholders and teams within an organization. Additionally, a standard does not have to address everything that is defined in a policy. Standards should be compulsory and must be enforced to be effective.

Baselines

Baselines are the application of a standard to a specific category or grouping. Examples of groups include platform (the operating system and its version), device type (laptops, servers, desktops, routers, switches, firewalls, mobile devices, and so on), ownership (employee-owned or corporate-owned), and location (onsite, remote workers, and so on).

The primary objective of a baseline is uniformity and consistency. An example of a baseline related to our password policy and standard example is the mandate that a specific Active Directory Group Policy configuration (the standard) be used on all Windows devices (the group) to technically enforce security requirements, as illustrated in Figure 2-2.

In this example, by applying the same Active Directory Group Policy to all Windows workstations and servers, the baseline was implemented throughout the organization. In this case, there is also assurance that new devices will be configured accordingly.

Figure 2-3 shows another example of how different baselines can be enforced in the infrastructure with more sophisticated systems, such as the Cisco Identity Service Engine (ISE). Network Access Control (NAC) is a multipart solution that validates the security posture of an endpoint system before entering the network. With NAC, you can also define what resources the endpoint has access to, based on the results of its security posture. The main goal of any NAC solution is to improve the capability of the network to identify, prevent, and adapt to threats. The Cisco ISE shown in Figure 2-3 centralizes network access control based on business role and security policy to provide a consistent network access policy for end users, whether they connect through wired, wireless, or VPN. All this can be done from a centralized ISE console that then distributes enforcement across the entire network and security infrastructure.

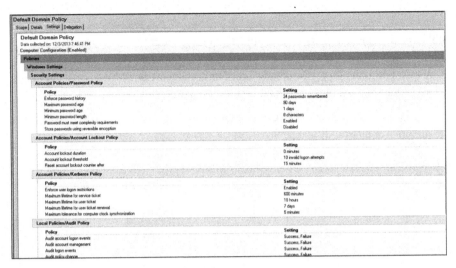

FIGURE 2-2   Windows Group Policy Settings

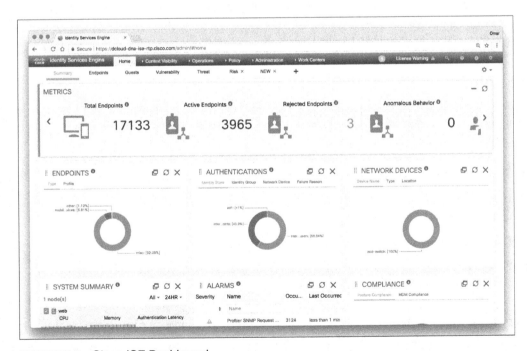

FIGURE 2-3   Cisco ISE Dashboard

In Figure 2-3, three different endpoint systems were denied or rejected access to the network because they didn't comply with a corporate baseline.

Guidelines

Guidelines are best thought of as teaching tools. The objective of a guideline is to help people conform to a standard. In addition to using softer language than standards, guidelines are customized for the intended audience and are not mandatory. Guidelines are akin to suggestions or advice. A guideline related to the password standard in the previous example might read like this:

"A good way to create a strong password is to think of a phrase, song title, or other group of words that is easy to remember and then convert it, like this:

- "The phrase 'Up and at 'em at 7!' can be converted into a strong password such as **up&atm@7!**.

- "You can create many passwords from this one phrase by changing the number, moving the symbols, or changing the punctuation mark."

This guideline is intended to help readers create easy-to-remember, yet strong passwords.

Guidelines are recommendations and advice to users when certain standards do not apply to your environment. Guidelines are designed to streamline certain processes according to best practices and must be consistent with the cybersecurity policies. On the other hand, guidelines often are open to interpretation and do not need to be followed to the letter.

Procedures

Procedures are instructions for how a policy, a standard, a baseline, and guidelines are carried out in a given situation. Procedures focus on actions or steps, with specific starting and ending points. There are four commonly used procedure formats:

- **Simple Step:** Lists sequential actions. There is no decision making.

- **Hierarchical:** Includes both generalized instructions for experienced users and detailed instructions for novices.

- **Graphic:** This format uses either pictures or symbols to illustrate the step.

- **Flowchart:** Used when a decision-making process is associated with the task. Flowcharts are useful when multiple parties are involved in separate tasks.

In keeping with our previous password example, the following is a Simple Step procedure for changing a user's Windows password (Windows 7 and earlier):

1. Press and hold the Ctrl+Alt+Delete keys.

2. Click the **Change Password** option.

3. Type your current password in the top box.

4. Type your new password in both the second and third boxes. (If the passwords don't match, you will be prompted to reenter your new password.)

5. Click **OK**, and then log in with your new password.

The following is the procedure to change your Windows password (Windows 10 and later):

1. Click **Start**.

2. Click your user account on the top, and select **Change Account Settings**.

3. Select **Sign-in Options** on the left panel.

4. Click the **Change** button under Password.

5. Enter your current password, and hit **Next**.

6. Type your new password and reenter it. Enter a password hint that will help you in case you forget your password.

> **Note**
>
> As with guidelines, it is important to know both your audience and the complexity of the task when designing procedures. In Chapter 8, "Communications and Operations Security," we discuss in detail the use of cybersecurity playbooks and standard operating procedures (SOPs).

Procedures should be well documented and easy to follow to ensure consistency and adherence to policies, standards, and baselines. Like policies and standards, they should be well reviewed to ensure that they accomplish the objective of the policy and that they are accurate and still relevant.

Plans and Programs

The function of a plan is to provide strategic and tactical instructions and guidance on how to execute an initiative or how to respond to a situation, within a certain time frame, usually with defined stages and with designated resources. Plans are sometimes referred to as programs. For our purposes, the terms are interchangeable. Here are some examples of information security–related plans we discuss in this book:

- Vendor Management Plan
- Incident Response Plan
- Business Continuity Plan
- Disaster Recovery Plan

Policies and plans are closely related. For example, an Incident Response Policy will generally include the requirement to publish, maintain, and test an Incident Response Plan. Conversely, the Incident Response Plan gets its authority from the policy. Quite often, the policy will be included in the plan document.

In Practice

Policy Hierarchy Review

Let's look at an example of how standards, guidelines, and procedures support a policy statement:

- The policy requires that all media should be encrypted.

- The standard specifies the type of encryption that must be used.

- The guideline might illustrate how to identify removable media.

- The procedure would provide the instructions for encrypting the media.

Writing Style and Technique

Style is critical. The first impression of a document is based on its style and organization. If the reader is immediately intimidated, the contents become irrelevant. Keep in mind that the role of policy is to guide behavior. That can happen only if the policy is clear and easy to use. How the document flows and the words you use will make all the difference as to how the policy is interpreted. Know your intended reader and write in a way that is understandable. Use terminology that is relevant. Most important, keep it simple. Policies that are overly complex tend to be misinterpreted. Policies should be written using plain language.

Using Plain Language

The term *plain language* means using the simplest, most straightforward way to express an idea.

No single technique defines plain language. Rather, plain language is defined by results—it is easy to read, understand, and use. Studies have proven that documents created using plain-language techniques are effective in a number of ways:[1]

- Readers understand documents better.

- Readers prefer plain language.

- Readers locate information faster.

- Documents are easier to update.

- It is easier to train people.

- Plain language saves time and money.

Even confident readers appreciate plain language. It enables them to read more quickly and with increased comprehension. The use of plain language is spreading in many areas of American culture, including governments at all levels, especially the federal government, health care, the sciences, and the legal system.

FYI: Warren Buffet on Using Plain Language

The following is excerpted from the preface to the Securities and Exchange Commission's *A Plain English Handbook:*

"For more than forty years, I've studied the documents that public companies file. Too often, I've been unable to decipher just what is being said or, worse yet, had to conclude that nothing was being said.

"Perhaps the most common problem, however, is that a well-intentioned and informed writer simply fails to get the message across to an intelligent, interested reader. In that case, stilted jargon and complex constructions are usually the villains.

"One unoriginal but useful tip: Write with a specific person in mind. When writing Berkshire Hathaway's annual report, I pretend that I'm talking to my sisters. I have no trouble picturing them: Though highly intelligent, they are not experts in accounting or finance. They will understand plain English, but jargon may puzzle them. My goal is simply to give them the information I would wish them to supply me if our positions were reversed. To succeed, I don't need to be Shakespeare; I must, though, have a sincere desire to inform.

"No siblings to write to? Borrow mine: Just begin with 'Dear Doris and Bertie.'"

Source: Securities and Exchange Commission, "A Plain English Handbook: How to Create Clear SEC Disclosure Documents," www.sec.gov/news/extra/handbook.htm.

The Plain Language Movement

It seems obvious that everyone would want to use plain language, but as it turns out, that is not the case. There is an enduring myth that to appear official or important, documents should be verbose. The result has been a plethora of complex and confusing regulations, contracts, and, yes, policies. In response to public frustration, the Plain Language Movement began in earnest in the early 1970s.

In 1971, the National Council of Teachers of English in the United States formed the Public Double-speak Committee. In 1972, U.S. President Richard Nixon created plain language momentum when he decreed that the "Federal Register be written in 'layman's terms.'" The next major event in the U.S. history of plain language occurred in 1978, when U.S. President Jimmy Carter issued Executive Orders 12,044 and 12,174. The intent was to make government regulations cost-effective and easy to understand. In 1981, U.S. President Ronald Reagan rescinded Carter's executive orders. Nevertheless, many continued their efforts to simplify documents; by 1991, eight states had passed statutes related to plain language.

In 1998, then-President Clinton issued a Presidential Memorandum requiring government agencies to use plain language in communications with the public. All subsequent administrations have supported this memorandum. In 2010, plain-language advocates achieved a major victory when the Plain Writing Act was passed. This law requires federal government agencies to write publications and forms in a "clear, concise, well-organized" manner using plain language guidelines.

We can take a cue from the government and apply these same techniques when writing policies, standards, guidelines, and plans. The easier a policy is to understand, the better the chance of compliance.

FYI: Plain Language Results

Here's an example of using plain language that involves the Pacific Offshore Cetacean Take Reduction Plan: Section 229.31. Not only did the National Marine Fisheries Service (NMFS) improve the language of this regulation, it turned the critical points into a user-friendly quick reference card, made it bright yellow so it's easy to find, and laminated it to stand up to wet conditions.

Before

After notification of NMFS, this final rule requires all CA/OR DGN vessel operators to have attended one Skipper Education Workshop after all workshops have been convened by NMFS in September 1997. CA/OR DGN vessel operators are required to attend Skipper Education Workshops at annual intervals thereafter, unless that requirement is waived by NMFS. NMFS will provide sufficient advance notice to vessel operators by mail prior to convening workshops.

After

After notification from NMFS, vessel operators must attend a skipper education workshop before commencing fishing each fishing season.

Source: www.plainlanguage.gov/examples/before_after/regfisheries.cfm

---

Plain Language Techniques for Policy Writing

The Plain Language Action and Information Network (PLAIN) describes itself on its website (http://plainlanguage.gov) as a group of federal employees from many agencies and specialties, who support the use of clear communication in government writing. In March of 2011, PLAIN published the Federal Plain Language Guidelines. Some of the guidelines are specific to government publications. Many are applicable to both government and industry. The ten guidelines, listed here, are pertinent to writing policies and companion documents:

1. Write for your audience. Use language your audience knows and is familiar with.

2. Write short sentences. Express only one idea in each sentence.

3. Limit a paragraph to one subject. Aim for no more than seven lines.

4. Be concise. Leave out unnecessary words. Instead of "for the purpose of," use "to." Instead of "due to the fact that," use "because."

5. Don't use jargon or technical terms when everyday words have the same meaning.

6. Use active voice. A sentence written in the active voice shows the subject acting in standard English sentence order: subject–verb–object. Active voice makes it clear who is supposed to do what. It eliminates ambiguity about responsibilities. Not "it must be done" but "you must do it."

7. Use "must," not "shall," to indicate requirements. "Shall" is imprecise. It can indicate either an obligation or a prediction. The word "must" is the clearest way to convey to your audience that they have to do something.

8. Use words and terms consistently throughout your documents. If you use the term "senior citizens" to refer to a group, continue to use this term throughout your document. Don't substitute another term, such as "the elderly" or "the aged." Using a different term may cause the reader to wonder if you are referring to the same group.

9. Omit redundant pairs or modifiers. For example, instead of "cease and desist," use either "cease" or "desist." Even better, use a simpler word such as "stop." Instead of saying "the end result was the honest truth," say "the result was the truth."

10. Avoid double negatives and exceptions to exceptions. Many ordinary terms have a negative meaning, such as unless, fail to, notwithstanding, except, other than, unlawful ("un-" words), disallowed ("dis-" words), terminate, void, insufficient, and so on. Watch out for them when they appear after "not." Find a positive word to express your meaning.

Want to learn more about using plain language? The official website of PLAIN has a wealth of resources, including the Federal Plain Language Guidelines, training materials and presentations, videos, posters, and references.

In Practice

Understanding Active and Passive Voice

Here are some key points to keep in mind concerning active and passive voice:

- Voice refers to the relationship of a subject and its verb.
- Active voice refers to a verb that shows the subject acting.
- Passive voice refers to a verb that shows the subject being acted upon.

Active Voice

A sentence written in the active voice shows the subject acting in standard English sentence order: subject–verb–object. The subject names the agent responsible for the action, and the verb identifies the action the agent has set in motion. Example: "George threw the ball."

Passive Voice

A sentence written in the passive voice reverses the standard sentence order. Example: "The ball was thrown by George." George, the agent, is no longer the subject but now becomes the object of the preposition "by." The ball is no longer the object but now becomes the subject of the sentence, where the agent preferably should be.

Conversion Steps

To convert a passive sentence into an active one, take these steps:

1. Identify the agent.
2. Move the agent to the subject position.
3. Remove the helping verb (to be).
4. Remove the past participle.
5. Replace the helping verb and participle with an action verb.

Examples of Conversion

Original: The report has been completed.

Revised: Stefan completed the report.

Original: A decision will be made.

Revised: Omar will decide.

In Practice

U.S. Army Clarity Index

The Clarity Index was developed to encourage plain writing. The index has two factors: average number of words per sentence and percentage of words longer than three syllables. The index adds together the two factors. The target is an average of 15 words per sentence and with 15% of the total text composed of three syllables or less. A resulting index between 20 and 40 is ideal and indicates the right balance of words and sentence length. In the following example (excerpted from Warren Buffet's SEC introduction), the index is composed of an average of 18.5 words per sentence, and 11.5% of the words are three syllables or less. An index of 30 falls squarely in the ideal range!

Sentence	Number of Words per Sentence	Number and Percentage of Words with Three or More Syllables
For more than forty years, I've studied the documents that public companies file.	13	Two words: 2/13 = 15%
Too often, I've been unable to decipher just what is being said or, worse yet, had to conclude that nothing was being said.	23	One word: 1/23 = 4%
Perhaps the most common problem, however, is that a well-intentioned and informed writer simply fails to get the message across to an intelligent, interested reader.	26	Three words: 3/26= 11%
In that case, stilted jargon and complex constructions are usually the villains.	12	One word 2/12= 16%
Total	74	46%
Average	18.5	11.5%
Clarity Index	**18.5 + 11.5 = 30**	

Policy Format

Writing policy documents can be challenging. Policies are complex documents that must be written to withstand legal and regulatory scrutiny and at the same time be easily read and understood by the reader. The starting point for choosing a format is identifying the policy audience.

Understand Your Audience

Who the policy is intended for is referred to as the *policy audience*. It is imperative, during the planning portion of the security policy project, to clearly define the audience. Policies may be intended for a particular group of employees based on job function or role. For example, an application development policy is targeted to developers. Other policies may be intended for a particular group or individual based on organizational role, such as a policy defining the responsibility of the Chief Information Security Officer (CISO). The policy, or portions of it, can sometimes apply to people outside of the company, such as business partners, service providers, contractors, or consultants. The policy audience is a potential resource during the entire policy life cycle. Indeed, who better to help create and maintain an effective policy than the very people whose job it is to use those policies in the context of their everyday work?

Policy Format Types

Organize, before you begin writing! It is important to decide how many sections and subsections you will require before you put pen to paper. Designing a template that allows the flexibility of editing will save considerable time and reduce aggravation. In this section you will learn the different policy sections and subsections, as well as the policy document formation options.

There are two general ways to structure and format your policy:

- **Singular policy:** You write each policy as a discrete document.

- **Consolidated policy:** Grouping similar and related policies together.

Consolidated policies are often organized by section and subsection.

Table 2-1 illustrates policy document format options.

TABLE 2-1   Policy Document Format Options

Description	Example
Singular policy	Chief Information Security Officer (CISO) Policy: Specific to the role and responsibility of the Information Security Officer.
Consolidated policy section	Governance Policy: Addresses the role and responsibilities of the Board of Directors, executive management, Chief Risk Officer, CISO, Compliance Officer, legal counsel, auditor, IT Director, and users.

The advantage to individual policies is that each policy document can be short, clean, and crisp, and targeted to its intended audience. The disadvantage is the need to manage multiple policy documents and the chance that they will become fragmented and lose consistency. The advantage to consolidation is that it presents a composite management statement in a single voice. The disadvantage is the potential size of the document and the reader challenge of locating applicable sections.

In the first edition of this book, we limited our study to singular documents. Since then, both the use of technology and the regulatory landscape have increased exponentially—only outpaced by escalating threats. In response to this ever-changing environment, the need for and number of policies has grown. For many organizations, managing singular policies has become unwieldy. The current trend is toward consolidation. Throughout this edition, we are going to be consolidating policies by security domain.

Regardless of which format you choose, do not include standards, baselines, guidelines, or procedures in your policy document. If you do so, you will end up with one big unruly document. And you will undoubtedly encounter one or more of the following problems:

- **Management challenge:** Who is responsible for managing and maintaining a document that has multiple contributors?

- **Difficulty of updating:** Because standards, guidelines, and procedures change far more often than policies, updating this whale of a document will be far more difficult than if these elements were properly treated separately. Version control will become a nightmare.

- **Cumbersome approval process:** Various regulations as well as the Corporate Operating Agreement require that the Board of Directors approve new policies as well as changes. Mashing it all together means that every change to a procedure, guideline, or standard will potentially require the Board to review and approve. This will become very costly and cumbersome for everyone involved.

Policy Components

Policy documents have multiple sections or components (see Table 2-2). How the components are used and in what order will depend on which format—singular or consolidated—you choose. In this section, we examine the composition of each component. Consolidated policy examples are provided in the "In Practice" sidebars.

TABLE 2-2   Policy Document Components

Component	Purpose
Version control	To track changes
Introduction	To frame the document
Policy heading	To identify the topic
Policy goals and objectives	To convey intent
Policy statement	Mandatory directive
Policy exceptions	To acknowledge exclusions
Policy enforcement clause	Violation sanctions
Administrative notations	Additional information
Policy definitions	Glossary of terms

Version Control

Best practices dictate that policies are reviewed annually to ensure they are still applicable and accurate. Of course, policies can (and should) be updated whenever there is a relevant change driver. Version control, as it relates to policies, is the management of changes to the document. Versions are usually identified by a number or letter code. Major revisions generally advance to the next letter or digit (for example, from 2.0 to 3.0). Minor revisions generally advance as a subsection (for example, from 2.0 to 2.1). Version control documentation should include the change date, name of the person or persons making the change, a brief synopsis of the change, the name of the person, committee, or board that authorized the change, and the effective date of the change.

- For singular policy documents, this information is split between the policy heading and the administrative notation sections.

- For consolidated policy documents, a version control table is included either at the beginning of the document or at the beginning of a section.

In Practice

Version Control Table

Version control tables are used in consolidated policy documents. The table is located after the title page, before the table of contents. Version control provides the reader with a history of the document. Here's an example:

V.	Editor	Purpose	Change Description	Authorized By	Effective Date
1.0	S. Ford, EVP		Original.	Sr. management committee	01/17/18
1.1	S. Ford, EVP	Subsection addition	2.5: Disclosures to Third Parties.	Sr. management committee	03/07/18
1.2	S. Ford, EVP	Subsection update	4.4: Border Device Management. 5.8: Wireless Networks.	Sr. management committee	01/14/19
--	S. Ford, EVP	Annual review	No change.	Sr. management committee	01/18/19
2.0	B. Lin, CIO	Section revision	Revised "Section 1.0: Governance and Risk Management" to reflect internal reorganization of roles and responsibilities.	Acme, Board of Directors	05/13/19

Introduction

Think of the introduction as the opening act. This is where we first meet the readers and have the opportunity to engage them. Here are the objectives of the introduction:

- To provide context and meaning
- To convey the importance of understanding and adhering to the policy
- To acquaint the reader with the document and its contents
- To explain the exemption process as well as the consequence of noncompliance
- To reinforce the authority of the policy

The first part of the introduction should make the case for why policies are necessary. It is a reflection of the guiding principles, defining for the reader the core values the company believes in and is committed to. This is also the place to set forth the regulatory and contractual obligations that the company has—often by listing which regulations, such as GLBA, HIPAA, or MA CMR 17 201, pertain to the organization as well as the scope of the policy.

The second part of the introduction should leave no doubt that compliance is mandatory. A strong statement of expectation from a senior authority, such as the Chairman of the Board, CEO, or President, is appropriate. Users should understand that they are unequivocally and directly responsible for following the policy in the course of their normal employment or relationship with the company. It should also make clear that questions are welcome and a resource is available who can clarify the policy and/or assist with compliance.

The third part of the introduction should describe the policy document, including the structure, categories, and storage location (for example, the company intranet). It should also reference companion documents such as standards, guidelines, programs, and plans. In some cases, the introduction includes a revision history, the stakeholders that may have reviewed the policy, and who to contact to make any modifications.

The fourth part of the introduction should explain how to handle situations where compliance may not be feasible. It should provide a high-level view of the exemption and enforcement process. The section should also address the consequences of willful noncompliance.

- For singular policy documents, the introduction should be a separate document.

- For consolidated policy documents, the introduction serves as the preface and follows the version control table.

In Practice

Introduction

The introduction has five objectives: to provide context and meaning, to convey the importance of understanding and adhering to the policy, to acquaint the reader with the document, to explain the exemption process and the consequence of noncompliance, and, last, to thank the reader and reinforce the authority of the policy. Each objective is called out in the following example:

[Objective 1: Provide context and meaning]

The 21st century environment of connected technologies offers us many exciting present and future opportunities. Unfortunately, there are those who seek to exploit these opportunities for personal, financial, or political gain. We, as an organization, are committed to protecting our clients, employees, stakeholders, business partners, and community from harm and to providing exceptional service.

The objective of our Cybersecurity Policy is to protect and respect the confidentiality, integrity, and availability of client information, company proprietary data, and employee data, as well as the infrastructure that supports our services and business activities.

This policy has been designed to meet or exceed applicable federal and state information security–related regulations, including but not limited to sections 501 and 505(b) of the Gramm-Leach-Bliley Act (GLBA) and MA CMR 17 201 as well as our contractual obligations.

The scope of the Cybersecurity Policy extends to all functional areas and all employees, directors, consultants, contractors, temporary staff, co-op students, interns, partners and third-party employees, and joint venture partners, unless explicitly excluded.

[Objective 2: Convey the importance of understanding and adhering to the policy]

Diligent information security practices are a civic responsibility and a team effort involving the participation and support of every employee and affiliate who deals with information and/or information systems. It is the responsibility of every employee and affiliate to know, understand, and adhere to these policies, and to conduct their activities accordingly. If you have any questions or would like more information, I encourage you to contact our Compliance Officer at x334.

[Objective 3: Acquaint the reader with the document and its contents]

At first glance, the policy [or policies, if you are using singular policy documents] may appear daunting. If you take a look at the table of contents [or list, if you are using singular policy documents] you will see that the Cybersecurity Policy is organized by category. These categories form the framework of our Cybersecurity Program. Supporting the policies are implementation standards, guidelines, and procedures. You can find these documents in the Governance section of our online company library.

[Objective 4: Explain the consequence of noncompliance as well as the exception process]

Where compliance is not technically feasible or justified by business needs, an exemption may be granted. Exemption requests must be submitted in writing to the Chief Operating Officer (COO), including justification and benefits attributed to the exemption. Unless otherwise stated, the COO and the President have the authority to grant waivers.

Willful violation of this policy [or policies, if you are using singular policy documents] may result in disciplinary action, which may include termination for employees and temporaries, a termination of employment relations in the case of contractors and consultants, and dismissal for interns and volunteers. Additionally, individuals may be subject to civil and criminal prosecution.

[Objective 5: Thank the reader and provide a seal of authority]

I thank you in advance for your support, as we all do our best to create a secure environment and to fulfill our mission.

—Anthony Starks, Chief Executive Officer (CEO)

Policy Heading

A *policy heading* identifies the policy by name and provides the reader with an overview of the policy topic or category. The format and contents of the heading significantly depend on the format (singular or consolidated) you are using.

- Singular policies must be able to stand on their own, which means it is necessary to include significant logistical detail in each heading. The information contained in a singular policy heading may include the organization or division name, category (section), subsection, policy number, name of the author, version number, approval authority, effective date of the policy, regulatory cross-reference, and a list of supporting resources and source material. The topic is generally self-explanatory and does not require an overview or explanation.

■ In a consolidated policy document, the heading serves as a section introduction and includes an overview. Because the version number, approval authority, and effective date of the policy have been documented in the version control table, it is unnecessary to include them in section headings. Regulatory cross-reference (if applicable), lead author, and supporting documentation are found in the Administrative Notation section of the policy.

In Practice

Policy Heading

A consolidated policy heading serves as the introduction to a section or category.

Section 1: Governance and Risk Management

Overview

Governance is the set of responsibilities and practices exercised by the Board of Directors and management team with the goal of providing strategic direction, ensuring that organizational objectives are achieved, risks are managed appropriately, and enterprise resources are used responsibly. The principal objective of an organization's risk management process is to provide those in leadership and data steward roles with the information required to make well-informed decisions.

Policy Goals and Objectives

Policy goals and objectives act as a gateway to the content to come and the security principle they address. This component should concisely convey the intent of the policy. Note that even a singular policy can have multiple objectives. We live in a world where business matters are complex and interconnected, which means that a policy with a single objective might risk not covering all aspects of a particular situation. It is therefore important, during the planning phase, to pay appropriate attention to the different objectives the security policy should seek to achieve.

■ Singular policies list the goals and objectives either in the policy heading or in the body of the document.

■ In a consolidated policy document, the goals and objectives are grouped and follow the policy heading.

In Practice

Policy Goals and Objectives

Goals and objectives should convey the intent of the policy. Here's an example:

Goals and Objectives for Section 1: Governance and Risk Management

- To demonstrate our commitment to information security
- To define organizational roles and responsibilities
- To provide the framework for effective risk management and continuous assessment
- To meet regulatory requirements

Policy Statement

Up to this point in the document, we have discussed everything but the actual policy statement. The *policy statement* is best thought of as a high-level directive or strategic roadmap. This is the section where we lay out the rules that need to be followed and, in some cases, reference the implementation instructions (standards) or corresponding plans. Policy statements are intended to provide action items as well as the framework for situational responses. Policies are mandatory. Deviations or exceptions must be subject to a rigorous examination process.

In Practice

Policy Statement

The bulk of the final policy document is composed of policy statements. Here is an example of an excerpt from a governance and risk management policy:

1.1. Roles and Responsibilities

    1.1.1. The Board of Directors will provide direction for and authorize the Cybersecurity Policy and corresponding program.

    1.1.2. The Chief Operating Officer (COO) is responsible for the oversight of, communication related to, and enforcement of the Cybersecurity Policy and corresponding program.

    1.1.3. The COO will provide an annual report to the Board of Directors that provides them with the information necessary to measure the organizations' adherence to the Cybersecurity Policy objectives and to gauge the changing nature of risk inherent in lines of business and operations.

1.1.4. The Chief Information Security Officer (CISO) is charged with the implementation of the Cybersecurity Policy and standards including but not limited to:

- Ensuring that administrative, physical, and technical controls are selected, implemented, and maintained to identify, measure, monitor, and control risks, in accordance with applicable regulatory guidelines and industry best practices
- Managing risk assessment–related remediation
- Authorizing access control permissions to client and proprietary information
- Reviewing access control permissions in accordance with the audit standard
- Responding to security incidents

1.1.5. In-house legal counsel is responsible for communicating to all contracted entities the information security requirements that pertain to them as detailed within the Cybersecurity Policy and the Vendor Management Program.

Policy Exceptions and the Exemption Process

Realistically, there will be situations where it is not possible or practical, or perhaps may even be harmful, to obey a policy directive. This does not invalidate the purpose or quality of the policy. It just means that some special situations will call for *exceptions* to the rule. *Policy exceptions* are agreed waivers that are documented within the policy. For example, in order to protect its intellectual property, Company A has a policy that bans digital cameras from all company premises. However, a case could be made that the HR department should be equipped with a digital camera to take pictures of new employees to paste them on their ID badges. Or maybe the Security Officer should have a digital camera to document the proceedings of evidence gathering after a security breach has been detected. Both examples are valid reasons why a digital camera might be needed. In these cases, an exception to the policy could be added to the document. If no exceptions are ever to be allowed, this should be clearly stated in the Policy Statement section as well.

An *exemption* or *waiver process* is required for exceptions identified after the policy has been authorized. The exemption process should be explained in the introduction. The criteria or conditions for exemptions should not be detailed in the policy, only the method or process for requesting an exemption. If we try to list all the conditions to which exemptions apply, we risk creating a loophole in the exemption itself. It is also important that the process follow specific criteria under which exemptions are granted or rejected. Whether an exemption is granted or rejected, the requesting party should be given a written report with clear reasons either way.

Finally, it is recommended that you keep the number of approved exceptions and exemptions low, for several reasons:

- Too many built-in exceptions may lead employees to perceive the policy as unimportant.
- Granting too many exemptions may create the impression of favoritism.
- Exceptions and exemptions can become difficult to keep track of and successfully audit.

If there are too many built-in exceptions and/or exemption requests, it may mean that the policy is not appropriate in the first place. At that point, the policy should be subject to review.

In Practice

Policy Exception

Here's a policy exception that informs the reader who is not required to conform to a specific clause and under what circumstances and whose authorization:

"At the discretion of in-house legal counsel, contracted entities whose contracts include a confidentiality clause may be exempted from signing nondisclosure agreements."

The process for granting post-adoption exemptions should be included in the introduction. Here's an example:

"Where compliance is not technically feasible or as justified by business needs, an exemption may be granted. Exemption requests must be submitted in writing to the COO, including justification and benefits attributed to the exemption. Unless otherwise stated, the COO and the President have the authority to grant waivers."

Policy Enforcement Clause

The best way to deliver the message that policies are mandatory is to include the penalty for violating the rules. The *policy enforcement clause* is where the sanctions for non-adherence to the policy are unequivocally stated to reinforce the seriousness of compliance. Obviously, you must be careful with the nature of the penalty. It should be proportional to the rule that was broken, whether it was accidental or intentional, and the level of risk the company incurred.

An effective method of motivating compliance is proactive training. All employees should be trained in the acceptable practices presented in the security policy. Without training, it is hard to fault employees for not knowing they were supposed to act in a certain fashion. Imposing disciplinary actions in such situations can adversely affect morale. We take a look at various training, education, and awareness tools and techniques in later chapters.

In Practice

Policy Enforcement Clause

This example of a policy enforcement clause advises the reader, in no uncertain terms, what will happen if they do not obey the rules. It belongs in the introduction and, depending on the circumstances, may be repeated within the policy document.

"Violation of this policy may result in disciplinary action, which may include termination for employees and temporaries, a termination of employment relations in the case of contractors and consultants, and dismissal for interns and volunteers. Additionally, individuals are subject to civil and criminal prosecution."

Administrative Notations

The purpose of *administrative notations* is to refer the reader to additional information and/or provide a reference to an internal resource. Notations include regulatory cross-references, the name of corresponding documents such as standards, guidelines, and programs, supporting documentation such as annual reports or job descriptions, and the policy author's name and contact information. You should include only notations that are applicable to your organization. However, you should be consistent across all policies.

- Singular policies incorporate administrative notations either in the heading, at the end of the document, or split between the two locations. How this is handled depends on the policy template used by the company.

- In a consolidated policy document, the administrative notations are located at the end of each section.

In Practice

Administrative Notations

Administrative notations are a reference point for additional information. If the policy is distributed in electronic format, it is a great idea to hyperlink the notations directly to the source document.

Regulatory Cross Reference

Section 505(b) of the Gramm-Leach-Bliley Act

MA CMR 17 201

Lead Author

B. Lin, Chief Information Officer

b.lin@example.com

Corresponding Documents

Risk Management Standards

Vendor Management Program

Supporting Documentation

Job descriptions as maintained by the Human Resources Department.

Policy Definitions

The Policy Definition section is a glossary of terms, abbreviations, and acronyms used in the document that the reader may be unfamiliar with. Adding definitions to the overall document will aid the target audience in understanding the policy, and will therefore make the policy a much more effective document.

The general rule is to include definitions for any instance of industry-specific, technical, legal, or regulatory language. When deciding what terms to include, it makes sense to err on the side of caution. The purpose of the security policy as a document is communication and education. The target audience for this document usually encompasses all employees of the company, and sometimes outside personnel. Even if some technical topics are well known to all in-house employees, some of those outside individuals who come in contact with the company—and therefore are governed by the security policy—may not be as well versed in the policy's technical aspects.

Simply put, before you begin writing down definitions, it is recommended that you first define the target audience for whom the document is crafted, and cater to the lowest common denominator to ensure optimum communication efficiency.

Another reason why definitions should not be ignored is for the legal ramification they represent. An employee cannot pretend to have thought that a certain term used in the policy meant one thing when it is clearly defined in the policy itself. When you're choosing which words will be defined, therefore, it is important not only to look at those that could clearly be unknown, but also those that should be defined to remove any and all ambiguity. A security policy could be an instrumental part of legal proceedings and should therefore be viewed as a legal document and crafted as such.

In Practice

Terms and Definitions

Any term that may not be familiar to the reader or is open to interpretation should be defined.

Here's an example of an abbreviation:

- MOU—Memorandum of Understanding

Here's an example of a regulatory reference:

- MA CMR 17 201—Standards for the Protection of Personal Information of Residents of the Commonwealth establishes minimum standards to be met in connection with the safeguarding of personal information of Massachusetts residents.

And, finally, here are a few examples of security terms:

- **Distributed Denial of Service (DDoS):** An attack in which there is a massive volume of IP packets from multiple sources. The flood of incoming packets consumes available resources resulting in the denial of service to legitimate users.

- **Exploit:** A malicious program designed to "exploit" or take advantage of a single vulnerability or set of vulnerabilities.

- **Phishing:** Where the attacker presents a link that looks like a valid, trusted resource to a user. When the user clicks it, he is prompted to disclose confidential information such as his username and password.

- **Pharming:** The attacker uses this technique to direct a customer's URL from a valid resource to a malicious one that could be made to appear as the valid site to the user. From there, an attempt is made to extract confidential information from the user.

- **Malvertising:** The act of incorporating malicious ads on trusted websites, which results in users' browsers being inadvertently redirected to sites hosting malware.

- **Logic bomb:** A type of malicious code that is injected into a legitimate application. An attacker can program a logic bomb to delete itself from the disk after it performs the malicious tasks on the system. Examples of these malicious tasks include deleting or corrupting files or databases and executing a specific instruction after certain system conditions are met.

- **Trojan horse:** A type of malware that executes instructions determined by the nature of the Trojan to delete files, steal data, or compromise the integrity of the underlying operating system. Trojan horses typically use a form of social engineering to fool victims into installing such software on their computers or mobile devices. Trojans can also act as backdoors.

- **Backdoor:** A piece of malware or configuration change that allows attackers to control the victim's system remotely. For example, a backdoor can open a network port on the affected system so that the attacker can connect and control the system.

Summary

You now know that policies need supporting documents to give them context and meaningful application. Standards, guidelines, and procedures provide a means to communicate specific ways to implement our policies. We create our organizational standards, which specify the requirements for each policy. We offer guidelines to help people comply with standards. We create sets of instructions known as procedures so tasks are consistently performed. The format of our procedure—Simple Step, Hierarchical, Graphic, or Flowchart—depends on the complexity of the task and the audience. In addition to our policies, we create plans or programs to provide strategic and tactical instructions and guidance on how to execute an initiative or how to respond to a situation, within a certain time frame, usually with defined stages and with designated resources.

Writing policy documents is a multistep process. First, we need to define the audience for which the document is intended. Then, we choose the format. Options are to write each policy as a discrete document (singular policy) or to group like policies together (consolidated policy). Last, we need to decide upon the structure, including the components to include and in what order.

The first and arguably most important section is the introduction. This is our opportunity to connect with the reader and to convey the meaning and importance of our policies. The introduction should be written by the "person in charge," such as the CEO or President. This person should use the introduction to reinforce company-guiding principles and correlate them with the rules introduced in the security policy.

Specific to each policy are the heading, goals and objectives, the policy statement, and (if applicable) exceptions. The ***heading*** identifies the policy by name and provides the reader with an overview of the policy topic or category. The goals and objectives convey what the policy is intended to accomplish. The policy statement is where we lay out the rules that need to be followed and, in some cases, reference the implementation instructions (standards) or corresponding programs. Policy exceptions are agreed waivers that are documented within the policy.

An exemption or waiver process is required for exceptions identified after a policy has been authorized. The ***policy enforcement clause*** is where the sanctions for willful non-adherence to the policy are unequivocally stated to reinforce the seriousness of compliance. Administrative notations refer the reader to additional information and/or provide a reference to an internal resource. ***The policy definition section*** is a glossary of terms, abbreviations, and acronyms used in the document that the reader may be unfamiliar with.

Recognizing that the first impression of a document is based on its style and organization, we studied the work of the Plain Language Movement. Our objective for using plain language is to produce documents that are easy to read, understand, and use. We looked at ten techniques from the Federal Plain Language Guideline that we can (and should) use for writing effective policies. In the next section of the book, we put these newfound skills to use.

Test Your Skills

MULTIPLE CHOICE QUESTIONS

1. The policy hierarchy is the relationships between which of the following?

   A. Guiding principles, regulations, laws, and procedures

   B. Guiding principles, standards, guidelines, and procedures

   C. Guiding principles, instructions, guidelines, and programs

   D. None of the above

2. Which of the following statements best describes the purpose of a standard?

   A. To state the beliefs of an organization

   B. To reflect the guiding principles

   C. To dictate mandatory requirements

   D. To make suggestions

3. Which of the following statements best describes the purpose of a guideline?

   A. To state the beliefs of an organization

   B. To reflect the guiding principles

   C. To dictate mandatory requirements

   D. To help people conform to a standard

4. Which of the following statements best describes the purpose of a baseline?

   A. To measure compliance

   B. To ensure uniformity across a similar set of devices

   C. To ensure uniformity and consistency

   D. To make suggestions

5. Simple Step, Hierarchical, Graphic, and Flowchart are examples of which of the following formats?

   A. Policy

   B. Program

   C. Procedure

   D. Standard

6. Which of the following terms best describes instructions and guidance on how to execute an initiative or how to respond to a situation, within a certain time frame, usually with defined stages and with designated resources?

   A. Plan

   B. Policy

   C. Procedure

   D. Package

7. Which of the following statements best describes a disadvantage to using the singular policy format?

   A. The policy can be short.

   B. The policy can be targeted.

   C. You may end up with too many policies to maintain.

   D. The policy can easily be updated.

8. Which of the following statements best describes a disadvantage to using the consolidated policy format?

   A. Consistent language is used throughout the document.

   B. Only one policy document must be maintained.

   C. The format must include a composite management statement.

   D. The potential size of the document.

9. Policies, standards, guidelines, and procedures should all be in the same document.

   A. True

   B. False

   C. Only if the company is multinational

   D. Only if the documents have the same author

10. Version control is the management of changes to a document and should include which of the following elements?

    A. Version or revision number

    B. Date of authorization or date that the policy took effect

    C. Change description

    D. All of the above

11. What is an exploit?

    A. A phishing campaign

    B. A malicious program or code designed to "exploit" or take advantage of a single vulnerability or set of vulnerabilities

C. A network or system weakness

D. A protocol weakness

12. The name of the policy, policy number, and overview belong in which of the following sections?

   A. Introduction

   B. Policy Heading

   C. Policy Goals and Objectives

   D. Policy Statement

13. The aim or intent of a policy is stated in the _____.

   A. introduction

   B. policy heading

   C. policy goals and objectives

   D. policy statement

14. Which of the following statements is true?

   A. A security policy should include only one objective.

   B. A security policy should not include any exceptions.

   C. A security policy should not include a glossary.

   D. A security policy should not list all step-by-step measures that need to be taken.

15. The _____ contains the rules that must be followed.

   A. policy heading

   B. policy statement

   C. policy enforcement clause

   D. policy goals and objectives

16. A policy should be considered _____.

   A. mandatory

   B. discretionary

   C. situational

   D. optional

17. Which of the following best describes policy definitions?

   A. A glossary of terms, abbreviations, and acronyms used in the document that the reader may be unfamiliar with

   B. A detailed list of the possible penalties associated with breaking rules set forth in the policy

    C. A list of all the members of the security policy creation team

    D. None of the above

18. The _____ contains the penalties that would apply if a portion of the security policy were to be ignored by an employee.

    A. policy heading

    B. policy statement

    C. policy enforcement clause

    D. policy statement of authority

19. What component of a security policy does the following phrase belong to? "Wireless networks are allowed only if they are separate and distinct from the corporate network."

    A. Introduction

    B. Administrative notation

    C. The policy heading

    D. The policy statement

20. There may be situations where it is not possible to comply with a policy directive. Where should the exemption or waiver process be explained?

    A. Introduction

    B. The policy statement

    C. The policy enforcement clause

    D. The policy exceptions

21. The name of the person/group (for example, executive committee) that authorized the policy should be included in _____.

    A. the version control table or the policy statement

    B. the heading or the policy statement

    C. the policy statement or the policy exceptions

    D. the version control table or the policy heading

22. When you're drafting a list of exceptions for a security policy, the language should _____.

    A. be as specific as possible

    B. be as vague as possible

    C. reference another, dedicated document

    D. None of the above

23. If supporting documentation would be of use to the reader, it should be _____.

    A. included in full in the policy document

    B. ignored because supporting documentation does not belong in a policy document

    C. listed in either the Policy Heading or Administrative Notation section

    D. included in a policy appendix

24. When writing a policy, standard, guideline, or procedure, you should use language that is _____.

    A. technical

    B. clear and concise

    C. legalese

    D. complex

25. Readers prefer "plain language" because it _____.

    A. helps them locate pertinent information

    B. helps them understand the information

    C. saves time

    D. All of the above

26. Which of the following is not a characteristic of plain language?

    A. Short sentences

    B. Using active voice

    C. Technical jargon

    D. Seven or fewer lines per paragraph

27. Which of the following terms is best to use when indicating a mandatory requirement?

    A. must

    B. shall

    C. should not

    D. may not

28. A company that uses the term "employees" to refer to workers who are on the company payroll should refer to them throughout their policies as _____.

    A. workforce members

    B. employees

    C. hired hands

    D. workers

29. Which of the following statements is true regarding policy definitions?

    A. They should be defined and maintained in a separate document.

    B. The general rule is to include definitions for any topics except technical, legal, or regulatory language.

    C. The general rule of policy definitions is to include definitions for any instance of industry-specific, technical, legal, or regulatory language.

    D. They should be created before any policy or standards.

30. Even the best-written policy will fail if which of the following is true?

    A. The policy is too long.

    B. The policy is mandated by the government.

    C. The policy doesn't have the support of management.

    D. All of the above.

EXERCISES

EXERCISE 2.1: Creating Standards, Guidelines, and Procedures

The University System has a policy that states, "All students must comply with their campus attendance standard."

1. You are tasked with developing a standard that documents the mandatory requirements (for example, how many classes can be missed without penalty). Include at least four requirements.

2. Create a guideline to help students adhere to the standard you created.

3. Create a procedure for requesting exemptions to the policy.

EXERCISE 2.2: Writing Policy Statements

1. Who would be the target audience for a policy related to campus elections?

2. Keeping in mind the target audience, compose a policy statement related to campus elections.

3. Compose an enforcement clause.

EXERCISE 2.3: Writing a Policy Introduction

1. Write an introduction to the policy you created in Exercise 2.2.

2. Generally an introduction is signed by an authority. Who would be the appropriate party to sign the introduction?

3. Write an exception clause.

EXERCISE 2.4: **Writing Policy Definitions**

1. The purpose of policy definitions is to clarify ambiguous terms. If you were writing a policy for an on-campus student audience, what criteria would you use to determine which terms should have definitions?

2. What are some examples of terms you would define?

EXERCISE 2.5: **Using Clear Language**

1. Identify the passive verb in each of the following lines. Hint: Test by inserting a subject (for example, he or we) before the verb.

a) was written	will write	has written	is writing
b) shall deliver	may deliver	is delivering	is delivered
c) has sent	were sent	will send	is sending
d) should revoke	will be revoking	has revoked	to be revoked
e) is mailing	have been mailed	having mailed	will mail
f) may be requesting	are requested	have requested	will request

2. Shorten the following phrases (for example, "consideration should be given to" can be shortened to "consider").

Original	**Modified**
a) For the purpose of	To
b) Due to the fact that	Because
c) Forwarded under separate cover	Sent separately

3. Delete the redundant modifiers (for example, for "actual facts," you would delete the word "actual"):

   a) Honest truth

   b) End result

   c) Separate out

   d) Start over again

   e) Symmetrical in form

   f) Narrow down

PROJECTS

PROJECT 2.1: Comparing Security Policy Templates

1. Search online for "cybersecurity policy templates."

2. Read the documents and compare them.

3. Identify the policy components that were covered in this chapter.

4. Search now for a real-world policy, such as Tuft's University Two-factor Authentication Policy at https://it.tufts.edu/univ-pol.

5. Choose a couple terms in the policy that are not defined in the Policy Definitions section and write a definition for each.

PROJECT 2.2: Analyzing the Enterprise Security Policy for the State of New York

1. Search online for the "State of New York Cybersecurity Policy P03-002" document.

2. Read the policy. What is your overall opinion of the policy?

3. What is the purpose of the italic format? In your opinion, is it useful or distracting?

4. The policy references standards and procedures. Identify at least one instance of each. Can you find any examples of where a standard, guideline, or procedure is embedded in the policy document?

PROJECT 2.3: Testing the Clarity of a Policy Document

1. Locate your school's cybersecurity policy. (It may have a different name.)

2. Select a section of the policy and use the U.S. Army's Clarity Index to evaluate the ease of reading (reference the "In Practice: U.S. Army Clarity Index" sidebar for instructions).

3. Explain how you would make the policy more readable.

Case Study

Clean Up the Library Lobby

The library includes the following exhibition policy:

"Requests to utilize the entrance area at the library for the purpose of displaying posters and leaflets gives rise to the question of the origin, source, and validity of the material to be displayed. Posters, leaflets, and other display materials issued by the Office of Campus Security, Office of Student Life, the Health Center, and other authoritative bodies are usually displayed in libraries, but items of a fractious or controversial kind, while not necessarily excluded, are considered individually."

The lobby of the school library is a mess. Plastered on the walls are notes, posters, and cards of all sizes and shapes. It is impossible to tell current from outdated messages. It is obvious that no one is paying any attention to the library exhibition policy. You have been asked to evaluate the policy and make the necessary changes needed to achieve compliance.

1. Consider your audience. Rewrite the policy using plain language guidelines. You may encounter resistance to modifying the policy, so document the reason for each change, such as changing passive voice to active voice, eliminating redundant modifiers, and shortening sentences.

2. Expand the policy document to include goals and objectives, exceptions, and a policy enforcement clause.

3. Propose standards and guidelines to support the policy.

4. Propose how you would suggest introducing the policy, standards, and guidelines to the campus community.

References

1. Baldwin, C. *Plain Language and the Document Revolution*. Washington, D.C.: Lamplighter, 1999.

Regulations and Directives Cited

Carter, J. "Executive Order—Improving Government Regulations," accessed 05/2018, www.presidency.ucsb.edu/ws/?pid=30539.

Clinton, W. "President Clinton's Memorandum on Plain Language in Government Writing," accessed 05/2018, www.plainlanguage.gov/whatisPL/govmandates/memo.cfm.

Obama, B. "Executive Order 13563—Improving Regulation and Regulatory Review," accessed 05/2018, https://obamawhitehouse.archives.gov/the-press-office/2011/01/18/executive-order-13563-improving-regulation-and-regulatory-review.

"Plain Writing Act of 2010" PUBLIC LAW 111–274, Oct. 13, 2010, accessed 05/2018, https://www.gpo.gov/fdsys/pkg/PLAW-111publ274/pdf/PLAW-111publ274.pdf.

Other References

Krause, Micki, CISSP, and Harold F. Tipton, CISSP. 2004. *Information Security Management Handbook*, Fifth Edition. Boca Raton, FL: CRC Press, Auerbach Publications.

Chapter | **3**

Cybersecurity Framework

Chapter Objectives

After reading this chapter and completing the exercises, you will be able to do the following:

- Understand confidentiality, integrity, and availability (the CIA security model).
- Describe the security objectives of confidentiality, integrity, and availability.
- Discuss why organizations choose to adopt a security framework.
- Understand the intent of the National Institute of Standards and Technology (NIST) Cybersecurity Framework.
- Understand the intent of the ISO/IEC 27000-series of information security standards.
- Outline the domains of an information security program.

Our focus in this chapter on information security objectives and framework will answer the following (and many other) questions associated with the need to maintain secure data storage and communications among and between government, public, and private sectors. In context, our efforts to sustain reliable and secure communications has become a worldwide global effort with cybersecurity.

- What are we trying to achieve in pursuit of cybersecurity?
- What is the ultimate goal of writing cybersecurity policies?
- What tangible benefit will come to our customers, our employees, our partners, and our organizations from our Herculean effort?

To organize the effort, a framework is required. A framework lends itself to many easily related metaphors. The most obvious is that of any building: no foundation, no building. More specifically, the better the framing of any building, the longer it will last, the more it can hold, and the more functional it becomes. Of course, with any building there must first be a plan. We hire architects and engineers to design our buildings, to think about what is possible, and relay the best way to achieve those possibilities.

In the same way, we need a framework for our information security program. Much like the many rooms in a building, each with its own functions, we segment our information security program into logical and tangible units called domains. *Security domains* are associated with designated groupings of related activities, systems, or resources. For example, the Human Resources Security Management domain includes topics related to personnel, such as background checks, confidentiality agreements, and employee training. Without the framework, every new situation will see us repeating, redesigning, and reacting, which all together can be referred to as "unplanned," or spending time in crisis. Fortunately, in the information security arena there is absolutely no reason to choose crisis over preparedness. Strategies involving proactive, rather than reactive, procedures have become the ad hoc standard for systems of cybersecurity governance. A number of public and private organizations, including the International Organization for Standardization (ISO) and the National Institute of Standards and Technology (NIST), have all invested considerable time and energy to develop standards that enable proactive cybersecurity frameworks.

In this chapter, you are introduced to the standards developed by both organizations. Before we begin building our information security program and policies, we need to first identify what we are trying to achieve and why. We begin this chapter by discussing the three basic tenets of information security. We then look at the escalating global threat, including who is behind the attacks, their motivation, and how they attack. We apply this knowledge to building the framework of our information security program and how we write our policies.

Confidentiality, Integrity, and Availability

The elements of confidentiality, integrity, and availability are often described as the CIA model. It is easy to guess that the first thing that popped into your mind when you read those three letters was the United States Central Intelligence Agency. In the world of cybersecurity, these three letters represent something we strive to attain and protect. Confidentiality, integrity, and availability (CIA) are the unifying attributes of an information security program. Collectively referred to as the *CIA triad* or *CIA security model*, each attribute represents a fundamental objective of information security.

You may be wondering which is most important: confidentiality, integrity, or availability? The answer requires an organization to assess its mission, evaluate its services, and consider regulations and contractual agreements. As Figure 3-1 illustrates, organizations may consider all three components of the CIA triad equally important, in which case resources must be allocated proportionately.

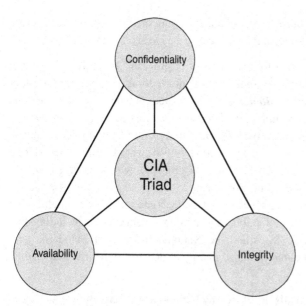

FIGURE 3-1 CIA Triad

What Is Confidentiality?

When you tell a friend something in confidence, you expect them to keep the information private and not share what you told them with anyone else without your permission. You also hope that they will never use this against you. Likewise, *confidentiality* is the requirement that private or confidential information not be disclosed to unauthorized individuals.

There are many attempts to define what confidentiality is. As an example, the ISO 2700 standard provides a good definition of confidentiality as "the property that information is not made available or disclosed to unauthorized individuals, entities, or processes."

Confidentiality relies on three general concepts, as illustrated in Figure 3-2.

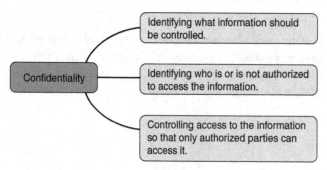

FIGURE 3-2 Confidentiality General Concepts

There are several ways to protect the confidentiality of a system or its data; one of the most common is to use encryption. This includes encryption of data in transit with the use of site-to-site and remote access virtual private networks (VPNs), or by deploying server and client-side encryption using Transport Layer Security (TLS).

Another important element of confidentiality is that all sensitive data needs to be controlled, audited, and monitored at all times. This is often done by *encrypting data at rest*. Here are some examples of sensitive data:

- Social security numbers
- Bank and credit card account information
- Criminal records
- Patient and health records
- Trade secrets
- Source code
- Military secrets

The following are examples of security mechanisms designed to preserve confidentiality:

- Logical and physical access controls
- Encryption (in motion and at rest)
- Database views
- Controlled traffic routing

Data classification is important when you're deciding how to protect data. By having a good data classification methodology, you can enhance the way you secure your data across your network and systems.

Not only has the amount of information stored, processed, and transmitted on privately owned networks and the public Internet increased dramatically, so has the number of ways to potentially access the data. The Internet, its inherent weaknesses, and those willing (and able) to exploit vulnerabilities are the main reasons why protecting confidentiality has taken on a new urgency. The technology and accessibility we take for granted would have been considered magic just 10 years ago. The amazing speed at which we arrived here is also the reason we have such a gap in security. The race to market often means that security is sacrificed. So although it may seem that information security requirements are a bit extreme at times, it is really a reaction to the threat environment.

You also have to pay attention to confidentiality laws. For example, information exchanged between doctors and patients or lawyers and clients is protected by confidentiality laws called the "doctor-patient privilege" and the "attorney-client privilege," respectively.

As it pertains to information security, confidentiality is the protection of information from unauthorized people and processes. Federal Code 44 U.S.C., Sec. 3542 defines confidentiality as "preserving authorized restrictions on access and disclosure, including means for protecting personal privacy and proprietary information."

None of us likes the thought of our private health information or financial information falling into some stranger's hands. No business owner likes the thought of her proprietary business information being disclosed to competitors. Information is valuable. Social security numbers are used for identity theft. Bank account credentials are used to steal money. Medical insurance information can be used to fraudulently obtain services or to make counterfeit claims. Military secrets can be used to build weaponry, track troop movements, or expose counterintelligence agents. The list goes on and on.

Because there is value in confidential information, it is often a target of cybercriminals. For instance, many breaches involve the theft of credit card information or other personal information useful for identity theft. Criminals look for and are prepared to exploit weaknesses in network designs, software, communication channels, and people to access confidential information. The opportunities are plentiful.

Criminals are not always outsiders. Insiders can be tempted to "make copies" of information they have access to for financial gain, notoriety, or to "make a statement." The most recent threat to confidentiality is *hacktivism*, which is a combination of the terms "hack" and "activism." Hacktivism has been described as the fusion of hacking and activism, politics, and technology. Hacktivist groups or collectives expose or hold hostage illegally obtained information to make a political statement or for revenge.

FYI: Examples of Cybersecurity Vulnerabilities Impacting Confidentiality and How to Assess Their Associated Risk

The Common Vulnerability Scoring System (CVSS) uses the CIA triad principles within the metrics used to calculate the CVSS base score. Let's take a look at two examples of security vulnerabilities that have an effect on confidentiality:

- Cisco WebEx Meetings Server Information Disclosure Vulnerability: https://tools.cisco.com/security/center/content/CiscoSecurityAdvisory/cisco-sa-20180117-wms3

- Cisco Adaptive Security Appliance Remote Code Execution and Denial of Service Vulnerability: https://tools.cisco.com/security/center/content/CiscoSecurityAdvisory/cisco-sa-20180129-asa1

The first vulnerability (Cisco WebEx Meetings Server Information Disclosure Vulnerability) is a medium-severity vulnerability that has a CVSS base score of 5.3. The CVSSv3 base score vector and parameters can be seen at the CVSS calculator at the following link:

https://tools.cisco.com/security/center/cvssCalculator.x?version=3.0&vector=CVSS:3.0/AV:N/AC:L/PR:N/UI:N/S:U/C:L/I:N/A:N

The vulnerability affects confidentiality, but it does not affect integrity or availability.

The second vulnerability (Cisco Adaptive Security Appliance Remote Code Execution and Denial of Service Vulnerability) is a critical vulnerability that has a CVSS base score of 10. The CVSSv3 base score vector and parameters can be seen at the CVSS calculator at the following link:

https://tools.cisco.com/security/center/cvssCalculator.x?version=3&vector=CVSS:3.0/AV:N/AC:L/PR:N/UI:N/S:C/C:H/I:H/A:H

This vulnerability has a direct impact on confidentiality, integrity, and availability.

FYI: Hacktivism

Throughout the years, hacktivists have used tools to perform website defacements, redirects, denial of service (DoS) attacks, information theft, website parodies, virtual sit-ins, typosquatting, and virtual sabotage. Examples include the "hacker group" that goes by the name Anonymous and their infamous hacks, and Lulzec attacks, which had a direct impact on organizations like Fox.com, the Sony PlayStation Network, and the CIA. The Lulzec hacker group leaked several passwords, stole private user data, and took networks offline. Another example is the attacks against numerous network infrastructure devices around the globe, where attackers left United States flags on the screens and configurations of those devices after abusing the Smart Install protocol.

The ability to obtain unauthorized access is often opportunistic. In this context, opportunistic means taking advantage of identified weaknesses or poorly protected information. Criminals (and nosy employees) care about the work factor, which is defined as how much effort is needed to complete a task. The longer it takes to obtain unauthorized access, the greater the chance of being caught. Complexity also plays a part—the more complex, the more opportunity to screw up, the more difficulty to cover tracks. The more a "job" costs to successfully complete, the less profit earned. The information security goal of confidentiality is to protect information from unauthorized access and misuse. The best way to do this is to implement safeguards and processes that increase the work factor and the chance of being caught. This calls for a spectrum of access controls and protections as well as ongoing monitoring, testing, and training.

What Is Integrity?

Whenever the word integrity comes to mind, so does Brian De Palma's classic 1987 film *The Untouchables*, starring Kevin Costner and Sean Connery. The film is about a group of police officers who could not be "bought off" by organized crime. They were incorruptible. Integrity is certainly one of the highest ideals of personal character. When we say someone has integrity, we mean she lives her life according to a code of ethics; she can be trusted to behave in certain ways in certain situations. It is interesting to note that those to whom we ascribe the quality of integrity can be trusted with our confidential information. As for information security, integrity has a very similar meaning. *Integrity* is basically the ability to make sure that a system and its data has not been altered or compromised. It ensures that the data is an accurate and unchanged representation of the original secure data. Integrity applies not only to data, but also to systems. For instance, if a threat actor changes the configuration of a server, firewall, router, switch, or any other infrastructure device, it is considered that he or she impacted the integrity of the system.

Data integrity is a requirement that information and programs are changed only in a specified and authorized manner. In other words, is the information the same as it was intended to be? For example, if you save a file with important information that must be relayed to members of your organization, but someone opens the file and changes some or all of the information, the file has lost its integrity. The consequences could be anything from co-workers missing a meeting you planned for a specific date and time, to 50,000 machine parts being produced with the wrong dimensions.

System integrity is a requirement that a system "performs its intended function in an unimpaired manner, free from deliberate or inadvertent unauthorized manipulation of the system." A computer virus that corrupts some of the system files required to boot the computer is an example of deliberate unauthorized manipulation.

Errors and omissions are an important threat to data and system integrity. These errors are caused not only by data entry clerks processing hundreds of transactions per day, but also by all types of users who create and edit data and code. Even the most sophisticated programs cannot detect all types of input errors or omissions. In some cases, the error is the threat, such as a data entry error or a programming error that crashes a system. In other cases, the errors create vulnerabilities. Programming and development errors, often called "bugs," can range in severity from benign to catastrophic.

To make this a bit more personal, let's talk about medical and financial information. What if you are injured, unconscious, and taken to the emergency room of a hospital, and the doctors need to look up your health information. You would want it to be correct, wouldn't you? Consider what might happen if you had an allergy to some very common treatment, and this critical information had been deleted from your medical records. Or think of your dismay if you check your bank balance after making a deposit and find that the funds have not been credited to your account!

Integrity and confidentiality are interrelated. If a user password is disclosed to the wrong person, that person could in turn manipulate, delete, or destroy data after gaining access to the system with the password he obtained. Many of the same vulnerabilities that threaten integrity also threaten confidentiality. Most notable, though, is human error. Safeguards that protect against the loss of integrity include access controls, such as encryption and digital signatures; process controls, such as code testing; monitoring controls, such as file integrity monitoring and log analysis; and behavioral controls, such as separation of duties, rotation of duties, and training.

What Is Availability?

The last component of the CIA triad is availability, which states that systems, applications, and data must be available to authorized users when needed and requested. The most common attack against availability is a denial-of-service (DoS) attack. User productivity can be greatly affected, and companies can lose a lot of money if data is not available. For example, if you are an online retailer or a cloud service provider and your ecommerce site or service is not available to your users, you could potentially lose current or future business, thus impacting revenue.

In fact, availability is generally one of the first security issues addressed by Internet service providers (ISPs). You may have heard the expressions "uptime" and "5-9s" (99.999% uptime). This means the systems that serve Internet connections, web pages, and other such services will be available to users who need them when they need them. Service providers frequently utilize *service level agreements (SLAs)* to assure their customers of a certain level of availability.

Just like confidentiality and integrity, we prize availability. We want our friends and family to "be there when we need them," we want food and drink available, we want our money available, and so forth. In some cases, our lives depend on the availability of these things, including information. Ask yourself how you would feel if you needed immediate medical care and your physician could not access your medical records. Not all threats to availability could be malicious. For example, human error or a misconfigured server or infrastructure device can cause a network outage that will have a direct impact to availability.

Figure 3-3 shows a few additional examples of threats to availability.

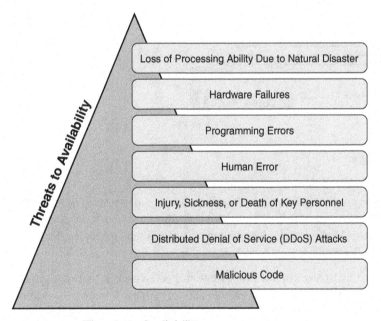

FIGURE 3-3   Threats to Availability

We are more vulnerable to availability threats than to the other components of the CIA triad. We are certain to face some of them. Safeguards that address availability include access controls, monitoring, data redundancy, resilient systems, virtualization, server clustering, environmental controls, continuity of operations planning, and incident response preparedness.

Talking About Availability, What Is a Denial of Service (DoS) Attack?

Denial-of-service (DoS) and distributed DoS (DDoS) attacks have been around for quite some time now, but there has been heightened awareness of them over the past few years. A DoS attack typically uses one system and one network connection to perform a denial of service condition to a targeted system, network, or resource. DDoS attacks use multiple computers and network connections that can be geographically dispersed (that is, distributed) to perform a denial of service condition against the victim.

DDoS attacks can generally be divided into the following three categories:

- Direct DDoS attacks
- Reflected DDos attacks
- Amplification DDoS attacks

Direct DDoS attacks occur when the source of the attack generates the packets, regardless of protocol, application, and so on, that are sent directly to the victim of the attack.

Figure 3-4 illustrates a direct DDoS attack.

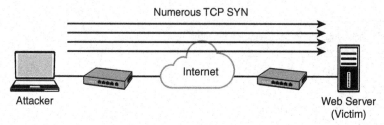

FIGURE 3-4 A Direct DDoS Attack

In Figure 3-4, the attacker launches a direct DoS to a web server (the victim) by sending numerous TCP SYN packets. This type of attack is aimed at flooding the victim with an overwhelming number of packets, oversaturating its connection bandwidth, or depleting the target's system resources. This type of attack is also known as a "SYN flood attack."

Reflected DDoS attacks occur when the sources of the attack are sent spoofed packets that appear to be from the victim, and then the sources become unwitting participants in the DDoS attacks by sending the response traffic back to the intended victim. UDP is often used as the transport mechanism because it is more easily spoofed because of the lack of a three-way handshake. For example, if the attacker (A) decides he wants to attack a victim (V), he will send packets (for example, Network Time Protocol [NTP] requests) to a source (S) that thinks these packets are legitimate. The source then responds to the NTP requests by sending the responses to the victim, who was never expecting these NTP packets from the source, as shown in Figure 3-5.

An amplification attack is a form of reflected attack in which the response traffic (sent by the unwitting participant) is made up of packets that are much larger than those that were initially sent by the attacker (spoofing the victim). An example is when DNS queries are sent, and the DNS responses are much larger in packet size than the initial query packets. The end result is that the victim's machine gets flooded by large packets for which it never actually issued queries.

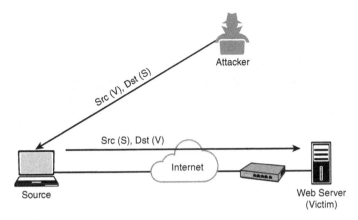

FIGURE 3-5 Reflected DDoS Attacks

Another type of DoS is caused by exploiting vulnerabilities such as buffer overflows to cause a server or even network infrastructure device to crash, subsequently causing a denial-of-service condition.

Many attackers use botnets to launch DDoS attacks. A botnet is a collection of compromised machines that the attacker can manipulate from a command and control (CnC) system to participate in a DDoS, send spam emails, and perform other illicit activities. Figure 3-6 shows how a botnet is used by an attacker to launch a DDoS attack.

In Practice

The "Five A's" of Information Security

Supporting the CIA triad of information security are five key information security principles, commonly known as the *Five A's.* Here is a quick explanation of each:

- **Accountability:** The process of tracing actions to their source. Nonrepudiation techniques, intrusion detection systems (IDS), and forensics all support accountability. This can help protect integrity and also confidentiality.

- **Assurance:** The processes, policies, and controls used to develop confidence that security measures are working as intended. Auditing, monitoring, testing, and reporting are the foundations of assurance that all three elements in CIA are protected.

- **Authentication:** The positive identification of the person or system seeking access to secured information or systems. Password, Kerberos, token, and biometric are forms of authentication. This also allows you to create control mechanisms to protect all CIA elements.

- **Authorization:** Granting users and systems a predetermined level of access to information resources.

- **Accounting:** The logging of access and usage of information resources.

CIA plus the Five A's are fundamental objectives and attributes of a cybersecurity program.

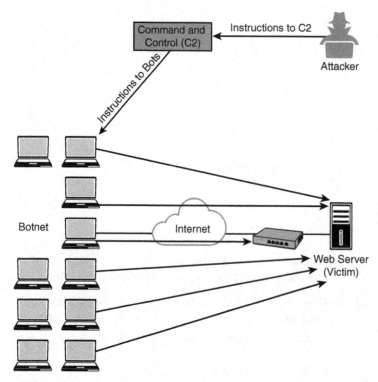

FIGURE 3-6   Botnets and Command and Control Systems

In Figure 3-6, the attacker sends instructions to the CnC; subsequently, the CnC sends instructions to the bots within the botnet to launch the DDoS attack against the victim.

Who Is Responsible for CIA?

It is the information owners' responsibility to ensure confidentiality, integrity, and availability. What does it mean to be an information owner? Under FISMA, an information owner is an official with statutory or operational authority for specified information and responsibility for establishing the criteria for its creation, collection, processing, dissemination, or disposal, which may extend to interconnected systems or groups of interconnected systems. More simply, an *information owner* has the authority and responsibility for ensuring that information is protected, from creation through destruction. For example, a bank's senior loan officer might be the owner of information pertaining to customer loans. The senior loan officer has the responsibility to decide who has access to customer loan information, the policies for using this information, and the controls to be established to protect this information.

Information technology (IT) or information systems (IS) departments are widely perceived as owning the information and information systems. Perhaps this is due to the word "information" being part of the department title. For the record, with the exception of information specific to their department, IT and IS departments should not be considered information owners. Rather, they are the people charged with maintaining the systems that store, process, and transmit the information. They are known as *information custodians*—those responsible for implementing, maintaining, and monitoring safeguards and systems. They are better known as system administrators, webmasters, and network engineers. We will be taking a closer look at each of these roles in the next chapter.

NIST's Cybersecurity Framework

Before discussing the NIST Cybersecurity Framework in detail, let's define a security framework. *Security framework* is a collective term given to guidance on topics related to information systems security, predominantly regarding the planning, implementing, managing, and auditing of overall information security practices. One of the most comprehensive frameworks for cybersecurity is the NIST Cybersecurity Framework, https://www.nist.gov/cyberframework. NIST's guidance into the trustworthiness of systems covers various technical areas. These areas include general cybersecurity guidance, cloud computing, big data, and physical systems. These efforts and guidance focus on the security objectives of confidentiality, integrity, and availability (CIA).

What Is NIST's Function?

Founded in 1901, NIST is a nonregulatory federal agency within the U.S. Commerce Department's Technology Administration. NIST's mission is to develop and promote measurement, standards, and technology to enhance productivity, facilitate trade, and improve quality of life. The Computer Security Division (CSD) is one of seven divisions within NIST's Information Technology Laboratory. The mission of NIST's CSD is to improve information systems security as follows:

- By raising awareness of IT risks, vulnerabilities, and protection requirements, particularly for new and emerging technologies.

- By researching, studying, and advising agencies of IT vulnerabilities and devising techniques for the cost-effective security and privacy of sensitive federal systems.

- By developing standards, metrics, tests, and validation programs

  - to promote, measure, and validate security in systems and services, and

  - to educate consumers and to establish minimum security requirements for federal systems.

- By developing guidance to increase secure IT planning, implementation, management, and operation.

The 2002 E-Government Act [Public Law 107-347] assigned the NIST the mission of developing an Information Assurance Framework (standards and guidelines) designed for federal information systems that are not designated as national security systems. The NIST Information Assurance Framework includes the Federal Information Processing Standards (FIPS) and Special Publications (SP). Although developed for government use, the framework is applicable to the private sector and addresses the management, operational, and technical aspects of protecting the CIA of information and information systems.

NIST defines information security as the protection of information and information systems from unauthorized access, use, disclosure, disruption, modification, or destruction in order to provide CIA. Currently, there are more than 500 NIST information security–related documents. This number includes FIPS, the SP 800 series, information, Information Technology Laboratory (ITL) bulletins, and NIST interagency reports (NIST IR):

- **Federal Information Processing Standards (FIPS):** This is the official publication series for standards and guidelines.

- **Special Publication (SP) 800 series:** This series reports on ITL research, guidelines, and outreach efforts in information system security and its collaborative activities with industry, government, and academic organizations. SP 800 series documents can be downloaded from https://csrc.nist.gov/publications/sp800.

- **Special Publication (SP) 1800 series:** This series focuses on cybersecurity practices and guidelines. SP 1800 series documents can be downloaded from https://csrc.nist.gov/publications/sp1800.

- **NIST Internal or Interagency Reports (NISTIR):** These reports focus on research findings, including background information for FIPS and SPs.

- **ITL bulletins:** Each bulletin presents an in-depth discussion of a single topic of significant interest to the information systems community. Bulletins are issued on an as-needed basis.

From access controls to wireless security, the NIST publications are truly a treasure trove of valuable and practical guidance.

So, What About ISO?

ISO is a network of the national standards institutes of more than 160 countries. Each member country is allowed one delegate, and a Central Secretariat in Geneva, Switzerland, coordinates the system. In 1946, delegates from 25 countries met in London and decided to create a new international organization, whose objective would be "to facilitate the international coordination and unification of industrial standards." The new organization, ISO, officially began operations on February 23, 1947.

ISO is a nongovernmental organization. Unlike the United Nations, its members are not delegations of national governments. Nevertheless, ISO occupies a special position between the public and private sectors. This is because, on the one hand, many of its member institutes are part of the governmental structure of their countries, or are mandated by their government. On the other hand, other members have their roots uniquely in the private sector, having been set up by national partnerships of industry associations. ISO has developed more than 13,000 International Standards on a variety of subjects, ranging from country codes to passenger safety.

The ISO/IEC 27000 series (also known as the ISMS Family of Standards, or ISO27k for short) comprises information security standards published jointly by ISO and the International Electrotechnical Commission (IEC).

The first six documents in the ISO/IEC 27000 series provide recommendations for "establishing, implementing, operating, monitoring, reviewing, maintaining, and improving an Information Security Management System." In all, there are 22 documents in the series, and several more are still under development.

- ISO 27001 is the specification for an Information Security Management System (ISMS).

- ISO 27002 describes the Code of Practice for information security management.

- ISO 27003 provides detailed implementation guidance.

- ISO 27004 outlines how an organization can monitor and measure security using metrics.

- ISO 27005 defines the high-level risk management approach recommended by ISO.

- ISO 27006 outlines the requirements for organizations that will measure ISO 27000 compliance for certification.

The framework is applicable to public and private organizations of all sizes. According to the ISO website, "the ISO standard gives recommendations for information security management for use by those who are responsible for initiating, implementing or maintaining security in their organization. It is intended to provide a common basis for developing organizational security standards and effective security management practice and to provide confidence in inter-organizational dealings."

NIST Cybersecurity Framework

NIST's Cybersecurity Framework is a collection of industry standards and best practices to help organizations manage cybersecurity risks. This framework is created in collaboration between the United States government, corporations, and individuals. The NIST Cybersecurity Framework is developed with a common taxonomy, and one of the main goals is to address and manage cybersecurity risk in a cost-effective way to protect critical infrastructure.

Private sector organizations are often using the NIST Cybersecurity Framework to enhance their cybersecurity programs

One of the goals of NIST's Cybersecurity Framework is to not only help the United States government, but provide guidance to any organization regardless of size, degree of cybersecurity risk, or maturity.

> **Note**
>
> Chapter 16 covers the NIST Cybersecurity Framework in detail.

ISO Standards

The ISO 27002 standard has its origins in Great Britain. In 1989, the UK Department of Trade and Industry's (DTI's) Commercial Computer Security Centre (CCSC) developed the "Users Code of Practice," designed to help computer users employ sound security practices and ensure the CIA of information systems. Further development came from the National Computing Centre (NCC), and later a group formed from British industry, to ensure that the Code was applicable and practical from a user's point of view. The document was originally published as British Standards guidance document PD 0003: A Code of Practice for Information Security Management. After more input was received from private sector organizations, the document was reintroduced as British Standard BS7799:1995. After two revisions in 1997 and 1999, BS7799 was proposed as an ISO standard. Though the first revisions were defeated, it was eventually adopted by the ISO after an international ballot closed in August 2000 and was published with minor amendments as ISO/IEC 17799:2000 on December 1, 2000. A new version, ISO 17799:2005, was published in 2005. In 2007, this version was renamed as 27002:2005 and incorporated into the 27000 series. The most significant difference between the 17799 series and the 27000 series is an optional certification process. Organizations' ISMS may be certified compliant with ISO/IEC 27001 by a number of Accredited Registrars worldwide.

In October 2013, ISO 27002:2005 was replaced with ISO 27002:2013. Two categories were added: Cryptography and Supplier Relationships. The Operations and Communications domain was split into two separate categories. Most important, a decision was made to remove the risk assessment guidance because it was a subset of ISO 27005, which specifically addresses information security risk management, including risk assessment, risk treatment, risk acceptance, risk communication, risk monitoring, and risk review. More information about ISO can be found at www.iso.org.

The ISO 27002:2013 Code of Practice is a comprehensive set of information security recommendations comprising best practices in information security. It is intended to serve as a single reference point for identifying the range of controls needed for most situations where information systems are used in industry and commerce as well as by large, medium, and small organizations. The term "organization" is used throughout this standard to mean both commercial and nonprofit organizations, such as public sector and government agencies. 27002:2013 does not mandate specific controls but leaves it to the organization to select and implement controls that suit them, using a risk-assessment process to identify the most appropriate controls for their specific requirements. The recommended practices are organized into the following "domains" or categories:

- Information Security Policies
- Organization of Information Security

- Human Resources Security

- Asset Management

- Access Control

- Cryptography

- Physical and Environmental Security

- Operations Security

- Communications Security

- Systems Acquisition, Development, and Maintenance

- Supplier Relationships

- Information Security Incident Management

- Business Continuity Management

- Compliance Management

We will use both the ISO 27002:2013 Code of Practice and the NIST guidance as a framework for developing procedures and policies. Using this framework will allow us to organize our approach to developing policies; it provides a structure for development and a method of grouping similar policies. The first step is to become familiar with the goals and intent of each of the security domains (or categories). In subsequent chapters, we examine each domain in depth, evaluate security practices, and develop policy.

Information Security Policies (ISO 27002:2013 Section 5)

The Information Security Policies domain focuses on information security policy requirements and the need to align policy with organizational objectives. The domain stresses the importance of management participation and support. This domain is covered in Chapter 4, "Governance and Risk Management."

The corresponding NIST Special Publications are as follows:

- **SP 800-12, R1:** "An Introduction to Information Security"

- **SP 800-100:** "Information Security Handbook: A Guide for Managers"

Organization of Information Security (ISO 27002:2013 Section 6)

The Organization of Information Security domain focuses on establishing and supporting a management structure to implement and manage information security within, across, and outside the organization. Inward-facing governance concentrates on employee and stakeholder relationships. Outward-facing governance concentrates on third-party relationships. Third parties include vendors, trading partners, customers, and service providers. This domain is covered in Chapter 4.

The corresponding NIST Special Publications are as follows:

- **SP 800-12, R1:** "An Introduction to Information Security"

- **SP 800-14:** "Generally Accepted Principles and Practices for Securing Information Technology Systems"

- **SP 800-100:** "Information Security Handbook: A Guide for Managers"

Human Resources Security Management (ISO 27002:2013 Section 7)

The Human Resources Security Management domain focuses on integrating security into the employee life cycle, agreements, and training. Human nature is to be trusting. This domain reminds us that there are both good and bad people and that we need to keep our eyes wide open. Chapter 6, "Human Resources Security," covers this domain in more detail.

The corresponding NIST Special Publications are as follows:

- **SP 800-12:** "An Introduction to Computer Security—The NIST Handbook"

- **SP 800-16:** "Information Technology Security Training Requirements: A Role- and Performance-Based Model"

- **SP 800-50:** "Building an Information Technology Security Awareness and Training Program"

- **SP 800-100:** "Information Security Handbook: A Guide for Managers"

Asset Management (ISO 27002:2013 Section 8)

The Asset Management domain focuses on developing classification schema, assigning classification levels, and maintaining accurate inventories of data and devices. The importance of documented handling standards to protect information is stressed. This domain is covered in Chapter 5, "Asset Management and Data Loss Prevention."

The corresponding NIST Special Publications are as follows:

- **SP 800-60:** "Guide for Mapping Types of Information and Information Systems to Security Categories" (two volumes)

- **SP 800-88, R1:** "Guidelines for Media Sanitization"

Access Control (ISO 27002:2013 Section 9)

The Access Control domain focuses on managing authorized access and preventing unauthorized access to information systems. This domain extends to remote locations, home offices, and mobile access. This domain is covered in Chapter 9, "Access Control Management."

The corresponding NIST Special Publications are as follows:

- **SP 800-41, R1:** "Guidelines on Firewalls and Firewall Policy"

- **SP 800-46, R2:** "Guide to Enterprise Telework, Remote Access, and Bring Your Own Device (BYOD) Security"

- **SP 800-63-3:** "Digital Identity Guidelines"

- **SP 800-63A:** "Enrollment and Identity Proofing"

- **SP 800-63B:** "Authentication and Life Cycle Management"

- **SP 800-63C:** "Federation and Assertions"

- **SP 800-77:** "Guide to IPsec VPNs"

- **SP 800-113:** "Guide to SSL VPNs"

- **SP 80 0-114:** "User's Guide to Telework and Bring Your Own Device (BYOD) Security"

- **SP 800-153:** "Guidelines for Securing Wireless Local Area Networks (WLANs)"

Cryptography (ISO 27002:2013 Section 10)

The Cryptography domain was added in the 2013 update. The domain focuses on proper and effective use of cryptography to protect the confidentiality, authenticity, and/or integrity of information. Special attention is paid to key management. This domain is included in Chapter 10, "Information Systems Acquisition, Development, and Maintenance."

The corresponding NIST Special Publications are as follows:

- **800-57:** "Recommendations for Key Management—Part 1: General (Revision 3)"

- **800-57:** "Recommendations for Key Management—Part 2: Best Practices for Key Management Organization"

- **800-57:** "Recommendations for Key Management—Part 3: Application-Specific Key Management Guidance"

- **800-64:** "Security Considerations in the System Development Life Cycle"

- **800-111:** "Guide to Storage Encryption Technologies for End User Devices"

Physical and Environmental Security (ISO 27002:2013 Section 11)

The Physical and Environmental Security domain focuses on designing and maintaining a secure physical environment to prevent unauthorized access, damage, and interference to business premises.

Special attention is paid to disposal and destruction. This domain is covered in Chapter 7, "Physical and Environmental Security."

The corresponding NIST Special Publications are as follows:

- **SP 800-12:** "An Introduction to Computer Security—The NIST Handbook"
- **SP 800-14:** "Generally Accepted Principles and Practices for Securing Information Technology Systems"
- **SP 800-88:** "Guidelines for Media Sanitization"
- **SP 800-100:** "Information Security Handbook: A Guide for Managers"

Operations Security (ISO 27002:2013 Section 12)

The Operations Security domain focuses on data center operations, integrity of operations, vulnerability management, protection against data loss, and evidence-based logging. This domain is covered in Chapter 8, "Communications and Operations Security."

The corresponding NIST Special Publications are as follows:

- **SP 800-40, R3:** "Guide to Enterprise Patch Management Technologies"
- **SP 800-115:** "Technical Guide to Information Security Testing and Assessment"
- **SP 800-83, R1:** "Guide to Malware Incident Prevention and Handling for Desktops and Laptops"
- **SP 800-92:** "Guide to Computer Security Log Management"
- **SP 800-100:** "Information Security Handbook: A Guide for Managers"

Communications Security (ISO 27002:2013 Section 13)

The Communications Security domain focuses on the protection of information in transit. The domain incorporates internal and external transmission as well as Internet-based communication. This domain is covered in Chapter 8.

The corresponding NIST Special Publications are as follows:

- **SP 800-14:** "Generally Accepted Principles and Practices for Securing Information Technology Systems"
- **SP 800-45:** "Guidelines on Electronic Mail Security"
- **SP 800-92:** "Guide to Computer Security Log Management"

Information Systems Acquisition, Development, and Maintenance (ISO 27002:2013 Section 14)

The Information Systems Acquisition, Development, and Maintenance domain focuses on the security requirements of information systems, applications, and code from conception to destruction. This sequence is referred to as the systems development life cycle. This domain is covered in Chapter 10.

The corresponding NIST Special Publication is SP 800-23: "Guidelines to Federal Organizations on Security Assurance and Acquisition/Use of Tested/Evaluated Products."

Supplier Relationships (ISO 27002:2013 Section 15)

The Supplier Relationship domain was added in the 2013 update. The domain focuses on service delivery, third-party security requirements, contractual obligations, and oversight. This domain is included in Chapter 8.

There is no corresponding NIST Special Publication.

Information Security Incident Management (ISO 27002:2013 Section 16)

The Information Security Incident Management domain focuses on a consistent and effective approach to the management of information security incidents, including detection, reporting, response, escalation, and forensic practices. This domain is covered in Chapter 11, "Cybersecurity Incident Response."

The corresponding NIST Special Publications are as follows:

- **SP 800-61, R2:** "Computer Security Incident Handling Guide"
- **SP 800-83:** "Guide to Malware Incident Prevention and Handling"
- **SP 800-86:** "Guide to Integrating Forensic Techniques into Incident Response"

Business Continuity (ISO 27002:2013 Section 17)

The Business Continuity Management domain focuses on availability and the secure provision of essential services during a disruption of normal operating conditions. ISO 22301 provides a framework to plan, establish, implement, operate, monitor, review, maintain, and continually improve a business continuity management system (BCMS). This domain is covered in Chapter 12, "Business Continuity Management."

The corresponding NIST Special Publications are as follows:

- **SP 800-34:** "Contingency Planning Guide for Information Technology System, Revision 1"
- **SP 800-84:** "Guide to Test, Training and Exercise Programs for Information Technology Plans and Capabilities"

Compliance Management (ISO 2700:2013 Section 18)

The Compliance Management domain focuses on conformance with internal policy; local, national, and international criminal and civil laws; regulatory or contractual obligations; intellectual property rights (IPR); and copyrights. This domain relates to Part III, "Regulatory Compliance" (covered in Chapters 13, 14, and 15).

The corresponding NIST Special Publications are as follows:

- **SP 800-60 Volume I:** "Guide for Mapping Types of Information and Information Systems to Security Categories"

- **SP 800-60 Volume II:** "Appendices to Guide for Mapping Types of Information and Information Systems to Security"

- **SP 800-66:** "An Introductory Resource Guide for Implementing the Health Insurance Portability and Accountability Act (HIPAA) Security Rule"

- **SP 800-122:** "Guide to Protecting the Confidentiality of Personally Identifiable Information (PII)"

Too Many Domains?

As with policies, for an information security program to be effective, it must be meaningful and relevant as well as appropriate to the size and complexity of the organization. Not all organizations will need all the policies referenced in the ISO 27002 Code of Practice. The key is to understand what domains are applicable to a given environment and then develop, adopt, and implement the controls and policies that make sense for the organization. Remember, policies must support, not hinder, the mission and goals of an organization.

Section 4.1 of the 27002:2013 Code of Practice document informs us that the order of the domains does not imply their importance, nor are they listed in priority order. As such, this book takes the liberty of reordering the sections and, where applicable, combining domains. Starting with Chapter 4 and continuing through Chapter 12, we map the security objectives of each domain to realistic, relevant, and usable practices and policies. We define goals and objectives, explore in detail relevant security issues, and discuss the applicability of the standard.

> **Note**
>
> Within each chapter, you will find "In Practice" sidebars that contain relevant policy statements. Each policy statement is preceded by a synopsis. The synopsis is included only as explanatory text and would not normally be included in a policy document. At the end of the book, you will find a comprehensive information security policy document that includes all the policy statements as well as the supporting policy elements discussed in Chapter 2, "Cybersecurity Policy Organization, Format, and Styles."

Summary

Ensuring confidentiality, integrity, and availability is the unifying principle of every information security program. Collectively referred to as the *CIA triad* or *CIA security model*, each attribute represents a fundamental objective and corresponding action related to the protection of information, processes, or systems. *Confidentiality* is protection from unauthorized access or disclosure. *Integrity* is protection from manipulation. *Availability* is protection from denial of service (DoS). In support of the CIA triad are the security principles known as the *Five A's*: accountability, assurance, authentication, accounting, and authorization.

An *information owner* is one who has been assigned the authority and responsibility for ensuring that information and related systems are protected from creation through destruction. This includes making decisions on information classification, safeguards, and controls. *Information custodians* are those responsible for implementing, maintaining, and monitoring the safeguards based on decisions made by information owners. Cohesive decision making requires a framework.

A *security framework* is a collective term given to guidance on topics related to information systems security, predominantly regarding the planning, implementing, managing, and auditing of overall information security practices. In this chapter you learned highlights of *NIST's Cybersecurity Framework*. Chapter 16 covers the NIST Cybersecurity Framework in detail. The *International Organization for Standardization* (ISO) has published a technology-neutral Code of Standards for Information Security known as the ISO/IEC 27002:2013. This standard has been internationally adopted by both private and public organizations of all sizes. ISO 27002:2013 is divided into 14 domains. Each of these categories has a control objective, compliance requirements, and recommended policy components. NIST has a number of Special Publications that complement the ISO Code of Practice. The publications provide in-depth research, recommendations, and guidance that can be applied to security domains and specific technologies. The ISO standards and the NIST Cybersecurity Framework could also be used by regulatory organizations to provide assurance that a cyber policy is robust and complete. In this book, we use both to build our information security policy and program.

Test Your Skills

MULTIPLE CHOICE QUESTIONS

1. Which of the following are the three principles in the CIA triad?

    A. Confidence, integration, availability

    B. Consistency, integrity, authentication

    C. Confidentiality, integrity, availability

    D. Confidentiality, integrity, awareness

2. Which of the following is an example of acting upon the goal of integrity?

   A. Ensuring that only authorized users can access data

   B. Ensuring that systems have 99.9% uptime

   C. Ensuring that all modifications go through a change-control process

   D. Ensuring that changes can be traced back to the editor

3. Which of the following is a control that relates to availability?

   A. Disaster recovery site

   B. Data loss prevention (DLP) system

   C. Training

   D. Encryption

4. Which of the following is an objective of confidentiality?

   A. Protection from unauthorized access

   B. Protection from manipulation

   C. Protection from denial of service

   D. Protection from authorized access

5. Which of the following is a good definition for confidentiality?

   A. The property that information is not made available or disclosed to unauthorized individuals, entities, or processes

   B. The processes, policies, and controls used to develop confidence that security measures are working as intended

   C. The positive identification of the person or system seeking access to secured information or systems

   D. The logging of access and usage of information resources

6. An important element of confidentiality is that all sensitive data needs to be controlled, audited, and monitored at all times. Which of the following provides an example about how data can be protected?

   A. Ensuring availability

   B. Encrypting data in transit and at rest

   C. Deploying faster servers

   D. Taking advantage of network programmability

7. Which of the following statements identify threats to availability? (Select all that apply.)

   A. Loss of processing capabilities due to natural disaster or human error

   B. Loss of confidentiality due to unauthorized access

C. Loss of personnel due to accident

D. Loss of reputation from unauthorized event

8. Which of the following terms best describes the logging of access and usage of information resources?

A. Accountability

B. Acceptance

C. Accounting

D. Actuality

9. Which of the following combinations of terms best describes the Five A's of information security?

A. Awareness, acceptance, availability, accountability, authentication

B. Awareness, acceptance, authority, authentication, availability

C. Accountability, assurance, authorization, authentication, accounting

D. Acceptance, authentication, availability, assurance, accounting

10. An information owner is responsible for _____.

A. maintaining the systems that store, process, and transmit information

B. protecting the business reputation and results derived from use of that information

C. protecting the people and processes used to access digital information

D. ensuring that information is protected, from creation through destruction

11. Which of the following terms best describes ISO?

A. Internal Standards Organization

B. International Organization for Standardization

C. International Standards Organization

D. Internal Organization of Systemization

12. Which of the following statements best describes opportunistic crime?

A. Crime that is well planned

B. Crime that is targeted

C. Crime that takes advantage of identified weaknesses or poorly protected information

D. Crime that is quick and easy

13. Which of the following terms best describes the motivation for hacktivism?

A. Financial

B. Political

C. Personal

E. Fun

14. The longer it takes a criminal to obtain unauthorized access, the _____

    A. more time it takes

    B. more profitable the crime is

    C. better chance of success

    D. better chance of getting caught

15. Which of the following terms best describes an attack whose purpose is to make a machine or network resource unavailable for its intended use?

    A. Man-in-the-middle

    B. Data breach

    C. Denial of service

    D. SQL injection

16. Information custodians are responsible for _____

    A. writing policy

    B. classifying data

    C. approving budgets

    D. implementing, maintaining, and monitoring safeguards

17. The National Institute of Standards and Technology (NIST) is a(n) _____

    A. international organization

    B. privately funded organization

    C. U.S. government institution, part of the U.S. Department of Commerce

    D. European Union agency

18. The International Organization for Standardization (ISO) is _____

    A. a nongovernmental organization

    B. an international organization

    C. headquartered in Geneva

    D. all of the above

19. The current ISO family of standards that relates to information security is _____.

    A. BS 7799:1995

    B. ISO 17799:2006

C. ISO/IEC 27000

D. None of the above

20. Which of the following terms best describes the security domain that relates to managing authorized access and preventing unauthorized access to information systems?

A. Security policy

B. Access control

C. Compliance

D. Risk assessment

21. Which of the following terms best describes the security domain that relates to how data is classified and valued?

A. Security policy

B. Asset management

C. Compliance

D. Access control

22. Which of the following terms best describes the security domain that includes HVAC, fire suppression, and secure offices?

A. Operations

B. Communications

C. Risk assessment

D. Physical and environmental controls

23. Which of the following terms best describes the security domain that aligns most closely with the objective of confidentiality?

A. Access control

B. Compliance

C. Incident management

D. Business continuity

24. The primary objective of the _____ domain is to ensure conformance with GLBA, HIPAA, PCI/DSS, and FERPA.

A. Security Policy

B. Compliance

C. Access Control

D. Contract and Regulatory

25. Processes that include responding to a malware infection, conducting forensics investigations, and reporting breaches are included in the _____ domain.

    A. Security Policy

    B. Operations and Communications

    C. Incident Management

    D. Business Continuity Management

26. Which of the following terms best describes a synonym for business continuity?

    A. Authorization

    B. Authentication

    C. Availability

    D. Accountability

27. Which domain focuses on service delivery, third-party security requirements, contractual obligations, and oversight?

    A. Incident Handling and Forensics

    B. Security Policy

    C. Supplier Relationships

    D. Information Security Incident Management

28. Which domain focuses on proper and effective use of cryptography to protect the confidentiality, authenticity, and/or integrity of information?

    A. Cryptography

    B. Cryptanalysis

    C. Encryption and VPN Governance

    D. Legal and Compliance

29. Which domain focuses on integrating security into the employee life cycle, agreements, and training?

    A. Operations and Communications

    B. Human Resources Security Management

    C. Governance

    D. Legal and Compliance

30. Which of the following security objectives is most important to an organization?

    A. Confidentiality

    B. Integrity

    C. Availability

    D. The answer may vary from organization to organization

31. Which of the following are some of the components of NIST's Cybersecurity Framework core functions? (Choose all that apply.)

    A. Identify

    B. Integrity

    C. Detect

    D. Protect

    E. All of the above

EXERCISES

EXERCISE 3.1: Understanding CIA

1. Define the security term "confidentiality." Provide an example of a business situation where confidentiality is required.

2. Define the security term "integrity." Provide an example of a business situation in which the loss of integrity could result in significant harm.

3. Define the security term "availability." Provide an example of a business situation in which availability is more important than confidentiality.

EXERCISE 3.2: Understanding Opportunistic Cybercrime

1. Define what is meant by an "opportunistic" crime.

2. Provide an example.

3. Locate (online) a copy of the most recent Verizon Data Breach Incident Report. What percentage of cybercrimes are considered "opportunistic"?

EXERCISE 3.3: Understanding Hacktivism or DDoS

1. Find a recent news article relating to either hacktivism or a distributed denial of service (DDoS) attack.

2. Summarize the attack.

3. Explain why the attacker was successful (or not).

EXERCISE 3.4: Understanding NIST and ISO

1. At their respective websites, read the Mission and About sections of both ISO (www.iso.org) and the NIST Computer Security Resource Center (http://csrc.nist.gov/). Describe the similarities and differences between the organizations.

2. Which do you think is more influential, and why?

3. Identify how they complement each other.

EXERCISE 3.5: Understanding ISO 27002

1. Choose one of the ISO 27002:2013 categories and explain why this domain is of particular interest to you.

2. ISO 27002 Supplier Relationships (Section 15) was added in the 2013 version. Why do you think this section was added?

3. 27002:2013 does not mandate specific controls but leaves it to the organization to select and implement controls that suit them. NIST Special Publications provide specific guidance. In your opinion, which approach is more useful?

PROJECTS

PROJECT 3.1: Conducting a CIA Model Survey

1. Survey 10 people about the importance of the CIA model to them. Use the following table as a template. Ask them to name three types of data they have on their phone or tablet. For each data type, ask which is more important—that the information on their device be kept confidential (C), be correct (I), or be available (A).

#	Participant Name	Device Type	Data Type 1	CIA	Data Type 2	CIA	Data Type 3	CIA
1.	Sue Smith	iPhone	Phone numbers	I	Pictures	A	Text messages	C
2.								
3.								

2. Summarize the responses.

3. Are the responses in line with your expectations? Why or why not?

PROJECT 3.2: **Preparing a Report Based on the NIST Special Publications 800 Series Directory**

1. Locate the NIST Special Publications 800 Series directory.

2. Read through the list of documents. Choose one that interests you and read it.

3. Prepare a report that addresses the following:

   a. Why you chose this topic

   b. What audience the document was written for

   c. Why this document would be applicable to other audiences

   d. The various sections of the document

   e. Whether the document addresses confidentiality, integrity, or availability

PROJECT 3.3: **Preparing a Report on ISO 27001 Certification**

1. Research how many organizations are currently ISO 27001–certified.

2. Prepare a report on how an organization achieves ISO 27001 certification.

PROJECT 3.4: **NIST's Cybersecurity Framework Spreadsheet**

1. Download NIST's Cybersecurity Framework spreadsheet from: https://www.nist.gov/cyberframework.

   Familiarize yourself with the different components, categories, subcategories, and informative references of the NIST Cybersecurity Framework.

2. Download NIST's CSF tool from https://www.nist.gov/cyberframework/csf-reference-tool. Familiarize yourself with all the capabilities of the tool and how it may allow you to start developing your own cybersecurity program.

3. Prepare a report that explains how an enterprise or private sector organization can leverage the framework to help with the following:

   ■ Identify assets and associated risks.

   ■ Protect against threat actors.

   ■ Detect and respond to any cybersecurity events and incidents.

   ■ Recover after a cybersecurity incident happened.

Case Study

Policy Writing Approach

Regional Bank has been growing rapidly. In the past two years, it has acquired six smaller financial institutions. The long-term strategic plan is for the bank to keep growing and to "go public" within the next three to five years. FDIC regulators have told management that they will not approve any additional acquisitions until the bank strengthens its information security program. The regulators commented that Regional Bank's information security policy is confusing, lacking in structure, and filled with discrepancies. You have been tasked with "fixing" the problems with the policy document.

1. Consider the following questions: Where do you begin this project? Would you use any material from the original document? What other materials should you request? Would you want to interview the author of the original policy? Who else would you interview? Should the bank work toward ISO certification? Which ISO 27002:2013 domains and sections would you include? Should you use NIST's Cybersecurity Framework and related tools? What other criteria should you consider?

2. Create a project plan of how you would approach this project.

References

Regulations Cited

"NIST Cybersecurity Framework," accessed 04/2018, https://www.nist.gov/cyberframework.

"Federal Code 44 U.S.C., Sec. 3542," accessed 04/2018, https://www.gpo.gov/fdsys/pkg/CFR-2002-title44-vol1/content-detail.html.

"The Cybersecurity Framework: Implementation Guidance for Federal Agencies," accessed 04/2018, https://csrc.nist.gov/publications/detail/nistir/8170/draft.

"Public Law 107–347–E-Government Act of 2002," official website of the U.S. Government Printing Office, accessed 04/2018, www.gpo.gov/fdsys/pkg/PLAW-107publ347/content-detail.html.

ISO Research

"International Standard ISO/IEC 27001," First Edition 2005-10-15, published by ISO, Switzerland.

"International Standard ISO/IEC 27000," Second Edition 2012-12-01, published by ISO, Switzerland.

"International Standard ISO/IEC 27002:2013," Second Edition 2013-10-01, published by ISO, Switzerland.

"About ISO," official website of the International Organization for Standardization (ISO), accessed on 04/2018, https://www.iso.org/about-us.html.

"A Short History of the ISO 27000 Standards: Official," *The ISO 27000 Directory*, accessed on 04/2018, www.27000.org/thepast.htm.

"An Introduction to ISO 27001, ISO 27002, ... ISO 27008," *The ISO 27000 Directory*, accessed on 04/2018, www.27000.org.

"The ISO/IEC 27000 Family of Information Security Standards," IT Governance, accessed 04/2018, https://www.itgovernance.co.uk/iso27000-family.

"ISO/IEC 27000 Series," Wikipedia, accessed 04/2018, https://en.wikipedia.org/wiki/ISO/IEC_27000-series.

NIST Research

"NIST General Information," official website of the National Institute of Standards and Technology, accessed 04/2018, https://www.nist.gov/director/pao/nist-general-information.

"NIST Computer Security Division," official website of the NIST Computer Security Resource Center, accessed 04/2018, https://csrc.nist.gov.

"Federal Information Processing Standards (FIPS) Publications," official website of the NIST Computer Security Resource Center, accessed 04/2018, https://www.nist.gov/itl/fips-general-information.

"Special Publications (800 Series) Directory," official website of the NIST Computer Security Resource Center, accessed 04/2018, https://csrc.nist.gov/publications.

Other References

"Distributed Denial of Service Attack (DDoS)," Security Search, accessed 05/2018, http://searchsecurity.techtarget.com/definition/distributed-denial-of-service-attack.

"Hacktivism," Wikipedia, accessed 05/2018, http://en.wikipedia.org/wiki/index.html?curid=162600.

Poulen, K., and Zetter, K. "U.S. Intelligence Analyst Arrested in WikiLeaks Video Probe," *Wired Magazine*, accessed 05/2018, http://www.wired.com/threatlevel/2010/06/leak/.

"Edward Snowden," accessed 05/2018, https://www.biography.com/people/edward-snowden-21262897.

"What Is WikiLeaks," WikiLeaks, accessed 05/2018, https://wikileaks.org.

"Cisco security: Russia, Iran switches hit by attackers who leave US flag on screens," ZDNet, accessed on 05/2018.

Chapter | **4**

Governance and Risk Management

Chapter Objectives

After reading this chapter and completing the exercises, you will be able to do the following:

- Define governance.
- Explain cybersecurity governance and NIST's Cybersecurity Framework.
- Explain the importance of strategic alignment.
- Know how to manage cybersecurity policies.
- Describe cybersecurity-related roles and responsibilities.
- Identify the components of risk management.
- Create policies related to cybersecurity policy, governance, and risk management.

NIST's Cybersecurity Framework provides guidelines around the governance structure necessary to implement and manage cybersecurity policy operations, risk management, and incident handling across and outside of the organization. The framework was created to help protect the United States critical infrastructure, but it is used by many nongovernment organizations to build a strong cybersecurity program.

This chapter also includes a discussion of risk management because it is a fundamental aspect of governance, decision making, and policy. The NIST Cybersecurity Framework includes several references to ISO/IEC standards, as well as other sources for organizations to help create an appropriate risk management process. In the case of the ISO/IEC standards, risk management is important enough that it warrants two sets of standards: ISO/IEC 27005 and ISO/IEC 31000. In addition, the Information Security Policies (ISO 27002:2013 Section 5) and Organization of Information Security (ISO 27002:2013 Section 6) are closely related, so we address all of these domains in this chapter.

Understanding Cybersecurity Policies

As described in Chapter 2, cybersecurity policies, standards, procedures, and plans exist for one reason—to protect the organization and, by extension, its constituents from harm. The objective of cybersecurity policies is threefold:

- Cybersecurity directives should be codified in a written policy document.

- It is important that management participate in policy development and visibly support the policy.

- Management must strategically align cybersecurity with business requirements and relevant laws and regulations.

Internationally recognized security standards such as ISO 27002:2013 and the NIST Cybersecurity Framework can provide a framework, but ultimately each organization must construct its own security strategy and policy taking into consideration organizational objectives and regulatory requirements.

What Is Governance?

NIST defines *governance* as "the process of establishing and maintaining a framework and supporting management structure and processes to provide assurance that information security strategies are aligned with and support business objectives, are consistent with applicable laws and regulations through adherence to policies and internal controls, and provide assignment of responsibility, all in an effort to manage risk."

What Is Meant by Strategic Alignment?

The two approaches to cybersecurity are silo-based and integrated. A *silo-based approach* to cybersecurity assigns responsibility for *being secure* to the IT department, views compliance as discretionary, and has little or no organizational accountability. The silo-based approach is illustrated in Figure 4-1.

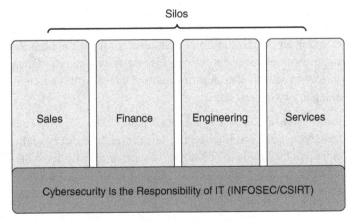

FIGURE 4-1   Silo-Based Approach to Cybersecurity

An ***integrated approach*** recognizes that security and success are intertwined. The integrated approach is illustrated in Figure 4-2.

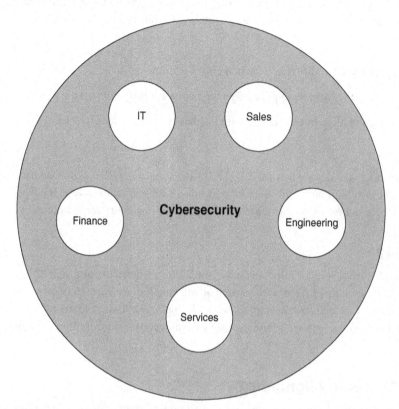

FIGURE 4-2   Integrated Approach to Cybersecurity

One of the drawbacks of a silo-based approach is that organizational silos do not share the same priorities, goals, or even the same tools, so each silo or department operates as individual business units or entities within the enterprise. Silos occur because of how an organization is structured. Managers are responsible for one specific department within an organization, and each manager has different priorities, responsibilities, and vision. This can be problematic for a good cybersecurity program. Often, stakeholders are not aware of the priorities and goals of other departments, and there is little communication, collaboration, and teamwork among these business units.

When strategically aligned, security functions as a business enabler that adds value. Security is an expected topic of discussion among decision makers and is given the same level of respect as other fundamental drivers and influencing elements of the business. This doesn't happen magically. It requires leadership that recognizes the value of cybersecurity, invests in people and processes, encourages discussion and debate, and treats security in the same fashion as every other business requirement.

It also requires that cybersecurity professionals recognize that the true value of cybersecurity is protecting the business from harm and achieving organizational objectives. Visible management support coupled with written policy formalizes and communicates the organizational commitment to cybersecurity.

Regulatory Requirements

In an effort to protect the citizens of the United States, legislators recognized the importance of written cybersecurity policies. The following are a few examples of regulations that are related to cybersecurity and privacy:

- Gramm-Leach-Bliley Act (GLBA)

- Health Insurance Portability and Accountability Act (HIPAA)

- Sarbanes-Oxley (SOX)

- Family Educational Rights and Privacy Act (FERPA)

- Federal Information Systems Management Act (FISMA)

- Payment Card Industry Data Security Standard (PCI DSS)—not a government regulation, but very relevant and with an international audience

- The New York Department of Financial Services (DFS) Cybersecurity Regulation 23 NYCRR 500.

All the listed regulations and standards require covered entities to have in place written policies and procedures that protect their information assets. They also require the policies to be reviewed on a regular basis. Each of these legislative acts better secured each person's private information and introduced governance to reduce fraudulent reporting of corporate earnings.

Many organizations find that they are subject to more than one set of regulations. For example, publicly traded banks are subject to both GLBA and SOX requirements, whereas medical billing companies find themselves subject to both HIPAA and GLBA. Organizations that try to write their policies to match federal state regulations find the task daunting. Fortunately, the regulations published to date have enough in common that a well-written set of cybersecurity policies based on a framework such as the ISO 27002 can be mapped to multiple regulatory requirements. Policy administrative notations often include a cross-reference to specific regulatory requirements.

A good governance program examines the organization's environment, operations, culture, and threat landscape against industry standard frameworks. It also aligns compliance to organization risk and incorporates business processes. In addition, having a good governance and appropriate tools allows you to measure progress against mandates and achieve compliance standards.

To have a strong cybersecurity program, you need to ensure business objectives take into account risk tolerance and that the resulting policies are accountable. Governance includes many types of policies. The sections that follow cover examples of the most relevant policies.

User-Level Cybersecurity Policies

Cybersecurity policies are governance statements written with the intent of directing the organization. Correctly written, policies can also be used as teaching documents that influence behavior. An Acceptable Use Policy document and corresponding agreement should be developed specifically for distribution to the user community. The Acceptable Use Policy should include only pertinent information and, as appropriate, explanations and examples. The accompanying agreement requires users to acknowledge that they understand their responsibilities and affirm their individual commitment.

Vendor Cybersecurity Policies

As we discuss in Chapter 8, "Communications and Operations Security," companies can outsource work but not responsibility or liability. Vendors or business partners (often referred to as "third parties") that store, process, transmit, or access information assets should be required to have controls that meet or, in some cases, exceed organizational requirements. One of the most efficient ways to evaluate vendor security is to provide them with a vendor version of organizational security policies and require them to attest to their compliance. The vendor version should contain only policies that are applicable to third parties and should be sanitized as to not disclose any confidential information.

Cybersecurity Vulnerability Disclosure Policies

Vendors often create and publicly publish a vulnerability disclosure policy. This is a common practice among mature vendors (especially in the technology sector). In this policy the vendor explains how it receives, manages, fixes, and discloses security vulnerabilities in the products and services that could impact its customers. As an example, the following URL includes Cisco's public security vulnerability policy:

https://www.cisco.com/c/en/us/about/security-center/security-vulnerability-policy.html

The following URL is another example—the CERT/CC vulnerability disclosure policy:

http://www.cert.org/vulnerability-analysis/vul-disclosure.cfm

Client Synopsis of Cybersecurity Policies

In this context, *client* refers to companies to which an organization provides services. A synopsis of the cybersecurity policy should be available upon request to clients. As applicable to the client base, the synopsis could be expanded to incorporate incident response and business continuity procedures, notifications, and regulatory cross-references. The synopsis should not disclose confidential business information unless the recipients are required to sign a nondisclosure agreement.

In Practice

Cybersecurity Policy

Synopsis: The organization is required to have a written cybersecurity policy and supporting documents.

Policy Statement:

- The company must have written cybersecurity policies.

- Executive management is responsible for establishing the mandate and general objectives of the cybersecurity policy.

- The policies must support organizational objectives.

- The policies must comply with relevant statutory, regulatory, and contractual requirements.

- The policies must be communicated to all relevant parties both within and external to the company.

- As applicable, standards, guidelines, plans, and procedures must be developed to support the implementation of policy objectives and requirements.

- For the purpose of educating the workforce, user-level documents will be derived from the cybersecurity policy, including but not limited to Acceptable Use Policy, Acceptable Use Agreement, and Information Handling Instructions.

- Any cybersecurity policy distributed outside the organization must be sanitized.

- All documentation will be retained for a period of six years from the last effective date.

FYI: Policy Hierarchy Refresher

- *Guiding principles* are the fundamental philosophy or beliefs of an organization and reflect the kind of company an organization seeks to be. The policy hierarchy represents the implementation of guiding principles.

- *Policies* are directives that codify organizational requirements.

- *Standards* are implementation specifications.

- *Baselines* are an aggregate of minimum implementation standards and security controls for a specific category or grouping.

- *Guidelines* are suggested actions or recommendations.

- *Procedures* are instructions.

- *Plans* are strategic and tactical guidance used to execute an initiative or respond to a situation, within a certain timeframe, usually with defined stages and with designated resources.

Who Authorizes Cybersecurity Policy?

A policy is a reflection of the organization's commitment, direction, and approach. Cybersecurity policies should be authorized by executive management. Depending on the size, legal structure, and/or regulatory requirements of the organization, executive management may be defined as owners, directors, or executive officers.

Because executive management is responsible for and can be held legally liable for the protection of information assets, it is incumbent upon those in leadership positions to remain invested in the proper execution of the policy as well as the activities of oversight that ensure it. The National Association of Corporate Directors (NACD), the leading membership organization for Boards and Directors in the U.S., recommends five essential principles:

- Approach cybersecurity as an enterprise-wide risk management issue, not just an IT issue.

- Understand the legal implications of cyber risks.

- Boards should have adequate access to cybersecurity expertise; cyber-risk management should be given adequate time on board agendas.

- Directors should set expectations that management will establish an enterprise cyber-risk management framework.

- Boards need to discuss details of cyber-risk management and risk treatment.

Policies should be reviewed at planned intervals to ensure their continuing suitability, adequacy, and effectiveness.

FYI: Director's Liability and Duty of Care

In tort law, duty of care is a legal standard applied to directors and officers of a corporation. In 1996, the shareholders of Caremark International, Inc., brought a derivative action, alleging that the Board of Directors breached its duty of care by failing to put in place adequate internal control systems. In response, the Delaware court defined a multifactor test designed to determine when duty of care is breached:

- The directors knew or should have known that violations of the law were occurring, and

- The directors took no steps in a good faith effort to prevent or remedy the situation, and

- Such failure proximately resulted in the losses complained of.

According to the firm of Orrick, Herrington, and Sutcliffe, LLP, "in short, as long as a director acts in good faith, as long as she exercises proper due care and does not exhibit gross negligence, she cannot be held liable for failing to anticipate or prevent a cyber-attack. However, if a plaintiff can show that a director failed to act in the face of a known duty to act, thereby demonstrating a conscious disregard for [her] responsibilities, it could give rise to a claim for breach of fiduciary duty."

What Is a Distributed Governance Model?

It is time to bury the myth that "security is an IT issue." Security is not an isolated discipline and should not be siloed. Designing and maintaining a secure environment that supports the mission of the organization requires enterprise-wide input, decision making, and commitment. The foundation of a distributed governance model is the principle that stewardship is an organizational responsibility. Effective security requires the active involvement, cooperation, and collaboration of stakeholders, decision makers, and the user community. Security should be given the same level of respect as other fundamental drivers and influencing elements of the business.

Chief Information Security Officer (CISO)

Even in the most security-conscious organization, someone still needs to provide expert leadership. That is the role of the CISO. As a member of the executive team, the CISO is positioned to be a leader, teacher, and security champion. The CISO coordinates and manages security efforts across the company, including IT, human resources (HR), communications, legal, facilities management, and other groups, as shown in Figure 4-3.

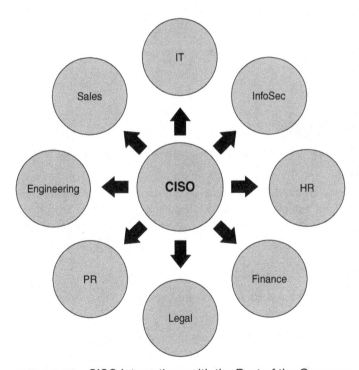

FIGURE 4-3   CISO Interactions with the Rest of the Company

The most successful CISOs successfully balance security, productivity, and innovation. The CISO must be an advocate for security as a business enabler while being mindful of the need to protect the organization from unrecognized harm. The CISO must be willing to not be the most popular person in the room. This position generally reports directly to a senior functional executive (CEO, COO, CFO, General Counsel) and should have an unfiltered communication channel to the Board of Directors.

In smaller organizations, this function is often vested in the non-executive-level position of Information Security Officer (ISO). A source of conflict in many companies is whom the ISO should report to and if the ISO should be a member of the IT team. It is not uncommon or completely out of the question for the position to report to the CIO. However, this chain of command can raise questions concerning adequate levels of independence. To ensure appropriate segregation of duties, the ISO should report directly to the Board or to a senior officer with sufficient independence to perform assigned tasks. Security officers should not be assigned operational responsibilities within the IT department. They should have sufficient knowledge, background, and training, as well as a level of authority that enables them to adequately and effectively perform their assigned tasks. Security decision making should not be a singular task. Supporting the CISO or ISO should be a multidisciplinary committee that represents functional and business units.

In Practice

CISO Policy

Synopsis: To define the role of the CISO as well as the reporting structure and lines of communication.

Policy Statement:

- The COO will appoint the CISO.

- The CISO will report directly to the COO.

- At his or her discretion, the CISO may communicate directly with members of the Board of Directors.

- The CISO is responsible for managing the cybersecurity program, ensuring compliance with applicable regulations and contractual obligations, and working with business units to align cybersecurity requirements and business initiatives.

- The CISO will function as an internal consulting resource on cybersecurity issues.

- The CISO will chair the Cybersecurity Steering Committee.

- The CISO will be a standing member of the Incident Response Team and the Continuity of Operations Team.

- Quarterly, the CISO will report to the executive management team on the overall status of the cybersecurity program. The report should discuss material matters, including such issues as risk assessment, risk management, control decisions, service provider arrangements, results of testing, security breaches or violations, and recommendations for policy changes.

Cybersecurity Steering Committee

Creating a culture of security requires positive influences at multiple levels within an organization. Having a Cybersecurity Steering Committee provides a forum to communicate, discuss, and debate security requirements and business integration. Typically, members represent a cross-section of business lines or departments, including operations, risk, compliance, marketing, audit, sales, HR, and legal. In addition to providing advice and counsel, their mission is to spread the gospel of security to their colleagues, coworkers, subordinates, and business partners.

In Practice

Cybersecurity Steering Committee Policy

Synopsis: The Cybersecurity Steering Committee (ISC) is tasked with supporting the cybersecurity program.

Policy Statement:

- The Cybersecurity Steering Committee serves in an advisory capacity in regard to the implementation, support, and management of the cybersecurity program, alignment with business objectives, and compliance with all applicable state and federal laws and regulations.

- The Cybersecurity Steering Committee provides an open forum to discuss business initiatives and security requirements. Security is expected to be given the same level of respect as other fundamental drivers and influencing elements of the business.

- Standing membership will include the CISO (Chair), the COO, the Director of Information Technology, the Risk Officer, the Compliance Officer, and business unit representatives. Adjunct committee members may include but are not limited to representatives of HR, training, and marketing.

- The Cybersecurity Steering Committee will meet on a monthly basis.

Organizational Roles and Responsibilities

In addition to the CISO and the Cybersecurity Steering Committee, distributed throughout the organization are a variety of roles that have cybersecurity-related responsibilities. For example:

- **Compliance Officer:** Responsible for identifying all applicable cybersecurity-related statutory, regulatory, and contractual requirements.

- **Privacy Officer:** Responsible for the handling and disclosure of data as it relates to state, federal, and international law and customs.

- **Internal audit:** Responsible for measuring compliance with Board-approved policies and to ensure that controls are functioning as intended.

- **Incident response team:** Responsible for responding to and managing security-related incidents.

- **Data owners:** Responsible for defining protection requirements for the data based on classification, business need, legal, and regulatory requirements; reviewing the access controls; and monitoring and enforcing compliance with policies and standards.

- **Data custodians:** Responsible for implementing, managing, and monitoring the protection mechanisms defined by data owners and notifying the appropriate party of any suspected or known policy violations or potential endangerments.

- **Data users:** Are expected to act as agents of the security program by taking reasonable and prudent steps to protect the systems and data they have access to.

Each of these responsibilities should be documented in policies, job descriptions, or employee manuals.

Evaluating Cybersecurity Policies

Directors and executive management have a fiduciary obligation to manage the company in a responsible manner. It is important that they be able to accurately gauge adherence to policy directives, the effectiveness of cybersecurity policies, and the maturity of the cybersecurity program. Standardized methodologies such as audits and maturity models can be used as evaluation and reporting mechanisms. Organizations may choose to conduct these evaluations using in-house personnel or engage independent third parties. The decision criteria include the size and complexity of the organization, regulatory requirements, available expertise, and segregation of duties. To be considered *independent*, assessors should not be responsible for, benefit from, or have in any way influenced the design, installation, maintenance, and operation of the target, or the policies and procedures that guide its operation.

Audit

A *cybersecurity audit* is a systematic, evidence-based evaluation of how well the organization conforms to such established criteria as Board-approved policies, regulatory requirements, and internationally recognized standards, such as the ISO 27000 series. Audit procedures include interviews, observation, tracing documents to management policies, review of practices, review of documents, and tracing data to source documents. An *audit report* is a formal opinion (or disclaimer) of the audit team based on predefined scope and criteria. Audit reports generally include a description of the work performed, any inherent limitations of the work, detailed findings, and recommendations.

FYI: Certified Cybersecurity Auditor (CISA)

The CISA certification is granted by ISACA (previously known as the Information Systems Audit and Control Association) to professionals who have demonstrated a high degree of audit-related knowledge and have verifiable work experience. The CISA certification is well respected across the globe, and the credibility of its continuing professional education (CPE) program ensures that CISA-certified professionals maintain their skill set. The American National Standards Institute (ANSI) accredited the CISA certification program under ISO/IEC 17024:2003: General Requirements for Bodies Operating Certification Systems of Persons. For more information about ISACA certification, visit www.isaca.org.

Capability Maturity Model

A *capability maturity model (CMM)* is used to evaluate and document process maturity for a given area. The term "maturity" relates to the degree of formality and structure, ranging from ad hoc to optimized processes. Funded by the United States Air Force, the CMM was developed in the mid 1980s at the Carnegie Mellon University Software Engineering Institute. The objective was to create a model for the military to use to evaluate software development. It has since been adopted for subjects as diverse as cybersecurity, software engineering, systems engineering, project management, risk management, system acquisition, information technology (IT) services, and personnel management. The NIST Cybersecurity Framework in some cases can be considered as a maturity model or as a "framework" to measure the maturity of your cybersecurity program.

As documented in Table 4-1, a variation of the CMM can be used to evaluate enterprise cybersecurity maturity. Contributors to the application of the model should possess intimate knowledge of the organization and expertise in the subject area.

TABLE 4-1   Capability Maturity Model (CMM) Scale

Level	State	Description
0	Nonexistent	The organization is unaware of the need for policies or processes.
1	Ad hoc	There are no documented policies or processes; there is sporadic activity.
2	Repeatable	Policies and processes are not fully documented; however, the activities occur on a regular basis.
3	Defined process	Policies and processes are documented and standardized; there is an active commitment to implementation.
4	Managed	Policies and processes are well defined, implemented, measured, and tested.
5	Optimized	Policies and process are well understood and have been fully integrated into the organizational culture.

As Figure 4-4 illustrates, the result is easily expressed in a graphic format and succinctly conveys the state of the cybersecurity program on a per-domain basis. The challenge with any scale-based model is that sometimes the assessment falls in between levels, in which case it is perfectly appropriate to use gradations (such as 3.5). This is an effective mechanism for reporting to those responsible for oversight, such as the Board of Directors or executive management. Process improvement objectives are a natural outcome of a CMM assessment.

The Board of Directors (or organizational equivalent) is generally the authoritative policy-making body and is responsible for overseeing the development, implementation, and maintenance of the cybersecurity program. The use of the term "oversee" is meant to convey the Board's conventional supervisory role, leaving day-to-day responsibilities to management. Executive management should be tasked with providing support and resources for proper program development, administration, and maintenance, as well as ensuring strategic alignment with organizational objectives.

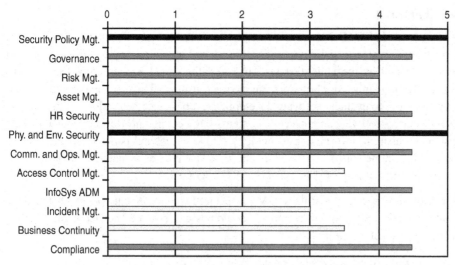

Information Security Program Maturity Assessment

FIGURE 4-4   Capability Maturity Model (CMM) Assessment

Cybersecurity Policy Authorization and Oversight Policy

Synopsis: Cybersecurity policies must be authorized by the Board of Directors. The relevancy and the effectiveness of the policy must be reviewed annually.

Policy Statement:

- The Board of Directors must authorize the cybersecurity policy.

- An annual review of the cybersecurity policy must be conducted.

- The Chief Information Security Officer (CISO) is responsible for managing the review process.

- Changes to the policy must be presented to and approved by a majority of the Board of Directors.

- The Chief Operating Officer (COO) and the CISO typically jointly present an annual report to the Board of Directors that provides them the information necessary to measure the organizations' adherence to the cybersecurity policy objectives and the maturity of the cybersecurity program.

- When in-house knowledge is not sufficient to review or audit aspects of the cybersecurity policy, or if circumstances dictate independence, third-party professionals must be engaged.

Revising Cybersecurity Policies: Change Drivers

Because organizations change over time, policies need to be revisited. Change *drivers* are events that modify how a company does business. Change drivers can be any of the following:

- Demographic

- Economic

- Technological

- Regulatory

- Personnel related

Examples of change drivers include company acquisition, new products, services or technology, regulatory updates, entering into a contractual obligation, and entering a new market. Change can introduce new vulnerabilities and risks. Change drivers should trigger internal assessments and ultimately a review of policies. Policies should be updated accordingly and subject to reauthorization.

Let's take a look at the example illustrated in Figure 4-5.

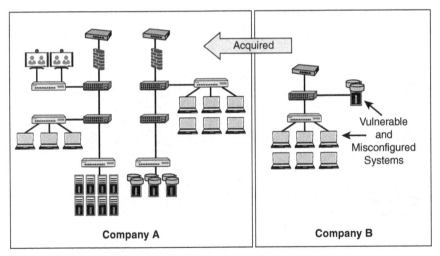

FIGURE 4-5   Example of Change Drivers in Cybersecurity Policies

In Figure 4-5, two companies are shown (Company A and Company B). Company A acquired Company B. Company B never had the resources to create an appropriate cybersecurity governance and had never updated its cybersecurity policies. As a result, several vulnerable systems now present a risk for Company A. In this example, Company A extends its cybersecurity policies and program to completely replace those of Company B.

NIST Cybersecurity Framework Governance Subcategories and Informative References

The NIST Cybersecurity Framework includes several subcategories related to governance. The following are those subcategories:

- **ID.GV-1:** Organizational information security policy is established.

- **ID.GV-2:** Information security roles and responsibilities are coordinated and aligned with internal roles and external partners.

- **ID.GV-3:** Legal and regulatory requirements regarding cybersecurity, including privacy and civil liberties obligations, are understood and managed.

- **ID.GV-4:** Governance and risk management processes address cybersecurity risks.

Each subcategory related to governance has several informative references that can be beneficial to you when establishing your cybersecurity program and governance. The informative references (standards and guidelines) related to ID.GV-1 (organizational information security policy is established) are shown in Figure 4-6. The informative references include the standards and guidelines that you learned in Chapter 3, "Cybersecurity Framework," except the Control Objectives for Information and Related Technologies (COBIT). COBIT is a framework created by international professional association ISACA for IT management and governance. It defines a set of controls organized around a logical framework of IT processes and enablers.

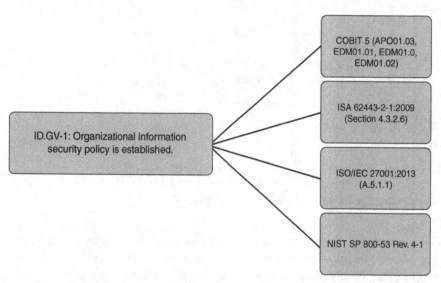

FIGURE 4-6   NIST Cybersecurity Framework ID.GV-1 Informative References

Figure 4-7 shows the informative references related to the ID.GV-2 subcategory.

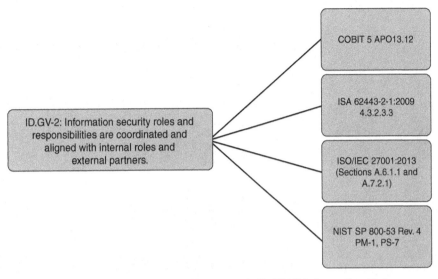

FIGURE 4-7   NIST Cybersecurity Framework ID.GV-2 Informative References

Figure 4-8 shows the informative references related to the ID.GV-3 subcategory.

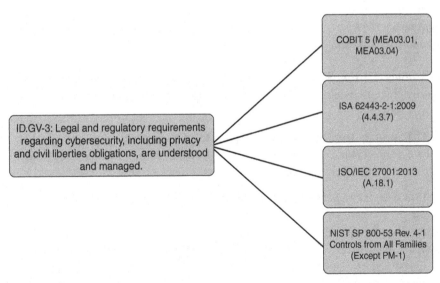

FIGURE 4-8   NIST Cybersecurity Framework ID.GV-3 Informative References

Figure 4-9 shows the informative references related to the ID.GV-4 subcategory.

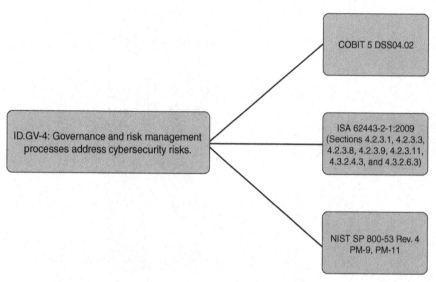

FIGURE 4-9   NIST Cybersecurity Framework ID.GV-4 Informative References

Regulatory Requirements

The necessity of formally assigning cybersecurity-related roles and responsibilities cannot be overstated. The requirement has been codified in numerous standards, regulations, and contractual obligations—most notably the following:

- **Gramm-Leach-Bliley (GLBA) Section 314-4:** "In order to develop, implement, and maintain your cybersecurity program, you shall (a) Designate an employee or employees to coordinate your cybersecurity program."

- **HIPAA/HITECH Security Rule Section 164-308(a):** "Identify the security official who is responsible for the development and implementation of the policies and procedures required by this subpart [the Security Rule] for the entity."

- **Payment Card Industry Data Security Standard (PCI DSS) Section 12.5:** "Assign to an individual or team the following cybersecurity management responsibilities: establish, document, and distribute security policies and procedures; monitor and analyze security alerts and information, and distribute to appropriate personnel; establish, document, and distribute security incident response and escalation procedures to ensure timely and effective handling of all situations; administer user accounts, including additions, deletions, and modifications; monitor and control all access to data."

- **23 NYCRR 500: Cybersecurity Requirements for Financial Services Companies—Section 500.02:** "Cybersecurity Program. Each Covered Entity shall maintain a cybersecurity program designed to protect the confidentiality, integrity and availability of the Covered Entity's Information Systems."

- **European Global Data Protection Regulation (GDPR):** "The principles of data protection should apply to any information concerning an identified or identifiable natural person. Personal data which have undergone pseudonymisation, which could be attributed to a natural person by the use of additional information should be considered to be information on an identifiable natural person. To determine whether a natural person is identifiable, account should be taken of all the means reasonably likely to be used, such as singling out, either by the controller or by another person to identify the natural person directly or indirectly. To ascertain whether means are reasonably likely to be used to identify the natural person, account should be taken of all objective factors, such as the costs of and the amount of time required for identification, taking into consideration the available technology at the time of the processing and technological developments."

- **European Directive on Security of Network and Information Systems (NIS Directive):** "Member States preparedness by requiring them to be appropriately equipped, e.g. via a Computer Security Incident Response Team (CSIRT) and a competent national NIS authority, cooperation among all the Member States, by setting up a cooperation group, in order to support and facilitate strategic cooperation and the exchange of information among Member States. They will also need to set a CSIRT Network, in order to promote swift and effective operational cooperation on specific cybersecurity incidents and sharing information about risks, a culture of security across sectors which are vital for our economy and society and moreover rely heavily on ICTs, such as energy, transport, water, banking, financial market infrastructures, healthcare and digital infrastructure. Businesses in these sectors that are identified by the Member States as operators of essential services will have to take appropriate security measures and to notify serious incidents to the relevant national authority. Also key digital service providers (search engines, cloud computing services and online marketplaces) will have to comply with the security and notification requirements under the Directive."

- **201 CMR 17: Standards for the Protection of Personal Information of the Residents of the Commonwealth – Section 17.0.2:** "Without limiting the generality of the foregoing, every comprehensive cybersecurity program shall include, but shall not be limited to: (a) Designating one or more employees to maintain the comprehensive cybersecurity program."

Creating a culture of security requires positive influences at multiple levels within an organization. Security champions reinforce by example the message that security policies and practices are important to the organization. The regulatory requirement to assign security responsibilities is a de facto mandate to create security champions.

Cybersecurity Risk

Three factors influence cybersecurity decision making and policy development:

- Guiding principles
- Regulatory requirements
- Risks related to achieving their business objectives

Risk is the potential of an undesirable or unfavorable outcome resulting from a given action, activity, and/or inaction. The motivation for taking a risk is a favorable outcome. *Managing risk* implies that other actions are being taken to either mitigate the impact of the undesirable or unfavorable outcome and/or enhance the likelihood of a positive outcome.

The following are a few key concepts of the governance of cybersecurity risk:

- An organization's assessment of cybersecurity risk and potential risk responses considers the privacy implications of its cybersecurity program.
- Individuals with cybersecurity-related privacy responsibilities report to appropriate management and are appropriately trained.
- Process is in place to support compliance of cybersecurity activities with applicable privacy laws, regulations, and Constitutional requirements.
- Process is in place to assess implementation of the foregoing organizational measures and controls.

These key concepts are categorized and illustrated in Figure 4-10.

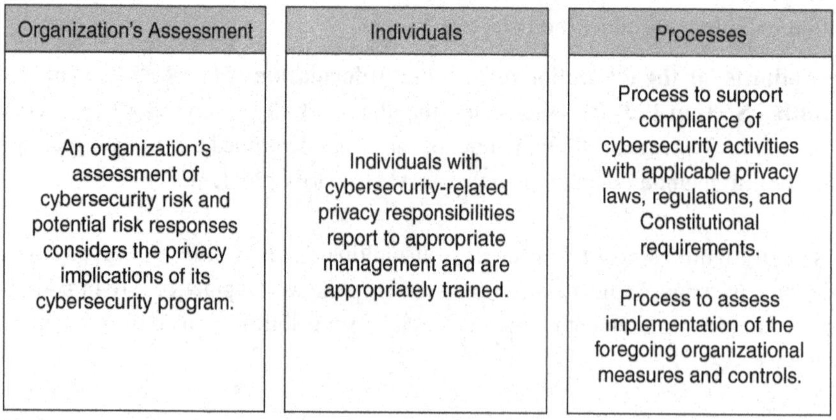

Organization's Assessment	Individuals	Processes
An organization's assessment of cybersecurity risk and potential risk responses considers the privacy implications of its cybersecurity program.	Individuals with cybersecurity-related privacy responsibilities report to appropriate management and are appropriately trained.	Process to support compliance of cybersecurity activities with applicable privacy laws, regulations, and Constitutional requirements. Process to assess implementation of the foregoing organizational measures and controls.

FIGURE 4-10   Governance of Cybersecurity Risk Key Concepts

For example, a venture capitalist (VC) decides to invest a million dollars in a startup company. The risk (undesirable outcome) in this case is that the company will fail and the VC will lose part or all of her investment. The motivation for taking this risk is that the company could become wildly successful and the initial backers make a great deal of money. To influence the outcome, the VC may require a seat on the Board of Directors, demand frequent financial reports, and mentor the leadership team. Doing these things, however, does not guarantee success.

Risk tolerance is how much of the undesirable outcome the risk taker is willing to accept in exchange for the potential benefit—in this case, how much money the VC is willing to lose. Certainly, if the VC believed that the company was destined for failure, the investment would not be made. Conversely, if the VC determined that the likelihood of a three-million-dollar return on investment was high, she may be willing to accept the tradeoff of a potential $200,000 loss.

The NIST Cybersecurity Framework includes several references under the subcategory "ID.GV-4: Governance and risk management processes address cybersecurity risks."

Is Risk Bad?

Inherently, risk is neither good nor bad. All human activity carries some risk, although the amount varies greatly. Consider this: Every time you get in a car you are risking injury or even death. You manage the risk by keeping your car in good working order, wearing a seat beat, obeying the rules of the road, not texting, not being impaired, and paying attention. Your risk tolerance is that the reward for reaching your destination outweighs the potential harm.

Risk taking can be beneficial and is often necessary for advancement. For example, entrepreneurial risk taking can pay off in innovation and progress. Ceasing to take risks would quickly wipe out experimentation, innovation, challenge, excitement, and motivation. Risk taking can, however, be detrimental when it is considered or influenced by ignorance, ideology, dysfunction, greed, or revenge. The key is to balance risk against rewards by making informed decisions and then managing the risk commensurate with organizational objectives. The process of managing risk requires organizations to assign risk-management responsibilities, establish the organizational risk appetite and tolerance, adopt a standard methodology for assessing risk, respond to risk levels, and monitor risk on an ongoing basis.

Understanding Risk Management

Risk management is the process of determining an acceptable level of risk (risk appetite and tolerance), calculating the current level of risk (risk assessment), accepting the level of risk (risk acceptance), or taking steps to reduce risk to the acceptable level (risk mitigation). We discussed the first two components in the previous sections.

Risk Acceptance

Risk acceptance indicates that the organization is willing to accept the level of risk associated with a given activity or process. Generally, but not always, this means that the outcome of the risk assessment is within tolerance. There may be times when the risk level is not within tolerance, but the organization will still choose to accept the risk because all other alternatives are unacceptable. Exceptions should always be brought to the attention of management and authorized by either the executive management or the Board of Directors.

Risk Mitigation

Risk mitigation implies one of four actions:

- Reducing the risk by implementing one or more countermeasures (risk reduction)
- Sharing the risk with another entity (risk sharing)
- Transferring the risk to another entity (risk transference)
- Modifying or ceasing the risk-causing activity (risk avoidance), or a combination thereof

Risk reduction is accomplished by implementing one or more offensive or defensive controls to lower the residual risk. An *offensive control* is designed to reduce or eliminate vulnerability, such as enhanced training or applying a security patch. A *defensive control* is designed to respond to a threat source (for example, a sensor that sends an alert if an intruder is detected). Prior to implementation, risk reduction recommendations should be evaluated in terms of their effectiveness, resource requirements, complexity impact on productivity and performance, potential unintended consequences, and cost. Depending on the situation, risk reduction decisions may be made at the business unit level, by management or by the Board of Directors.

Risk transfer or *risk sharing* is undertaken when organizations desire and have the means to shift risk liability and responsibility to other organizations. This is often accomplished by purchasing insurance.

Risk sharing shifts a portion of risk responsibility or liability to other organizations. The caveat to this option is that regulations such as GLBA (financial institutions) and HIPAA/HITECH (health-care organizations) prohibit covered entities from shifting compliance liability.

Risk avoidance may be the appropriate risk response when the identified risk exceeds the organizational risk appetite and tolerance, and a determination has been made not to make an exception. *Risk avoidance* involves taking specific actions to eliminate or significantly modify the process or activities that are the basis for the risk. It is unusual to see this strategy applied to critical systems and processes, because both prior investment and opportunity costs need to be considered. However, this strategy may be very appropriate when evaluating new processes, products, services, activities, and relationships.

In Practice

Cybersecurity Risk Response Policy

Synopsis: To define cybersecurity risk response requirements and authority.

Policy Statement:

- The initial results of all risk assessments must be provided to executive management and business process owners within seven days of completion.

- Low risks can be accepted by business process owners.

- Elevated risks and severe risks (or comparable rating) must be responded to within 30 days. Response is the joint responsibility of the business process owner and the CISO. Risk reduction recommendations can include risk acceptance, risk mitigation, risk transfer, risk avoidance, or a combination thereof. Recommendations must be documented and include an applicable level of detail.

- Severe and elevated risks can be accepted by executive management.

- The Board of Directors must be informed of accepted severe risk. At its discretion, it can choose to overrule acceptance.

FYI: Cyber-Insurance

Two general categories of risks and potential liabilities are covered by cyber-insurance: first-party risks and third-party risks:

- First-party risks are potential costs for loss or damage to the policyholder's own data, or lost income or business.

- Third-party risks include the policyholder's potential liability to clients or to various governmental or regulatory entities.

- A company's optimal cybersecurity policy would contain coverage for both first- and third-party claims. A 2013 Ponemon Institute Study commissioned by Experian Data Breach Resolution found that of 683 surveys completed by risk management professionals across multiple business sectors that have considered or adopted cyber-insurance, 86% of policies covered notification costs, 73% covered legal defense costs, 64% covered forensics and investigative costs, and 48% covered replacement of lost or damaged equipment. Not everything was always covered, though, as companies said only 30% of policies covered third-party liability, 30% covered communications costs to regulators, and 8% covered brand damages.

> ### FYI: Small Business Note
>
> Policy, governance, and risk management are important regardless of the size of the organization. The challenge for small organizations is who is going to accomplish these tasks. A small (or even a mid-size) business may not have a Board of Directors, C-level officers, or directors. Instead, as illustrated in Table 4-2, tasks are assigned to owners, managers, and outsourced service providers. What does not change regardless of size is the responsibilities of data owners, data custodians, and data users.
>
> **TABLE 4-2**   Organizational Roles and Responsibilities
>
> | Role | Small Business Equivalent |
> | --- | --- |
> | Board of Directors | Owner(s). |
> | Executive management | Owner(s) and/or management. |
> | Chief Security Officer | A member of the management team whose responsibilities include cybersecurity. If internal expertise does not exist, external advisors should be engaged. |
> | Chief Risk Officer | A member of the management team whose responsibilities include evaluating risk. If internal expertise does not exist, external advisors should be engaged. |
> | Compliance Officer | A member of the management team whose responsibilities include ensuring compliance with applicable laws and regulations. If internal expertise does not exist, external advisors should be engaged. |
> | Director of IT | IT manager. If internal expertise does not exist, external service providers should be engaged. |
> | Internal audit | If this position is required, it is generally outsourced. |

Risk Appetite and Tolerance

Risk appetite is defined by the ISO 31000 risk management standard as the "amount and type of risk that an organization is prepared to pursue, retain or take." In other words, how much risk you are willing to accept within your organization. Risk tolerance is tactical and specific to the target being evaluated. Risk tolerance levels can be qualitative (for example, low, elevated, severe) or quantitative (for example, dollar loss, number of customers impacted, hours of downtime). It is the responsibility of the Board of Directors and executive management to establish risk-tolerance criteria, set standards for acceptable levels of risk, and disseminate this information to decision makers throughout the organization.

There is no silver bullet to accept and set risk appetite; however, the method used should be owned by the Board of Directors executives and should reflect the collective informed views of the Board. The risk appetite should be defined in measurable terms. The use of subjective measures such as high, medium, and low are not a proper way of classifying such risk because these measurements mean different things to different people. The risk appetite and tolerance should be articulated in terms of acceptable variance in the organization's objectives (including its budget). For instance, the company executives may be willing to tolerate a minimum return on capital of 3% against a budget of 15%. Subsequently, the executives need to determine the risk categories for which an appetite will be set, including all material risks.

In Practice

Cybersecurity Risk Management Oversight Policy

Synopsis: To assign organizational roles and responsibilities with respect to risk management activities.

Policy Statement:

- Executive management, in consultation with the Board of Directors, is responsible for determining the organizational risk appetite and risk tolerance levels.

- Executive management will communicate the above to decision makers throughout the company.

- The CISO, in consultation with the Chief Risk Officer, is responsible for determining the cybersecurity risk assessment schedule, managing the risk assessment process, certifying results, jointly preparing risk reduction recommendations with business process owners, and presenting the results to executive management.

- The Board of Directors will be apprised by the COO of risks that endanger the organization, stakeholders, employees, or customers.

What Is a Risk Assessment?

An objective of a risk assessment is to evaluate what could go wrong, the likelihood of such an event occurring, and the harm if it did. In cybersecurity, this objective is generally expressed as the process of (a) identifying the *inherent risk* based on relevant *threats*, *threat sources*, and related *vulnerabilities*; (b) determining the *impact* if the threat source was successful; and (c) calculating the *likelihood of occurrence*, taking into consideration the *control* environment in order to determine *residual* risk.

- *Inherent risk* is the level of risk before security measures are applied.

- A *threat* is a natural, environmental, technical, or human event or situation that has the potential for causing undesirable consequences or impact. Cybersecurity focuses on the threats to confidentiality (unauthorized use or disclosure), integrity (unauthorized or accidental modification), and availability (damage or destruction).

- A *threat source* is either (1) intent and method targeted at the intentional exploitation of a vulnerability, such as criminal groups, terrorists, bot-net operators, and disgruntled employees, or (2) a situation and method that may accidentally trigger a vulnerability, such as an undocumented process, severe storm, and accidental or unintentional behavior.

- NIST provides several definitions for what is a *vulnerability*:

  - A weakness in an information system, system security procedures, internal controls, or implementation that could be exploited or triggered by a threat source.

  - A weakness in a system, application, or network that is subject to exploitation or misuse.

  - A weakness in an information system, system security procedures, internal controls, or implementation that could be exploited by a threat source.

- Vulnerabilities can be physical (for example, unlocked door, insufficient fire suppression), natural (for example, facility located in a flood zone or in a hurricane belt), technical (for example, misconfigured systems, poorly written code), or human (for example, untrained or distracted employee).

- *Impact* is the magnitude of harm.

- The *likelihood of occurrence* is a weighted factor or probability that a given threat is capable of exploiting a given vulnerability (or set of vulnerabilities).

- A *control* is a security measure designed to prevent, deter, detect, or respond to a threat source.

- *Residual risk* is the level of risk after security measures are applied. In its most simple form, residual risk can be defined as the likelihood of occurrence after controls are applied, multiplied by the expected loss. Residual risk is a reflection of the actual state. As such, the risk level can run the gamut from severe to nonexistent.

Let's consider the threat of obtaining unauthorized access to protected customer data. A threat source could be a cybercriminal. The vulnerability is that the information system that stores the data is Internet facing. We can safely assume that if no security measures were in place, the criminal would have unfettered access to the data (inherent risk). The resulting harm (impact) would be reputational damage, cost of responding to the breach, potential lost future revenue, and perhaps regulatory penalties. The security measures in place include data access controls, data encryption, ingress and egress filtering, an intrusion detection system, real-time activity monitoring, and log review. The residual risk calculation is based on the likelihood that the criminal (threat source) would be able to successfully penetrate the security measures, and if so, what the resulting harm would be. In this example, because the stolen or accessed data are encrypted, one could assume that the residual risk would be low (unless, of course, they were also able to access the decryption key). However, depending on the type of business, there still might be an elevated reputation risk associated with a breach.

FYI: Business Risk Categories

In a business context, risk is further classified by category, including strategic, financial, operational, personnel, reputational, and regulatory/compliance risk:

- Strategic risk relates to adverse business decisions.

- Financial (or investment) risk relates to monetary loss.

- Reputational risk relates to negative public opinion.

- Operational risk relates to loss resulting from inadequate or failed processes or systems.

- Personnel risk relates to issues that affect morale, productivity, recruiting, and retention.

- Regulatory/compliance risk relates to violations of laws, rules, regulations, or policy.

Risk Assessment Methodologies

Components of a risk assessment methodology include a defined process, a risk model, an assessment approach, and standardized analysis. The benefit of consistently applying a risk assessment methodology is comparable and repeatable results. The three most well-known cybersecurity risk assessment methodologies are the following:

- OCTAVE (Operationally Critical Threat, Asset, and Vulnerability Evaluation).

- Factor Analysis of Information Risk (FAIR).

- NIST Risk Management Framework (RMF). The NIST Risk Management Framework includes both risk assessment and risk management guidance.

OCTAVE

OCTAVE was originally developed at the CERT Coordination Center at Carnegie Mellon University. They developed this specification as a self-directed guideline, which means that stakeholders assume responsibility for specifying the organization's security strategy. OCTAVE relies on individual knowledge of the organization's security practices and processes to classify risk to the most critical assets. The OCTAVE approach is driven by two of the aspects: operational risk and security practices. OCTAVE was originally developed in the early 2000s, and most folks that adopted it have migrated to the NIST Risk Assessment Methodology.

FAIR

FAIR provides a model for understanding, analyzing, and quantifying information risk in quantitative financial and business terms. This is a bit different from risk assessment frameworks that focus their output on qualitative color-based charts or numerical weighted scales. The FAIR creators and maintainers goal was to build a foundation for developing a scientific approach to information risk management.

The original development of FAIR led to the creation of the FAIR Institute, which is an expert nonprofit organization that is helping the members to mature by providing learning opportunities, sharing of best practices, and exploration of possible new applications of the FAIR standard. Information about FAIR and the FAIR Institute can be obtained at https://www.fairinstitute.org. The Open Group adopted FAIR and is also evangelizing its use among the community.

NIST Risk Assessment Methodology

Federal regulators and examiners historically refer to NIST SP 800-30 and SP 800-39 in their commentary and guidance and, more recently, to the NIST Cybersecurity Framework (because, as you learned earlier, it provides a comprehensive list of guidelines and references).

The NIST Risk Assessment methodology, as defined in SP 800-30: Guide to Conducting Risk Assessments, is divided into four steps:

STEP 1.   Prepare for the assessment.

STEP 2.   Conduct the assessment.

STEP 3.   Communicate the results.

STEP 4.   Maintain the assessment.

These steps are illustrated in Figure 4-11.

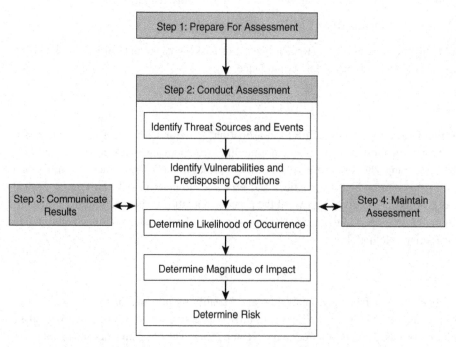

FIGURE 4-11   NIST Risk Assessment Methodology as Defined in SP-800-30

It is unrealistic that a single methodology would be able to meet the diverse needs of private and public-sector organizations. The expectation set forth in NIST SP 800-39 and 800-30 is that each organization will adapt and customize the methodology based on size, complexity, industry sector, regulatory requirements, and threat vector.

In Practice

Cybersecurity Risk Assessment Policy

Synopsis: To assign responsibility for and set parameters for conducting cybersecurity risk assessments.

Policy Statement:

- The company must adopt a cybersecurity risk assessment methodology to ensure consistent, repeatable, and comparable results.

- Cybersecurity risk assessments must have a clearly defined and limited scope. Assessments with a broad scope become difficult and unwieldy in both their execution and the documentation of the results.

- The CISO is charged with developing a cybersecurity risk assessment schedule based on the information system's criticality and information classification level.

- In addition to scheduled assessments, cybersecurity risk assessments must be conducted prior to the implementation of any significant change in technology, process, or third-party agreement.

- The CISO and the business process owner are jointly required to respond to risk assessment results and develop risk reduction strategies and recommendations.

- Risk assessment results and recommendations must be presented to executive management.

Summary

Cybersecurity is not an end unto itself. Cybersecurity is a business discipline that exists to support business objectives, add value, and maintain compliance with externally imposed requirements. This type of relationship is known as "strategic alignment." Organizational commitment to cybersecurity practices should be codified in a written policy. The cybersecurity policy is an authoritative document that informs decision making and practices. As such, it should be authorized by the Board of Directors or equivalent body. Derivative documents for specific audiences should be published and distributed. This includes an Acceptable Use Policy and Agreement for users, a third-party version for vendors and service providers, and a synopsis for business partners and clients.

It is essential that cybersecurity policies remain relevant and accurate. At a minimum, policies should be reviewed and reauthorized annually. Change drivers are events that modify how a company operates and are a trigger for policy review. Compliance with policy requirements should be assessed and reported to executive management.

A *cybersecurity audit* is a systematic evidence-based evaluation of how well the organization conforms to established criteria. Audits are generally conducted by independent auditors, which implies that the auditor is not responsible for, has not benefited from, and is not in any way influenced by the audit target. A *capability maturity model (CMM) assessment* is an evaluation of process maturity for a given area. In contrast to an audit, the application of a CMM is generally an internal process. Audits and maturity models are good indicators of policy acceptance and integration.

Governance is the process of managing, directing, controlling, and influencing organizational decisions, actions, and behaviors. The Board of Directors is the authoritative policy-making body. Executive management is tasked with providing support and resources. Endorsed by the Board of Directors and executive management, the CISO (or equivalent role) is vested with cybersecurity program management responsibility and accountability. The chain of command for the CISO should be devoid of conflict of interest. The CISO should have the authority to communicate directly with the Board of Directors.

Discussion, debate, and thoughtful deliberation result in good decision making. Supporting the CISO should be a Cybersecurity Steering Committee, whose members represent a cross-section of the organization. The steering committee serves in an advisory capacity with particular focus on the alignment of business and security objectives. Distributed throughout the organization are a variety of roles that have cybersecurity-related responsibilities. Most notably, data owners are responsible for defining protection requirements, data custodians are responsible for managing the protection mechanisms, and data users are expected to act in accordance with the organization's requirements and to be stewards of the information in their care.

Three factors influence cybersecurity decision making and policy development: guiding principles, regulatory requirements, and risks related to achieving their business objectives. *Risk* is the potential of an undesirable or unfavorable outcome resulting from a given action, activity, and/or inaction. *Risk tolerance* is how much of the undesirable outcome the risk taker is willing to accept in exchange for the potential benefit. *Risk management* is the process of determining an acceptable level of risk, identifying the level of risk for a given situation, and determining if the risk should be accepted or mitigated. A *risk assessment* is used to calculate the level of risk. A number of publicly available risk assessment methodologies are available for organizations to use and customize. Risk acceptance indicates that the organization is willing to accept the level of risk associated with a given activity or process. Risk mitigation implies that one of four actions (or a combination of actions) will be undertaken: risk reduction, risk sharing, risk transference, or risk avoidance.

Risk management, governance, and information policy are the basis of an information program. Policies related to these domains include the following policies: Cybersecurity Policy, Cybersecurity Policy Authorization and Oversight, CISO, Cybersecurity Steering Committee, Cybersecurity Risk Management Oversight, Cybersecurity Risk Assessment, and Cybersecurity Risk Management.

Test Your Skills

MULTIPLE CHOICE QUESTIONS

1. What does it indicate when a cybersecurity program is said to be "strategically aligned"?

    A. It supports business objectives.

    B. It adds value.

    C. It maintains compliance with regulatory requirements.

    D. All of the above.

2. How often should cybersecurity policies be reviewed?

    A. Once a year

    B. Only when a change needs to be made

    C. At a minimum, once a year and whenever there is a change trigger

    D. Only as required by law

3. Cybersecurity policies should be authorized by _____.

    A. the Board of Directors (or equivalent)

    B. business unit managers

    C. legal counsel

    D. stockholders

4. Which of the following statements best describes policies?

    A. Policies are the implementation of specifications.

    B. Policies are suggested actions or recommendations.

    C. Policies are instructions.

    D. Policies are the directives that codify organizational requirements.

5. Which of the following statements best represents the most compelling reason to have an employee version of the comprehensive cybersecurity policy?

   A. Sections of the comprehensive policy may not be applicable to all employees.

   B. The comprehensive policy may include unknown acronyms.

   C. The comprehensive document may contain confidential information.

   D. The more understandable and relevant a policy is, the more likely users will positively respond to it.

6. Which of the following is a common element of all federal cybersecurity regulations?

   A. Covered entities must have a written cybersecurity policy.

   B. Covered entities must use federally mandated technology.

   C. Covered entities must self-report compliance.

   D. Covered entities must notify law enforcement if there is a policy violation.

7. Organizations that choose to adopt the ISO 27002:2103 framework must _____.

   A. use every policy, standard, and guideline recommended

   B. create policies for every security domain

   C. evaluate the applicability and customize as appropriate

   D. register with the ISO

8. Evidence-based techniques used by cybersecurity auditors include which of the following elements?

   A. Structured interviews, observation, financial analysis, and documentation sampling

   B. Structured interviews, observation, review of practices, and documentation sampling

   C. Structured interviews, customer service surveys, review of practices, and documentation sampling

   D. Casual conversations, observation, review of practices, and documentation sampling

9. Which of the following statements best describes independence in the context of auditing?

   A. The auditor is not an employee of the company.

   B. The auditor is certified to conduct audits.

   C. The auditor is not responsible for, has not benefited from, and is not in any way influenced by the audit target.

   D. Each auditor presents his or her own opinion.

10. Which of the following states is *not* included in a CMM?

   A. Average

   B. Optimized

C. Ad hoc

D. Managed

11. Which of the following activities is not considered a governance activity?

A. Managing

B. Influencing

C. Evaluating

D. Purchasing

12. To avoid conflict of interest, the CISO could report to which of the following individuals?

A. The Chief Information Officer (CIO)

B. The Chief Technology Officer (CTO)

C. The Chief Financial Officer (CFO)

D. The Chief Compliance Officer (CCO)

13. Which of the following statements best describes the role of the Cybersecurity Steering Committee?

A. The committee authorizes policy.

B. The committee helps communicate, discuss, and debate on security requirements and business integration.

C. The committee approves the InfoSec budget.

D. None of the above.

14. Defining protection requirements is the responsibility of _____.

A. the ISO

B. the data custodian

C. data owners

D. the Compliance Officer

15. Designating an individual or team to coordinate or manage cybersecurity is required by _____.

A. GLBA

B. 23 NYCRR 500

C. PCI DSS

D. All of the above

16. Which of the following terms best describes the potential of an undesirable or unfavorable outcome resulting from a given action, activity, and/or inaction?

    A. Threat

    B. Risk

    C. Vulnerability

    D. Impact

17. Inherent risk is the state before _____.

    A. an assessment has been conducted

    B. security measures have been implemented

    C. the risk has been accepted

    D. None of the above

18. Which of the following terms best describes the natural, environmental, technical, or human event or situation that has the potential for causing undesirable consequences or impact?

    A. Risk

    B. Threat source

    C. Threat

    D. Vulnerability

19. Which of the following terms best describes a disgruntled employee with intent to do harm?

    A. Risk

    B. Threat source

    C. Threat

    D. Vulnerability

20. Which of the following activities is *not* considered an element of risk management?

    A. The process of determining an acceptable level of risk

    B. Assessing the current level of risk for a given situation

    C. Accepting the risk

    D. Installing risk-mitigation technologies and cybersecurity products

21. How much of the undesirable outcome the risk taker is willing to accept in exchange for the potential benefit is known as _____.

    A. risk acceptance

    B. risk tolerance

    C. risk mitigation

    D. risk avoidance

22. Which of the following statements best describes a vulnerability?

    A. A vulnerability is a weakness that could be exploited by a threat source.

    B. A vulnerability is a weakness that can never be fixed.

    C. A vulnerability is a weakness that can only be identified by testing.

    D. A vulnerability is a weakness that must be addressed regardless of the cost.

23. Which of the following are benefits of security controls?

    A. Detect threats

    B. Deter threats

    C. Prevent cyber-attacks and breaches

    D. All of the above

24. Which of the following is not a risk-mitigation action?

    A. Risk acceptance

    B. Risk sharing or transference

    C. Risk reduction

    D. Risk avoidance

25. Which of the following risks is best described as the expression of (the likelihood of occurrence after controls are applied) × (expected loss)?

    A. Inherent risk

    B. Expected risk

    C. Residual risk

    D. Accepted risk

26. Which of the following risk types best describes an example of insurance?

    A. Risk avoidance

    B. Risk transfer

    C. Risk acknowledgement

    D. Risk acceptance

27 Which of the following risk types relates to negative public opinion?

    A. Operational risk

    B. Financial risk

    C. Reputation risk

    D. Strategic risk

28. Which of the following is not true about compliance risk as it relates to federal and state regulations?

    A. Compliance risk cannot be avoided

    B. Compliance risk cannot be transferred

    C. Compliance risk cannot be accepted

    D. None of these answers are correct

29. Which of the following statements best describes organizations that are required to comply with multiple federal and state regulations?

    A. They must have different policies for each regulation.

    B. They must have multiple ISOs.

    C. They must ensure that their cybersecurity program includes all applicable requirements.

    D. They must choose the one regulation that takes precedence.

30. Which of the following are subcategories of the NIST Cybersecurity Framework that are related to cybersecurity governance?

    A. ID.GV-1: Organizational information security policy is established.

    B. ID.GV-2: Information security roles and responsibilities are coordinated and aligned with internal roles and external partners.

    C. ID.GV-3: Legal and regulatory requirements regarding cybersecurity, including privacy and civil liberties obligations, are understood and managed.

    D. ID.GV-4: Governance and risk management processes address cybersecurity risks.

    E. All of these answers are correct.

EXERCISES

EXERCISE 4-1: Understanding ISO 27002:2005

The introduction to ISO 27002:2005 includes this statement: "This International Standard may be regarded as a starting point for developing organization-specific guidelines. Not all of the controls and guidance in this code of practice may be applicable. Furthermore, additional controls and guidelines not included in this standard may be required."

1. Explain how this statement relates to the concept of strategic alignment.

2. The risk assessment domain was included in the ISO 27002:2005 edition and then removed in ISO 27002:2013. Why do you think they made this change?

3. What are the major topics of ISO 27005?

EXERCISE 4-2: **Understanding Policy Development and Authorization**

Three entrepreneurs got together and created a website design hosting company. They will be creating websites and social media sites for their customers, from simple "Hello World" pages to full-fledged e-commerce solutions. One entrepreneur is the technical guru, the second is the marketing genius, and the third is in charge of finances. They are equal partners. The entrepreneurs also have five web developers working for them as independent contractors on a per-project basis. Customers are requesting a copy of their security policies.

1. Explain the criteria they should use to develop their policies. Who should authorize the policies?

2. Should the policies apply to the independent contractors? Why or why not?

3. What type of documentation should they provide their customers?

EXERCISE 4-3: **Understanding Cybersecurity Officers**

1. ISOs are in high demand. Using online job hunting sites (such as Monster.com, Dice.com, and TheLadders.com), research available positions in your geographic area.

2. Is there a common theme in the job descriptions?

3. What type of certifications, education, and experience are employers seeking?

EXERCISE 4-4: **Understanding Risk Terms and Definitions**

1. Define each of the following terms: inherent risk, threat, threat source, vulnerability, likelihood, impact, and residual risk.

2. Provide examples of security measures designed to (a) deter a threat source, (b) prevent a threat source from being successful, and (c) detect a threat source.

3. Explain risk avoidance and why that option is generally not chosen.

EXERCISE 4-5: **Understanding Insurance**

1. What is cyber-insurance and what does it generally cover?

2. Why would an organization purchase cyber-insurance?

3. What is the difference between first-party coverage and third-party coverage?

PROJECTS

PROJECT 4-1: Analyzing a Written Policy

1. Many organizations rely on institutional knowledge rather than written policy. Why do you think all major cybersecurity regulations require a written cybersecurity policy? Do you agree? Explain your opinion.

2. We are going to test the conventional wisdom that policy should be documented by conducting an experiment.

   a. Write down or print out these three simple policy statements. Or, if you prefer, create your own policy statements.

      The Board of Directors must authorize the Cybersecurity Policy.

      An annual review of the Cybersecurity Policy must be conducted.

      The CISO is responsible for managing the review process.

   b. Enlist four subjects for your experiment.

      Give two of the subjects the written policy. Ask them to read the document. Have them keep the paper.

      Read the policy to the two other subjects. Do not give them a written copy.

   c. Within 24 hours, contact each subject and ask them to recall as much of the policy as possible. If they ask, let the first two subjects know that they can consult the document you gave them. Document your findings. Does the outcome support your answer to Question 1?

PROJECT 4-2: Analyzing Cybersecurity Management

1. Does your school or workplace have a CISO or an equivalent position? Who does the CISO (or equivalent) report to? Does he or she have any direct reports? Is this person viewed as a security champion? Is he or she accessible to the user community?

2. It is important that CISOs stay current with security best practices, regulations, and peer experiences. Research and recommend (at least three) networking and educational resources.

3. If you were tasked with selecting a Cybersecurity Steering Committee at your school or workplace to advise the CISO (or equivalent), who would you choose and why?

PROJECT 4-3: Using Risk Assessment Methodologies

The three most well-known cybersecurity risk assessment methodologies are OCTAVE (Operationally Critical Threat, Asset, and Vulnerability Evaluation, developed at the CERT Coordination Center at Carnegie Mellon University), FAIR (Factor Analysis of Information Risk), and the NIST Risk Management Framework (RMF).

1. Research and write a description of each (including pros and cons).

2. Are they in the public domain, or is there a licensing cost?

3. Is training available?

Case Study

Determining the Likelihood and Impact of Occurrence

One of the most challenging aspects of a risk assessment is determining the likelihood of occurrence and impact. NIST SP 800-30 defines the likelihood of occurrence as follows: A weighted risk factor based on an analysis of the probability that a given threat source is capable of exploiting a given vulnerability (or set of vulnerabilities). For adversarial threats, an assessment of likelihood of occurrence is typically based on: (i) adversary *intent*; (ii) adversary *capability*; and (iii) adversary *targeting*. For other than adversarial threat events, the likelihood of occurrence is estimated using historical evidence, empirical data, or other factors. Organizations typically employ a three-step process to determine the overall likelihood of threat events:

- Organizations assess the likelihood that threat events will be initiated (for adversarial threat events) or will occur (for non-adversarial threat events).

- Organizations assess the likelihood that the threat events, once initiated or occurring, will result in adverse impacts or harm to organizational operations and assets, individuals, other organizations, or the nation.

- Organizations assess the overall likelihood as a combination of likelihood of initiation/occurrence and likelihood of resulting in adverse impact.

Identify two threat sources—one adversarial and one non-adversarial—that could exploit a vulnerability at your school or workplace and would result in disruption of service. An adversarial event is the *intentional* exploitation of a vulnerability by criminal groups, terrorists, bot-net operators, or disgruntled employees. A non-adversarial event is the *accidental* exploit of a vulnerability, such as an undocumented process, a severe storm, or accidental or unintentional behavior.

1. For each (using your best judgment), answer the following questions:

    a. What is the threat?

    b. What is the threat source?

    c. Is the source adversarial or non-adversarial?

    d. What vulnerability could be exploited?

    e. How likely is the threat source to be successful and why?

    f. If the threat source is successful, what is the extent of the damage caused?

2. Risk assessments are rarely conducted by one individual working alone. If you were hosting a workshop to answer the preceding questions, who would you invite and why?

References

Regulations Cited

"Appendix B to Part 364—Interagency Guidelines Establishing Cybersecurity Standards," accessed 04/2018, https://www.fdic.gov/regulations/laws/rules/2000-8660.html.

"201 CMR 17.00: Standards for the Protection of Personal Information of Residents of the Commonwealth," official website of the Office of Consumer Affairs & Business Regulation (OCABR), accessed 04/2018, http://www.mass.gov/ocabr/docs/idtheft/201cmr1700reg.pdf.

"Family Educational Rights and Privacy Act (FERPA)," official website of the US Department of Education, accessed 04/2018, https://www2.ed.gov/policy/gen/guid/fpco/ferpa/index.html.

"HIPAA Security Rule," official website of the Department of Health and Human Services, accessed 04/2018, https://www.hhs.gov/hipaa/for-professionals/security/index.html.

European Global Data Protection Regulation (GDPR) website, accessed 04/2018, https://ec.europa.eu/info/strategy/justice-and-fundamental-rights/data-protection_en.

"The Directive on Security of Network and Information Systems (NIS Directive)," accessed 04/2018, https://ec.europa.eu/digital-single-market/en/network-and-information-security-nis-directive.

"New York State 23 NYCRR 500: Cybersecurity Requirements for Financial Services Companies," accessed 04/2018, http://www.dfs.ny.gov/legal/regulations/adoptions/dfsrf500txt.pdf.

Other References

Allen, Julia, "Governing for Enterprise Security: CMU/SEI-2005-TN-023 2005," Carnegie Mellon University, June 2005.

Bejtlich, Richard, "Risk, Threat, and Vulnerability 101," accessed 04/2018, http://taosecurity.blogspot.com/2005/05/risk-threat-and-vulnerability-101-in.html.

NIST's Glossary of Key Information Security Terms, accessed 04/2018, http://nvlpubs.nist.gov/nistpubs/ir/2013/NIST.IR.7298r2.pdf.

DeMauro, John, "Filling the Cybersecurity Officer Role within Community Banks," accessed 04/2018, www.practicalsecuritysolutions.com/articles/.

"Duty of Care," Legal Information Institute, Cornell University Law School, accessed 04/2018, https://www.law.cornell.edu/wex/duty_of_care.

AIG Study, "Is Cyber Risk Systemic?", accessed 04/2018, https://www.aig.com/content/dam/aig/america-canada/us/documents/business/cyber/aig-cyber-risk-systemic-final.pdf.

Godes, Scott, Esq., and Kristi Singleton, Esq. "Top Ten Tips for Companies Buying Cybersecurity Insurance Coverage," accessed 04/2018, http://www.acc.com/legalresources/publications/topten/tttfcbcsic.cfm.

"Cybersecurity Governance: Guidance for Boards of Directors and Executive Management, Second Edition," IT Governance Institute, 2006.

Matthews, Chris, "Cybersecurity Insurance Picks Up Steam," *Wall Street Journal/Risk & Compliance Journal*, August 7, 2013, accessed 04/2018, https://blogs.wsj.com/riskandcompliance/2013/08/07/cybersecurity-insurance-picks-up-steam-study-finds/.

"PCI DDS Requirements and Security Assessment Procedures," accessed 04/2018, https://www.pcisecuritystandards.org/pci_security/standards_overview.

"Process & Performance Improvement," Carnegie Mellon Software Engineering Institute, accessed 04/2018, www.sei.cmu.edu/process/.

Swenson, David, Ph.D., "Change Drivers," accessed 04/2018, http://faculty.css.edu/dswenson/web/Chandriv.htm.

"The Security Risk Management Guide," Microsoft, accessed 04/2018, https://technet.microsoft.com/en-us/library/cc163143.aspx.

"What Is the Capability Maturity Model (CMM)?" accessed 04/2018, http://www.selectbs.com/process-maturity/what-is-the-capability-maturity-model.

"European Union Cybersecurity-Related Legislation," accessed 04/2018, https://www.securityroundtable.org/wp-content/uploads/2017/05/eu-cybersecurity-legislation-executive-advisory-report.pdf.

NIST Computer Security Resource Center Publications, accessed 04/2018, https://csrc.nist.gov/publications.

NIST Cybersecurity Framework, accessed 04/2018, https://www.nist.gov/cyberframework.

FAIR and The FAIR Institute, accessed 04/2018, https://www.fairinstitute.org.

Chapter 5

Asset Management and Data Loss Prevention

Chapter Objectives

After reading this chapter and completing the exercises, you will be able to do the following:

- Assign information ownership responsibilities.
- Develop and use information classification guidelines.
- Understand information handling and labeling procedures.
- Identify and inventory information systems.
- Create and implement asset classification policies.
- Understand data loss prevention technologies.

Is it possible to properly protect information if we do not know how much it is worth and how sensitive it is? Until we classify the information, how do we know the level of protection required? Unless we determine the value to the organization, how can we decide the amount of time, effort, or money that we should spend securing the asset? Who is responsible for making these decisions? How do we communicate the value of our information assets to our employees, business partners, and vendors?

Identification and classification of information assets and systems is essential to the proper selection of security controls to *protect against loss* of confidentiality, integrity, and availability (CIA):

- A *loss of confidentiality* is the unauthorized disclosure of information.
- A *loss of integrity* is the unauthorized or unintentional modification or destruction of information.
- A *loss of availability* is the accidental or intentional disruption of access to or use of information or an information system.

In this chapter, we look at the various methods and rating methodologies that organizations use to define, inventory, and classify information and information systems. We examine public and private sector classification systems that are used to communicate value and handling instructions. We will determine who is responsible for these activities. Last, we will put these best practices into policy.

FYI: ISO/IEC 27002:2013 and NIST Cybersecurity Framework

Section 8 of ISO 27002:2013 focuses on asset management with the objective of developing classification schemas, assigning classification levels, and developing handling standards to protect information.

The Asset Management category of the NIST Cybersecurity Framework defines asset management as the "data, personnel, devices, systems, and facilities that enable the organization to achieve business purposes that are identified and managed consistently with their relative importance to business objectives and the organization's risk strategy."

The ID.AM-5: Resources subcategory includes hardware, devices, data, time, and software. These resources are prioritized based on their classification, criticality, and business value. The following are the additional resources included in the NIST Cybersecurity Framework for the Asset Management category:

- COBIT 5 APO03.03, APO03.04, BAI09.02

- ISA 62443-2-1:2009 4.2.3.6

- ISO/IEC 27001:2013 A.8.2.1

- NIST SP 800-53 Rev. 4 CP-2, RA-2, SA-14

Information Assets and Systems

What exactly is an information asset and why protect it? An *information asset* is a definable piece of information, stored in any manner, that is recognized as having value to the organization. Information assets include raw, mined, developed, and purchased data. If the information is damaged, compromised, or stolen, the consequences could include embarrassment, legal liability, financial ruin, and even loss of life.

Examples of organizational information include the following:

- Data stores or warehouses of information about customers, personnel, production, sales, marketing, or finances

- Intellectual property (IP) such as drawings, schematics, patents, music scores, or other publications that have commercial value

- Operational and support procedures

- Research documentation or proprietary information based on experimentation or exploration

- Strategic and operational plans, processes, and procedures that uniquely define the organization

Information systems are the supporting players. *Information systems* provide a way and a place to process, store, transmit, and communicate the information. These systems are generally a combination of hardware and software assets and associated services. Information systems can be garden-variety off-the-shelf products or highly customized equipment and code. Support services may be technical services (voice communication and data communication) or environmental (heating, lighting, air conditioning, and power). The location of information systems may be "on premises," at a contracted data center, or in the cloud.

Who Is Responsible for Information Assets?

This brings us to the question of ownership. Every information asset must be assigned an owner. The success of an information security program is directly related to the defined relationship between the data owner and the information. In the best-case scenario, the data owner also functions as a security champion enthusiastically embracing the goals of CIA.

In Chapter 3, "Cybersecurity Framework," we defined information ownership as being liable and responsible for protecting the information and the business results derived from using that information. For example, you have a medical file at your doctor's office that may contain your medical history, digital scans, lab results, and physician notes. The clinicians in the office use that information to provide you with medical care. Because the information is all about you, are you the owner? No. The medical staff uses the information to provide care, so are they the owner? No. The information owner is the one responsible for protecting the *confidentiality* of your medical record, ensuring the *integrity* of the information in your records, and making sure that it is *available* to the clinicians whenever you need care. In a small medical practice, the owner is generally a physician. In a clinic or hospital, the owner is a member of senior management. Although it may seem obvious that every information asset needs an owner, it is not always apparent who should be or who is willing to assume the responsibility of ownership.

The Role of the Data Owner

The ISO 27002:2013 standard recommends that we have a policy that specifically addresses the need to account for our information assets and to assign an owner to the asset. The goal of an Information Ownership policy is to ensure that appropriate protection is maintained. Owners should be identified for all major information assets and be given the responsibility for the safeguarding of the information system. The owner is responsible for the security of the asset.

Figure 5-1 shows the data owner responsibilities.

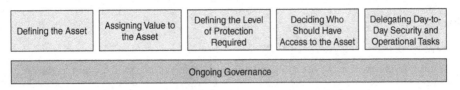

FIGURE 5-1 Data Owner Responsibilities

As illustrated in Figure 5-1, the data owner responsibilities include the following:

- Defining what is an asset

- Assigning the economic or business value to the asset

- Defining the level of protection required for such asset

- Deciding who should have access to the asset and who should grant such access

- Delegating day-to-day security and operational tasks

Owners perform the ongoing governance of all asset management, as well as the authorization of any disclosure of information.

However, the owner is not the one who will be tasked with implementing security controls. That responsibility can be delegated to the information custodians, such as system administrators.

Asset (system, data, and resource) custodian responsibilities include the following:

- Being a subject matter expert

- Implementing protection mechanisms

- Monitoring for problems or violations

- Reporting suspected incidents

Common custodian roles include network administrators, IT specialists, database administrators, application developers, application administrators, and librarians.

The Role of the Information Security Officer

The information owner is accountable for the protection of the information asset. The information custodian is responsible for managing the day-to-day controls. The role of the Information Security Officer (ISO) is to provide direction and guidance as to the appropriate controls and to ensure that controls are applied consistently throughout the organization. Whereas information owners and custodians focus on specific information assets, the ISO is responsible for the security of the entire organization. As such, the office of the ISO is the central repository of security information. The ISO publishes the classification criteria, maintains the information system inventories, and implements broad strategic and tactical security initiatives.

Information Ownership Policy Statement

Synopsis: A data owner is responsible for the protection of assigned information and systems. Inclusive in this responsibility are decisions about classification of information, protection of information and information systems, and access to information and information systems.

Policy Statement:

- All information assets and systems must have an assigned owner.

- The Office of Information Security will maintain an inventory of information ownership.

- Owners are required to classify information and information systems in accordance with the organizational classification guidelines.

- Owners are responsible for determining the required level of protection.

- Owners must authorize internal information and information system access rights and permissions. Access rights and permissions must be reviewed and approved annually.

- Owners must authorize third-party access to information or information systems. This includes information provided to a third party.

- Implementation and maintenance of controls is the responsibility of the Office of Information Security; however, accountability will remain with the owner of the asset.

Information Classification

As discussed in the previous section, the information or data owner is responsible for classifying information using the criteria established by the ISO. The objective of an *information classification system* is to differentiate data types to enable organizations to safeguard CIA based on content. The natural outcome of the classification process is instructions on who can access the asset, how the asset is to be used, what security measures need to be in place, and ultimately the method in which the asset should be destroyed or disposed of. Classification systems have their genesis in two seminal security models designed in the 1970s for the U.S. military: Bell-Lapadula and Biba. Both models are based on the assumption that an information system may contain information that requires different levels of security and that users of various clearance levels would be accessing the information system. The objective of the Bell-Lapadula model is to ensure confidentiality by restricting read access to data above what a user has permission to read and to restrict write access to data at a level below to minimize potential exposure. This is generally expressed as "no read up, no write down." The objective of the Biba model is to ensure data integrity. The Biba model restricts users from reading data at a lower level and writing information to a higher level. The theory is that data at a lower level may be incomplete and/or inaccurate and if read could unduly influence what is written at a higher level. This is generally expressed as "no read down, no write up." The implementation of Bell-Lapadula, Biba, and subsequent models required that a structured data classification system be developed.

When using Bell-LaPadula, users can create content only at or above their own security level. On the other hand, users can view content only at or below their own security level. You can use the Biba model to address the concerns of integrity, but it addresses only the first goal of integrity—protecting the system from access by unauthorized users. Availability and confidentiality are not examined. The Biba model also expects that internal threats are being protected by good coding practices, and this is why it focuses on external threats.

Classification systems are now used in the private sector, the government, and the military. A financial institution will allow a teller to view general account information and cash checks of reasonable amounts. That same teller is not allowed to view information about internal bank assets and most definitely cannot access systems that would allow her to transfer millions of dollars. A hospital will allow a lab technician to access patient demographics and physician instructions but will not allow him to read or edit the complete patient record. The military, based on national security concerns, makes decisions about to whom and how to make information accessible. They certainly do not want battle plans shared with the enemy. In fact, the military is a vivid example of an organization that relies extensively on a well-defined classification system. They classify not only information systems but people as well. Military and supporting civilian personnel are assigned clearance levels. The clearance level of the individual must match the classification of the data in order to be granted access. In this section, we examine different approaches to information classification.

In Practice

Information Classification Life Cycle Process

An information classification life cycle begins with the assignment of classification and ends with declassification. The information owner is responsible for managing this process, which is as follows:

- Document the information asset and the supporting information systems.
- Assign a classification level.
- Apply the appropriate labeling.
- Document "special" handling procedures (if different from organizational standards).
- Conduct periodic classification reviews.
- Declassify information when (and if) appropriate.

How Does the Federal Government Classify Data?

Let's start with looking at how federal agencies categorize information and systems and then compare how the private sector classifies information. The United States government has enormous amounts of data and has a vested responsibility in protecting the CIA of the information and information systems. To this end, federal guidelines require that federal agencies categorize information and information systems. Federal Information Processing Standard 199 (FIPS-199) requires that information owners classify information and information systems as *low*, *moderate*, or *high security* based on CIA criteria. The generalized format for expressing the security category (SC) of an information type is as follows: The SC of information type = {(confidentiality, impact), (integrity, impact), (availability, impact)}, where the acceptable values for potential impact are low, moderate, high, or not applicable:

- *Low potential impact* means the loss of CIA could be expected to have a *limited* adverse effect on organizational operations, organizational assets, or individuals.

- *Moderate potential impact* means the loss of CIA could be expected to have a *serious* adverse effect on organizational operations, organizational assets, or individuals.

- *High potential impact* means the loss of CIA could be expected to have a severe or catastrophic adverse effect on organizational operations, organizational assets, or individuals.

Confidentiality Factors

Information is evaluated for confidentiality with respect to the impact of unauthorized disclosure as well as the use of the information. Federal guidelines suggest that agencies consider the following:

- How can a malicious adversary use the unauthorized disclosure of information to do limited/serious/severe harm to agency operations, agency assets, or individuals?

- How can a malicious adversary use the unauthorized disclosure of information to gain control of agency assets that might result in unauthorized modification of information, destruction of information, or denial of system services that would result in limited/serious/severe harm to agency operations, agency assets, or individuals?

- Would unauthorized disclosure/dissemination of elements of the information type violate laws, executive orders (EOs), or agency regulations?

Integrity Factors

Information is evaluated for integrity with respect to the impact associated with unauthorized modification or destruction. Federal guidelines suggest that agencies consider the following:

- How does unauthorized or unintentional modification of information harm agency operations, agency assets, or individuals?
- What is the impact of actions taken, decisions made based on modified information, or if the modified information is disseminated to other organizations or the public?
- Does modification/destruction of elements of the information type violate laws, EOs, or agency regulations?

Availability Factors

Information is evaluated for availability with respect to the impact of disruption of access to or use of the information. Federal guidelines suggest that agencies consider the following:

- How does the disruption of access to or use of information do harm to agency operations, agency assets, or individuals?
- What is the impact of destruction and/or permanent loss of information?
- Does disruption of access to or use of elements of the information type violate laws, EOs, or agency regulations?

FYI: Examples of FIPS-199 Classification

Example 1: An organization managing *public information* on its web server determines that there is no potential impact from a loss of confidentiality (that is, confidentiality requirements are not applicable), a moderate potential impact from a loss of integrity, and a moderate potential impact from a loss of availability. The resulting SC of this information type is expressed as follows:

SC *public information* = {(confidentiality, n/a), (integrity, moderate), (availability, moderate)}.

Example 2: A law enforcement organization managing extremely sensitive investigative information determines that the potential impact from a loss of confidentiality is high, the potential impact from a loss of integrity is moderate, and the potential impact from a loss of availability is moderate. The resulting SC for this type of information is expressed as follows:

SC *investigative information* = {(confidentiality, high), (integrity, moderate), (availability, moderate)}.

Example 3: A power plant contains an SCADA (supervisory control and data acquisition) system controlling the distribution of electric power for a large military installation. The SCADA system contains both real-time sensor data and routine administrative information. The management at the power plant determines that: (i) for the sensor data being acquired by the SCADA system, there is moderate impact from a loss of confidentiality, a high potential impact from a loss of integrity, and a high potential impact from a loss of availability; and (ii) for the administrative information being processed by the system, there is a low potential impact from a loss of confidentiality, a low potential impact from a loss of integrity, and a low potential impact from a loss of availability. The resulting SCs of these information types are expressed as follows:

SC sensor data = {(confidentiality, moderate), (integrity, high), (availability, high)}, and

SC administrative information = {(confidentiality, low), (integrity, low), (availability, low)}.

The resulting SC of the information system is expressed as

SC SCADA system = {(confidentiality, moderate), (integrity, high), (availability, high)},

thus representing the high-water mark or maximum potential impact values for each security objective from the information types resident on the SCADA system.

Why Is National Security Information Classified Differently?

The Unites States government and the military process, store, and transmit information directly related to national security. It is important that everyone who interacts with these data recognize the significance. The first EO specifically defining and classifying government information was issued by President Harry S. Truman in 1952. Subsequent EOs were issued by Presidents Eisenhower, Nixon, Carter, Reagan, Clinton, and Bush. In December 2009, President Barack Obama issued Executive Order 13526 (Classified National Security Information), which revoked and replaced previous EOs:

"This order prescribes a uniform system for classifying, safeguarding, and declassifying national security information, including information relating to defense against transnational terrorism. Our democratic principles require that the American people be informed of the activities of their Government. Also, our Nation's progress depends on the free flow of information. Nevertheless, throughout our history, the national defense has required that certain information be maintained in confidence in order to protect our citizens, our democratic institutions, our homeland security, and our interactions with foreign nations. Protecting information critical to our Nation's security and demonstrating our commitment to open Government through accurate and accountable application of classification standards and routine, secure, and effective declassification are equally important priorities." (President Barack Obama, December 29, 2009)

The following three special classifications defined in Executive Order 13526 denote special access and handling requirements. Information extraneous to the classification system is considered unclassified. Sensitive But Unclassified (SBU) is a Department of Defense–specific classification category. Authorization to assign classification level is restricted to specific U.S. Government officials:

- **Top Secret (TS):** Any information or material the unauthorized disclosure of which reasonably could be expected to cause exceptionally grave damage to the national security. Examples of exceptionally grave damage include armed hostilities against the United States or its allies;

disruption of foreign relations vitally affecting the national security; the compromise of vital national defense plans or complex cryptology and communications intelligence systems; the revelation of sensitive intelligence operations; and the disclosure of scientific or technological developments vital to national security.

- **Secret (S):** Any information or material the unauthorized disclosure of which reasonably could be expected to cause serious damage to the national security. Examples of serious damage include disruption of foreign relations significantly affecting the national security; significant impairment of a program or policy directly related to the national security; revelation of significant military plans or intelligence operations; compromise of significant military plans or intelligence operations; and compromise of significant scientific or technological developments relating to national security.

- **Confidential (C):** Any information or material the unauthorized disclosure of which reasonably could be expected to cause damage to the national security. Examples of damage include the compromise of information that indicates strength of ground, air, and naval forces in the United States and overseas areas; disclosure of technical information used for training, maintenance, and inspection of classified munitions of war; and revelation of performance characteristics, test data, design, and production data on munitions of war.

- **Unclassified (U):** Any information that can generally be distributed to the public without any threat to national interest. Note: This category is not specifically defined in EO 13526.

- **Sensitive But Unclassified (SBU):** This classification is a Department of Defense subcategory and is applied to "any information of which the loss, misuse or unauthorized access to, or modification of might *adversely affect* U.S. National Interests, the conduct of the Department of Defense (DoD) programs or the privacy of DoD personnel." Labeling in this category includes "For Official Use Only," "Not for Public Release," and "For Internal Use Only." Note that this category is not specifically defined in EO 13526.

Who Decides How National Security Data Is Classified?

National security data is classified in one of two ways:

- *Original classification* is the initial determination that information requires protection. Only specific U.S. Government officials who have been trained in classification requirements have the authority to make the classification decisions. Original classification authorities issue security classification guides that others use in making derivative classification decisions. Most government employees and contractors make derivative classification decisions.

- *Derivative classification* is the act of classifying a specific item of information or material based on an original classification decision already made by an authorized original classification authority. The source of authority for derivative classification ordinarily consists of a previously classified document or a classification guide issued by an original classification authority. There are two primary sources of policy guidance for derivative classification. Within the Department of Defense, DoD Manual 5200.01, Volumes 1-4, the Information Security Program, provides the basic guidance and regulatory requirements for the DoD Information Security Program. Volume 1, Enclosure 4, discusses derivative classifier responsibilities. For the private sector the DoD 5220.22-M, the National Industrial Security Program Operating Manual, or NISPOM, details the derivative classification responsibilities.

How Does the Private Sector Classify Data?

There are no legally mandated private sector data classifications, so organizations are free to develop a classification system appropriate to their organization. Commonly used classifications include Legally Protected, Confidential, Internal Use, and Public. Information owners are responsible for classifying data and systems. Based on the classification, information custodians can apply the appropriate controls and, importantly, users know how to interact with the data.

- **Protected:** Data that is protected by law, regulation, memorandum of agreement, contractual obligation, or management discretion. Examples include nonpublic personal information (NPPI), such as social security number, driver's license or state-issued identification number, bank account or financial account numbers, payment card information (PCI), which is credit or debit cardholder information, and personal health information (PHI).

- **Confidential:** Data that is essential to the mission of an organization. Loss, corruption, or un-authorized disclosure would cause *significant* financial or legal damage to the organization and its reputation. Examples include business strategies, financial positions, employee records, up-coming sales or advertising campaigns, laboratory research, and product schematics.

- **Internal Use:** Data that is necessary for conducting ordinary company business. Loss, corruption, or unauthorized disclosure *may* impair the business or result in business, financial, or legal loss. Examples include policy documents, procedure manuals, nonsensitive client or vendor information, employee lists, or organizational announcements.

- **Public:** Information that is specifically intended for the public at large. Public information requires discretionary treatment and should be cleared for release prior to public distribution. This category includes annual reports, product documentation, list of upcoming trade shows, and published white papers.

If the appropriate classification is not inherently obvious, a conservative approach is generally used and the data is classified in the more restrictive category.

FYI: What Is NPPI and Why Protect It?

Nonpublic personal information (NPPI) is data or information considered to be personal in nature, subject to public availability, and if disclosed is an invasion of privacy. Compromise of NPPI is often a precursor to identity theft. NPPI is protected from disclosure and/or requires notification of disclosure by a variety of federal and state laws and regulations.

NPPI in the private sector is also referred to as personally identifiable information (PII), or sensitive personal information (SPI).

NPPI is defined as an individual's first name (or first initial) and last name linked with any one or more of the following data elements:

- Social security number

- Driver's license number

- Date of birth

- Credit or debit card numbers

- State identification card number

- Financial account number, in combination with any required security code, access code, or password that would permit access to the account

In Practice

Information Classification Policy

Synopsis: An information classification system will be used to categorize information and information systems. The classification will be used to design and communicate baseline security controls.

Policy Statement:

- The company will use a four-tiered data classification schema consisting of protected, confidential, restricted, and public.

- The company will publish definitions for each classification.

- The criteria for each level will be maintained by and be available from the Office of Information Security.

- All information will be associated with one of the four data classifications. It is the responsibility of information owners to classify data.

- Information systems containing information from multiple classification levels will be secured in accordance with the requirements of the highest classification level.

- Data classification will remain in force regardless of the location or state of the data at any given time. This includes backup and archive mediums and locations.

- The classification system will allow that classifications of information assets may change over time.

- Each classification will have handling and protection rules. The Office of Information Security is responsible for the development and enforcement of the handling and protection rules.

Can Information Be Reclassified or Even Declassified?

Over a period of time, the need to protect information may change. An example of this can be found in the auto industry. Prior to a new car introduction, the design information is considered confidential. Disclosure would have serious ramifications to the automaker. After introduction, the same information is considered public and is published in the automotive manual. The process of downgrading sensitivity levels is known as *declassification*.

Conversely, organizations may choose to strengthen the classification level if they believe that doing so is for the benefit of the organization or required by evolving regulations. For example, in 2013, HIPAA regulations were extended to cover data maintained by business associates. In this case, business associates need to revisit the classification of data they access, store, process, or transmit. The process of upgrading a classification is known as *reclassification*. If the information owner knows ahead of time when the information should be reclassified, then that date should be noted on the original classification label (for example, "Confidential until [date]"). At the time an organization is establishing the criteria for classification levels, it should also include a mechanism for reclassifying and declassifying information. This responsibility may be assigned to the information owner or be subject to an internal review process.

Labeling and Handling Standards

Information owners classify information to identify the level of protection necessary. As we defined in Chapter 2, "Cybersecurity Policy Organization, Format and Styles," standards serve as specifications for the implementation of policy and dictate mandatory requirements. Handling standards dictate by classification level how information must be stored, transmitted, communicated, accessed, retained, and destroyed. *Labeling* is the vehicle for communicating the assigned classification to information custodians and users.

Why Label?

Labels make it easy to identify the data classification. Labels can take many forms: electronic, print, audio, and visual. Information may need to be labeled in many ways, depending on the audience. The labels you are probably most familiar with are safety labels. You recognize poison from the skull-and-crossbones symbol. You instinctively know to stop when you see a red stop sign. You know to pull over when you hear a police siren. To protect information, classification level labels need to be as clear and universally understood as a skull-and-crossbones symbol or a stop sign. Labels transcend institutional knowledge and provide stability in environments that experience personnel turnover.

In electronic form, the classification should be a part of the document name (for example, "Customer Transaction History–PROTECTED"). On written or printed documents, the classification label should be clearly marked on the outside of the document, as well as in either the document header or footer. Media, such as backup tapes, should be clearly labeled with words and (where appropriate) symbols.

Why Handling Standards?

Information needs to be handled in accordance with its classification. *Handling standards* inform custodians and users how to treat the information they use and the systems they interact with. Handling standards generally include storage, transmission, communication, access, retention, destruction, and disposal, and may extend to incident management and breach notification.

As illustrated in Table 5-1, it is important that handling standards be succinctly documented in usable format. The handling standards should be introduced during the orientation period and reintroduced as part of an Acceptable Use Policy and Agreement.

TABLE 5-1   Sample Handling Standards Matrix

Data-Handling Standard	Protected	Confidential	Internal
Data Storage (Servers)	Allowed as required for business purposes.	Allowed as required for business purposes.	Allowed as required for business purposes.
Data Storage (Workstations–Internal)	Not allowed.	Not allowed.	Allowed as required for business purposes.
Data Storage (Mobile Devices and Media)	Allowed as required for business purposes. Encryption required.	Allowed as required for business purposes. Encryption required.	Allowed as required for business purposes. Encryption highly recommended.
Data Storage (Workstations–Home)	Not allowed.	Not allowed.	Allowed as required for business purposes.
Data Storage (Removable Media for Backup Purposes)	Storage allowed as required for business purposes. Encryption required.	Allowed as required for business purposes. Encryption required.	Allowed as required for business purposes.
Internal Email	Should be avoided if possible.	Should be avoided if possible.	Allowed.
Instant Message or Chat	Not allowed.	Not allowed.	Allowed, but strongly discouraged.
External Email	Text allowed as required for business purposes. Encryption required. No attachments. Footer must indicate that the content is legally protected.	Text allowed as required for business purposes. Encryption required. No attachments.	Allowed. Encryption optional but strongly recommended.
External File Transfer	Must be pre-authorized by a SVP. Encryption required.	Must be pre-authorized by a SVP. Encryption required.	Allowed. Encryption optional but strongly recommended.
Remote Access	Multifactor authentication required.	Multifactor authentication required.	Multifactor authentication required.

Data-Handling Standard	"Protected"	"Confidential"	"Internal"
Data Retention	Refer to Legal Record Retention and Destruction Guidelines.	Refer to Company Record Retention and Destruction Guidelines.	Refer to Departmental Record Retention and Destruction Guidelines.
Electronic Data Disposal/ Destruction	Must be irrevocably destroyed. Destruction certification required.	Must be irrevocably destroyed.	Recommend irrevocable destruction.
Paper Document Disposal	Must be cross-shredded. Destruction certification required.	Must be cross-shredded.	Recommend cross-shred.
Paper Document Storage	Maintained in a secure storage area or locked cabinet.	Maintained in a secure storage area or locked cabinet.	No special requirements.
External Mail Carriers	Use commercial carrier or courier service. Envelope/box should be sealed in such a way that tampering would be obvious. Packages must be signed for.	Use commercial carrier or courier service. Envelope/box should be sealed in such a way that tampering would be obvious. Packages must be signed for.	No special requirements.
Outgoing Fax	Cover page should indicate the faxed information is legally protected.	Cover page should indicate the faxed information is confidential.	Cover page should indicate the faxed information is internal use.
Incoming Fax	Incoming faxes should be directed to the closest fax machine, and removed from the machine immediately.	Incoming faxes should be directed to closest fax machine, and removed from the machine immediately.	No special requirements.
Suspected Breach, Unauthorized Disclosure, or Compliance Violation Should Be Reported To:	Reported immediately to the ISO or Compliance Officer.	Reported immediately to the ISO or Supervisor.	Reported immediately to Supervisor.
Data Handling Questions Should Be Directed To:	ISO or Compliance Officer.	ISO or Supervisor.	Supervisor.

In Practice

Information Classification Handling and Labeling Requirements Policy

Synopsis: The classification and handling requirements of information assets should be clearly identified.

Policy Statement:

- Each classification will have labeling standards.

- Data and information systems will be labeled in accordance with their classification.

- Each classification of data will have documented handling standards for the following categories: storage, transmission, communication, access, logging, retention, destruction, disposal, incident management, and breach notification.

- The Office of Information Security is responsible for the development and implementation of the labeling and handling standards.

- All employees, contractors, and affiliates will be provided or have access to written documentation that clearly describes the labeling and handling standards.

- All employees, contractors, and affiliates will be provided with a resource to whom questions can be directed.

- All employees, contractors, and affiliates will be provided with a resource to whom violations can be reported.

Information Systems Inventory

As amazing as it may seem, many organizations do not have an up-to-date inventory of information systems. This happens for any number of reasons. The most prevalent is a lack of centralized management and control. Departments within organizations are given the autonomy to make individual decisions, bring in systems, and create information independent of the rest of the organization. Corporate cultures that encourage entrepreneurial behavior are particularly vulnerable to this lack of structure. Another reason is the growth of corporations through acquisitions and mergers. Sometimes companies change so rapidly it becomes nearly impossible to manage information effectively. Generally, the plan is to consolidate or merge information and systems, but in reality, they often end up cohabitating.

Why an Inventory Is Necessary and What Should Be Inventoried

An information systems inventory is necessary because without it, it will be very challenging to efficiently and accurately keep track of all the items that need to be secured, and also the elements that can introduce risk to the organization.

Putting together and maintaining a comprehensive physical inventory of information systems is a major task. The critical decision is choosing what attributes and characteristics of the information asset you want to record. The more specific and detailed the inventory, the more useful the inventory will be. Bear in mind that over time your inventory may have multiple purposes, including being used for criticality and risk analysis, business impact, disaster recovery planning insurance coverage, and business valuation.

Hardware Assets

Hardware assets are visible and tangible pieces of equipment and media, such as the following:

- **Computer equipment:** Mainframe computers, servers, desktops, laptops, tablets, and smartphones

- **Printers:** Printers, copiers, scanners, fax machines, and multifunction devices

- **Communication and networking equipment:** IDS/IPSs, firewalls, modems, routers, access points, cabling, DSU/CSUs, and transmission lines

- **Storage media:** Magnetic tapes, disks, CDs, DVDs, and USB thumb drives

- **Infrastructure equipment:** Power supplies, air conditioners, and access control devices

Software Assets

Software assets are programs or code that provide the interface between the hardware, the users, and the data. Software assets generally fall into three categories:

- **Operating system software:** Operating systems are responsible for providing the interface between the hardware, the user, and the application. Examples include Microsoft Windows, Apple iOS, Linux, UNIX, and FreeBSD.

- **Productivity software:** The objective of productivity software is to provide basic business functionality and tools. Examples include mobile apps, the Microsoft Office Suite (Word, Excel, Publisher, and PowerPoint), Adobe Reader, Intuit Quick Books, and TurboTax.

- **Application software:** Application software is designed to implement the business rules of the organization and is often custom-developed. Examples include programs that run complex machinery, process bank transactions, or manage lab equipment.

Asset Inventory Characteristics and Attributes

Each asset should have a ***unique identifier***. The most significant identifier is the device or program name. Although you may assume that the name is obvious, you'll often find that different users, departments, and audiences refer to the same information, system, or device differently. Best practices dictate that the organization chooses a naming convention for its assets and apply the standard consistently. The naming convention may include the location, vendor, instance, and date of service. For example, a Microsoft Exchange server located in New York City and connected to the Internet may be named MS_EX_NYC_1. A SQL database containing inventory records of women's shoes might be named SQL_SHOES_W. The name should also be clearly labeled on the device. The key is to be consistent so that the names themselves become pieces of information. This is, however, a double-edged sword. We risk exposing asset information to the public if our devices are accessible or advertise them in any way. We need to protect this information consistent with all other valuable information assets.

An *asset description* should indicate what the asset is used for. For example, devices may be identified as computers, connectivity, or infrastructure. Categories can (and should) be subdivided. Computers can be broken down into domain controllers, application servers, database servers, web servers, proxy servers' workstations, laptops, tablets, smartphones, and smart devices. Connectivity equipment might include IDS/IPSs, firewalls, routers, satellites, and switches. Infrastructure might include HVAC, utility, and physical security equipment.

For hardware devices, the manufacturer name, model number, part number, serial number, and host name or alias should be recorded. The physical and logical addresses should also be documented. The physical address refers to the geographic location of the device itself or the device that houses the information. This should be as specific as possible. For example, APPS1_NYC is located at the East 21st Street office's second floor data center. The logical address is where the asset can be found on the organization's network. The logical address should reference the host name, the Internet Protocol (IP) address, and, if applicable, the Media Access Control (MAC) address. Host names are "friendly names" given to systems. The host name may be the actual name of the system or an alias used for easy reference. The IP address is the unique network address location assigned to this system. Last, the MAC address is a unique identifier assigned to network connectivity devices by the manufacturer of the device.

FYI: Logical Addresses

Every device connected to a network or the Internet must be uniquely identified. The MAC address, the IP address, and the domain name are all used to identify a device. These addresses are known as "logical" rather than "physical" because they have little or no relationship to the geographic location of the device.

- **MAC Address:** A Media Access Control (MAC) address is a hardware identification number that uniquely identifies a device. The MAC address is manufactured into every network card, such as an Ethernet card or Wi-Fi card. MAC addresses are made up of six two-digit hexadecimal numbers, separated by colon. Example: 9c:d3:6d:b9:ff:5e.

- **IPv4 Address:** A numeric label that uniquely identifies a device on the Internet and/or on an internal network. The label consists of four groups of numbers between 0 and 255, separated by periods (dots). Example: 195.112.56.75.

- **IPv6 Address:** Similar in function to IPv4, IPv6 is a 128-bit identifier. An IPv6 address is represented as eight groups of four hexadecimal digits. Example: FE80:0000:0000:0000: 0202:B3FF:FE1E:8329.

- **IP Domain Name:** Domain names serve as humanly memorable names for Internet connected devices (for example, www.yourschool.edu). The "yourschool.edu" section of the name is assigned by an Internet registrar and uniquely describes a set of devices. The "www" is an alias for a specific device. When you access a website, the full domain name is actually translated to an IP address, which defines the server where the website is located. This translation is performed dynamically by a service called a domain name system (DNS).

Software should be recorded by publisher or developer, version number, revision, the department or business that purchased or paid for the asset number, and, if applicable, patch level. Software vendors often assign a serial number or "software key," which should be included in the record.

Last but not least, the controlling entity should be recorded. The controlling entity is the department or business that purchased or paid for the asset and/or is responsible for the ongoing maintenance and upkeep expense. The controlling entity's capital expenditures and expenses are reflected in its budgets, balance sheets, and profit and loss statements.

There are many tools in the market that can accelerate and automate asset inventory. Some of these tools and solutions can be cloud-based or installed on-premise. Asset management software and solutions help you to monitor the complete asset life cycle from procurement to disposal. Some of these solutions support the automated discovery and management of all hardware and software inventory deployed in your network. Some also allow you to categorize and group your assets so that you can understand the context easily. These asset management solutions can also help you keep track of all your software assets and licenses so you can remain compliant. The following are a few examples of asset management solutions:

- ServiceNOW

- SolarWinds Web Help Desk

- InvGate Assets

- ManageEngine AssetExplorer

Removing, Disposing Of, or Destroying Company Property

Company assets should be accounted for at all times. If company property needs to move from its assigned location or be destroyed, there should be an asset management procedure. Documentation should be maintained so that at any time an audit will account for the location and possession of every piece of equipment or information. Asset disposal and destruction is discussed in Chapter 7, "Physical and Environmental Security."

In Practice

Inventory of Information System Assets Policy

Synopsis: All information systems should be inventoried and tracked.

Policy Statement:

- All information system assets will be identified and documented with their classification, owner, location, and other details according to standards published by the Office of Information Security.

- Company assets must be accounted for at all times.

- The Office of Information Security will maintain the inventory documentation.

- Copies of all inventory documentation will be included in the Business Continuity Plan.

FYI: Small Business Note

Is it necessary for small businesses to classify data? Emphatically, yes! It is very likely that a small business stores, processes, or transmits legally protected financial or medical data and/or is contractually obligated to protect debit and credit card information. At the very least, the company has information that for reasons related to either privacy or competition should not become public knowledge. Table 5-2 shows a combination three-tier data classification description and data-handling instructions for small businesses.

TABLE 5-2 Small Business Data Classification and Handling Instructions

Data Classification and Data Handling Instructions

I. Data Classification Definitions

Protected	Data that is protected by law, regulation, contractual obligation, or management discretion.
Confidential	Data that should not be publicly disclosed.
Public	Data that is specifically intended for the public at large.

II. Data Handling Instructions

	Protected	*Confidential*	*Public*
Data Storage Servers	Allowed as required for business purposes.	Allowed as required for business purposes.	Allowed as required for business purposes.
Data Storage Workstations	Not allowed.	Not allowed.	Allowed as required for business purposes.
Data Storage Mobile Devices	Allowed as required for business purposes. Encryption required.	Allowed as required for business purposes. Encryption required.	Allowed as required for business purposes.

	Protected	Confidential	Public
Data Storage Home Workstations	Not allowed.	Not allowed.	Allowed as required for business purposes.
Internal Email	Should be avoided if possible.	Allowed.	Allowed.
External Email	Must be sent using secure email.	Allowed.	Allowed.
External File Transfer	Must be sent using a secure file transfer program.	Must be sent using a secure file transfer program.	Allowed.
Remote Access	Requires multifactor authentication.	Requires multifactor authentication.	N/A
Disposal/ Destruction	Must be irrevocably destroyed.	Must be irrevocably destroyed.	N/A
Paper Documents	Maintained in a secure storage area or in a locked cabinet.	Maintained in a secure storage area or in a locked cabinet.	N/A
Questions and Concerns	Please direct all questions or concerns to your direct supervisor.		

Understanding Data Loss Prevention Technologies

Data loss prevention (DLP) is the capability to detect any sensitive emails, documents, or information leaving your organization. These solutions typically protect the following data types:

- **Personally Identifiable Information (PII):** Date of birth, employee numbers, social security numbers, national and local government identification numbers, credit card information, personal health information, and so on

- **Intellectual Property (IP):** Patent applications, product design documents, the source code of software, research information, and customer data

- **Nonpublic Information (NPI):** Financial information, acquisitions-related information, corporate policies, legal and regulatory matters, executive communication, and so on

Figure 5-2 lists the three states in which data can exist and the related protections.

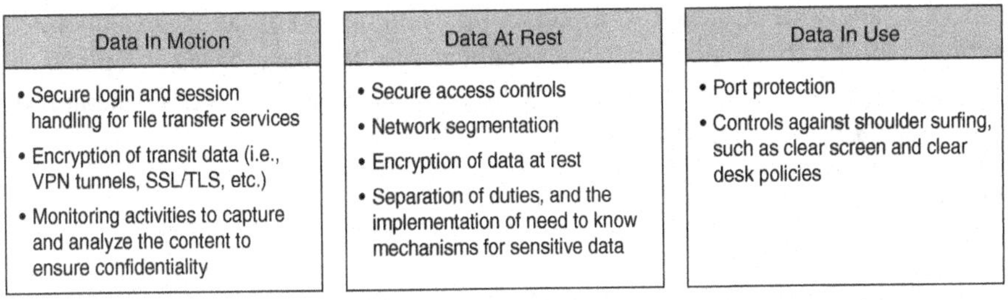

Data In Motion	Data At Rest	Data In Use
• Secure login and session handling for file transfer services • Encryption of transit data (i.e., VPN tunnels, SSL/TLS, etc.) • Monitoring activities to capture and analyze the content to ensure confidentiality	• Secure access controls • Network segmentation • Encryption of data at rest • Separation of duties, and the implementation of need to know mechanisms for sensitive data	• Port protection • Controls against shoulder surfing, such as clear screen and clear desk policies

FIGURE 5-2 Data States and Related Protections

What is data exfiltration? This is often referred to as data extrusion. Data exfiltration is the unauthorized transfer of data from a system or network manually (carried out by someone with physical access to such system), or it may be automated and carried out through malware or system compromise over a network.

Several products in the industry inspect for traffic to prevent data loss in an organization. Several industry security products integrate with third-party products to provide this type of solution.

For example, the Cisco ESA and the Cisco WSA integrate RSA email DLP for outbound email and web traffic. These DLP solutions allow network security administrators to remain compliant and to maintain advanced control with encryption, DLP, and onsite identity-based integration. These solutions also allow deep content inspection for regulatory compliance and data exfiltration protection. It enables an administrator to inspect web content by title, metadata, and size, and even to prevent users from storing files to cloud services such as Dropbox, Box, and Google Drive.

CloudLock is also another DLP solution. CloudLock is designed to protect organizations of any type against data breaches in any type of cloud environment or application (app) through a highly configurable cloud-based DLP architecture.

Several of these solutions provide application programming interfaces (APIs) that provide a deep level of integration with monitored SaaS, IaaS, PaaS, and IDaaS solutions. They provide advanced cloud DLP functionality that includes out-of-the-box policies designed to help administrators maintain compliance.

An important benefit of cloud-based DLP solutions is that they allow you to monitor data at rest within platforms via APIs and provide a comprehensive picture of user activity through retroactive monitoring capabilities. Security administrators can mitigate risk efficiently using configurable, automated response actions, including encryption, quarantine, and end-user notification.

Data loss doesn't always take place because of a complex attack carried out by an external attacker; many data loss incidents have been carried out by internal (insider) attacks. Data loss can also happen because of human negligence or ignorance—for example, an internal employee sending sensitive corporate email to a personal email account, or uploading sensitive information to an unapproved cloud provider. This is why maintaining visibility into what's coming as well as leaving the organization is so important.

Data loss prevention (DLP) tools are designed to detect and prevent data exfiltration (unauthorized release or removal of data). DLP technologies locate and catalogue sensitive data (based on a predetermined set of rules or criteria), and DLP tools monitor target data while in use, in motion, and at rest. Table 5-3 summarizes some DLP tools and where they are placed in the network.

TABLE 5-3   DLP Location/Placement

DLP Tool	Description/Placement
Network-based (on premise)	Network-based (hardware or virtual appliance) deals with data in motion and is usually located on the network perimeter.
Storage-based	Storage-based (software) operates on long-term storage (archive).
End-point based	End-point based (software) operates on a local device and focuses on data-in-use.
Cloud-based (off premise)	Cloud-based operates in the cloud, with data in use, motion, and at rest.

DLP solutions can be used to identify and control end-point ports as well as block access to removable media.

- Identify removable devices / media connected to your network by type (for example, USB thumb drive, CD burner, smart phone), manufacturer, model number, and MAC address.

- Control and manage removable devices through endpoint ports, including USB, FireWire, Wi-Fi, Modem / Network NIC, and Bluetooth.

- Require encryption, limit file types, limit file size.

- Provide detailed forensics on device usage and data transfer by person, time, file type, and amount.

Summary

You may have heard the phrase "security through obscurity." This phrase implies that there is a proportional relationship between keeping an asset hidden and its safety. The problem with this concept is that it is not practical, or even desirable, to keep our information and systems locked up. Information assets have value to the organization and are often used in day-to-day operations to accomplish its mission. The inverse to "security through obscurity" is "security through classification and labeling." The best way to protect an information asset or system is to identify the confidentiality, integrity, and availability (CIA) requirements, and then apply the appropriate safeguards and handling standards. The process of identification and differentiation is known as *classification*. Information owners are responsible for properly identifying and classifying the information for which they are responsible. Information custodians are tasked with implementing security controls.

FISMA requires that federal agency information owners classify their information and information systems as low, moderate, or high security based on criteria outlined in the FIPS-199. Information is evaluated for confidentiality with respect to the impact of unauthorized disclosure as well as the use of the information, integrity with respect to the impact associated with unauthorized modification or destruction, and availability with respect to the impact of disruption of access to or use of the information. Five special classifications are reserved for national security–related information that denotes special access and handling requirements: Top Secret, Secret, Confidential, Unclassified, and Sensitive But Unclassified (SBU). The process of downgrading a classification is known as *declassification*. The process of upgrading a classification is known as *reclassification*.

There are no comparable classification requirements for the private sector. However, multiple state and federal statutes require all organizations to protect specific categories of information. The broadest category is nonpublic personal information (NPPI). NPPI is information considered to be personal in nature, subject to public availability, and if disclosed is an invasion of privacy. It is common for private sector organizations to adopt a three- or four-tier classification system that takes into account legal, privacy, and business confidentiality requirements. Labeling is the vehicle for communicating the assigned classification to information custodians and users. Handling standards inform custodians and users how to treat the information they use and the systems they interact with.

Information systems provide a way and a place to process, store, and transmit information assets. It is important to maintain an up-to-date inventory of hardware and software assets. Hardware assets are visible and tangible pieces of equipment and media. Software assets are programs or code that provide the interface between the hardware, the users, and the data. Descriptors may include what the asset is used for, its location, the unique hardware identification number known as a MAC address, the unique network identifier known as an IP address, host name, and domain name.

Organizational Asset Management policies include Information Ownership, Information Classification, Handling and Labeling Requirements, and Information Systems Inventory.

In this chapter, you learned that DLP is the technology and capability to detect any sensitive emails, documents, or information leaving your organization. This is often referred to as *data exfiltration* or *data extrusion*. Data exfiltration is the unauthorized transfer of data from a system or network manually (carried out by someone with physical access to such system), or it may be automated and carried out through malware or system compromise over a network.

Test Your Skills

MULTIPLE CHOICE QUESTIONS

1. Which of the following terms best describes a definable piece of information, stored in any manner, that is recognized as having value to the organization?

    A. NPPI

    B. Information asset

    C. Information system

    D. Classified data

2. Information systems _____, _____, and _____ information.

    A. create, modify, and delete

    B. classify, reclassify, and declassify

    C. store, process, and transmit

    D. use, label, and handle

3. Information owners are responsible for which of the following tasks?

    A. Classifying information

    B. Maintaining information

    C. Using information

    D. Registering information

4. Which of the following roles is responsible for implementing and maintaining security controls and reporting suspected incidents?

    A. Information owner

    B. Information vendor

    C. Information user

    D. Information custodian

5. FIPS-199 requires that federal government information and information systems be classified as _____.

   A. low, moderate, high security

   B. moderate, critical, low security

   C. high, critical, top-secret security

   D. none of the above

6. Information classification systems are used in which of the following organizations?

   A. Government

   B. Military

   C. Financial institutions

   D. All of the above

7. FIPS requires that information be evaluated for _____ requirements with respect to the impact of unauthorized disclosure as well as the use of the information.

   A. integrity

   B. availability

   C. confidentiality

   D. secrecy

8. Which of the following National Security classifications requires the most protection?

   A. Secret

   B. Top Secret

   C. Confidential

   D. Unclassified

9. Which of the following National Security classifications requires the least protection?

   A. Secret

   B. Unclassified

   C. Confidential

   D. Sensitive But Unclassified (SBU)

10. The Freedom of Information Act (FOIA) allows anyone access to which of the following?

   A. Access to all government information just by asking

   B. Access to all classified documents

    C. Access to classified documents on a "need to know" basis

    D. Access to any records from federal agencies unless the documents can be officially declared exempt

11. Which of the following terms best describes the CIA attribute associated with the modification of information?

    A. Classified

    B. Integrity

    C. Availability

    D. Intelligence

12. Is it mandatory for all private businesses to classify information?

    A. Yes.

    B. Yes, but only if they want to pay less tax.

    C. Yes, but only if they do business with the government.

    D. No.

13. Which of the following is not a criterion for classifying information?

    A. The information is not intended for the public domain.

    B. The information has no value to the organization.

    C. The information needs to be protected from those outside of the organization.

    D. The information is subject to government regulations.

14. Data that is considered to be personal in nature and, if disclosed, is an invasion of privacy and a compromise of security is known as which of the following?

    A. Nonpersonal public information

    B. Nonprivate personal information

    C. Nonpublic personal information

    D. None of the above

15. Most organizations restrict access to protected, confidential, and internal-use data to which of the following roles within the organization?

    A. Executives

    B. Information owners

    C. Users who have a "need to know"

    D. Vendors

16. Labeling is the vehicle for communicating classification levels to which of the following roles within the organization?

    A. Employees

    B. Information custodians

    C. Contractors

    D. All of the above

17. Which of the following terms best describes rules for how to store, retain, and destroy data based on classification?

    A. Handling standards

    B. Classification procedures

    C. Use policies

    D. Material guidelines

18. Which of the following terms best describes the process of removing restricted classification levels?

    A. Declassification

    B. Classification

    C. Reclassification

    D. Negative classification

19. Which of the following terms best describes the process of upgrading or changing classification levels?

    A. Declassification

    B. Classification

    C. Reclassification

    D. Negative classification

20. The impact of destruction and/or permanent loss of information is used to determine which of the following safeguards?

    A. Authorization

    B. Availability

    C. Authentication

    D. Accounting

21. Which of the following terms best describes an example of a hardware asset?

    A. Server

    B. Database

    C. Operating system

    D. Radio waves

22. Which of the following statements best describes a MAC address?

    A. A MAC address is a dynamic network address.

    B. A MAC address is a unique host name.

    C. A MAC address is a unique hardware identifier.

    D. A MAC address is a unique alias.

23. 10.1.45.245 is an example of which of the following?

    A. A MAC address

    B. A host name

    C. An IP address

    D. An IP domain name

24. Source code and design documents are examples of which of the following?

    A. Software assets

    B. Proprietary information

    C. Internal-use classification

    D. Intellectual property (IP)

25. Which of the following terms best describes the act of classifying information based on an original classification decision already made by an authorized original classification authority?

    A. Reclassification

    B. Derivative classification

    C. Declassification

    D. Original classification

26. Which of the following types of information would not be considered NPPI?

    A. Social security number

    B. Date of birth

    C. Debit card PIN

    D. Car manufacturer's name

27. In keeping with best practices and regulatory expectations, legally protected data that is stored on mobile devices should be _____.

    A. masked

    B. encrypted

    C. labeled

    D. segregated

28. Which of the following statements best describes how written documents that contain NPPI should be handled?

    A. Written documents that contain NPPI should be stored in locked areas or in a locked cabinet.

    B. Written documents that contain NPPI should be destroyed by cross-cut shredding.

    C. Written documents that contain NPPI should be subject to company retention policies.

    D. All of the above.

29. Which of the following address types represents a device location on a network?

    A. A physical address

    B. A MAC address

    C. A logical address

    D. A static address

30. What is DLP?

    A. An email inspection technology used to prevent phishing attacks

    B. A software or solution for making sure that corporate users do not send sensitive or critical information outside the corporate network

    C. A web inspection technology used to prevent phishing attacks

    D. A cloud solution used to provide dynamic layer protection

EXERCISES

EXERCISE 5.1: Assigning Ownership

Owners are responsible for the protection of assets. For each of the following assets, assign an owner and list the owner's responsibilities in regard to protecting the asset:

1. The house you live in.

2. The car you drive.

3. The computer you use.

4. The city you live in.

EXERCISE 5.2: Differentiating Between Ownership and Custodianship

A smartphone is an information system. As with any information system, data ownership and custodianship must be assigned.

1. If a company provides a smartphone to an employee to use for work-related communications:

   a. Who would you consider the information system owner? Why?

   b. Who would you consider the information system custodian? Why?

2. If a company allows an employee to use a personally owned device for work-related communications:

   a. Who would you consider the information system owner? Why?

   b. Who would you consider the information system custodian? Why?

   c. In regard to protecting data, should there be a distinction between company data and personal data?

EXERCISE 5.3: Creating an Inventory

You have been tasked with creating an inventory system for the computer lab at your school.

1. For the hardware in the lab, list at least five characteristics you will use to identify each asset.

2. For the software in the lab, list at least five characteristics you will use to identify each asset.

3. Create an inventory template. Use either a spreadsheet or database application.

4. Visit a classroom or lab and inventory a minimum of three hardware and three software assets.

EXERCISE 5.4: Reviewing a Declassified Document

Go to either http://FOIA.gov or the CIA FOIA Electronic Reading Room at www.foia.cia.gov.

1. Find a document that has been recently declassified.

2. Write a brief report explaining why and when the document was declassified.

EXERCISE 5.5: Understanding Color-Coded National Security

The Department of Homeland Security uses a color-coded advisory system to communicate threat levels to the public. This is an example of labeling.

1. What colors are used in the Threat Advisory System?

2. What does each of the colors mean?

3. Do you think these labels are an effective way to communicate threat information to the general public? Why or why not?

PROJECTS

PROJECT 5.1: Developing an Email Classification System and Handling Standards

Data classification categories and handling standards are necessary to properly protect information. Email is a good example of an information system that processes, stores, and transmits many types of information.

1. Develop a three-level classification system for your email communications. Consider the type of emails you send and receive. Take into consideration who should be able to view, save, print, or forward your email. For each classification, decide how you will label your emails to communicate the assigned classification. For each classification, develop handling standards.

2. Multiple information systems are used to process, transmit, store, and back up email. Identify as many systems as possible involved in each step. For each system identified, document the person or position you would expect to be the information system owner. Is it necessary to provide them with a copy of your classification system or handling standards? Why or why not?

3. Sometimes information system owners have different priorities. For example, your Internet service provider (ISP) by law has the right to view/open all documents that are stored on or passed through its systems. The ISP may choose to exercise this right by scanning for viruses or checking for illegal content. Suppose you have sent emails that could cause you harm if they were disclosed or compromised. As the information owner, what are your options?

PROJECT 5.2: Classifying Your School Records

Over time, your school has accumulated a great deal of information about you and your family, including your medical records, finances (including tax returns), transcripts, and student demographic data (name, address, date of birth, and so on). It is important that access to this information be restricted to authorized users.

1. Create a table listing each of these information categories. Classify each one as either Protected, Confidential, Internal Use, or Public.

2. Include in your table a column defining the "need to know" criteria. (Hint: This is the reason someone should be granted access to the information.)

3. Even though the information pertains to you, you are not the owner. Include in your table a column listing who you would expect to be the information owner.

4. Choose one of the categories you have listed and find out where the information is actually stored, who is responsible for it, who has access to it, and what policies are in place to protect it. Compare this information with your answers to items 1, 2, and 3 of this project.

PROJECT 5.3: Locating and Using Special Publications

The National Institute of Standards and Technology (NIST) special publications contain a wealth of information applicable to both private and public sector organizations. In this exercise, you will familiarize yourself with locating and using special publications.

1. Download a copy of NIST SP 800-88, R1: Guidelines for Media Sanitization.

2. Read through the document.

3. To whom do they assign ultimate responsibility for media sanitization?

4. In regard to media sanitization, explain the differences between clear, purge, and destroy?

Case Study

Assessing Classification and Authorization at SouthEast Healthcare

SouthEast Healthcare was founded in 1920. It is headquartered in Atlanta, Georgia and has 15 patient care sites located throughout the state. SouthEast Healthcare provides a full range of health-care services. The organization is a leader in electronic medical records and telemedicine services delivered via the Web. Over the years, they have made significant information security investments, including advanced intrusion detection systems; programs that audit, monitor, and report access; biometric devices; and training. Although their information technology (IT) and security staff is small, they are a dedicated team of professionals. SouthEast Healthcare appeared to be a model of security and was selected to participate in a HIPAA security study. At first, the audit team was very impressed. Then they began to wonder how protection decisions were made. It appeared to them that all information assets were being treated with equal protection, which meant that some were perhaps protected too much, whereas others were under-protected. They approached the CEO and asked her to explain how the organization made protection decisions. She replied that she left it up to the IT and security team. The auditors then went to the members of the team and asked them the same question. They enthusiastically replied that the importance of the various information assets was "institutional knowledge." They were puzzled when the auditors asked if the information owners classified the information and authorized the protection levels. No, they replied, it had always been left to them. The auditors were not happy with this answer and expressed their displeasure in their interim report. The auditors are coming back in three months to complete the study. SouthEast Healthcare's CEO wants this problem fixed before they return.

1. Who should take responsibility for the classification and authorization project?

2. Is this one project or two separate projects?

3. Who should be involved in this project(s)?

4. Would you engage external resources? Why or why not?

5. How would you gain consensus?

6. What involvement should the Board of Directors have?

References

Regulations Cited

FIPS PUB 199 Standards for the Security Categorization of Federal Information and Information Systems, February 2004, accessed 05/2018, http://nvlpubs.nist.gov/nistpubs/FIPS/NIST.FIPS.199.pdf.

Freedom of Information Act, official website of the U.S. Department of Justice, FOIA, accessed 05/2018, www.foia.gov/.

Modifications to the HIPAA Privacy, Security, Enforcement, and Breach Notification Rules 45 CFR Parts 160 and 164 Under the Health Information Technology for Economic and Clinical Health Act and the Genetic Information Nondiscrimination Act; Other Modifications to the HIPAA Rules; Final Rule Federal Register, Volume 78, No. 17, January 25, 2013, accessed 05/2018, https://www.hhs.gov/hipaa/for-professionals/privacy/laws-regulations/combined-regulation-text/omnibus-hipaa-rulemaking/index.html.

"Instructions for Developing Security Classification Guides," accessed 05/2018, http://www.esd.whs.mil/Portals/54/Documents/DD/issuances/dodm/520045m.pdf.

Chapter | **6**

Human Resources Security

Chapter Objectives

After reading this chapter and completing the exercises, you will be able to do the following:

- Define the relationship between cybersecurity and personnel practices.
- Recognize the stages of the employee life cycle.
- Describe the purpose of confidentiality and acceptable use agreements.
- Understand appropriate security education, training, and awareness programs.
- Create personnel-related security policies and procedures.

Is it possible that people are simultaneously an organization's most valuable asset and their most dangerous threat? Study after study cites people as the weakest link in cybersecurity. Because cybersecurity is primarily a people-driven process, it is imperative that the cybersecurity program be faithfully supported by information owners, custodians, and users.

For an organization to function, employees need access to information and information systems. Because we are exposing valuable assets, we must know our employees' backgrounds, education, and weaknesses. Employees must also know what is expected of them; from the very first contact, the organization needs to deliver the message that security is taken seriously. Conversely, candidates and employees provide employers with a great deal of personal information. It is the organization's responsibility to protect employee-related data in accordance with regulatory and contractual obligations.

Before employees are given access to information and information systems, they must understand organizational expectations, policies, handling standards, and consequences of noncompliance. This information is generally codified into two agreements: a confidentiality agreement and an acceptable use agreement. Acceptable use agreements should be reviewed and updated annually and redistributed to employees for signature. An orientation and training program should be designed to explain and expand upon the concepts presented in the agreements. Even long-standing employees continually need to be reeducated about security issues. NIST has invested significant resources in developing a role-based Security Education, Training, and Awareness (SETA) model. Although designed for government, the model is on target for the private sector.

We begin this chapter with examining the security issues associated with employee recruitment, onboarding, user provisioning, career development, and termination. We then discuss the importance of confidentiality and acceptable use agreements. Last, we focus on the SETA training methodology. Throughout the chapter, we codify best practices into human resources security policy.

FYI: NIST Cybersecurity Framework and ISO/IEC 27002:2013

The PR.IP-11 subcategory of the NIST Cybersecurity Framework describes human resources practices (including deprovisioning, personnel screening, and so on).

Section 7 of ISO 27002:2013 is dedicated to Human Resources Security Management with the objective of ensuring that security is integrated into the employee life cycle.

Corresponding NIST guidance is provided in the following documents and other references:

- SP 800-12: An Introduction to Computer Security—The NIST Handbook
- SP 800-16: Information Technology Security Training Requirements: A Role- and Performance-Based Model
- SP 800-50: Building an Information Technology Security Awareness and Training Program
- SP 800-100: Information Security Handbook: A Guide for Managers
- SP 800-53 Rev. 4 PS Family
- COBIT 5 APO07.01, APO07.02, APO07.03, APO07.04, APO07.05

The Employee Life Cycle

The *employee life cycle 1* model (shown in Figure 6-1) represents stages in an employee's career. Specific employee life cycle models vary from company to company, but common stages include the following:

- **Recruitment:** This stage includes all the processes leading up to and including the hiring of a new employee.
- **Onboarding:** In this stage, the employee is added to the organization's payroll and benefits systems.
- **User provisioning:** In this stage, the employee is assigned equipment as well as physical and technical access permissions. The user provisioning process is also invoked whenever there is a change in the employee's position, level of access required, or termination.

- **Orientation:** In this stage, the employee settles into the job, integrates with the corporate culture, familiarizes himself with co-workers and management, and establishes his role within the organization.

- **Career development:** In this stage, the employee matures in his role in the organization. Professional development frequently means a change in roles and responsibilities.

- **Termination:** In this stage, the employee leaves the organization. The specific processes are somewhat dependent on whether the departure is the result of resignation, firing, or retirement. Tasks include removing the employee from the payroll and benefits system, recovering information assets such as his smartphone, and deleting or disabling user accounts and access permissions.

- **Off-boarding:** The process for transitioning employees out of an organization. This includes documenting the separation or termination details, tasks and responsibilities prior to departure, knowledge transfer, an exit interview (if applicable), the deletion of all user credentials and any other access the user had.

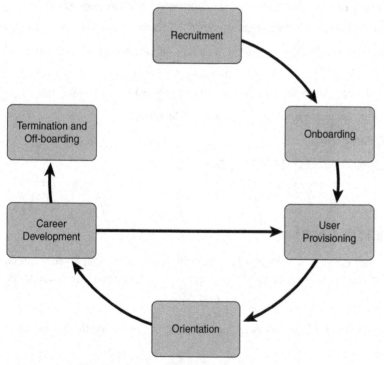

FIGURE 6-1   The Employee Life Cycle

With the exception of career development, we are going to examine each of these stages in relation to cybersecurity concepts, safeguards, and policies.

What Does Recruitment Have to Do with Security?

The recruitment stage includes developing and publishing job descriptions, actively seeking potential employees, collecting and assessing candidate data, interviewing, conducting background checks, and either making an offer or rejecting a candidate. A significant flow of information occurs during the recruitment stage. In hopes of attracting the most qualified candidate, information about the organization is publicly revealed. In turn, potential candidates respond with a plethora of personal information.

Job Postings

The first direct contact many potential candidates have with their future employer is a help-wanted advertisement. Historically, this advertisement was either published in a newspaper or trade journal or provided to a "headhunter" who specialized in finding potential candidates. In either case, the circulation was limited in scope and time. Today, a majority of recruiting is Internet-based. Companies may post jobs on their website, use online employment search engines such as Monster. com, or use social media such as LinkedIn. The upside to this trend is reaching a wider audience of talent. The downside is that this exposure also reaches a wider audience of potential intruders and may have the unintended consequence of exposing information about an organization. Job postings are one of the sources that intruders often look to use. Why? Because job postings can be a wealth of information about an organization: personnel changes, product development, new services, opening of offices, as well as basic information such as the name and phone number of the hiring manager. All these items can be used in social engineering attacks and provide a path to more in-depth knowledge. An idea to consider is having two versions of a job description. Version A is posted and/or published and has enough information to attract the attention and interest of a potential employee. Version B is more detailed and is posted internally and/or shared with candidates that have made the "first cut." Version B of a job description needs to be detailed enough to convey the facets of the position and has the following characteristics:

- It conveys the mission of the organization.

- It describes the position in general terms.

- It outlines the responsibilities of the position.

- It details the necessary skill set.

- It states the organization's expectations regarding confidentiality, safety, and security. The goal of this characteristic is to deliver the message that the organization has a commitment to security and that all employees are required to honor that commitment.

What should not be in either version of the job description is information regarding specific systems, software versions, security configurations, or access controls.

Candidate Application Data

The intent of posting a job is to have candidates respond with pertinent information. Collecting candidate data is a double-edged sword. On one hand, companies need personal information to properly select potential employees. On the other hand, once this information is collected, companies are responsible for protecting the data as well as the privacy of the job seeker. *Candidate data* generally collected during this phase includes demographic, contact, work history, accomplishments, education, compensation, previous employer feedback, references, clearances, and certifications. If possible, legally protected *nonpublic personal information (NPPI)*, such as social security number, date of birth, driver's license or state identification number, and financial information should not be collected at this stage.

The Interview

Top-tier candidates are often invited to one or more interviews with a cross-section of personnel. Invariably, interviewers share more information than they should with job candidates. They do so for a variety of reasons. Sometimes they are trying to impress a sought-after candidate. They may be proud of (or dismayed with) the organization. Sometimes they simply do not realize the confidentiality of the information they are sharing. For example, an interviewer might reveal that the organization is about to launch a new mobile app and that they know little about how to secure it! Creating and following an interview script (that has been vetted by cybersecurity personnel) can minimize the risk of disclosure. One of the worst mistakes that an interviewer can make is taking an early-stage job candidate on a tour of the facility. A candidate should never be allowed access to secure areas without prior authorization by the information system owner. Even then, caution should be exercised.

In Practice

Job Recruitment Policy

Synopsis: In support of cybersecurity, the purpose of this policy is to ensure that company and candidate resources are protected during the recruitment process.

Policy Statement:

- Any information that is classified as "protected" or "confidential" must *not* be included in job postings or job descriptions.

- Candidates will not be allowed access to any secure area unless authorized in writing by the information owner.

- All nonpublic information submitted by candidates must be classified as "protected" and handled in accordance with company handling standards.

- Under no circumstances will the company request that candidates provide a password to social media, blog, web, or personal email accounts.

- The Office of Information Security and the Office of Human Resources will be jointly responsible for the implementation and enforcement of this policy.

Screening Prospective Employees

You are a business owner. You have spent the past 10 years toiling night and day to build your business. You have invested your personal financial resources. Your reputation in the community is intertwined with the actions of the business. How much do you need to know about your newest salesperson?

You are the Chief Executive Officer (CEO) of a Fortune 1000 financial services company. You are responsible to the stockholders and accountable to the government for the actions of your business. How much do you need to know about your new Chief Financial Officer (CFO)?

You are the Head of Medicine at your local hospital. You are responsible for maintaining the health of your patients and for guaranteeing their right to privacy. How much do you need to know about the new emergency room intake nurse?

In all three cases, the information owner wants assurance that the user will treat the information appropriately in accordance with its classification. One of the standards in determining who should have access is defining the user criteria. These criteria extend to their background: education, experience, certification/license, criminal record, and financial status. In addition, we must consider the amount of power or influence the employee will have in the organization.

For example, we expect that a CFO will have access to confidential financial records and sensitive corporate strategy documents. In addition, the CFO has the power to potentially manipulate the data. In this case, we need to be concerned about both the confidentiality and the integrity of the information. It seems obvious that the CFO needs to be held to a high standard. He should have a spotless criminal record and not be under any financial pressure that may lead to inappropriate activities such as embezzlement. Unfortunately, as corporate scandals such as Enron, Adelphia, HealthSouth, and Tyco have shown us, those in power do not always act in the best interest of the organization. The organization needs to proactively protect itself by conducting background and reference checks on potential employees and directors. The same holds true for positions of less prominence, such as a salesperson or intake nurse. Although these positions may have less power, the potential for misuse still exists.

Not all potential employees need to undergo the same level of scrutiny. It is the responsibility of the information owner to set standards based on level of information access and position.

The various types of background checks are as follows:

- **Educational:** Verification that all educational credentials listed on the application, resume, or cover letter are valid and have been awarded.

- **Employment:** Verification of all relevant previous employment as listed on the application, resume, or cover letter.

- **License/certification:** Verification of all relevant licenses, certifications, or credentials.

- **Credit history:** Checking the credit history of the selected applicant or employee. Federal laws prohibit discrimination against an applicant or employee because of bankruptcy. Federal law also requires that applicants be notified if their credit history influences the employment decision.

- **Criminal history:** Verification that the selected applicant or employee does not have any un-disclosed criminal history.

It is important to have a policy that sets the minimum standards for the organization yet affords information owners the latitude to require additional or more in-depth background checks or investigations. This is an example of a policy that in the development stage may need to involve outsiders, such as legal counsel or employee representatives. Many organizations have union labor. The union contract may forbid the background checks. This policy would need to be incorporated into the next round of negotiations. The following are rules you should be aware of:

- **Employee's right to privacy:** There are legal limits on the information you can gather and use when making employment decisions. Workers have a right to privacy in certain personal matters, a right they can enforce by suing you if you pry too deeply. Make sure your inquiries are related to the job. Stick to information that is relevant to the job for which you are considering the worker. Different regulatory bodies such as Article 88 of the European Union General Data Protection Regulation (GDPR) include strict rules around the processing of data and privacy in the context of employment.

- **Getting consent:** Although not universally required by law, conventional wisdom recommends asking candidates to agree to a background check. Most organizations include this request on their application forms and require the applicant to agree in writing. By law, if a candidate refuses to agree to a reasonable request for information, you may decide not to hire the worker on that basis.

- **Using social media:** Social media sites are increasingly being used to "learn more" about a candidate. They are also used as recruiting platforms. According to HireRight's 2017 Benchmark Report, several organizations use social media to conduct pre-hire background checks. However, according to the same report, "in the transportation sector, only nine percent of companies surveyed turn to social media when conducting pre-hire background checks. The decline in the practice is becoming widespread throughout other industries as well." Social media profiles include information such as gender, race, and religious affiliation. The law prohibits the use of this information for hiring. Access to this info could have the organization subject to discrimination charges. Legal experts recommend that organizations have a non-decision maker conduct the search and provide to the decision maker(s) only relevant job-related information.

- **Educational records:** Under the *Family Educational Rights and Privacy Act (FERPA)*, schools must have written permission to release any information from a student's education record. For more information on obtaining records under FERPA, go to www.ed.gov.

- **Motor vehicle records:** Under the federal *Drivers Privacy Protection Act (DPPA)*, the release or use by any state DMV (or any officer, employee, or contractor thereof) of personal information about an individual obtained by the department in connection with a motor vehicle record is prohibited. The latest amendment to the DPPA requires states to get permission from individuals before their personal motor vehicle record may be sold or released to third-party marketers.

- **Financial history:** According to the Federal Trade Commission (FTC), you may use credit reports when you hire new employees and when you evaluate employees for promotion, reassignment, and retention, as long as you comply with the *Fair Credit Reporting Act (FCRA)*. Sections 604, 606, and 615 of the FCRA spell out employer responsibilities when using credit reports for employment purposes. These responsibilities include the requirement of notification if the information obtained may result in a negative employment decision. The *Fair and Accurate Credit Transaction Act of 2003 (FACTA)* added new sections to the federal FCRA, intended primarily to help consumers fight the growing crime of identity theft. Accuracy, privacy, limits on information sharing, and new consumer rights to disclosure are included in FACTA. For more information on using credit reports and the FCRA, go to www.ftc.gov.

- **Bankruptcies:** Under *Title 11 of the U.S. Bankruptcy Code*, employers are prohibited from discriminating against someone who has filed for bankruptcy. Although employers can use a negative credit history as a reason not to hire, employers cannot use bankruptcy as a sole reason.

- **Criminal record:** The law on how this information can be used varies extensively from state to state.

- **Workers' Compensation history:** In most states, when an employee's claim goes through Workers' Compensation, the case becomes public record. An employer may use this information only if an injury might interfere with one's ability to perform required duties. Under the federal *Americans with Disabilities Act*, employers cannot use medical information or the fact an applicant filed a Workers' Compensation claim to discriminate against applicants.

In Practice

Personnel Screening Policy

Synopsis: Background checks must be conducted on employees, temporaries, and contractors.

Policy Statement:

- As a condition of employment, all employees, temporaries, and contractors must agree to and are subject to background screening that includes identity verification, confirmation of educational and professional credentials, credit check, and state and federal criminal check.

- Comprehensive background screening will be conducted pre-hire. Criminal check will be conducted annually thereafter.

- Background screening will be conducted in accordance with local, state, and federal law and regulations.

- If the person will have access to "protected" or highly confidential information, additional screening may be required at the discretion of the information owner. This includes new personnel as well as employees who might be moved into such a position.

- Background screening will be conducted and/or managed by the Human Resources department.

- If temporary or contractor staff is provided by an agency or third party, the contract must clearly specify the agency or third-party responsibility for conducting background checks in accordance with this policy. Results must be submitted to the Human Resources department for approval.

- The Office of Information Security (or Cybersecurity Office) and the Office of Human Resources will be jointly responsible for the implementation and enforcement of this policy.

- All information obtained in the screening process will be classified as "protected" and handled in accordance with company handling standards.

Government Clearance

Many U.S. government jobs require that the prospective employee have the requisite security clearance. Although each government agency has its own standards, in general, a **security clearance** investigation is an inquiry into an individual's loyalty, character, trustworthiness, and reliability to ensure that he or she is eligible for access to national security–related information. The process to obtain clearance is both costly and time-consuming.

Obtaining a U.S. government security clearance involves a four-phase process:

1. **Application phase:** This phase includes verification of U.S. citizenship, fingerprinting, and completion of the Personnel Security Questionnaire (SF-86).

2. **Investigative phase:** This phase includes a comprehensive background check.

3. **Adjudication phase:** During this phase, the findings from the investigation are reviewed and evaluated based on 13 factors determined by the Department of Defense. Examples of these factors include criminal and personal conduct, substance abuse, and any mental disorders.

4. **Granting (or denial) of clearance at a specific level:** To obtain access to data, clearance and classification must match. For example, to view Top Secret information, the person must hold Top Secret clearance. However, merely having a certain level of security clearance does not mean one is authorized to access the information. To have access to the information, one must possess two elements: a level of security clearance at least equal to the classification of the information and an appropriate "need to know" the information in order to perform one's duties.

What Happens in the Onboarding Phase?

Once hired, a candidate transitions from a potential hire to an employee. At this stage, he or she is added to the organization's payroll and benefits systems. To accomplish these tasks, the employee must provide a full spectrum of personal information. It is the responsibility of the organization to properly classify and safeguard employee data.

Payroll and Benefits Employee Data

When an employee is hired in the United States, he or she must provide proof of identity, work authorization, and tax identification. The two forms that must be completed are the Department of Homeland Security/U.S. Citizenship and Immigration Services Form I-9 Employment Eligibility Verification and the Internal Revenue Service Form W-4 Employee's Withholding Allowance Certificate.

The purpose of Form I-9 is to prove that each new employee (both citizen and noncitizen) is authorized to work in the United States. Employees are required to provide documentation that (a) establishes both identity and employment authorization *or* (b) documents and establishes identity *and* (c) documents and establishes employment authorization. Employees provide original documentation to the employer, who then copies the documents, retains a copy, and returns the original to the employee. Employers who hire undocumented workers are subject to civil and criminal penalties per the Immigration Reform and Control Act of 1986. For an example of an I-9 form, visit https://www.uscis.gov/i-9. As shown on page 9 of this document, the required documents may contain NPPI and must be safeguarded by the employer.

Completion of Form W-4 is required in order for employers to withhold the correct amount of income tax from employee pay. Information on this form includes complete address, marital status, social security number, and number of exemptions. Additionally, according to the W-4 Privacy Act Notice, routine uses of this information include giving it to the Department of Justice for civil and criminal litigation; to cities, states, the District of Columbia, and U.S. commonwealths and possessions for use in administering their tax laws; and to the Department of Health and Human Services for use in the National Directory of New Hires. They may also disclose this information to other countries under a tax treaty, to federal and state agencies to enforce federal nontax criminal laws, or to federal law enforcement and intelligence agencies to combat terrorism. The confidentiality of information provided on Form W-4 is legally protected under 26 USC § 6103: Confidentiality and Disclosure of Returns and Return Information.

What Is User Provisioning?

User provisioning is the name given to the process of creating user accounts and group membership, providing company identification, and assigning access rights and permissions as well as access devices, such as a token or smartcard. This process may be manual, automated (commonly referred to as an identity management system), or a combination thereof. Prior to granting access, the user should be provided with and acknowledge the terms and conditions of an acceptable use agreement. We examine this agreement later in the chapter. The permissions and access rights a user is granted should match his or her role and responsibilities. The information owner is responsible for defining who should be granted access and under what circumstances. Supervisors generally request access on behalf of their employees. Depending on the organization, the provisioning process is managed by the Human Resources department, the Cybersecurity department, or the Information Technology (IT) department.

One important step toward securing your infrastructure and effective identity management practices is to ensure that you can manage user accounts from one single location regardless of where these accounts were created. Although the majority of organizations will have their primary account directory on-premise, hybrid cloud deployments are on the rise, and it is important that you understand how to integrate on-premise and cloud directories and provide a seamless experience to the end user, and to also manage onboarding of new employees and deleting accounts for departing employees. To accomplish this hybrid identity scenario, it is recommended that you synchronize and federate your on-premise directory with your cloud directory. A practical example of this is using Active Directory Federation Services (ADFS). We discuss role-based access controls and other identity management topics later in the book.

In Practice

User Provisioning Policy

Synopsis: The company must have an enterprise-wide user provisioning process.

Policy Statement:

- There will be defined and documented a user provisioning process for granting and revoking access to information resources that includes but is not limited to account creation, account management (including assignment of access rights and permissions), periodic review of access rights and permissions, and account termination.

- The Office of Human Resources and the Office of Information or Cybersecurity are jointly responsible for the user provisioning process.

What Should an Employee Learn During Orientation?

In this stage, the employee begins to learn about the company, the job, and co-workers. Before having access to information systems, it is important that the employee understand his or her responsibilities, learn the information-handling standards and privacy protocols, and have an opportunity to ask questions. Organizational orientation is usually a Human Resources department responsibility. Departmental orientation is usually conducted by a supervisor or departmental trainer. Employee orientation training is just the beginning. Every employee should participate in SETA programs throughout his or her tenure. We'll examine the importance of SETA later in this chapter.

Privacy Rights

The standard in most private sector organizations is that employees should have *no expectation of privacy* in respect to actions taken on company time or with company resources. This extends to electronic monitoring, camera monitoring, and personal searches.

- Electronic monitoring includes phone, computer, email, mobile, text, Internet access, and location (GPS-enabled devices).

- Camera monitoring includes on-premise locations, with the exception of cameras in restrooms or locker rooms where employees change clothes, which is prohibited by law.

- Personal searches extend to searching an employee, an employee's workspace, or an employee's property, including a car, if it is on company property. Personal searches must be conducted in accordance with state regulations.

A company should disclose its monitoring activities to employees and get written acknowledgment of the policy. According to the American Bar Association, "an employer that fails to adopt policies or warnings or acts inconsistently with its policies or warnings may find that the employee still has a reasonable expectation of privacy." The lesson is that companies must have clear policies and be consistent in their application. Privacy expectations should be defined in the cybersecurity policy, acknowledged in the signed acceptable use agreement, and included in login banners and warnings.

In Practice

Electronic Monitoring Policy

Synopsis: It is necessary to have the ability to monitor certain employee activities. Employee expectation of privacy must be clearly defined and communicated.

Policy Statement:

- The company reserves the right to monitor electronic activity on company-owned information systems, including but not limited to voice, email, text and messaging communications sent, received, or stored, computer and network activity, and Internet activity, including sites visited and actions taken.

- The policy must be included in the employee acceptable use agreement, and employees must acknowledge the policy by signing the agreement.

- Whenever technically feasible, login banners and warning messages will remind users of this policy.

- The Office of Human Resources and the Office of Information or Cybersecurity are jointly responsible for developing and managing electronic monitoring and employee notification.

Why Is Termination Considered the Most Dangerous Phase?

In this stage, the employee leaves the organization. This is an emotionally charged event. Depending on the circumstances, the terminated employee may seek revenge, create havoc, or take information with him. Don't assume that a termination is friendly even if the employee resigns for personal reasons or is retiring. Many organizations have painfully discovered that employees who left their company voluntarily or because of layoffs have retained access to corporate applications, and some have logged in to corporate resources after leaving the company. In a perfect world, you would like to trust everyone to do the right thing after leaving your organization, but unfortunately, that is not the case.

How termination is handled depends on the specific circumstances and transition arrangements that have been made with the employee. However, in situations where there is any concern that an employee may react negatively to being terminated or laid off, access to the network, internal, and web-based application, email, and company owned social media should be disabled prior to informing the employee. Similarly, if there is any cause for concern associated with a resignation or retirement, all access should be disabled. If the employee is leaving to work for a competitor, the best bet is to escort them off the property immediately. In all cases, make sure not to forget about remote access capabilities.

FYI: The Insider Threat

The insider threat has never been more real. Insiders have a significant advantage over external threat actors. They not only have access to internal resources and information, but they are also aware of the organization's policies, procedures, and technology (and potential gaps in those policies, procedures, and technologies). The risk of insider threats requires a different strategy from other cybersecurity challenges. This is because of their inherent nature. The Computer Emergency Response Team (CERT) Insider Threat Center at Carnegie Mellon's Software Engineering Institute (SEI) has many resources that were created to help you identify potential and realized insider threats in your organization, institute ways to prevent and detect them, and establish processes to deal with them if they do happen.

You can obtain more information about CERT's Insider Threat Center at: https://resources.sei.cmu.edu/library/asset-view.cfm?assetid=91513.

In Practice

Employee Termination Policy

Synopsis: Information assets and systems must be protected from terminated employees.

Policy Statement:

- Upon the termination of the relationship between the company and any employee, all access to facilities and information resources shall cease.

- In the case of unfriendly termination, all physical and technical access will be disabled pre-notification.

- In the case of a friendly termination, including retirement, the Office of Human Resources is responsible for determining the schedule for disabling access.

- Termination procedures are to be included in the user provisioning process.

- The Office of Human Resources and the Office of Information or Cybersecurity are jointly responsible for the user provisioning process.

The Importance of Employee Agreements

It is common practice to require employees, contractors, and outsourcers to sign two basic agreements: a confidentiality agreement (also known as a *nondisclosure agreement*) and an acceptable use agreement. Confidentiality agreements are in place to protect from unauthorized disclosure of information and are generally a condition of work, regardless of access to information systems. Acceptable use agreements traditionally focus on the proper use of information systems and cover such topics as password management, Internet access, remote access, and handling standards. A growing trend is to augment the agreement-distribution process with training and explanation; the ultimate goal of the acceptable use agreement is to teach the employee the importance of security, obtain commitment, and install organizational values.

What Are Confidentiality or Nondisclosure Agreements?

Confidentiality or non-disclosure agreements are contracts entered into by the employee and the organization in which the parties agree that certain types of information remain confidential. The type of information that can be included is virtually unlimited. Any information can be considered confidential—data, expertise, prototypes, engineering drawings, computer software, test results, tools, systems, and specifications.

Confidentiality agreements perform several functions. First and most obviously, they protect confidential, technical, or commercial information from disclosure to others. Second, they can prevent the forfeiture of valuable patent rights. Under U.S. law and in other countries as well, the public disclosure of an invention can be deemed as a forfeiture of patent rights in that invention. Third, confidentiality agreements define exactly what information can and cannot be disclosed. This is usually accomplished by specifically classifying the information as such and then labeling it appropriately (and clearly). Fourth, confidentiality agreements define how the information is to be handled and for what length of time. Last, they state what is to happen to the information when employment is terminated or, in the case of a third party, when a contract or project ends.

What Is an Acceptable Use Agreement?

An **acceptable use agreement** is a policy contract between the company and information systems user. By signing the agreement, the user acknowledges and agrees to the rule regarding how he or she must interact with information systems and handle information. It is also a teaching document that should reinforce the importance of cybersecurity to the organization. Another way to think about an acceptable use agreement is that it is a condensed version of the entire cybersecurity policy document specifically crafted for employees. It contains only the policies and standards that pertain to them and is written in language that can be easily and unequivocally understood. SANS has a sample acceptable use policy in its Information Security Policy Templates website at https://www.sans.org/security-resources/policies.

Components of an Acceptable Use Agreement

An acceptable use agreement should include an introduction, information classifications, categorized policy statements, data-handling standards, sanctions for violations, contacts, and an employee acknowledgment:

- The *introduction* sets the tone for the agreement and emphasizes the commitment of the leadership of the organization.

- *Data classifications* define (and include examples of) the classification schema adopted by the organization.

- *Applicable policy statements* include Authentications & Password Controls, Application Security, Messaging Security (including email, instant message, text, and video conferencing), Internet Access Security, Remote Access Security, Mobile Device Security, Physical Access Security, Social Media, Incident Use of Information Resources, Expectation of Privacy, and Termination.

- *Handling standards* dictate by classification level how information must be stored, transmitted, communicated, accessed, retained, and destroyed.

- *Contacts* should include to whom to address questions, report suspected security incidents, and report security violations.

- The *Sanctions for Violations* section details the internal process for violation as well as applicable civil and criminal penalties for which the employee could be liable.

- The *Acknowledgment* states that the user has read the agreement, understands the agreement and the consequences of violation, and agrees to abide by the policies presented. The agreement should be dated, signed, and included in the employee permanent record.

In Practice

Employee Agreements Policy

Synopsis: All employees and third-party personnel not otherwise covered by contractual agreement are required to agree to Confidentiality and Acceptable Use requirements.

Policy Statement:

- All employees must be provided with and sign a confidentiality agreement as a condition of employment and prior to being provided any company information classified as protected, confidential, or internal use.

- All employees must be provided with and sign an acceptable use agreement as a condition of employment and prior to being granted access to any company information or systems.

- The documents provided to the employee will clearly state the employees' responsibilities during both employment and post-employment.

- The employee's legal rights and responsibilities will be included in the document.

- Legal counsel is responsible for developing, maintaining, and updating the confidentiality agreement.

- The Office of Information or Cybersecurity is responsible for developing, maintaining, and updating the acceptable use agreement.

- The Office of Human Resources is responsible for distributing the agreement and managing the acknowledgment process.

The following is a real-life example of a Confidentiality and Acceptable Use Policy of the City of Chicago: https://www.cityofchicago.org/content/dam/city/depts/doit/supp_info/Confidentiality-andAcceptableUsePolicyV50Accessible.pdf.

The Importance of Security Education and Training

NIST Special Publication 800-50: Building an Information Technology Security Awareness and Training Program succinctly defines why security education and training is so important:

"Federal agencies and organizations cannot protect the confidentiality, integrity, and availability of information in today's highly networked systems environment without ensuring that all people involved in using and managing IT:

- Understand their roles and responsibilities related to the organizational mission;

- Understand the organization's IT security policy, procedures, and practices;

- Have at least adequate knowledge of the various management, operational, and technical controls required and available to protect the IT resources for which they are responsible.

"The 'people factor'—not technology—is key to providing an adequate and appropriate level of security. If people are the key, but are also a weak link, more and better attention must be paid to this 'asset.'

"A strong IT security program cannot be put in place without significant attention given to training agency IT users on security policy, procedures, and techniques, as well as the various management, operational, and technical controls necessary and available to secure IT resources. In addition, those in the agency who manage the IT infrastructure need to have the necessary skills to carry out their assigned duties effectively. Failure to give attention to the area of security training puts an enterprise at great risk because security of agency resources is as much a *human issue* as it is a technology issue.

"Everyone has a role to play in the success of a security awareness and training program, but agency heads, Chief Information Officers (CIOs), program officials, and IT security program managers have key responsibilities to ensure that an effective program is established agency wide. The scope and content of the program must be tied to existing security program directives and established agency security policy. Within agency IT security program policy, there must exist clear requirements for the awareness and training program."

In addition, NIST created the National Initiative for Cybersecurity Education (NICE) and defined it NIST Special Publication 800-181. The NICE Cybersecurity Workforce Framework (NICE Framework) is designed to provide guidance on how to identify, recruit, develop, and retain cybersecurity talent. According to NIST, "it is a resource from which organizations or sectors can develop additional publications or tools that meet their needs to define or provide guidance on different aspects of workforce development, planning, training, and education."

Details about the NICE Cybersecurity Workforce Framework can be obtained at the NIST Special Publication 800-181, https://nvlpubs.nist.gov/nistpubs/SpecialPublications/NIST.SP.800-181.pdf, and at the NICE Framework website: https://www.nist.gov/itl/applied-cybersecurity/nice/resources/nice-cybersecurity-workforce-framework.

Influencing Behavior with Security Awareness

Security awareness is defined in NIST Special Publication 800-16 as follows: "Awareness is not training. The purpose of awareness presentations is simply to focus attention on security. Awareness presentations are intended to allow individuals to recognize IT security concerns and respond accordingly." *Security awareness* programs are designed to remind the user of appropriate behaviors. In our busy world, sometimes it is easy to forget why certain controls are in place. For example, an organization may have access control locks to secure areas. Access is granted by entering a PIN on the lock pad or perhaps using a swipe card. If the door doesn't click shut or someone enters at the same time, the control is effectively defeated. A poster reminding us to check to make sure the door is shut completely is an example of an awareness program.

Teaching a Skill with Security Training

Security training is defined in NIST Special Publication 800-16 as follows: "Training seeks to teach skills, which allow a person to perform a specific function." Examples of training include teaching a system administrator how to create user accounts, training a firewall administrator how to close ports, or training an auditor how to read logs. Training is generally attended by those tasked with implementing and monitoring security controls. You may recall from previous chapters that the person charged with implementing and maintaining security controls is referred to as the **information custodian**.

Security Education Is Knowledge Driven

Security education is defined in NIST Special Publication 800-16 as follows: "The 'Education' level integrates all of the security skills and competencies of the various functional specialties into a common body of knowledge, adds a multidisciplinary study of concepts, issues, and principles (technological and social), and strives to produce IT security specialists and professionals capable of vision and pro-active response."

Education is management-oriented. In the field of cybersecurity, education is generally targeted to those who are involved in the decision-making process: classifying information, choosing controls, and evaluating and reevaluating security strategies. The person charged with these responsibilities is often the information owner.

In Practice

Cybersecurity Training Policy

Synopsis: All employees, contractors, interns, and designated third parties must receive training appropriate to their position throughout their tenure.

Policy Statement:

- The Human Resources department is responsible for cybersecurity training during the employee orientation phase. The training must include compliance requirements, company policies, and handling standards.

- Subsequent training will be conducted at the departmental level. Users will be trained on the use of departmental systems appropriate to their specific duties to ensure that the confidentiality, integrity, and availability (CIA) of information is safeguarded.

- Annual cybersecurity training will be conducted by the Office of Information or Cybersecurity. All staff is required to participate, and attendance will be documented. At a minimum, training will include the following topics: current cybersecurity-related threats and risks, security policy updates, and reporting of security incidents.

- The company will support the ongoing education of cybersecurity personnel by funding attendance at conferences, tuition at local colleges and universities, subscriptions to professional journals, and membership in professional organizations.

FYI: Small Business Note

Many small businesses treat employees like family. They are uncomfortable with the idea of background checks, confidentiality agreements, or acceptable use agreements. They don't want to give the impression that their employees are not trusted. Small business owners need to recognize human resources security practices as positive safeguards designed to protect the long-term health of the company and, in turn, their employees.

Background verification, confidentiality agreements, and acceptable use agreements may be even more important in small organizations than in a large one. Small business employees often wear many hats and have access to a wide range of company information and system. Misuse, disclosure, or actions that result in compromise or exposure could easily devastate a small business. Small businesses don't have to go it alone. A number of reputable and affordable third-party service providers can assist with recruiting, conduct background checks, and craft appropriate agreements on behalf of the organization.

Summary

Personnel security needs to be embedded in each stage of the employee life cycle—recruitment, onboarding, user provisioning, orientation, career development, and termination. It is the responsibility of the organization to deliver the message that security is a priority even before an employee joins the organization. Job postings, job descriptions, and even the interview process need to reflect an organizational culture committed to cybersecurity. Most important, companies need to protect candidate data, including NPPI, demographics, work history, accomplishments, education, compensation, previous employer feedback, references, clearances, and certifications. If the candidate is hired, the obligation extends to employee information.

Prior to hire, candidates should be subject to background checks, which may include criminal record, credit record, and licensure verification. Employers should request consent prior to conducting background checks. There are legal limits on the information that can be used to make employment decisions. Rules to be aware of include worker's right to privacy, social media restrictions, and regulatory restraints related to credit, bankruptcy, workers compensation, and medical information.

Many U.S. government jobs require that the prospective employee have the requisite security clearance and, in addition to the standard screening, the employer will investigate an individual's loyalty, character, trustworthiness, and reliability to ensure that he or she is eligible for access to national security–related information.

Confidentiality and acceptable use agreements should be a condition of employment. A *confidentiality agreement* is a legally binding obligation that defines what information can be disclosed, to whom, and within what time frame.

An *acceptable use agreement* is an acknowledgment of organization policy and expectations. An acceptable use agreement should include information classifications, categorized policy statements, data-handling standards, sanctions for violations, and contact information for questions. The agreement should disclose and clearly explain the organization's privacy policy and the extent of monitoring the employee should expect. Training and written acknowledgment of rights and responsibilities should occur prior to being granted access to information and information systems. Organizations will reap significant benefits from training users throughout their tenure. Security awareness programs, security training, and security education all serve to reinforce the message that security is important. Security awareness programs are designed to remind the user of appropriate behaviors. Security training teaches specific skills. Security education is the basis of decision making.

From a security perspective, termination is fraught with danger. How termination is handled depends on the specific circumstances and transition arrangements that have been made with the employee. Regardless of the circumstance, organizations should err on the side of caution and disable or remove network, internal, web-based application, email, and company-owned social media rights as soon as possible.

Human Resources policies include job recruitment, personnel screening, employee agreements, user provisioning, electronic monitoring, cybersecurity training, and employee termination.

Test Your Skills

MULTIPLE CHOICE QUESTIONS

1. Which of the following statements best describes the employee life cycle?

    A. The employee life cycle spans recruitment to career development.

    B. The employee life cycle spans onboarding to orientation.

    C. The employee life cycle spans user provision to termination.

    D. The employee life cycle spans recruitment to termination.

2. At which of the following phases of the hiring process should personnel security practices begin?

    A. Interview

    B. Offer

    C. Recruitment

    D. Orientation

3. A published job description for a web designer should not include which of the following?

    A. Job title

    B. Salary range

    C. Specifics about the web development tool the company is using

    D. Company location

4. Data submitted by potential candidates must be _____.

    A. protected as required by applicable law and organizational policy

    B. not protected unless the candidate is hired

    C. stored only in paper form

    D. publicly accessible

5. During the course of an interview, a job candidate should be given a tour of which of the following locations?

    A. The entire facility

    B. Public areas only (unless otherwise authorized)

    C. The server room

    D. The wiring closet

6. Which of the following facts is an interviewer permitted to reveal to a job candidate?

    A. A detailed client list

    B. The home phone numbers of senior management

    C. The organization's security weaknesses

    D. The duties and responsibilities of the position

7. Which of the following statements best describes the reason for conducting background checks?

    A. To verify the truthfulness, reliability, and trustworthiness of the applicant

    B. To find out if the applicant ever got in trouble in high school

    C. To find out if the applicant has a significant other

    D. To verify the applicant's hobbies, number of children, and type of house

8. Which of the following is not a background check type?

    A. Credit history

    B. Criminal history

    C. Education

    D. Religious or Political

9. Social media profiles often include gender, race, and religious affiliation. Which of the following statements best describes how this information should be used in the hiring process?

    A. Gender, race, and religious affiliation can legally be used in making hiring decisions.

    B. Gender, race, and religious affiliation cannot legally be used in making hiring decisions.

    C. Gender, race, and religious affiliation are useful in making hiring decisions.

    D. Gender, race, and religious affiliation listed in social media profiles should not be relied upon because they may be false.

10. Under the Fair Credit Reporting Act (FCRA), which of the following statements is true?

    A. Employers cannot request a copy of an employee's credit report under any circumstances.

    B. Employers must get the candidate's consent to request a credit report.

    C. Employers cannot use credit information to deny a job.

    D. Employers are required to conduct credit checks on all applicants.

11. Candidate and employee NPPI must be protected. NPPI does not include which of the following?

    A. Social security number

    B. Credit card number

C. Published telephone number

D. Driver's license number

12. Which of the following statements best describes the purpose of completing Department of Homeland Security/U.S. Citizenship and Immigration Services Form I-9 and providing supporting documentation?

   A. The purpose is to establish identity and employment authorization.

   B. The purpose is to determine tax identification and withholding.

   C. The purpose is to document educational achievements.

   D. The purpose is to verify criminal records.

13. The permissions and access rights a user is granted should match the user's role and responsibilities. Who is responsible for defining to whom access should be granted?

   A. The data user

   B. The data owner

   C. The data custodian

   D. The data author

14. Network administrators and help desk personnel often have elevated privileges. They are examples of which of the following roles?

   A. The data owners

   B. The data custodians

   C. The data authors

   D. The data sellers

15. Which of the following statements is *not* true of confidentiality agreements?

   A. Confidentiality/nondisclosure agreements are legal protection against unauthorized use of information.

   B. Confidentiality/nondisclosure agreements are generally considered a condition of work.

   C. Confidentiality/nondisclosure agreements are legally binding contracts.

   D. Confidentiality agreements should be required only of top-level executives.

16. Which of the following elements would you expect to find in an acceptable use agreement?

   A. Handling standards

   B. A lunch and break schedule

   C. A job description

   D. An evacuation plan

17. Which of the following statements best describes when acceptable use agreements should be reviewed, updated, and distributed?

    A. Acceptable use agreements should be reviewed, updated, and distributed only when there are organizational changes.

    B. Acceptable use agreements should be reviewed, updated, and distributed annually.

    C. Acceptable use agreements should be reviewed, updated, and distributed only during the merger and acquisition due diligence phase.

    D. Acceptable use agreements should be reviewed, updated, and distributed at the discretion of senior management.

18. Which of the following is true about the NICE Cybersecurity Workforce Framework (NICE Framework)?

    A. NICE is designed to provide guidance on how to implement the NIST Cybersecurity Framework.

    B. NICE is designed to provide guidance on how to identify, recruit, develop, and retain cybersecurity talent.

    C. NICE is designed to provide guidance on how to onboard new employees and delete accounts for departing personnel.

    D. NICE is designed to provide guidance on how to create cybersecurity programs to maintain compliance with regulations.

19. Posters are placed throughout the workplace reminding users to log off when leaving their workstations unattended. This is an example of which of the following programs?

    A. A security education program

    B. A security training program

    C. A security awareness program

    D. None of the above

20. A network engineer attends a one-week hands-on course on firewall configuration and mainte-nance. This is an example of which of the following programs?

    A. A security education program

    B. A security training program

    C. A security awareness program

    D. None of the above

21. The Board of Directors has a presentation on the latest trends in security management. This is an example of which of the following programs?

    A. A security education program

    B. A security training program

   C. A security awareness program

   D. None of the above

22. Companies have the legal right to perform which of the following activities?

   A. Monitor user Internet access from the workplace

   B. Place cameras in locker rooms where employees change clothes

   C. Conduct a search of an employee's home

   D. None of the above

23. Sanctions for policy violations should be included in which of the following documents?

   A. The employee handbook

   B. A confidentiality/nondisclosure agreement

   C. An acceptable use agreement

   D. All of the above

24. Studies often cite _____ as the weakest link in cybersecurity.

   A. policies

   B. people

   C. technology

   D. regulations

25. Which of the following is not a component of an Acceptable Use Agreement?

   A. Handling standards

   B. Sanctions for violations

   C. Acknowledgment

   D. Social media monitoring

26. Which of the following is a privacy regulation that has a goal to protect citizens' personal data and simplify the regulatory environment for international business by unifying the regulation within the European Union?

   A. European Union General Data Protection Regulation (GDPR)

   B. European Union PCI Council

   C. European Union Gramm-Leach-Bliley Act (GLBA)

   D. Privacy Data Protection of the European Union (PDPEU)

27. Which of the following regulations specifically stipulates that schools must have written permission to release any information from a student's education record?

    A. FERPA

    B. HIPAA

    C. DPPA

    D. FISMA

28. Best practices dictate that employment applications should *not* ask prospective employees to provide which of the following information?

    A. Last grade completed

    B. Current address

    C. Social security number

    D. Email address

29. After a new employee's retention period has expired, completed paper employment applications should be _____.

    A. cross-cut shredded

    B. recycled

    C. put in the trash

    D. stored indefinitely

30. Threat actors might find job posting information useful for which of the following attacks?

    A. A distributed denial of service attack (DDoS) attack

    B. A social engineering attack

    C. A man-in-the-middle attack

    D. An SQL injection attack

EXERCISES

EXERCISE 6.1: Analyzing Job Descriptions

1. Access an online job-posting service such as Monster.com.

2. Find two IT-related job postings.

3. Critique the postings. Do they reveal any information that a potential intruder could use in designing an attack, such as the specific technology or software used by the organization, security controls, or organizational weaknesses?

4. Document your findings.

EXERCISE 6.2: Assessing Background Checks

1. Go online and locate one company that provides background checks.

2. What types of investigative services does it offer?

3. What information do you have to provide to it?

4. What is the promised delivery time?

5. Does the company require permission from the target of the investigation?

EXERCISE 6.3: Learning What Your Social Media Says About You

1. What can a potential employer learn about you from your social media activities?

2. Look at the profile of a friend or acquaintance. What can a potential employer learn about him or her?

3. Investigate what recent events have led to more privacy regulations and scrutiny.

EXERCISE 6.4: Evaluating the Actions of Bad Employees

1. Locate a news article about a terminated or disgruntled employee who stole, exposed, compromised, or destroyed company information.

2. What could the company have done to prevent the damage?

3. In your opinion, what should be the consequences of the employee action?

EXERCISE 6.5: Evaluating Security Awareness Training

1. Either at your school or your place of work, locate and document at least one instance of a security awareness reminder.

2. In your opinion, is the reminder effective? Explain why or why not.

3. If you can't locate an example of a security awareness reminder, compose a memo to senior management suggesting one.

EXERCISE 6.6: Protecting Job Candidate Data

1. Companies have an obligation to protect the information provided by job seekers. The General Electric (GE) Candidate Privacy Notice (found at https://www.ge.com/careers/privacy) is a good example of how multinational companies approach the handling of candidate data. Read the Candidate Privacy Notice.

2. In your opinion, does the privacy notice cover all items that will make you feel comfortable sharing information with GE? Explain why or why not.

3. The notice reads "GE may transfer Candidate Data to external third-party providers performing certain services for GE. Such third-party providers have access to Candidate Data solely for the purposes of performing the services specified in the applicable service contract, and GE requires the providers to undertake security measures consistent with the protections specified in this Notice." As a job applicant, will this make you comfortable? Explain why or why not.

4. Try to find similar job candidate privacy notices from other companies, and write a report comparing the approach of these companies.

PROJECTS

PROJECT 6.1: Evaluating the Hiring Process

1. Contact a local business and ask to speak with the Human Resources manager or hiring manager. Explain you are a college student working on a report and explain the information you need (see step 4) to complete the report. Request a 15-minute meeting.

2. At the meeting, ask the manager to explain the company's hiring process. Be sure to ask what (if any) background checks the company does and why. Also ask for a copy of a job application form. Don't forget to thank the person for his or her time.

3. After the meeting, review the application form. Does it include a statement authorizing the company to conduct background checks? Does it ask for any NPPI?

4. Write a report that covers the following:

   - Summary of meeting logistics (whom you met with, where, and when)

   - Summary of hiring practices

   - Summary of any information shared with you that you would classify as protected or confidential (do not include specifics in your summary).

PROJECT 6.2: **Evaluating an Acceptable Use Agreement**

1. Locate a copy of your school or workplace acceptable use agreement (or equivalent document).

2. Write a critique of the agreement. Do you think that it includes enough detail? Does it explain why certain activities are prohibited or encouraged? Does it encourage users to be security conscious? Does it include sanction policy? Does it clearly explain the employee expectation of privacy? Can you tell when it was last updated? Are there any statements that are out of date?

3. Go back to Chapter 2, "Cybersecurity Policy Organization, Format, and Styles," and review the sections on using plain language. Edit the agreement so that it conforms with plain language guidelines.

PROJECT 6.3: **Evaluating Regulatory Training**

1. Go online and locate an example of HIPAA security awareness training and GLBA security awareness training. (Note: You can use the actual training or an outline of topics.)

2. Document the similarities and differences.

Case Study: The NICE Challenge Project and CyberSeek

NIST has created a project called the NICE Challenge Project (https://nice-challenge.com/) with the goal of developing "virtual challenges and environments to test students and professionals alike on their ability to perform NICE Cybersecurity Workforce Framework tasks and exhibit their knowledge, skills, and abilities." The NICE Challenge Project has dozens of unique challenges available for students and cybersecurity professionals.

In addition, NIST has created a website called CyberSeek (cyberseek.org). CyberSeek provides "detailed, actionable data about supply and demand in the cybersecurity job market." One of the main features of the CyberSeek website is the ability to track data on cybersecurity job demand overall and within the public and private sectors. The CyberSeek career pathway helps both students and professionals interested in cybersecurity careers and employers looking to fill job openings.

1. Assume that you are working in a large corporation and that you have been tasked with the following:

   a. Create a security awareness campaign focused on this topic. Include in this plan specifics on how you intend to deliver the message.

   b. Create at least one piece of supporting collateral.

   c. Design a way to test the effectiveness of your message.

2. Before launching the campaign, you want to make sure you have the full support of the executive management.

   a. What type of "educational" program would you develop for management?

   b. What would the message be?

3. Explain how the NICE Framework can be used to develop employees from your organization and how you can also benefit from CyberSeek to recruit new talent. Provide examples.

References

"Employee Life Cycle," Search Financial Applications, accessed 05/2018, http://searchhrsoftware.techtarget.com/definition/employee-life-cycle.

"Obtaining Security Clearance," Monster.com, accessed 05/2018, http://govcentral.monster.com/security-clearance-jobs/articles/413-how-to-obtain-a-security-clearance.

Changes to employee data management under the GDPR, accessed 05/2018, https://www.taylorwessing.com/globaldatahub/article-changes-to-employee-data-management-under-the-gdpr.html.

"2017 Trends in Recruiting via Social Media," HireRight, accessed 05/2018, http://www.hireright.com/blog/2017/05/2017-trends-in-recruiting-via-social-media/.

The CERT Insider Threat Center at Carnegie Mellon's Software Engineering Institute (SEI), accessed 05/2018, https://resources.sei.cmu.edu/library/asset-view.cfm?assetid=91513.

The NICE Framework, accessed 05/2018, https://www.nist.gov/itl/applied-cybersecurity/nice.

CyberSeek, NIST, accessed 05/2018, http://cyberseek.org.

Regulations Cited

The European Union General Data Protection Regulation (GDPR), accessed 05/2018, https://www.eugdpr.org.

"26 U.S.C. 6103: Confidentiality and Disclosure of Returns and Return Information," accessed 05/2018, https://www.gpo.gov/fdsys/granule/USCODE-2011-title26/USCODE-2011-title26-subtitleF-chap61-subchapB-sec6103/content-detail.html.

"Americans with Disabilities Act (ADA)," official website of the United States Department of Justice, Civil Rights Division, accessed 05/2018, https://www.ada.gov/2010_regs.htm.

"Fair Credit Reporting Act (FCRA). 15 U.S.C. 1681," accessed 05/2018, https://www.ecfr.gov/cgi-bin/text-idx?SID=2b1fab8de5438fc52f2a326fc6592874&mc=true&tpl=/ecfrbrowse/Title16/16CIsubchapF.tpl.

"Family Educational Rights and Privacy Act (FERPA)," official website of the U.S. Department of Education, accessed 05/2018, https://www2.ed.gov/policy/gen/guid/fpco/ferpa/index.html.

"Immigration Reform and Control Act of 1986 (IRCA)," official website of the U.S. Department of Homeland Security, U.S. Citizenship and Immigration Services, accessed 05/2018, https://www.uscis.gov/.

"Public Law 108–159: Dec. 4, 2003 Fair and Accurate Credit Transactions Act of 2003," accessed 05/2018, www.gpo.gov/fdsys/pkg/PLAW-108publ159/.../PLAW-108publ159.pdf.

"Public Law No. 91-508: The Fair Credit Reporting Act," accessed 05/2018, https://www.ecfr.gov/cgi-bin/text-idx?SID=2b1fab8de5438fc52f2a326fc6592874&mc=true&tpl=/ecfrbrowse/Title16/16CIsubchapF.tpl.

"Sarbanes-Oxley Act—SoX," accessed 05/2018, http://uscode.house.gov/download/pls/15C98.txt https://www.sec.gov/about/laws/soa2002.pdf.

"U.S. Department of Homeland Security and U.S. Citizenship and Immigration Services, Instructions for Employment Eligibility Verification," accessed 05/2018, https://www.uscis.gov/i-9.

"U.S. Department of the Treasury and Internal Revenue Service, 2017 General Instructions for Forms W-2 and W-3," accessed 05/2018, https://www.irs.gov/pub/irs-pdf/iw2w3.pdf.

Chapter | 7

Physical and Environmental Security

Chapter Objectives

After reading this chapter and completing the exercises, you will be able to do the following:

- Define the concept of physical security and how it relates to information security.
- Evaluate the security requirements of facilities, offices, and equipment.
- Understand the environmental risks posed to physical structures, areas within those structures, and equipment.
- Enumerate the vulnerabilities related to reusing and disposing of equipment.
- Recognize the risks posed by the loss or theft of mobile devices and media.
- Develop policies designed to ensure the physical and environmental security of information, information systems, and information-processing and storage facilities.

In the beginning of the computer age, it was easy to protect the systems; they were locked away in a lab, weighed thousands of pounds, and only a select few were granted access. Today, computing devices are ubiquitous. We are tasked with protecting devices that range from massive cloud-based multiplex systems to tiny handheld devices. The explosion of both distributed and mobile computing means that computing devices can be located anywhere in the world and are subject to local law and custom. Possession requires that each individual user take responsibility for mobile device security.

Security professionals are often so focused on technical controls that they overlook the importance of physical controls. The simple reality is that physical access is the most direct path to malicious activity, including unauthorized access, theft, damage, and destruction. Protection mechanisms include controlling the physical security perimeter and physical entry, creating secure offices, rooms, and facilities, and implementing barriers to access, such as monitoring, and alerting. Section 11 of ISO 27002:2013 encompasses both physical and environmental security. Environmental security refers to the workplace environment, which includes the design and construction of the facilities, how and where people move, where equipment is stored, how the equipment is secured, and protection from natural and man-made disasters.

In previous chapters, you learned that to properly protect organizational information, we must first know where it is and how critical it is to the organization. Just as we shouldn't spend as much money or resources to protect noncritical information as we would to protect critical information, so it goes that we shouldn't spend the same amount to protect a broom closet as we should to protect information-processing facilities such as data centers, server rooms, or even offices containing client information.

Information security professionals rarely have the expertise to address this security domain on their own. It is critical to involve facilities and physical security personnel in strategic and tactical decisions, policies, and procedures. For example, the information security expert designs a server room with a double steel door, card-reading lock, and a camera outside the door. A facilities expert may question the construction of the walls, floor, vents, and ceilings, the capability of the HVAC and fire suppression systems, as well as the potential for a natural disaster, such as an earthquake, fire, or flood. A physical security expert may question the location, the topography, and even the traffic patterns of pedestrians, automobiles, and airplanes. Creating and maintaining physical and environmental security is a team effort.

In this chapter, we focus on design, obstacles, monitoring, and response as they relate to secure areas, equipment security, and environmental controls. We examine the security issues, related best practices, and of course, physical and environmental security policies.

FYI: ISO/IEC 27002:2013 and NIST Cybersecurity Framework

Section 11 of ISO 27002:2013 is dedicated to physical and environmental security, with the objective of maintaining a secure physical environment to prevent unauthorized access, damage, and interference to business premises. Special attention is paid to disposal and destruction.

The NIST Cybersecurity Framework addresses physical security in three areas:

- Under the Protect Identity Management, Authentication and Access Control (PR.AC) Category stating that physical access to assets must be managed and protected

- Under the Information Protection Processes and Procedures (PR.IP) Category stating that policy and regulations regarding the physical operating environment for organizational assets must be met

- Under the Security Continuous Monitoring (DE.CM) Category stating that the physical environment needs to be monitored to detect potential cybersecurity events

Corresponding NIST guidance is provided in the following documents:

- **SP 800-12:** "An Introduction to Computer Security—The NIST Handbook"

- **SP 800-14:** "Generally Accepted Principles and Practices for Securing Information Technology Systems"

- **SP 800-88:** "Guidelines for Media Sanitization"

- **SP 800-100:** "Information Security Handbook: A Guide for Managers"

- **SP 800-116 Rev. 1:** "A Recommendation for the Use of PIV Credentials in Physical Access Control Systems (PACS)"

- **SP 800-116:** "A Recommendation for the Use of PIV Credentials in Physical Access Control Systems (PACS)"

- **SP 800-183:** "Networks of 'Things'"

Understanding the Secure Facility Layered Defense Model

The premise of a *layered defense model* is that if an intruder can bypass one layer of controls, the next layer of controls should provide additional deterrence or detection capabilities. Layered defense is both physical and psychological. The mere fact that an area *appears* to be secure is in itself a deterrent. Imagine the design of a medieval castle. The castle itself was built of stone. It was sited high on a hill within a walled property. There may have been a moat and an entry drawbridge. There were certainly lookouts and guards. For intruders to launch a successful attack, they had to overcome and penetrate each of these obstacles. The same concept is used in designing secure buildings and areas.

FYI: How Can You Ensure Physical Security of Assets When Your Data and Applications are in the Cloud?

Mature cloud providers such as Amazon Web Services (AWS) provide detailed explanations of their physical and operational security processes for the network and server infrastructure. These are the servers that will host your applications and data in the cloud that you do not have any control over. AWS details all their physical security practices at the following white paper:

https://d1.awsstatic.com/whitepapers/Security/AWS_Security_Whitepaper.pdf

The white paper details:

"AWS's data centers are state of the art, utilizing innovative architectural and engineering approaches. Amazon has many years of experience in designing, constructing, and operating large-scale data centers. This experience has been applied to the AWS platform and infrastructure. AWS data centers are housed in nondescript facilities. Physical access is strictly controlled both at the perimeter and at building ingress points by professional security staff utilizing video surveillance, intrusion detection systems, and other electronic means.

Authorized staff must pass two-factor authentication a minimum of two times to access data center floors. All visitors and contractors are required to present identification and are signed in and continually escorted by authorized staff. AWS only provides data center access and information to employees and contractors who have a legitimate business need for such privileges. When an employee no longer has a business need for these privileges, his or her access is immediately revoked, even if they continue to be an employee of Amazon or Amazon Web Services. All physical access to data centers by AWS employees is logged and audited routinely."

The paper describes their methodologies and capabilities for the following:

- Fire detection and suppression systems to reduce risk of fire.

- Data center electrical power systems are designed to be fully redundant and maintainable without impact to operations, 24 hours a day, and seven days a week. This includes the use of uninterruptible power supply (UPS) units to provide back-up power and the use of generators.

- Climate and temperature control required to maintain a constant operating temperature for servers and other hardware.

- Management and monitoring of electrical, mechanical, and life support systems and equipment so that any issues are immediately identified.

- Storage device decommissioning when a storage device has reached the end of its useful life, to prevent customer data from being exposed to unauthorized individuals. AWS states that it follows the NIST SP 800-88 ("Guidelines for Media Sanitization") as part of their decommissioning process.

How Do We Secure the Site?

Depending on the size of the organization, information-processing facilities can range from a closet with one server to an entire complex of buildings with several thousand or even hundreds of thousands of computers. In addressing site physical security, we need to think of the most obvious risks, such as theft and other malicious activity, but we also must consider accidental damage and destruction related to natural disasters.

Location

The design of a secure site starts with the location. Location-based threats that need to be evaluated include political stability, susceptibility to terrorism, the crime rate, adjacent buildings, roadways, flight paths, utility stability, and vulnerability to natural disasters. Historical and predictive data can be used to establish both criminal and natural disaster chronology for a geographic area. The outcome will influence the type of security measures that an organization should implement. Best practices dictate that critical information-processing facilities be inconspicuous and unremarkable. They should not have signage relating to their purpose, nor should their outward appearance hint at what may be inside.

Perimeter Security

The three elements to security are obstacles that deter trivial attackers and delay serious ones, detection systems that make it more likely that the attack will be noticed, and a response capability to repel or catch attackers. Obstacles include physical elements such as berms, fences, gates, and bollards. Lighting is also a valuable deterrent. Entrances, exits, pathways, and parking lots should be illuminated. Fences should be at least eight feet in height, with a two-foot parameter of light used to illuminate along the top portion of the fence. The candlepower of the lighting must meet security standards. Detection systems include IP cameras, closed-circuit TV, alarms, motion sensors, and security guards. Response systems include locking gates and doors, on-site or remote security personnel notification, and direct communication with local, county, or state police.

In Practice

Physical Security Perimeter Policy

Synopsis: Securing the perimeter is the first line of defense against external physical attacks. Perimeter controls are required to prevent unauthorized access and damage to facilities.

Policy Statement:

- The company will establish physical security perimeters around business premises.

- An annual risk assessment of all existing business premises and information-processing facilities will be performed to determine the type and strength of the security perimeter that is appropriate and prudent.

- A risk assessment must be conducted on all new sites under consideration prior to building plans being finalized.

- The Office of Facilities Management in conjunction with the Office of Information Security will conduct the risk assessment.

- Risk assessment results and recommendations are to be submitted to the Chief Operating Officer (COO).

- The Office of Facilities Management is responsible for the implementation and maintenance of all physical security perimeter controls.

How Is Physical Access Controlled?

Our next area to consider is physical entry and exit controls. What does it take to get in and out? How is trouble detected and reported? Depending on the site and level of security required, a plethora of access controls are available, including cameras, security guards, mantraps, locks, barriers, metal detectors, biometric scanners, fire-resistant exterior walls that are solid and heavy, and unbreakable/shatterproof glass. The biggest challenge is authorized entry.

Authorizing Entry

How does a company identify authorized personnel, such as employees, contractors, vendors, and visitors? Of greatest concern are the fraudulent or forged credentials obtained through careful profiling or the carelessness of authenticated employees. One commonly used option is a badging system. Badges may also function as access cards. Visitors to secure areas should be credentialed and authorized. Tailgating is one of the most common physical security challenges of all time. In some cases, it might be done innocently by an authorized individual opening a door and holding it open for others, visitors without badges, or someone who looks to be an employee. A number of visitor management systems facilitate ID scanning and verification, photo storage, credentialing, check in and check out, notifications, and monitoring. Visitors should be required to wear some kind of identification that can be evaluated from a distance. For instance, we might choose to have three different colored badges for visitors, which tell our employees what level of supervision should be expected, even if they view the person from across a 100-foot room. If a blue badge denotes close supervision, and you see someone wearing a blue badge without any supervision, you would know immediately to report the visitor or perhaps activate a silent alarm without having to confront or even come within close proximity of the individual. You can install the most advanced security system in the industry, but your security measures will fail if your employees are not educated about the associated security risks. You need to create a secure building culture and good security awareness campaigns.

Background Checks

Your organization should also establish formal policies and procedures to delineate the minimum standards for logical and physical access to your premises and infrastructure hosts. Typically, enterprise organizations conduct criminal background checks, as permitted by law, as part of pre-employment screening practices for employees and matching with the employee's position within the company and required level of access. The policies also identify functional responsibilities for the administration of physical access during working hours and after hours (including weekends and holidays).

Physical Entry Controls Policy

Synopsis: Authorization and identification are required for entry to all nonpublic company locations.

Policy Statement:

- Access to all nonpublic company locations will be restricted to authorized persons only.
- The Office of Human Resources is responsible for providing access credentials to employees and contractors.
- The Office of Facilities Management is responsible for visitor identification, providing access credentials, and monitoring access. All visitor management activities will be documented.
- Employees and contractors are required to visibly display identification in all company locations.
- Visitors are required to display identification in all nonpublic company locations.
- Visitors are to be escorted at all times.
- All personnel must be trained to immediately report unescorted visitors.

Securing Offices, Rooms, and Facilities

In addition to securing building access, the organization needs to secure the workspaces within the building. Workspaces should be classified based on the level of protection required. The classification system should address personnel security, information systems security, and document security. The security controls must take into consideration workplace violence, intentional crime, and environmental hazards.

Secure design controls for spaces within a building include (but are not limited to) the following:

- Structural protection, such as full-height walls, fireproof ceilings, and restricted vent access
- Alarmed solid, fireproof, lockable, and observable doors
- Alarmed locking, unbreakable windows
- Monitored and recorded entry controls (keypad, biometric, card swipe)
- Monitored and recorded activity

Workspace Classification

Synopsis: A classification system will be used to categorize workspaces. Classifications will be used to design and communicate baseline security controls.

Policy Statement:

- The company will use a four-tiered workspace classification schema consisting of secure, restricted, nonpublic, and public.

- The company will publish definitions for each classification.

- The criteria for each level will be maintained by and available from the Office of Facilities Management.

- All locations will be associated with one of the four data classifications. Classification assignment is the joint responsibility of the Office of Facilities Management and the Office of Information Security.

- Each classification must have documented security requirements.

- The COO must authorize exceptions.

Working in Secure Areas

It is not enough to just physically secure an area. Close attention must be paid to who is allowed to access the area and what they are allowed to do. Access control lists should be reviewed frequently. If the area is continually monitored, there should be guidelines specifying what is considered "suspicious" activity. If the area is videoed and not continually monitored, then there should be documented procedures regarding how often and by whom the video should be reviewed. Depending on the circumstances, it may be prudent to restrict cameras or recording devices, including smartphones, tablets, and USB drives, from being taken into the area.

In Practice

Working in Secure Areas Policy

Synopsis: Areas classified as "secure" will be continually monitored. Use of recording devices will be forbidden.

Policy Statement:

- All access to areas classified as "secure" will be continually monitored.

- All work in areas classified as "secure" will be recorded. The recordings will be maintained for a period of 36 months.

- Mobile data storage devices are prohibited and may not be allowed in areas classified as "secure" without the authorization of the system owner or Information Security Officer (ISO).

- Audio- and video-recording equipment is prohibited and may not be allowed in areas classified as "secure" without the authorization of the system owner or the Office of Information Security.

- This policy is in addition to workspace classification security protocols.

Ensuring Clear Desks and Clear Screens

Documents containing protected and confidential information are subject to intentional or accidental unauthorized disclosure unless secured from viewing by unauthorized personnel when not in use. The same holds true for computer screens. Companies have a responsibility to protect physical and digital information both during the workday and during nonbusiness hours. All too often, organizations make it *easy* for unauthorized users to view information. Unauthorized access can be the result of viewing a document left unattended or in plain sight, removing (or reprinting) a document from a printer, copier, or fax machine, stealing digital media, such as a DVD or USB drive, and even *shoulder surfing*, which is the act of looking over someone's shoulder to see what is displayed on a monitor or device.

Protected or confidential documents should never be viewable by unauthorized personnel. When not in use, documents should be locked in file rooms, cabinets, or desk drawers. Copiers, scanners, and fax machines should be located in nonpublic areas and require use codes. Printers should be assigned to users with similar access rights and permissions and located close to the designated users. Users should be trained to retrieve printed documents immediately. Monitors and device screens should be situated to ensure privacy. Password-protected screen savers should be set to engage automatically. Users should be trained to lock their screens when leaving devices unattended. Physical security expectations and requirements should be included in organizational acceptable use agreements.

In Practice

Clear Desk and Clear Screen Policy

Synopsis: User controls are required to prevent the unauthorized viewing or taking of information.

Policy Statement:

- When left unattended during business hours, desks shall be clear of all documents classified as "protected" or "confidential."

- During nonbusiness hours, all documents classified as "protected" or "confidential" will be stored in a secure location.

- While in use, device displays of any type must be situated to not allow unauthorized viewing.

- When left unattended during business hours, device displays should be cleared and locked to prevent viewing.

- Protected and confidential documents should be printed only to assigned printers. Print jobs should be retrieved immediately.

- Scanners, copiers, and fax machines must be locked when not in use and require user codes to operate.

Protecting Equipment

Now that we have defined how facilities and work areas will be secured, we must address the security of the equipment within these facilities. Traditionally, protection controls were limited to company-owned equipment. This is no longer the case. Increasingly, organizations are encouraging employees and contractors to "bring your own device" to work (referred to as BYOD). These devices may store, process, or transmit company information. In developing policies, we need to consider how best to protect both company- and employee-owned equipment from unauthorized access, theft, damage, and destruction.

No Power, No Processing?

No power, no processing—it's that simple. Long before computers took over the business world, organizations have been taking steps to ensure that power is available. Of course, it is now more important than ever. All information systems rely on clean, consistent, and abundant supplies of electrical power. Even portable devices that run on battery power require electricity for replenishment. Power is not free. Quite the contrary: Power can be very expensive, and excessive use has an environmental and geopolitical impact.

Power Protection

To function properly, our systems need consistent power delivered at the correct voltage level. Systems need to be protected from power loss, power degradation, and even from too much power, all of which can damage equipment. Common causes of voltage variation include lightning; damage to overhead lines from storms, trees, birds, or animals; vehicles striking poles or equipment; and load changes or equipment failure on the network. Heat waves can also contribute to power interruptions because the demand in electricity (that is, air conditioners) can sometimes exceed supply. The variation may be minor or significant.

Power fluctuations are categorized by changes in voltage and power loss. Figure 7-1 shows the difference between a *power surge* and a *power spike*.

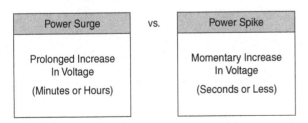

FIGURE 7-1   Power Surge vs. Power Spike

Figure 7-2 shows the difference between a *brownouts* and a *sag*.

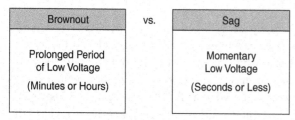

FIGURE 7-2   Brownout vs. Sag

Figure 7-3 shows the difference between a *blackout* and a *fault*.

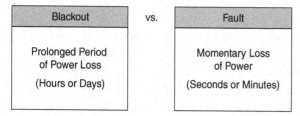

FIGURE 7-3   Blackout vs. Fault

Companies can install protective devices to help guard their premises and assets, such as installing surge protection equipment, line filters, isolation transformers, voltage regulators, power conditioners, uninterruptible power supplies (UPSs), and back-up power supplies or generators. These power protection devices can condition the feed for consistency, provide continuous power for critical systems, and manage a controlled shutdown in the event of total loss of power.

In Practice

Power Consumption Policy

Synopsis: Power conditioning and redundancy protections must be in place to maintain the availability and performance of information systems and infrastructure. Power consumption should be minimized.

Policy Statement:

- The company is committed to sustainable computing and the minimization of power consumption.

- All computing devices purchased must be Energy Star (or equivalent)–certified.

- All computing devices must be configured in power saver mode unless the setting degrades performance.

- A biannual assessment must be conducted by the Office of Facilities Management to determine the best method(s) to provide clean, reliable data center power.

■ Data center equipment must be protected from damage caused by power fluctuations or interruptions.

■ Data center power protection devices must be tested on a scheduled basis for functionality and load capacity. A log must be kept of all service and routine maintenance.

■ Data center generators must be tested regularly according to manufacturer's instructions. A log must be kept of all service and routine maintenance.

How Dangerous Is Fire?

Imagine the impact of a data center fire—equipment and data irrevocably destroyed, internal communications damaged, and external connectivity severed. On November 2017, Data Center Dynamics reported that a faulty battery in a UPS caused a fire in a health center in Cairns, Australia, causing two hospitals and several of the city's health service systems to fail.

Fire protection is composed of the three elements shown in Figure 7-4.

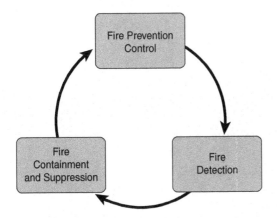

FIGURE 7-4 Fire Protection Elements

Active and passive *fire prevention controls* are the first line of defense. Fire prevention controls include hazard assessments and inspections, adhering to building and construction codes, using flame-retardant materials, and proper handling and storage procedures for flammable/combustible materials. *Fire detection* is recognizing that there is a fire. Fire detection devices can be smoke activated, heat activated, or flame activated. *Fire containment and suppression* involve actually responding to the fire. Containment and suppression equipment is specific to fire classification. Data center environments are typically at risk of Class A, B, or C fires:

■ **Class A:** Fire with combustible materials as its fuel source, such as wood, cloth, paper, rubber, and many plastics

- **Class B:** Fire in flammable liquids, oils, greases, tars, oil-based paints, lacquers, and flammable gases

- **Class C:** Fire that involves electrical equipment

- **Class D:** Combustibles that involve metals

Facilities must comply with standards to test fire-extinguishing methods annually to validate full functionality.

The best-case scenario is that data centers and other critical locations are protected by an automatic fire-fighting system that spans multiple classes. Like all other major investments, it's prudent to do a cost/benefit analysis before making a decision. In any emergency situation, human life always takes precedence. All personnel should know how to quickly and safely evacuate an area.

In Practice

Data Center and Communications Facilities Environmental Safeguards Policy

Synopsis: Data center and communications facilities must have controls designed to minimize the impact of power fluctuations, temperature, humidity, and fire.

Policy Statement:

- Smoking, eating, and drinking are not permitted in data center and communications facilities.

- Servers and communications equipment must be located in areas free from physical danger.

- Servers and communications must be protected by uninterruptable power supplies and back-up power sources.

- Appropriate fire detection, suppression, and fighting equipment must be installed and/or available in all data center and communications facilities.

- Appropriate climate control systems must be installed in all data center and communications facilities.

- Emergency lighting must engage automatically during power outages at all data center and communications facilities.

- The Office of Facilities Management is responsible for assessing the data center and communications facilities environmental requirements and providing the recommendations to the COO.

- The Office of Facilities Management is responsible for managing and maintaining the data center and communications facilities' climate-control, fire, and power systems.

What About Disposal?

What do servers, workstations, laptops, tablets, smartphones, firewalls, routers, copiers, scanners, printers, memory cards, cameras, and flash drives have in common? They all store data that should be permanently removed before handing down, recycling, or discarding.

The data can be apparent, hidden, temporary, cached, browser-based, or metadata:

- *Apparent data files* are files that authorized users can view and access.

- *Hidden files* are files that the operating system by design does not display.

- *Temporary files* are created to hold information temporarily while a file is being created.

- A *web cache* is the temporary storage of web documents, such as HTML pages, images, and downloads.

- A *data cache* is the temporary storage of data that has recently been read and, in some cases, adjacent data areas that are likely to be accessed next.

- *Browser-based data* includes the following items:

    - Browsing history, which is the list of sites visited

    - Download history, which is the list of files downloaded

    - Form history, which includes the items entered into web page forms

    - Search bar history, which includes items entered into the search engines

    - Cookies, which store information about websites visited, such as site preferences and login status

- *Metadata* is details about a file that describes or identifies it, such as title, author name, subject, and keywords that identify the document's topic or contents.

Removing Data from Drives

A common misconception is that deleting a file will permanently remove its data. *Deleting* (or trashing) a file removes the operating system pointer to the file. *Formatting* a disk erases the operating system address tables. In both cases, the files still reside on the hard drive, and system recovery software can be used to restore the data. To give you an idea of how easy it is to recover information from a formatted hard drive, simply Google the phrase "data recovery" and see what comes back to you. Utilities are available for less than $50 that are quite capable of recovering data from formatted drives. Even if a drive has been formatted and a new operating system installed, the data is recoverable.

NIST Special Publication 800-88 Revision 1 defines ***data destruction*** as "the result of actions taken to ensure that media cannot be reused as originally intended and that information is virtually impossible to recover or prohibitively expensive." There are two methods of permanently removing data from a drive—disk wiping (also known as scrubbing) and degaussing. The ***disk wiping*** process will overwrite the master boot record (MBR), partition table, and every sector of the hard drive with the numerals 0 and 1 several times. Then the drive is formatted. The more times the disk is over-written and formatted, the more secure the disk wipe is. The government medium security standard (DoD 5220.22-M) specifies three iterations to completely overwrite a hard drive six times. Each iteration makes two write passes over the entire drive; the first pass inscribes ones (1) over the drive surface and the second inscribes zeros (0) onto the surface. After the third iteration, a government-designated code of 246 is written across the drive, and then it is verified by a final pass that uses a read-verify process. There are several commercially available applications that follow this standard. Disk wiping does not work reliably on solid-state drives, USB thumb drives, compact flash, and MMC/SD cards.

Degaussing is the process wherein a magnetic object, such as a computer tape, hard disk drive, or CRT monitor, is exposed to a magnetic field of greater, fluctuating intensity. As applied to magnetic media, such as video, audio, computer tape, or hard drives, the movement of magnetic media through the degaussing field realigns the particles, resetting the magnetic field of the media to a near-zero state, in effect erasing all the data previously written to the tape or hard drive. In many instances, degaussing resets the media to a like-new state so that it can be reused and recycled. In some instances, this simply wipes the media in preparation for safe and secure disposal. The National Security Agency (NSA) approves powerful degaussers that meet their specific standards and that in many cases utilize the latest technology for top-secret erasure levels.

Cryptographic Erase is a technique that uses the encryption of target data by enabling sanitization of the target data's encryption key. This is done to leave only the cipher text on the media and preventing read-access, because no one should have the encryption key. It is common for storage manufacturers to include integrated encryption and access control capabilities, also known as self-encrypting drives (SEDs). SEDs feature always-on encryption that ensures that all data in the storage device is encrypted. In practice, cryptographic erase can be executed in a fraction of a second. This is a great benefit because nowadays other sanitization methods take more time in large storage devices. Cryptographic erase can also be used in addition to other data destruction methods. You should not use cryptographic erase to sanitize data if the encryption was enabled after sensitive data was stored on the device without having been sanitized first. In addition, you should not use cryptographic erase if you are not certain if sensitive data was stored on the device without being sanitized prior to encryption.

Destroying Materials

The objective of physical *destruction* is to render the device and/or the media unreadable and unusable. Devices and media can be crushed, shredded, or, in the case of hard drives, drilled in several locations perpendicular to the platters and penetrating clear through from top to bottom.

Cross-cut shredding technology, which reduces material to fine, confetti-like pieces, can be used on all media, ranging from paper to hard drives.

It is common for organizations to outsource the destruction process. Companies that offer destruction services often have specialized equipment and are cognizant of environmental and regulatory requirements. The downside is that the organization is transferring responsibility for protecting information. The media may be transported to off-site locations. The data is being handled by non-employees over whom the originating organization has no control. Selecting a destruction service is serious business, and thorough due diligence is in order.

Both in-house and outsourced destruction procedures should require that an unbroken predestruction *chain of custody* be maintained and documented and that an itemized post-destruction certificate of destruction be issued that serves as evidence of destruction in the event of a privacy violation, complaint, or audit. NIST Special Publication 800-88 Revision 1 mentions that destructive techniques also render a "device purged when effectively applied to the appropriate media type, including incineration, shredding, disintegrating, degaussing, and pulverizing."

In Practice

Secure Disposal Policy

Synopsis: All media must be disposed of in a secure and environmentally sound manner.

Policy Statement:

- The Office of Facilities Management and the Office of Information Security are jointly responsible for determining the disposal standards for each classification of information.

- Devices or media containing "protected" or "confidential" information must not be sent off-site for repair and/or maintenance.

- The standards for the highest classification must be adhered to when the device or media contains multiple types of data.

- A chain of custody must be maintained for the destruction of "protected" and "confidential" information.

- A certificate of destruction is required for third-party destruction of devices or media that contains "protected" and "confidential" information.

- Disposal of media and equipment will be done in accordance with all applicable state and federal environmental disposal laws and regulations.

Stop, Thief!

According to the Federal Bureau of Investigation (FBI), on average, a laptop is stolen every 53 seconds, and one in ten individuals will have their laptop stolen at some point. The recovery statistics of stolen laptops is even worse, with only 3% ever being recovered. This means 97% of laptops stolen will never be returned to their rightful owners. The Ponemon Institute has conducted several studies and reported that almost half of laptops were lost or stolen off-site (working from a home office or hotel room) and one third were lost or stolen in travel or transit. The statistics for mobile phones and tablets is even worse.

The cost of lost and stolen devices is significant. The most obvious loss is the device itself. The cost of the device pales in comparison to the cost of detection, investigation, notification, after-the-fact response, and economic impact of lost customer trust and confidence, especially if the device contained legally protected information. The Ponemon Institute "2017 Cost of Data Breach Study: Global Overview" (https://www-01.ibm.com/common/ssi/cgi-bin/ssialias?htmlfid=SEL03130WWEN) calculated the average business cost of a breach in the United States to be $141 per record across all industries.

Consider this scenario: A laptop valued at $1,500 is stolen. A file on the laptop has information about 2,000 individuals. Using the Ponemon conclusion of $141 per record, the cost of the compromise would be $282,000! That cost doesn't include potential litigation or fines.

Additional examples of things that are attractive to thieves are modern portable media theft, such as thumb or pen drives and SD cards. This is why it is important that you have a good asset inventory. In Chapter 5, "Asset Management and Data Loss Prevention," you learned that asset management is crucial. In addition, you learned that every information asset must be assigned an owner. The success of an information security program is directly related to the defined relationship between the data owner and the information. In the best-case scenario, the data owner also functions as a security champion enthusiastically embracing the goals of confidentiality, integrity, and availability (CIA).

You should also have an established and effective process for individuals to report lost or stolen devices. Additionally, you should have mitigations in place in case of theft. These mitigations include encryption and remote wipe capabilities for mobile devices. Typically, remote wipe is a function of a mobile device management (MDM) application.

In Practice

Mobile Device and Media Security

Synopsis: Safeguards must be implemented to protect information stored on mobile devices and media.

Policy Statement:

- All company-owned and employee-owned mobile devices and media that store or have the potential to store information classified as "protected" or "confidential" must be encrypted.

- Whenever feasible, an antitheft technology solution must be deployed that enables remote locate, remote lock, and remote delete/wipe functionality.

- Loss or theft of a mobile device or media must be reported immediately to the Office of Information Security.

FYI: Small Business Note

Two physical security issues are specific to small business and/or remote offices: location and person identification. A majority of small business and remote offices are located in multitenant buildings, where occupants do not have input into or control of perimeter security measures. In this case, the organization must treat their entry doors as the perimeter and install commensurate detective and preventative controls. Often, tenants are required to provide access mechanisms (for example, keys, codes) to building personnel, such as maintenance and security. Unique entry codes should be assigned to third-party personnel so that entry can be audited. Rarely are employee identification badges used in a small office. This makes it all the more important that visitors be clearly identified. Because there is little distinction between public and private spaces, visitors should be escorted whenever they need to go on the premises.

Summary

The objective of physical and environmental security is to prevent unauthorized access, damage, and interference to business premises and equipment. In this chapter, with a focus on the physical environment, we discussed the three elements to security—obstacles that deter trivial attackers and delay serious ones, detection systems that make it more likely that the attack will be noticed, and a response capability to repel or catch attackers. We began at the security perimeter, worked our way gradually inward to the data center, and then back out to mobile devices. Starting at the perimeter, we saw the importance of having a layered defense model as well as incorporating CPTED (crime prevention through environmental design) concepts. Moving inside the building, we looked at entry controls and the challenge of authorized access and identification. We acknowledged that not all access is equal. Workspaces and areas need to be classified so that levels of access can be determined and appropriate controls implemented. Equipment needs to be protected from damage, including natural disasters, voltage variations (such as surges, brownouts, and blackouts), fire, and theft. Purchasing Energy Star–certified equipment and proactively reducing energy consumption supports the long-term security principle of availability.

We explored the often-overlooked risks of device and media disposal and how important it is to permanently remove data before handing down, recycling, or discarding devices. Even the most innocuous devices or media may contain business or personal data in metadata, hidden or temporary files, web or data caches, or the browser history. Deleting files or formatting drives is not sufficient. DoD-approved disk-wiping software or a degaussing process can be used to permanently remove data. The most secure method of disposal is destruction, which renders the device and/or the media unreadable and unusable.

Mobile devices that store, process, or transmit company data are the newest challenge to physical security. These devices travel the world and in some cases are not even company-owned. Threats run the gamut from nosy friends and colleagues to targeted theft. The detection, investigation, notification, and after-the-fact response cost of a lost or stolen mobile device is astronomical. The economic impact of lost customer trust and confidence is long-lasting. Encryption and antitheft technology solutions that enable remote locate, remote lock, and remote delete/wipe functionality must be added to the protection arsenal.

Physical and environmental security policies include perimeter security, entry controls, workspace classification, working in secure areas, clean desk and clean screen, power consumption, data center and communications facilities environmental safeguards, secure disposal, and mobile device and media security.

Test Your Skills

MULTIPLE CHOICE QUESTIONS

1. Which of the following groups should be assigned responsibility for physical and environmental security?

    A. Facilities management

    B. Information security management

    C. Building security

    D. A team of experts including facilities, information security, and building security

2. Physical and environmental security control decisions should be driven by a(n) _____.

    A. educated guess

    B. industry survey

    C. risk assessment

    D. risk management

3. Which of the following terms best describes CPTED?

    A. Crime prevention through environmental design

    B. Crime prevention through environmental designation

    C. Criminal prevention through energy distribution

    D. Criminal prosecution through environmental design

4. The design of a secure site starts with the _____.

    A. natural surveillance

    B. territorial reinforcement

    C. natural access control

    D. location

5. Which of the following models is known as the construct that if an intruder can bypass one layer of controls, the next layer of controls should provide additional deterrence or detection capabilities?

    A. Layered defense model

    B. Perimeter defense model

    C. Physical defense model

    D. Security defense model

6. The mere fact that an area appears to be secure is in itself a _____.

   A. deterrent

   B. layer

   C. defense

   D. signature

7. Best practices dictate that data centers should be _____.

   A. well marked

   B. located in urban areas

   C. inconspicuous and unremarkable

   D. built on one level

8. Which of the following would be considered a "detection" control?

   A. Lighting

   B. Berms

   C. Motion sensors

   D. Bollards

9. Badging or an equivalent system at a secure facility should be used to identify _____.

   A. everyone who enters the building

   B. employees

   C. vendors

   D. visitors

10. Which of the following statements best describes the concept of shoulder surfing?

    A. Shoulder surfing is the use of a keylogger to capture data entry.

    B. Shoulder surfing is the act of looking over someone's shoulder to see what is on a computer screen.

    C. Shoulder surfing is the act of positioning one's shoulders to prevent fatigue.

    D. None of the above.

11. The term BYOD is used to refer to devices owned by _____.

    A. the company

    B. a vendor

    C. the employee

    D. a contractor

12. Which of the following statements is *not* true about data center best practices?

    A. Data center equipment must be protected from damage caused by power fluctuations or interruptions.

    B. Data center power protection devices must be tested on a scheduled basis for functionality and load capacity.

    C. Data center generators must be tested regularly according to manufacturer's instructions.

    D. You can optionally log all service and routine maintenance.

13. Which of the following terms best describes a prolonged increase in voltage?

    A. Power spike

    B. Power surge

    C. Power hit

    D. Power fault

14. Common causes of voltage variations include _____.

    A. lightning, storm damage, and electric demand

    B. using a power conditioner

    C. turning on and off computers

    D. using an uninterruptable power supply

15. Adhering to building and construction codes, using flame-retardant materials, and properly grounding equipment are examples of which of the following controls?

    A. Fire detection controls

    B. Fire containment controls

    C. Fire prevention controls

    D. Fire suppression controls

16. A Class C fire indicates the presence of which of the following items?

    A. Electrical equipment

    B. Flammable liquids

    C. Combustible materials

    D. Fire extinguishers

17. Confidential data can reside on which of the following items?

    A. Smartphones

    B. Cameras

    C. Scanners

    D. All of the above

18. Which of the following data types includes details about a file or document?

    A. Apparent data

    B. Hidden data

    C. Metadata

    D. Cache data

19. URL history, search history, form history, and download history are stored by the device
    _____.

    A. operating system

    B. browser

    C. BIOS

    D. ROMMON

20. Which of the following statements about formatting a drive is not true?

    A. Formatting a drive creates a bootable partition.

    B. Formatting a drive overwrites data.

    C. Formatting a drive fixes bad sectors.

    D. Formatting a drive permanently deletes files.

EXERCISES

EXERCISE 7.1: Researching Data Destruction Services

1. Research companies in your area that offer data destruction services.

2. Document the services they offer.

3. Make a list of questions you would ask them if you were tasked with selecting a vendor for data destruction services.

EXERCISE 7.2: **Assessing Data Center Visibility**

1. Locate the data center at your school or workplace.

2. Is the facility or area marked with signage? How easy was it to find? What controls are in place to prevent unauthorized access? Document your findings.

EXERCISE 7.3: **Reviewing Fire Containment**

1. Find at least three on-campus fire extinguishers (do not touch them). Document their location, what class fire they can be used for, and when they were last inspected.

2. Find at least one fire extinguisher (do not touch it) in your dorm, off-campus apartment, or home. Document the location, what class fire it can be used for, and when it was last inspected.

EXERCISE 7.4: **Assessing Identification Types**

1. Document what type of identification is issued to students, faculty, staff, and visitors at your school. If possible, include pictures of these types of documentation.

2. Describe the process for obtaining student identification.

3. Describe the procedure for reporting lost or stolen identification.

EXERCISE 7.5: **Finding Data**

1. Access a public computer in either the library, a computer lab, or a classroom.

2. Find examples of files or data that other users have left behind. The files can be apparent, temporary, browser based, cached, or document metadata. Document your findings.

3. What should you do if you discover "personal" information?

PROJECTS

PROJECT 7.1: **Assessing Physical and Environmental Security**

1. You are going to conduct a physical assessment of a computing device you own. This could be a desktop computer, a laptop, a tablet, or a smartphone. Use the following table as a template to document your findings. You can add additional fields.

Device Description	Laptop Computer								
							Safeguard		
Threats/ Danger	Impact	Safeguard 1	Safeguard 2	Safeguard 3	Assessment	Recommendation	Initial Cost	Annual Cost	Cost/Benefit Analysis
Lost or forgotten	Need laptop for schoolwork	Pink case	Labeled with owner's contact info		Inadequate	Install remote find software	$20.00	$20.00	$20 per year vs. the cost of replacing the laptop

2. Determine the physical and environmental dangers (threats); for example, losing or forgetting your laptop at school. Document your findings.

3. For each danger (threat), identify the controls that you have implemented; for example, your case is pink (recognizable) and the case and laptop are labeled with your contact information. It is expected that not all threats will have corresponding safeguards. Document your findings.

4. For threats that do not have a corresponding safeguard or ones for which you feel the current safeguards are inadequate, research the options you have for mitigating the danger. Based on your research, make recommendations. Your recommendation should include initial and ongoing costs. Compare the costs of the safeguard to the cost impact of the danger. Document your findings.

PROJECT 7.2: Assessing Data Center Design

1. You have been tasked with recommending environmental and physical controls for a *new* data center to be built at your school. You are expected to present a report to the Chief Information Officer. The first part of your report should be a synopsis of the importance of data center physical and environmental security.

2. The second part of your report should address three areas: location, perimeter security, and power.

   a. Location recommendations should include where the data center should be built and a description of the security of the surrounding area (for example, location-based threats include political stability, susceptibility to terrorism, the crime rate, adjacent buildings, roadways, pedestrian traffic, flight paths, utility stability, and vulnerability to natural disasters).

   b. Access control recommendations should address who will be allowed in the building and how they will be identified and monitored.

   c. Power recommendations should take into account power consumption as well as normal and emergency operating conditions.

PROJECT 7.3: **Securing the Perimeter**

1. The security perimeter is a barrier of protection from theft, malicious activity, accidental damage, and natural disaster. Almost all buildings have multiple perimeter controls. We have become so accustomed to perimeter controls that they often go unnoticed (that is, security guards). Begin this project with developing a comprehensive list of perimeter controls.

2. Conduct a site survey by walking around your city or town. You are looking for perimeter controls. Include in your survey results the address of the building, a summary of building occupants, type(s) of perimeter controls, and your opinion as to the effectiveness of the controls. To make your survey valid, you must include at least 10 properties.

3. Choose one property to focus on. Taking into consideration the location, the depth of security required by the occupants, and the geography, comment in detail on the perimeter controls. Based on your analysis, recommend additional physical controls to enhance perimeter security.

Case Study

Physical Access Social Engineering

In your role of ISO at Anywhere USA University Teaching Hospital, you commissioned an independent security consultancy to test the hospital's physical security controls using social engineering impersonation techniques. At the end of the first day of testing, the tester submitted a preliminary report.

Physical Access to Facilities

Dressed in blue scrubs, wearing a stethoscope, and carrying a clipboard, the tester was able to access the lab, the operating room, and the maternity ward. In one case, another staff member buzzed him in. In the two other cases, the tester walked in with other people.

Physical Access to the Network

Dressed in a suit, the tester was able to walk into a conference room and plug his laptop into a live data jack. Once connected, he was able to access the hospital's network.

Physical Access to a Computer

Wearing a polo shirt with a company name, the tester was able to sit down at an unoccupied office cubicle and remove a hard disk from a workstation. When questioned, he answered that he had been hired by John Smith, IT Manager, to repair the computer.

Physical Access to Patient Files

Wearing a lab coat, the tester was able to walk up to a printer in the nursing station and remove recently printed documents.

Based on these findings, you request that the consultancy suspend the testing. Your immediate response is to call a meeting to review the preliminary report.

1. Determine who should be invited to the meeting.
2. Compose a meeting invitation explaining the objective of the meeting.
3. Prepare an agenda for the meeting.
4. Identify what you see as the most immediate issues to be remediated.

References

Regulations Cited

DoD 5220.22-M: National Industrial Security Program Operating Manual, February 28, 2006, revised March 28, 2013.

Other References

"About Energy Star," Energy Star, accessed 04/2018, https://www.energystar.gov.

Amazon Web Services Physical Security Whitepaper, accessed 04/2018, https://d1.awsstatic.com/whitepapers/Security/AWS_Security_Whitepaper.pdf.

The Ponemon Institute, "2017 Cost of Data Breach Study: Global Overview," accessed 04/2018, https://www-01.ibm.com/common/ssi/cgi-bin/ssialias?htmlfid=SEL03130WWEN.

Destruct Data, "Department of Defense (DoD) Media Sanitization Guidelines 5220.22M," accessed 04/2018, http://www.destructdata.com/dod-standard/.

Bray, Megan, "Review of Computer Energy Consumption and Potential Savings," December 2006, accessed 04/2018, www.dssw.co.uk/research/computer_energy_consumption.html.

"Efficiency: How We Do It," Google, accessed 04/2018, https://www.google.com/about/datacenters/efficiency/internal/index.html#temperature.

"Facilities Services Sustainable Computing Guide," Cornell University, accessed 04/2018, http://www.ictliteracy.info/rf.pdf/FSSustainableComputingGuide.pdf.

"Foundations Recovery Network Notifying Patients After a Laptop with PHI Was Stolen from an Employee's Car," PHIprivacy.net, June 24, 2013, accessed 04/2018, https://www.databreaches.net/foundations-recovery-network-notifying-patients-after-a-laptop-with-phi-was-stolen-from-an-employees-car/.

"Google Data Centers," Google.com, accessed 04/2018, https://www.google.com/about/datacenters.

Jeffery, C. Ray. 1977. *Crime Prevention Through Environmental Design*, Second Edition, Beverly Hills: Sage Publications.

"Your Guide To Degaussers," Degausser.com, accessed 04/2018, http://degausser.com/.

"Data Center Battery Incident Causes Fire in Australian Hospital," Data Center Dynamics, accessed 04/2018, http://www.datacenterdynamics.com/content-tracks/security-risk/data-center-battery-incident-causes-fire-in-australian-hospital/99357.fullarticle.

Chapter 8

Communications and Operations Security

Chapter Objectives

After reading this chapter and completing the exercises, you will be able to do the following:

- Create useful and appropriate standard operating procedures.
- Implement change control processes.
- Understand the importance of patch management.
- Protect information systems against malware.
- Consider data backup and replication strategies.
- Recognize the security requirements of email and email systems.
- Appreciate the value of log data and analysis.
- Evaluate service provider relationships.
- Understand the importance of threat intelligence and information sharing.
- Write policies and procedures to support operational and communications security.

Section 3.3 of the NIST Cybersecurity Framework, "Communicating Cybersecurity Requirements with Stakeholders," provides guidance to organizations to learn how to communicate requirements among interdependent stakeholders responsible for the delivery of essential critical infrastructure services.

Section 12 of ISO 27002:2013, "Operations Security," and Section 13 of ISO 27002:2013, "Communications Security," focus on information technology (IT) and security functions, including standard operating procedures, change management, malware protection, data replication, secure messaging, and activity monitoring. These functions are primarily carried out by IT and information security data custodians, such as network administrators and security engineers. Many companies outsource some aspect of their operations. Section 15 of ISO 27002:2013, "Supplier Relationships," focuses on service delivery and third-party security requirements.

The NICE Framework introduced in Chapter 6, "Human Resources Security," is particularly appropriate for this domain. Data owners need to be educated on operational risk so they can make informed decisions. Data custodians should participate in training that focuses on operational security threats so that they understand the reason for implementing safeguards. Users should be surrounded by a security awareness program that fosters everyday best practices. Throughout the chapter, we cover policies, processes, and procedures recommended to create and maintain a secure operational environment.

FYI: NIST Cybersecurity Framework and ISO/IEC 27002:2013

As previously mentioned in this chapter, Section 3.3 of the NIST Cybersecurity Framework, "Communicating Cybersecurity Requirements with Stakeholders," provides guidance to organizations to learn how to communicate requirements among interdependent stakeholders. Examples include how organizations could use a Target Profile to express cybersecurity risk management requirements to an external service provider. These external service providers could be a cloud provider, such as Amazon Web Services (AWS), Google Cloud, or Microsoft Azure; or it can be a cloud service, such as Box, Dropbox, or any other service.

In addition, the NIST Framework suggests that an organization may express its cybersecurity state through a Current Profile to report results or to compare with acquisition requirements. Also, a critical infrastructure owner or operator may use a Target Profile to convey required Categories and Subcategories.

A critical infrastructure sector may establish a Target Profile that can be used among its constituents as an initial baseline Profile to build their tailored Target Profiles.

Section 12 of ISO 27002:2013, "Operations Security," focuses on data center operations, integrity of operations, vulnerability management, protection against data loss, and evidence-based logging. Section 13 of ISO 27002:2013, "Communications Security," focuses on protection of information in transit. Section 15 of ISO 27002:2013, "Supplier Relationships," focuses on service delivery and third-party security requirements.

Additional NIST guidance is provided in the following documents:

- "NIST Cybersecurity Framework" (covered in detail in Chapter 16)
- **SP 800-14:** "Generally Accepted Principles and Practices for Securing Information Technology Systems"
- **SP 800-53:** "Recommended Security Controls for Federal Information Systems and Organizations"
- **SP 800-100:** "Information Security Handbook: A Guide for Managers"
- **SP 800-40:** "Creating a Patch and Vulnerability Management Program"
- **SP 800-83:** "Guide to Malware Incident Prevention and Handling for Desktops and Laptops'
- **SP 800-45:** "Guidelines on Electronic Mail Security"
- **SP 800-92:** "Guide to Computer Security Log Management"
- **SP 800-42:** "Guideline on Network Security Testing"

Standard Operating Procedures

Standard operating procedures (SOPs) are detailed explanations of how to perform a task. The objective of an SOP is to provide standardized direction, improve communication, reduce training time, and improve work consistency. An alternate name for SOPs is *standard operating protocols*. An effective SOP communicates who will perform the task, what materials are necessary, where the task will take place, when the task will be performed, and how the person will execute the task.

Why Document SOPs?

The very process of creating SOPs requires us to evaluate what is being done, why it is being done that way, and perhaps how we could do it better. SOPs should be written by individuals knowledgeable about the activity and the organization's internal structure. Once written, the details in an SOP standardize the target process and provide sufficient information that someone with limited experience or knowledge of the procedure, but with a basic understanding, can successfully perform the procedure unsupervised. Well-written SOPs reduce organizational dependence on individual and institutional knowledge.

It is not uncommon for an employee to become so important that losing that individual would be a huge blow to the company. Imagine that this person is the only one performing a critical task; no one has been cross-trained, and no documentation exists as to how the employee performs this task. The employee suddenly becoming unavailable could seriously injure the organization. Having proper documentation of operating procedures is not a luxury: It is a business requirement.

SOPs should be authorized and protected accordingly, as illustrated in Figure 8-1 and described in the following sections.

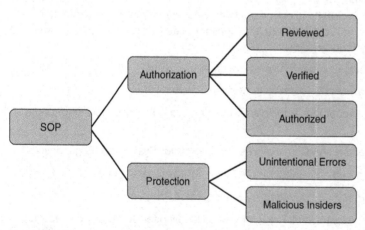

FIGURE 8-1 Authorizing and Protecting SOPs

Authorizing SOP Documentation

After a procedure has been documented, it should be reviewed, verified, and authorized before being published. The reviewer analyzes the document for clarity and readability. The verifier tests the procedure to make sure it is correct and not missing any steps. The process owner is responsible for authorization, publication, and distribution. Post-publication changes to the procedures must be authorized by the process owner.

Protecting SOP Documentation

Access and version controls should be put in place to protect the integrity of the document from both unintentional error and malicious insiders. Imagine a case where a disgruntled employee gets hold of a business-critical procedure document and changes key information. If the tampering is not discovered, it could lead to a disastrous situation for the company. The same holds true for revisions. If multiple revisions of the same procedure exist, there is a good chance someone is going to be using the wrong version.

Developing SOPs

SOPs should be understandable to everyone who uses them. SOPs should be written in a concise, step-by-step, *plain language* format. If not well written, SOPs are of limited value. It is best to use short, direct sentences so that the reader can quickly understand and memorize the steps in the procedure. Information should be conveyed clearly and explicitly to remove any doubt as to what is required. The steps must be in logical order. Any exceptions must be noted and explained. Warnings must stand out.

The four common SOP formats are Simple Step, Hierarchical, Flowchart, and Graphic. As shown in Table 8-1, two factors determine what type of SOP to use: how many decisions the user will need to make and how many steps are in the procedure. Routine procedures that are short and require few decisions can be written using the simple step format. Long procedures consisting of more than 10 steps, with few decisions, should be written in a hierarchical format or in a graphic format. Procedures that require many decisions should be written in the form of a flowchart. It is important to choose the correct format. The best-written SOPs will fail if they cannot be followed.

TABLE 8-1 SOP Methods

Many Decisions?	More Than Ten Steps?	Recommended SOP Format
No	No	Simple Step
No	Yes	Hierarchical or Graphic
Yes	No	Flowchart
Yes	Yes	Flowchart

As illustrated in Table 8-2, the simple step format uses sequential steps. Generally, these rote procedures do not require any decision making and do not have any substeps. The simple step format should be limited to 10 steps.

TABLE 8-2   Simple Step Format

Procedure	Completed
Note: These procedures are to be completed by the night operator by 6:00 a.m., Monday–Friday. Please initial each completed step.	

1. Remove backup tape from tape drive.

2. Label with the date.

3. Place tape in tape case and lock.

4. Call ABC delivery at 888-555-1212.

5. Tell ABC that the delivery is ready to be picked up.

6. When ABC arrives, require driver to present identification.

7. Note in pickup log the driver's name.

8. Have the driver sign and date the log.

As illustrated in the New User Account Creation Procedure example, shown in Table 8-3, the hierarchical format is used for tasks that require more detail or exactness. The hierarchical format allows the use of easy-to-read steps for experienced users while including substeps that are more detailed as well. Experienced users may refer to the substeps only when they need to, whereas beginners will use the detailed substeps to help them learn the procedure.

TABLE 8-3   Hierarchical Format

New User Account Creation Procedure

Note: You must have the HR New User Authorization Form before starting this process.

Procedures	Detail
Launch Active Directory Users and Computers (ADUC).	a. Click on the TS icon located on the administrative desktop. b. Provide your login credentials. c. Click the ADUC icon.
Create a new user.	a. Right-click the Users OU folder. b. Choose New User.
Enter the required user information.	a. Enter user first, last, and full name. b. Enter user login name and click Next. c. Enter user's temporary password. d. Choose User Must Change Password at Next Login and click Next.
Create an Exchange mailbox.	a. Make sure Create an Exchange Mailbox is checked. b. Accept the defaults and click Next.
Verify account information.	a. Confirm that all information on the summary screen is correct. b. Choose Finish.
Complete demographic profile.	a. Double-click the username. b. Complete the information on the General, Address, Telephone, and Organization tabs. (Note: Info should be on the HR request sheet.)

Procedures	Detail
Add users to groups.	a. Choose the Member Of tab. b. Add groups as listed on the HR request sheet. c. Click OK when completed.
Set remote control permissions.	a. Click the Remote Control tab. b. Make sure the Enable Remote Control and Require User's Permission boxes are checked. c. Level of control should be set to Interact with the Session.
Advise HR regarding account creation.	a. Sign and date the HR request form. b. Send it to HR via interoffice mail.

Pictures truly are worth a thousand words. The graphic format, shown in Figure 8-2, can use photographs, icons, illustrations, or screenshots to illustrate the procedure. This format is often used for configuration tasks, especially if various literacy levels or language barriers are involved.

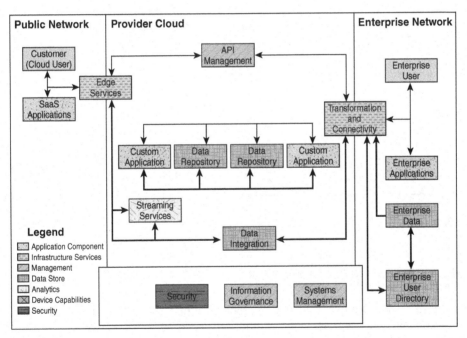

FIGURE 8-2   Example of the Graphic Format

A *flowchart*, shown in Figure 8-3, is a diagrammatic representation of steps in a decision-making process. A flowchart provides an easy-to-follow mechanism for walking a worker through a series of logical decisions and the steps that should be taken as a result. When developing flowcharts, you should use the generally accepted flowchart symbols. ISO 5807:1985 defines symbols to be used in flowcharts and gives guidance for their use.

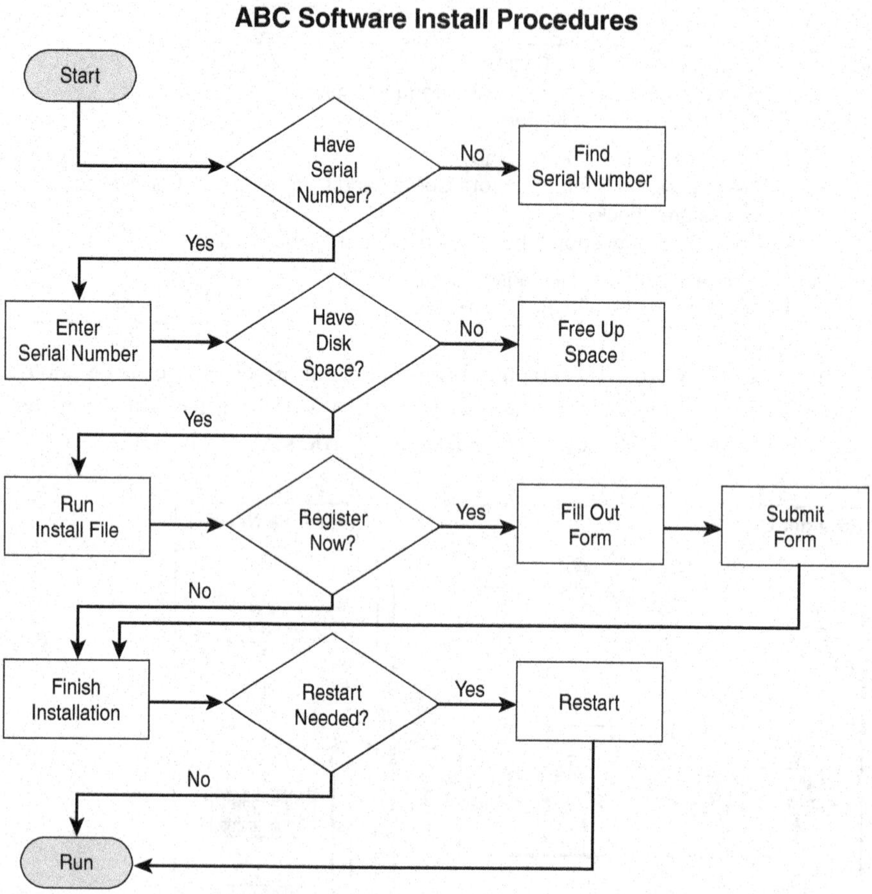

ABC Software Install Procedures

FIGURE 8-3   Flowchart Format

FYI: A Recommended Writing Resource

There are several resources for learning how to write procedures that, even if they are not related to cybersecurity, could be very beneficial to get started. An example is the North Carolina State University's Produce Safety SOP template at: https://ncfreshproducesafety.ces.ncsu.edu/wp-content/uploads/2014/03/how-to-write-an-SOP.pdf.

Another example is the Cornell University "Developing Effective Standard Operating Procedures" by David Grusenmeyer.

Standard Operating Procedures Documentation Policy

Synopsis: Standard operating procedures (SOPs) are required to ensure the consistent and secure operation of information systems.

Policy Statement:

- SOPs for all critical information processing activities will be documented.

- Information system custodians are responsible for developing and testing the procedures.

- Information system owners are responsible for authorization and ongoing review.

- The Office of Information Technology is responsible for the publication and distribution of information systems-related SOPs.

- SOPs for all critical information security activities will be documented, tested, and maintained.

- Information security custodians are responsible for developing and testing the procedures.

- The Office of Information Security is responsible for authorization, publication, distribution, and review of information security–related SOPs.

- Internal auditors will inspect actual practice against the requirements of the SOPs. Each auditor or an audit team creates audit checklists of the items to be covered. Corrective actions and suggestions for remediation may be raised following an internal or regulatory audit where discrepancies have been observed.

Operational Change Control

Operational change is inevitable. *Change control* is an internal procedure by which authorized changes are made to software, hardware, network access privileges, or business processes. The information security objective of change control is to ensure the stability of the network while maintaining the required levels of confidentiality, integrity, and availability (CIA). A *change management process* establishes an orderly and effective mechanism for submission, evaluation, approval, prioritization, scheduling, communication, implementation, monitoring, and organizational acceptance of change.

Why Manage Change?

The process of making changes to systems in production environments presents risks to ongoing operations and data that are effectively mitigated by consistent and careful management. Consider this scenario: Windows 8 is installed on a mission-critical workstation. The system administrator installs a service pack. A service pack often will make changes to system files. Now imagine that for a reason beyond the installer's control, the process fails halfway through. What is the result? An operating system that is neither the original version, nor the updated version. In other words, there could be a mix of new and old system files, which would result in an unstable platform. The negative impact on the process that depends on the workstation would be significant. Take this example to the next level and imagine the impact if this machine were a network server used by all employees all day long. Consider the impact on the productivity of the entire company if this machine were to become unstable because of a failed update. What if the failed change impacted a customer-facing device? The entire business could come grinding to a halt. What if the failed change also introduced a new vulnerability? The result could be loss of confidentiality, integrity, and/or availability (CIA).

Change needs to be controlled. Organizations that take the time to assess and plan for change spend considerably less time in crisis mode. Typical change requests are a result of software or hardware defects or bugs that must be fixed, system enhancement requests, and changes in the underlying architecture such as a new operating system, virtualization hypervisor, or cloud provider.

The change control process starts with an *RFC (Request for Change)*. The RFC is submitted to a decision-making body (generally senior management). The change is then evaluated and, if approved, implemented. Each step must be documented. Not all changes should be subject to this process. In fact, doing so would negate the desired effect and in the end significantly impact operations. There should be an organization policy that clearly delineates the type(s) of change that the change control process applies to. Additionally, there needs to be a mechanism to implement "emergency" changes. Figure 8-4 illustrates the RFC process and divides it into three primary milestones or phases: evaluate, approve, and verify.

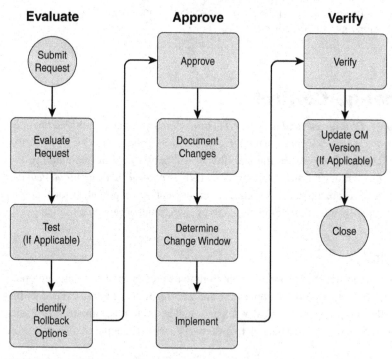

FIGURE 8-4   Flowchart Format

Submitting an RFC

The first phase of the change control process is an RFC submission. The request should include the following items:

- Requestor name and contact information
- Description of the proposed change
- Justification of why the proposed changes should be implemented
- Impact of not implementing the proposed change
- Alternatives to implementing the proposed change
- Cost
- Resource requirements
- Time frame

Figure 8-5 shows a template of the aforementioned RFC.

REQUESTOR Name: _____ Email :_____ Address:_____ Phone: _____	DESCRIPTION OF THE PROPOSED CHANGE:	
JUSTIFICATION:	IMPACT IF NOT IMPLEMENTED:	COST:
ALTERNATIVES TO IMPLEMENTING THE PROPOSED CHANGE:	RESOURCE REQUIREMENTS:	TIMEFRAME:

FIGURE 8-5 RFC Template

Taking into consideration the preceding information as well as organizational resources, budget, and priorities, the decision makers can choose to continue to evaluate, approve, reject, or defer until a later date.

Developing a Change Control Plan

After a change is approved, the next step is for the requestor to develop a *change control plan*. The complexity of the change as well as the risk to the organization will influence the level of detail required. Standard components of a change control plan include a security review to ensure that new vulnerabilities are not being introduced.

Communicating Change

The need to communicate to all relevant parties that a change will be taking place cannot be over-emphasized. Different research studies have found that communicating the reason for change was identified as the number-one most important message to share with employees and the second most important message for managers and executives (with the number-one message being about their role and expectations). The messages to communicate to impacted employees fell into two categories: messages about the change and how the change impacts them.

Messages about the change include the following:

- The current situation and the rationale for the change
- A vision of the organization after the change takes place
- The basics of what is changing, how it will change, and when it will change
- The expectation that change will happen and is not a choice
- Status updates on the implementation of the change, including success stories

Messages about how the change will affect the employee include the following:

- The impact of the change on the day-to-day activities of the employee
- Implications of the change on job security
- Specific behaviors and activities expected from the employee, including support of the change
- Procedures for getting help and assistance during the change

Projects that fail to communicate are doomed to fail.

Implementing and Monitoring Change

After the change is approved, planned, and communicated, it is time to implement. Change can be unpredictable. If possible, the change should first be applied to a test environment and monitored for impact. Even minor changes can cause havoc. For example, a simple change in a shared database's filename could cause all applications that use it to fail. For most environments, the primary implementation objective is to minimize stakeholder impact. This includes having a plan to roll back or recover from a failed implementation.

Throughout the implementation process, all actions should be documented. This includes actions taken before, during, and after the changes have been applied. Changes should not be "set and forget." Even a change that appears to have been flawlessly implemented should be monitored for unexpected impact.

Some emergency situations require organizations to bypass certain change controls to recover from an outage, incident, or unplanned event. Especially in these cases, it is important to document the change thoroughly, communicate the change as soon as possible, and have it approved post implementation.

Operational Change Control Policy

Synopsis: To minimize harm and maximize success associated with making changes to information systems or processes.

Policy Statement:

- The Office of Information Technology is responsible for maintaining a documented change control process that provides an orderly method in which changes to the information systems and processes are requested and approved prior to their installation and/or implementation. Changes to information systems include but are not limited to:
  - Vendor-released operating system, software application, and firmware patches, updates, and upgrades
  - Updates and changes to internally developed software applications
  - Hardware component repair/replacement
- Implementations of security patches are exempt from this process as long as they follow the approved patch management process.
- The change control process must take into consideration the criticality of the system and the risk associated with the change.
- Changes to information systems and processes considered critical to the operation of the company must be subject to preproduction testing.
- Changes to information systems and processes considered critical to the operation of the company must have an approved rollback and/or recovery plan.
- Changes to information systems and processes considered critical to the operation of the company must be approved by the Change Management Committee. Other changes may be approved by the Director of Information Systems, Chief Technology Officer (CTO), or Chief Information Officer (CIO).
- Changes must be communicated to all impacted stakeholders.
- In an emergency scenario, changes may be made immediately (business system interruption, failed server, and so on) to the production environment. These changes will be verbally approved by a manager supervising the affected area at the time of change. After the changes are implemented, the change must be documented in writing and submitted to the CTO.

Why Is Patching Handled Differently?

A *patch* is software or code designed to fix a problem. Applying *security patches* is the primary method of fixing security vulnerabilities in software. The vulnerabilities are often identified by researchers or ethical hackers who then notify the software company so that they can develop and distribute a patch. A function of change management, patching is distinct in how often and how quickly patches need to be applied. The moment a patch is released, attackers make a concerted effort to reverse engineer the patch swiftly (measured in days or even hours), identify the vulnerability, and develop and release exploit code. The time immediately after the release of a patch is ironically a particularly vulnerable moment for most organizations because of the time lag in obtaining, testing, and deploying a patch.

FYI: Patch Tuesday and Exploit Wednesday

Microsoft releases new security updates and their accompanying bulletins on the second Tuesday of every month at approximately 10 a.m. Pacific Time, hence the name *Patch Tuesday*. The following day is referred to as *Exploit Wednesday*, signifying the start of exploits appearing in the wild. Many security researchers and threat actors reverse engineer the fixes (patches) to create exploits, in some cases within hours after disclosure.

Cisco also releases bundles of Cisco IOS and IOS XE Software Security Advisories at 1600 GMT on the fourth Wednesday in March and September each year. Additional information can be found on Cisco's Security Vulnerability Policy at: https://www.cisco.com/c/en/us/about/security-center/security-vulnerability-policy.html.

Understanding Patch Management

Timely patching of security issues is generally recognized as critical to maintaining the operational CIA of information systems. *Patch management* is the process of scheduling, testing, approving, and applying security patches. Vendors who maintain information systems within a company network should be required to adhere to the organizational patch management process.

The patching process can be unpredictable and disruptive. Users should be notified of potential downtime due to patch installation. Whenever possible, patches should be tested prior to enterprise deployment. However, there may be situations where it is prudent to waive testing based on the severity and applicability of the identified vulnerability. If a critical patch cannot be applied in a timely manner, senior management should be notified of the risk to the organization.

Today's cybersecurity environment and patching dependencies call for substantial improvements in the area of vulnerability coordination. Open source software vulnerabilities like Heartbleed, protocol vulnerabilities like the WPA KRACK attacks, and others highlight coordination challenges among software and hardware providers.

The Industry Consortium for Advancement of Security on the Internet (ICASI) proposed to the FIRST Board of Directors that a Special Interest Group (SIG) be considered on vulnerability disclosure to review and update vulnerability coordination guidelines. Later, the National Telecommunications and Information Association (NTIA) convened a multistakeholder process to investigate cybersecurity vulnerabilities. The NTIA multiparty effort joined the similar effort underway within the FIRST Vulnerability Coordination SIG. Stakeholders created a document that derives multiparty disclosure guidelines and practices from common coordination scenarios and variations. This document can be found at https://first.org/global/sigs/vulnerability-coordination/multiparty/guidelines-v1.0.

Figure 8-6 shows the FIRST Vulnerability Coordination stakeholder roles and communication paths.

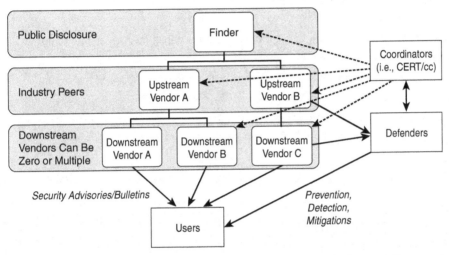

FIGURE 8-6   FIRST Vulnerability Coordination Stakeholder Roles and Communication Paths

The definitions of the different stakeholders used in the FIRST "Guidelines and Practices for Multi-Party Vulnerability Coordination and Disclosure" document are based on the definitions available in ISO/IEC 29147:2014 and used with minimal modification.

NIST Special Publication 800-40 Revision 3, *Guide to Enterprise Patch Management Technologies*, published July 2013, is designed to assist organizations in understanding the basics of enterprise patch management technologies. It explains the importance of patch management and examines the challenges inherent in performing patch management. The publication also provides an overview of enterprise patch management technologies and discusses metrics for measuring the technologies' effectiveness and for comparing the relative importance of patches.

Security Patch Management Policy

Synopsis: The timely deployment of security patches will reduce or eliminate the potential for exploitation.

Policy Statement:

- Implementations of security patches are exempt from the organizational change management process as long as they follow the approved patch management process.

- The Office of Information Security is responsible for maintaining a documented patch management process.

- The Office of Information Technology is responsible for the deployment of all operating system, application, and device security patches.

- Security patches will be reviewed and deployed according to applicability of the security vulnerability and/or identified risk associated with the patch or hotfix.

- Security patches will be tested prior to deployment in the production environment. The CIO and the CTO have authority to waive testing based on the severity and applicability of the identified vulnerability.

- Vendors who maintain company systems are required to adhere to the company patch management process.

- If a security patch cannot be successfully applied, the COO must be notified. Notification must detail the risk to the organization.

Malware Protection

Malware, short for "malicious software," is software (or script or code) designed to disrupt computer operation, gather sensitive information, or gain unauthorized access to computer systems and mobile devices. Malware is operating-system agnostic. Malware can infect systems by being bundled with other programs or self-replicating; however, the vast majority of malware requires user interaction, such as clicking an email attachment or downloading a file from the Internet. It is critical that *security awareness* programs articulate individual responsibility in fighting malware.

Malware has become the tool of choice for cybercriminals, hackers, and hacktivists. It has become easy for attackers to create their own malware by acquiring malware toolkits, such as Zeus, Shadow Brokers leaked exploits, and many more, and then customizing the malware produced by those toolkits to meet their individual needs. Examples are ransomware such as WannaCry, Nyetya, Bad Rabbit, and many others. Many of these toolkits are available for purchase, whereas others are open source, and most have user-friendly interfaces that make it simple for unskilled attackers to create customized, high-capability malware. Unlike most malware several years ago, which tended to be easy to notice, much of today's malware is specifically designed to quietly and slowly spread to other hosts, gathering information over extended periods of time and eventually leading to exfiltration of sensitive data and other negative impacts. The term *advanced persistent threats (APTs)* is generally used to refer to this approach.

NIST Special Publication 800-83, Revision 1, *Guide to Malware Incident Prevention and Handling for Desktops and Laptops*, published in July 2012, provides recommendations for improving an organization's malware incident prevention measures. It also gives extensive recommendations for enhancing an organization's existing incident response capability so that it is better prepared to handle malware incidents, particularly widespread ones.

Are There Different Types of Malware?

Malware categorization is based on infection and propagation characteristics. The categories of malware include viruses, worms, Trojans, bots, ransomware, rootkits, and spyware/adware. *Hybrid malware* is code that combines characteristics of multiple categories—for example, combining a virus's ability to alter program code with a worm's ability to reside in live memory and to propagate without any action on the part of the user.

A *virus* is malicious code that attaches to and becomes part of another program. Generally, viruses are destructive. Almost all viruses attach themselves to executable files. They then execute in tandem with the host file. Viruses spread when the software or document they are attached to is transferred from one computer to another using the network, a disk, file sharing, or infected email attachments.

A *worm* is a piece of malicious code that can spread from one computer to another without requiring a host file to infect. Worms are specifically designed to exploit known vulnerabilities, and they spread by taking advantage of network and Internet connections. An early example of a worm was W32/SQL Slammer (aka Slammer and Sapphire), which was one of the fastest spreading worms in history. It infected the process space of Microsoft SQL Server 2000 and Microsoft SQL Desktop Engine (MSDE) by exploiting an unpatched buffer overflow. Once running, the worm tried to send itself to as many other Internet-accessible SQL hosts as possible. Microsoft had released a patch six months prior to the Slammer outbreak. Another example of a "wormable" malware was the WannaCry ransomware, which is discussed later in this chapter.

A *Trojan* is malicious code that masquerades as a legitimate benign application. For example, when a user downloads a game, he may get more than he expected. The game may serve as a conduit for a malicious utility such as a keylogger or screen scraper. A *keylogger* is designed to capture and log keystrokes, mouse movements, Internet activity, and processes in memory such as print jobs. A *screen scraper* makes copies of what you see on your screen. A typical activity attributed to Trojans is to open connections to a *command and control server* (known as a C&C). Once the connection is made, the machine is said to be "owned." The attacker takes control of the infected machine. In fact, cybercriminals will tell you that after they have successfully installed a Trojan on a target machine, they actually have more control over that machine than the very person seated in front of and interacting with it. Once "owned," access to the infected device may be sold to other criminals. Trojans do not reproduce by infecting other files, nor do they self-replicate. Trojans must spread through user interaction, such as opening an email attachment or downloading and running a file from the Internet. Examples of Trojans include Zeus and SpyEye. Both Trojans are designed to capture financial website login credentials and other personal information.

Bots (also known as *robots*) are snippets of code designed to automate tasks and respond to instructions. Bots can self-replicate (like worms) or replicate via user action (like Trojans). A malicious bot is installed in a system without the user's permission or knowledge. The bot connects back to a central server or command center. An entire network of compromised devices is known as a *botnet*. One of the most common uses of a botnet is to launch distributed denial of service (DDoS) attacks. An example of a botnet that caused major outages in the past is the Mirai botnet, which is often referred to as the IoT Botnet. Threat actors were able to successfully compromise IoT devices, including security cameras and consumer routing devices, to create one of the most devastating botnets in history, launching numerous DDoS attacks against very high-profile targets.

Ransomware is a type of malware that takes a computer or its data hostage in an effort to extort money from victims. There are two types of ransomware: *Lockscreen ransomware* displays a full-screen image or web page that prevents you from accessing anything in your computer. *Encryption ransomware* encrypts your files with a password, preventing you from opening them. The most common ransomware scheme is a notification that authorities have detected illegal activity on your computer and you must pay a "fine" to avoid prosecution and regain access to your system. Examples of popular ransomware include WannaCry, Nyetya, Bad Rabbit, and others. Ransomware typically spreads or is delivered by malicious emails, malvertising (malicious advertisements or ads), and other drive-by downloads. However, in the case of WannaCry, this ransomware was the first one that spread in similar ways as worms (as previously defined in this chapter). Specifically, it used the EternalBlue exploit.

EternalBlue is an SMB exploit affecting various Windows operating systems from XP to Windows 7 and various flavors of Windows Server 2003 & 2008. The exploit technique is known as HeapSpraying and is used to inject shellcode into vulnerable systems, allowing for the exploitation of the system. The code is capable of targeting vulnerable machines by IP address and attempting exploitation via SMB port 445. The EternalBlue code is closely tied with the DoublePulsar backdoor and even checks for the existence of the malware during the installation routine.

Cisco Talos has created numerous articles covering in-depth technical details of numerous types of ransomware at http://blog.talosintelligence.com/search/label/ransomware.

A *rootkit* is a set of software tools that hides its presence in the lower layers of the operating system's application layer, the operating system kernel, or in the device basic input/output system (BIOS) with privileged access permissions. *Root* is a UNIX/Linux term that denotes administrator-level or privileged access permissions. The word "kit" denotes a program that allows someone to obtain root/admin-level access to the computer by executing the programs in the kit—all of which is done without end-user consent or knowledge. The intent is generally remote C&C. Rootkits cannot self-propagate or replicate; they must be installed on a device. Because of where they operate, they are very difficult to detect and even more difficult to remove.

Spyware is a general term used to describe software that without a user's consent and/or knowledge tracks Internet activity, such as searches and web surfing, collects data on personal habits, and displays advertisements. Spyware sometimes affects the device configuration by changing the default browser, changing the browser home page, or installing "add-on" components. It is not unusual for an application or online service license agreement to contain a clause that allows for the installation of spyware.

A *logic bomb* is a type of malicious code that is injected into a legitimate application. An attacker can program a logic bomb to delete itself from the disk after it performs the malicious tasks on the system. Examples of these malicious tasks include deleting or corrupting files or databases and executing a specific instruction after certain system conditions are met.

A *downloader* is a piece of malware that downloads and installs other malicious content from the Internet to perform additional exploitation on an affected system.

A *spammer* is a piece of malware that sends spam, or unsolicited messages sent via email, instant messaging, newsgroups, or any other kind of computer or mobile device communications. Spammers send these unsolicited messages with the primary goal of fooling users into clicking malicious links, replying to emails or other messages with sensitive information, or performing different types of scams. The attacker's main objective is to make money.

How Is Malware Controlled?

The IT department is generally tasked with the responsibility of employing a strong antimalware defense-in-depth strategy. In this case, *defense-in-depth* means implementing prevention, detection, and response controls, coupled with a security awareness campaign.

Using Prevention Controls

The goal of *prevention control* is to stop an attack before it even has a chance to start. This can be done in a number of ways:

- Impact the distribution channel by training users not to clink links embedded in email, open unexpected email attachments, irresponsibly surf the Web, download games or music, participate in peer-to-peer (P2P) networks, and allow remote access to their desktop.

- Configure the firewall to restrict access.

- Do not allow users to install software on company-provided devices.

- Do not allow users to make changes to configuration settings.

- Do not allow users to have administrative rights to their workstations. Malware runs in the security context of the logged-in user.

- Do not allow users to disable (even temporarily) anti-malware software and controls.

- Disable remote desktop connections.

- Apply operating system and application security patches expediently.

- Enable browser-based controls, including pop-up blocking, download screening, and automatic updates.

- Implement an enterprise-wide antivirus/antimalware application. It is important that the antimalware solutions be configured to update as frequently as possible because many new pieces of malicious code are released daily.

You should also take advantage of sandbox-based solutions to provide a controlled set of resources for guest programs to run in. In a sandbox network, access is typically denied to avoid network-based infections.

Using Detection Controls

Detection controls should identify the presence of malware, alert the user (or network administrator), and in the best-case scenario stop the malware from carrying out its mission. Detection should occur at multiple levels—at the entry point of the network, on all hosts and devices, and at the file level. Detection controls include the following:

- Real-time firewall detection of suspicious file downloads.

- Real-time firewall detection of suspicious network connections.

- Host and network-based intrusion detection systems (IDS) or intrusion prevention systems (IPS).

- Review and analysis of firewalls, IDS, operating systems, and application logs for indicators of compromise.

- User awareness to recognize and report suspicious activity.

- Antimalware and antivirus logs.

- Help desk (or equivalent) training to respond to malware incidents.

What Is Antivirus Software?

Antivirus (AV) software is used to detect, contain, and in some cases eliminate malicious software. Most AV software employs two techniques—signature-based recognition and behavior-based (heuristic) recognition. A common misconception is that AV software is 100% effective against malware intrusions. Unfortunately, that is not the case. Although AV applications are an essential control, they are increasingly limited in their effectiveness. This is due to three factors—the sheer volume of new malware, the phenomenon of "single-instance" malware, and the sophistication of blended threats.

The core of AV software is known as the "engine." It is the basic program. The program relies on virus definition files (known as DAT files) to identify malware. The definition files must be continually updated by the software publisher and then distributed to every user. This was a reasonable task when the number and types of malware were limited. New versions of malware are increasing exponentially, thus making research, publication, and timely distribution a next-to-impossible task. Complicating this problem is the phenomenon of single-instance malware—that is, variants only used one time. The challenge here is that DAT files are developed using historical knowledge, and it is impossible to develop a corresponding DAT file for a single instance that has never been seen before. The third challenge is the sophistication of malware—specifically, blended threats. A *blended threat* occurs when multiple variants of malware (worms, viruses, bots, and so on) are used in concert to exploit system vulnerabilities. Blended threats are specifically designed to circumvent AV and behavioral-based defenses.

Numerous antivirus and antimalware solutions on the market are designed to detect, analyze, and protect against both known and emerging endpoint threats. The following are the most common types of antivirus and antimalware software:

- ZoneAlarm PRO Antivirus+, ZoneAlarm PRO Firewall, and ZoneAlarm Extreme Security
- F-Secure Anti-Virus
- Kaspersky Anti-Virus
- McAfee AntiVirus
- Panda Antivirus
- Sophos Antivirus
- Norton AntiVirus
- ClamAV
- Immunet AntiVirus

There are numerous other antivirus software companies and products.

ClamAV is an open source antivirus engine sponsored and maintained by Cisco and non-Cisco engineers. You can download ClamAV from www.clamav.net. Immunet is a free community-based antivirus software maintained by Cisco Sourcefire. You can download Immunet from www.immunet.com

Personal firewalls and host intrusion prevention systems (HIPSs) are software applications that you can install on end-user machines or servers to protect them from external security threats and intrusions. The term *personal firewall* typically applies to basic software that can control Layer 3 and Layer 4 access to client machines. HIPS provide several features that offer more robust security than a traditional personal firewall, such as host intrusion prevention and protection against spyware, viruses, worms, Trojans, and other types of malware.

FYI: What Are the OSI and TCP/IP Models?

Two main models are currently used to explain the operation of an IP-based network. These are the TCP/IP model and the Open System Interconnection (OSI) model. The TCP/IP model is the foundation for most modern communication networks. Every day, each of us uses some application based on the TCP/IP model to communicate. Think, for example, about a task we consider simple: browsing a web page. That simple action would not be possible without the TCP/IP model.

The TCP/IP model's name includes the two main protocols we discuss in the course of this chapter: Transmission Control Protocol (TCP) and Internet Protocol (IP). However, the model goes beyond these two protocols and defines a layered approach that can map nearly any protocol used in today's communication.

In its original definition, the TCP/IP model included four layers, where each of the layers would provide transmission and other services for the level above it. These are the link layer, internet layer, transport layer, and application layer.

In its most modern definition, the link layer is split into two additional layers to clearly demark the physical and data link type of services and protocols included in this layer. The internet layer is also sometimes called the networking layer, which is based on another well-known model, the Open System Interconnection (OSI) model.

The OSI reference model is another model that uses abstraction layers to represent the operation of communication systems. The idea behind the design of the OSI model is to be comprehensive enough to take into account advancement in network communications and to be general enough to allow several existing models for communication systems to transition to the OSI model.

The OSI model presents several similarities with the TCP/IP model described above. One of the most important similarities is the use of abstraction layers. As with TCP/IP, each layer provides service for the layer above it within the same computing device while it interacts at the same layer with other computing devices. The OSI model includes seven abstract layers, each representing a different function and service within a communication network:

- **Physical layer—Layer 1 (L1):** Provides services for the transmission of bits over the data link.

- **Data link layer—Layer 2 (L2):** Includes protocols and functions to transmit information over a link between two connected devices. For example, it provides flow control and L1 error detection.

- **Network layer—Layer 3 (L3):** This layer includes the function necessary to transmit information across a network and provides abstraction on the underlying means of connection. It defines L3 addressing, routing, and packet forwarding.

- **Transport layer—Layer 4 (L4):** This layer includes services for end-to-end connection establishment and information delivery. For example, it includes error detection, retransmission capabilities, and multiplexing.

- **Session layer—Layer 5 (L5):** This layer provides services to the presentation layer to establish a session and exchange presentation layer data.

- **Presentation layer—Layer 6 (L6):** This layer provides services to the application layer to deal with specific syntax, which is how data is presented to the end user.

- **Application layer—Layer 7 (L7):** This is the last (or first) layer of the OSI model (depending on how you see it). It includes all the services of a user application, including the interaction with the end user.

Figure 8-7 illustrates how each layer of the OSI model maps to the corresponding TCP/IP layer.

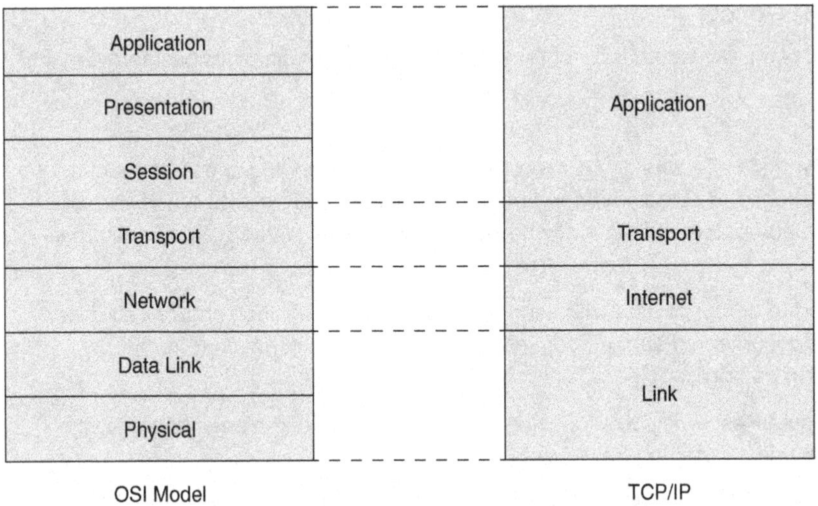

OSI Model   TCP/IP

FIGURE 8-7   OSI and TCP/IP Models

Attacks are getting very sophisticated and can evade detection of traditional systems and endpoint protection. Today, attackers have the resources, knowledge, and persistence to beat point-in-time detection. These solutions provide mitigation capabilities that go beyond point-in-time detection. It uses threat intelligence to perform retrospective analysis and protection. These malware protection solutions also provide device and file trajectory capabilities to allow a security administrator to analyze the full spectrum of an attack.

FYI: CCleaner Antivirus Supply Chain Backdoor

Security researchers at Cisco Talos found a backdoor that was included with version 5.33 of the CCleaner antivirus application. During the investigation and when analyzing the delivery code from the command and control server, they found references to several high-profile organizations including Cisco, Intel, VMWare, Sony, Samsung, HTC, Linksys, Microsoft, and Google Gmail that were specifically targeted through delivery of a second-stage loader. Based on a review of the command and control tracking database, they confirmed that at least 20 victims were served specialized secondary payloads. Interestingly, the array specified contains different domains of high-profile technology companies. This would suggest a very focused actor after valuable intellectual property.

Another example of potential supply chain attacks are the allegations against security products like the Kaspersky antivirus. The United States Department of Homeland Security (DHS) issued a Binding Operational Directive 17-01 strictly calling on all U.S. government departments and agencies to identify any use or presence of Kaspersky products on their information systems and to develop detailed plans to remove and discontinue present and future use of these products. This directive can be found at https://www.dhs.gov/news/2017/09/13/dhs-statement-issuance-binding-operational-directive-17-01.

In Practice

Malicious Software Policy

Synopsis: To ensure a companywide effort to prevent, detect, and contain malicious software.

Policy Statement:

- The Office of Information Technology is responsible for recommending and implementing prevention, detection, and containment controls. At a minimum, antimalware software will be installed on all computer workstations and servers to prevent, detect, and contain malicious software.

- Any system found to be out of date with vendor-supplied virus definition and/or detection engines must be documented and remediated immediately or disconnected from the network until it can be updated.

- The Office of Human Resources is responsible for developing and implementing malware awareness and incident reporting training.

- All malware-related incidents must be reported to the Office of Information Security.

- The Office of Information Security is responsible for incident management.

Data Replication

The impact of malware, computer hardware failure, accidental deletion of data by users, and other eventualities is reduced with an effective data backup or replication process that includes periodic testing to ensure the integrity of the data as well as the efficiency of the procedures to restore that data in the production environment. Having multiple copies of data is essential for both data integrity and availability. **Data replication** is the process of copying data to a second location that is available for immediate or near-time use. **Data backup** is the process of copying and storing data that can be restored to its original location. A company that exists without a tested backup-and-restore or data replication solution is like a flying acrobat working without a net.

When you perform data replication, you copy and then move data between different sites. Data replication is typically measured as follows:

- **Recovery Time Objective (RTO):** The targeted time frame in which a business process must be restored after a disruption or a disaster.

- **Recovery Point Objective (RPO):** The maximum amount of time in which data might be lost from an organization due to a major incident.

Is There a Recommended Backup or Replication Strategy?

Making the decision to back up or to replicate, and how often, should be based on the impact of not being able to access the data either temporarily or permanently. Strategic, operational, financial, transactional, and regulatory requirements must be considered. You should consider several factors when designing a replication or data backup strategy. Reliability is paramount; speed and efficiency are also very important, as are simplicity, ease of use, and, of course, cost. These factors will all define the criteria for the type and frequency of the process.

Data backup strategies primarily focus on compliance and granular recovery—for example, recovering a document created a few months ago or a user's email a few years ago.

Data replication and recovery focus on business continuity and the quick or easy resumption of operations after a disaster or corruption. One of the key benefits of data replication is minimizing the recovery time objective (RTO). Additionally, data backup is typically used for everything in the organization, from critical production servers to desktops and mobile devices. On the other hand, data replication is often used for mission-critical applications that must always be available and fully operational.

Backed-up or replicated data should be stored at an off-site location, in an environment where it is secure from theft, the elements, and natural disasters such as floods and fires. The backup strategy and associated procedures must be documented.

Figure 8-8 shows an example of data replication between two geographical locations. In this example, data stored at an office in New York, NY, is replicated to a site in Raleigh, North Carolina.

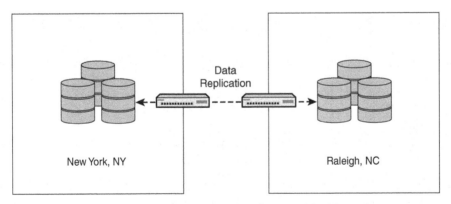

FIGURE 8-8   Data Replication Between Two Geographical Locations

Organizations also can use data backups or replication to the cloud. *Cloud storage* refers to using Internet-based resources to store your data. A number of the cloud-based providers, such as Google, Amazon, Microsoft Azure, Box, Dropbox, and others offer scalable, affordable storage options that can be used in place of (or in addition to) local backup.

Figure 8-9 shows an example of an organization that has an office in San Juan, Puerto Rico, backing up its data in the cloud.

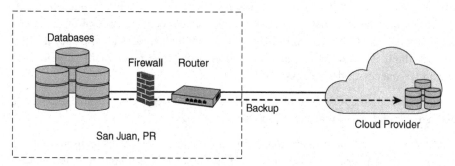

FIGURE 8-9   Cloud-Based Data Backup Example

Different data backup recovery types can be categorized as follows:

- Traditional recovery

- Enhanced recovery

- Rapid recovery

- Continuous availability

Figure 8-10 lists the benefits and elements of each data backup recovery type.

Good ───▶ Best

Traditional Recovery	Enhanced Recovery	Rapid Recovery	Continuous Availability
• Tape Backup • Low Complexity • Low Cost • Recovery Measured in Hours to Days	• Automated Solutions • Medium Complexity • Low Cost • Recovery Measured in Hours to Days • More Recoverable Data	• Asynchronous Replication • High Complexity • Moderate Cost • Recovery Measured in Hours	• Synchronous Replication • High Complexity • High Cost • Recovery Measured in Seconds

FIGURE 8-10   Data Backup Types

Understanding the Importance of Testing

The whole point of replicating or backing up data is that it can be accessed or restored if the data is lost or tampered with. In other words, the value of the backup or replication is the assurance that running a restore operation will yield success and that the data will again be available for production and business-critical application systems.

Just as proper attention must be paid to designing and testing the replication or backup solution, the accessibility or restore strategy must also be carefully designed and tested before being approved. Accessibility or restore procedures must be documented. The only way to know whether a replication or backup operation was successful and can be relied upon is to test it. It is recommended that testing access or restores of random files be conducted at least monthly.

In Practice

Data Replication Policy

Synopsis: Maintain the availability and integrity of data in the case of error, compromise, failure, or disaster.

Policy Statement:

- The Office of Information Security is responsible for the design and oversight of the enterprise replication and backup strategy. Factors to be considered include but are not limited to impact, cost, and regulatory requirements.

- Data contained on replicated or backup media will be protected at the same level of access control as the data on the originating system.

- The Office of Information Technology is responsible for the implementation, maintenance, and ongoing monitoring of the replication and backup/restoration strategy.

- The process must be documented.

- The procedures must be tested on a scheduled basis.

- Backup media no longer in rotation for any reason will be physically destroyed so that the data is unreadable by any means.

Secure Messaging

In 1971, Ray Tomlinson, a Department of Defense (DoD) researcher, sent the first ARPANET email message to himself. The *ARPANET*, the precursor to the Internet, was a United States (U.S.) Advanced Research Project Agency (ARPA) project intended to develop a set of communications protocols to transparently connect computing resources in various geographical locations. Messaging applications were available on ARPANET systems; however, they could be used only for sending messages to users with local system accounts. Tomlinson modified the existing messaging system so that users could send messages to users on other ARPANET-connected systems. After Tomlinson's modification was available to other researchers, email quickly became the most heavily used application on the ARPANET. Security was given little consideration because the ARPANET was viewed as a trusted community.

Current email architecture is strikingly similar to the original design. Consequently, email servers, email clients, and users are vulnerable to exploit and are frequent targets of attack. Organizations need to implement controls that safeguard the CIA of email hosts and email clients. NIST Special Publication 800-177, *Trustworthy Email*, recommends security practices for improving the trustworthiness of email. NIST's recommendations are aimed to help you reduce the risk of spoofed email being used as an attack vector and the risk of email contents being disclosed to unauthorized parties. The recommendations in the special publication apply to both the email sender and receiver.

What Makes Email a Security Risk?

When you send an email, the route it takes in transit is complex, with processing and sorting occurring at several intermediary locations before arriving at the final destination. In its native form, email is transmitted using clear-text protocols. It is almost impossible to know if anyone has read or manipulated your email in transit. Forwarding, copying, storing, and retrieving email is easy (and commonplace); preserving confidentiality of the contents and metadata is difficult. Additionally, email can be used to distribute malware and to exfiltrate company data.

Understanding Clear Text Transmission

Simple Mail Transfer Protocol (SMTP) is the de facto message transport standard for sending email messages. Jon Postel of the University of Southern California developed SMTP in August 1982. At the most basic level, SMTP is a minimal language that defines a communications protocol for delivering email messages. After a message is delivered, users need to access the mail server to retrieve the message. The two most widely supported mailbox access protocols are *Post Office Protocol (now POP3)*, developed in 1984, and *Internet Message Access Protocol (IMAP)*, developed in 1988. The designers never envisioned that someday email would be ubiquitous, and as with the original ARPANET communications, reliable message delivery, rather than security, was the focus. SMTP, POP, and IMAP are all clear-text protocols. This means that the delivery instructions (including access passwords) and email contents are transmitted in a human readable form. Information sent in clear text may be captured and read by third parties, resulting in a breach of confidentiality. Information sent in clear text may be captured and manipulated by third parties, resulting in a breach of integrity.

Encryption protocols can be used to protect both authentication and contents. *Encryption* protects the privacy of the message by converting it from (readable) plain text into (scrambled) cipher text. Late implementation of POP and IMAP support encryption. RFC 2595, "Using TLS with IMAP, POP3 and ACAP" introduces the use of encryption in these popular email standards.

We examine encryption protocols in depth in Chapter 10, "Information Systems Acquisition, Development, and Maintenance." Encrypted email is often referred to as "secure email." As we discussed in Chapter 5, "Asset Management and Data Loss Prevention," email-handling standards should specify the email encryption requirements for each data classification. Most email encryption utilities can be configured to auto-encrypt based on preset criteria, including content, recipient, and email domain.

Understanding Metadata

Documents sent as email attachments or via any other communication or collaboration tools might contain more information than the sender intended to share. The files created by many office programs contain hidden information about the creator of the document, and may even include some content that has been reformatted, deleted, or hidden. This information is known as *metadata*.

Keep this in mind in the following situations:

- If you recycle documents by making changes and sending them to new recipients (that is, using a boilerplate contract or a sales proposal).

- If you use a document created by another person. In programs such as Microsoft Office, the document might list the original person as the author.

- If you use a feature for tracking changes. Be sure to accept or reject changes, not just hide the revisions.

Understanding Embedded Malware

Email is an effective method to attack and ultimately infiltrate an organization. Common mechanisms include embedding malware in an attachment and directing the recipient to click a hyperlink that connects to a malware distribution site (unbeknownst to the user). Increasingly, attackers are using email to deliver zero-day attacks at targeted organizations. A *zero-day exploit* is one that takes advantage of a security vulnerability on the same day that the vulnerability becomes publicly or generally known.

Malware can easily be embedded in common attachments, such as PDF, Word, and Excel files, or even a picture. Not allowing any attachments would simplify email security; however, it would dramatically reduce the usefulness of email. Determining which types of attachments to allow and which to filter out must be an organizational decision. Filtering is a mail server function and is based on the file type. The effectiveness of filtering is limited because attackers can modify the file extension. In keeping with a defense-in-depth approach, allowed attachments should be scanned for malware at the mail gateway, email server, and email client.

A *hyperlink* is a word, phrase, or image that is programmatically configured to connect to another document, bookmark, or location. Hyperlinks have two components—the text to display (such as www.goodplace.com) and the connection instructions. Genuine-looking hyperlinks are used to trick email recipients into connecting to malware distribution sites. Most email client applications have the option to disable active hyperlinks. The challenge here is that hyperlinks are often legitimately used to direct the recipient to additional information. In both cases, users need to be taught to not click on links or open any attachment associated with an unsolicited, unexpected, or even mildly suspicious email.

Controlling Access to Personal Email Applications

Access to personal email accounts should not be allowed from a corporate network. Email that is delivered via personal email applications such as Gmail bypass all the controls that the company has invested in, such as email filtering and scanning. A fair comparison would be that you install a lock, lights, and an alarm system on the front door of your home but choose to leave the back door wide open all the time based on the assumption that the back door is really just used occasionally for friends and family.

In addition to outside threats, consideration needs to be given to both the malicious and unintentional insider threat. If an employee decides to correspond with a customer via personal email, or if an employee chooses to exfiltrate information and send it via personal email, there would be no record of the activity. From both an HR and a forensic perspective, this would hamper an investigation and subsequent response.

Understanding Hoaxes

Every year, a vast amount of money is lost, in the form of support costs and equipment workload, due to hoaxes sent by email. A *hoax* is a deliberately fabricated falsehood. An email hoax may be a fake virus warning or false information of a political or legal nature and often borders on criminal mischief. Some hoaxes ask recipients to take action that turns out to be damaging—deleting supposedly malicious files from their local computer, sending uninvited mail, randomly boycotting organizations for falsified reasons, or defaming an individual or group by forwarding the message.

Understanding the Risks Introduced by User Error

The three most common user errors that impact the confidentiality of email are sending email to the wrong person, choosing Reply All instead of Reply, and using Forward inappropriately.

It is easy to mistakenly send email to the wrong address. This is especially true with email clients that autocomplete addresses based on the first three or four characters entered. All users must be made aware of this and must pay strict attention to the email address entered in the To field, along with the CC and BCC fields when used.

The consequence of choosing Reply All instead of Reply can be significant. The best-case scenario is embarrassment. In the worst cases, confidentiality is violated by distributing information to those who do not have a "need to know." In regulated sectors such as health care and banking, violating the privacy of patients and/or clients is against the law.

Forwarding has similar implications. Assume that two people have been emailing back and forth using the Reply function. Their entire conversation can be found online. Now suppose that one of them decides that something in the last email is of interest to a third person and forwards the email. In reality, what that person just did was forward the entire thread of emails that had been exchanged between the two original people. This may well have not been the person's intent and may violate the privacy of the other original correspondent.

Are Email Servers at Risk?

Email servers are hosts that deliver, forward, and store email. Email servers are attractive targets because they are a conduit between the Internet and the internal network. Protecting an email server from compromise involves hardening the underlying operating system, the email server application, and the network to prevent malicious entities from directly attacking the mail server. Email servers should be single-purpose hosts, and all other services should be disabled or removed. Email server threats include relay abuse and DoS attacks.

Understanding Relay Abuse and Blacklisting

The role of an email server is to process and relay email. The default posture for many email servers is to process and relay *any* mail sent to the server. This is known as *open mail relay*. The ability to relay mail through a server can (and often is) taken advantage of by those who benefit from the illegal use of the resource. Criminals conduct Internet searches for email servers configured to allow relay. After they locate an open relay server, they use it for distributing spam and malware. The email appears to come from the company whose email server was misappropriated. Criminals use this technique to hide their identity. This is not only an embarrassment but can also result in legal and productivity ramifications.

In a response to the deluge of spam and email malware distribution, blacklisting has become a standard practice. A *blacklist* is a list of email addresses, domain names, or IP addresses known to send unsolicited commercial email (spam) or email-embedded malware. The process of blacklisting is to use the blacklist as an email filter. The receiving email server checks the incoming emails against the blacklist, and when a match is found, the email is denied.

Understanding Denial of Service Attacks

The SMTP protocol is especially vulnerable to DDoS attacks because, by design, it accepts and queues incoming emails. To mitigate the effects of email DoS attacks, the mail server can be configured to limit the amount of operating system resources it can consume. Some examples include configuring the mail server application so that it cannot consume all available space on its hard drives or partitions, limiting the size of attachments that are allowed, and ensuring log files are stored in a location that is sized appropriately.

Other Collaboration and Communication Tools

In addition, nowadays organizations use more than just email. Many organizations use Slack, Cisco Spark, WebEx, Telepresence, and many other collaboration tools that provide a way for internal communications. Most of these services or products provide different encryption capabilities. This includes encryption during the transit of the data and encryption of the data at rest. Most of these are also cloud services. You must have a good strategy when securing and understanding the risk of each of these solutions, including knowing the risks that you can control and the ones that you cannot.

Are Collaboration and Communication Services at Risk?

Absolutely! Just like email, collaboration tools like WebEx, Slack, and others need to be evaluated. This is why the United States Federal Government created the Federal Risk and Authorization Management Program, or FedRAMP. FedRAMP is a program that specifies a standardized approach to security assessment, authorization, and continuous monitoring for cloud products and services. This includes cloud services such as Cisco WebEx.

According to its website (https://www.fedramp.gov) the following are the goals of FedRAMP:

- Accelerate the adoption of secure cloud solutions through reuse of assessments and authorizations

- Increase confidence in security of cloud solutions

- Achieve consistent security authorizations using a baseline set of agreed-upon standards to be used for cloud product approval in or outside of FedRAMP

- Ensure consistent application of existing security practice

- Increase confidence in security assessments

- Increase automation and near real-time data for continuous monitoring

Also as defined in its website, the following are the benefits of FedRAMP:

- Increase re-use of existing security assessments across agencies

- Save significant cost, time, and resources—"do once, use many times"

- Improve real-time security visibility

- Provide a uniform approach to risk-based management

- Enhance transparency between government and Cloud Service Providers (CSPs)

- Improve the trustworthiness, reliability, consistency, and quality of the Federal security authorization process

Email and Email Systems Security Policy

Synopsis: To recognize that email and messaging platforms are vulnerable to unauthorized disclosure and attack, and to assign responsibility to safeguarding said systems.

Policy Statement:

- The Office of Information Security is responsible for assessing the risk associated with email and email systems. Risk assessments must be performed at a minimum biannually or whenever there is a change trigger.

- The Office of Information Security is responsible for creating email security standards, including but not limited to attachment and content filtering, encryption, malware inspection, and DDoS mitigation.

- External transmission of data classified as "protected" or "confidential" must be encrypted.

- Remote access to company email must conform to the corporate remote access standards.

- Access to personal web-based email from the corporate network is not allowed.

- The Office of Information Technology is responsible for implementing, maintaining, and monitoring appropriate controls.

- The Office of Human Resources is responsible for providing email security user training.

Activity Monitoring and Log Analysis

NIST defines a *log* as a record of the events occurring within an organization's systems and networks. Logs are composed of log entries; each entry contains information related to a specific event that has occurred within a system or network. Security logs are generated by many sources, including security software, such as AV software, firewalls, and IDS/IPS systems; operating systems on servers, workstations, and networking equipment; and applications. Another example of "records" from network activity is NetFlow. NetFlow was initially created for billing and accounting of network traffic and to measure other IP traffic characteristics, such as bandwidth utilization and application performance. NetFlow has also been used as a network-capacity planning tool and to monitor network availability. Nowadays, NetFlow is used as a network security tool because its reporting capabilities provide nonrepudiation, anomaly detection, and investigative capabilities. As network traffic traverses a NetFlow-enabled device, the device collects traffic flow information and provides a network administrator or security professional with detailed information about such flows. The Internet Protocol Flow Information Export (IPFIX) is a network flow standard led by the Internet Engineering Task Force (IETF). IPFIX was created to create a common, universal standard of export for flow information from routers, switches, firewalls, and other infrastructure devices. IPFIX defines how flow information should be formatted and transferred from an exporter to a collector.

Logs are a key resource when performing auditing and forensic analysis, supporting internal investigations, establishing baselines, and identifying operational trends and long-term problems. Routine log analysis is beneficial for identifying security incidents, policy violations, fraudulent activity, and operational problems. Third-party security specialists should be engaged for log analysis if in-house knowledge is not sufficient.

Big data analytics is the practice of studying large amounts of data of a variety of types and a variety of courses to learn interesting patterns, unknown facts, and other useful information. Big data analytics can play a crucial role in cybersecurity. Many in the industry are changing the tone of their conversation, saying that it is no longer if or when your network will be compromised, but the assumption is that your network has already been hacked or compromised. They suggest focusing on minimizing the damage and increasing visibility to aid in identification of the next hack or compromise.

Advanced analytics can be run against very large diverse data sets to find indicators of compromise (IOCs). These data sets can include different types of structured and unstructured data processed in a "streaming" fashion or in batches. Any organization can collect data just for the sake of collecting data; however, the usefulness of such data depends on how actionable such data is to make any decisions (in addition to whether the data is regularly monitored and analyzed).

What Is Log Management?

Log management activities involve configuring the log sources, including log generation, storage, and security, performing analysis of log data, initiating appropriate responses to identified events, and managing the long-term storage of log data. Log management infrastructures are typically based on one of the two major categories of log management software: syslog-based centralized logging software and security information and event management software (SIEM). *Syslog* provides an open framework based on message type and severity. *Security information and event management* (SIEM) software includes commercial applications and often uses proprietary processes. NIST Special Publication SP 800-92, *Guide to Computer Security Log Management*, published September 2006, provides practical, real-world guidance on developing, implementing, and maintaining effective log management practices throughout an enterprise. The guidance in SP 800-92 covers several topics, including establishing a log management infrastructure.

Prioritizing and Selecting Which Data to Log

Ideally, data would be collected from every significant device and application on the network. The challenge is that network devices and applications can generate hundreds of events per minute. A network with even a small number of devices can generate millions of events per day. The sheer volume can overwhelm a log management program. Prioritization and inclusion decisions should be based on system or device criticality, data protection requirements, vulnerability to exploit, and regulatory requirements. For example, websites and servers that serve as the public face of the company are vulnerable specifically because they are Internet accessible. E-commerce application and database servers may drive the company's revenue and are targeted because they contain valuable information, such as credit card information. Internal devices are required for day-to-day productivity; access makes them vulnerable to insider attacks. In addition to identifying suspicious activity, attacks, and compromises, log data can be used to better understand normal activity, provide operational oversight, and provide a historical record of activity. The decision-making process should include information system owners as well as information security, compliance, legal, HR, and IT personnel.

Systems within an IT infrastructure are often configured to generate and send information every time a specific event happens. An event, as described in NIST SP 800-61 revision 2, "Computer Security Incident Handling Guide," is any observable occurrence in a system or network, whereas a security incident is an event that violates the security policy of an organization. One important task of a security operation center analyst is to determine when an event constitutes a security incident. An event log (or simply a log) is a formal record of an event and includes information about the event itself. For example, a log may contain a timestamp, an IP address, an error code, and so on.

Event management includes administrative, physical, and technical controls that allow for the proper collection, storage, and analysis of events. Event management plays a key role in information security because it allows for the detection and investigation of a real-time attack, enables incident response, and allows for statistical and trending reporting. If an organization lacks information about past events and logs, this may reduce its ability to investigate incidents and perform a root-cause analysis.

An additional important function of monitoring and event management is compliance. Many compliance frameworks (for example, ISO and PCI DSS) mandate log management controls and practices. One of the most basic tasks of event management is log collection. Many systems in the IT infrastructure are in fact capable of generating logs and sending them to a remote system that will store them. Log storage is a critical task for maintaining log confidentiality and integrity. Confidentiality is needed because the logs may contain sensitive information. In some scenarios, logs may need to be used as evidence in court or as part of an incident response. The integrity of the logs is fundamental for them to be used as evidence and for attribution.

The facilities used to store logs need to be protected against unauthorized access, and the logs' integrity should be maintained. Enough storage should be allocated so that the logs are not missed due to lack of storage.

The information collected via logs usually includes, but is not limited to, the following:

- User ID
- System activities
- Timestamps

- Successful or unsuccessful access attempts
- Configuration changes
- Network addresses and protocols
- File access activities

Different systems may send their log messages in various formats, depending on their implementation.

According to NIST SP 800-92, "Guide to Computer Security Log Management," three categories of logs are of interest for security professionals:

- Logs generated by security software: This includes logs and alerts generated by the following software and devices:
  - Antivirus/antimalware
  - IPS and IDS
  - Web proxies
  - Remote access software
  - Vulnerability management software
  - Authentication servers
  - Infrastructure devices (including firewalls, routers, switches, and wireless access points)
- Logs generated by the operating system: This includes the following:
  - System events
  - Audit records
- Logs generated by applications: This includes the following:
  - Connection and session information
  - Usage information
  - Significant operational action

Once collected, the logs need to be analyzed and reviewed to detect security incidents and to make sure security controls are working properly. This is not a trivial task, because the analyst may need to analyze an enormous amount of data. It is important for the security professional to understand which logs are relevant and should be collected for the purpose of security administration and event and incident management.

Systems that are used to collect and store the logs usually offer a management interface through which the security analyst is able to view the logs in an organized way, filter out unnecessary entries, and produce historical reporting. At some point, logs may not be needed anymore. The determination of how long a log needs to be kept is included in the log retention policy. Logs can be deleted from the system or archived in separate systems. One of the most used protocols for event notification is syslog, which is defined in RFC 5424.

The syslog protocol specifies three main entities:

- **Originator:** The entity that generates a syslog message (for example, a router).

- **Collector:** The entity that receives information about an event in syslog format (for example, a syslog server).

- **Relay:** An entity that can receive messages from originators and forward them to other relays or collectors.

What Are Security Information and Event Managers?

The Security Information and Event Manager (SIEM) is a specialized device or software for security event management. It typically allows for the following functions:

- **Log collection:** This includes receiving information from devices with multiple protocols and formats, storing the logs, and providing historical reporting and log filtering.

- **Log normalization:** This function extracts relevant attributes from logs received in different formats and stores them in a common data model or template. This allows for faster event classification and operations. Non-normalized logs are usually kept for archive, historical, and forensic purposes.

- **Log aggregation:** This function aggregates information based on common information and reduces duplicates.

- **Log correlation:** This is probably one of most important functions of an SIEM. It refers to the ability of the system to associate events gathered by various systems, in different formats and at different times, and create a single actionable event for the security analyst or investigator. Often the quality of an SIEM is related to the quality of its correlation engine.

- **Reporting:** Event visibility is also a key functionality of an SIEM. Reporting capabilities usually include real-time monitoring and historical base reports.

Most modern SIEMs also integrate with other information systems to gather additional contextual information to feed the correlation engine. For example, they can integrate with an identity management system to get contextual information about users or with NetFlow collectors to get additional flow-based information.

Analyzing Logs

Done correctly and consistently, log analysis is a reliable and accurate way to discover potential threats, identify malicious activity, and provide operational oversight. Log analysis techniques include correlation, sequencing, signature, and trend analysis:

- *Correlation* ties individual log entries together based on related information.

- *Sequencing* examines activity based on patterns.

- *Signature* compares log data to "known bad" activity.

- *Trend analysis* identifies activity over time that in isolation might appear normal.

A common mistake made when analyzing logs is to focus on "denied" activity. Although it is important to know what was denied, it is much more important to focus on allowed activity that may put the organization at risk.

FYI: Log Review Regulatory Requirements and Contractual Obligations

Monitoring event and audit logs is an integral part of complying with a variety of federal regulations, including the Gramm-Leach-Bliley Act. In addition, as of July 2013, at least 48 states and U.S. territories have instituted security breach notification laws that require businesses to monitor and protect specific sets of consumer data:

- **Gramm-Leach-Bliley Act (GLBA)** requires financial institutions to protect their customers' information against security threats. Log management can be helpful in identifying possible security violations and resolving them effectively.

- **Health Insurance Portability and Accountability Act of 1996 (HIPAA)** includes security standards for certain health information, including the need to perform regular reviews of audit logs and access reports. Section 4.22 specifies that documentation of actions and activities needs to be retained for at least six years.

- **Federal Information Security Management Act of 2002 (FISMA)** requirements found in NIST SP 800-53, *Recommended Security Controls for Federal Information Systems*, describes several controls related to log management, including the generation, review, protection, and retention of audit records, as well as the actions to be taken because of audit failure.

- **Payment Card Industry Data Security Standard (PCI DSS)** applies to organizations that store, process, or transmit cardholder data for payment cards. The fifth core PCI DSS principle, *Regulatory Monitor and Test Networks*, includes the requirement to track and monitor all access to network resources and cardholder data.

Firewall logs can be used to detect security threats, such as network intrusion, virus attacks, DoS attacks, anomalous behavior, employee web activities, web traffic analysis, and malicious insider activity. Reviewing log data provides oversight of firewall administrative activity and change management, including an audit trail of firewall configuration changes. Bandwidth monitoring can provide information about sudden changes that may be indicative of an attack.

Web server logs are another rich source of data to identify and thwart malicious activity. HTTP status codes indicating redirection, client error, or server error can indicate malicious activity as well as malfunctioning applications or bad HTML code. Checking the logs for Null Referrers can identify hackers who are scanning the website with automated tools that do not follow proper protocols. Log data can also be used to identify web attacks, including SQL injection, cross-site scripting (XSS), and directory traversal. As with the firewall, reviewing web server log data provides oversight of web server/website administrative activity and change management, including an audit trail of configuration changes.

Authentication server logs document user, group, and administrative account activity. Activity that should be mined and analyzed includes account lockouts, invalid account logons, invalid passwords, password changes, and user management changes, including new accounts and changed accounts, computer management events (such as when audit logs are cleared or computer account names are changed), group management events (such as the creation or deletion of groups and the addition of users to high-security groups), and user activity outside of logon time restrictions. Operational activity, such as the installation of new software, the success/failure of patch management, server reboots, and policy changes, should be on the radar as well.

In Practice

Security Log Management Policy

Synopsis: To require that devices, systems, and applications support logging and to assign responsibility for log management.

Policy Statement:

- Devices, systems, and applications implemented by the company must support the capability to log activities, including data access and configuration modifications. Exceptions must be approved by the COO.

- Access to logs must be restricted to individuals with a need to know.

- Logs must be retained for a period of 12 months.

- Log analysis reports must be retained for 36 months.

- The Office of Information Security is responsible for the following:

  - Developing log management standards, procedures, and guidelines

  - Prioritizing log management appropriately throughout the organization

  - Creating and maintaining a secure log management infrastructure

  - Establishing log analysis incident response procedures

  - Providing proper training for all staff with log management responsibilities

- The Office of Information Technology is responsible for the following:

  - Managing and monitoring the log management infrastructure

  - Proactively analyzing log data to identify ongoing activity and signs of impending problems

  - Providing reports to the Office of Information Security

Service Provider Oversight

Many companies outsource some aspect of their operations. These relationships, however beneficial, have the potential to introduce vulnerabilities. From a regulatory perspective, you can outsource the work, but you cannot outsource the legal responsibility. Organizational CIA requirements must extend to all service providers and business partners that store, process, transmit, or access company data and information systems. Third-party controls must be required to meet or, in some cases, exceed internal requirements. When working with service providers, organizations need to exercise due diligence in selecting providers, contractually obligate providers to implement appropriate security controls, and monitor service providers for ongoing compliance with contractual obligations.

FYI: Strengthening the Resilience of Outsourced Technology Services

The Federal Financial Institutions Examination Council (FFIEC) Information Technology Examination Handbook (IT Handbook) *Business Continuity Booklet,* Appendix J, "Strengthening the Resilience of Outsourced Technology Services," provides guidance and examination procedures to assist examiners and bankers in evaluating a financial institution's risk management processes to establish, manage, and monitor IT outsourcing and third-party relationships. However, the guidance is useful for organizations of all types and sizes. A number of the recommendations in this section are from the FFIEC guidance. To download the booklet from the FFIEC site, visit https://ithandbook.ffiec.gov/it-booklets/business-continuity-planning/appendix-j-strengthening-the-resilience-of-outsourced-technology-services.aspx.

What Is Due Diligence?

Vendor *due diligence* describes the process or methodology used to assess the adequacy of a service provider. The depth and formality of the due diligence performed may vary based on the risk of the outsourced relationship. Due diligence investigation may include the following:

- Corporate history

- Qualifications, backgrounds, and reputations of company principals

- Financial status, including reviews of audited financial statements

- Service delivery capability, status, and effectiveness

- Technology and systems architecture

- Internal controls environment, security history, and audit coverage

- Legal and regulatory compliance, including any complaints, litigation, or regulatory actions

- Reliance on and success in dealing with third-party service providers

- Insurance coverage

- Incident response capability

- Disaster recovery and business continuity capability

Documentation requested from a service provider generally includes financial statements, security-related policies, proof of insurance, subcontractor disclosure, disaster recovery, and continuity of operations plan, incident notification, and response procedures, security testing results, and independent audit reports, such as an SSAE16.

Understanding Independent Audit Reports

The objective of an independent audit is to objectively evaluate the effectiveness of operational, security, and compliance controls. Standards for Attestation Engagements (SSAE) 18, known as *SSAE18 audit reports*, have become the most widely accepted due diligence documentation. SSAE18 was developed by the American Institute of CPAs (AICPA). The SSAE defines controls at a service organization (SOC). SOC reports specifically address one or more of the following five key system attributes:

- **Security:** The system is protected against unauthorized access (both physical and logical).

- **Availability:** The system is available for operation and use as committed or agreed.

- **Processing integrity:** System processing is complete, accurate, timely, and authorized.

- **Confidentiality:** Information designated as confidential is protected as committed or agreed.

- **Privacy:** Personal information is collected, used, retained, disclosed, and disposed of in conformity with the commitments in the entity's privacy notice, and with criteria set forth in Generally Accepted Privacy Principles (GAPP) issued by the AICPA and Canadian Institute of Chartered Accountants.

SSAE audits must be attested to by a certified public accounting (CPA) firm. SSAE Service organizations that had an SOC engagement within the past year may register with the AICPA to display the applicable logo.

What Should Be Included in Service Provider Contracts?

Service provider contracts should include a number of information security–related clauses, including performance standards, security and privacy compliance requirements, incident notification, business continuity, disaster recovery commitments, and auditing options. The objective is to ensure that the service provider exercises *due care*, which is the expectation that reasonable efforts will be made to avoid harm and minimize risk.

Performance standards define minimum service-level requirements and remedies for failure to meet standards in the contract—for example, system uptime, deadlines for completing batch processing, and number of processing errors. MTTR (mean time to repair) may be a clause condition in a service level agreement (SLA), along with a standard reference to Tier 1, Tier 2, and Tier 3 performance factors. All support service requests begin in Tier 1. This is where the issue is identified, triaged, and initially documented. Any support service requests that cannot be resolved with Tier 1 support are escalated to Tier 2. Advanced support staff is assigned for higher level troubleshooting of software or hardware issues. Similarly, any support service requests that cannot be resolved with Tier 2 support are escalated to Tier 3. How effective your staff is at each tier should be measured and analyzed to improve performance.

Security and privacy compliance requirements address the service provider stewardship of information and information systems, as well as organizational processes, strategies, and plans. At a minimum, the service provider control environment should be consistent with organizational policies and standards. The agreement should prohibit the service provider and its agents from using or disclosing the information, except as necessary for or consistent with providing the contracted services, and to protect against unauthorized use. If the service provider stores, processes, receives, or accesses nonpublic personal information (NPPI), the contract should state that the service provider will comply with all applicable security and privacy regulations.

Incident notification requirements should be clearly spelled out. In keeping with state breach notification laws, unless otherwise instructed by law enforcement, the service provider must disclose both verified security breaches and suspected incidents. The latter is often a point of contention. The contract should specify the time frame for reporting, as well as the type of information that must be included in the incident report.

Last, the contract should include the types of audit reports it is entitled to receive (for example, financial, internal control, and security reviews). The contract should specify the audit frequency, any charges for obtaining the audits, as well as the rights to obtain the results of the audits in a timely manner. The contract may also specify rights to obtain documentation of the resolution of any deficiencies and to inspect the processing facilities and operating practices of the service provider. For Internet-related services, the contract should require periodic control reviews performed by an independent party with sufficient expertise. These reviews may include penetration testing, intrusion detection, reviews of firewall configuration, and other independent control reviews.

Managing Ongoing Monitoring

The due diligence is done, the contract is signed, and the service is being provided—but it's not yet time to relax. Remember that you can outsource the work but not the responsibility. Ongoing monitoring should include the effectiveness of the service providers' security controls, financial strength, ability to respond to changes in the regulatory environment, and the impact of external events. Business process owners should establish and maintain a professional relationship with key service provider personnel.

In Practice

Service Provider Management Policy

Synopsis: To establish the information security–related criteria for service provider relationships.

Policy Statement:

- *Service provider* is defined as a vendor, contractor, business partner, or affiliate who stores, processes, transmits, or accesses company information or company information systems.

- The Office of Risk Management is responsible for overseeing the selection, contract negotiations, and management of service providers.

- The Office of Risk Management will be responsible for conducting applicable service provider risk assessments.

- Due diligence research must be conducted on all service providers. Depending on risk assessment results, due diligence research may include but is not limited to the following:

  - Financial soundness review
  - Internal information security policy and control environment review
  - Review of any industry standard audit and/or testing of information security–related controls

- Service provider systems are required to meet or exceed internal security requirements. Safeguards must be commensurate with the classification of data and the level of inherent risk.

- Contracts and/or agreements with service providers will specifically require them to protect the CIA of all company, customer, and proprietary information that is under their control.

- Contracts and/or agreements must include notification requirements for suspected or actual compromise or system breach.

- Contracts and/or agreements must include the service provider's obligation to comply with all applicable state and federal regulations.

- As applicable, contracts and/or agreements must include a clause related to the proper destruction of records containing customer or proprietary information when no longer in use or if the relationship is terminated.

- Contracts and/or agreements must include provisions that allow for periodic security reviews/audits of the service provider environment.

- Contracts and/or agreements must include a provision requiring service providers to disclose the use of contractors.

- To the extent possible and practical, contractual performance will be monitored and/or verified. Oversight is the responsibility of the business process owner.

FYI: Small Business Note

The majority of small businesses do not have dedicated IT or information security staff. They rely on outside organizations or contractors to perform a wide range of tasks, including procurement, network management and administration, web design, and off-site hosting. Rarely are the "IT guys" properly vetted. A common small business owner remark is, "I wouldn't even know what to ask. I don't know anything about technology." Rather than being intimidated, small business owners and managers need to recognize that they have a responsibility to evaluate the credentials of everyone who has access to their information systems. Peer and industry groups such as the Chamber of Commerce, Rotary, ISC2, and ISACA chapters can all be a source for references and recommendations. As with any service provider, responsibilities and expectations should be codified in a contract.

Threat Intelligence and Information Sharing

It is very common that organizations use threat intelligence to better know how threat actors carry out their attacks and to gain insights about the current threat landscape. Threat intelligence and cybersecurity are relatively new concepts; the use of intelligence to learn how the enemy is operating is a very old concept. Adopting intelligence to the field of cybersecurity makes complete sense, mainly because now the threat landscape is so broad and the adversaries vary widely, from state-sponsored actors to cybercriminals extorting money from their victims.

Threat intelligence can be used to understand which attack profile is most likely to target your organization. For example, a hacktivist group may be against you if your organization supports certain social or political tendencies. By using threat intelligence, you also would like to understand what assets that you own are most likely desired by the threat actor. You may also be able to take advantage of threat intelligence to scope data based on the adversary. If you have a full understanding of the types of assets that you are trying to protect, it can also help identify the threat actors that you should be worried about. The information that you obtain from threat intelligence can be categorized as

- Technical
- Tactical
- Operational
- Strategical

> **FYI: Open Source Intelligence (OSINT)**
>
> Various commercial threat intelligence companies provide threat intelligence feeds to their customers. However, there are also free open source feeds and publicly available sources. I have published a GitHub repository that includes several open source intelligence (OSINT) resources at https://github.com/The-Art-of-Hacking/art-of-hacking/tree/master/osint. The same GitHub repository includes numerous cybersecurity and ethical hacking references.
>
> The Cisco Computer Security Incident Response Team (CSIRT) created an open source tool that can be used for collecting, processing, and exporting high-quality indicators of compromise (IOCs) called GOSINT. GOSINT allows a security analyst to collect and standardize structured and unstructured threat intelligence. The tool and additional documentation can be found at https://github.com/ciscocsirt/gosint.

How Good Is Cyber Threat Intelligence if It Cannot Be Shared?

No organization can have enough information to create and maintain accurate situational awareness of the cyber threat landscape. The sharing of relevant cyber threat information among trusted partners and communities is a must to effectively defend your organization. Through cyber threat intelligence information sharing, organizations and industry peers can achieve a more complete understanding of the threats they face and how to defeat them.

Trust is the major barrier among organizations to effectively and openly share threat intelligence with one another. This is why the Information Sharing and Analysis Centers (ISACs) were created. According to the National Council of ISACs, each ISAC will "collect, analyze and disseminate actionable threat information to their members and provide members with tools to mitigate risks and enhance resiliency."

ISACs were created after the Presidential Decision Directive-63 (PDD-63), signed May 22, 1998. The United States federal government asked each critical infrastructure sector to establish sector-specific organizations to share information about threats and vulnerabilities. Most ISACs have threat warning and incident reporting capabilities. The following are examples of the different ISACs that exist today, along with a link to their website:

- Automotive ISAC: www.automotiveisac.com

- Aviation ISAC: www.a-isac.com

- Communications ISAC: www.dhs.gov/national-coordinating-center-communications

- Defense Industrial Base ISAC: www.dibisac.net

- Downstream Natural Gas ISAC: www.dngisac.com

- Electricity ISAC: www.eisac.com

- Emergency Management and Response ISAC: www.usfa.dhs.gov/emr-isac

- Financial Services ISAC: www.fsisac.com

- Healthcare Ready: www.healthcareready.org

- Information Technology ISAC: www.it-isac.org

- Maritime ISAC: www.maritimesecurity.org

- Multi-State ISAC: www.ms-isac.org

- National Defense ISAC: www.ndisac.org

- National Health ISAC: www.nhisac.org

- Oil & Natural Gas ISAC: www.ongisac.org

- Real Estate ISAC: www.reisac.org

- Research and Education Network ISAC: www.ren-isac.net

- Retail Cyber Intelligence Sharing Center: www.r-cisc.org

- Surface Transportation, Public Transportation and Over-The-Road Bus ISACS: www.surfacetransportationisac.org

- Water ISAC: www.waterisac.org

FYI: Technical Standards for Cyber Threat Intelligence Sharing

There are technical standards that define a set of information representations and protocols to model, analyze, and share cyber threat intelligence. Standardized representations have been created to exchange information about cyber campaigns, threat actors, incidents, tactics techniques and procedures (TTPs), indicators, exploit targets, observables, and courses of action. Two of the most popular standards for cyber threat intelligence information exchange are the Structured Threat Information Expression (STIX) and the Trusted Automated Exchange of Indicator Information (TAXII). Additional information about STIX and TAXII can be obtained at https://oasis-open.github.io/cti-documentation.

Another related standard is the OASIS Open Command and Control (OpenC2). The standard documents and provides specifications, lexicons, and other artifacts to describe cybersecurity command and control (C2) in a standardized manner. Additional information about OpenC2 can be obtained at https://www.oasis-open.org/committees/tc_home.php?wg_abbrev=openc2.

Summary

This security domain is all about day-to-day operational activities. We started the chapter by looking at SOPs. We discussed that well-written SOPs provide direction, improve communication, reduce training time, and improve work consistency. Routine procedures that are short and require few decisions can be written using the simple step format. Long procedures consisting of more than 10 steps, with few decisions, should be written in hierarchical steps format or in a graphic format. Procedures that require many decisions should be written in the form of a flowchart.

Organizations are dynamic, and change is inevitable. The objective of change control is to ensure that only authorized changes are made to software, hardware, network access privileges, or business processes. A change management process establishes an orderly and effective mechanism for submission, evaluation, approval, prioritization, scheduling, communication, implementation, monitoring, and organizational acceptance of change.

Two mandatory components of a change management process are an RFC (Request for Change) document and a change control plan. Scheduled changes can be exempt from the process as long as they have a preapproved procedure. A good example of this is patch management. A patch is software or code designed to fix a problem. Applying security patches is the primary method of fixing security vulnerabilities in software. Patch management is the process of scheduling, testing, approving, and applying security patches.

Criminals design malware, short for *malicious software* (or script or code), to exploit devices, operating systems, applications, and user vulnerabilities with the intent of disrupting computer operations, gathering sensitive information, or gaining unauthorized access. A zero-day exploit is one that takes advantage of security vulnerability on the same day that the vulnerability becomes publicly or generally known. Malware categorization is based on infection and propagation characteristics. A virus is malicious code that attaches to and becomes part of another program. A worm is a piece of malicious code that can spread from one computer to another without requiring a host file to infect. A Trojan is malicious code that masquerades as a legitimate benign application. Bots (also known as robots) are snippets of code designed to automate tasks and respond to instructions. An entire network of compromised devices is known as a botnet. Ransomware is a type of malware that takes a computer or its data hostage in an effort to extort money from victims. A rootkit is set of software tools that hides its presence in the lower layers of the operating system application layer, operating system kernel, or in the device BIOS with privileged access permissions. Spyware is a general term used to describe software that, without a user's consent and/or knowledge, tracks Internet activity, such as searches and web surfing, collects data on personal habits, and displays advertisements. Hybrid malware is code that combines characteristics of multiple categories. A blended threat is when multiple variants of malware (worms, viruses, bots, and so on) are used in concert to exploit system vulnerabilities. An antimalware defense-in-depth arsenal includes both prevention and detection controls. The most familiar of these is AV software that is designed to detect, contain, and in some cases eliminate malicious software.

Malware, user error, and system failure are among the many threats that can render data unusable. Having multiple copies of data is essential for both data integrity and availability. Data replication is the process of copying data to a second location that is available for immediate or near-time use. Data backup is the process of copying and storing data that can be restored to its original location. In both cases, it is essential to have SOPs for both replication/backup and restoration/recovery. Restoration and recovery processes should be tested to ensure that they work as anticipated.

Email is a primary malware distribution channel. Criminals embed malware in attachments or include a hyperlink to a malware distribution site. Email systems need to be configured to scan for malware and to filter attachments. Users need to be trained not to click email links and not to open unexpected attachments. Organizations should also restrict access to personal web mail applications because they bypass internal email controls. Criminals take advantage of the inherent weaknesses in the email communication system.

Cloud services including collaboration and unified communications solutions are used by many organizations nowadays. Performing threat modeling of cloud services and understanding the risk of such services is crucial for any organization. Encryption protects the privacy of the message by converting it from (readable) plain text into (scrambled) cipher text. The default posture for many email servers is to process and relay any mail sent to the server; this feature is known as *open mail relay*. Criminals exploit open mail relay to distribute malware, spam, and illegal material such as pornography. A blacklist is a list of email addresses, domain names, or IP addresses known to be compromised or intentionally used as a distribution platform. The process of blacklisting is to use the blacklist as an email filter. Because email servers are Internet-facing and are open to receiving packets, they are easy targets for distributed denial of service (DDoS) attacks. The objective of a DDoS attack is to render the service inoperable.

Almost every device and application on a network can record activity. This record of events is known as a log. Logs can be processed either using standard syslog protocols or using SIEM applications. Syslog provides an open framework based on message type and severity. Security information and event management software (SIEM) are commercial applications and often use proprietary processes. Analysis techniques include correlation, sequencing, signature comparison, and trend analysis. Correlation ties individual log entries together based on related information. Sequencing examines activity based on patterns. Signature compares log data to "known bad" activity. Trend analysis identifies activity over time that in isolation might appear normal. The process of configuring the log sources, including log generation, storage, and security, performing analysis of log data, initiating appropriate responses to identified events, and managing the long-term storage of log data is known as log management.

Operational security extends to service providers. Service providers are vendors, contractors, business partners, and affiliates who store, process, transmit, or access company information or company information systems. Service provider internal controls should meet or exceed those of the contracting organization. The conventional wisdom (and in some cases, the regulatory requirement) is that you can outsource the work but not the liability. Due diligence describes the process or methodology used to assess the adequacy of a service provider. SSAE18 audit reports have become the most widely accepted due diligence documentation. SSAE18 reports are independent audits certified by CPA firms.

Service provider contracts should include a number of information security–related clauses, including performance standards, security and privacy compliance requirements, incident notification, business continuity and disaster recovery commitments, and auditing and ongoing monitoring options.

Threat intelligence can be used to understand which attack profile is most likely to target your organization. You may also be able to take advantage of threat intelligence to scope data based on the adversary. If you have a full understanding of the types of assets that you are trying to protect, it can also help identify the threat actors that you should be worried about. The sharing of relevant cyber threat information among trusted partners and communities is a must to effectively defend your organization. Through cyber threat intelligence information sharing, organizations and industry peers can achieve a more complete understanding of the threats they face and how to defeat them.

Test Your Skills

MULTIPLE CHOICE QUESTIONS

1. Which of the following is true about documenting SOPs?

    A. It promotes business continuity.

    B. The documentation should be approved before publication and distribution.

    C. Both A and B.

    D. Neither A nor B.

2. Which of the following is an alternative name for SOPs?

    A. System operating protocols

    B. Standard operating protocols

    C. Standard objective protocols

    D. Standard objective procedures

3. After a procedure has been documented, it should be_____.

    A. reviewed, verified, and authorized before being published

    B. triaged, tested, and authenticated before being published

    C. reviewed, authorized, and archived before being published

    D. reviewed, verified, and deleted before being published

4. The change control process starts with which of the following?

    A. Budget

    B. RFC submission

    C. Vendor solicitation

    D. Supervisor authorization

5. What is the most important message to share with the workforce about "change"?

   A. The reason for the change

   B. The cost of the change

   C. Who approved the change

   D. Management's opinion of the change

6. When protecting SOP documentation, _____ should be put in place to protect the integrity of the document from both unintentional error and malicious insiders.

   A. access and version controls

   B. access and authorization

   C. triage functions and enforcement controls

   D. access, log accounting, and parsing.

7. _____ is an internal procedure by which authorized changes are made to software, hardware, network access privileges, or business processes.

   A. Engineering management

   B. Engineering control

   C. Change management

   D. Change control

8. Which of the following statements best describes a security patch?

   A. A security patch is designed to fix a security vulnerability.

   B. A security patch is designed to add security features.

   C. A security patch is designed to add security warnings.

   D. A security patch is designed to fix code functionality.

9. Which of the following is a component of an AV application?

   A. Definition files

   B. Handler

   C. Patch

   D. Virus

10. Which of the following statements best describes the testing of security patches?

   A. Security patches should never be tested because waiting to deploy is dangerous.

   B. Security patches should be tested prior to deployment, if possible.

   C. Security patches should be tested one month after deployment.

   D. Security patches should never be tested because they are tested by the vendor.

11. Which of the following operating systems are vulnerable to malware?

    A. Apple OS only.

    B. Android OS only.

    C. Microsoft Windows OS only.

    D. Malware is operating system–agnostic.

12. Which of the following terms best describes malware that is specifically designed to hide in the background and gather info over an extended period of time?

    A. Trojan

    B. APT

    C. Ransomware

    D. Zero-day exploit

13. A _____ can spread from one computer to another without requiring a host file to infect.

    A. virus

    B. Trojan

    C. worm

    D. rootkit

14. _____ wait for remote instructions and are often used in DDoS attacks.

    A. APTs

    B. Bots

    C. DATs

    D. Command and Control servers

15. Which of the following is a type of malware that takes a computer or its data hostage in an effort to extort money from victims?

    A. Virus

    B. Trojan

    C. APT

    D. Ransomware

16. Which of the following OSI Layers provides services for the transmission of bits over the data link?

    A. Layer 1: Physical Layer

    B. Layer 2: Data Link Layer

    C. Layer 3: Network Layer

    D. Layer 7: Application Layer

17. Which of the following OSI Layers includes services for end-to-end connection establishment and information delivery? For example, it includes error detection, retransmission capabilities, and multiplexing.

    A. Layer 4: Transport Layer

    B. Layer 2: Data Link Layer

    C. Layer 3: Network Layer

    D. Layer 7: Application Layer

18. Which of the following is the targeted time frame in which a business process must be restored after a disruption or a disaster?

    A. Recovery time objective (RTO)

    B. Recovery point objective (RPO)

    C. Recovery trusted objective (RTO)

    D. Recovery disruption objective (RDO)

19. Which of the following terms best describes the Department of Defense project to develop a set of communications protocols to transparently connect computing resources in various geographical locations?

    A. DoDNet

    B. ARPANET

    C. EDUNET

    D. USANET

20. Which of the following terms best describes the message transport protocol used for sending email messages?

    A. SMTP

    B. SMNP

    C. POP3

    D. MIME

21. In its native form, email is transmitted in _____.

    A. cipher text

    B. clear text

    C. hypertext

    D. meta text

22. Which of the following statements best describes how users should be trained to manage their email?

    A. Users should click embedded email hyperlinks.

    B. Users should open unexpected email attachments.

    C. Users should access personal email from the office.

    D. Users should delete unsolicited or unrecognized emails.

23. The default posture for many email servers is to process and relay any mail sent to the server. The ability to relay mail through a server can (and often is) taken advantage of by those who benefit from the illegal use of the resource. Which of the following are attractive to criminals to send unsolicited emails (spam)?

    A. Open mail proxies

    B. Open mail relays

    C. Closed mail relays

    D. Blacklist relay servers

24. NetFlow is used as a network security tool because _____.

    A. its reporting capabilities provide nonrepudiation, anomaly detection, and investigative capabilities

    B. it is better than IPFIX

    C. it is better than SNMP

    D. it is better than IPSEC

25. Which of the following statements best describes trend analysis?

    A. Trend analysis is used to tie individual log entries together based on related information.

    B. Trend analysis is used to examine activity over time that in isolation might appear normal.

    C. Trend analysis is used to compare log data to known bad activity.

    D. Trend analysis is used to identify malware only.

26. It is very common that organizations use threat intelligence to _____.

    A. maintain competitive advantage

    B. configure their antivirus to be less invasive

    C. hire new employees for their cybersecurity teams

    D. better know how threat actors carry out their attacks and to gain insights about the current threat landscape

27. Which of the following is a standard used for cyber threat intelligence?

    A. STIX

    B. CSAF

    C. XIT

    D. TIX

28. SSAE18 audits must be attested to by a _____.

    A. Certified Information System Auditor (CISA)

    B. Certified Public Accountant (CPA)

    C. Certified Information Systems Manager (CISM)

    D. Certified Information System Security Professional (CISSP)

29. Why were Information Sharing and Analysis Centers (ISACs) created?

    A. To disclose vulnerabilities to the public

    B. To disclose vulnerabilities to security researchers

    C. To combat ransomware and perform reverse engineering

    D. To effectively and openly share threat intelligence with one another

30. Which of the following reasons best describes why independent security testing is recommended?

    A. Independent security testing is recommended because of the objectivity of the tester.

    B. Independent security testing is recommended because of the expertise of the tester.

    C. Independent security testing is recommended because of the experience of the tester.

    D. All of the above.

EXERCISES

EXERCISE 8.1: Documenting Operating Procedures

1. SOPs are not restricted to use in IT and information security. Cite three non-IT or security examples where SOP documentation is important.

2. Choose a procedure that you are familiar enough with that you can write SOP documentation.

3. Decide which format you are going to use to create the SOP document.

EXERCISE 8.2: **Researching Email Security**

1. Does your personal email application you are currently using have an option for "secure messaging"? If so, describe the option. If not, how does this limit what you can send via email?

2. Does the email application you are using have an option for "secure authentication" (this may be referred to as secure login or multifactor authentication)? If so, describe the option. If not, does this concern you?

3. Does the email application scan for malware or block attachments? If so, describe the option. If not, what can you do to minimize the risk of malware infection?

EXERCISE 8.3: **Researching Metadata**

1. Most applications include metadata in the document properties. What metadata does the word processing software you currently use track?

2. Is there a way to remove the metadata from the document?

3. Why would you want to remove metadata before distributing a document?

EXERCISE 8.4: **Understanding Patch Management**

1. Do you install operating system or application security patches on your personal devices such as laptops, tablets, and smartphone? If yes, how often? If not, why not?

2. What method do you use (for example, Windows Update)? Is the update automatic? What is the update schedule? If you do not install security patches, research and describe your options.

3. Why is it sometimes necessary to reboot your device after applying security patches?

EXERCISE 8.5: **Understanding Malware Corporate Account Takeovers**

1. Hundreds of small businesses across the country have been victims of corporate account takeovers. To learn more, visit the Krebs on Security blog, https://krebsonsecurity.com/category/smallbizvictims.

2. Should financial institutions be required to warn small business customers of the dangers associated with cash management services such as ACH and wire transfers? Explain your reasoning.

3. What would be the most effective method of teaching bank customers about corporate account takeover attacks?

PROJECTS

PROJECT 8.1: Performing Due Diligence with Data Replication and Backup Service Providers

1. Do you store your schoolwork on your laptop? If not, where is the data stored? Write a memo explaining the consequences of losing your laptop, or if the alternate location or device becomes unavailable. Include the reasons why having a second copy will contribute to your success as a student. After you have finished step 2 of this project, complete the memo with your recommendations.

2. Research "cloud-based" backup or replication options. Choose a service provider and answer the following questions:

   What service/service provider did you choose?

   How do you know they are reputable?

   What controls do they have in place to protect your data?

   Do they reveal where the data will be stored?

   Do they have an SSAE18 or equivalent audit report available for review?

   Do they have any certifications, such as McAfee Secure?

   How much will it cost?

   How often are you going to update the secondary copy?

   What do you need to do to test the restore/recovery process?

   How often will you test the restore/recovery process?

PROJECT 8.2: Developing an Email and Malware Training Program

You are working as an information security intern for Best Regional Bank, who has asked you to develop a PowerPoint training module that explains the risks (including malware) associated with email. The target audience is all employees.

1. Create an outline of the training to present to the training manager.

2. The training manager likes your outline. She just learned that the company would be monitoring email to make sure that data classified as "protected" is not being sent insecurely and that access to personal web-based email is going to be restricted. You need to add these topics to your outline.

3. Working from your outline, develop a PowerPoint training module. Be sure to include email "best practices." Be prepared to present the training to your peers.

PROJECT 8.3: Developing Change Control and SOPs

The Dean of Academics at ABC University has asked your class to design a change control process specifically for mid-semester faculty requests to modify the day, the time, or the location where their class meets. You need to do the following:

1. Create an RFC form.

2. Develop an authorization workflow that specifies who (for example, the department chair) needs to approve the change and in what order.

3. Develop an SOP flowchart for faculty members to use that includes submitting the RFC, authorization workflow, and communication (for example, students, housekeeping, campus security, registrar).

Case Study

Using Log Data to Identify Indicators of Compromise

Log data offer clues about activities that have unexpected—and possibly harmful—consequences. The following parsed and normalized firewall log entries indicate a possible malware infection and data exfiltration. The entries show a workstation making connections to Internet address 93.177.168.141 and receiving and sending data over TCP port 16115.

```
id=firewall sn=xxxxxxxxxxxx time="2018-04-02 11:53:12 UTC"
fw=255.255.255.1 pri=6 c=262144

m=98 msg="Connection Opened" n=404916 src=10.1.1.1 (workstation)
:49427:X0 dst=93.177.168.141 :16115:X1 proto=tcp/16115

id=firewall sn=xxxxxxxxxxxx time="2018-04-02 11:53:29 UTC"
fw=255.255.255.1 pri=6 c=1024

m=537 msg="Connection Closed" n=539640 src=10.1.1.1 (workstation)
:49427:X0 dst=93.177.168.141 :16115:X1 proto=tcp/16115 sent=735 rcvd=442

id=firewall sn=xxxxxxxxxxxx time="2018-04-02 11:53:42 UTC"
fw=255.255.255.1 pri=6 c=262144

m=98 msg="Connection Opened" n=404949 src=10.1.1.1 (workstation)
:49430:X0 dst=93.177.168.141 :16115:X1 proto=tcp/16115

id=firewall sn=xxxxxxxxxxxx time="2018-04-02 11:54:30 UTC"
fw=255.255.255.1 pri=6 c=1024

m=537 msg="Connection Closed" n=539720 src=10.1.1.1 (workstation)
:49430:X0 dst=93.177.168.141 :16115:X1 proto=tcp/16115 sent=9925
rcvd=639
```

1. Describe what is happening.

2. Is the log information useful? Why or why not?

3. Research the destination IP address (dst) and the protocol/port (proto) used for communication.

4. Can you find any information that substantiates a malware infection and data exfiltration?

5. What would you recommend as next steps?

References

Regulations Cited

"16 CFR Part 314: Standards for Safeguarding Customer Information; Final Rule, Federal Register," accessed 04/2018, https://ithandbook.ffiec.gov/it-workprograms.aspx.

"Federal Information Security Management Act (FISMA)," accessed 04/2018, https://csrc.nist.gov/topics/laws-and-regulations/laws/fisma.

"Gramm-Leach-Bliley Act," the official website of the Federal Trade Commission, Bureau of Consumer Protection Business Center, accessed 04/2018, https://www.ftc.gov/tips-advice/business-center/privacy-and-security/gramm-leach-bliley-act.

"DHS Statement on the Issuance of Binding Operational Directive 17-01," accessed 04/2018, https://www.dhs.gov/news/2017/09/13/dhs-statement-issuance-binding-operational-directive-17-01.

"HIPAA Security Rule," the official website of the Department of Health and Human Services, accessed 04/2018, https://www.hhs.gov/hipaa/for-professionals/security/index.html.

Other References

NIST Cybersecurity Framework version 1.11, accessed 04/2018, https://www.nist.gov/sites/default/files/documents/draft-cybersecurity-framework-v1.11.pdf.

NIST article "A Framework for Protecting Our Critical Infrastructure," accessed 04/2018, https://www.nist.gov/blogs/taking-measure/framework-protecting-our-critical-infrastructure.

FFIEC IT Examination Handbook, accessed 04/2018, https://ithandbook.ffiec.gov/.

"ISO 5807:1985," ISO, accessed 04/2018, https://www.iso.org/standard/11955.html.

NIST Special Publication 800-115: Technical Guide to Information Security Testing and Assessment, accessed 04/2018, https://csrc.nist.gov/publications/detail/sp/800-115/final.

"Project Documentation Guidelines, Virginia Tech," accessed 04/2018, www.itplanning.org.vt.edu/pm/documentation.html.

"The State of Risk Oversight: An Overview of Enterprise Risk Management Practices," American Institute of CPAs and NC State University, accessed 04/2018, https://www.aicpa.org/content/dam/aicpa/interestareas/businessindustryandgovernment/resources/erm/downloadabledocuments/aicpa-erm-research-study-2017.pdf.

Cisco Talos Ransomware Blog Posts, accessed 04/2018, http://blog.talosintelligence.com/search/label/ransomware.

Skoudis, Ed. *Malware: Fighting Malicious Code*, Prentice Hall, 2003.

Still, Michael, and Eric Charles McCreath. "DDoS Protections for SMTP Servers." *International Journal of Computer Science and Security*, Volume 4, Issue 6, 2011.

"What Is the Difference: Viruses, Worms, Trojans, and Bots," accessed 04/2018, https://www.cisco.com/c/en/us/about/security-center/virus-differences.html.

Wieringa, Douglas, Christopher Moore, and Valerie Barnes. *Procedure Writing: Principles and Practices, Second Edition*, Columbus, Ohio: Battelle Press, 1988.

"Mirai IoT Botnet Co-Authors Plead Guilty", Krebs on Security, accessed 04/2018, https://krebsonsecurity.com/2017/12/mirai-iot-botnet-co-authors-plead-guilty/.

National Council of ISACs, accessed 04/2018, https://www.nationalisacs.org.

OASIS Cyber Threat Intelligence (CTI) Technical Committee, accessed 04/2018, https://www.oasis-open.org/committees/tc_home.php?wg_abbrev=cti.

Chapter | 9

Access Control Management

Chapter Objectives

After reading this chapter and completing the exercises, you will be able to do the following:

- Explain access control fundamentals.
- Apply the concepts of default deny, need-to-know, and least privilege.
- Understand secure authentication.
- Protect systems from risks associated with Internet connectivity, remote access, and telework environments.
- Manage and monitor user and administrator access.
- Develop policies to support access control management.

What could be more essential to security than managing access to information and information systems? The primary objective of access controls is to protect information and information systems from unauthorized access (confidentiality), modification (integrity), or disruption (availability). The access control management domain incorporates the most fundamental precepts in information security: default deny, least privilege, and need-to-know.

We begin this chapter with a broad discussion of access control concepts and security models with a focus on authentication and authorization. We examine the factors of authentication with an emphasis on the importance of multifactor authentication. We look at the mandatory and discretionary authorization options for granting access rights and permission. We consider the risks associated with administrative and privileged accounts. Reaching past the boundaries of the internal network, we apply these concepts to the infrastructure, including border security, Internet access, remote access, and the teleworking environment. We will be mindful of the need to audit and monitor entry and exit points and to be prepared to respond to security violations. Throughout the chapter, we develop policies designed to support user access and productivity while simultaneously mitigating the risk of unauthorized access.

FYI: ISO/IEC 27002:2013 and NIST Guidance

Section 9 of ISO 27002:2013 is dedicated to access control, with the objective of managing authorized access and preventing unauthorized access to information systems. This domain extends to remote locations, home offices, and mobile access.

Corresponding NIST guidance is provided in the following documents:

- **SP 800-94:** "Guide to Intrusion Detection and Prevention Systems"

- **SP 800-41, R1:** "Guidelines on Firewalls and Firewall Policy"

- **SP 800-46, R1:** "Guide to Enterprise Telework and Remote Access Security"

- **SP 800-77:** "Guide to IPsec VPNs"

- **SP 800-114:** "User's Guide to Securing External Devices for Telework and Remote Access"

- **SP 800-113:** "Guide to SSL VPNs"

- **SP 800-225:** "Guidelines for Securing Wireless Local Area Networks (WLANs)"

- **SG 800-46, R2:** "Guide to Enterprise Telework, Remote Access and Bring Your Own Device Security"

- **SG 800-114:** "User's Guide to Telework and Bring Your Own Device (BYOD) Security"

Access Control Fundamentals

Access controls are security features that govern how users and processes communicate and interact with systems and resources. The primary objective of access controls is to protect information and information systems from unauthorized access (confidentiality), modification (integrity), or disruption (availability). When we're discussing access controls, the active entity (that is, the user or system) that requests access to a resource or data is referred to as the *subject*, and the passive entity being accessed or being acted upon is referred to as the *object*.

An identification scheme, an authentication method, and an authorization model are the three common attributes of all access controls. An *identification scheme* is used to identify unique records in a set, such as a username. *Identification* is the process of the subject supplying an identifier to the object. The *authentication method* is how identification is proven to be genuine. *Authentication* is the process of the subject supplying verifiable credentials to the object. The *authorization model* defines how access rights and permission are granted. *Authorization* is the process of assigning authenticated subjects the permission to carry out a specific operation.

The process for identifying, authenticating and authorizing users or groups of users to have access to applications, systems or networks is referred to as *identity management*. This is done by associating user permissions with established identities. These managed identities can also refer to systems and applications that need access to organizational systems. Identity management is focused on authentication, whereas access management is aimed at authorization. The purpose of having a good identity management solution is to enforce that only authenticated and authorized users are granted access to the specific applications, systems, or networks within your organization. Identity management is certainly an important part of cybersecurity and it also provides benefits for the overall productivity of the organization.

The security posture of an organization determines the default settings for access controls. Access controls can be technical (such as firewalls or passwords), administrative (such as separation of duties or dual controls), or physical (such as locks, bollards, or turnstiles).

What Is a Security Posture?

A *security posture* is an organization's approach to access controls based on information about an object, such as a host (end system) or network. There is a concept called network access control (NAC) in which networking devices such as switches, firewalls, wireless access points, and others can enforce policy based on the security posture of a subject, in this case a device trying to join the network. NAC can provide the following:

- Identity and trust
- Visibility
- Correlation
- Instrumentation and management
- Isolation and segmentation
- Policy enforcement

The two fundamental postures are open and secure. *Open*, also referred to as *default allow*, means that access not explicitly forbidden is permitted. *Secure*, also referred to as *default deny*, means that access not explicitly permitted is forbidden. In practical application, default deny means that access is unavailable until a rule, access control list (ACL), or setting is modified to allow access.

The challenge for organizations that adopt a secure posture is that a number of devices on the market today, including tablets and smartphones as well as software applications, come with an out-of-the-box setting of default allow. Why? Interoperability, ease of use, and productivity are the three reasons cited. The explosive growth in the use of technology, coupled with increasing awareness of vulnerabilities, is creating a shift in the industry. Organizations have become more security conscious and are beginning to demand more secure products from their vendors. Microsoft is an example of a company that has responded to market requirements. Early Windows server operating systems were configured as default allow. Current Windows server operating systems are configured as default deny.

There is also the concept of threat-centric network access control (TC-NAC), which enables identity systems to collect threat and vulnerability data from many third-party threat and vulnerability scanners and software. This gives the identity management system a threat and risk view into the hosts it is controlling access rights for. TC-NAC enables you to have visibility into any vulnerable hosts on your network and to take dynamic network quarantine actions when required. The identity management system can create authorization policies based on vulnerability attributes, such as Common Vulnerability Scoring System (CVSS) scores received from your third-party threat and vulnerability assessment software. Threat severity levels and vulnerability assessment results can be used to dynamically control the access level of an endpoint or a user.

You can configure the external vulnerability and threat software to send high-fidelity Indications of Compromise (IoC), Threat Detected events, and CVSS scores to a central identity management system. This data can then be used in authorization policies to dynamically or manually change an endpoint's network access privileges accordingly. The following are examples of threat software and vulnerability scanners:

- Cisco Advanced Malware Protection (AMP) for Endpoints

- Cisco Cognitive Threat Analytics (CTA)

- Qualys

- Rapid7 Nexpose

- Tenable Security Center

Principle of Least Privilege and Separation of Duties

The *principle of least privilege* states that all users—whether they are individual contributors, managers, directors, or executives—should be granted only the level of privilege they need to do their jobs, and no more. For example, a sales account manager really has no business having administrator privileges over the network, or a call center staff member over critical corporate financial data.

The same concept of principle of least privilege can be applied to software. For example, programs or processes running on a system should have the capabilities they need to get their job done, but no root access to the system. If a vulnerability is exploited on a system that runs everything as root, the damage could extend to a complete compromise of the system. This is why you should always limit users, applications, and processes to access and run as the least privilege they need.

Somewhat related to the principle of least privilege is the concept of need-to-know, which means that users should get access only to data and systems that they need to do their job, and no other.

Separation of duties is an administrative control that dictates that a single individual should not perform all critical- or privileged-level duties. Additionally, important duties must be separated or divided among several individuals within the organization. The goal is to safeguard against a single individual performing sufficiently critical or privileged actions that could seriously damage a system or the organization as a whole. For instance, security auditors responsible for reviewing security logs should not necessarily have administrative rights over the systems. Another example is that a network administrator should not have the ability to alter logs on the system. This is to prevent such individuals from carrying out unauthorized actions and then deleting evidence of such action from the logs (in other words, covering their tracks).

Think about two software developers in the same organization ultimately working toward a common goal, but one is tasked with developing a portion of a critical application and the other is tasked with creating an application programming interface (API) for other critical applications. Each developer has the same seniority and working grade level; however, they do not know or have access to each other's work or systems.

How Is Identity Verified?

Identification is the process of providing the identity of a subject or user. This is the first step in the authentication, authorization, and accounting process. Providing a username, a passport, an IP address, or even pronouncing your name is a form of identification. A secure identity should be unique in the sense that two users should be able to identify themselves unambiguously. This is particularly important in the context of account monitoring. Duplication of identity is possible if the authentication systems are not connected. For example, a user can use the same user ID for his corporate account and for his personal email account. A secure identity should also be nondescriptive, so that information about the user's identity cannot be inferred. For example, using "Administrator" as the user ID is generally not recommended. An identity should also be issued in a secure way. This includes all processes and steps in requesting and approving an identity request. This property is usually referred to as secure issuance.

The list that follows highlights the key concepts of identification.

- Identities should be unique. Two users with the same identity should not be allowed.

- Identities should be nondescriptive. It should not be possible to infer the role or function of the user. For example, a user called "Admin" represents a descriptive identity, whereas a user called "o1337ms1" represents a nondescriptive identity.

- Identities should be securely issued. A secure process for issuing an identity to a user needs to be established.

- Identities can be location-based. A process for authenticating someone based on his or her location.

There are three categories of factors: knowledge (something the user knows), possession (something a user has), and inherence or characteristics (something the user is).

Authentication by Knowledge

Authentication by knowledge is where the user provides a secret that is only known by him or her. An example of authentication by knowledge would be a user providing a password, a personal identification number (PIN) code, or answering security questions.

The disadvantage of using this method is that once the information is lost or stolen (for example, if a user's password is stolen), an attacker would be able to successfully authenticate. Nowadays, a day does not pass without hearing about a new breach in retailers, service providers, cloud services, and social media companies. If you look at the VERIS community database, you will see thousands of breach cases where users' passwords were exposed (https://github.com/vz-risk/VCDB). Websites like "Have I been pwned" (https://haveibeenpwned.com) include a database of billions of usernames and passwords from past breaches and even allow you to search for your email address to see if your account or information has potentially been exposed.

Something you know is knowledge-based authentication. It could be a string of characters, referred to as a password or PIN, or it could be an answer to a question. Passwords are the most commonly used single-factor network authentication method. The authentication strength of a password is a function of its length, complexity, and unpredictability. If it is easy to guess or deconstruct, it is vulnerable to attack. Once known, it is no longer useful as a verification tool. The challenge is to get users to create, keep secret, and remember secure passwords. Weak passwords can be discovered within minutes or even seconds using any number of publicly available password crackers or social engineering techniques. Best practices dictate that passwords be a minimum of eight characters in length (preferably longer), include a combination of at least three upper and/or lowercase letters, punctuation, symbols, and numerals (referred to as complexity), be changed frequently, and be unique. Using the same password to log in to multiple applications and sites significantly increases the risk of exposure.

NIST Special Publication 800-63B, "Digital Identity Guidelines: Authentication and Lifecycle Management" provides guidelines for authentication and password strengths. NIST confirms that the length of a password has been found to be a primary factor in characterizing password strength. The longer the password the better. Passwords that are too short are very susceptible to brute force and dictionary attacks using words and commonly chosen passwords.

NIST suggests that "the minimum password length that should be required depends to a large extent on the threat model being addressed. Online attacks where the attacker attempts to log in by guessing the password can be mitigated by limiting the rate of login attempts permitted."

Generally, when users are granted initial access to an information system, they are given a temporary password. Most systems have a technical control that will force the user to change his or her password at first login. A password should be changed immediately if there is any suspicion that it has been compromised.

As any help desk person will tell you, users forget their passwords with amazing regularity. If a user forgets his password, there needs to be a process for reissuing passwords that includes verification that the requester is indeed who he says he is. Often cognitive passwords are used as secondary verification.

A *cognitive password* is a form of knowledge-based authentication that requires a user to answer a question based on something familiar to them. Common examples are mother's maiden name and favorite color. The problem, of course, is that this information is very often publicly available. This weakness can be addressed using sophisticated questions that are derived from subscription databases such as credit reports. These questions are commonly referred to as *out-of-wallet* challenge questions. The term was coined to indicate that the answers are not easily available to someone other than the user, and that the user is not likely to carry such information in his or her wallet. Out-of-wallet question systems usually require that the user correctly answer more than one question and often include a "red herring" question that is designed to trick an imposter but which the legitimate user will recognize as nonsensical.

It may seem very convenient when a website or application offers to remember a user's log on credentials or provide an automatic logon to a system, but this practice should be strictly prohibited. If a user allows websites or software applications to automate the authentication process, unattended devices can be used by unauthorized people to gain access to information resources.

FYI: Yahoo! Password Compromise

In October 2017, Yahoo confirmed that more than 3 billion accounts were compromised in its websites, including email, Tumblr, Fantasy, and Flickr. Prior to that, in July of 2012, the hacker group D33ds Company claimed responsibility for attacking Yahoo! Voice and exposing 453,492 plain text login credentials. The full data dump was made available on Pastebin and the passwords are well-known and weak. The top 10 most used passwords in order of popularity are listed here. Additional information is available at http://pastebin.com/2D6bHGTa.

1. 123456 (38%)

2. password (18%)

3. welcome (10%)

4. ninja (8%)

5. abc123 (6%)

6. 123456789 (5%)

7. 12345678 (5%)

8. sunshine (5%)

9. princess (5%)

10. qwerty (4%)

Authentication by Ownership or Possession

With this type of authentication, the user is asked to provide proof that he owns something specific—for example, a system might require an employee to use a badge to access a facility. Another example of authentication by ownership is the use of a token or smart card. Similar to the previous method, if an attacker is able to steal the object used for authentication, he will be able to successfully access the system.

Examples include a one-time passcode, memory cards, smartcard, and out-of-band communication. The most common of the four is the one-time passcode sent to a device in the user's possession. A *one-time passcode (OTP)* is a set of characteristics that can be used to prove a subject's identity one time and one time only. Because the OTP is valid for only one access, if captured, additional access would be automatically denied. OTPs are generally delivered through a hardware or software token device. The token displays the code, which must then be typed in at the authentication screen. Alternatively, the OTP may be delivered via email, text message, or phone call to a predetermined address or phone number.

A *memory card* is an authentication mechanism that holds user information within a magnetic strip and relies on a reader to process the information. The user inserts the card into the reader and enters a personal identification number (PIN). Generally, the PIN is hashed and stored on the magnetic strip. The reader hashes the inputted PIN and compares it to the value on the card itself. A familiar example of this is a bank ATM card. A *smartcard* works in a similar fashion. Instead of a magnetic strip, it has a microprocessor and integrated circuits. The user inserts the card into a reader, which has electrical contacts that interface with the card and power the processor. The user enters a PIN that unlocks the information. The card can hold the user's private key, generate an OTP, or respond to a challenge-response.

Out-of-band authentication requires communication over a channel that is distinct from the first factor. A cellular network is commonly used for out-of-band authentication. For example, a user enters her name and password at an application logon prompt (factor 1). The user then receives a call on her mobile phone; the user answers and provides a predetermined code (factor 2). For the authentication to be compromised, the attacker would have to have access to both the computer and the phone.

FYI: The Multifactor Authentication Gold Rush

In response to password insecurity, many organizations, such as Google, Facebook, Twitter, Valve, and Apple have deployed multifactor authentication options to their users. With multifactor authentication, accounts are protected by something you know (password) and something you have (one-time verification code provided to you). Google offers a variety of ways to get the code, including text message, phone call, Google authenticator app for Android and iOS devices, and a printable list of one-time codes.

Even gamers have been protecting their accounts using services and applications such as the Steam Guard Mobile Authenticator app. Millions of users have made their accounts stronger with multifactor verification. Have you?

Authentication by Characteristic

A system that uses authentication by characteristic authenticates the user based on some physical or behavioral characteristic, sometimes referred to as a biometric attribute. Here are the most used physical or physiological characteristics:

- Fingerprints
- Face recognition
- Retina and iris
- Palm and hand geometry
- Blood and vascular information
- Voice recognition

Here are examples of behavioral characteristics:

- Signature dynamic
- Keystroke dynamic/pattern

The drawback of a system based on this type of authentication is that it's prone to accuracy errors. For example, a signature-dynamic-based system would authenticate a user by requesting that the user write his signature and then comparing the signature pattern to a record in the system. Given that the way a person signs his name differs slightly every time, the system should be designed so that the user can still authenticate even if the signature and pattern is not exactly the one in the system. However, it should also not be too loose and thus authenticate an unauthorized user attempting to mimic the pattern.

Two types of errors are associated with the accuracy of a biometric system:

- A Type I error, also called false rejection, happens when the system rejects a valid user who should have been authenticated.
- A Type II error, also called false acceptance, happens when the system accepts a user who should have been rejected (for example, an attacker trying to impersonate a valid user).

The crossover error rate (CER), also called the equal error rate (EER), is the point where the rate of false rejection errors (FRR) and the rate of false acceptance error (FAR) are equal. This is generally accepted as an indicator of the accuracy (and hence the quality) of a biometric system.

Multi-Factor Authentication

The process of *authentication* requires the subject to supply verifiable credentials. The credentials are often referred to as *factors*.

Single-factor authentication is when only one factor is presented. The most common method of single-factor authentication is the password. *Multifactor authentication* is when two or more factors are presented. *Multilayer authentication* is when two or more of the same type of factors are presented. Data classification, regulatory requirements, the impact of unauthorized access, and the likelihood of a threat being exercised should all be considered when you're deciding on the level of authentication required. The more factors, the more robust the authentication process.

Identification and authentication are often performed together; however, it is important to understand that they are two different operations. Identification is about establishing who you are, whereas authentication is about proving you are the entity you claim to be.

What Is Authorization?

Once authenticated, a subject must be authorized. *Authorization* is the process of assigning authenticated subjects permission to carry out a specific operation. The *authorization model* defines how access rights and permission are granted. The three primary authorization models are object capability, security labels, and ACLs. *Object capability* is used programmatically and is based on a combination of an unforgeable reference and an operational message. *Security labels* are mandatory access controls embedded in object and subject properties. Examples of security labels (based on its classification) are "confidential", "secret", and "top secret." *Access control lists (ACLs)* are used to determine access based on some combination of specific criteria, such as a user ID, group membership, classification, location, address, and date.

Additionally, when granting access, the authorization process would check the permissions associated with the subject/object pair so that the correct access right is provided. The object owner and management usually decide (or give input on) the permission and authorization policy that governs the authorization process.

The authorization policy and rule should take various attributes into consideration, such as the identity of the subject, the location from where the subject is requesting access, the subject's role within the organization, and so on. Access control models, which are described in more detail later in this chapter, provide the framework for the authorization policy implementation.

An authorization policy should implement two concepts:

- **Implicit deny:** If no rule is specified for the transaction of the subject/object, the authorization policy should deny the transaction.

- **Need-to-know:** A subject should be granted access to an object only if the access is needed to carry out the job of the subject.

The three categories of ACLs are discretionary access controls, role-based access controls, and rule-based access controls.

Mandatory Access Control (MAC)

Mandatory access controls (MACs) are defined by policy and cannot be modified by the information owner. MACs are primarily used in secure military and government systems that require a high degree of confidentiality. In a MAC environment, objects are assigned a security label that indicates the classification and category of the resource. Subjects are assigned a security label that indicates a clearance level and assigned categories (based on need-to-know). The operating system compares the object's security label with the subject's security label. The subject's clearance must be equal to or greater than the object's classification. The category must match. For example, for a user to access a document classified as "Secret" and categorized as "Flight Plans," the user must have either Secret or Top Secret clearance and have been tagged to the Flight Plan category.

Discretionary Access Control (DAC)

Discretionary access controls (DACs) are defined by the owner of the object. DACs are used in commercial operating systems. The object owner builds an ACL that allows or denies access to the object based on the user's unique identity. The ACL can reference a user ID or a group (or groups) that the user is a member of. Permissions can be cumulative. For example, John belongs to the Accounting Group. The Accounting Group is assigned read permissions to the Income Tax folder and the files in the folder. John's user account is assigned write permissions to the Income Tax folder and the files in the folder. Because DAC permissions are cumulative, John can access, read, and write to the files in the tax folder.

Role-Based Access Control (RBAC)

Role-based access controls (RBACs) (also called "nondiscretionary controls") are access permissions based on a specific role or function. Administrators grant access rights and permissions to roles. Users are then associated with a single role. There is no provision for assigning rights to a user or group account.

Let's take a look at the example illustrated in Figure 9-1.

Omar is associated with the role of "Engineer" and inherits all the permissions assigned to the Engineer role. Omar cannot be assigned any additional permissions. Jeannette is associated with the role of "Sales" and inherits all the permissions assigned to the Sales role and cannot access engineering resources. Users can belong to multiple groups. RBAC enables you to control what users can do at both broad and granular levels.

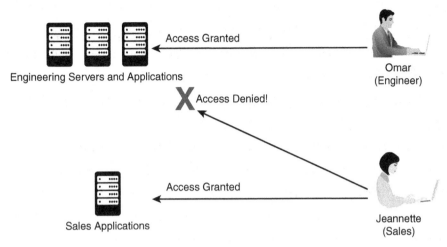

Engineering Servers and Applications

Access Granted

Omar
(Engineer)

Access Denied!

Sales Applications

Access Granted

Jeannette
(Sales)

FIGURE 9-1   RBAC Example

Rule-Based Access Control

In a *rule-based access controls* environment, access is based on criteria that are independent of the user or group account. The rules are determined by the resource owner. Commonly used criteria include source or destination address, geographic location, and time of day. For example, the ACL on an application requires that it be accessed from a specific workstation. Rule-based access controls can be combined with DACs and RBACs.

In Practice

Access Control Authorization Policy

Synopsis: To state the access control authorization principles of the organization.

Policy Statement:

- Default access privileges will be set to default deny (deny all).

- Access to information and information systems must be limited to personnel and processes with a need-to-know to effectively fulfill their duties.

- Access permissions must be based on the minimum required to perform the job or program function.

- Information and information system owners are responsible for determining access rights and permissions.

- The Office of Information Security is responsible for enforcing an authorization process.

- Permissions must not be granted until the authorization process is complete.

Attribute-Based Access Control

Attribute-based access control (ABAC) is a logical access control model that controls access to objects by evaluating rules against the attributes of entities (both subject and object), operations, and the environment relevant to a request.

- ABAC supports a complex Boolean rule set that can evaluate many different attributes.

- The policies that can be implemented in an ABAC model are limited only to the degree imposed by the computational language and the richness of the available attributes.

- An example of an access control framework that is consistent with ABAC is the Extensible Access Control Markup Language (XACML).

Accounting

Accounting is the process of auditing and monitoring what a user does once a specific resource is accessed. This process is sometimes overlooked; however, as a security professional, it is important to be aware of accounting and to advocate that it be implemented because of the great help it provides during detection and investigation of cybersecurity breaches.

When accounting is implemented, an audit trail log is created and stored that details when the user has accessed the resource, what the user did with that resource, and when the user stopped using the resource. Given the potential sensitive information included in the auditing logs, special care should be taken in protecting them from unauthorized access.

In Practice

Authentication Policy

Synopsis: To require the positive identification of the person or system seeking access to secured information, information systems, or devices.

Policy Statement:

- Access to and use of information technology (IT) systems must require an individual to uniquely identify and authenticate him/herself to the resource.

- Multiuser or shared accounts are allowed only when there is a documented and justified reason that has been approved by the Office of Information Security.

- The Office of Information Security is responsible for managing an annual user account audit of network accounts, local application accounts, and web application accounts.

- Data classification, regulatory requirements, the impact of unauthorized access, and the likelihood of a threat being exercised must all be considered when deciding upon the level of authentication required. The Office of Information Security will make this determination in conjunction with the information system owner.

- Operating systems and applications will at a minimum be configured to require single-factor complex password authentication:

- The inability to technically enforce this standard does not negate the requirement.

- Password length, complexity, and expiration will be defined in the company password standard.

- The password standard will be published, distributed, and included in the acceptable use agreement.

- Web applications that transmit, store, or process "protected" or "confidential" information must at a minimum be configured to require single-factor complex password authentication:

- The inability to technically enforce this standard does not negate the requirement.

- Password length, complexity, and expiration will be defined in the company password standard.

- If available, multifactor authentication must be implemented.

- Passwords and PINs must be unique to the application.

- Exceptions to this policy must be approved by the Office of Information Security.

- All passwords must be encrypted during transmission and storage. Applications that do not conform to this requirement may not be used.

- Any mechanism used for storing passwords must be approved by the Office of Information Security.

- If any authentication mechanism has been compromised or is suspected of being compromised, users must immediately contact the Office of Information Security and follow the instructions given.

Infrastructure Access Controls

A *network infrastructure* is defined as an interconnected group of hosts and devices. The infrastructure can be confined to one location or, as often is the case, widely distributed, including branch locations and home offices. Access to the infrastructure enables the use of its resources. *Infrastructure access controls* include physical and logical network design, border devices, communication mechanisms, and host security settings. Because no system is foolproof, access must be continually monitored; if suspicious activity is detected, a response must be initiated.

Why Segment a Network?

Network segmentation is the process of logically grouping network assets, resources, and applications. Segmentation provides the flexibility to implement a variety of services, authentication requirements, and security controls. Working from the inside out, network segments include the following types:

- **Enclave network:** A segment of an internal network that requires a higher degree of protection. Internal accessibility is further restricted through the use of firewalls, VPNs, VLANs, and network access control (NAC) devices.

- **Trusted network (wired or wireless):** The internal network that is accessible to authorized users. External accessibility is restricted through the use of firewalls, VPNs, and IDS/IPS devices. Internal accessibility may be restricted through the use of VLANs and NAC devices.

- **Semi-trusted network, perimeter network, or DMZ:** A network that is designed to be Internet accessible. Hosts such as web servers and email gateways are generally located in the DMZ. Internal and external accessibility is restricted through the use of firewalls, VPNs, and IDS/IPS devices.

- **Guest network (wired or wireless):** A network that is specifically designed for use by visitors to connect to the Internet. There is no access from the Guest network to the internal trusted network.

- **Untrusted network:** A network outside your security controls. The Internet is an untrusted network.

Figure 9-2 shows the topology of a network that has not been properly segmented.

The network topology in Figure 9-2 shows an enterprise that has a call center, a branch office, a warehouse, and a data center. The branch is a retail office where customers purchase their goods and the enterprise accepts credit cards. Users in the call center and the warehouse have access to the resources in the Branch office and vice versa. They also have access to resources in the data center. If any device is compromised, an attacker can pivot (or move laterally) in the network.

The topology in Figure 9-3 shows the same enterprise network topology, except that firewalls were installed to segment the network and to allow the traffic from the credit card readers to communicate only with specific servers in the data center.

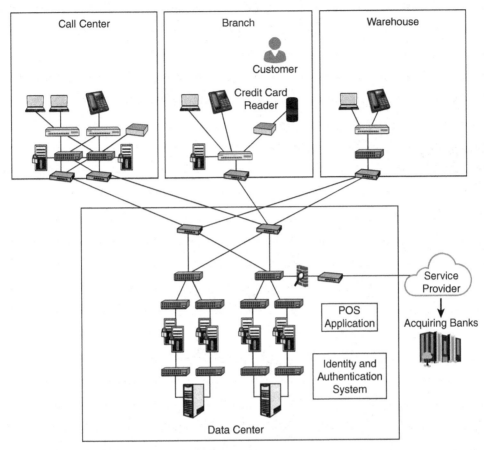

FIGURE 9-2 Network Without Segmentation

Several other technologies can be used to segment a network:

- Virtual LANs (VLANs)
- Security Group Tagging (SGT)
- VPN Routing and Forwarding (VRF)
- vMicro-segmentation at the virtual machine level
- Micro-segmentation for containers

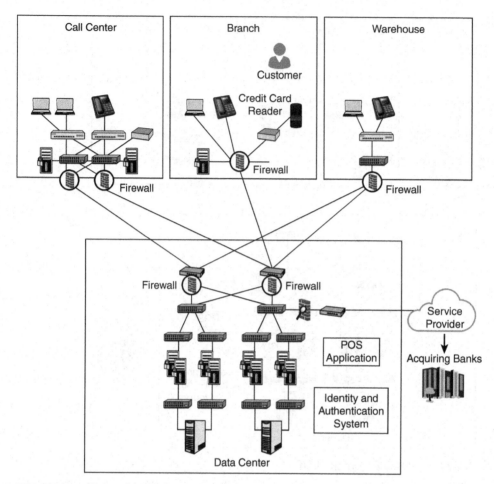

FIGURE 9-3 Network with Segmentation

Network Segmentation Policy

Synopsis: Directive to logically group network assets, resources, and applications for the purpose of applying security controls.

Policy Statement:

- The network infrastructure will be segregated into distinct segments according to security requirements and service function.

- The Office of Information Security and the Office of Information Technology are jointly responsible for conducting annual network segment risk assessments. The results of the assessments will be provided to the Chief Operating Officer (COO).

- Complete documentation of the network topology and architecture will be maintained by the Office of Information Technology, including an up-to-date network diagram showing all internal (wired and wireless) connections, external connections, and end points, including the Internet.

What Is Layered Border Security?

Layered security is the term applied to having different types of security measures designed to work in tandem with a single focus. The focus of *layered border security* is protecting the internal network from external threats. Layered border security access controls include firewall devices, intrusion detection systems (IDSs), and intrusion prevention systems (IPSs). To be effective, these devices must be properly configured and expertly managed. Due to the complexity of and resource requirements associated with maintaining and monitoring border security devices, many organizations have chosen to outsource the function to *managed security service providers* (referred to as MSSPs). Oversight of in-house administration or of the MSSP is a critical risk management safeguard.

So, What Are Firewalls?

Firewalls are devices or software that control the flow of traffic between networks. They are responsible for examining network entry and exit requests and enforcing organizational policy. Firewalls are a mandatory security control for any network connected to an untrusted network such as the Internet. Without a properly configured firewall, a network is completely exposed and could potentially be compromised within minutes, if not seconds. A firewall policy defines how the firewall should handle inbound and outbound network traffic for specific IP addresses and address ranges, protocols, ports, applications, and content types. The policy is codified in the rule set. The rule set is used by the firewall to evaluate *ingress* (incoming) and *egress* (outgoing) network traffic. In keeping with access control best practices, rule sets should be initially set to default deny (deny all) and then strict rules implemented that allow connectivity based on business need.

NIST SP-41, R1: Guidelines on Firewalls and Firewall Policy, provides an overview of firewall technologies and discusses their security capabilities and relative advantages and disadvantages in detail. It also provides examples of where firewalls can be placed within networks, and the implications of deploying firewalls in particular locations. The document also makes recommendations for establishing firewall policies and for selecting, configuring, testing, deploying, and managing firewall solutions.

FYI: IP Address, Ports, and Protocols Simplified

IP addresses, ports, and protocols form the basis of Internet communications:

- An *IP address* is how a specific network host or device is identified.

- A *port* is how an application or service is identified.

- A *protocol* is a standardized way for hosts and network devices to exchange information.

Let's compare IP addresses, ports, and protocols to mailing a letter.

If you want to mail a letter, you must follow the postal protocol, including how to address the letter to the recipient, the return address requirements, and where a letter can be mailed (such as the post office or mailbox).

The address must include the city (network), the street (network segment), and house number (host or device).

To be delivered to the right person (application or service), the address must include a unique name (port).

Network-based firewalls provide key features used for perimeter security. The primary task of a network firewall is to deny or permit traffic that attempts to enter or leave the network based on explicit preconfigured policies and rules. Firewalls are often deployed in several other parts of the network to provide network segmentation within the corporate infrastructure and also in data centers. The processes used to allow or block traffic may include the following:

- Simple packet-filtering techniques

- Application proxies

- Network address translation

- Stateful inspection firewalls

- Next-generation context-aware firewalls

The purpose of packet filters is simply to control access to specific network segments by defining which traffic can pass through them. They usually inspect incoming traffic at the transport layer of the Open System Interconnection (OSI) model. For example, packet filters can analyze Transmission Control Protocol (TCP) or User Datagram Protocol (UDP) packets and judge them against a set of predetermined rules called access control lists (ACLs). They inspect the following elements within a packet:

- Source IP address

- Destination IP address

- Source port

- Destination port

- Protocol

Packet filters do not commonly inspect additional Layer 3 and Layer 4 fields such as sequence numbers, TCP control flags, and TCP acknowledgment (ACK) fields. Various packet-filtering firewalls can also inspect packet header information to find out whether the packet is from a new or an existing connection. Simple packet-filtering firewalls have several limitations and weaknesses:

- Their ACLs or rules can be relatively large and difficult to manage.

- They can be deceived into permitting unauthorized access of spoofed packets. Attackers can orchestrate a packet with an IP address that is authorized by the ACL.

- Numerous applications can build multiple connections on arbitrarily negotiated ports. This makes it difficult to determine which ports are selected and used until after the connection is completed. Examples of this type of application are multimedia applications such as streaming audio and video applications. Packet filters do not understand the underlying upper-layer protocols used by this type of application, and providing support for this type of application is difficult because the ACLs need to be manually configured in packet-filtering firewalls.

Application proxies, or proxy servers, are devices that operate as intermediary agents on behalf of clients that are on a private or protected network. Clients on the protected network send connection requests to the application proxy to transfer data to the unprotected network or the Internet. Consequently, the application proxy sends the request on behalf of the internal client. The majority of proxy firewalls work at the application layer of the OSI model. Most proxy firewalls can cache information to accelerate their transactions. This is a great tool for networks that have numerous servers that experience high usage. Additionally, proxy firewalls can protect against some web-server-specific attacks; however, in most cases, they do not provide any protection against the web application itself.

Several Layer 3 devices can supply network address translation (NAT) services. The Layer 3 device translates the internal host's private (or real) IP addresses to a publicly routable (or mapped) address.

NAT is often used by firewalls; however, other devices, such as routers and wireless access points, provide support for NAT. By using NAT, the firewall hides the internal private addresses from the unprotected network, and exposes only its own address or public range. This enables a network professional to use any IP address space as the internal network. A best practice is to use the address spaces that are reserved for private use (see RFC 1918, "Address Allocation for Private Internets").

The white paper titled "A Security-Oriented Approach to IP Addressing" provides numerous tips on planning and preparing your network IP address scheme. This white paper is posted at the following link: www.cisco.com/web/about/security/intelligence/security-for-ip-addr.html.

Normally, firewalls perform a technique called port address translation (PAT). This feature is a subset of the NAT feature that allows many devices on the internal protected network to share one IP address by inspecting the Layer 4 information on the packet. This shared address is usually the firewall's public address; however, it can be configured to any other available public IP address.

Intrusion Detection Systems and Intrusion Prevention Systems

It is possible for malicious activity to masquerade as legitimate traffic. *Intrusion detection systems (IDSs)* are passive devices designed to analyze network traffic to detect unauthorized access or malevolent activity. Most IDSs use multiple methods to detect threats, including signature-based detection, anomaly-based detection, and stateful protocol analysis. If suspicious activity is detected, IDSs generate an onscreen, email, and/or text alert. *Intrusion prevention systems (IPSs)* are active devices that sit inline with traffic flow and can respond to identified threats by disabling the connection, dropping the packet, or deleting the malicious content.

There are four types of IDS/IPS technologies:

- **Network-based IDS/IPS:** Monitors network traffic for particular network segments or devices and analyzes the network and application protocol activity to identify suspicious activity.

- **Wireless IDS/IPS:** Monitors wireless network traffic and analyzes it to identify suspicious activity involving the wireless networking protocols themselves.

- **Network behavior analysis IDS/IPS:** Examines network traffic to identify threats that generate unusual traffic flows, such as distributed denial of service (DDoS) attacks, certain forms of malware, and policy violations (for example, a client system providing network services to other systems).

- **Host-based IDS/IPS:** Monitors the characteristics of a single host and the events occurring within that host for suspicious activity.

IDS/IPS has four decision states. *True positive* occurs when the IDS/IPS correctly identifies an issue. *True negative* occurs when the IDS/IPS correctly identifies normal traffic. *False positive* occurs when the IDS/IPS incorrectly identifies normal activity as an issue. *False negative* occurs when the IDS/ISP incorrectly identifies an issue as normal activity.

Network-based IDS and IPS use several detection methodologies, such as the following:

- Pattern-matching and stateful pattern-matching recognition

- Protocol analysis

- Heuristic-based analysis

- Anomaly-based analysis

- Correlation protection capabilities based on threat intelligence

NIST SP-94: "Guide to Intrusion Detection and Prevention Systems" describes the characteristics of IDS and IPS technologies and provides recommendations for designing, implementing, configuring, securing, monitoring, and maintaining them. The types of IDS/IPS technologies are differentiated primarily by the types of events they monitor and the ways in which they are deployed.

Content Filtering and Whitelisting/Blacklisting

Controls are required to protect the internal network from insider requests that could result in malware distribution, data exfiltration, participation in peer-to-peer (P2P) networks, and viewing of inappropriate or illegal content. The insider request could come from authenticated authorized users or could be a response to a malicious command or instruction. As discussed earlier, border device egress filters can and should be used to restrict outbound traffic by source and destination address, port, and protocol. The filters can be supplemented by self-generated, open source, or subscription-based IP whitelists and/or blacklists. *Whitelists* are addresses (IP and/or Internet domain names) of known "good" sites to which access should be allowed. Conversely, *blacklists* are addresses (IP and/or Internet domain names) of known "bad" sites to which access should be denied. It is common practice to block entire ranges of IP addresses specific to geographic regions. *Content-filtering* applications can be used to restrict access by content category (such as violence, gaming, shopping, or pornography), time factors, application type, bandwidth use, and media.

Border Device Administration and Management

Border device administration and management is a 24/7/365 responsibility. On a daily basis, performance needs to be monitored to enable potential resource issues to be identified and addressed before components become overwhelmed. Logs and alerts must be monitored and analyzed to identify threats—both successful and unsuccessful. Administrators need to be on the watch for security patches and apply them expediently. Border device policies, configurations, and rule sets must be backed up or replicated.

Policy rules and rule sets need to be updated as the organization's requirements change or when new threats are identified. Changes should be closely monitored because unauthorized or incorrect modifications to the rule set can put the organization at risk. Modifications should be subject to the organization's change management process. This includes a separation of approval and implementation duties. Configuration and rule set reviews as well as testing should be performed periodically to ensure continued compliance with the organization's policies. Internal reviews can uncover configuration settings and rules that are outdated, redundant, or harmful. The review should include a detailed examination of all changes since the last regular review, particularly who made the changes and under what circumstances. External penetration testing can be used to verify that the devices are performing as intended.

FYI: Blue, Red, and Purple Teams

The defenders of the corporate network are typically referred to as *blue teams*. These blue teams include analysts in a security operation center (SOC), computer security incident response teams (CSIRTs), and other information security (InfoSec) teams. Offensive security teams such as ethical hackers or penetration testers are often referred to as the *red team*. The objective of red teams is to identify vulnerabilities as well as an organization's attack detection and response capabilities. There is another concept called *purple teaming*. Purple teaming is when both the red and blue teams align forces to completely defend the organization and collaborate closely. In the past, most of these teams did not collaborate with each other.

In Practice

Border Device Security Access Control Policy

Synopsis: Requirements for the secure design, configuration, management, administration, and oversight of border devices.

Policy Statement:

- Border security access control devices will be implemented and securely maintained to restrict access between networks that are trusted to varying degrees.

- The default policy for handling inbound and outbound traffic should be to default deny (deny all).

- If any situation renders the Internet-facing border security devices inoperable, Internet service must be disabled.

- The Office of Information Security is responsible for approving border security access control architecture, configuration, and rule sets.

- The Office of Information Technology is responsible for designing, maintaining, and managing border security access control devices.

- At the discretion of the COO, this function or part of it may be outsourced to an MSSP.

- Oversight of internal or MSSP border security device administrators is assigned to the Office of Information Security.

- The types of network traffic that must always be denied without exception will be documented in the border device security standards.

- Rule sets must be as specific and simple as possible. Rule set documentation will include the business justification for allowed traffic.

- All configuration and rule set changes are subject to the organizational change management process.

- All rule set modifications must be approved by the Office of Information Security.

- All border security access control devices must be physically located in a controlled environment, with access limited to authorized personnel.

- To support recovery after failure or natural disaster, the border security device configuration, policy, and rules must be backed up or replicated on a scheduled basis, as well as before and after every configuration change.

- Border devices must be configured to log successful and failed activity as well as configuration changes.

- Border device logs must be reviewed daily by the Office of Information Technology or MSSP, and an activity report must be submitted to the Office of Information Security.

- Configuration and rule set reviews must be conducted annually:

  - The review is to be conducted by an external, independent entity.

  - Selection of the vendor is the responsibility of the Audit Committee.

  - Testing results are to be submitted to the COO.

- External penetration testing must, at a minimum, be performed semi-annually:

  - The testing is to be conducted by an external, independent entity.

  - Selection of the vendor is the responsibility of the Audit Committee.

  - Testing results are to be submitted to the COO.

Remote Access Security

The need to access internal corporate network resources from external locations has become increasingly common. In fact, for companies with a remote or mobile workforce, remote access has become the norm. The nature of remote access technologies—permitting access to protected resources from external networks and often external hosts as well—is fraught with risk. Companies should start with the assumption that external facilities, networks, and devices contain hostile threats that will, if given the opportunity, attempt to gain access to the organization's data and resources. Controls, including authentication, must be carefully evaluated and chosen based on the network segment's information systems and the classification of information that will be accessible. Consideration must be given to ensuring that the remote access communication and stored user data cannot be accessed or read by unauthorized parties (confidentiality), detecting intentional or unintentional modifications to data in transit (integrity), and ensuring that users can access the resources as required (availability). Remote access security controls that must be considered include the physical security of the client devices, the use of cryptography in transit, the method of authentication and authorization, and the risks associated with local storage.

NIST SP 800-46, R2 "Guide to Enterprise Telework, Remote Access and Bring Your Own Device Security," provides information on security considerations for several types of remote access solutions, and it makes recommendations for securing a variety of telework and remote access technologies. The publication also provides recommendations for creating telework-related policies and for selecting, implementing, and maintaining the necessary security controls for remote access servers and clients.

Remote Access Technologies

The two most common remote access technologies are virtual private networks (VPNs) and remote access portals. VPNs are generally used to extend the resources of a network to a remote location. Portals are generally used to provide access to specific applications.

A *virtual private network (VPN)* provides a secure tunnel for transmitting data through an unsecured network such as the Internet. This is achieved using tunneling and encryption in combination to provide high security remote access without the high cost of dedicated private lines. *IPsec* (short for IP security) is a set of protocols developed by the Internet Engineering Task Force (IETF) to support secure exchange of packets at the IP layer. IPsec is most commonly associated with VPNs as the protocol providing tunneling and encryption for VPN connections between physical sites or between a site and a remote user. The tunnel can be thought of as a virtual pathway between systems within the larger pathway of the Internet. The popularity of VPN deployments is a result of worldwide low-cost accessibility to the Internet, in contrast to private circuits that are expensive, require long-term contracts, and must be implemented between specific locations. More information on IPsec VPNs is available from NIST SP 800-77, "Guide to IPsec VPNs," and more information on SSL tunnel VPNs is available from NIST SP 800-113, "Guide to SSL VPNs."

A *remote access portal* offers access to one or more applications through a single centralized interface. A portal server transfers data to the client device as rendered desktop screen images or web pages, but data is typically stored on the client device temporarily. Portals limit remote access to specific portal-based applications. Another type of portal solution is terminal server access, which gives each remote user access to a separate standardized virtual desktop. The terminal server simulates the look and feel of a desktop operating system and provides access to applications. Terminal server access requires the remote user either to install a special terminal server client application or to use a web-based interface, often with a browser plug-in or other additional software provided by the organization. What's more, applications such as Teamview and Joinme are specifically designed to create remote desktop sessions.

Remote Access Authentication and Authorization

Whenever feasible, organizations should implement *mutual authentication* so that a remote access user can verify the legitimacy of a remote access server before providing authentication credentials to it. The presentation of a preselected picture is an example of server-side authentication. Best practices dictate that multifactor authentication be required for remote access authentication. For an attacker to gain unauthorized access, he would have to compromise two authentication factors—one of which would either be something the user has or something the user is. Significantly increasing the work factor is a powerful deterrent! Additionally, users should be required to reauthenticate periodically during long remote access sessions or after a period of inactivity.

In addition to authenticating the user, remote access devices such as workstations and tablets should be evaluated to ensure they meet the baseline standards required for internal systems. *Network access control (NAC)* systems can be used to check a remote access device based on defined criteria, such as operating system version, security patches, antivirus software version, and wireless and firewall configurations, before it is allowed to connect to the infrastructure. If the device does not meet the predefined criteria, the device is denied access.

In Practice

Remote Access Security

Synopsis: To assign responsibility and set the requirements for remote access connections to the internal network.

Policy Statement:

- The Office of Information Security is responsible for approving remote access connections and security controls.

- The Office of Information Technology is responsible for managing and monitoring remote access connection.

- Remote access connections must use 128-bit or greater encryption to protect data in transit (such as VPN, SSL, or SSH).

- Multifactor authentication must be used for remote access. Whenever technically feasible, one factor must be out-of-band.

- Remote equipment must be company-owned and configured in accordance with company workstation security standards.

- Business partners and vendors wanting to obtain approval for remote access to computing resources must have access approved by the COO. Their company sponsor is required to provide a valid business reason for the remote access to be authorized.

- Employees, business partners, and vendors approved for remote access must be presented with and sign a Remote Access Agreement that acknowledges their responsibilities prior to being granted access.

- Remote access devices must be configured to log successful and failed activity as well as configuration changes.

- Remote access logs must be reviewed daily by the Office of Information Technology or designee, and an activity report must be submitted to the Office of Information Security.

- Remote access user lists must be reviewed quarterly by the Office of Human Resources.

- The result of the review must be reported to both the Office of Information Security and the Office of Information Technology.

- External penetration testing must, at a minimum, be performed semi-annually:

  - The testing is to be conducted by an external independent entity.

  - Selection of the vendor is the responsibility of the Audit Committee.

  - Testing results are to be submitted to the COO.

Teleworking Access Controls

The Telework Enhancement Act of 2010, Public Law 111-292, defines *teleworking* as "a work flexibility arrangement under which an employee performs the duties and responsibilities of such employee's position, and other authorized activities, from an approved worksite other than the location from which the employee would otherwise work." In plain language, teleworking allows employees to work offsite, often from their home. The Telework Coalition (TelCoa) list of teleworking benefits includes "increased employee productivity and motivation, reduced vehicular pollution, traffic reduction, improved work-life balance, a reduced dependency on imported oil, providing new employment opportunities for the disabled, rural, and older worker, as well as spouses of those in the military and a means to efficiently and effectively establish a decentralized and distributed work force that is necessary as a critical component in business continuity and disaster recovery planning."[1]

Remote locations must be thought of as logical and physical extensions of the internal network and secured appropriately. Controls to ensure the confidentiality, integrity, and availability (CIA) of the information assets and information systems, including monitoring, must be commensurate with the on-premise environment.

NIST SP 800-114, "User's Guide to Telework and Bring Your Own Device (BYOD) Security," provides practical, real-world recommendations for securing telework computers' operating systems (OS) and applications, as well as the home networks that the computers use. It presents basic recommendations for securing consumer devices used for telework. The document also presents advice on protecting the information stored on telework computers and removable media. In addition, it provides tips on considering the security of a device owned by a third party before deciding whether it should be used for telework.

---

1. Our Vision and Mission, © 2011, The Telework Coalition

> ### In Practice
>
> #### Teleworking Policy
> **Synopsis:** To assign responsibility and set the requirements for teleworking.
>
> **Policy Statement:**
> - Teleworking schedules must be requested in writing by management and authorized by the Office of Human Resources.
> - The Office of Human Resources is responsible for notifying the Office of Information Security and Office of Information Technology when a user is granted or denied teleworking privileges.
> - Teleworking equipment, including connectivity devices, must be company-owned and configured in accordance with company security standards.
> - The Office of Information Technology is responsible for managing, maintaining, and monitoring the configuration of and the connection to the teleworking location.
> - Remote access will be granted in accordance with the remote access policy and standards.
> - The teleworker is responsible for the physical security of the telecommuting location.
> - Local storage of information classified as "protected" or "confidential" must be authorized by the Office of Information Security.
> - Monitoring the teleworker is the responsibility of his or her immediate supervisor.

User Access Controls

The objective of *user access controls* is to ensure that authorized users are able to access information and resources while unauthorized users are prevented from access to the same. User access control and management is an enterprise-wide security task. NIST recommends that organizations manage information system accounts, including the following:

- Identifying account types (individual, group, system, application, guest, and temporary)
- Establishing conditions for group membership
- Identifying authorized users of the information system and specifying access privileges
- Requiring appropriate approvals for requests to establish accounts
- Establishing, activating, modifying, disabling, and removing accounts
- Specifically authorizing and monitoring the use of guest/anonymous and temporary accounts

- Notifying account managers when temporary accounts are no longer required and when information system users are terminated, transferred, or information system usage or need-to-know/need-to-share changes

- Deactivate temporary accounts that are no longer required and accounts of terminated or transferred users

- Granting access to the system based on

  - A valid access authorization
  - Intended system usage
  - Other attributes as required by the organization or associated business functions
  - Reviewing accounts periodically

Why Manage User Access?

User access must be managed to maintain confidentiality and data integrity. In keeping with the *least privilege* and *need-to-know* security precepts, users should be provided access to the information and systems needed to do their job and no more. Humans are naturally curious beings. Given unfettered access, we will peek at that which we know we should not. Moreover, user accounts are the first target of a hacker who has gained access to an organization's network. Diligent care must be used when designing procedures for creating accounts and granting access to information.

As discussed in Chapter 6, "Human Resources Security," user provisioning is the process of creating user accounts and group membership, providing company identification and authentication mechanisms, and assigning access rights and permissions. Regardless of the department tasked with the user provisioning process, the information owner is ultimately responsible for authorization and oversight of access. The information owner or designee should review application, folder, or file access controls on a periodic basis. Factors that influence how often reviews should be conducted include the classification of the information being accessed, regulatory requirements, and rate of turnover and/or reorganization of duties. The review should be documented. Issues or inaccuracies should be responded to expediently.

In Practice

User Access Control and Authorization Policy

Synopsis: To define user access control and authorization parameters and responsibilities.

Policy Statement:

- Default user access permissions will be set to default deny (deny all) prior to the appropriation of specific permissions based on role and/or job function.

- Access to company information and systems will be authorized only for workforce personnel with a need-to-know to perform their job function(s).

- Access will be restricted to the minimal amount required to carry out the business requirement of the access.

- An authorization process must be maintained. Permissions must not be granted until the authorization process is complete.

- Information owners are responsible for annually reviewing and reauthorizing user access permissions to data classified as "protected" or "confidential":

- The Office of Information Security is responsible for managing the review and reauthorization process.

- An annual report of completion will be provided to the Audit Committee.

Administrative Account Controls

Networks and information systems must be implemented, configured, managed, and monitored. Doing so requires accounts with elevated privileges. Common privileged accounts include network administrators, system administrators, database administrators, firewall administrators, and webmasters. This concentration of power can be dangerous. Mitigating controls include segregation of duties and dual controls. *Segregation of duties* requires that tasks be assigned to individuals in such a manner that no one individual can control a process from start to finish. *Dual control* requires that two individuals must both complete their half of a specific task. An example of segregation of duties is allowing a security engineer to modify a firewall configuration file but not upload the configuration into the production environment. An example of dual control is requiring two separate keys to unlock a door. Each key is assigned to an individual user. The theory of both controls is that in order to act maliciously, two or more individuals would need to work together. All administrative or privileged account activity should be logged and reviewed.

Administrative accounts should be used only when the activity being performed requires elevated rights and permissions. There is no need to use this type of account to perform routine activities such as checking email, writing reports, performing research on the Internet, and other activities for which a basic user account will suffice. This is important because viruses, worms, and other malicious code will run in the security context of the logged-in user. If a user is logged in as a system administrator and her computer is infected with malicious code, the criminal that controls the malware has administrative privilege as well. To address this very real risk, every person with a special privilege account should also have a basic user account with which to perform duties that do not require administrative access.

FYI: User Account Controls in Windows, MAC OS X, and Linux

Microsoft Windows User Account Control (UAC) can be configured so that applications and tasks always run in the security context of a non-administrator account, unless an administrator specifically authorizes administrator-level access to the system. Microsoft takes this to the next level since Windows 10. The UAC privilege elevation prompts are color-coded to be app-specific. This is done to allow you to quickly identify an application's potential security risk. Detailed information about Windows UAC can be obtained at

https://docs.microsoft.com/en-us/windows/security/identity-protection/user-account-control/how-user-account-control-works.

Linux-based systems and MAC OS X have implemented a similar approach since the early 1980s. There are two ways to run administrative applications in Linux and MAC OS X. You can either switch to the super user (root) with the **su** command, or you can take advantage of **sudo**. For example, to be able to install an application in Debian or Ubuntu you can run the **sudo apt-get install** command followed by the application or package name that you would like to install. If you are not familiar with Linux, you can learn additional details about Linux users and groups at https://linode.com/docs/tools-reference/linux-users-and-groups/.

In Practice

Administrative and Privileged Account Policy

Synopsis: To ensure the proper assignment, use, management, and oversight of accounts with administrative or elevated privileges.

Policy Statement:

- Request for assignment of administrator-level accounts or changes to privileged group membership must be submitted to the Office of Information Security and approved by the COO.

- The Office of Information Security is responsible for determining the appropriate use of administrator segregation of duties and dual controls.

- Administrative and privileged user accounts will be used only when performing duties requiring administrative or privileged access.

- All administrative and privileged account holders will have a second user account for performing any function where administrative or privileged access is not required.

- User accounts assigned to contractors, consultants, or service providers who require administrative or privileged access will be enabled according to documented schedule and/or formal request, and be disabled at all other times.

- Administrative and privileged account activity will be logged daily and reviewed by the Office of Information Security.

- Administrative and privileged account assignments will be reviewed quarterly by the Office of Information Security.

What Types of Access Should Be Monitored?

Monitoring access and use is a critical component of information security. What is most unfortunate is that many organizations deploy elaborate systems to gather data from many sources and then never look at the data. Mining log data results in a wealth of information that can be used to protect your organization. Log data offers clues about activities that have unexpected and possibly harmful consequences, including the following:

- At-risk events, such as unauthorized access, malware, data leakage, and suspicious activity

- Oversight events, such as reporting on administrative activity, user management, policy changes, remote desktop sessions, configuration changes, and unexpected access

- Security-related operational events, such as reporting on patch installation, software installation, service management, system reboots, bandwidth utilization, and DNS/DHCP traffic

At a minimum, three categories of user access should be logged and analyzed: successful access, failed access, and privileged operations. *Successful access* is a record of user activity. Reporting should include date, time, and action (for example, authenticate, read, delete, or modify). *Failed access* is indicative of either unauthorized attempts or authorized user issues. In the first instance, it is important to know whether an intruder is "testing" the system or has launched an attack. In the second, from an operational standpoint, it is important to know if users are having problems logging in, accessing information, or doing their jobs. Oversight of administrative or privileged accounts is critical. Administrators hold the keys to the kingdom. In many organizations, they have unfettered access. Compromise or misuse of administrator accounts can have disastrous consequences.

Is Monitoring Legal?

As we discussed in Chapter 6, employees should have *no expectation of privacy* in respect to actions taken on company time or with company resources. The United States judiciary system has favored employers' right to monitor to protect their interests. Among the reasons given in the *Defense Counsel Journal* are the following:

- The work is done at the employer's place of business.

- The employer owns the equipment.

- The employer has an interest in monitoring employee activity to ensure the quality of work.

- The employer has the right to protect property from theft and fraud.

Court rulings suggest that reasonableness is a standard applying to surveillance and monitoring activities. Electronic monitoring is reasonable when there is a business purpose, policies exist to set the privacy expectations of employees, and employees are informed of organizational rules regarding network activities and understand the means used to monitor the workplace.

Acceptable use agreements should include a clause informing users that the company will and does monitor system activity. A commonly accepted practice is to present this statement to system users as a legal warning during the authentication process. Users must agree to company monitoring as a condition of logging on.

In Practice

Monitoring System Access and Use Policy

Synopsis: Monitoring of network activity is necessary to detect unauthorized, suspicious, or at-risk activity.

Policy Statement:

- The Office of Information Technology, the Office of Information Security, and the Office of Human Resources are jointly responsible for determining the extent of logging and analysis required for information systems storing, processing, transmitting, or providing access to information classified as "confidential" or "protected." However, at a minimum the following must be logged:

  - Successful and failed network authentication
  - Successful and failed authentication to any application that stores or processes information classified as "protected"
  - Network and application administrative or privileged account activity

- Exceptions to this list must be authorized by the COO.

- Access logs must be reviewed daily by the Office of Information Technology or designee, and an activity report must be submitted to the Office of Information Security.

FYI: Small Business Note

One of the most significant information security challenges that small businesses face is not having dedicated IT or information security personnel. Very often, someone in the organization with "IT skills" is tapped to install and support critical devices, such as firewalls, wireless access points, and networking components. The result is that these devices are often left in their default mode and are not properly configured. Of particular concern is when the administrative account password is not changed. Attackers can easily obtain default passwords and take over the device. Passwords can be found in product documentation, and compiled lists are available on the Internet from sites such as www.defaultpassword.com/ and www.routerpasswords.com/.

Summary

Access controls are security features that govern how users and processes communicate and interact with systems and resources. The objective of implementing access controls is to ensure that authorized users and processes are able to access information and resources while unauthorized users and processes are prevented from access to the same. Access control models refer to the active entity that requests access to an object or data as the *subject* and the passive entity being accessed or being acted upon as the *object*.

An organization's approach to access controls is referred to as its *security posture*. There are two fundamental approaches—open and secure. Open, also referred to as *default allow*, means that access not explicitly forbidden is permitted. Secure, also referred to as *default deny*, means that access not explicitly permitted is forbidden. Access decisions should consider the security principles of need-to-know and least privilege. *Need-to-know* means having a demonstrated and authorized reason for being granted access to information. *Least privilege* means granting subjects the minimum level of access required to perform their job or function.

Gaining access is a three-step process. The first step is for the object to recognize the subject. *Identification* is the process of the subject supplying an identifier such as a username to the object. The next step is to prove that the subjects are who they say they are. *Authentication* is the process of the subject supplying verifiable credentials to the object. The last step is determining the actions a subject can take. *Authorization* is the process of assigning authenticated subjects the rights and permissions needed to carry out a specific operation.

Authentication credentials are called *factors*. There are three categories of factors: knowledge (something the user knows), possession (something a user has), and inherence (something the user is). *Single-factor authentication* is when only one factor is presented. *Multifactor authentication* is when two or more factors are presented. *Multilayer authentication* is when two or more of the same type of factor are presented. *Out-of-band authentication* requires communication over a channel that is distinct from the first factor. Data classification, regulatory requirement, the impact of unauthorized access, and the likelihood of a threat being exercised must all be considered when deciding on the level of authentication required.

Once authentication is complete, an authorization model defines how subjects access objects. *Mandatory access controls (MACs)* are defined by policy and cannot be modified by the information owner. *Discretionary access controls (DACs)* are defined by the owner of the object. *Role-based access controls (RBACs)* (also called *nondiscretionary*) are access permissions based on a specific role or function. In a *rule-based access controls* environment, access is based on criteria that are independent of the user or group account, such as time of day or location.

A *network infrastructure* is defined as an interconnected group of hosts and devices. The infrastructure can be confined to one location or, as often is the case, widely distributed, including branch locations and home offices. *Network segmentation* is the process of logically grouping network assets, resources, and applications to stratify authentication requirements and security controls. Segments include enclaves, trusted networks, guest networks, perimeter networks (also referred to as DMZs), and untrusted networks (including the Internet).

Layered security is the term applied to having different types of security measures designed to work in tandem with a single focus. The focus of layered border security is protecting the internal network from external threats. Firewalls are devices or software that control the flow of traffic between networks using ingress and egress filters. Egress filters can be supplemented by self-generated, open source, or subscription-based IP whitelists or blacklists. *Whitelists* are addresses (IP and/or Internet domain names) of known "good" sites. Conversely, *blacklists* are addresses (IP and/or Internet domain names) of known "bad" sites. Content-filtering applications can be used to restrict access by content category (such as violence, gaming, shopping, or pornography), time factors, application type, bandwidth use, and media. *Intrusion detection systems (IDSs)* are passive devices designed to analyze network traffic to detect unauthorized access or malevolent activity. *Intrusion prevention systems (IPSs)* are active devices that sit inline with traffic flow and can respond to identified threats by disabling the connection, dropping the packet, or deleting the malicious content.

The need to access internal corporate network resources from remote locations has become increasingly common. Users who work remotely (often from home) on a scheduled basis are referred to as *teleworkers*. VPNs and remote access portals can be used to provide secure remote access for authorized users. A *virtual private network (VPN)* provides a secure tunnel for transmitting data through an unsecured network such as the Internet. *IPsec* (short for IP security) is a set of protocols developed by the Internet Engineering Task Force (IETF) to support secure exchange of packets at the IP layer and is used by VPN devices.

A remote access portal offers access to one or more applications through a single centralized interface. Both mechanisms authenticate and authorize subjects. Best practices dictate that multifactor authentication be used for remote access connections. *Network access control (NAC)* systems can be used to check a remote access device based on defined criteria, such as operating system version, security patches, antivirus software and DAT files, and wireless and firewall configurations, before it is allowed to connect to the infrastructure.

Organizations are dynamic. New employees are hired, others change roles, some leave under friendly conditions, and others are involuntarily terminated. The objective of user access controls is to ensure that authorized users are able to access information and resources while unauthorized users are prevented from access to the same. Information owners are responsible for the authorization of access and ongoing oversight. Access control reviews should be conducted periodically, commensurate with the classification of the information being accessed, regulatory requirements, and the rate of turnover and/or reorganization of duties.

Access controls are configured and managed by users with administrative or elevated privileges. Although this is necessary, the concentration of power can be dangerous. Mitigating controls include segregation of duties and dual controls. *Segregation of duties* requires that tasks be assigned to individuals in such a manner that no one individual can control a process from start to finish. *Dual control* requires that two individuals must both complete their half of a specific task.

Oversight of user and administrator access reflects best practices and, in many cases, a regulatory requirement. At a minimum, three categories of user access should be logged and analyzed: successful access, failed access, and privileged operations. It is incumbent on the organization to institute a log review process as well as incident-responsive procedures for at-risk or suspicious activity.

Access control management policies include Authentication Policy, Access Control Authorization Policy, Network Segmentation Policy, Border Device Security Policy, Remote Access Security Policy, Teleworking Policy, User Access Control and Authorization Policy, Administrative and Privileged Account Policy, and Monitoring System Access and Use Policy.

Test Your Skills

MULTIPLE CHOICE QUESTIONS

1. Which of the following terms best describes access controls that are security features that govern how users and processes interact?

    A. Objects

    B. Resources

    C. Processes

    D. All of the above

2. Which of the following terms best describes the process of verifying the identity of a subject?

    A. Accountability

    B. Authorization

    C. Access model

    D. Authentication

3. Which of the following terms best describes the process of assigning authenticated subjects permission to carry out a specific operation?

    A. Accountability

    B. Authorization

    C. Access model

    D. Authentication

4. Which of the following terms best describes the active entity that requests access to an object or data?

  A. Subject

  B. Object

  C. Resource

  D. Factor

5. Which of the following security principles is best described as giving users the minimum access required to do their jobs?

  A. Least access

  B. Less protocol

  C. Least privilege

  D. Least process

6. Which of the following security principles is best described as prohibiting access to information not required for one's work?

  A. Access need security principle

  B. Need-to-monitor security principle

  C. Need-to-know security principle

  D. Required information process security principle

7. Which type of access is allowed by the security principle of default deny?

  A. Basic access is allowed.

  B. Access that is not explicitly forbidden is permitted.

  C. Access that is not explicitly permitted is forbidden.

  D. None of the above.

8. Which of the following statements best describes security posture?

  A. An organization's approach to access controls based on information about an object, such as a host (end system) or network

  B. An organization's approach to access controls based on information about a network switch or router

  C. An organization's approach to access controls based on information about a router

  D. An organization's approach to access controls based on information about a firewall

9. Who is responsible for defining discretionary access controls (DACs)?

   A. Data owners

   B. Data administrators

   C. Data custodians

   D. Data users

10. Which of the following terms best describes the control that is used when the SOP for user provisioning requires the actions of two systems administrators—one who can create and delete accounts and the other who assigns access permissions?

    A. Least privilege

    B. Segregation of duties

    C. Need-to-know

    D. Default deny

11. Which of the following types of network, operating system, or application access controls is user-agnostic and relies on specific criteria, such as source IP address, time of day, and geographic location?

    A. Mandatory

    B. Role-based

    C. Rule-based

    D. Discretionary

12. Which of the following is not considered an authentication factor?

    A. Knowledge

    B. Inheritance

    C. Possession

    D. Biometric

13. Which of the following terms best describes authentication that requires two or more factors?

    A. Dual control

    B. Multifactor

    C. Multilabel

    D. Multilayer

14. Which of the following statements provides examples of good password management?

    A. Passwords should be changed to increase the complexity and the length of the password.

    B. Passwords should be changed when there is a suspicion that the password has been compromised.

    C. Passwords should be changed to create a unique password after a user initially logs on to a system using a default or basic password.

    D. All of the above.

15. Which of the following terms best describes a type of password that is a form of knowledge-based authentication that requires users to answer a question based on something familiar to them?

    A. Categorical

    B. Cognitive

    C. Complex

    D. Credential

16. Which of the following types of authentication requires two distinct and separate channels to authenticate?

    A. In-band authentication

    B. Mobile authentication

    C. Out-of-band authentication

    D. Out-of-wallet authentication

17. Which of the following terms best describes the internal network that is accessible to authorized users?

    A. Trusted network

    B. DMZ

    C. The Internet

    D. Semi-trusted network

18. Rules related to source and destination IP address, port, and protocol are used by a(n) _____ to determine access.

    A. Firewall

    B. IPS

    C. IDS

    D. VPN

19. Which of the following statements is true of an intrusion detection system (IDS)?

    A. An IDS can disable a connection.

    B. An IDS can respond to identified threats.

    C. An IDS uses signature-based detection and/or anomaly-based detection techniques.

    D. An IDS can delete malicious content.

20. Which of the following terms best describes a VPN?

    A. A VPN provides an encrypted tunnel for transmitting data through an untrusted network.

    B. A VPN is a cost-effective solution for securing remote access.

    C. Both A and B.

    D. Neither A nor B.

EXERCISES

EXERCISE 9.1: Understanding Access Control Concepts

1. Define the following access control management terminology:

	Term	Definition
1.1	Access control	
1.2	Authentication	
1.3	Authorization	
1.4	Default deny	
1.5	Default allow	
1.6	Least privilege	
1.7	Need-to-know	
1.8	Mandatory access control (MAC)	
1.9	Discretionary access control (DAC)	
1.10	Network access control (NAC)	

2. Provide an example of an authentication control that affects you.

3. Provide an example of an authorization control that affects you.

EXERCISE 9.2: **Managing User Accounts and Passwords**

1. How many authentication factors does the email program you use require?

2. What are the required password characteristics for the email program you use? Include length, complexity, expiration, and banned words or phrases.

3. In your opinion, are the requirements adequate?

EXERCISE 9.3: **Understanding Multifactor and Mutual Authentication**

1. Find an image of or take a picture of a possession or inherence authentication device.

2. Find and describe an example of mutual authentication.

3. Explain how one of the preceding works.

EXERCISE 9.4: **Analyzing Firewall Rule Sets**

Firewall rule sets use source IP addresses, destination addresses, ports, and protocols.

1. Describe the function of each.

2. What is the purpose of the following rule?

   Allow Src=10.1.23.54 dest=85.75.32.200 Proto=tcp 21

3. What is the purpose of the following rule?

   Deny Src=ANY dest=ANY Proto=tcp 23

EXERCISE 9.5: **Granting Administrative Access**

1. Do you have administrative rights on your laptop, workstation, or tablet?

2. If yes, do you have the option to also have a normal user account? If no, who does?

3. Explain what is meant by the phrase "security context of the currently logged-in user."

PROJECTS

PROJECT 9.1: **Creating an RFP for Penetration Testing**

You have been asked to send out a red team penetration testing Request for Proposal (RFP) document.

1. Explain what is often referred to as a "red team."

2. What is the difference between a red team and a blue team?

3. Find three companies to send the RFP to. Explain why you chose them.

4. The selected vendor will potentially have access to your network. What due diligence criteria should be included in the vendor selection process? Select one of the companies from the previous step and find out as much as you can about them (for example, reputation, history, credentials).

PROJECT 9.2: **Reviewing User Access Permissions**

Reviewing user access permissions can be a time-consuming and resource-intensive process and is generally reserved for applications or systems that have information classified as "protected" or "confidential."

1. Should the student portal at your school be subject to an annual user access permission audit? If yes, why? If no, why not?

2. Automating review processes contributes to efficiency and accuracy. Research options for automating the user access review process and make a recommendation.

PROJECT 9.3: **Developing Telecommuting Best Practices**

Your organization has decided to allow users the option of working from home.

1. Make a list of six security issues that must be considered.

2. Note your recommendations for each issue and detail any associated security control.

3. Assume that your recommendations have been accepted. You have now been tasked with training teleworkers. Create a presentation that explains "work from home" security best practices.

Case Study

Assessing a Current Security Breach

It often feels like every week there is a major breach. In early 2018 Facebook suffered from a privacy breach. Research this incident and answer the following questions:

1. How did the Facebook breach happen? How did it impact its reputation?

2. Research another breach that is more current. How does it compare to the Facebook breach?

3. Why was the attack successful? What controls were missing that may have prevented or detected the attack?

4. How much did the breach cost each company?

References

Regulations Cited

"Supplement to Authentication in an Internet Banking Environment," issued by the Federal Institutions Examination Council, 6/28/2011.

"The Telework Enhancement Act of 2010, Public Law 111-292," official website of the Government Printing Office, accessed 11/2017, https://www.gpo.gov/fdsys/pkg/BILLS-111hr1722enr/pdf/BILLS-111hr1722enr.pdf.

Other References

Kampanakis, Panos, Omar Santos, and Aaron Woland, *Cisco Next-Generation Security Solutions: All-in-One Cisco ASA Firepower Services, NGIPS, and AMP*, Indianapolis: Cisco Press, 2016.

Santos, Omar, Joseph Muniz, and Stefano De Crescenzo, *CCNA Cyber Ops SECFND 210-250 Official Cert Guide*, First Edition, Indianapolis: Cisco Press, 2017.

"Statistics of 450,000 Leaked Yahoo Accounts," Pastebin, accessed 04/2018, http://pastebin.com/2D6bHGTa.

Larson, Selena, "Every Single Yahoo Account Was Hacked—3 Billion in All," *CNN,* October 4, 2017, accessed 04/2018, http://money.cnn.com/2017/10/03/technology/business/yahoo-breach-3-billion-accounts/index.html.

Saltzer, J. H., and M. D. Schroeder, "The Protection of Information in Computer Systems." Proceedings of the IEEE, vol. 63, no. 9 (Sept. 1975).

"The Telecommuter Infographic, An Analysis of the World's Remote Workforce," MySammy LLC, accessed 04/2018, https://www.mysammy.com/infographics-telecommuter.

"What Is Telecommuting?" Emory University WorkLife Resource Center, accessed 04/2018, www.worklife.emory.edu/workplaceflexibility/telecommuting/whatis.html.

Chapter 10

Information Systems Acquisition, Development, and Maintenance

Chapter Objectives

After reading this chapter and completing the exercises, you will be able to do the following:

- Understand the rationale for the systems development life cycle (SDLC).
- Recognize the stages of software releases.
- Appreciate the importance of developing secure code.
- Be aware of the most common application development security faults.
- Explain cryptographic components.
- Develop policies related to systems acquisition, development, and maintenance.

Section 14 of ISO 27002:2013: "Information Systems Acquisition, Development, and Maintenance (ISADM)" focuses on the security requirements of information systems, application, and code from conception to destruction. This sequence is referred to as the systems development life cycle (SDLC). Particular emphasis is put on vulnerability management to ensure integrity, cryptographic controls to ensure integrity and confidentiality, and security of system files to ensure confidentiality, integrity, and availability (CIA). The domain constructs apply to in-house, outsourced, and commercially developed systems, applications, and code. Section 10 of ISO 27002:2013: "Cryptography," focuses on proper and effective use of cryptography to protect the confidentiality, authenticity, and/or integrity of information. Because cryptographic protection mechanisms are closely related to information systems development and maintenance, it is included in this chapter.

Of all the security domains we have discussed so far, this one has the most widespread implications. Most cybercrime is opportunistic, meaning that the criminals take advantage of the system vulnerabilities. Information systems, applications, and code that does not have embedded security controls all expose the organization to undue risk. Consider a company that relies on a web-based application linked to a back-end database. If the code used to create the web-based application was not thoroughly vetted, it may contain vulnerabilities that would allow a hacker to bring down the application with a denial of service (DoS) attack, run code on the server hosting the application, or even trick the database into publishing classified information. These events harm an organization's reputation, create compliance and legal issues, and significantly impact the bottom line.

FYI: ISO/IEC 27002:2013 and NIST Guidance

Section 10 of ISO 27002:2013, the cryptography domain, focuses on proper and effective use of cryptography to protect the confidentiality, authenticity, and/or integrity of information. Section 14 of ISO 27002:2013, the ISADM domain, focuses on the security requirements of information systems, applications, and code, from conception to destruction.

Corresponding NIST guidance is provided in the following documents:

- **SP 800-23:** "Guidelines to Federal Organizations on Security Assurance and Acquisition/Use of Tested/Evaluated Products"

- **SP 800-57:** "Recommendations for Key Management—Part 1: General (Revision 3)"

- **SP 800-57:** "Recommendations for Key Management—Part 2: Best Practices for Key Management Organization"

- **SP 800-57:** "Recommendations for Key Management—Part 3: Application-Specific Key Management Guidance"

- **SP 800-64:** "Security Considerations in the System Development Life Cycle"

- **SP 800-111:** "Guide to Storage Encryption Technologies for End User Devices"

System Security Requirements

Security should be a priority objective during the design and acquisition phases of any new information system, application, or code development. Attempting to retrofit security is expensive, resource-intensive, and all too often does not work. Productivity requirements and/or the rush to market often preclude a thorough security analysis, which is unfortunate because it has been proven time and time again that early-stage identification of security requirements is both cost-effective and efficient. Utilizing a structured development process increases the probability that security objectives will be achieved.

What Is SDLC?

The *systems development life cycle (SDLC)* provides a standardized process for all phases of any system development or acquisition effort. Figure 10-1 shows the SDLC phases defined by NIST in their Special Publication (SP) 800-64 Revision 2, "Security Considerations in the System Development Life Cycle."

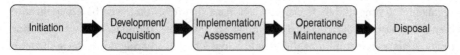

FIGURE 10-1   The Five Phases of SDLC

- During the ***initiation*** phase, the need for a system is expressed, and the purpose of the system is documented.

- During the ***development/acquisition*** phase, the system is designed, purchased, programmed, developed, or otherwise constructed.

- The ***implementation/assessment*** phase includes system testing, modification if necessary, retesting if modified, and finally acceptance.

- During the ***operations/maintenance*** phase, the system is put into production. The system is almost always modified by the addition of hardware and software and by numerous other events. Monitoring, auditing, and testing should be ongoing.

- Activities conducted during the ***disposal*** phase ensure the orderly termination of the system, safeguarding vital system information, and migrating data processed by the system to a new system.

Each phase includes a minimum set of tasks needed to effectively incorporate security in the system development process. Phases may continue to be repeated throughout a system's life prior to disposal.

Initiation Phase

During the initiation phase, the organization establishes the need for a system and documents its purpose. Security planning must begin in the initiation phase. The information to be processed, transmitted, or stored is evaluated for CIA security requirements, as well as the security and criticality requirements of the information system. It is essential that all stakeholders have a common understanding of the security considerations. This early involvement will enable the developers or purchasing managers to plan security requirements and associated constraints into the project. It also reminds project leaders that many decisions being made have security implications that should be weighed appropriately, as the project continues. Other tasks that should be addressed in the initiation phase include assignment of roles and responsibilities, identification of compliance requirements, decisions on security metrics and testing, and the systems acceptance process.

Development/Acquisition Phase

During this phase, the system is designed, purchased, programmed, developed, or otherwise constructed. A key security activity in this phase is conducting a risk assessment. In addition, the organization should analyze security requirements, perform functional and security testing, and design the security architecture. Both the ISO standard and NIST emphasize the importance of conducting risk assessments to evaluate the security requirements for new systems and upgrades. The aim is to identify potential risks associated with the project and to use this information to select baseline security controls. The risk assessment process is iterative and needs to be repeated whenever a new functional requirement is introduced. As they are determined, security control requirements become part of the project security plan. Security controls must be tested to ensure they perform as intended.

Implementation/Assessment Phase

In the implementation phase, the organization configures and enables system security features, tests the functionality of these features, installs or implements the system, and obtains a formal authorization to operate the system. Design reviews and system tests should be performed before placing the system into operation to ensure that it meets all required security specifications. It is important that adequate time be built into the project plan to address any findings, modify the system or software, and retest.

The final task in this phase is authorization. It is the responsibility of the system owner or designee to green light the implementation and allow the system to be placed in production mode. In the federal government, this process is known as *certification and accreditation (C&A)*. OMB Circular A-130 requires the security authorization of an information system to process, store, or transmit information. The authorizing official relies primarily on the completed system security plan, the inherent risk as determined by the risk assessment, and the security test results.

Operations/Maintenance Phase

In this phase, systems and products are in place and operating, enhancements and/or modifications to the system are developed and tested, and hardware and software components are added or replaced. Configuration management and change control processes are essential to ensure that required security controls are maintained. The organization should continuously monitor performance of the system to ensure that it is consistent with pre-established user and security requirements, and that needed system modifications are incorporated. Periodic testing and evaluation of the security controls in an information system must be conducted to ensure continued effectiveness and to identify any new vulnerabilities that may have been introduced or recently discovered. Vulnerabilities identified after implementation cannot be ignored. Depending on the severity of the finding, it may be possible to implement compensating controls while fixes are being developed. There may be situations that require the system to be taken offline until the vulnerabilities can be mitigated.

Disposal Phase

Often, there is no definitive end or retirement of an information system or code. Systems normally evolve or transition to the next generation because of changing requirements or improvements in technology. System security plans should continually evolve with the system. Much of the environmental, management, and operational information for the original system should still be relevant and useful when the organization develops the security plan for the follow-on system. When the time does come to discard system information, hardware, and software, it must not result in the unauthorized disclosure of protected or confidential data. Disposal activities archiving information, sanitization of media, and disposal of hardware components must be done in accordance with the organization's destruction and disposal requirements and policies.

In Practice

Systems Development Life Cycle (SDLC) Policy

Synopsis: Ensure a structured and standardized process for all phases of system development/acquisition efforts, which includes security considerations, requirements, and testing.

Policy Statement:

- The Office of Information Technology is responsible for adopting, implementing, and requiring compliance with an SDLC process and workflow. The SDLC must define initiation, development/acquisition, implementation, operations, and disposal requirements.

- At each phase, security requirements must be evaluated and, as appropriate, security controls tested.

- The system owner, in conjunction with the Office of Information Security, is responsible for defining system security requirements.

- The system owner, in conjunction with the Office of Information Security, is responsible for authorizing production systems prior to implementation.

- If necessary, independent experts may be brought in to evaluate the project or any component thereof.

What About Commercially Available or Open Source Software?

SDLC principles apply to commercially available software—sometimes referred to as *commercial off-the-shelf software (COTS)*—and to open source software. The primary difference is that the development is not done in-house. Commercial software should be evaluated to make sure it meets or exceeds the organization's security requirement. Because software is often released in stages, it is important to be aware of and understand the release stages. Only stable and tested software releases should be deployed on production servers to protect data availability and data integrity. Operating system and application updates should not be deployed until they have been thoroughly tested in a lab environment and declared safe to be released in a production environment. After installation, all software and applications should be included in internal vulnerability testing. Open source software included in in-house applications or any products created by the organization should be registered in a central database for the purpose of licensing requirements and disclosures, as well as to track any vulnerabilities that affect such open source components or software.

Software Releases

The *alpha phase* is the initial release of software for testing. Alpha software can be unstable and can cause crashes or data loss. External availability of alpha software is uncommon in proprietary software. However, open source software, in particular, often has publicly available alpha versions, often distributed as the raw source code of the software. *Beta phase* indicates that the software is feature complete and the focus is usability testing. A *release candidate (RC)* is a hybrid of a beta and a final release version. It has the potential to be the final release unless significant issues are identified. *General availability* or *go live* is when the software has been made commercially available and is in general distribution. Alpha, beta, and RCs have a tendency to be unstable and unpredictable and are not suitable for a production environment. This unpredictability can have devastating consequences, including data exposures, data loss, data corruption, and unplanned downtime.

Software Updates

During its supported lifetime, software is sometimes updated. Updates are different from security patches. *Security patches* are designed to address a specific vulnerability and are applied in accordance with the patch management policy. *Updates* generally include functional enhancements and new features. Updates should be subject to the organization's change management process and should be thoroughly tested before being implemented in a production environment. This is true for both operating systems and applications. For example, a new system utility might work perfectly with 99% of applications, but what if a critical line-of-business application deployed on the same server falls in the remaining 1%? This can have a disastrous effect on the availability, and potentially on the integrity, of the data. This risk, however minimal it may appear, must not be ignored. Even when an update has been thoroughly tested, organizations still need to prepare for the unforeseen and make sure they have a documented *rollback strategy* to return to the previous stable state in case problems occur.

If an update requires a system reboot, it should be delayed until the reboot will have the least impact on business productivity. Typically, this means after hours or on weekends, although if a company is international and has users who rely on data located in different time zones, this can get a bit tricky. If an update does not require a system reboot, but will still severely impact the level of system performance, it should also be delayed until it will have the least impact on business productivity.

Security vulnerability patching for commercial and open source software is one of the most important processes of any organization. An organization may use the following technologies and systems to maintain an appropriate vulnerability management program:

- Vulnerability management software and scanners (such as Qualys, Nexpose, Nessus, etc.)

- Software composition analysis tools (such as BlackDuck Hub, Synopsys Protecode (formerly known as AppCheck), FlexNet Code Insight (formerly known as Palamida), SourceClear, etc.)

- Security vulnerability feeds (such as NIST's National Vulnerability Database (NVD), VulnDB, etc.)

The Testing Environment

The worst-case scenario for a testing environment is that a company does not have one and is willing to have production servers double as test servers. The best-case scenario is that the testing environment is set up as a mirror image of the production environment, software and hardware included. The closer to the production environment the test environment is, the more the test results can be trusted. A cost/benefit analysis that takes into consideration the probability and associated costs of downtime, data loss, and integrity loss will determine how much should be invested in a test or staging environment.

Protecting Test Data

Consider a medical practice with an electronic medical records (EMR) database replete with patient information. Imagine the security measures that have been put in place to make sure the CIA of the data is protected. Because this database is pretty much the lifeblood of this practice and is protected under law, it is to be expected that those security measures are extensive. Live data should never be used in a test environment because it is highly unlikely that the same level of data protection has been implemented, and exposure of protected data would be a serious violation of patient confidentiality and regulatory requirements. Instead, either de-identified data or dummy data should be used. *De-identification* is the process of removing information that would identify the source or subject of the data. Strategies include deleting or masking the name, social security number, date of birth, and demographics. *Dummy data* is, in essence, fictional. For example, rather than using actual patient data to test an EMR database, the medical practice would enter fake patient data into the system. That way, the application could be tested with no violation of confidentiality.

In Practice

System Implementation and Update Policy

Synopsis: Define the requirements for the implementation and maintenance of commercial and open source software.

Policy Statement:

- Operating systems and applications (collectively referred to as "system") implementation and updates must follow the company's change management process.

- Without exception, alpha, beta, or prerelease applications must not be deployed on production systems.

- It is the joint responsibility of the Office of Information Security and the Office of Information Technology to test system implementation and updates prior to deployment in the production environment.

- The Office of Information Technology is responsible for budgeting for and maintaining a test environment that is representative of the production environment.

- Without exception, data classified as "protected" must not be used in a test environment unless it has been de-identified. It is the responsibility of the Office of Information Security to approve the de-identification schema.

FYI: The Open Software Assurance Maturity Model

The **Software Assurance Maturity Model (SAMM)** is an open framework to help organizations formulate and implement a strategy for software security that is tailored to the specific risks facing the organization. The resources provided by SAMM (www.opensamm.org/) will aid in the following:

- Evaluating an organization's existing software security practices

- Building a balanced software security assurance program in well-defined iterations

- Demonstrating concrete improvements to a security assurance program

- Defining and measuring security-related activities throughout an organization

SAMM was defined with flexibility in mind so that it can be utilized by small, medium, and large organizations using any style of development. Additionally, this model can be applied organizationwide, for a single line of business, or even for an individual project. Beyond these traits, SAMM was built on the following principles:

- *An organization's behavior changes slowly over time.* A successful software security program should be specified in small iterations that deliver tangible assurance gains while incrementally working toward long-term goals.

- *There is no single recipe that works for all organizations.* A software security framework must be flexible and allow organizations to tailor their choices based on their risk tolerance and the way in which they build and use software.

- *Guidance related to security activities must be prescriptive.* All the steps in building and assessing an assurance program should be simple, well defined, and measurable. This model also provides roadmap templates for common types of organizations.

Secure Code

The two types of code are insecure code (sometimes referred to as "sloppy code") and secure code. *Insecure code* is sometimes the result of an amateurish effort, but more often than not, it reflects a flawed process. *Secure code*, however, is always the result of a deliberate process that prioritized security from the beginning of the design phase onward. It is important to note that software developers and programmers are human and they will always make mistakes. Having a good secure code program and ways to verify and mitigate the creation of insecure code is paramount for any organization. Examples of mitigations and detection mechanisms include source code and static analysis.

The Open Web Application Security Project (OWASP)

Deploying secure code is the responsibility of the system owner. A number of secure coding resources are available for system owners, project managers, developers, programmers, and information security professionals. One of the most well respected and widely utilized is OWASP (owasp.org). The *Open Web Application Security Project (OWASP)* is an open community dedicated to enabling organizations to develop, purchase, and maintain applications that can be trusted. Everyone is free to participate in OWASP, and all its materials are available under a free and open software license. On a three-year cycle, beginning in 2004, OWASP releases the OWASP Top Ten. The OWASP Top Ten (https://www.owasp.org/index.php/Category:OWASP_Top_Ten_Project) represents a broad consensus about what the most critical web application security flaws are. The information is applicable to a spectrum of nonweb applications, operating systems, and databases. Project members include a variety of security experts from around the world who have shared their expertise to produce this list.

OWASP also has created source code analysis tools (often referred to as Static Application Security Testing (SAST) tools). These tools are designed to analyze source code and/or compiled versions of code to help find security flaws. The following are examples of these tools and projects:

- **OWASP SonarQube Project:** https://www.owasp.org/index.php/OWASP_SonarQube_Project

- **OWASP Orizon Project:** https://www.owasp.org/index.php/Category:OWASP_Orizon_Project

- **OWASP LAPSE Project:** https://www.owasp.org/index.php/OWASP_LAPSE_Project

- **OWASP O2 Platform:** https://www.owasp.org/index.php/OWASP_O2_Platform

- **OWASP WAP-Web Application Protection:** https://www.owasp.org/index.php/OWASP_WAP-Web_Application_Protection

---

FYI: The Common Weakness Enumeration

MITRE led the creation of the Common Weakness Enumeration (CWE), which is a community-driven list of common security weaknesses. Its main purpose is to provide common language and a baseline for weakness identification, mitigation, and prevention efforts. Many organizations use CWE to measure and understand the common security problems introduced in their software and hardware and how to mitigate them. You can obtain more information about CWE at https://cwe.mitre.org.

There are numerous types of vulnerabilities.

What Is Injection?

The most common web application security flaw is the failure to properly validate input from the client or environment. OWASP defines *injection* as when untrusted data is sent to an interpreter as part of a command or query. The attacker's hostile data can trick the interpreter into executing an unintended command or accessing data without proper authorization. The attacker can be anyone who can send data to the systems, including internal users, external users, and administrators. The attack is simply a data string designed to exploit the code vulnerability. Injection flaws are particularly common in older code. A successful attack can result in data loss, corruption, compromise, or a denial of service condition. Preventing injection requires keeping untrusted data separate from commands and queries. The following are examples of injection vulnerabilities:

- Code Injection
- Command Injection
- Comment Injection Attack
- Content Spoofing
- Cross-site Scripting (XSS)
- Custom Special Character Injection
- Function Injection
- Resource Injection
- Server-Side Includes (SSI) Injection
- Special Element Injection
- SQL Injection
- XPATH Injection

Input Validation

Input validation is the process of validating all the input to an application before using it. This includes correct syntax, length, characters, and ranges. Consider a web page with a simple form that contains fields corresponding to your physical address information, such as street name, ZIP code, and so on. After you click the Submit button, the information you entered in the fields is sent to the web server and entered into a back-end database. The objective of input validation is to evaluate the format of entered information and, when appropriate, deny the input. To continue our example, let's focus on the ZIP code field. ZIP codes consist of numbers only, and the basic ones include only five digits. Input validation would look at how many and what type of characters are entered in the field. In this case, the first section of the ZIP code field would require five numeric characters. This limitation would prevent the user from entering more or less than five characters as well as nonnumeric characters. This strategy is known as *whitelist* or *positive validation*.

You may wonder, why bother to go through all this? Who cares if a user sends the wrong ZIP code? Who cares if the information entered in the ZIP code field includes letters and/or ASCII characters? Hackers care. Hackers attempt to pass code in those fields to see how the database will react. They want to see if they can bring down the application (DoS attack against that application), bring down the server on which it resides (DoS against the server, and therefore against all the applications that reside on that server), or run code on the target server to manipulate or publish sensitive data. Proper input validation is therefore a way to limit the ability of a hacker to try to abuse an application system.

Dynamic Data Verification

Many application systems are designed to rely on outside parameter tables for dynamic data. *Dynamic data* is defined as data that changes as updates become available—for example, an e-commerce application that automatically calculates sales tax based on the ZIP code entered. The process of checking that the sales tax rate entered is indeed the one that matches the state entered by the customer is another form of input validation. This is a lot harder to track than when the data input is clearly wrong, such as when a letter is entered in a ZIP code field.

Dynamic data is used by numerous application systems. A simple example is the exchange rate for a particular currency. These values continually change, and using the correct value is critical. If the transaction involves a large sum, the difference can translate into a fair amount of money! Data validation extends to verification that the business rule is also correct.

Output Validation

Output validation is the process of validating (and in some cases, masking) the output of a process before it is provided to the recipient. An example is substituting asterisks for numbers on a credit card receipt. Output validation controls what information is exposed or provided. You need to be aware of output validation, however, especially as it relates to hacker discovery techniques. Hackers look for clues and then use this information as part of the footprinting process. One of the first things a hacker looks to learn about a targeted application is how it reacts to systematic abuse of the interface. A hacker will learn a lot about how the application reacts to errors if the developers did not run output validation tests prior to deployment. They may, for example, learn that a certain application is vulnerable to SQL injection attacks, buffer overflow attacks, and so on. The answer an application gives about an error is potentially a pointer that can lead to vulnerability, and a hacker will try to make that application "talk" to better customize the attack.

Developers test applications by feeding erroneous data into the interface to see how it reacts and what it reveals. This feedback is used to modify the code with the objective of producing a secure application. The more time spent on testing, the less likely hackers will gain the advantage.

Runtime Defenses and Address Randomization

Several runtime defenses and address randomization techniques exist nowadays to prevent threat actors from performing code execution even if a buffer (stack or heap-based) overflow takes place. The most popular technique is address space layout randomization (ASLR). ASRL was created to prevent exploitation of memory corruption vulnerabilities by randomly arranging the address space positions of key data areas of a process. This randomization includes the base of the executable and the positions of the stack, heap and respective libraries.

Another related technique is a position-independent executable (PIE). PIE provides a random base address for the main binary that is being executed. PIE is typically used for network-facing daemons. There is another implementation called the kernel address space layout randomization (KASLR). KASLR's main purpose is to provide address space randomization to running Linux kernel images by randomizing where the kernel code is placed at boot time.

Why Is Broken Authentication and Session Management Important?

If session management assets such as user credentials and session IDs are not properly protected, the session can be hijacked or taken over by a malicious intruder. When authentication credentials are stored or transmitted in clear text, or when credentials can be guessed or overwritten through weak account management functions (for example, account creation, change password, recover password, weak session IDs), the identity of the authorized user can be impersonated. If session IDs are exposed in the URL, do not time out, or are not invalidated after successful logoff, malicious intruders have the opportunity to continue an authenticated session. A critical security design requirement must be strong authentication and session management controls. A common control for protecting authentication credentials and session IDs is encryption. We discussed authentication in Chapter 9, "Access Control Management." We examine encryption and the field of cryptography in the next section of this chapter.

In Practice

Application Development Policy

Synopsis: Define code and application development security requirements.

Policy Statement:

- System owners are responsible for oversight of secure code development.
- Security requirements must be defined and documented during the application development initiation phase.
- Code development will be done in accordance with industry best practices.

- Developers will be provided with adequate training, resources, and time.

- At the discretion of the system owner and with the approval of the Office of Information Security, third parties may be engaged to design, develop, and test internal applications.

- All code developed or customized must be tested and validated during development, prior to release, and whenever a change is implemented.

- The Office of Information Security is responsible for certifying the results of testing and accreditation to move to the next phase.

Cryptography

The art and science of writing secret information is called *cryptography*. The origin of the term involves the Greek words *kryptos*, meaning "hidden," and *graphia*, meaning "writing." Three distinct goals are associated with cryptography:

- **Confidentiality:** Unauthorized parties cannot access the data. Data can be *encrypted*, which provides confidentiality.

- **Integrity:** Assurance is provided that the data was not modified. Data can be *hashed*, which provides integrity.

- **Authenticity/nonrepudiation:** The source of the data is validated. Data can be *digitally signed*, which ensures authentication/nonrepudiation and integrity.

Data can be encrypted and digitally signed, which provides for confidentiality, authentication, and integrity.

Encryption is the conversion of plain text into what is known as *cipher text*, using an algorithm called a *cipher*. **Cipher text** is text that is unreadable by a human or computer. Literally hundreds of encryption algorithms are available, and there are likely many more that are proprietary and used for special purposes, such as for governmental use and national security.

Common methods that ciphers use include the following:

- **Substitution:** This type of cipher substitutes one character for another.

- **Polyalphabetic:** This is similar to substitution, but instead of using a single alphabet, it can use multiple alphabets and switch between them by some trigger character in the encoded message.

- **Transposition:** This method uses many different options, including the rearrangement of letters. For example, if we have the message "This is secret," we could write it out (top to bottom, left to right) as shown in Figure 10-2.

FIGURE 10-2   Transposition Example

We then encrypt it as RETCSIHTSSEI, which involves starting at the top right and going around like a clock, spiraling inward. For someone to know how to encrypt/decrypt this correctly, the correct key is needed.

Decryption, the inverse of encryption, is the process of turning cipher text back into readable plain text. Encryption and decryption require the use of a secret key. The *key* is a value that specifies what part of the algorithm to apply, in what order, and what variables to input. Similar to authentication passwords, it is critical to use a strong key that cannot be discovered and to protect the key from unauthorized access. Protecting the key is generally referred to as *key management*. We examine the use of symmetric and asymmetric keys, as well as key management, later in this chapter.

Ensuring that a message has not been changed in any way during transmission is referred to as *message integrity*. *Hashing* is the process of creating a numeric value that represents the original text. A hash function (such as SHA or MD5) takes a variable size input and produces a fixed size output. The output is referred to as a hash value, message digest, or fingerprint. Unlike encryption, hashing is a one-way process, meaning that the hash value is never turned back into plain text. If the original data has not changed, the hash function should always produce the same value. Comparing the values confirms the integrity of the message. Used alone, hashing provides message integrity and not confidentiality or authentication.

A *digital signature* is a hash value (message digest) that has been encrypted with the sender's private key. The hash must be decrypted with the corresponding key. This proves the identity of the sender. The hash values are then compared to prove the message integrity. Digital signatures provide authenticity/nonrepudiation and message integrity. Nonrepudiation means that the sender cannot deny that the message came from them.

Why Encrypt?

Encryption protects the confidentiality of data at rest and in transit. There are a wide variety of encryption algorithms, techniques, and products. Encryption can be applied granularly, such as to an individual file, or broadly, such as encrypting all stored or transmitted data. Per NIST, the appropriate encryption solution for a particular situation depends primarily on the type of storage, the amount of information that needs to be protected, the environments where the storage will be located, and the threats that need to be mitigated. The three classes of storage ("at rest") encryption techniques are full disk encryption, volume and virtual disk encryption, and file/folder encryption. The array of in-transit encryption protocols and technologies include TLS/SSL (HTTPS), WPA2, VPN, and IPsec. Protecting information in transit safeguards the data as it traverses a wired or wireless network. The current standard specification for encrypting electronic data is the Advanced Encryption Standard (AES). Almost all known attacks against AES's underlying algorithm are computationally infeasible.

Regulatory Requirements

In addition to being a best practice, the need for encryption is cited in numerous federal regulations, including the Gramm-Leach-Bliley Act (GLBA) and HIPAA/HITECH. At the state level, multiple states (including Massachusetts, Nevada, and Washington) have statutes requiring encryption. Massachusetts 201 CMR17 requires encryption of all transmitted records and files containing personal information that will travel across public networks, encryption of all data containing personal information to be transmitted wirelessly, as well as encryption of all personal information stored on laptops or other portable devices. Nevada NRS 603A requires encryption of credit and debit card data as well as encryption of mobile devices and media. Washington HB 2574 requires that personal information, including name combined with social security number, driver's license number, and financial account information, be encrypted if it is transmitted or stored on the Internet.

Another example is the General Data Protection Regulation (GDPR) by the European Commission. One of the GDPR's main goals is to strengthen and unify data protection for individuals within the European Union (EU), while addressing the export of personal data outside the EU. In short, the primary objective of the GDPR is to give citizens back control of their personal data.

What Is a "Key"?

A *key* is a secret code that is used by a cryptographic algorithm. It provides the instructions that result in the functional output. Cryptographic algorithms themselves are generally known. It is the secrecy of the key that provides for security. The number of possible keys that can be used with an algorithm is known as the *keyspace*, which is a large set of random values that the algorithm chooses from when it needs to make a key. The larger the keyspace, the more possibilities for different keys. For example, if an algorithm uses a key that is a string of 10 bits, then its key space is the set of all binary strings of length 10, which results in a keyspace size of 2^{10} (or 1,024); a 40-bit key results in 2^{40} possible values; and a 256-bit key results in 2^{256} possible values. Longer keys are harder to break, but require more computation and processing power. Two factors must be taken into consideration when deciding upon the key length: the desired level of protection and the amount of resources available.

Symmetric Keys

A *symmetric key* algorithm uses a single secret key, which must be shared in advance and be kept private by both the sender and the receiver. Symmetric keys are often referred to as *shared keys*. Because the keys are shared, symmetric algorithms cannot be used to provide nonrepudiation or authenticity. One of the most popular symmetric algorithms of recent years is AES. The strength of symmetric keys is that they are computationally efficient. The weakness is that key management is inherently insecure and that it is not scalable, because a unique key set must be used to protect the secrecy of the key.

Asymmetric Keys

Asymmetric key cryptography, also as known as *public key* cryptography, uses two different but mathematically related keys known as *public* and *private* keys. Think of public and private keys as two keys to the same lock—one used to lock and the other to unlock. The private key never leaves the owner's possession. The public key is given out freely. The public key is used to encrypt plain text or to verify a digital signature, whereas the private key is used to decrypt cipher text or to create a digital signature. Asymmetric key technologies allow for efficient, scalable, and secure key distribution; however, they are computationally resource-intensive.

What Is PKI?

Public key infrastructure (PKI) is the framework and services used to create, distribute, manage, and revoke public keys. PKI is made up of multiple components, including a certification authority (CA), a registration authority (RA), client nodes, and the digital certificate itself:

- The *certification authority (CA)* issues and maintains digital certificates.

- The *registration authority (RA)* performs the administrative functions, including verifying the identity of users and organizations requesting a digital certificate, renewing certificates, and revoking certificates.

- *Client nodes* are interfaces for users, devices, and applications to access PKI functions, including the requesting of certificates and other keying material. They may include cryptographic modules, software, and procedures necessary to provide user access to the PKI.

- A *digital certificate* is used to associate a public key with an identity. Certificates include the certificate holder's public key, serial number of the certificate, certificate holder's distinguished name, certificate validity period, unique name of the certificate issuer, digital signature of the issuer, and signature algorithm identifier.

FYI: Viewing a Digital Certificate

If you are using an Apple Mac operating system, the certificates are stored in the Keychain Access utility. If you are using a Microsoft Windows operating system, digital certificates are stored in the Internet Browser application. Figure 10-3 shows the digital certificate for twitter.com, as an example.

FIGURE 10-3   Example of a Digital Certificate

Why Protect Cryptographic Keys?

As mentioned earlier in the chapter, the usefulness of a cryptographic system is entirely dependent on the secrecy and management of the key. This is so important that NIST has published a three-part document devoted to cryptographic key management guidance. SP 800-67: Recommendations for Key Management, Part 1: General (Revision 3) provides general guidance and best practices for the management of cryptographic keying material. Part 2: Best Practices for Key Management Organization provides guidance on policy and security planning requirements for U.S. government agencies. Part 3: Application Specific Key Management Guidance provides guidance when using the cryptographic features of current systems. In the Overview of Part 1, NIST describes the importance of key management as follows: "The proper management of cryptographic keys is essential to the effective use of cryptography for security. Keys are analogous to the combination of a safe. If a safe combination is known to an adversary, the strongest safe provides no security against penetration. Similarly, poor key management may easily compromise strong algorithms. Ultimately, the security of information protected by cryptography directly depends on the strength of the keys, the effectiveness of mechanisms and protocols associated with keys, and the protection afforded to the keys. All keys need to be protected against modification, and secret and private keys need to be protected against unauthorized disclosure. Key management provides the foundation for the secure generation, storage, distribution, use, and destruction of keys."

Best practices for key management include the following:

- The key length should be long enough to provide the necessary level of protection.

- Keys should be transmitted and stored by secure means.

- Key values should be random, and the full spectrum of the keyspace should be used.

- The key's lifetime should correspond with the sensitivity of the data it is protecting.

- Keys should be backed up in case of emergency. However, multiple copies of keys increase the chance of disclosure and compromise.

- Keys should be properly destroyed when their lifetime ends.

- Keys should never be presented in clear text.

Key management policy and standards should include assigned responsibility for key management, the nature of information to be protected, the classes of threats, the cryptographic protection mechanisms to be used, and the protection requirements for the key and associated processes.

Digital Certificate Compromise

Certification Authorities (CAs) have increasingly become targets for sophisticated cyber attacks. An attacker who breaches a CA to generate and obtain fraudulent certificates can then use the fraudulent certificates to impersonate an individual or organization. In July of 2012, NIST issued an ITL bulletin titled "Preparing for and Responding to Certification Compromise and Fraudulent Certificate Issue." The bulletin primarily focuses on guidance for Certification and Registration Authorities. The bulletin does, however, include the guidance for any organization impacted by the fraud.

The built-in defense against a fraudulently issued certificate is certificate revocation. When a rogue or fraudulent certificate is identified, the CA will issue and distribute a certificate revocation list. Alternatively, a browser may be configured to use the Online Certificate Status Protocol (OCSP) to obtain revocation status.

In Practice

Key Management Policy

Synopsis: To assign responsibility for key management and cryptographic standards.

Policy Statement:

- The Office of Information Security is responsible for key management, including but not limited to algorithm decisions, key length, key security and resiliency, requesting and maintaining digital certificates, and user education. The Office of Information Security will publish cryptographic standards.

- The Office of Information Technology is responsible for implementation and operational management of cryptographic technologies.

- Without exception, encryption is required whenever protected or confidential information is transmitted externally. This includes email and file transfer. The encryption mechanism must be NIST-approved.

- Without exception, all portable media that stores or has the potential to store protected or confidential information must be encrypted. The encryption mechanism must be NIST-approved.

- Data at rest must be encrypted regardless of media when required by state and/or federal regulation or contractual agreement.

- At all times, passwords and PINs must be stored and transmitted as cipher text.

FYI: Small Business Note

Encryption keeps valuable data safe. Every organization, irrespective of size, should encrypt the following if there is any chance that legally protected or company confidential data will be stored or transmitted:

- Mobile devices, such as laptops, tablets, smartphones

- Removable media, such as USB drives and backup tapes

- Internet traffic, such as file transfer or email

- Remote access to the company network

- Wireless transmission

When creating the secure key, make sure to use a long random string of numbers, letters, and special characters.

Summary

Whether they are developed in-house, purchased, or open source, companies rely on line-of-business applications. This reliance implies that the availability of those solutions must be protected to avoid severe losses in revenue; the integrity must be protected to avoid unauthorized modification; and the confidentiality must be protected to honor the public trust and maintain compliance with regulatory requirements.

Custom applications should be built with security in mind from the start. Adopting an SDLC methodology that integrates security considerations ensures that this objective is met. The SDLC provides a structured and standardized process for all phases of any system development effort. During the initiation phase, the need for a system is expressed and the purpose of the system is documented. During the development/acquisition phase, the system is designed, purchased, programmed, developed, or otherwise constructed. During the implementation phase, the system is tested, modified if necessary, retested if modified, and finally accepted. During the operational phase, the system is put into production. Monitoring, auditing, and testing should be ongoing. Activities conducted during the disposal phase ensure the orderly termination of the system, safeguarding vital system information, and migrating data processed by the system to a new system.

SDLC principles extend to COTS (commercial off-the-shelf) software as well as open source software. It is important to recognize the stages of software releases. The alpha phase is the initial release of software for testing. Beta phase indicates that the software is feature-complete and the focus is usability testing. A release candidate (RC) is a hybrid of a beta and a final release version. General availability or "go live" is when the software has been made commercially available and is in general distribution. Alpha, beta, and RCs should never be implemented in a production environment. Over the course of time, publishers may release updates and security patches. Updates generally include enhancements and new features. Updates should be thoroughly tested before release to a production environment. Even tested applications should have a rollback strategy in case the unexpected happens. Live data should never be used in a test environment; instead, de-identified or dummy data should be used.

The Open Web Application Security Project (OWASP) is an open community dedicated to enabling organizations to develop, purchase, and maintain applications that can be trusted.

The Software Assurance Maturity Model (SAMM) is an open framework to help organizations formulate and implement a strategy for software security that is tailored to the specific risks facing the organization. Throughout recent years, OWASP rated injection flaws as the number-one software and database security issue. Injection is when untrusted data is sent to an interpreter as part of a command or query. Input and output validation minimizes injection vulnerabilities. Input validation is the process of validating all the input to an application before using it. This includes correct syntax, length, characters, and ranges. Output validation is the process of validating (and in some cases, masking) the output of a process before it is provided to the recipient.

Data at rest and in transit may require cryptographic protection. Three distinct goals are associated with cryptography: Data can be encrypted, which provides confidentiality. Data can be hashed, which provides integrity. Data can be digitally signed, which provides authenticity/nonrepudiation and integrity. Also, data can be encrypted and digitally signed, which provides for confidentiality, authentication, and integrity. Encryption is the conversion of plain text into what is known as cipher text, using an algorithm called a cipher. Decryption, the inverse of encryption, is the process of turning cipher text back into readable plain text. Hashing is the process of creating a fixed-length value known as a fingerprint that represents the original text. A digital signature is a hash value (also known as a message digest) that has been encrypted with the sender's private key.

A key is a value that specifies what part of the cryptographic algorithm to apply, in what order, and what variables to input. The keyspace is a large set of random values that the algorithm chooses from when it needs to make a key. Symmetric key algorithms use a single secret key, which must be shared in advance and kept private by both the sender and the receiver. Asymmetric key cryptography, also known as public key cryptography, uses two different but mathematically related keys known as public and private keys. A digital certificate is used to associate a public key with an identity.

A public key infrastructure (PKI) is used to create, distribute, manage, and revoke asymmetric keys. A certification authority (CA) issues and maintains digital certificates. A registration authority (RA) performs the administrative functions, including verifying the identity of users and organizations requesting a digital certificate, renewing certificates, and revoking certificates. Client nodes are interfaces for users, devices, and applications to access PKI functions, including the requesting of certificates and other keying material. They may include cryptographic modules, software, and procedures necessary to provide user access to the PKI.

Information Systems Acquisition, Development, and Maintenance (ISADM) policies include SDLC, Application Development, and Key Management.

Test Your Skills

MULTIPLE CHOICE QUESTIONS

1. When is the best time to think about security when building an application?

   A. Build the application first and then add a layer of security.

   B. From the planning and design phase and through the whole development life cycle.

   C. Start the application development phase, and when you reach the halfway point, you have enough of a basis to look at to decide where and how to set up the security elements.

   D. No security needs to be developed inside of the code itself. It will be handled at the operating system level.

2. Which of the following statements best describes the purpose of the systems development life cycle (SDLC)?

    A. The purpose of the SDLC is to provide a framework for system development efforts.

    B. The purpose of the SDLC is to provide a standardized process for system development efforts.

    C. The purpose of the SDLC is to assign responsibility.

    D. All of the above.

3. In which phase of the SDLC is the need for a system expressed and the purpose of the system documented?

    A. The initiation phase

    B. The implementation phase

    C. The operational phase

    D. The disposal phase

4. In which phase of the SDLC should design reviews and system tests be performed to ensure that all required security specifications are met?

    A. The initiation phase

    B. The implementation phase

    C. The operational phase

    D. The disposal phase

5. Which of the following statements is true?

    A. Retrofitting security controls to an application system after implementation is normal; this is when security controls should be added.

    B. Retrofitting security controls to an application system after implementation is sometimes necessary based on testing and assessment results.

    C. Retrofitting security controls to an application system after implementation is always a bad idea.

    D. Retrofitting security controls to an application system after implementation is not necessary because security is handled at the operating system level.

6. Which phase of software release indicates that the software is feature-complete?

    A. Alpha

    B. Beta

    C. Release candidate

    D. General availability

7. Which phase of software release is the initial release of software for testing?

   A. Alpha

   B. Beta

   C. Release candidate

   D. General availability

8. Which of the following statements best describes the difference between a security patch and an update?

   A. Patches provide enhancements; updates fix security vulnerabilities.

   B. Patches should be tested; updates do not need to be tested.

   C. Patches fix security vulnerabilities; updates add features and functionality.

   D. Patches cost money; updates are free.

9. The purpose of a rollback strategy is to _____.

   A. make backing up easier

   B. return to a previous stable state in case problems occur

   C. add functionality

   D. protect data

10. Which of the following statements is true?

   A. A test environment should always be exactly the same as the live environment.

   B. A test environment should be as cheap as possible, no matter what.

   C. A test environment should be as close to the live environment as possible.

   D. A test environment should include live data for true emulation of the real-world setup.

11. Which of the following statements best describes when dummy data should be used?

   A. Dummy data should be used in the production environment.

   B. Dummy data should be used in the testing environment.

   C. Dummy data should be used in both test and production environments.

   D. Dummy data should not be used in either test or production environments.

12. Which of the following terms best describes the process of removing information that would identify the source or subject?

   A. Detoxification

   B. Dumbing down

   C. Development

   D. De-identification

13. Which of the following terms best describes the open framework designed to help organizations implement a strategy for secure software development?

   A. OWASP

   B. SAMM

   C. NIST

   D. ISO

14. Which of the following statements best describes an injection attack?

   A. An injection attack occurs when untrusted data is sent to an interpreter as part of a command.

   B. An injection attack occurs when trusted data is sent to an interpreter as part of a query.

   C. An injection attack occurs when untrusted email is sent to a known third party.

   D. An injection attack occurs when untrusted data is encapsulated.

15. Input validation is the process of _____.

   A. masking data

   B. verifying data syntax

   C. hashing input

   D. trusting data

16. Which of the following types of data change as updates become available?

   A. Moving data

   B. Mobile data

   C. Dynamic data

   D. Delta data

17. The act of limiting the characters that can be entered into a web form is known as
_____.

    A. output validation

    B. input validation

    C. output testing

    D. input testing

18. Which statement best describes a distinguishing feature of cipher text?

    A. Cipher text is unreadable by a human.

    B. Cipher text is unreadable by a machine.

    C. Both A and B.

    D. Neither A nor B.

19. Which term best describes the process of transforming plain text to cipher text?

    A. Decryption

    B. Hashing

    C. Validating

    D. Encryption

20. Which of the following statements is true?

    A. Digital signatures guarantee confidentiality only.

    B. Digital signatures guarantee integrity only.

    C. Digital signatures guarantee integrity and nonrepudiation.

    D. Digital signatures guarantee nonrepudiation only.

21. Hashing is used to ensure message integrity by _____.

    A. comparing hash values

    B. encrypting data

    C. encapsulating data

    D. comparing algorithms and keys

22. When unauthorized data modification occurs, which of the following tenets of security is directly being threatened?

    A. Confidentiality

    B. Integrity

    C. Availability

    D. Authentication

23. Which of the following statements about encryption is true?

    A. All encryption methods are equal: Just choose one and implement it.

    B. The security of the encryption relies on the key.

    C. Encryption is not needed for internal applications.

    D. Encryption guarantees integrity and availability, but not confidentiality.

24. Which of the following statements about a hash function is true?

    A. A hash function takes a variable-length input and turns it into a fixed-length output.

    B. A hash function takes a variable-length input and turns it into a variable-length output.

    C. A hash function takes a fixed-length input and turns it into a fixed-length output.

    D. A hash function takes a fixed-length input and turns it into a variable-length output.

25. Which of the following values represents the number of available values in a 256-bit keyspace?

    A. 2×2^{256}

    B. 2×256

    C. 256^2

    D. 2^{256}

26. Which of the following statements is *not* true about a symmetric key algorithm?

    A. Only one key is used.

    B. It is computationally efficient.

    C. The key must be publicly known.

    D. AES is widely used.

27. The contents of a _____ include the issuer, subject, valid dates, and public key.

   A. digital document

   B. digital identity

   C. digital thumbprint

   D. digital certificate

28. Two different but mathematically related keys are referred to as _____.

   A. public and private keys

   B. secret keys

   C. shared keys

   D. symmetric keys

29. In cryptography, which of the following is *not* publicly available?

   A. Algorithm

   B. Public key

   C. Digital certificate

   D. Symmetric key

30. A hash value that has been encrypted with the sender's private key is known as a _____.

   A. message digest

   B. digital signature

   C. digital certificate

   D. cipher text

EXERCISES

EXERCISE 10.1: Building Security into Applications

1. Explain why security requirements should be considered at the beginning stages of a development project.

2. Who is responsible for ensuring that security requirements are defined?

3. In which phases of the SDLC should security be evaluated?

EXERCISE 10.2: **Understanding Input Validation**

1. Define input validation.

2. Describe the type of attack that is related to poor input validation.

3. In the following scenario, what should the input validation parameters be?
   A class registration web form requires that students enter their current year. The entry options are numbers from 1 to 4 that represent the following: freshmen=1, sophomores=2, juniors=3, and seniors=4.

EXERCISE 10.3: **Researching Software Releases**

1. Find an example of commercially available software that is available as either a beta version or a release candidate.

2. Find an example of open source software that is available as either an alpha, beta, or release candidate.

3. For each, does the publisher include a disclaimer or warning?

EXERCISE 10.4: **Learning About Cryptography**

1. Access the National Security Agency's CryptoKids website.

2. Play at least two of the games.

3. Explain what you learned.

EXERCISE 10.5: **Understanding Updates and Systems Maintenance**

1. Microsoft bundles feature and function updates and refers to them as "service packs." Locate a recently released service pack.

2. Does the service pack have a rollback option?

3. Explain why a rollback strategy is important when upgrading an operating system or application.

PROJECTS

PROJECT 10.1: Creating a Secure App

You have obtained financing to design a mobile device app that integrates with your school's student portal so that students can easily check their grades from anywhere.

1. Create a list of security concerns. For each concern, indicate if the issue is related to confidentiality, integrity, availability (CIA), or any combination thereof.

2. Create a project plan using the SDLC framework as a guide. Describe your expectations for each phase. Be sure to include roles and responsibilities.

3. Research and recommend an independent security firm to test your application. Explain why you chose them.

PROJECT 10.2: Researching the Open Web Application Security Project (OWASP)

The OWASP Top Ten has become a must-read resource. Go to https://www.owasp.org and access the current OWASP Top Ten Web Application report.

1. Read the entire report.

2. Write a memo addressed to Executive Management on why they should read the report. Include in your memo what OWASP means by "It's About Risks, Not Weaknesses" on page 20.

3. Write a second memo addressed to developers and programmers on why they should read the report. Include in your memo references to other OWASP resources that would be of value to them.

PROJECT 10.3: Researching Digital Certificates

You have been tasked with obtaining an extended validation SSL digital certificate for an online shopping portal.

1. Research and choose an issuing CA. Explain why you chose the specific CA.

2. Describe the process and requirements for obtaining a digital certificate.

3. Who in the organization should be tasked with installing the certificate and why?

References

Regulations Cited

"201 Cmr 17.00: Standards for the Protection of Personal Information of Residents of the Commonwealth," official website of the Office of Consumer Affairs & Business Regulation (OCABR), accessed 04/2017, www.mass.gov/ocabr/docs/idtheft/201cmr1700reg.pdf.

"HIPAA Security Rule," official website of the Department of Health and Human Services, accessed 04/2017, https://www.hhs.gov/hipaa/for-professionals/security/index.html.

State of Nevada, "Chapter 603A—Security of Personal Information," accessed 04/2017, https://www.leg.state.nv.us/NRS/NRS-603A.html.

State of Washington, "HB 2574, An Act Relating to Securing Personal Information Accessible Through the Internet," accessed 04/2017, http://apps.leg.wa.gov/documents/billdocs/2007-08/Pdf/Bills/House%20Bills/2574.pdf.

Other References

"Certificate," Microsoft Technet, accessed 04/2017, https://technet.microsoft.com/en-us/library/cc700805.aspx.

Santos, Omar, Joseph Muniz, and Stefano De Crescenzo, *CCNA Cyber Ops SECFND 210-250 Official Cert Guide*, Cisco Press: Indianapolis, 2017.

Kak, Avi, "Lecture 15: Hashing for Message Authentication, Lecture Notes on Computer and Network Security," Purdue University, accessed 04/2017, https://engineering.purdue.edu/kak/compsec/NewLectures/Lecture15.pdf.

"OpenSAMM: Software Assurance Maturity Model," accessed 04/2017, www.opensamm.org.

"RFC 6960, X.509 Internet Public Key Infrastructure Online Certificate Status Protocol—OCSP," June 2013, Internet Engineering Task Force, accessed 04/2017, https://tools.ietf.org/html/rfc6960.

"RFC 5280, Internet X.509 Public Key Infrastructure Certificate and Certificate Revocation List (CRL) Profile," May 2008, Internet Engineering Task Force, accessed 04/2017, https://tools.ietf.org/html/rfc5280.

Chapter 11

Cybersecurity Incident Response

Chapter Objectives

After reading this chapter and completing the exercises, you will be able to do the following:

- Prepare for a cybersecurity incident.
- Identify a cybersecurity incident.
- Understand the incident response plan.
- Understand the incident response process.
- Understand information sharing and coordination.
- Identify incident response team structure.
- Understand federal and state data breach notification requirements.
- Consider an incident from the perspective of the victim.
- Create policies related to security incident management.

Incidents happen. Security-related incidents have become not only more numerous and diverse but also more damaging and disruptive. A single incident can cause the demise of an entire organization. In general terms, incident management is defined as a predicable response to damaging situations. It is vital that organizations have the practiced capability to respond quickly, minimize harm, comply with breach-related state laws and federal regulations, and maintain their composure in the face of an unsettling and unpleasant experience.

Incident Response

Incidents drain resources, can be very expensive, and can divert attention from the business of doing business. Keeping the number of incidents as low as possible should be an organizational priority. That means as much as possible identifying and remediating weaknesses and vulnerabilities before they are exploited. As we discussed in Chapter 4, "Governance and Risk Management," a sound approach to improving an organizational security posture and preventing incidents is to conduct periodic risk assessments of systems and applications. These assessments should determine what risks are posed by combinations of threats, threat sources, and vulnerabilities. Risks can be mitigated, transferred, or avoided until a reasonable overall level of acceptable risk is reached. However, it is important to realize that users will make mistakes, external events may be out of an organization's control, and malicious intruders are motivated. Unfortunately, even the best prevention strategy isn't always enough, which is why preparation is key.

Incident preparedness includes having policies, strategies, plans, and procedures. Organizations should create written guidelines, have supporting documentation prepared, train personnel, and engage in mock exercises. An actual incident is not the time to learn. Incident handlers must act quickly and make far-reaching decisions—often while dealing with uncertainty and incomplete information. They are under a great deal of stress. The more prepared they are, the better the chance that sound decisions will be made.

Computer security incident response is a critical component of information technology (IT) programs. The incident response process and incident handling activities can be very complex. To establish a successful incident response program, you must dedicate substantial planning and resources. Several industry resources were created to help organizations establish a computer security incident response program and learn how to handle cybersecurity incidents efficiently and effectively. One of the best resources available is NIST Special Publication 800-61, which can be obtained from the following URL:

http://nvlpubs.nist.gov/nistpubs/SpecialPublications/NIST.SP.800-61r2.pdf

NIST developed Special Publication 800-61 due to statutory responsibilities under the Federal Information Security Management Act (FISMA) of 2002, Public Law 107-347.

The benefits of having a practiced incident response capability include the following:

- Calm and systematic response

- Minimization of loss or damage

- Protection of affected parties

- Compliance with laws and regulations

- Preservation of evidence

- Integration of lessons learned

- Lower future risk and exposure

FYI: United States Computer Emergency Readiness Team (US-CERT)

US-CERT is the 24-hour operational arm of the Department of Homeland Security's National Cybersecurity and Communications Integration Center (NCCIC). US-CERT accepts, triages, and collaboratively responds to incidents; provides technical assistance to information system operators; and disseminates timely notifications regarding current and potential security threats and vulnerabilities.

US-CERT also distributes vulnerability and threat information through its National Cyber Awareness System (NCAS). There are four mailing lists that anyone can subscribe to:

- **Alerts:** Timely information about current security issues, vulnerabilities, and exploits.

- **Bulletins:** Weekly summaries of new vulnerabilities. Patch information is provided when available.

- **Tips:** Advice about common security issues for the general public.

- **Current Activity:** Up-to-date information about high-impact types of security activity affecting the community at large.

To subscribe, visit https://public.govdelivery.com/accounts/USDHSUSCERT/subscriber/new.

What Is an Incident?

A *cybersecurity incident* is an adverse event that threatens business security and/or disrupts service. Sometimes confused with a disaster, an information security incident is related to loss of confidentiality, integrity, or availability (CIA), whereas a disaster is an event that results in widespread damage or destruction, loss of life, or drastic change to the environment. Examples of incidents include exposure of or modification of legally protected data, unauthorized access to intellectual property, or disruption of internal or external services. The starting point of incident management is to create an organization-specific definition of the term *incident* so that the scope of the term is clear. Declaration of an incident should trigger a mandatory response process.

Not all security incidents are the same. For example, a breach of personally identifiable information (PII) typically requires strict disclosure under many circumstances. The OMB Memorandum M-07-16, "Safeguarding Against and Responding to the Breach of Personally Identifiable Information," requires Federal agencies to develop and implement a breach notification policy for PII. Another example is Article 33 of the GDPR, "Notification of a personal data breach to the supervisory authority," which specifies that any organization under regulation must report a data breach within 72 hours. NIST defines a privacy breach as follows: "when sensitive PII of taxpayers, employees, beneficiaries, etc. was accessed or exfiltrated." NIST also defines a proprietary breach as when "unclassified proprietary information, such as protected critical infrastructure information (PCII), was accessed or exfiltrated." An integrity breach is when sensitive or proprietary information was changed or deleted.

Before you learn the details about how to create a good incident response program within your organization, you must understand the difference between security *events* and security *incidents*. The following is from NIST Special Publication 800-61:

"An event is any observable occurrence in a system or network. Events include a user connecting to a file share, a server receiving a request for a web page, a user sending email, and a firewall blocking a connection attempt. Adverse events are events with a negative consequence, such as system crashes, packet floods, unauthorized use of system privileges, unauthorized access to sensitive data, and execution of malware that destroys data."

According to the same document, "a computer security incident is a violation or imminent threat of violation of computer security policies, acceptable use policies, or standard security practices."

The definition and criteria should be codified in policy. Incident management extends to third-party environments. As we discussed in Chapter 8, "Communications and Operations Security," business partners and vendors should be contractually obligated to notify the organization if an actual or suspected incident occurs.

Table 11-1 lists a few examples of cybersecurity incidents.

TABLE 11-1   Cybersecurity Incident Examples

Incident	Description
1	Attacker sends a crafted packet to a router and causes a denial of service condition.
2	Attacker compromises a point-of-sale (POS) system and steals credit card information.
3	Attacker compromises a hospital database and steals thousands of health records.
4	Ransomware is installed in a critical server and all files are encrypted by the attacker.

In Practice

Incident Definition Policy

Synopsis: To define organizational criteria pertaining to an information security incident.

Policy Statement:

- An information security incident is an event that has the potential to adversely impact the company, our clients, our business partners, and/or the public-at-large.

- An information security incident is defined as the following:

  - Actual or suspected unauthorized access to, compromise of, acquisition of, or modification of protected client or employee data, including but not limited to:

    - Personal identification numbers, such as social security numbers (SSNs), passport numbers, driver's license numbers

    - Financial account or credit card information, including account numbers, card numbers, expiration dates, cardholder names, and service codes

    - Health care/medical information

  - Actual or suspected event that has the capacity to disrupt the services provided to our clients.

  - Actual or suspected unauthorized access to, compromise of, acquisition of, or modification of company intellectual property.

  - Actual or suspected event that has the capacity to disrupt the company's ability to provide internal computing and network services.

  - Actual or suspected event that is in violation of legal or statutory requirements.

  - Actual or suspected event not defined above that warrants incident classification as determined by management.

- All employees, contractors, consultants, vendors, and business partners are required to report known or suspected information security incidents.

- This policy applies equally to internal and third-party incidents.

Although any number of events could result in an incident, a core group of attacks or situations are most common. Every organization should understand and be prepared to respond to intentional unauthorized access, distributed denial of service (DDoS) attacks, malicious code (malware), and inappropriate usage.

Intentional Unauthorized Access or Use

An intentional unauthorized access incident occurs when an insider or intruder gains logical or physical access without permission to a network, system, application, data, or other resource. Intentional unauthorized access is typically gained through the exploitation of operating system or application vulnerabilities using malware or other targeted exploits, the acquisition of usernames and passwords, the physical acquisition of a device, or social engineering. Attackers may acquire limited access through one vector and use that access to move to the next level.

Denial of Service (DoS) Attacks

A *denial of service (DoS) attack* is an attack that successfully prevents or impairs the normal authorized functionality of networks, systems, or applications by exhausting resources or in some way obstructs or overloads the communication channel. This attack may be directed at the organization or may be consuming resources as an unauthorized participant in a DoS attack. DoS attacks have become an increasingly severe threat, and the lack of availability of computing and network services now translates to significant disruption and major financial loss.

> **Note**
>
> Refer to Chapter 8 for a description of DOS attacks.

> **FYI: The Mirai Botnet**
>
> The Mirai botnet has been called the Internet of Things (IoT) Botnet responsible for launching the historically large distributed denial-of-service (DDoS) attack against KrebsOnSecurity and several other victims. Mirai is basically malware that compromises networking devices running Linux into remotely controlled bots that can be used as part of a botnet in large-scale DDoS attacks. This malware mostly targets online consumer devices such as IP cameras and home routers. You can access several articles about this botnet and malware at: https://krebsonsecurity.com/tag/mirai-botnet.

> **FYI: False Positives, False Negatives, True Positives, and True Negatives**
>
> The term *false positive* is a broad term that describes a situation in which a security device triggers an alarm but there is no malicious activity or an actual attack taking place. In other words, false positives are "false alarms," and they are also called "benign triggers." False positives are problematic because by triggering unjustified alerts, they diminish the value and urgency of real alerts. If you have too many false positives to investigate, it becomes an operational nightmare, and you most definitely will overlook real security events.
>
> There are also false negatives, which is the term used to describe a network intrusion device's inability to detect true security events under certain circumstances—in other words, a malicious activity that is not detected by the security device.

A true positive is a successful identification of a security attack or a malicious event. A true negative is when the intrusion detection device identifies an activity as acceptable behavior and the activity is actually acceptable.

Traditional IDS and IPS devices need to be tuned to avoid false positives and false negatives. Next-generation IPSs do not need the same level of tuning compared to a traditional IPS. Also, you can obtain much deeper reports and functionality, including advanced malware protection and retrospective analysis to see what happened after an attack took place.

Traditional IDS and IPS devices also suffer from many evasion attacks. The following are some of the most common evasion techniques against traditional IDS and IPS devices:

- **Fragmentation:** When the attacker evades the IPS box by sending fragmented packets.

- **Using low-bandwidth attacks:** When the attacker uses techniques that use low-bandwidth or a very small number of packets in order to evade the system.

- **Address spoofing/proxying:** Using spoofed IP addresses or sources, as well as using intermediary systems such as proxies to evade inspection.

- **Pattern change evasion:** Attackers may use polymorphic techniques to create unique attack patterns.

- **Encryption:** Attackers can use encryption to hide their communication and information.

Malware

Malware has become the tool of choice for cybercriminals, hackers, and hacktivists. *Malware* (malicious software) refers to code that is covertly inserted into another program with the intent of gaining unauthorized access, obtaining confidential information, disrupting operations, destroying data, or in some manner compromising the security or integrity of the victim's data or system. Malware is designed to function without the user's knowledge. There are multiple categories of malware, including virus, worm, Trojans, bots, ransomware, rootkits, and spyware/adware. Suspicion of or evidence of malware infection should be considered an incident. Malware that has been successfully quarantined by antivirus software should not be considered an incident.

Note

Refer to Chapter 8 for an extensive discussion of malware.

Inappropriate Usage

An inappropriate usage incident occurs when an authorized user performs actions that violate internal policy, agreement, law, or regulation. Inappropriate usage can be internal facing, such as accessing data when there is clearly not a "need to know." An example would be when an employee or contractor views a patient's medical records or a bank customer's financial records purely for curiosity's sake, or when the employee or contractor shares information with unauthorized users. Conversely, the perpetrator can be an insider, and the victim can be a third party (for example, the downloading of music or video in violation of copyright laws).

Incident Severity Levels

Not all incidents are equal in severity. Included in the incident definition should be severity levels based on the operational, reputational, and legal impact to the organization. Corresponding to the level should be required response times as well as minimum standards for internal notification. Table 11-2 illustrates this concept.

TABLE 11-2   Incident Severity Level Matrix

An information security incident is any adverse event whereby some aspect of an information system or information itself is threatened. Incidents are classified by severity relative to the impact they have on an organization. This severity level is typically assigned by an incident manager or a cybersecurity investigator. How it is validated depends on the organizational structure and the incident response policy. Each level has a maximum response time and minimum internal notification requirements.

Severity Level = 1	
Explanation	Level 1 incidents are defined as those that could cause significant harm to the business, customers, or the public and/or are in violation of corporate law, regulation, or contractual obligation.
Required Response Time	Immediate.
Required Internal Notification	Chief Executive Officer. Chief Operating Officer. Legal counsel. Chief Information Security Officer. Designated incident handler.
Examples	Compromise or suspected compromise of protected customer information. Theft or loss of any device or media on any device that contains legally protected information. A denial of service attack. Identified connection to "command and control" sites. Compromise or suspected compromise of any company website or web presence. Notification by a business partner or vendor of a compromise or potential compromise of a customer or customer-related information. Any act that is in direct violation of local, state, or federal law or regulation.

Severity Level = 2	
Explanation	Level 2 incidents are defined as compromise of or unauthorized access to noncritical systems or information; detection of a precursor to a focused attack; a believed threat of an imminent attack; or any act that is a potential violation of law, regulation, or contractual obligation.
Required Response Time	Within four hours.
Required Internal Notification	Chief Operating Officer. Legal counsel. Chief Information Security Officer. Designated incident handler.
Examples	Inappropriate access to legally protected or proprietary information. Malware detected on multiple systems. Warning signs and/or reconnaissance detected related to a potential exploit. Notification from a third party of an imminent attack.
Severity Level = 3	
Explanation	Level 3 incidents are defined as situations that can be contained and resolved by the information system custodian, data/process owner, or HR personnel. There is no evidence or suspicion of harm to customer or proprietary information, processes, or services.
Required Response Time	Within 24 hours.
Required Internal Notification	Chief Information Security Officer. Designated incident handler.
Examples	Malware detected and/or suspected on a workstation or device, with no external connections identified. User access to content or sites restricted by policy. User's excessive use of bandwidth or resources.

How Are Incidents Reported?

Incident reporting is best accomplished by implementing simple, easy-to-use mechanisms that can be used by all employees to report the discovery of an incident. Employees should be required to report all actual and suspected incidents. They should not be expected to assign a severity level, because the person who discovers an incident may not have the skill, knowledge, or training to properly assess the impact of the situation.

People frequently fail to report potential incidents because they are afraid of being wrong and looking foolish, they do not want to be seen as a complainer or whistleblower, or they simply don't care enough and would prefer not to get involved. These objections must be countered by encouragement from management. Employees must be assured that even if they were to report a perceived incident that ended up being a false positive, they would not be ridiculed or met with annoyance. On the contrary, their willingness to get involved for the greater good of the company is exactly the type of behavior the company needs! They should be supported for their efforts and made to feel valued and appreciated for doing the right thing.

Digital forensic evidence is information in digital form found on a wide range of endpoint, server, and network devices—basically, any information that can be processed by a computing device or stored on other media. Evidence tendered in legal cases, such as criminal trials, is classified as witness testimony or direct evidence, or as indirect evidence in the form of an object, such as a physical document, the property owned by a person, and so forth.

Cybersecurity forensic evidence can take many forms, depending on the conditions of each case and the devices from which the evidence was collected. To prevent or minimize contamination of the suspect's source device, you can use different tools, such as a piece of hardware called a write blocker, on the specific device so you can copy all the data (or an image of the system).

The imaging process is intended to copy all blocks of data from the computing device to the forensics professional evidentiary system. This is sometimes referred to as a "physical copy" of all data, as distinct from a "logical copy," which copies only what a user would normally see. Logical copies do not capture all the data, and the process will alter some file metadata to the extent that its forensic value is greatly diminished, resulting in a possible legal challenge by the opposing legal team. Therefore, a full bit-for-bit copy is the preferred forensic process. The file created on the target device is called a *forensic image file*.

Chain of custody is the way you document and preserve evidence from the time that you started the cyber forensics investigation to the time the evidence is presented in court. It is extremely important to be able to show clear documentation of the following:

- How the evidence was collected
- When it was collected
- How it was transported
- How is was tracked
- How it was stored
- Who had access to the evidence and how it was accessed

A method often used for evidence preservation is to work only with a copy of the evidence—in other words, you do not want to work directly with the evidence itself. This involves creating an image of any hard drive or any storage device. Additionally, you must prevent electronic static or other discharge from damaging or erasing evidentiary data. Special evidence bags that are antistatic should be used to store digital devices. It is very important that you prevent electrostatic discharge (ESD) and other electrical discharges from damaging your evidence. Some organizations even have cyber forensic labs that control access to only authorized users and investigators. One method often used involves constructing what is called a *Faraday cage*. This cage is often built out of a mesh of conducting material that prevents electromagnetic energy from entering into or escaping from the cage. Also, this prevents devices from communicating via Wi-Fi or cellular signals.

What's more, transporting the evidence to the forensics lab or any other place, including the court-house, has to be done very carefully. It is critical that the chain of custody be maintained during this transport. When you transport the evidence, you should strive to secure it in a lockable container. It is also recommended that the responsible person stay with the evidence at all times during transportation.

In Practice

Information Security Incident Classification Policy

Synopsis: Classify incidents by severity and assigned response and notification requirements.

Policy Statement:

- Incidents are to be classified by severity relative to the impact they have on an organization. If there is ever a question as to which level is appropriate, the company must err on the side of caution and assign the higher severity level.

- Level 1 incidents are defined as those that could cause significant harm to the business, customers, or the public and/or are in violation of corporate law, regulation, or contractual obligation:

  - Level 1 incidents must be responded to immediately upon report.

  - The Chief Executive Officer, Chief Operating Officer, legal counsel, and Chief Information Security Officer must be informed of Level 1 incidents.

- Level 2 incidents are defined as a compromise of or unauthorized access to noncritical systems or information; detection of a precursor to a focused attack; a believed threat of an imminent attack; or any act that is a potential violation of law, regulation, or contractual obligation:

  - Level 2 incidents must be responded to within four hours.

  - The Chief Operating Officer, legal counsel, and Chief Information Security Officer must be informed of Level 2 incidents.

- Level 3 incidents are defined as situations that can be contained and resolved by the information system custodian, data/process owner, or HR personnel. There is no evidence or suspicion of harm to customer or proprietary information, processes, or services:

  - Level 3 incidents must be responded to within 24 business hours.

  - The Information Security Officer must be informed of Level 3 incidents.

What Is an Incident Response Program?

An *incident response program* is composed of policies, plans, procedures, and people. Incident response policies codify management directives. Incident response plans (IRPs) provide a well-defined, consistent, and organized approach for handling internal incidents as well as taking appropriate action when an external incident is traced back to the organization. Incident response procedures are detailed steps needed to implement the plan.

The Incident Response Plan

Having a good incident response plan and incident response process will help you minimize loss or theft of information and disruption of services caused by incidents. It will also help you enhance your incident response program by using lessons learned and information obtained during the security incident.

Section 2.3 of NIST Special Publication 800-61 Revision 2 goes over the incident response policies, plans, and procedures, including information on how to coordinate incidents and interact with outside parties. The policy elements described in NIST Special Publication 800-61 Revision 2 include the following:

- Statement of management commitment
- Purpose and objectives of the incident response policy
- The scope of the incident response policy
- Definition of computer security incidents and related terms
- Organizational structure and definition of roles, responsibilities, and levels of authority
- Prioritization or severity ratings of incidents
- Performance measures
- Reporting and contact forms

NIST's incident response plan elements include the following:

- Incident response plan's mission
- Strategies and goals of the incident response plan
- Senior management approval of the incident response plan
- Organizational approach to incident response
- How the incident response team will communicate with the rest of the organization and with other organizations
- Metrics for measuring the incident response capability and its effectiveness

- Roadmap for maturing the incident response capability

- How the program fits into the overall organization

NIST also defines standard operating procedures (SOPs) as "a delineation of the specific technical processes, techniques, checklists, and forms used by the incident response team. SOPs should be reasonably comprehensive and detailed to ensure that the priorities of the organization are reflected in response operations." You learned details about SOP in Chapter 8, "Communications and Operations Security."

In Practice

Cybersecurity Incident Response Program Policy

Synopsis: To ensure that information security incidents are responded to, managed, and reported in a consistent and effective manner.

Policy Statement:

- An incident response plan (IRP) will be maintained to ensure that information security incidents are responded to, managed, and reported in a consistent and effective manner.

- The Office of Information Security is responsible for the establishment and maintenance of an IRP.

- The IRP will, at a minimum, include instructions, procedures, and guidance related to

  - Preparation

  - Detection and investigation

  - Initial response

  - Containment

  - Eradication and recovery

  - Notification

  - Closure and post-incident activity

  - Documentation and evidence handling

- In accordance with the Information Security Incident Personnel Policy, the IRP will further define personnel roles and responsibilities, including but not limited to incident response coordinators, designated incident handlers, and incident response team members.

- All employees, contractors, consultants, and vendors will receive incident response training appropriate to their role.

- The IRP must be annually authorized by the Board of Directors.

The Incident Response Process

NIST Special Publication 800-61 goes over the major phases of the incident response process in detail. You should become familiar with that publication because it provides additional information that will help you succeed in your security operations center (SOC). The important key points are summarized here.

NIST defines the major phases of the incident response process as illustrated in Figure 11-1.

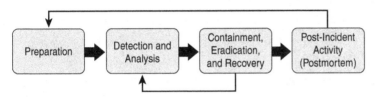

FIGURE 11-1   NIST Incident Response Process

The Preparation Phase

The preparation phase includes creating and training the incident response team, as well as deploying the necessary tools and resources to successfully investigate and resolve cybersecurity incidents. In this phase, the incident response team creates a set of controls based on the results of risk assessments. The preparation phase also includes the following tasks:

- Creating processes for incident handler communications and the facilities that will host the security operation center (SOC) and incident response team

- Making sure that the organization has appropriate incident analysis hardware and software as well as incident mitigation software

- Creating risk assessment capabilities within the organization

- Making sure the organization has appropriately deployed host security, network security, and malware prevention solutions

- Developing user awareness training

The Detection and Analysis Phase

The detection and analysis phase is one of the most challenging phases. Although some incidents are easy to detect (for example, a denial-of-service attack), many breaches and attacks are left unde-tected for weeks or even months. This is why detection may be the most difficult task in incident response. The typical network is full of blind spots where anomalous traffic goes undetected. Imple-menting analytics and correlation tools is critical to eliminating these network blind spots. As a result, the incident response team must react quickly to analyze and validate each incident. This is done by following a predefined process while documenting each step the analyst takes. NIST provides various recommendations for making incident analysis easier and more effective:

- Profile networks and systems

- Understand normal behaviors

- Create a log retention policy

- Perform event correlation

- Maintain and use a knowledge base of information

- Use Internet search engines for research

- Run packet sniffers to collect additional data

- Filter the data

- Seek assistance from others

- Keep all host clocks synchronized

- Know the different types of attacks and attack vectors

- Develop processes and procedures to recognize the signs of an incident

- Understand the sources of precursors and indicators

- Create appropriate incident documentation capabilities and processes

- Create processes to effectively prioritize security incidents

- Create processes to effectively communicate incident information (internal and external communications)

Containment, Eradication, and Recovery

The containment, eradication, and recovery phase includes the following activities:

- Evidence gathering and handling

- Identifying the attacking hosts

- Choosing a containment strategy to effectively contain and eradicate the attack, as well as to successfully recover from it

NIST Special Publication 800-61 Revision 2 also defines the following criteria for determining the appropriate containment, eradication, and recovery strategy:

- The potential damage to and theft of resources

- The need for evidence preservation

- Service availability (for example, network connectivity as well as services provided to external parties)

- Time and resources needed to implement the strategy

- Effectiveness of the strategy (for example, partial containment or full containment)

- Duration of the solution (for example, emergency workaround to be removed in four hours, temporary workaround to be removed in two weeks, or permanent solution)

Post-Incident Activity (Postmortem)

The post-incident activity phase includes lessons learned, how to use collected incident data, and evidence retention. NIST Special Publication 800-61 Revision 2 includes several questions that can be used as guidelines during the lessons learned meeting(s):

- Exactly what happened, and at what times?

- How well did the staff and management perform while dealing with the incident?

- Were the documented procedures followed? Were they adequate?

- What information was needed sooner?

- Were any steps or actions taken that might have inhibited the recovery?

- What would the staff and management do differently the next time a similar incident occurs?

- How could information sharing with other organizations be improved?

- What corrective actions can prevent similar incidents in the future?

- What precursors or indicators should be watched for in the future to detect similar incidents?

- What additional tools or resources are needed to detect, analyze, and mitigate future incidents?

Tabletop Exercises and Playbooks

Many organizations take advantage of tabletop (simulated) exercises to further test their capabilities. These tabletop exercises are an opportunity to practice and also perform gap analysis. In addition, these exercises may allow them to create playbooks for incident response. Developing a playbook framework makes future analysis modular and extensible. A good playbook typically contains the following information:

- Report identification

- Objective statement

- Result analysis

- Data query/code

- Analyst comments/notes

There are significant long-term advantages for having relevant and effective playbooks. When developing playbooks, focus on organization and clarity within your own framework. Having a playbook and detection logic is not enough. The playbook is only a proactive plan. Your plays must actually run to generate results, those results must be analyzed, and remedial actions must be taken for malicious events. This is why tabletop exercises are very important.

Table-top exercises could be technical and also at the executive level. You can create technical simulations for your incident response team and also risk-based exercises for your executive and management staff. A simple methodology for an incident response tabletop exercise includes the following steps:

1. **Preparation:** Identify the audience, what you want to simulate, and how the exercise will take place.

2. **Execution:** Execute the simulation and record all findings to identify all areas for improvement in your program.

3. **Report:** Create a report and distribute it to all the respective stakeholders. Narrow your assessment to specific facets of incident response. You can compare the results with the existing incident response plans. You should also measure the coordination among different teams within the organization and/or external to the organization. Provide a good technical analysis and identify gaps.

Information Sharing and Coordination

During the investigation and resolution of a security incident, you may also need to communicate with outside parties regarding the incident. Examples include, but are not limited to, contacting law enforcement, fielding media inquiries, seeking external expertise, and working with Internet service providers (ISPs), the vendor of your hardware and software products, threat intelligence vendor feeds, coordination centers, and members of other incident response teams. You can also share relevant incident indicator of compromise (IoC) information and other observables with industry peers. A good example of information-sharing communities includes the Financial Services Information Sharing and Analysis Center (FS-ISAC).

Your incident response plan should account for these types of interactions with outside entities. It should also include information about how to interact with your organization's public relations (PR) department, legal department, and upper management. You should also get their buy-in when sharing information with outside parties to minimize the risk of information leakage. In other words, avoid leaking sensitive information regarding security incidents with unauthorized parties. These actions could potentially lead to additional disruption and financial loss. You should also maintain a list of all the contacts at those external entities, including a detailed list of all external communications for liability and evidentiary purposes.

Computer Security Incident Response Teams

There are different incident response teams. The most popular is the Computer Security Incident Response Team (CSIRT). Others include the following:

■ Product Security Incident Response Team (PSIRT)

■ National CSIRT and Computer Emergency Response Team (CERT)

■ Coordination center

■ The incident response team of a security vendor and Managed Security Service Provider (MSSP)

In this section, you learn about CSIRTs. The rest of the incident response team types are covered in the subsequent sections in this chapter.

The CSIRT is typically the team that works hand in hand with the information security teams (often called InfoSec). In smaller organizations, InfoSec and CSIRT functions may be combined and provided by the same team. In large organizations, the CSIRT focuses on the investigation of computer security incidents, whereas the InfoSec team is tasked with the implementation of security configurations, monitoring, and policies within the organization.

Establishing a CSIRT involves the following steps:

STEP 1. Defining the CSIRT constituency.

STEP 2. Ensuring management and executive support.

STEP 3. Making sure that the proper budget is allocated.

STEP 4. Deciding where the CSIRT will reside within the organization's hierarchy.

STEP 5. Determining whether the team will be central, distributed, or virtual.

STEP 6. Developing the process and policies for the CSIRT.

It is important to recognize that every organization is different, and these steps can be accomplished in parallel or in sequence. However, defining the constituency of a CSIRT is certainly one of the first steps in the process. When defining the constituency of a CSIRT, one should answer the following questions:

■ Who will be the "customer" of the CSIRT?

■ What is the scope? Will the CSIRT cover only the organization or also entities external to the organization? For example, at Cisco, all internal infrastructure and Cisco's websites and tools (that is, cisco.com) are a responsibility of the Cisco CSIRT, and any incident or vulnerability concerning a Cisco product or service is the responsibility of the Cisco PSIRT.

- Will the CSIRT provide support for the complete organization or only for a specific area or segment? For example, an organization may have a CSIRT for traditional infrastructure and IT capabilities and a separate one dedicated to cloud security.

- Will the CSIRT be responsible for part of the organization or all of it? If external entities will be included, how will they be selected?

Determining the value of a CSIRT can be challenging. One of the main questions that executives will ask is, what is the return on investment for having a CSIRT? The main goals of the CSIRT are to minimize risk, contain cyber damage, and save money by preventing incidents from happening—and when they do occur, to mitigate them efficiently. For example, the smaller the scope of the damage, the less money you need to spend to recover from a compromise (including brand reputation). Many studies in the past have covered the cost of security incidents and the cost of breaches. Also, the Ponemon Institute periodically publishes reports covering these costs. It is a good practice to review and calculate the "value add" of the CSIRT. This calculation can be used to determine when to invest more, not only in a CSIRT, but also in operational best practices. In some cases, an organization might even outsource some of the cybersecurity functions to a managed service provider, if the organization cannot afford or retain security talent.

An incident response team must have several basic policies and procedures in place to operate satisfactorily, including the following:

- Incident classification and handling

- Information classification and protection

- Information dissemination

- Record retention and destruction

- Acceptable usage of encryption

- Engaging and cooperating with external groups (other IRTs, law enforcement, and so on)

Also, some additional policies or procedures can be defined, such as the following:

- Hiring policy

- Using an outsourcing organization to handle incidents

- Working across multiple legal jurisdictions

Even more policies can be defined depending on the team's circumstances. The important thing to remember is that not all policies need to be defined on the first day.

The following are great sources of information from the International Organization for Standardization/ International Electrotechnical Commission (ISO/IEC) that you can leverage when you are constructing your policy and procedure documents:

- **ISO/IEC 27001:2005:** "Information Technology—Security Techniques—Information Security Management Systems—Requirements"

- **ISO/IEC 27002:2005:** "Information Technology—Security Techniques—Code of Practice for Information Security Management"

- **ISO/IEC 27005:2008:** "Information Technology—Security techniques—Information Security Risk Management"

- **ISO/PAS 22399:2007:** "Societal Security—Guidelines for Incident Preparedness and Operational Continuity Management"

- **ISO/IEC 27033:** "Information Technology—Security Techniques—Information Security Incident Management"

CERT provides a good overview of the goals and responsibilities of a CSIRT at the following site: https://www.cert.org/incident-management/csirt-development/csirt-faq.cfm.

Product Security Incident Response Teams (PSIRTs)

Software and hardware vendors may have separate teams that handle the investigation, resolution, and disclosure of security vulnerabilities in their products and services. Typically, these teams are called Product Security Incident Response Teams (PSIRTs). Before you can understand how a PSIRT operates, you must understand what constitutes security vulnerability.

The U.S. National Institute of Standards and Technology (NIST) defines a security vulnerability as follows:

"A flaw or weakness in system security procedures, design, implementation, or internal controls that could be exercised (accidentally triggered or intentionally exploited) and result in a security breach or a violation of the system's security policy."

There are many more definitions, but they tend to be variations on the one from the NIST.

Security Vulnerabilities and Their Severity

Why are product security vulnerabilities a concern? Because each vulnerability represents a potential risk that threat actors can use to compromise your systems and your network. Each vulnerability carries an associated amount of risk with it. One of the most widely adopted standards to calculate the severity of a given vulnerability is the Common Vulnerability Scoring System (CVSS), which has three components: base, temporal, and environmental scores. Each component is presented as a score on a scale from 0 to 10.

CVSS is an industry standard maintained by FIRST that is used by many PSIRTs to convey information about the severity of vulnerabilities they disclose to their customers.

In CVSS, a vulnerability is evaluated under three aspects and a score is assigned to each of them:

- The base group represents the intrinsic characteristics of a vulnerability that are constant over time and do not depend on a user-specific environment. This is the most important information and the only one that's mandatory to obtain a vulnerability score.

- The temporal group assesses the vulnerability as it changes over time.

- The environmental group represents the characteristics of a vulnerability, taking into account the organizational environment.

The score for the base group is between 0 and 10, where 0 is the least severe and 10 is assigned to highly critical vulnerabilities. For example, a highly critical vulnerability could allow an attacker to remotely compromise a system and get full control. Additionally, the score comes in the form of a vector string that identifies each of the components used to make up the score.

The formula used to obtain the score takes into account various characteristics of the vulnerability and how the attacker is able to leverage these characteristics.

CVSSv3 defines several characteristics for the base, temporal, and environmental groups.

The base group defines Exploitability metrics that measure how the vulnerability can be exploited, as well as Impact metrics that measure the impact on confidentiality, integrity, and availability. In addition to these two metrics, a metric called Scope Change (S) is used to convey impact on systems that are impacted by the vulnerability but do not contain vulnerable code.

The Exploitability metrics include the following:

- Attack Vector (AV) represents the level of access an attacker needs to have to exploit a vulnerability. It can assume four values:

    - Network (N)

    - Adjacent (A)

    - Local (L)

    - Physical (P)

- Attack Complexity (AC) represents the conditions beyond the attacker's control that must exist in order to exploit the vulnerability. The values can be the following:

    - Low (L)

    - High (H)

- Privileges Required (PR) represents the level of privileges an attacker must have to exploit the vulnerability. The values are as follows:

  - None (N)

  - Low (L)

  - High (H)

- User Interaction (UI) captures whether a user interaction is needed to perform an attack. The values are as follows:

  - None (N)

  - Required (R)

- Scope (S) captures the impact on systems other than the system being scored. The values are as follows:

  - Unchanged (U)

  - Changed (C)

The Impact metrics include the following:

- Confidentiality (C) measures the degree of impact to the confidentiality of the system. It can assume the following values:

  - Low (L)

  - Medium (M)

  - High (H)

- Integrity (I) measures the degree of impact to the integrity of the system. It can assume the following values:

  - Low (L)

  - Medium (M)

  - High (H)

- Availability (A) measures the degree of impact to the availability of the system. It can assume the following values:

  - Low (L)

  - Medium (M)

  - High (H)

The temporal group includes three metrics:

- Exploit Code Maturity (E), which measures whether or not public exploit is available
- Remediation Level (RL), which indicates whether a fix or workaround is available
- Report Confidence (RC), which indicates the degree of confidence in the existence of the vulnerability

The environmental group includes two main metrics:

- Security Requirements (CR, IR, AR), which indicate the importance of confidentiality, integrity, and availability requirements for the system
- Modified Base Metrics (MAV, MAC, MAPR, MUI, MS, MC, MI, MA), which allow the organization to tweak the base metrics based on specific characteristics of the environment

For example, a vulnerability that might allow a remote attacker to crash the system by sending crafted IP packets would have the following values for the base metrics:

- Access Vector (AV) would be Network because the attacker can be anywhere and can send packets remotely.
- Attack Complexity (AC) would be Low because it is trivial to generate malformed IP packets (for example, via the Scapy Python tool).
- Privilege Required (PR) would be None because there are no privileges required by the attacker on the target system.
- User Interaction (UI) would also be None because the attacker does not need to interact with any user of the system to carry out the attack.
- Scope (S) would be Unchanged if the attack does not cause other systems to fail.
- Confidentiality Impact (C) would be None because the primary impact is on the availability of the system.
- Integrity Impact (I) would be None because the primary impact is on the availability of the system.
- Availability Impact (A) would be High because the device could become completely unavailable while crashing and reloading.

Additional examples of CVSSv3 scoring are available at the FIRST website (https://www.first.org/cvss).

Vulnerability Chaining Role in Fixing Prioritization

In numerous instances, security vulnerabilities are not exploited in isolation. Threat actors exploit more than one vulnerability in a chain to carry out their attack and compromise their victims. By leveraging different vulnerabilities in a chain, attackers can infiltrate progressively further into the system or network and gain more control over it. This is something that PSIRT teams must be aware of. Developers, security professionals, and users must be aware of this because chaining can change the order in which a vulnerability needs to be fixed or patched in the affected system. For instance, multiple low-severity vulnerabilities can become a severe one if they are combined.

Performing vulnerability chaining analysis is not a trivial task. Although several commercial companies claim that they can easily perform chaining analysis, in reality the methods and procedures that can be included as part of a chain vulnerability analysis are pretty much endless. PSIRT teams should utilize an approach that works for them to achieve the best end result.

Fixing Theoretical Vulnerabilities

Exploits cannot exist without a vulnerability. However, there isn't always an exploit for a given vulnerability. Earlier in this chapter you were reminded of the definition of a vulnerability. As another reminder, an exploit is not a vulnerability. An exploit is a concrete manifestation, either a piece of software or a collection of reproducible steps, that leverage a given vulnerability to compromise an affected system.

In some cases, users call vulnerabilities without exploits "theoretical vulnerabilities." One of the biggest challenges with "theoretical vulnerabilities" is that there are many smart people out there capable of exploiting them. If you do not know how to exploit a vulnerability today, it does not mean that someone else will not find a way in the future. In fact, someone else may already have found a way to exploit the vulnerability and perhaps is even selling the exploit of the vulnerability in underground markets without public knowledge.

PSIRT personnel should understand there is no such thing as an "entirely theoretical" vulnerability. Sure, having a working exploit can ease the reproducible steps and help to verify whether that same vulnerability is present in different systems. However, because an exploit may not come as part of a vulnerability, you should not completely deprioritize it.

Internally Versus Externally Found Vulnerabilities

A PSIRT can learn about a vulnerability in a product or service during internal testing or during the development phase. However, vulnerabilities can also be reported by external entities, such as security researchers, customers, and other vendors.

The dream of any vendor is to be able to find and patch all security vulnerabilities during the design and development phases. However, that is close to impossible. On the other hand, that is why a secure development life cycle (SDL) is extremely important for any organization that produces software and hardware. Cisco has an SDL program that is documented at the following URL: www.cisco.com/c/en/us/about/security-center/security-programs/secure-development-lifecycle.html.

Cisco defines its SDL as "a repeatable and measurable process we've designed to increase the resiliency and trustworthiness of our products." Cisco's SDL is part of Cisco Product Development Methodology (PDM) and ISO 9000 compliance requirements. It includes, but is not limited to, the following:

- Base product security requirements

- Third-party software (TPS) security

- Secure design

- Secure coding

- Secure analysis

- Vulnerability testing

The goal of the SDL is to provide tools and processes that are designed to accelerate the product development methodology, by developing secure, resilient, and trustworthy systems. TPS security is one of the most important tasks for any organization. Most of today's organizations use open source and third-party libraries. This approach creates two requirements for the product security team. The first is to know what TPS libraries are used, reused, and where. The second is to patch any vulnerabilities that affect such library or TPS components. For example, if a new vulnerability in OpenSSL is disclosed, what do you have to do? Can you quickly assess the impact of such a vulnerability in all your products?

If you include commercial TPS, is the vendor of such software transparently disclosing all the security vulnerabilities, including in their software? Nowadays, many organizations are including security vulnerability disclosure SLAs in their contracts with third-party vendors. This is very important because many TPS vulnerabilities (both commercial and open source) go unpatched for many months—or even years.

TPS software security is a monumental task for any company of any size. To get a feeling of the scale of TPS code usage, visit the third-party security bulletins published by Cisco at https://tools.cisco.com/security/center/publicationListing.x?product=NonCisco#~Vulnerabilities. Another good resource is CVE Details (www.cvedetails.com).

Many tools are available on the market today to enumerate all open source components used in a product. These tools either interrogate the product source code or scan binaries for the presence of TPS. The following are a few examples:

- BlackDuck by Synopsys Software: https://www.blackducksoftware.com

- Synopsys Protecode (formerly known as AppCheck): https://www.synopsys.com/software-integrity/security-testing/software-composition-analysis.html

- Palamida: www.palamida.com

- SRC:CLR: https://www.sourceclear.com

National CSIRTs and Computer Emergency Response Teams (CERTS)

Numerous countries have their own Computer Emergency Response (or Readiness) Teams. Examples include the US-CERT (https://www.us-cert.gov), Indian Computer Emergency Response Team (http://www.cert-in.org.in), CERT Australia (https://cert.gov.au), and the Australian Computer Emergency Response Team (https://www.auscert.org.au/). The Forum of Incident Response and Security Teams (FIRST) website includes a list of all the national CERTS and other incident response teams at https://www.first.org/members/teams.

These national CERTS and CSIRTs aim to protect their citizens by providing security vulnerability information, security awareness training, best practices, and other information. For example, the following is the US-CERT mission posted at https://www.us-cert.gov/about-us:

"US-CERT's critical mission activities include:

- Providing cybersecurity protection to Federal civilian executive branch agencies through intrusion detection and prevention capabilities.

- Developing timely and actionable information for distribution to federal departments and agencies; state, local, tribal and territorial (SLTT) governments; critical infrastructure owners and operators; private industry; and international organizations.

- Responding to incidents and analyzing data about emerging cyber threats.

- Collaborating with foreign governments and international entities to enhance the nation's cybersecurity posture."

Coordination Centers

Several organizations around the world also help with the coordination of security vulnerability disclosures to vendors, hardware and software providers, and security researchers.

One of the best examples is the CERT Division of the Software Engineering Institute (SEI). CERT provides security vulnerability coordination and research. It is an important stakeholder of multi-vendor security vulnerability disclosures and coordination. Additional information about CERT can be obtained at their website at https://www.sei.cmu.edu/about/divisions/cert/index.cfm#cert-division-what-we-do.

Incident Response Providers and Managed Security Service Providers (MSSPs)

Cisco, along with several other vendors, provides incident response and managed security services to its customers. These incident response teams and outsourced CSIRTs operate a bit differently because their task is to provide support to their customers. However, they practice the tasks outlined earlier in this chapter for incident response and CSIRTs.

The following are examples of these teams and their services:

- The Cisco Incident Response Service: Provides Cisco customers with readiness or proactive services and post-breach support. The proactive services include infrastructure breach preparedness assessments, security operations readiness assessments, breach communications assessment, and security operations and incident response training. The post-breach (or reactive) services include the evaluation and investigation of the attack, countermeasure development and deployment, as well as the validation of the countermeasure effectiveness.

- FireEye Incident Response Services.

- Crowdstrike Incident Response Services.

- SecureWorks Managed Security Services.

- Cisco's Active Threat Analytics (ATA) managed security service.

Managed services, such as the SecureWorks Managed Security Services, Cisco ATA, and others, offer customers 24-hour continuous monitoring and advanced-analytics capabilities, combined with threat intelligence as well as security analysts and investigators to detect security threats in customer networks. Outsourcing has long been a practice for many companies, but the onset of the complexity of cybersecurity has allowed it to bloom and become bigger as the years go by in the world of incident response.

Key Incident Management Personnel

Key incident management personnel include incident response coordinators, designated incident handlers, incident response team members, and external advisors. In various organizations, they may have different titles, but the roles are essentially the same.

The *incident response coordinator (IRC)* is the central point of contact for all incidents. Incident reports are directed to the IRC. The IRC verifies and logs the incident. Based on predefined criteria, the IRC notifies appropriate personnel, including the designated incident handler (DIH). The IRC is a member of the incident response team (IRT) and is responsible for maintaining all non-evidence-based incident-related documentation.

Designated incident handlers (DIHs) are senior-level personnel who have the crisis management and communication skills, experience, knowledge, and stamina to manage an incident. DIHs are responsible for three critical tasks: incident declaration, liaison with executive management, and managing the incident response team (IRT).

The *incident response team (IRT)* is a carefully selected and well-trained team of professionals that provides services throughout the incident life cycle. Depending on the size of the organization, there may be a single team or multiple teams, each with its own specialty. The IRT members generally represent a cross-section of functional areas, including senior management, information security, information technology (IT), operations, legal, compliance, HR, public affairs and media relations, customer service, and physical security. Some members may be expected to participate in every response effort, whereas others (such as compliance) may restrict involvement to relevant events. The team as directed by the DIH is responsible for further analysis, evidence handling and documentation, containment, eradication and recovery, notification (as required), and post-incident activities.

Tasks assigned to the IRT include but are not limited to the following:

- Overall management of the incident

- Triage and impact analysis to determine the extent of the situation

- Development and implementation of containment and eradication strategies

- Compliance with government and/or other regulations

- Communication and follow-up with affected parties and/or individuals

- Communication and follow-up with other external parties, including the Board of Directors, business partners, government regulators (including federal, state, and other administrators), law enforcement, representatives of the media, and so on, as needed

- Root cause analysis and lessons learned

- Revision of policies/procedures necessary to prevent any recurrence of the incident

Figure 11-2 illustrates the incident response roles and responsibilities.

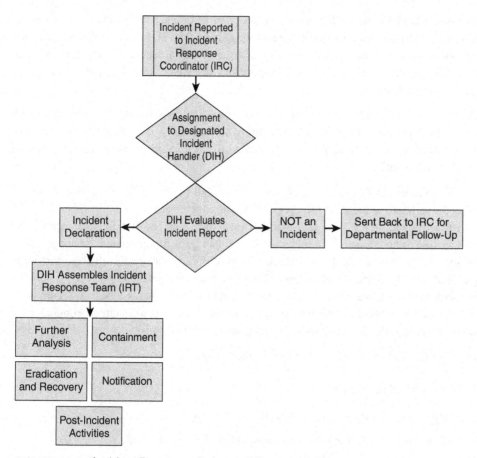

FIGURE 11-2   Incident Response Roles and Responsibilities

Incident Response Training and Exercises

Establishing a robust response capability ensures that the organization is prepared to respond to an incident swiftly and effectively. Responders should receive training specific to their individual and collective responsibilities. Recurring tests, drills, and challenging incident response exercises can make a huge difference in responder ability. Knowing what is expected decreases the pressure on the responders and reduces errors. It should be stressed that the objective of incident response exercises isn't to get an "A" but rather to honestly evaluate the plan and procedures, to identify missing resources, and to learn to work together as a team.

In Practice

Incident Response Authority Policy

Synopsis: To vest authority in those charged with responding to and/or managing an information security incident.

Policy Statement:

- The Chief Information Security Officer has the authority to appoint IRC, DIHs, and IRT members:

    - All responders must receive training commensurate with their role and responsibilities.

    - All responders must participate in recurring drills and exercises.

- During a security incident, as well as during drills and exercises, incident management and incident response–related duties supersede normal duties.

- The Chief Operating Office and/or legal counsel have the authority to notify law enforcement or regulatory officials.

- The Chief Operating Officer, Board of Directors, and/or legal counsel have the authority to engage outside personnel, including but not limited to forensic investigators, experts in related fields (such as security, technology, and compliance), and specialized legal counsel.

What Happened? Investigation and Evidence Handling

The primary reason for gathering evidence is to figure out what happened in order to contain and resolve the incident as quickly as possible. As an incident responder, it is easy to get caught up in the moment. It may not be apparent that careful evidence acquisition, handling, and documentation are important or even necessary. Consider the scenario of a workstation malware infection. The first impression may be that the malware download was inadvertent. This could be true, or perhaps it was the work of a malicious insider or careless business vendor. Until you have the facts, you don't know. Regardless of the source, if the malware infection resulted in a compromise of legally protected information, the company could be a target of a negligence lawsuit or regulatory action, in which case evidence of how the infection was contained and eradicated could be used to support the company's position. Because there are so many variables, by default, data handlers should treat every investigation as if it would lead to a court case.

Documenting Incidents

The initial documentation should create an incident profile. The profile should include the following:

- How was the incident detected?
- What is the scenario for the incident?
- What time did the incident occur?
- Who or what reported the incident?
- Who are the contacts for involved personnel?
- A brief description of the incident.
- Snapshots of all on-scene conditions.

All ongoing incident response–related activity should be logged and time-stamped. In addition to actions taken, the log should include decisions, record of contact (internal and external resources), and recommendations.

Documentation specific to computer-related activity should be kept separate from general documentation because of the confidential nature of what is being performed and/or found. All documentation should be sequential and time/date stamped, and should include exact commands entered into systems, results of commands, actions taken (for example, logging on, disabling accounts, applying router filters) as well as observations about the system and/or incident. Documentation should occur as the incident is being handled, not after.

Incident documentation should not be shared with anyone outside the team without the express permission of the DIH or executive management. If there is any expectation that the network has been compromised, documentation should not be saved on a network-connected device.

Working with Law Enforcement

Depending on the nature of the situation, it may be necessary to contact local, state, or federal law enforcement. The decision to do so should be discussed with legal counsel. It is important to recognize that the primary mission of law enforcement is to identify the perpetrators and build a case. There may be times when the law enforcement agency requests that the incident or attack continue while they work to gather evidence. Although this objective appears to be at odds with the organizational objective to contain the incident, it is sometimes the best course of action. The IRT should become acquainted with applicable law enforcement representatives before an incident occurs to discuss the types of incidents that should be reported to them, who to contact, what evidence should be collected, and how it should be collected.

If the decision is made to contact law enforcement, it is important to do so as early in the response life cycle as possible while the trail is still hot. On a federal level, both the Secret Service and the Federal

Bureau of Investigation (FBI) investigate cyber incidents. The Secret Service's investigative responsibilities extend to crimes that involve financial institution fraud, computer and telecommunications fraud, identity theft, access device fraud (for example, ATM or point of sale systems), electronic funds transfers, money laundering, corporate espionage, computer system intrusion, and Internet-related child pornography and exploitation. The FBI's investigation responsibilities include cyber-based terrorism, espionage, computer intrusions, and major cyber fraud. If the missions appear to overlap, it is because they do. Generally, it is best to reach out to the local Secret Service or FBI office and let them determine jurisdiction.

FYI: The Authors of the Mirai Botnet Plead Guilty

In late 2017, the authors of the Mirai malware and botnet (21-year-old Paras Jha from Fanwood, N.J., and Josiah White, 20, from Washington, Pennsylvania) pleaded guilty. Mirai is malware that compromised hundreds of thousands of Internet of Things devices, such as security cameras, routers, and digital video recorders for use in large-scale attacks.

KrebsOnSecurity published the results of that four-month inquiry, "Who Is Anna Senpai, the Mirai Worm Author?" The story is easily the longest in this site's history, and it cited a bounty of clues pointing back to Jha and White. Additional details can be found at: https://krebsonsecurity.com/2017/12/mirai-iot-botnet-co-authors-plead-guilty/.

Understanding Forensic Analysis

Forensics is the application of science to the identification, collection, examination, and analysis of data while preserving the integrity of the information. Forensic tools and techniques are often used to find the root cause of an incident or to uncover facts. In addition to reconstructing security incidents, digital forensic techniques can be used for investigating crimes and internal policy violations, troubleshooting operational problems, and recovering from accidental system damage.

As described in NIST Special Publication 800-87, the process for performing digital forensics includes collection, examination, analysis, and reporting:

- **Collection:** The first phase in the process is to identify, label, record, and acquire data from the possible sources of relevant data, while following guidelines and procedures that preserve the integrity of the data. Collection is typically performed in a timely manner because of the likelihood of losing dynamic data, such as current network connections, as well as losing data from battery-powered devices.

- **Examination:** Examinations involve forensically processing large amounts of collected data using a combination of automated and manual methods to assess and extract data of particular interest, while preserving the integrity of the data.

- **Analysis:** The next phase of the process is to analyze the results of the examination, using legally justifiable methods and techniques, to derive useful information that addresses the questions that were the impetus for performing the collection and examination.

- **Reporting:** The final phase is reporting the results of the analysis, which may include describing the actions used, explaining how tools and procedures were selected, determining what other actions need to be performed, and providing recommendations for improvement to policies, guidelines, procedures, tools, and other aspects of the forensic process. The formality of the reporting step varies greatly depending on the situation.

Incident handlers performing forensic tasks need to have a reasonably comprehensive knowledge of forensic principles, guidelines, procedures, tools, and techniques, as well as antiforensic tools and techniques that could conceal or destroy data. It is also beneficial for incident handlers to have expertise in information security and specific technical subjects, such as the most commonly used operating systems, file systems, applications, and network protocols within the organization. Having this type of knowledge facilitates faster and more effective responses to incidents. Incident handlers also need a general, broad understanding of systems and networks so that they can determine quickly which teams and individuals are well suited to providing technical expertise for particular forensic efforts, such as examining and analyzing data for an uncommon application.

FYI: CCFP—Certified Cyber Forensics Professional

The CCFP certification is offered by (ISC)². According to the ISC, "the Certified Cyber Forensics Professional (CCFP) credential indicates expertise in forensics techniques and procedures, standards of practice, and legal and ethical principles to assure accurate, complete, and reliable digital evidence admissible to a court of law. It also indicates the ability to apply forensics to other information security disciplines, such as e-discovery, malware analysis, or incident response." To learn more, go to https://www.isc2.org/ccfp/.

All (ISC)² certifications are accredited by the American National Standards Institute (ANSI) to be in compliance with the International Organization for Standardization and International Electrotechnical Commission (ISO/IEC) 17024 Standards.

Understanding Chain of Custody

Chain of custody applies to physical, digital, and forensic evidence. Evidentiary *chain of custody* is used to prove that evidence has not been altered from the time it was collected through production in court. This means that the moment evidence is collected, every transfer of evidence from person to person must be documented, and it must be provable that nobody else could have accessed that evidence. In the case of legal action, the chain of custody documentation will be available to opposing counsel through the information discovery process and may become public. Confidential information should be included in the document only if absolutely necessary.

To maintain an evidentiary chain, a detailed log should be maintained that includes the following information:

- Where and when (date and time) evidence was discovered.

- Identifying information such as the location, serial number, model number, host name, media access control (MAC) address, and/or IP address.

- Name, title, and phone number of each person who discovered, collected, handled, or examined the evidence.

- Where evidence was stored/secured and during what time period.

- If the evidence has changed custody, how and when the transfer occurred (include shipping numbers, and so on).

The relevant person should sign and date each entry in the record.

Storing and Retaining Evidence

It is not unusual to retain all evidence for months or years after the incident ends. Evidence, logs, and data associated with the incident should be placed in tamper-resistant containers, grouped together, and put in a limited-access location. Only incident investigators, executive management, and legal counsel should have access to the storage facility. If and when evidence is turned over to law enforcement, an itemized inventory of all the items should be created and verified with the law enforcement representative. The law enforcement representative should sign and date the inventory list.

Evidence needs to be retained until all legal actions have been completed. Legal action could be civil, criminal, regulatory, or personnel-related. Evidence-retention parameters should be documented in policy. Retention schedules should include the following categories: internal only, civil, criminal, regulatory, personnel-related incident, and to-be-determined (TBD). When categorization is in doubt, legal counsel should be consulted. If there is an organizational retention policy, a notation should be included that evidence-retention schedules (if longer) supersede operational or regulatory retention requirements.

In Practice

Evidence Handling and Use Policy

Synopsis: To ensure that evidence is handled in accordance with legal requirements.

Policy Statement:

- All evidence, logs, and data associated with the incident must be handled as follows:

  - All evidence, logs, and data associated with the incident must be labeled.

  - All evidence, logs, and data associated with the incident should be placed in tamper-resistant containers, grouped together, and put in a limited access location.

- All evidence handling must be recorded on a chain of custody.

- Unless otherwise instructed by legal counsel or law enforcement officials, all internal digital evidence should be handled in accordance with the procedures described in "Electronic Crime Scene Investigation: A Guide for First Responders, Second Edition" from the United States Department of Justice, National Institute of Justice (April 2008). If not possible, deviations must be noted.

- Unless otherwise instructed by legal counsel or law enforcement officials, subsequent internal forensic investigation and analysis should follow the guidelines provided in "Forensic Examination of Digital Evidence: A Guide for Law Enforcement" from the United States Department of Justice, National Institute of Justice (April 2004). If not possible, deviations must be noted.

- Executive management and the DIH have the authority to engage outside expertise for forensic evidence handling investigation and analysis.

- Exceptions to this policy can be authorized only by legal counsel.

Data Breach Notification Requirements

A component of incident management is to understand, evaluate, and be prepared to comply with the legal responsibility to notify affected parties. Most states have some form of data breach notification laws. Federal regulations, including but not limited to the Gramm-Leach-Bliley Act (GLBA), the Health Information Technology for Economic and Clinical Health (HITECH) Act, the Federal Information Security Management Act (FISMA), and the Federal Educational Rights and Privacy Act (FERPA), all address the protection of personally identifiable information (PII; also referred to as nonpublic personal information, or NPPI) and may potentially apply in an event of an incident.

A data breach is widely defined as an incident that results in compromise, unauthorized disclosure, unauthorized acquisition, unauthorized access, or unauthorized use or loss of control of legally protected PII, including the following:

- Any information that can be used to distinguish or trace an individual's identity, such as name, SSN, date and place of birth, mother's maiden name, or biometric records.

- Any other information that is linked or linkable to an individual, such as medical, educational, financial, and employment information.

- Information that is standing alone is not generally considered personally identifiable, because many people share the same trait, such as first or last name, country, state, ZIP code, age (without birth date), gender, race, or job position. However, multiple pieces of information, none of which alone may be considered personally identifiable, may uniquely identify a person when brought together.

Incidents resulting in unauthorized access to PII are taken seriously because the information can be used by criminals to make false identification documents (including drivers' licenses, passports, and insurance certificates), make fraudulent purchases and insurance claims, obtain loans or establish lines of credit, and apply for government and military benefits.

As we will discuss, the laws vary and sometimes even conflict in their requirements regarding the right of the individual to be notified, the manner in which they must be notified, and the information to be provided. What is consistent, however, is that notification requirements apply regardless of whether an organization stores and manages its data directly or through a third party, such as a cloud service provider.

FYI: Equifax Breach

A massive data breach at Equifax in 2017 raised the risk of identity theft for over 145 million U.S. consumers.

If you live in the United States and have a credit report, there's a good chance that you're one of those 145+ million American consumers whose sensitive personal information was exposed. Equifax is one of the nation's three major credit reporting agencies.

According to Equifax, the breach lasted from mid-May through July. Threat actors accessed consumer's names, social security numbers, birth dates, addresses and, in some instances, driver's license numbers. They also stole credit card numbers for about 209,000 people and dispute documents with personal identifying information for about 182,000 people. And they grabbed personal information of people in the UK and Canada, too. This breach highlighted the need of public disclosure of breaches.

The VERIS Community Database (VCDB) is an initiative that was launched to catalog security incidents in the public domain. VCDB contains raw data for thousands of security incidents shared under a creative commons license. You can download the latest release, follow the latest changes, and even help catalog and code incidents to grow the database at GitHub at: https://github.com/vz-risk/VCDB.

Is There a Federal Breach Notification Law?

The short answer is, there is not. Consumer information breach notification requirements have historically been determined at the state level. There are, however, federal statutes and regulations that require certain regulated sectors (such as health care, financial, and investment) to protect certain types of personal information, implement information security programs, and provide notification of security breaches. In addition, federal departments and agencies are obligated by memorandum to provide breach notification. The Veterans Administration is the only agency with its own law governing information security and privacy breaches.

GLBA Financial Institution Customer Information

Section 501(b) of the GLBA and FIL-27-2005 Guidance on Response Programs for Unauthorized Access to Customer Information and Customer Notice requires that a financial institution provide a notice to its customers whenever it becomes aware of an incident of unauthorized access to customer information and, at the conclusion of a reasonable investigation, determines that misuse of the information has occurred or it is reasonably possible that misuse will occur.

Customer notice should be given in a clear and conspicuous manner. The notice should include the following items:

- Description of the incident
- Type of information subject to unauthorized access
- Measures taken by the institution to protect customers from further unauthorized access
- Telephone number that customers can call for information and assistance
- A reminder to customers to remain vigilant over the next 12 to 24 months and to report suspected identity theft incidents to the institution

The guidance encourages financial institutions to notify the nationwide consumer reporting agencies prior to sending notices to a large number of customers that include contact information for the reporting agencies.

Customer notices are required to be delivered in a manner designed to ensure that a customer can reasonably be expected to receive them. For example, the institution may choose to contact all customers affected by telephone, by mail, or by electronic mail (for those customers for whom it has a valid email address and who have agreed to receive communications electronically).

Financial institutions must notify their primary federal regulator as soon as possible when the institution becomes aware of an incident involving unauthorized access to or use of nonpublic customer information. Consistent with the agencies' Suspicious Activity Report (SAR) regulations, institutions must file a timely SAR. In situations involving federal criminal violations requiring immediate attention, such as when a reportable violation is ongoing, institutions must promptly notify appropriate law enforcement authorities. Reference Chapter 12, "Business Continuity Management," for further discussion of financial institution–related security incidents.

HIPAA/HITECH Personal Healthcare Information (PHI)

The HITECH Act requires that covered entities notify affected individuals when they discover that their unsecured PHI has been, or is reasonably believed to have been, breached—even if the breach occurs through or by a business associate. A breach is defined as "impermissible acquisition, access, or use or disclosure of unsecured PHI...unless the covered entity or business associate demonstrates that there is a low probability that the PHI has been compromised."

The notification must be made without unreasonable delay and no later than 60 days after the discovery of the breach. The covered entity must also provide notice to "prominent media outlets" if the breach affects more than 500 individuals in a state or jurisdiction. The notice must include the following information:

- A description of the breach, including the date of the breach and date of discovery
- The type of PHI involved (such as full name, SSN, date of birth, home address, or account number)
- Steps individuals should take to protect themselves from potential harm resulting from the breach
- Steps the covered entity is taking to investigate the breach, mitigate losses, and protect against future breaches
- Contact procedures for individuals to ask questions or receive additional information, including a toll-free telephone number, email address, website, or postal address

Covered entities must notify the Department of Health and Human Services (HHS) of all breaches. Notice to HHS must be provided immediately for breaches involving more than 500 individuals and annually for all other breaches. Covered entities have the burden of demonstrating that they satisfied the specific notice obligations following a breach, or, if notice is not made following an unauthorized use or disclosure, that the unauthorized use or disclosure did not constitute a breach. See Chapter 13, "Regulatory Compliance for Financial Institutions," for further discussion of health-care–related security incidents.

Section 13407 of the HITECH Act directed the Federal Trade Commission (FTC) to issue breach notification rules pertaining to the exposure or compromise of personal health records (PHRs). A *personal health record* is defined by the FTC as an electronic record of "identifiable health information on an individual that can be drawn from multiple sources and that is managed, shared, and controlled by or primarily for the individual." Don't confuse PHR with PHI. PHI is information that is maintained by a covered entity as defined by HIPAA/HITECH. PHR is information provided by the consumer for the consumer's own benefit. For example, if a consumer uploads and stores medical information from many sources in one online location, the aggregated data would be considered a PHR. The online service would be considered a PHR vendor.

The FTC rule applies to both vendors of PHRs (which provide online repositories that people can use to keep track of their health information) and entities that offer third-party applications for PHRs. The requirements regarding the scope, timing, and content mirror the requirements imposed on covered entities. The enforcement is the responsibility of the FTC. By law, noncompliance is considered "unfair and deceptive trade practices."

Federal Agencies

Office of Management and Budget (OMB) Memorandum M-07-16: Safeguarding Against and Responding to the Breach of Personally Identifiable Information requires all federal agencies to implement a breach notification policy to safeguard paper and digital PII. Attachment 3, "External Breach Notification," identifies the factors agencies should consider in determining when notification outside the agency should be given and the nature of the notification. Notification may not be necessary for encrypted information. Each agency is directed to establish an agency response team. Agencies must assess the likely risk of harm caused by the breach and the level of risk. Agencies should provide notification without unreasonable delay following the detection of a breach, but are permitted to delay notification for law enforcement, national security purposes, or agency needs. Attachment 3 also includes specifics as to the content of the notice, criteria for determining the method of notification, and the types of notice that may be used. Attachment 4, "Rules and Consequences Policy," states that supervisors may be subject to disciplinary action for failure to take appropriate action upon discovering the breach or failure to take the required steps to prevent a breach from occurring. Consequences may include reprimand, suspension, removal, or other actions in accordance with applicable law and agency policy.

Veterans Administration

On May 3, 2006, a data analyst at Veterans Affairs took home a laptop and an external hard drive containing unencrypted information on 26.5 million people. The computer equipment was stolen in a burglary of the analyst's home in Montgomery County, Maryland. The burglary was immediately reported to both Maryland police and his supervisors at Veterans Affairs. The theft raised fears of potential mass identity theft. On June 29, the stolen laptop computer and hard drive were turned in by an unidentified person. The incident resulted in Congress imposing specific response, reporting, and breach notification requirements on the Veterans Administration (VA).

Title IX of P.L. 109-461, the Veterans Affairs Information Security Act, requires the VA to implement agency-wide information security procedures to protect the VA's "sensitive personal information" (SPI) and VA information systems. P.L. 109-461 also requires that in the event of a "data breach" of SPI processed or maintained by the VA, the Secretary must ensure that as soon as possible after discovery, either a non-VA entity or the VA's Inspector General conduct an independent risk analysis of the data breach to determine the level of risk associated with the data breach for the potential misuse of any SPI. Based on the risk analysis, if the Secretary determines that a reasonable risk exists of the potential misuse of SPI, the Secretary must provide credit protection services.

P.L. 109-461 also requires the VA to include data security requirements in all contracts with private-sector service providers that require access to SPI. All contracts involving access to SPI must include a prohibition of the disclosure of such information, unless the disclosure is lawful and expressly authorized under the contract, as well as the condition that the contractor or subcontractor notify the Secretary of any data breach of such information. In addition, each contract must provide for liquidated damages to be paid by the contractor to the Secretary in the event of a data breach with respect to any SPI, and that money should be made available exclusively for the purpose of providing credit protection services.

State Breach Notification Laws

All 50 states, the District of Columbia, Guam, Puerto Rico, and the Virgin Islands have enacted legislation requiring private or governmental entities to notify individuals of security breaches of information involving personally identifiable information.

- California was the first to adopt a security breach notification law. The California Security Breach Information Act (California Civil Code Section 1798.82), effective July 1, 2003, required companies based in California or with customers in California to notify them whenever their personal information may have been compromised. This groundbreaking legislation provided the model for states around the country.

- MA Chapter 93H Massachusetts Security Breach Notification Law, enacted in 2007, and the subsequent 201 CMR 17 Standards for the Protection of Personal Information of Residents of the Commonwealth, is widely regarded as the most comprehensive state information security legislation.

- The Texas Breach Notification Law was amended in 2011 to require entities doing business within the state to provide notification of data breaches to residents of states that have not enacted their own breach notification law. In 2013, this provision was removed. Additionally, in 2013, an amendment was added that notice provided to consumers in states that require notification can comply with either the Texas law or the law of the state in which the individual resides.

The basic premise of the state security breach laws is that consumers have a right to know if unencrypted personal information such as SSN, driver's license number, state identification card number, credit or debit card number, account password, PINs, or access codes have either been or are suspected to be compromised. The concern is that the listed information could be used fraudulently to assume or attempt to assume a person's identity. Exempt from legislation is publicly available information that is lawfully made available to the general public from federal, state, or local government records or by widely distributed media.

State security breach notification laws generally follow the same framework, which includes who must comply, a definition of personal information and breach, the elements of harm that must occur, triggers for notification, exceptions, and the relationship to federal law and penalties and enforcement authorities. Although the framework is standard, the laws are anything but. The divergence begins with the differences in how personal information is defined and who is covered by the law, and ends in aggregate penalties that range from $50,000 to $500,000. The variations are so numerous that compliance is confusing and onerous.

It is strongly recommended that any organization that experiences a breach or suspected breach of PII consult with legal counsel for interpretation and application of the myriad of sector-based, federal, and state incident response and notification laws.

Does Notification Work?

In the previous section, we discussed sector-based, federal, and state breach notification requirements. Notification can be resource-intensive, time-consuming, and expensive. The question that needs to be asked is, is it worth it? The resounding answer from privacy and security advocates, public relations (PR) specialists, and consumers is "yes." Consumers trust those who collect their personal information to protect it. When that doesn't happen, they need to know so that they can take steps to protect themselves from identity theft, fraud, and privacy violations.

Experian commissioned the Ponemon Institute to conduct a consumer study on data breach notification. The findings are instructive. When asked "What personal data if lost or stolen would you worry most about?", they overwhelmingly responded "password/PIN" and "social security number."

- Eighty-five percent believe notification about data breach and the loss or theft of their personal information is relevant to them.

- Fifty-nine percent believe a data breach notification means there is a high probability they will become an identity theft victim.

- Fifty-eight percent say the organization has an obligation to provide identity protection services, and 55% say they should provide credit-monitoring services.

- Seventy-two percent were disappointed in the way the notification was handled. A key reason for the disappointment is respondents' belief that the notification did not increase their understanding about the data breach.

In Practice

Data Breach Reporting and Notification Policy

Synopsis: To ensure compliance with all applicable laws, regulations, and contractual obligations, timely communications with customers, and internal support for the process.

Policy Statement:

- It is the intent of the company to comply with all information security breach–related laws, regulations, and contractual obligations.

- Executive management has the authority to engage outside expertise for legal counsel, crisis management, PR, and communications.

- Affected customer and business partners will be notified as quickly as possible of a suspected or known compromise of personal information. The company will provide regular updates as more information becomes known.

- Based on applicable laws, legal counsel in collaboration with the CEO will make the determination regarding the scope and content of customer notification.

- Legal counsel and the marketing/PR department will collaborate on all internal and external notifications and communications. All publications must be authorized by executive management.

- Customer service must staff appropriately to meet the anticipated demand for additional information.

- The COO is the official spokesperson for the organization. In his/her absence, the legal counsel will function as the official spokesperson.

The Public Face of a Breach

It's tempting to keep a data breach secret, but not reasonable. Consumers need to know when their information is at risk so they can respond accordingly. After notification has gone out, rest assured that the media will pick up the story. Breaches attract more attention than other technology-related topics, so reporters are more apt to cover them to drive traffic to their sites. If news organizations learn about these attacks through third-party sources while the breached organization remains silent, the fallout can be significant. Organizations must be proactive in their PR approach, using public messaging to counteract inaccuracies and tell the story from their point of view. Doing this right can save an organization's reputation and even, in some cases, enhance the perception of its brand in the eyes of customers and the general public. The PR professionals advise following these straightforward but strict rules when addressing the media and the public:

- Get it over with.
- Be humble.
- Don't lie.
- Say only what needs to be said.

Don't wait until a breach happens to develop a PR preparedness plan. Communications should be part of any incident preparedness strategy. Security specialists should work with PR people to identify the worst possible breach scenario so they can message against it and determine audience targets, including customers, partners, employees, and the media. Following a breach, messaging should be bulletproof and consistent.

Training users to use strong passwords, not click on email embedded links, not open unsolicited email attachments, properly identify anyone requesting information, and report suspicious activity can significantly reduce small business exposure and harm.

Summary

An information security incident is an adverse event that threatens business security and/or disrupts operations. Examples include intentional unauthorized access, DDoS attacks, malware, and inappropriate usage. The objective of an information security risk management program is to minimize the number of successful attempts and attacks. The reality is that security incidents happen even at the most security-conscious organizations. Every organization should be prepared to respond to an incident quickly, confidently, and in compliance with applicable laws and regulations.

The objective of incident management is a consistent and effective approach to the identification of and response to information security–related incidents. Meeting that objective requires situational awareness, incident reporting mechanisms, a documented IRP, and an understanding of legal obligations. Incident preparation includes developing strategies and instructions for documentation and evidence handling, detection and investigation (including forensic analysis), containment, eradication and recovery, notification, and closure. The roles and responsibilities of key personnel, including executive management, legal counsel, incident response coordinators (IRCs), designated incident handlers (DIHs), the incident response team (IRT), and ancillary personnel as well as external entities such as law enforcement and regulatory agencies, should be clearly defined and communicated. Incident response capabilities should be practiced and evaluated on an ongoing basis.

Consumers have a right to know if their personal data has been compromised. In most situations, data breaches of PII must be reported to the appropriate authority and affected parties notified. A data breach is generally defined as actual or suspected compromise, unauthorized disclosure, unauthorized acquisition, unauthorized access, or unauthorized use or loss of control of legally protected PII. All 50 states, the District of Columbia, Guam, Puerto Rico and the Virgin Islands have enacted legislation requiring private or governmental entities to notify individuals of security breaches of information involving personally identifiable information. In addition to state laws, there are sector- and agency-specific federal regulations that pertain to reporting and notification. Organizations that experience a breach or suspected breach of PII should consult with legal counsel for interpretation and application of often overlapping and contradictory rules and expectations.

Incident management policies include Incident Definition Policy, Incident Classification Policy, Information Response Program Policy, Incident Response Authority Policy, Evidence Handling and Use Policy, and Data Breach Reporting and Notification Policy. NIST Special Publication 800-61 goes over the major phases of the incident response process in detail. You should become familiar with that publication because it provides additional information that will help you succeed in your security operations center (SOC).

Many organizations take advantage of tabletop (simulated) exercises to further test their capabilities. These tabletop exercises are an opportunity to practice and also perform gap analysis. In addition, these exercises may also allow them to create playbooks for incident response. Developing a playbook framework makes future analysis modular and extensible.

During the investigation and resolution of a security incident, you may also need to communicate with outside parties regarding the incident. Examples include, but are not limited to, contacting law enforcement, fielding media inquiries, seeking external expertise, and working with Internet service providers (ISPs), the vendor of your hardware and software products, threat intelligence vendor feeds, coordination centers, and members of other incident response teams. You can also share relevant incident indicator of compromise (IoC) information and other observables with industry peers. A good example of information-sharing communities includes the Financial Services Information Sharing and Analysis Center (FS-ISAC).

Test Your Skills

MULTIPLE CHOICE QUESTIONS

1. Which of the following statements best defines incident management?

   A. Incident management is risk minimization.

   B. Incident management is a consistent approach to responding to and resolving issues.

   C. Incident management is problem resolution.

   D. Incident management is forensic containment.

2. Which of the following statements is true of security-related incidents?

   A. Over time, security-related incidents have become less prevalent and less damaging.

   B. Over time, security-related incidents have become more prevalent and more disruptive.

   C. Over time, security-related incidents have become less prevalent and more damaging.

   D. Over time, security-related incidents have become more numerous and less disruptive.

3. Which of the following CVSS score groups represents the intrinsic characteristics of a vulnerability that are constant over time and do not depend on a user-specific environment?

   A. Temporal

   B. Base

   C. Environmental

   D. Access vector

4. Which of the following aim to protect their citizens by providing security vulnerability information, security awareness training, best practices, and other information?

   A. National CERTs

   B. PSIRT

   C. ATA

   D. Global CERTs

5. Which of the following is the team that handles the investigation, resolution, and disclosure of security vulnerabilities in vendor products and services?

    A. CSIRT

    B. ICASI

    C. USIRP

    D. PSIRT

6. Which of the following is an example of a coordination center?

    A. PSIRT

    B. FIRST

    C. The CERT/CC division of the Software Engineering Institute (SEI)

    D. USIRP from ICASI

7. Which of the following is the most widely adopted standard to calculate the severity of a given security vulnerability?

    A. VSS

    B. CVSS

    C. VCSS

    D. CVSC

8. The CVSS base score defines Exploitability metrics that measure how a vulnerability can be exploited as well as Impact metrics that measure the impact on which of the following? (Choose three.)

    A. Repudiation

    B. Nonrepudiation

    C. Confidentiality

    D. Integrity

    E. Availability

9. Which of the following is true about cybersecurity incidents?

    A. Compromise business security

    B. Disrupt operations

    C. Impact customer trust

    D. All of the above

10. Which of the following statements is true when a cybersecurity-related incident occurs at a business partner or vendor that hosts or processes legally protected data on behalf of an organization?

    A. The organization does not need to do anything.

    B. The organization must be notified and respond accordingly.

    C. The organization is not responsible.

    D. The organization must report the incident to local law enforcement.

11. Which of the following can be beneficial to further test incident response capabilities?

    A. Phishing

    B. Legal exercises

    C. Tabletop exercises

    D. Capture the flag

12. A celebrity is admitted to the hospital. If an employee accesses the celebrity's patient record just out of curiosity, the action is referred to as _____.

    A. inappropriate usage

    B. unauthorized access

    C. unacceptable behavior

    D. undue care

13. Which of the following is true when employees report cybersecurity incidents?

    A. Prepared to respond to the incident

    B. Praised for their actions

    C. Provided compensation

    D. None of the above

14. Which of the following statements is true of an incident response plan?

    A. An incident response plan should be updated and authorized annually.

    B. An incident response plan should be documented.

    C. An incident response plan should be stress-tested.

    D. All of the above.

15. Which of the following terms best describes a signal or warning that an incident may occur in the future?

    A. A sign

    B. A precursor

    C. An indicator

    D. Forensic evidence

16. Which of the following terms best describes the process of taking steps to prevent the incident from spreading?

    A. Detection

    B. Containment

    C. Eradication

    D. Recovery

17. Which of the following terms best describes the addressing of the vulnerabilities related to the exploit or compromise and restoring normal operations?

    A. Detection

    B. Containment

    C. Testing

    D. Recovery

18. Which of the following terms best describes the eliminating of the components of the incident?

    A. Investigation

    B. Containment

    C. Eradication

    D. Recovery

19. Which of the following terms best describes the substantive or corroborating evidence that an incident may have occurred or may be occurring now?

    A. Indicator of compromise

    B. Forensic proof

    C. Heresy

    D. Diligence

20. Which of the following is not generally an incident response team responsibility?

    A. Incident impact analysis

    B. Incident communications

    C. Incident plan auditing

    D. Incident management

21. Documentation of the transfer of evidence is known as a _____.

    A. chain of evidence

    B. chain of custody

    C. chain of command

    D. chain of investigation

22. Data breach notification laws pertain to which of the following?

    A. Intellectual property

    B. Patents

    C. PII

    D. Products

23. HIPAA/HITECH requires _____ within 60 days of the discovery of a breach.

    A. notification be sent to affected parties

    B. notification be sent to law enforcement

    C. notification be sent to Department of Health and Human Services

    D. notification be sent to all employees

EXERCISES

EXERCISE 11.1: **Assessing an Incident Report**

1. At your school or workplace, locate information security incident reporting guidelines.

2. Evaluate the process. Is it easy to report an incident? Are you encouraged to do so?

3. How would you improve the process?

EXERCISE 11.2: **Evaluating an Incident Response Policy**

1. Locate an incident response policy document either at your school, workplace, or online. Does the policy clearly define the criteria for an incident?

2. Does the policy define roles and responsibilities? If so, describe the response structure (for example, who is in charge, who should investigate an incident, who can talk to the media). If not, what information is the policy missing?

3. Does the policy include notification requirements? If yes, what laws are referenced and why? If no, what laws should be referenced?

EXERCISE 11.3: **Researching Containment and Eradication**

1. Research and identify the latest strains of malware.

2. Choose one. Find instructions for containment and eradication.

3. Conventional risk management wisdom is that it is better to replace a hard drive than to try to remove malware. Do you agree? Why or why not?

EXERCISE 11.4: **Researching a DDoS Attack**

1. Find a recent news article about DDoS attacks.

2. Who were the attackers and what was their motivation?

3. What was the impact of the attack? What should the victim organization do to mitigate future damage?

EXERCISE 11.5: **Understanding Evidence Handling**

1. Create a worksheet that could be used by an investigator to build an incident profile.

2. Create an evidentiary chain of custody form that could be used in legal proceedings.

3. Create a log for documenting forensic or computer-based investigation.

PROJECTS

PROJECT 11.1: Creating Incident Awareness

1. One of the key messages to be delivered in training and awareness programs is the importance of incident reporting. Educating users to recognize and report suspicious behavior is a powerful deterrent to would-be intruders. The organization you work for has classified the following events as high priority, requiring immediate reporting:

- Customer data at risk of exposure or compromise

- Unauthorized use of a system for any purpose

- DoS attack

- Unauthorized downloads of software, music, or videos

- Missing equipment

- Suspicious person in the facility

You have been tasked with training all users to recognize these types of incidents.

1. Write a brief explanation of why each of the listed events is considered high priority. Include at least one example per event.

2. Create a presentation that can be used to train employees to recognize these incidents and how to report them.

3. Create a 10-question quiz that tests their post-presentation knowledge.

PROJECT 11.2: Assessing Security Breach Notifications

Access the State of New Hampshire, Department of Justice, Office of the Attorney General security breach notification web page. Sort the notifications by year.

1. Read three recent notification letters to the Attorney General as well as the corresponding notice that will be sent to the consumer (be sure to scroll through the document). Write a summary and timeline (as presented) of each event.

2. Choose one incident to research. Find corresponding news articles, press releases, and so on.

3. Compare the customer notification summary and timeline to your research. In your opinion, was the notification adequate? Did it include all pertinent details? What controls should the company put in place to prevent this from happening again?

PROJECT 11.3: **Comparing and Contrasting Regulatory Requirements**

The objective of this project is to compare and contrast breach notification requirements.

1. Create a grid that includes state, statute, definition of personal information, definition of a breach, time frame to report a breach, reporting agency, notification requirements, exemptions, and penalties for nonconformance. Fill in the grid using information from five states.

2. If a company that did business in all five states experienced a data breach, would it be able to use the same notification letter for consumers in all five states? Why or why not?

3. Create a single notification law using what you believe are the best elements of the five laws included in the grid. Be prepared to defend your choices.

Case Study

An Exercise in Cybercrime Incident Response

A cybercrime incident response exercise is one of the most effective ways to enhance organizational awareness. This cybercrime incident response exercise is designed to mimic a multiday event. Participants are challenged to find the clues, figure out what to do, and work as a team to minimize the impact. Keep the following points in mind:

- Although fictional, the scenarios used in the exercise are based on actual events.

- As in the actual events, there may be "unknowns," and it may be necessary to make some assumptions.

- The scenario will be presented in a series of situation vignettes.

- At the end of each day, you will be asked to answer a set of questions. Complete the questions before continuing on.

- At the end of Day 2, you will be asked to create a report.

This Case Study is designed to be a team project. You will need to work with at least one other member of your class to complete the exercise.

Background

BestBank is proudly celebrating its tenth anniversary year with special events throughout the year. Last year, BestBank embarked on a five-year strategic plan to extend its reach and offer services to municipalities and armed services personnel. Integral to this plan is the acquisition of U.S. Military Bank. The combined entity will be known as USBEST. The new entity will be primarily staffed by BestBank personnel.

USBEST is maintaining U.S. Military Bank's long-term contract with the Department of Defense to provide financial and insurance services to active-duty and retired military personnel. The primary delivery channel is via a branded website. Active-duty and retired military personnel can access the site directly by going to www.bankformilitary.org. USBEST has also put a link on its home page. The bankformilitary.org website is hosted by HostSecure, a private company located in the Midwest.

USBEST's first marketing campaign is a "We're Grateful" promotion, including special military-only certificate of deposit (CD) rates as well as discounted insurance programs.

Cast of Characters:

- Sam Smith, VP of Marketing
- Robyn White, Deposit Operations and Online Banking Manager
- Sue Jones, IT Manager
- Cindy Hall, Deposit Operations Clerk
- Joe Bench, COO

Day 1
Wednesday 7:00 A.M.

The marketing campaign begins with posts on Facebook and Twitter as well as emails to all current members of both institutions announcing the acquisition and the "We're Grateful" promotion. All communications encourage active-duty and retired military personnel to visit the www.bankformilitary.org website.

Wednesday 10:00 A.M.

IT sends an email to Sam Smith, VP of Marketing, reporting that they have been receiving alerts that indicate there is significant web traffic to http://www.bankformilitary.org. Smith is pleased.

Wednesday Late Morning/Early Afternoon

By late morning, the USBEST receptionist starts getting calls about problems accessing the bankformilitary.org site. After lunch, the calls escalate; the callers are angry about something on the website. As per procedure, she informs callers that the appropriate person will call them back as soon as possible and forwards the messages to Sam Smith's voicemail.

Wednesday 3:45 P.M.

Sam Smith returns to his office and retrieves his voice messages. Smith opens his browser and goes to bankformilitary.org. To his horror, he finds that "We're Grateful" has been changed to "We're Hateful" and that "USBEST will be charging military families fees for all services."

Sam immediately goes to the office of Robyn White, Deposit Operations and Online Banking Manager. Robyn's department is responsible for online services, including the bankformilitary.org website, and she has administrative access. He is told that Robyn is working remotely and that she has email access. Sam calls Robyn at home but gets her voicemail. He sends her an email asking her to call him ASAP!

Sam then contacts the bank's IT Manager, Sue Jones. Sue calls HostSecure for help in gaining access to the website. HostSecure is of little assistance. They claim that all they do is host, not manage the site. Sue insists upon talking to "someone in charge." After being transferred and put on hold numerous times, she speaks with the HostSecure Security Officer, who informs her that upon proper authorization, they can shut down the website. Jones inquires who is on the authorization list. The HostSecure Security Officer informs Sue that it would be a breach of security to provide that information.

Wednesday 4:40 P.M.

Sue Jones locates Robyn White's cell phone number and calls her to discuss what is happening. Robyn apologizes for not responding quicker to Sam's mail; she ducked out for her son's soccer game. Robyn tells Sue that she had received an email early this morning from HostSecure informing her that she needed to update her administrative password to a more secure version. The email had a link to a change password form. She was happy to learn that they were updating their password requirements. Robyn reported that she clicked the link, followed the instructions (which included verifying her current password), and changed her password to a secure, familiar one. She also forwarded the email to Cindy Hall, Deposit Operations Clerk, and asked her to update her password as well. Sue asks Robyn to log in to bankformilitary.org to edit the home page. Robyn complies and logs in with her new credentials. The login screen returns a "bad password" error. She logs in with her old credentials; they do not work either.

Wednesday 4:55 P.M.

Sue Jones calls HostSecure. She is put on hold. After waiting five minutes, she hangs up and calls again. This time she receives a message that regular business hours are 8:00 a.m. to 5:00 p.m. EST. The message indicates that for emergency service, customers should call the number on their service contract. Sue does not have a copy of the contract. She calls the Accounting and Finance Department Manager to see if they have a copy. Everyone in the department is gone for the day.

Wednesday 5:10 P.M.

Sue Jones lets Sam Smith know that she cannot do anything more until the morning. Sam decides to update Facebook and the USBEST website home page with an announcement of what is happening, reassuring the public that the bank is doing everything they can and apologizing profusely.

Day 1 Questions:

1. What do you suspect is happening or has happened?

2. What actions (if any) should be taken?

3. Who should be contacted and what should they be told?

4. What lessons can be learned from the day's events?

Day 2

Thursday 7:30 A.M.

Cindy Hall's first task of the day is to log in to the bankformilitary.org administrative portal to retrieve a report on the previous evening's transactional activity. She is surprised to see so many Bill Pay transactions. Upon closer inspection, the funds all seem to be going to the same account and they started a few minutes after midnight. She makes an assumption that the retailer must be having a midnight special and wonders what it is. She then opens Outlook and sees Robyn's forwarded email about changing her password. She proceeds to do so.

Thursday 8:00 A.M.

Customer Service opens at 8:00 a.m. Immediately they begin fielding calls from military personnel reporting fraudulent Bill Pay transactions. The CSR manager calls Cindy Hall in Deposit Operations to report the problem. Cindy accesses the bankformilitary.org administrative portal to get more information but finds she cannot log in. She figures she must have written down her new password incorrectly. She will ask Robyn to reset it when she gets in.

Thursday 8:30 A.M.

Robyn arrives for work and plugs in her laptop.

Thursday 9:00 A.M.

Sam Smith finally gets through to someone at HostSecure who agrees to work with him to remove the offending text. He is very relieved and informs Joe Bench, COO.

Thursday 10:10 A.M.

Sam Smith arrives 10 minutes late to the weekly senior management meeting. He is visibly shaken. He connects his iPad to a video projector and displays on the screen an anonymous blog that is describing the defacement, lists the URL for the bankformilitary.org administrative portal, the username and password for an administrative account, and member account information. He scrolls down to the next blog entry, which includes private internal bank correspondence.

Day 2 Questions:

1. What do you suspect is happening or has happened?

2. Who (if anyone) external to the organization should be notified?

3. What actions should be taken to contain the incident and minimize the impact?

4. What should be done post-containment?

5. What lessons can be learned from the day's events?

Day 2 Report

It is now 11:00 a.m. An emergency meeting of the Board of Directors has been called for 3:30 p.m. You are tasked with preparing a written report for the Board that includes a synopsis of the incident, detailing the response effort up to the time of the meeting, and recommending a timeline of next steps.

Day 2: Presentation to the Board of Directors 3:30 P.M.

1. Present your written report to the Board of Directors.

2. Be prepared to discuss next steps.

3. Be prepared to discuss law enforcement involvement (if applicable).

4. Be prepared to discuss consumer notification obligations (if applicable).

References

Regulations Cited

"Data Breach Response: A Guide for Business," Federal Trade Commission, accessed 04/2018, https://www.ftc.gov/tips-advice/business-center/guidance/data-breach-response-guide-business.

"Appendix B to Part 364—Interagency Guidelines Establishing Information Security Standards," accessed 04/2018, https://www.fdic.gov/regulations/laws/rules/2000-8660.html.

"201 CMR 17.00: Standards for the Protection of Personal Information of Residents of the Commonwealth," official website of the Office of Consumer Affairs & Business Regulation (OCABR), accessed 04/2018, www.mass.gov/ocabr/docs/idtheft/201cmr1700reg.pdf.

"Family Educational Rights and Privacy Act (FERPA)," official website of the U.S. Department of Education, accessed 04/2018, https://www2.ed.gov/policy/gen/guid/fpco/ferpa/index.html.

"Financial Institution Letter (FIL-27-2005), Final Guidance on Response Programs for Unauthorized Access to Customer Information and Customer Notice," accessed 04/2018, https://www.fdic.gov/news/news/financial/2005/fil2705.html.

"HIPAA Security Rule," official website of the Department of Health and Human Services, accessed 04/2018, https://www.hhs.gov/hipaa/for-professionals/security/index.html.

"Office of Management and Budget Memorandum M-07-16 Safeguarding Against and Responding to the Breach of Personally Identifiable Information," accessed 04/2018, https://www.whitehouse.gov/OMB/memoranda/fy2007/m07-16.pdf.

Other References

"The Vocabulary for Event Recording and Incident Sharing (VERIS)", accessed 04/2018, http://veriscommunity.net/veris-overview.html.

"Chain of Custody and Evidentiary Issues," eLaw Exchange, accessed 04/2018, www.elawexchange.com.

"Complying with the FTC's Health Breach Notification Rule," FTC Bureau of Consumer Protection, accessed 04/2018, https://www.ftc.gov/tips-advice/business-center/guidance/complying-ftcs-health-breach-notification-rule.

"Student Privacy," U.S. Department of Education, accessed 04/2018, https://studentprivacy.ed.gov/.

"Forensic Examination of Digital Evidence: A Guide for Law Enforcement," U.S. Department of Justice, National Institute of Justice, accessed 04/2018, https://www.nij.gov/publications/pages/publication-detail.aspx?ncjnumber=199408.

"VERIS Community Database, accessed 04/2018, http://veriscommunity.net/vcdb.html.

Mandia, Kevin, and Chris Prosise, *Incident Response: Investigating Computer Crime*, Berkeley, California: Osborne/McGraw-Hill, 2001.

Nolan, Richard, "First Responders Guide to Computer Forensics," 2005, Carnegie Mellon University Software Engineering Institute.

"United States Computer Emergency Readiness Team," US-CERT, accessed 04/2018, https://www.us-cert.gov.

"CERT Division of the Software Engineering Institute (SEI)," accessed 04/2018, https://cert.org.

Forum of Incident Response and Security Teams (FIRST), accessed 04/2018, https://first.org.

"The Common Vulnerability Scoring System: Specification Document," accessed 04/2018, https://first.org/cvss/specification-document.

Chapter | **12**

Business Continuity Management

Chapter Objectives

After reading this chapter and completing the exercises, you will be able to do the following:

- Define a disaster.
- Appreciate the importance of emergency preparedness.
- Analyze threats, risks, and business impact assessments.
- Explain the components of a business continuity plan and program.
- Develop policies related to business continuity management.

Section 17 of the ISO 27002:2013 is "Business Continuity Management." The objective of the Business Continuity Management domain is to ensure the continued operation and secure provision of essential services during a disruption of normal operating conditions. To support this objective, threat scenarios are evaluated, essential services and processes are identified, and response, contingency, and recovery and resumption strategies, plans, and procedures are developed, tested, and maintained. Business continuity is a component of organization risk management.

We have learned valuable lessons from the events of September 11, 2001, Hurricane Katrina, the 2013 Boston bombing, and Hurricane Maria's devastation in Puerto Rico. Preparation and business continuity plans do more than protect business assets; in the long run, they protect employees and their families, investors, business partners, and the community. Business continuity plans are, in essence, a civic duty.

FYI: ISO/IEC 27002:2013 and NIST Guidance

Section 17 of ISO 27002:2013, "Business Continuity Management," focuses on availability and the secure provision of essential services during a disruption of normal operating conditions. ISO 22301 provides a framework to plan, establish, implement, operate, monitor, review, maintain, and continually improve a business continuity management system (BCMS).

Corresponding NIST guidance is provided in the following documents:

- **SP 800-34:** "Contingency Planning Guide for Information Technology System, Revision 1"

- **SP 800-53:** "Security and Privacy Controls for Federal Information Systems and Organizations, Revision 5"

- **SP 800-84:** "Guide to Test, Training and Exercise Programs for Information Technology Plans and Capabilities"

Emergency Preparedness

A *disaster* is an event that results in damage or destruction, loss of life, or drastic change to the environment. In a business context, a disaster is an unplanned event that has the potential to disrupt the delivery of mission-critical services and functions, jeopardize the welfare of employees, customers, or business partners, and/or cause significant financial harm. From a security perspective, a disaster manifests itself as a sustained disruption of system availability and/or confidentiality or integrity controls. The cause can be environmental, operational, accidental, or willful, as illustrated in Figure 12-1.

Worldwide, a major disaster occurs almost daily. According to the Federal Emergency Management Agency (FEMA), a disaster has occurred, on average, every week in the United States for the past 10 years. The U.S. Department of Homeland Security (DHS) has identified the impact of 15 disaster scenarios that could take the country days (explosives) to weeks (food contamination) to months (pandemic, major hurricane) to years (nuclear detonation, major earthquake) to potentially recover from.

Preparing for a disaster can make the difference between life and death, success or failure, yet most businesses are not prepared. An Ad Council survey found that nearly two-thirds (62%) of respondents did not have an emergency plan in place for their business. When disaster inevitably strikes, without a plan, there is little chance of a successful response and recovery. The Insurance Information Institute reported that up to 40% of businesses affected by a natural or human-caused disaster never reopen.

The goal of emergency preparedness is to protect life and property. Disasters are unplanned; however, they should not be unanticipated. How much an organization should prepare depends on a number of factors, including risk tolerance, financial strength, regulatory requirements, and stakeholder impact. What we know for sure is that relying solely on insurance and post-disaster government assistance is shortsighted and, in some cases, negligent.

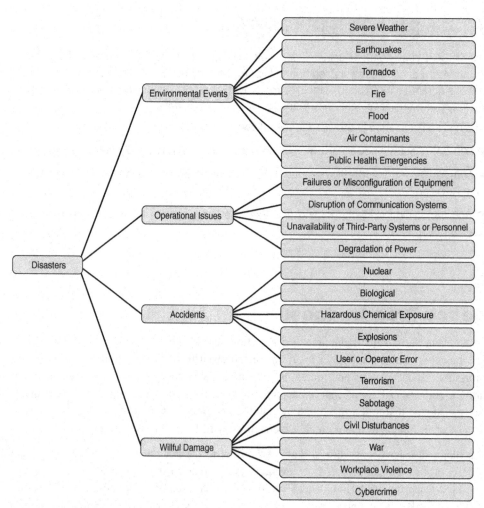

FIGURE 12-1   Disasters and Their Causes

What Is a Resilient Organization?

A *resilient* organization is one that has the ability to quickly adapt and recover from known or unknown changes to the environment. Resilience doesn't just happen. It requires management support, investment, planning, and layers of preparation. In their post-9/11 study, "The Five Principles of Organizational Resilience," Gartner reminds us that "organizational resilience has taken on a new urgency since the tragic events of Sept. 11. The ability to respond quickly, decisively and effectively to unforeseen and unpredictable forces is now an enterprise imperative." It cites leadership, culture, people, systems, and settings as the bedrock of an agile and adaptive organization.

- Resilience begins with enterprise leadership setting the priorities, allocating the resources, and making the commitments to establish organizational resilience throughout the enterprise.

- A resilient culture is built on principles of organizational empowerment, purpose, trust, and accountability.

- People who are properly selected, motivated, equipped, and led will overcome almost any obstacle or disruption.

- Organizations achieve agility and flexibility by combining a highly distributed workplace model with a highly robust and collaborative IT infrastructure.

- Alternative workplace techniques such as office hoteling, telecommuting, and desk sharing provide the level of workplace flexibility and agility that is essential for mitigating the risk of catastrophic or disruptive incidents.

Regulatory Requirements

Business disruption has an economic and societal ripple effect. Emergency preparedness is a civic duty and, in many cases, a regulatory requirement. In 1998, President Clinton issued *Presidential Decision Directive (PDD) 63 Critical Infrastructure Protection*. The first in a series of executive branch directives, PDD-63 outlined roles, responsibilities, and objectives for protecting the nation's utility, transportation, financial, and other essential infrastructure, and introduced the concept of public-private partnership. In 2003, President Bush issued *Presidential Directive HSPD-7 Critical Infrastructure Identification, Prioritization, and Protection*, which designates certain sectors of the national infrastructure as critical to the national and economic security of the United States and the well-being of its citizenry, and requires steps be taken to protect it, including emergency response and continuity measures.

Congress recognized the issue as well and included emergency preparedness in critical sector regulatory legislation. The Health Insurance Portability and Accountability Act (HIPAA) Contingency Plan Standard 164.308(a)(7) requires covered entities to "Establish (and implement as needed) policies and procedures for responding to an emergency or other occurrence (for example, fire, vandalism, system failure, and natural disaster) that damages systems that contain electronic protected health information." The standard includes implementation specifications for data backup, disaster recovery, and emergency mode operation plans. The Gramm-Leach-Bliley Safeguards Act requires financial institutions to "identify reasonably foreseeable internal and external threats that could result in unauthorized disclosure, misuse, alteration, or destruction of customer information or customer information systems" and to "take measures to protect against destruction, loss, or damage of customer information due to potential environmental hazards, such as fire and water damage or technological failures." Similar legislation has been issued by the Federal Energy Regulatory Commission (FERC) for utility companies, by the Nuclear Energy Regulatory Commission (NERC) for nuclear power plants, by the Federal Communications Commission (FCC) for telecom carriers, and by the Food and Drug Administration (FDA) for pharmaceutical companies.

In October 2012, the Department of Homeland Security issued *Federal Continuity Directive 1*. The directive states that "Federal Executive Branch organizations, regardless of their size or location, shall have in place a viable continuity capability to ensure resiliency and continued performance of their organization's essential functions under all conditions." Included in the directive was a restatement of the government's roles in creating public/private partnerships in order to create and sustain a "culture of continuity."

In May 2012, NIST released Special Publication 800-34, R1: Contingency Planning Guide for Federal Information Systems, which provides guidance for federal agencies. The guidance is applicable to public and private sector business continuity planning.

In Practice

Emergency Preparedness Policy

Policy Synopsis: Demonstrate the organization's commitment to emergency preparedness and business continuity.

Policy Statement:

- An emergency preparedness and business continuity strategy that ensures the safety of employees and customers, enables the company to perform essential functions absent normal operating conditions, protects organizational assets, and meets regulatory requirements is an organizational priority.

- The company will designate necessary resources to develop and maintain emergency preparedness and business continuity plans and procedures.

Business Continuity Risk Management

Continuity planning is simply the good business practice of ensuring the execution of essential functions. Continuity planning is an integral component of organizational risk management. In Chapter 4, "Governance and Risk Management," we defined risk management as the process of identifying, analyzing, assessing, and communicating risk and accepting, avoiding, transferring, or controlling it to an acceptable level considering associated costs and benefits of any actions taken. Risk management for continuity of operations requires that organizations identify threats (threat assessment), determine risk (risk assessment), and assess the internal and external impact of the disruption of mission-critical or essential services (business impact assessment). The two anticipated outcomes are (1) the identification and (if feasible) mitigation of significant threats and (2) the documentation of essential services. This information is then used to construct response, continuity, and recovery operations.

What Is a Business Continuity Threat Assessment?

A *business continuity threat* can best be defined as a potential danger to the organization. Threats can be business-specific, local, regional, national, or even global. The objective of a *business continuity threat assessment* is to identify viable threats and predict the likelihood of occurrence. Threat modeling takes into account historical and predictive geographic, technological, physical, environmental, third-party, and industry factors such as the following:

- What type of disasters have occurred in the community or at this location?
- What can happen due to the geographic location?
- What could cause processes or information systems to fail?
- What threats are related to service provider dependency?
- What disasters could result from the design or construction of the facility or campus?
- What hazards are particular to the industry sector?

Identified threats are rated in terms of the likelihood of occurrence and potential impact sans controls. The higher the rating, the more significant the threat. The challenge to this approach is the unexpected event. Sadly, as we saw on 9/11, threats are not always predictable. Table 12-1 presents threat assessments that take into account past occurrences.

TABLE 12-1   Threat Assessments: Historical

Threat Categories	Threat	Description	Likelihood Scale 1–5 [5=highest]	Impact Scale 1–5 [5=highest]	Impact Description	Inherent Risk (L*I)
Environmental	Wildfire	Wildfire consumed 15,000 acres, approximately 50 miles northwest of HQ	4	5	Campus fire.	20 HIGH
Service provider dependency	Disruption of Internet connectivity	Multiple periods of ISP downtime or extreme latency occurred.	4	5	Disruption of external mail, VPN connectivity, and cloud-based applications.	20 HIGH
Service provider dependency	Brownouts	Summer temperatures and corresponding air conditioning usage consistently results in brief periods of low power.	3	5	Power fluctuations have the potential to damage equipment.	15 MED
Location	Flood	Flash flooding is an annual occurrence on Highway 16.	5	2	Campus not affected; however, deliveries and personnel may be.	10 LOW

What Is a Business Continuity Risk Assessment?

The business continuity threat assessment identifies the most likely and significant business continuity–related threats to the organization. The ***business continuity risk assessment*** evaluates the sufficiency of controls to prevent a threat from occurring or to minimize its impact. The outcome is the residual risk associated with each threat. The residual risk level provides management with an accurate portrayal of what happens if the threat is exercised under current conditions.

In a best-case scenario, the residual risk is within organizational tolerance. If the residual risk is not within tolerance, the organization must decide to take action to lower the risk level, approve the risk, or share the risk. Table 12-2 illustrates risk assessment considerations for the specific threat of a wildfire. The actual process and calculations used should mirror the organizational risk assessment methodology.

TABLE 12-2   Sample Wildfire Risk Assessment

Threat	Area wildfires resulting in personnel evacuation and potential destruction.
Inherent Risk	High (as determined by the threat assessment).
Control Assessment	
Physical Controls	Fire berm around the campus. Contract with local firm for quarterly removal of flammable shrubs, leaves, dead limbs, and twigs within a 1,000-foot zone.
Building Controls	Fireproof construction. Sensor alarms with Fire Department (FD) notification. Fire and smoke sensors and sprinklers throughout the building. Fire safety maps throughout the building. Lighted emergency exits. No outside flammable substances stored near the building.
Data Center Controls	Sensor alarms with FD notification. Clean agent fire suppression system. Water mist system.
Personnel Controls	Evacuation plans. Fire drills conducted quarterly.
Technology Controls	Secondary data center 300 miles from primary campus. Near-time data replication. Secondary data center can support 200 concurrent remote users.
Financial Controls	Fire and hazard insurance policy. Business disruption insurance policy.
Control Assessment	Satisfactory.
Identified Vulnerabilities	Gas-powered generator. Gas fumes are combustible.
Residual Risk	Elevated.
Risk Reduction Recommendation	Replace gas-powered generator with diesel-powered generator.

Lowering the risk level requires the organization to implement additional controls and safeguards and/ or to modify existing ones. In general, preventative or mitigating controls that deter, detect, and/or reduce disruption and impact are preferable to contingency procedures or recovery activities. As new technologies become available, preventative controls should be reevaluated and recovery strategies modified. The widespread adoption of virtualization as a preventative control is a good example of how technological innovation can influence business continuity planning.

Approving the risk implies that the organization is willing to assume the level of risk even though it is not within an acceptable range. As we discussed in Chapter 4, approving elevated or severe risk level is an executive-level decision. The decision may be based on cost, market conditions, external pressures, or a willingness to play the odds.

Risk sharing is when the risk (and consequences) are distributed among two or more parties. Examples are outsourcing and insurance.

What Is a Business Impact Assessment?

The objective of a *business impact assessment (BIA)* is to identify *essential* services/processes and recovery time frames. In business continuity planning, *essential* means that the absence of, or disruption of the service/process, would result in significant, irrecoverable, or irreparable harm to the organization, employees, business partners, constituents, community, or country. Participants in the BIA process often incorrectly equate important with essential. There are a number of very important organization activities, such as marketing, recruiting, and auditing, that can be suspended in a disaster situation without impacting the viability of the organization, endangering constituents, or violating the law. On the other hand, there are mundane services, such as maintaining an ATM cash dispenser, that may be critical in a regional disaster. The key is to stay focused on the services required in the hours and days after a disaster strikes.

A business impact analysis is a multistep collaborative activity that should include business process owners, stakeholders, and corporate officers. This multistep collaborative activity is illustrated in Figure 12-2.

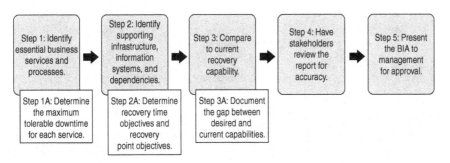

FIGURE 12-2 Business Impact Analysis

As noted in the previous steps, the BIA process incorporates three metrics:

- The ***maximum tolerable downtime (MTD)*** is the total length of time an essential business function can be unavailable without causing significant harm to the business.

- The ***recovery time objective (RTO)*** is the maximum amount of time a *system resource* can be unavailable before there is an unacceptable impact on other system resources or business processes.

- The ***recovery point objective (RPO)*** represents the point in time, prior to a disruption or system outage, that data can be recovered (in other words, the acceptable data loss).

In a perfect world, every essential system would be either redundant or available for immediate or near-time recovery. In reality, no organization has unlimited financial resources. The MTD, RTO, and RPO are useful in determining the optimum recovery investment and ancillary plans.

The outcome of a business impact analysis is a prioritized matrix of services, the required infrastructure, information systems, and dependencies for each service, recovery objectives, assessment of capabilities, and delta between the current and desired state. This information is then used by executive management to make investment decisions and to guide the development of disaster recovery and business contingency plans and procedures. Assuming an organization rated "Customer Communications" as an essential business process or service, Table 12-3 illustrates the components of a BIA.

TABLE 12-3   Business Impact Assessment: Customer Communications

Essential Business Process or Service: Customer Communications

Delivery Channels	Call Center	Website	Email
Required Infrastructure	Voice circuits. Wide area network power.	Internet access.	Internet access. Wide area network power.
Required Devices/ Information Systems	IP phone system. Call center system.	Hosted externally.	Email system, including email application servers and gateway filters. Authentication servers.
Third-Party Dependencies	Telco voice circuits.	Web hosting company. Internet service provider (ISP).	DNS propagation.
Maximum Tolerable Downtime (MTD)	5 minutes.	Need to update the site within 60 minutes.	60 minutes.
Recovery Time Objective (RTO)	Immediate.	30 minutes.	45 minutes.
Recovery Point Objective (RPO)	12 hours for historical data.	24 hours for website content.	No acceptable data loss.

Delivery Channels	Call Center	Website	Email
Current Capability	All calls will be automatically rerouted to the secondary data center. Redundant call center system located at secondary data center. Statistical data can be restored from backups. Data is replicated every 4 hours.	Localized disaster would not impact the website.	Redundant fully replicated email infrastructure located at the secondary data center. Assuming access to the secondary data center, external email will not be impacted. Incoming email will be delayed approximately 15 minutes, which is the time it takes for an MX record to be updated.
Identified Issues/Points of Failure	Call center staff is located at the primary location. Relocation will take a minimum of 8 hours.	Administrative access (required for updating) is restricted to specific IP addresses. Updating the access list is a third-party function. SLA is 30 minutes.	If the primary campus is available, the impact is minimal. If the primary campus is unavailable, only those users with remote access capability will be able to utilize email.
Capability Delta	755 minutes	0	+ 30 minutes
Data Loss Delta	0	0	0

In Practice

Business Impact Assessment

Synopsis: Require and assign responsibility for an annual BIA.

Policy Statement:

- The Chief Operating Officer is responsible for scheduling an enterprisewide annual BIA. System owner participation is required.

- The BIA will identify *essential* services and processes. *Essential* is defined as meeting one or more of the following criteria:

    - Required by law, regulation, or contractual obligation.
    - Disruption would be a threat to public safety.
    - Disruption would result in impact to the health and well-being of employees.
    - Disruption would result in irreparable harm to customers or business partners.
    - Disruption would result in significant or unrecoverable financial loss.

- For each essential service and/or process, the maximum tolerable downtime (MTD) will be documented. The MTD is the total length of time an essential function or process can be unavailable without causing significant harm to the business.

- For each essential service and/or process, supporting infrastructure, devices/information systems, and dependencies will be identified.

- Recovery time objectives (RTOs) and recovery point objectives (RPOs) for supporting infrastructure and devices/information systems will be documented.

- Current capability and capability delta will be identified. Deviations that put the organization at risk must be reported to the Board of Directors.

- The Chief Operating Officer, the Chief Information Officer, and the Business Continuity Team are jointly responsible for aligning the BIA outcome with the business continuity plan.

The Business Continuity Plan

The objective of business continuity planning is to ensure that organizations have the capability to respond to and recover from disaster situations. *Response plans* focus on the initial and near-term response and include such elements as authority, plan activation, notification, communication, evacuation, relocation, coordination with public authorities, and security. *Contingency plans* focus on immediate, near-term, and short-term alternate workforce and business processes. *Recovery plans* focus on the immediate, near-term, and short-term recovery of information systems, infrastructure, and facilities. *Resumption plans* guide the organization back to normalcy. Taken as a whole, this plan is referred to as the *business continuity plan (BCP)* or as the *continuity of operations plan (COOP)*. The discipline is referred to as *business continuity management*.

In Practice

Business Continuity Plan Policy

Synopsis: Require the organization to have a business continuity plan.

Policy Statement:

- The company's business continuity strategy will be documented in a business continuity plan. The plan will include plans, procedures, and ancillary documentation related to emergency preparedness, disaster preparation, response, contingency operations, recovery, resumption, training, testing, and plan maintenance.

Roles and Responsibilities

If we consider that the objective of business continuity management is to keep the business in business, it stands to reason that the responsibility must be distributed throughout the organization. Business continuity management involves the entire organization, from the Board member who approves the policy to the employee who carefully follows a related procedure. Depending on the size and complexity of the organizations as well as the nature of disaster, third parties such as public health and safety personnel, insurance representatives, legal counsel, service providers, and government agencies may all have a role to play. Business continuity responsibilities can be categorized as governance, operational, and tactical.

Governance

Governance is a continuing process in which diverse objectives, competing interests, and a range of ideas are evaluated, and ultimately binding decisions are made and supported. It is the responsibility of the Board of Directors (or equivalent) to provide oversight and guidance, authorize business continuity management–related policy, and be legally accountable for the actions of the organization.

Executive management is expected to provide leadership, demonstrate commitment, allocate budget, and devote resources to the development and continued upkeep of the BCP. In an emergency, they declare a disaster, activate the plan, and support the Business Continuity Team.

Operational Management

When disaster strikes, quick mobilization is essential to mitigate damages. It is imperative that there be designated leadership with the authority to act quickly. This is the primary role of the *Business Continuity Team (BCT)*, which is vested by the Board of Directors with the authority to make decisions related to disaster preparation, response, and recovery. BCT membership should represent a cross-section of the organization, including senior management, physical security, information technology (IT), human resources (HR), marketing/communications, information security, and business units. In concert, the team is responsible for the development, maintenance, testing, and updating of all related plans. The BCT may create subteams and assign responsibilities. Because the BCT will operate in unpredictable situations, second-in-command personnel should be trained and ready to assume their position. After executive management has declared a disaster and activated the plan, the BCT is responsible for assessing damage, managing the response, communications, continuity, and recovery activities, and providing status updates to executive management. It's also tasked with providing a post-disaster assessment of recovery and response efforts.

Tactical Activities

Tactical responsibilities are distributed throughout an enterprise. Depending on the size of the organization, some of these responsibilities may be consolidated. Unfortunately, it is all too common to encounter organizations that view the IT department as the owner of the business continuity process and expect IT to "take care of it." Although it is true that IT is a vital participant, business continuity management, as suggested by the following list, is an organization responsibility:

- The *IT department* is responsible for designing and supporting resilience systems and for the recovery of information and information systems in a disaster situation.

- *Department managers* are responsible for defining the operational needs of their department and for creating and maintaining functional departmental contingency procedures.

- The *HR department* is responsible for the communication with and welfare of personnel and provides emergency-related services and assistance.

- The *marketing or communications department* is responsible for crafting and releasing official statements, communicating with the media, and managing internal communication include updates.

- The *purchasing department* is responsible for expediently ordering necessary supplies and equipment.

- The *training department* is responsible for delivering business continuity–related training and ancillary materials.

- The *internal audit department* audits the BCP and procedures and reports its findings to executive management. The audit satisfies the best practice requirements of separation of duties and oversight.

In Practice

Business Continuity Management Policy

Synopsis: Assign business continuity management responsibilities.

Policy Statement:

- The Board of Directors is responsible for authorizing the business continuity plan. Reference to the business continuity plan is inclusive of plans, procedures, and ancillary documentation related to disaster preparation, response, contingency operations, recovery, resumption, training, testing, and plan maintenance. The Board must be apprised on a timely basis of any material changes to the business continuity strategy.

- The Chief Operating Officer or designee is responsible for the development, maintenance, and management of the business continuity strategy and plan.

- The Chief Financial Officer will include business continuity expenses in the annual operating budget.

- The Office of Information Technology is responsible for designing and supporting resilient systems and for the recovery of information and information systems in a disaster situation.

- Senior managers are responsible for defining the operational needs of their departments and for creating and maintaining functional departmental contingency procedures.

- The Chief Operating Officer will appoint the Business Continuity Team chairperson. The chairperson will appoint members of the Business Continuity Team. The team must include representatives of key functional areas, including but not limited to operations, communications, finance, IT, information security, physical security, and facilities management. Team members are responsible for designating backups to serve in their absence.

- Business Continuity Team responsibilities include active participation in business continuity preparation, response, recovery, and resumption activities. At its discretion, the Business Continuity Team may create subteams and assign responsibilities.

- The President/CEO has authority to declare an emergency, activate the plan, and contact/assemble the Business Continuity Team. In her absence, the COO has the authority to declare an emergency, activate the plan, and contact/assemble the Business Continuity Team. In his absence, the CFO has the authority to declare an emergency, activate the plan, and contact/assemble the Business Continuity Team. If none of the above listed are available, the Business Continuity Team chair in consultation with the Chairman of the Board of Directors has the authority to declare an emergency, activate the plan, and contact/assemble the Business Continuity Team.

- The Business Continuity Team will be the authoritative body during emergency response and recovery periods. Officers and employees will continue to conduct the affairs of the company under the guidance of the team leadership, except in matters that by statute require specific approval of the Board of Directors, or to conform to any governmental directives.

FYI: Business Continuity Management Education and Certification

DRI International (originally Disaster Recovery Institute International) is a nonprofit organization with the mission to make the world prepared. As the global education and certification body in business continuity and disaster recovery planning, DRI International sets the standard for professionalism. There are more than 11,000 active certified professionals worldwide. Continuity Professional certifications include Associate Business Continuity Professional (ABCP), Certified Functional Continuity Professional (CFCP), Certified Business Continuity Professional (CBCP), and Master Business Continuity Professional (MBCP). In addition, professionals may choose to specialize in audit, public sector, or health care. Learn more at www.drii.org.

Disaster Response Plans

What happens in those initial moments following a disaster has both an immediate impact and a note-worthy ripple effect. Disaster response can be either chaotic or orderly. The difference between these scenarios is established procedures and responsibilities. Think back to elementary school days. Hope-fully, you never experienced a fire at your school. But if you had, chances are that everyone would have evacuated the building safely. Why? Teachers and staff had specific assignments. Evacuation routes were mapped out. Students were taught not to panic, to line up single file, to follow a leader, and to gather at a specific location. All of these procedures and roles were reinforced through regularly scheduled fire drills. Similarly, organizations that have prepared for a disaster are able to focus on three immediate response goals:

1. Protecting the health and safety of employees, customers, first responders, and the public at large.

2. Minimizing damage to property and the environment.

3. Evaluating the situation and determining next steps.

The response plan should define the organizational structure, roles, and responsibilities, designated command and control, communications, and alternate work sites. Ancillary to the disaster response plan is the occupant emergency plan and procedures for immediate personnel safety. This plan is main-tained separately because it may be used in nondisaster situations.

Organizational Structure

An orderly response requires both disciplined leadership and acknowledgement of who is in charge. First and foremost, it is incumbent upon everyone to follow the instructions of first responders and public safety officials. Board-approved policy should vest corporate officers or executive management with the authority to declare an emergency and activate the plan. In a disaster situation, the organi-zational structure and/or chain of command may be affected by injury, death, travel restrictions, or personal circumstances. It is important to have a clearly defined Board-approved succession plan.

For decisions pertaining to the response, continuity, and recovery effort, the BCT is generally the authoritative body. Because this is a departure from normal operating conditions, it is critical that exec-utive management publicly support the authority of the BCT and that employees know who is in charge.

Command and Control Centers

Upon declaration of a disaster and the activation of the BCP, all BCT members should report to a desig-nated command and control center. Primary and alternate *command and control centers* (sometimes referred to as "war rooms") are predetermined locations equipped to support the work of the BCT. A conference room, a training room, or even a large office can quickly be transformed into a command and control center. The command and control center is initially used to direct operations and then may be used as a meeting center until normal business operations resume. At a minimum, the command

and control center should be prestocked with the BCP manuals, tables, chairs, whiteboards, phones, surge strips, and mobile device power cords. If available (and operational), having voice and video conferencing equipment on hand serves to facilitate communication. All BCT members should have directions to the location, keys, and access codes.

Communication

A disaster may occur with little or no advance warning. The importance of the capability to quickly alert and account for employees, service providers, and first responders cannot be overstated. Every organization should have an ***occupant emergency plan (OEP)***, which describes evacuation and shelter-in-place procedures in the event of a threat or incident to the health and safety of personnel. Such events include fire, bomb threat, chemical release, domestic violence in the workplace, or medical emergency. The OEP is distinct from the BCP and is often maintained by either the HR department or facilities management.

The business continuity response plan must assign responsibility for both internal and external communications and include instructions for using a variety of communications channels. To prevent miscommunication, a designated communications liaison and spokespersons should be appointed. All public statements should be authorized by the BCT. Employees should be instructed that all media requests and questions be referred to the designated spokesperson without comment (on or off the record). The widespread use of social media is both a blessing and a curse. Social media can be used to quickly disseminate information and misinformation. Particularly in an evolving situation, employees may not have all the facts and/or may inadvertently disclose confidential information; they should be strongly discouraged from posting any information about the event on personal social media accounts.

Relocation Strategies

In cases of natural, environmental, or physical disaster, relocation of critical business functions may be necessary. Relocation strategies need to consider both delivery and operational business functions. *Delivery functions* provide service or product to the customer. An example would be the teller line at a bank or a customer call center. *Operational business functions* provide the core infrastructure of the organization. They include accounting, marketing, HR, office services, security, and IT. It may not be practical to consider relocating all staff. The relocation plan should consider staffing levels for essential services, space considerations, utility and environmental needs, transportation, and logistics. Telecommuting, including mobile device access, may minimize personnel relocation requirements. Options for alternate operational locations include hot, warm, cold, and mobile sites. Alternate sites may be owned, leased, or even borrowed. Organizations that have multiple operational sites may be able to redirect the workload to a location that has not been impacted by the disaster situation.

- A ***hot site*** is a location that is fully operational and ready to move into; it has been configured with redundant hardware, software, and communications capability. Data has been replicated to the hot site on a real-time or near-time basis. Figure 12-3 shows an example of a hot site.

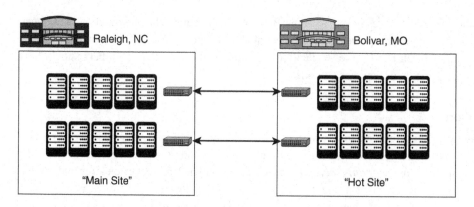

Data replicated to the hot site on a real-time or near-time basis.

FIGURE 12-3 A Hot Site Example

- A **warm site** is an environmentally conditioned workspace that is partially equipped with information systems and telecommunications equipment to support relocated operations. Computers and devices located at warm sites need to be configured and brought online. Data needs to be restored. Figure 12-4 shows an example of a warm site.

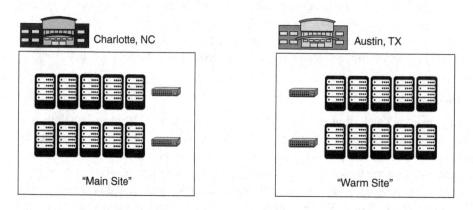

Computers and devices located at warm sites need to be configured and brought online. Data needs to be restored.

FIGURE 12-4 A Warm Site Example

- A **cold site** is a backup facility that has power, HVAC, and secure access. There is no staged equipment.

- **Mobile sites** are self-contained units. The units are provided by a third party and generally arrive equipped with the required hardware, software, and peripherals. Data needs to be restored.

- A *mirrored* site is fully redundant with real-time replication from the production site. Mirrored sites can assume processing with virtually no interruption.

- A *reciprocal* site is based on an agreement to have access to/use of another organization's facilities.

In addition to the previous options, it may be possible to offload operations to service bureaus or outsource operations to third parties.

In Practice

Emergency Response Plan Policy

Synopsis: Ensure that the organization is prepared to respond to an emergency situation.

Policy Statement:

- The Chief Operating Officer is responsible for developing and maintaining the emergency response plan. The emergency response plan is a component of the enterprise business continuity plan.

- The objective of the emergency response plan is to protect the health and safety of employees, customers, first responders, and the public at large, minimizing damage to property and the environment, and set in motion response, contingency, and recovery operations.

- The emergency response plan must, at a minimum, address organizational alerts and notification, disaster declaration, internal and external communication channels, command and control centers, relocation options, and decision making authority.

- Ancillary to the response plan are OEPs and the crisis communication plan (CCP). Both plans may be utilized in conjunction with and/or referenced by the response plan.

- The Office of Human Resources is responsible for maintaining the OEP.

- The Office of Communications and Marketing is responsible for maintaining a CCP.

- Personnel responsible for response operations must receive appropriate training.

- Response plans and procedures must be audited in accordance with the schedule set forth by the Business Continuity Team.

- Response procedures must be tested in accordance with the schedule set forth by the Business Continuity Team.

Operational Contingency Plans

Operational contingency plans address how an organization's essential business processes will be delivered during the recovery period. Let's consider some examples:

- Physical access to facilities at a maximum-security prison is regulated by a biometric fingerprint access control system. The access control system is managed and monitored by an information system. The back-end information system becomes unavailable due to power loss. The business contingency procedure would address an alternate method to lock and unlock doors. This may be a physical key or perhaps an access code. In either case, knowing where the key is or what the code is would be essential to operations.

- A financial institution offers its customers the option of telephone banking services. Due to a fire, the telebanking phone system is not operational. Contingency procedures would address rerouting telebanking calls to customer service and ensuring that the customer service representatives (CSRs) could service the customers or at the very least provide information while the telebanking system is being recovered.

- A federal agency is forced to vacate its premises due to a biochemical threat. The agency receives and processes unemployment claims. Its most critical task is producing unemployment checks based on the claims. Unemployed individuals depend on receiving these payments in a timely manner. Business contingency procedures address alternate methods to accept and process claims as well as to print and distribute checks. Procedures may include notifying recipients by phone that payments are delayed, estimating payments based on the previous week's claims, and/or coordinating with another agency for processing and postal services.

Operational contingency plans and procedures are developed at the departmental level. They are the responsibility of the business process owner.

Operational Contingency Procedures

Operational contingency documentation should follow the same form as standard operating procedures. As with standard operating procedures, operational contingency operating procedures are instructions that should be understandable to everyone who may need to use them. They should be written as simply as possible. It is best to use short, direct sentences so that the reader can easily understand the procedure. Chapter 8, "Communications and Operations Security," introduced four formats for writing procedural documentation: simple step, hierarchical, graphic, and flowchart. These same formats are recommended for writing operational contingency operating procedures.

In Practice

Operational Contingency Plan Policy

Synopsis: Ensure that the organization can continue to provide essential services during the recovery period.

Policy Statement:

- Business process owners are responsible for developing and maintaining operational contingency plans. Operational contingency plans are a component of the enterprise business continuity plan.

- The operational contingency plans must include strategies and procedures for providing essential services as determined by the business impact assessment during the recovery operations.

- The amount of procedural detail required should be enough that competent personnel familiar with the service or process could perform the alternate operation.

- External system dependencies and relevant contractual agreements must be reflected in the contingency plan.

- Personnel responsible for contingency operations must receive appropriate training.

- Contingency plans and procedures must be audited in accordance with the schedule set forth by the Business Continuity Team.

- Contingency procedures must be tested in accordance with the schedule set forth by the Business Continuity Team.

The Disaster Recovery Phase

In the *disaster recovery phase*, the organization begins the process of restoring or replacing damaged infrastructure, information systems, and facilities. Recovery activities can range from immediate failover to redundant systems to the significantly longer process of procuring equipment, restoring data, and potentially rebuilding facilities. Regardless of the strategy employed, it is critical that procedures have been documented and tested. Priorities for recovery operations should be consistent with the results of the business impact analysis.

Developing recovery plans and procedures can be a daunting task. A proven successful approach is to break the plan down into categories and assign responsibilities at the operational level, such as mainframe, network, communications, infrastructure, and facilities.

- *Mainframe recovery* is specific to the restoration of a mainframe computer (or equivalent capability) and corresponding data processing.

- *Network recovery* is specific to information systems (servers, workstations, mobile devices, applications, data stores, and supporting utilities) and includes the restoration of functionality and data.

- *Communications recovery* encompasses internal and external transmission systems, including local-area network (LAN), wide-area network (WAN), data circuits (T1, T3, MPLS), and Internet connectivity. Included in this category are connectivity devices such as switches, routers, firewalls, and IDSs.

- *Infrastructure recovery* encompasses those systems providing a general operating environment, including environmental and physical controls.

- *Facilities recovery* addresses the need to rebuild, renovate, or relocate the physical plant.

The criticality and priority determined by the business impact analysis provides the framework for choosing the appropriate strategy and level of investment.

Recovery Procedures

A disaster is not the time to figure out how to recover or restore a system, nor is it the time to determine inventory or search for vendor contacts. All these items need to be addressed beforehand and documented in recovery procedures and ancillary files. Recovery processes can be very technical. The procedures should explain in a logical progression what needs to be done, where it needs to be done, and how it needs to be done. Procedures may reference other documents. Table 12-4 illustrates a recovery procedure for an Active Directory domain controller.

TABLE 12-4   Active Directory Domain Controller Recovery Procedure

Active Directory Domain Controller Recovery	
Support Phone Numbers	Cisco Support: 800-553-2447 Microsoft Technical Support Regular Support: 888-888-9999 Business Critical: 888-888-7777
General Information	Active Directory domain controllers provide authentication, DNS, and DHCP services. If a domain controller fails, the remaining domain controllers will be able to authenticate user accounts, provide DNS resolution, and assign dynamic addresses. Note: Users may notice a degradation of service.
Configuration Information	There are four Windows Server domain controllers: Two are located at the data center in rack 7G. One is located in the Building A data closet rack. It is the second device from the top. One is located in the Building B data closet rack. It is the fourth device from the top. There are five FSMO roles that are server-specific: schema master, domain naming master, PDC emulator, RID master, and infrastructure master. Reference/recovery/server_roles.xls for server assignments. For more information on FMSO roles, refer to http://support.microsoft.com/kb/324801.

Active Directory Domain Controller Recovery

Recovery/ Resumption Instructions	1. If a domain controller fails, its objects and attributes will have to be removed from the Active Directory, and any FSMO roles that it held would have to be transferred to another domain controller. Follow the steps in http://support.microsoft.com/kb/216498 to remove the data. 2. After the failed domain controller has been removed from Active Directory, a replacement can be built. A virtual machine (VM) could be used to replace a (physical) server. Create a cloned VM from a template. Assign it the host name and static IP address of the failed domain controller. Patch the new server and install antivirus. From a run command, type DCPROMO to promote the member server to be a DC. 3. Accept the default setting and follow the prompts to complete the promotion. 4. Configure DNS for zone transfers and set the forwarders. Reference/recovery/DNS_recovery_procedures for DNS configuration instructions. 5. Configure DHCP scope information and restore assignments. Reference/recovery/DHCP_recovery_procedures for DHCP configuration instructions.

The key to disaster recovery is the ability to respond using validated, maintained, and tested procedures. All recovery procedures should be reviewed annually. Planning for recovery is a component of the systems development life cycle (SDLC) process.

Service Provider Dependencies

Recovery plans often depend on vendors to provide services, equipment, facilities, and personnel. This reliance should be reflected in contractual service agreements. Service level agreements (SLAs) should specify how quickly a vendor must respond, the type and quantity of replacement equipment guaranteed to be available, personnel and facility availability, and the status of the organization in the event of a major disaster involving multiple vendor clients. Service agreements should be referenced in the procedure as well as contact information, agreement numbers, and authorization requirements. Service provider dependencies should be included in the annual testing.

In Practice

Disaster Recovery Plan Policy

Synopsis: Ensure that the organization can recover infrastructure, systems, and facilities damaged during a disaster.

Policy Statement:

- The Office of Information Technology and the Office of Facilities Management are responsible for their respective disaster recovery plans. Disaster recovery plans are a component of the enterprise business continuity plan.

- The disaster recovery plan must include recovery strategies and procedures for systems and facilities as determined by the business impact assessment.

- Modifications to the recovery plan must be approved by the Chief Operating Officer.

- The amount of procedural detail required should be enough that competent personnel familiar with the environment could perform the recovery operation.

- External system dependencies and relevant contractual agreements must be reflected in the recovery plan.

- Personnel responsible for recovery operations must receive appropriate training.

- Recovery plans and procedures must be audited in accordance with the schedule set forth by the Business Continuity Team.

- Recovery procedures must be testing in accordance with the schedule set forth by the Business Continuity Team.

The Resumption Phase

The objective of the *resumption phase* is to transition to normal operations. Two major activities are associated with this phase: validation of successful recovery and deactivation of the BCP.

Validation is the process of verifying that recovered systems are operating correctly and that data integrity has been confirmed. Validation should be the final step of every recovery procedure.

Deactivation is the official notification that the organization is no longer operating in emergency or disaster mode. At this point, the BCT relinquishes authority, and normal operating procedures are reinstated. After the dust settles, figuratively and literally, an after-action report with lessons learned should be documented by the BCT. The BCP should be reviewed and revised based on the findings and recommendations of the BCT.

Plan Testing and Maintenance

A BCP should be maintained in a state of readiness, which includes having personnel trained to fulfill their roles and responsibilities within the plan, having plans exercised to validate their content, and having systems and system components tested to ensure their operability. NIST SP 800-84: Guide to Test, Training and Exercise Programs for Information Technology Plans and Capabilities provides guidelines on designing, developing, conducting, and evaluating test, training, and exercise (TT&E) events so that organizations can improve their ability to prepare for, respond to, manage, and recover from adverse events.

Why Is Testing Important?

It would be hard to overstate the importance of testing. Until tested, plans and procedures are purely theoretical. The objective of a testing program is to ensure that plans and procedures are accurate, relevant, and operable under adverse conditions. As important as demonstrating success is uncovering inadequacies. The worst time to find out that your plans were incomplete, outdated, or just plain wrong is in the midst of a disaster. The extent and complexity of the testing program should be commensurate with the criticality of the function or system. Prior to testing, a test plan should be developed that details the test objective, type of test, success criteria, and participants.

In addition to procedures being tested, the BCP should be audited. At a minimum, testing exercises and audits should be conducted annually. The results of both should be provided to the Board of Directors.

Testing Methodologies

There are three testing methodologies: tabletop exercises, functional exercises, and full-scale testing. *Tabletop exercises* can be conducted as structured reviews or simulations:

- A *structured review* focuses on a specific procedure or set of procedures. Representatives from each functional area participate in a systematic walkthrough of the procedures with the goal of verifying accuracy and completeness. A structured review can also be used as a training exercise with the objective of familiarization.

- A tabletop *simulation* focuses on participant readiness. A facilitator presents a scenario and asks the exercise participants' questions related to the scenario, including decisions to be made, procedures to use, roles, responsibilities, time frames, and expectations. A tabletop exercise is discussion-based only and does not involve deploying equipment or other resources.

Functional exercises allow personnel to validate plans, procedures, resource availability, and participant readiness. Functional exercises are scenario-driven and limited in scope, such as the failure of a critical business function or a specific hazard scenario. Functional exercises can be conducted in either a parallel or production environment.

Full-scale testing is conducted at the enterprise level. Based on a specific scenario, the business operates as if a disaster was declared. Normal operations are suspended. Recovery and contingency plans and procedures are implemented. Full-scale testing can be expensive and risky. It is, however, the most accurate test of plans and procedures.

Audits

A *business continuity plan audit* is an evaluation of how the business continuity program in its entirety is being managed. This includes policy, governance, assessments, documentation, testing, and maintenance. Audits are conducted by personnel independent of the response, contingency, or recovery efforts. Auditors will look at the quality and effectiveness of the organization's BCP process and determine whether the testing program is sufficient. At a minimum, you can anticipate they will ask the following questions:

- Is there a written business continuity policy and plan?
- Has the business continuity policy and plan been approved by the Board of Directors?
- How often is it reviewed and/or reauthorized?
- How often is a BIA conducted? By whom?
- Who is on the BCT?
- What training have they had?
- What training has the user community had?
- Is there a written test plan?
- How often is the plan tested?
- Are the results documented?
- If third parties are involved, what is the process for testing/verifying their procedures?
- Who is responsible for maintaining the plan?

As with all examinations and audits, independence must be maintained. Examiners and auditors must not be connected to the management or maintenance of related policies, plans, procedures, training, or testing.

Plan Maintenance

BCPs must stay in sync with organizational and personnel changes. At a minimum, on an annual basis, roles and responsibilities, including BCT membership, should be revisited, a BIA conducted, and recovery and contingency plans evaluated. Aside from the annual review, the BCP may need to be updated due to changes in regulatory requirements, technology, and the threat landscape.

FYI: Regulatory Expectations

The best way to know what to expect from an audit is to be privy to audit work papers. Fortunately, one of the best sets of work papers is in the public domain. The Federal Financial Institutions Examination Council (FFIEC) develops and publishes guides and audit work papers for use by field examiners in financial institution regulatory agencies. These resources are found in the *FFIEC Information Technology Examination Handbook InfoBase*. The handbooks are available to the public and can be downloaded from the FFIEC website at www.ffiec.gov.

Another example is the European Network and Information Security Agency (ENISA) IT Continuity website and underlying resources. Its main goal is to "Promote Risk Assessment and Risk Management methods to enhance the capability of dealing with network and information security threats" [ENISA Regulation]. Additional information can be found at ENISA's website at https://www.enisa.europa.eu/.

In Practice

Business Continuity Testing and Maintenance Policy

Synopsis: Codify testing and maintenance requirements and responsibility.

Policy Statement:

- Reference to the business continuity plan is inclusive of plans, procedures, and ancillary documentation related to disaster preparation, response, contingency operations, recovery, resumption, training, testing, and plan maintenance.

- The Chief Operating Officer or designee is responsible for maintenance of the business continuity plan.

- The Chief Operating Officer or designee will conduct an annual review of the business continuity plan.

- The Business Continuity Team is responsible for publishing an annual testing schedule and managing the test plan. The Chief Operating Officer will report the results to the Board of Directors.

- Internal audit is tasked with managing and selecting an independent firm to conduct an annual audit of the business continuity plan. The independent audit firm will report the results to the Board of Directors or designated committee.

FYI: Small Business Note

A disaster situation can be particularly devastating to a small business, yet few are prepared. According to David Paulison, former executive director of the Federal Emergency Management Agency (FEMA), "Small businesses that don't have a plan in place generally don't survive after a disaster, whether it's a flood or a tornado. We see that anywhere from 40–60 percent of those that are hit like that simply don't come back to business."

In response to the lack of preparedness, the Small Business Administration (SBA) has made available a number of general preparedness resources and specific disaster information designed to assist the small business community and support economic recovery.

General preparedness resources include an identifying critical business systems worksheet, creating a preparedness program template, and instructions on building a business disaster preparedness kit.

Specific disaster information includes hurricanes, winter weather, earthquakes, tornadoes, wildfires, floods, and cybersecurity.

The resources can be accessed at the following site: https://www.sba.gov/business-guide/manage/prepare-emergencies-disaster-assistance.

Summary

A disaster is an event that results in damage or destruction, loss of life, or drastic change to the environment. Preparing for a disaster can make the difference between life and death, success or failure. Preparedness is a regulatory requirement for industry sectors deemed critical to national security. Not investing the time and effort required to face disruptions is negligent and the consequences severe.

A resilient organization is one that has the ability to quickly adapt and recover from known or unknown changes to the environment. The objective of business continuity planning is to ensure that organizations have the capability to respond to and recover from disaster situations. Response plans focus on the initial and near-term response and include such elements as authority, plan activation, notification, communication, evacuation, relocation, coordination with public authorities, and security. Contingency plans focus on immediate, near-term, and short-term alternate workforce and business processes. Recovery plans focus on the immediate, near-term, and short-term recovery of information systems, infrastructure, and facilities. Resumption plans guide the organization back to normalcy. Taken as a whole, this is referred to as the business continuity plan (BCP) or as the continuity of operations plan (COOP). The discipline is referred to as business continuity management.

The precursor to developing a BCP is assessing the threat environment and organizational risk as well as determining essential business services and processes. A business continuity threat assessment identifies viable threats and predicts the likelihood of occurrence. Threat modeling takes into account historical and predictive geographic, technological, physical, environmental, third-party, and industry factors.

A business continuity risk assessment evaluates the sufficiency of controls to prevent the threat from occurring or to minimize its impact. A business impact assessment (BIA) identifies essential services/processes and recovery time frames. In BCP, *essential* means that the absence of, or disruption of, a service/process would result in significant, irrecoverable, or irreparable harm to the organization, employees, business partners, constituents, community, or country. The BIA process uses three prioritization metrics: MTD, recovery time objectives (RTOs), and recovery point objectives (RPOs). The MTD is the total length of time an essential business function can be unavailable without causing significant harm to the business. The RTO is the maximum amount of time a system resource can be unavailable before there is an unacceptable impact on other system resources or business process. The RPO represents the point in time, prior to a disruption or system outage, that data can be recovered; in other words, the acceptable data loss.

Business continuity management is a distributed responsibility. The Board of Directors or organizational equivalent is ultimately accountable for ensuring that the organization is prepared. It is the responsibility of executive management to ensure that threats are evaluated, impact to business processes recognized, and resources allocated. They are also charged with declaring a disaster and activating the BCP. The BCT, appointed by executive management, is expected to manage preparation and be the authoritative body in a declared disaster.

A BCP should be maintained in a state of readiness, which includes having personnel trained to fulfill their roles and responsibilities within the plan, having plans exercised to validate their content, and having systems and system components tested and audited to ensure their operability. The plan in its entirety should be reviewed on a scheduled basis. It should be reauthorized annually by the Board of Directors or organizational equivalent.

Business Continuity Management policies include Emergency Preparedness, Business Impact Assessment, Business Continuity Management, Emergency Response Plan, Operational Contingency Plan, Disaster Recovery Plan, and Business Continuity Testing and Maintenance.

Test Your Skills

MULTIPLE CHOICE QUESTIONS

1. Which of the following terms best describes the primary objective of business continuity?

   A. Assurance

   B. Availability

   C. Accounting

   D. Authentication

2. Which of the following statements best describes a disaster?

   A. A disaster is a planned activity.

   B. A disaster is an isolated incident.

   C. A disaster is a significant disruption of normal business functions.

   D. A disaster is a change in management structure.

3. Flood, fire, and wind are examples of which type of threat?

   A. Malicious act

   B. Environmental

   C. Logistical

   D. Technical

4. Which of the following terms best describes the process of identifying viable threats and likelihood of occurrence?

   A. Risk assessment

   B. Threat assessment

   C. Likelihood assessment

   D. Impact assessment

5. Which of the following terms best describes the process of evaluating the sufficiency of controls?

   A. Risk assessment

   B. Threat assessment

   C. Likelihood assessment

   D. Impact assessment

6. Which of the following statements best describes the outcome of a BIA?

   A. A BIA generates RTOs.

   B. A BIA produces an organizational agreement on essential processes and services.

   C. A BIA identifies the gap between current and desired recovery capabilities.

   D. All of the above

7. An acceptable length of time a business function or process can be unavailable is known as _____.

   A. maximum unavailability (MU)

   B. total acceptable time (TAT)

   C. maximum tolerable downtime (MTD)

   D. recovery time objective (RTO)

8. The recovery point objective (RPO) represents _____.

   A. acceptable data loss

   B. acceptable processing time loss

   C. acceptable downtime

   D. None of the above

9. Recovery time objectives relate to which of the following?

   A. The maximum amount of time a guest system can be unavailable

   B. The maximum amount of time a system resource can be unavailable

   C. The minimum amount of time a system resource can be unavailable

   D. None of the above

10. Which of the following plans are included in a BCP?

    A. Resumption plans

    B. Response plans

    C. Contingency plans

    D. All of the above

11. Legal and regulatory accountability for an organization's preparedness is assigned to
    _____.

    A. the BCT

    B. regulators

    C. the Board of Directors or organizational equivalent

    D. service providers

12. The authority to declare an emergency and activate the plan is owned by _____.

    A. the BCT

    B. executive management

    C. the Board of Directors or organizational equivalent

    D. service providers

13. Which of the following plans include evacuation and in-shelter procedures?

    A. The fire drill plan

    B. The occupant emergency plan

    C. The business contingency plan

    D. A FEMA directive

14. A _____ site is a backup facility that has power, HVAC, and secure access.

    A. hot

    B. cold

    C. replica

    D. mirror

15. _____ are self-contained units. The units are provided by a third-party and generally
    arrive equipped with the required hardware, software, and peripherals. Data need to be
    restored.

    A. Mobile sites

    B. Hot sites

    C. Cold sites

    D. Mirrored sites

16. A _____ site is fully redundant with real-time replication from the production site.

    A. mirrored

    B. hot

    C. cold

    D. replica

17. A _____ site is based on a agreement to have access to/use of another organization's facilities

    A. mirrored

    B. hot

    C. cold

    D. reciprocal

EXERCISES

EXERCISE 12.1: Assessing Threats

1. Based on historical occurrences, identify three environmental or location-based threats to your campus or workplace.

2. Choose one of the three threats and document how often the threat has occurred in the past 20 years.

3. Describe the factors you would take into consideration in predicting the likelihood of a reoccurrence within the next five years.

EXERCISE 12.2: Analyzing an Occupant Emergency Response Plan

1. Locate a copy of the occupant emergency response plan (note that it may go by a different name, such as evacuation plan) for your campus or workplace. If you cannot locate one, use the Internet to locate one from another school or organization.

2. When was the plan last updated?

3. Summarize the key components of the plan. In your opinion, does the plan provide adequate instructions?

EXERCISE 12.3: Assessing the Training and Testing of an Occupant Emergency Response Plan

1. Locate a copy of the occupant emergency response plan (note that it may go by a different name, such as evacuation plan) for your campus or workplace. If you cannot locate one, use the Internet to locate one from another school or organization. If you completed Exercise 12.2, you may use the same plan.

2. What type of exercises would you recommend to test the occupant emergency response plan?

3. What type of training would you recommend in order to educate personnel regarding the occupant emergency response plan?

4. If you were auditing the occupant emergency response plan, what questions would you ask?

EXERCISE 12.4: Researching Alternative Processing Sites

1. A number of companies specialize in offering hot site solutions. Locate at least three companies that offer this service.

2. Create a matrix comparing and contrasting options, such as technical support, available bandwidth, traffic redirection, managed security, and data center features (for example, power and connectivity and geographic location).

3. Recommend one of the sites. Be prepared to explain your recommendation.

EXERCISE 12.5: Researching the Federal Emergency Management Agency

1. Describe the FEMA resources available online to businesses to help them prepare for disasters.

2. Describe the FEMA resources available online to families to help them prepare for disasters.

3. What is FEMA Corps?

EXERCISE 12.6: Researching Similar Agencies or Programs in Europe, Canada, and Any Other Countries

1. Describe and compare non-U.S. programs and resources available to help businesses prepare and react for disasters.

2. What are the similarities with FEMA?

PROJECTS

PROJECT 12.1: **Assessing Disruptions in Business Continuity**

Disruption in service at a financial institution impacts both its customers and internal operations.

1. Listed here are various disruptions in banking service. Assign each event a rating of 1–5 (1 is the lowest, 5 is the highest) that best represents the impact on you (as the customer), and provide an explanation of your rating. Consider each event independently.

   A. ATM system unavailable, branches open.

   B. Closest local branch closed, others open.

   C. Internet banking unavailable, branches open.

   D. Core processing system unavailable, deposits accepted, withdrawals less than $100, other account information unavailable.

   E. Communications capabilities between branches disrupted, tellers work in offline mode.

2. Listed here are the same disruptions in banking service. Assign each event a rating of 1–5 (1 is the lowest, 5 is the highest) that best represents the impact on the bank from a financial, operational, legal, or regulatory perspective, and provide an explanation. Consider each event independently.

   A. ATM system unavailable, branches open.

   B. Closest local branch closed, others open.

   C. Internet banking unavailable, branches open.

   D. Core processing system unavailable, deposits accepted, withdrawals less than $100, other account information unavailable.

   E. Communications capabilities between branches disrupted, tellers work in offline mode.

3. Describe how business continuity planners should reconcile the differences in impact upon a business and its customers.

PROJECT 12.2: **Evaluating Business Continuity Plans**

The objective of this project is to evaluate your school or employer's BCP. You will need to obtain a copy of your school or employer's BCP (it may be known as a disaster response plan). If you cannot locate a copy, use the Internet to locate one from another school or organization.

1. Identify the sections related to preparation, response, contingency, recovery, resumption, testing, and maintenance. Is anything missing?

2. Identify roles and responsibilities referenced in the plan.

3. Critique the plan in terms of clarity and ease of use.

PROJECT 12.3: Assessing the Impact of the Cloud on Business Continuity

Infrastructure as a Service (IaaS) and Platform as a Service (PaaS) are changing how organizations design their technology environments.

1. How do IaaS and PaaS impact business continuity planning?

2. Have any of the cloud service providers (such as Google, Amazon, Rackspace, Savvis) experienced any major outages that would impact their customers?

3. Assuming an organization used the services of a cloud provider for business continuity services, explain the type of response, recovery, and continuity testing they could/should conduct.

Case Study

The Role of Social Media in a Disaster

Hurricane Maria is considered one of the worst natural disasters on record in Puerto Rico. Social media helped reunite families, friends, organize donation campaigns, and much more.

1. Document how social media was used as an emergency communication tool during the aftermath of Hurricane Maria.

2. Make a recommendation as to whether businesses should use social media as a communications tool during a disaster situation. Be sure to include both pros and cons.

3. Would your answer be different if the assignment was to make a recommendation as to whether colleges and universities should adopt social media for communicating about a disaster? Why or why not?

References

Regulations Cited

"16 CFR Part 314: Standards for Safeguarding Customer Information; Final Rule, Federal Register," accessed 06/2018, https://www.gpo.gov/fdsys/pkg/CFR-2016-title16-vol1/xml/CFR-2016-title16-vol1-part314.xml.

"HIPAA Security Rule," official website of the Department of Health and Human Services, accessed 06/2018, https://www.hhs.gov/hipaa/for-professionals/security/index.html.

Executive Orders Cited

"Federal Continuity Directives (FCD) 1 and 2," accessed 06/2018, https://www.fema.gov/guidance-directives.

"Presidential Decision Directive 63, Critical Infrastructure Protection," official website of the Government Printing Office, accessed 06/2018, https://www.gpo.gov/fdsys/granule/FR-1998-08-05/98-20865.

"Presidential Directive HSPD-7, Critical Infrastructure Identification, Prioritization, and Protection," official website of the Department of Homeland Security, accessed 06/2018, https://www.dhs.gov/homeland-security-presidential-directive-7.

Other References

Bell, Michael, "The Five Principles of Organizational Resilience," Gartner Group, January 7, 2002, accessed 06/2018, https://www.gartner.com/id=351410.

"Hurricane Maria News, Graphics, and Social Media", accessed 06/2018, https://www.fema.gov/disaster/updates/hurricane-maria-news-graphics-and-social-media.

"Puerto Ricans Organize on Social Media to Send Aid Back Home," accessed 06/2018, www.nola.com/hurricane/index.ssf/2017/09/puerto_rico_help_new_orleans_m.html.

"Business Testimonials: Aeneas," FEMA Ready, accessed 06/2018, https://www.ready.gov/business/business-testimonials.

"Emergency Preparedness," official website of the SBA, accessed 06/2018, https://www.sba.gov/business-guide/manage/prepare-emergencies-disaster-assistance.

Chapter | **13**

Regulatory Compliance for Financial Institutions

Chapter Objectives

After reading this chapter and completing the exercises, you will be able to do the following:

- Understand different financial institution cybersecurity regulatory compliance requirements.
- Understand the components of a GLBA-compliant information security program.
- Examine other financial services regulations, such as the New York Department of Financial Services (DFS) Cybersecurity Regulation.
- Prepare for a regulatory examination.
- Understand data privacy and new trends in international regulatory compliance.

Financial services institutions such as banks, credit unions, and lending institutions provide an array of solutions and financial instruments. You might think that money is their most valuable asset. On the other hand, the reality is that customer and transactional information is the heart of their business. Financial assets are material and can be replaced. Protection of customer information is necessary to establish and maintain trust between the financial institution and the community it serves. More specifically, institutions have a responsibility to safeguard the privacy of individual consumers and protect them from harm, including fraud and identity theft. On a broader scale, the industry is responsible for maintaining the nation's financial services critical infrastructure.

This chapter examines different examples of regulations applicable to the financial sector, focusing on the following topics:

- Title 5 Section 501(b) of the Gramm-Leach-Bliley Act (GLBA) and the corresponding interagency guidelines

- Federal Financial Institutions Examination Council (FFIEC)

- Federal Trade Commission (FTC) Safeguards Act, and Financial Institution Letters (FILs).

- New York's Department of Financial Services Cybersecurity Regulation (23 NYCRR Part 500)

Compliance with regulations such as the NYCRR and GLBA is mandatory. Noncompliance has significant penalties, including being forced to cease operations. As we examine the various regulations, we will look at how examiners assess compliance. We will conclude the chapter with a look at the most significant financial security issue of our time—personal and corporate identity theft—and the regulations that address this ever-growing problem.

The Gramm-Leach-Bliley Act

In a response to the massive bank failures of the Great Depression, the Banking Act of 1933 prohibited national and state banks from affiliating with securities companies. The specific provision is often referred to as the Glass-Steagall Act. Similar to the Glass-Steagall Act, the Bank Holding Company Act of 1956 prohibited banks from controlling a nonbank company. This act was amended by Congress in 1982 to further forbid banks from conducting general insurance underwriting or agency activities.

On November 11, 1999, the Glass-Steagall Act was repealed and the *Gramm-Leach-Bliley Act (GLBA)* was signed into law by President Bill Clinton. Also known as the *Financial Modernization Act of 1999,* GLBA effectively repealed the restrictions placed on banks during the six preceding decades, which prevented the merger of banks, stock brokerage companies, and insurance companies.

What Is a Financial Institution?

GLBA defines a *financial institution* as "Any institution the business of which is significantly engaged in financial activities as described in *Section 4(k) of the Bank Holding Company Act* (12 U.S.C. § 1843(k)." GLBA applies to all financial services organizations, regardless of size. This definition is important to understand, because these financial institutions include many companies that are not traditionally considered to be financial institutions, such as the following:

- Check cashing businesses

- Payday lenders

- Mortgage brokers

- Nonbank lenders (automobile dealers providing financial services)

- Technology vendors providing loans to their clients

- Educational institutions providing financial aid

- Debt collectors

- Real-estate settlement service providers

- Personal property or real-estate appraisers

- Retailers that issue branded credit cards

- Professional tax preparers

- Courier services

The law also applies to companies that receive information about customers of other financial institutions, including credit reporting agencies and ATM operators.

The Federal Trade Commission (FTC) is responsible for enforcing GLBA as it pertains to financial firms that are not covered by federal banking agencies, the SEC, the Commodity Futures Trading Commission, and state insurance authorities, which include tax preparers, debt collectors, loan brokers, real estate appraisers, and nonbank mortgage lenders.

Prior to GLBA, the insurance company that maintained health records was by law unrelated to the bank that financed mortgages and the brokerage house that traded stocks. Once merged, however, companies would have access to a cross-section of personal information. Using data-mining techniques, it is possible to build detailed customer and prospect profiles. Because of the potential for misuse of information, Title 5 of GLBA specifically addresses protecting both the privacy and the security of nonpublic personal information (NPPI).

GLBA's information protection directive is composed of the three main components shown in Figure 13-1.

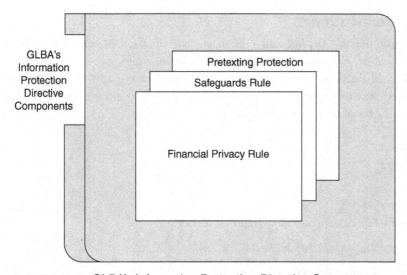

FIGURE 13-1   GLBA's Information Protection Directive Components

The following are the components illustrated in Figure 13-1:

- The *Privacy Rule* limits a financial institution's disclosure of nonpublic personal information (NPPI) to unaffiliated third parties, such as by selling the information to unaffiliated third parties. Subject to certain exceptions, the Privacy Rule prohibits disclosure of a consumer's NPPI to a nonaffiliated third party unless certain notice requirements are met and the consumer does not elect to prevent, or opt out of, the disclosure. The Privacy Rule requires that privacy notices provided to customers and consumers describe the financial institution's policies and practices to protect the confidentiality and security of that information. It does *not* impose any other obligations with respect to safeguarding customers or their information.

- The *Safeguards Rule* addresses the protection of the confidentiality and security of customer NPPI and ensuring the proper disposal of customer NPPI. It is directed toward preventing or responding to foreseeable threats to, or unauthorized access or use of, that information.

- *Pretexting* is also referred to as social engineering. It is a methodology by which an individual impersonates someone else to extract sensitive information from unsuspecting victims. GLBA encourages organizations to implement robust employee training programs to combat social engineering. One of the main entry points to cybersecurity breaches is by leveraging social engineering. Threat actors often impersonate legitimate customers of a financial institution to get more information about the customer they're pretending to be.

In addition, *nonpublic personal information (NPPI)* includes (but is not limited to) names, addresses, and phone numbers when linked to bank and credit card account numbers, income and credit histories, and social security numbers (SSNs). Regulatory language uses the terms *sensitive customer information* and *NPPI* interchangeably.

Regulatory Oversight

All financial institutions that conduct business in the United States are subject to GLBA. The regulation gives authority to various agencies to administer and enforce the privacy and security provisions. Table 13.1 lists the agencies, their charges, and the applicable public law. By law, the agencies are required to work together to issue consistent and comparable rules to implement the act's privacy provision. In contrast, the agencies are tasked with independently establishing minimum-security standards, as well as determining the type and severity of the penalties. Figure 13-2 lists several publications of standards and guidelines that have been published by different government agencies.

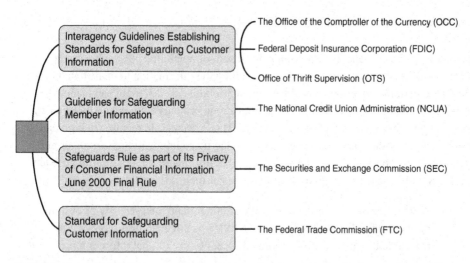

FIGURE 13-2   Publications by Federal Agencies Around the Safeguarding of Customer Information

Table 13-1 provides the GLBA regulatory agencies and their respective rules.

TABLE 13-1   GLBA Regulatory Agencies and Rules

Regulatory Agency	Institution Type	GLBA Rule Federal Register Designation
Federal Reserve Board (FRB)	Bank holding companies and member banks of the Federal Reserve System (FRS)	12 C.F.R. § 216
Office of the Comptroller of the Currency (OCC)	National banks, federal savings associations, and federal branches of foreign banks	12 C.F.R. § 40
Federal Deposit Insurance Corporation (FDIC)	State-chartered banks (that are not members of the FRS)	12 C.F.R. § 332
National Credit Union Administration (NCUA)	Federally chartered credit unions	NCUA: 12 C.F.R. § 716
Securities and Exchange Commission (SEC)	Securities brokers and dealers as well as investment companies	17 C.F.R. § 248
Commodity Futures Trading Commission (CFTC)	Futures and option markets	CFTC: 17 C.F.R. § 160
Federal Trade Commission (FTC)	Institutions not covered by the other agencies	16 C.F.R. § 313

> ### FYI: What Is the Federal Register?
>
> Published by the Office of the Federal Register, National Archives and Records Administration (NARA), the Federal Register is the official daily publication for rules, proposed rules, and notices of federal agencies and organizations, as well as executive orders and other presidential documents. It is updated daily by 6 a.m. and is published Monday through Friday, except on federal holidays. The official home page of the Federal Register is www.federalregister.gov.

The Federal Trade Commission (FTC) Safeguards Act

As noted earlier, a variety of companies are subject to GLBA regulations. Banks, credit unions, insurance agencies, and investment firms are subject to regulatory oversight by the agency that charters or licenses them. The FTC has jurisdiction over individuals or organizations that are significantly engaged in providing financial products or services to consumers and are not subject to regulatory oversight. Many of these organizations are small businesses. The FTC's implementation is known as the *Safeguards Act*. Overall, the requirements of the Safeguards Act are not as stringent as the Interagency Guidelines. The primary requirements are that covered entities must do the following:

- Designate the employee or employees to coordinate the safeguards.

- Identify and assess the risks to customer information in each relevant area of the company's operation, and evaluate the effectiveness of current safeguards for controlling these risks.

- Design a safeguards program, and detail the plans to monitor it.

- Select appropriate service providers and require them (by contract) to implement the safeguards.

- Evaluate the program and explain adjustments in light of changes to its business arrangements or the results of its security tests.

The FTC does not conduct regulatory compliance audits. Enforcement is complaint-driven. Consumers can file a complaint with the FTC. The FTC analyzes the complaints and if it detects a pattern of wrongdoing, it will investigate and prosecute, if appropriate. The FTC does not resolve individual consumer complaints.

The FTC has undertaken substantial efforts to promote cybersecurity in the private sector through the following:

- Civil law enforcement

- Business outreach and consumer education

- Policy initiatives

- Recommendations to Congress to enact legislation

Section 5 of The Federal Trade Commission (FTC) Safeguards Act is the primary enforcement tool that is used to prevent deceptive and unfair business practices. The FTC has been working with NIST and is aligning its practices with the NIST Cybersecurity Framework. FTC officials explain how the NIST Cybersecurity Framework relate to the FTC's work on data security on a blog posted at https://www.ftc.gov/news-events/blogs/business-blog/2016/08/nist-cybersecurity-framework-ftc.

As FTC officials describe in their blog and website:

> "The types of things the Framework calls for organizations to evaluate are the types of things the FTC has been evaluating for years in its Section 5 enforcement to determine whether a company's data security and its processes are reasonable. By identifying different risk management practices and defining different levels of implementation, the NIST Framework takes a similar approach to the FTC's long-standing Section 5 enforcement."

What Are the Interagency Guidelines?

As noted earlier, the financial services oversight agencies were tasked with independently establishing minimum-security standards as well as determining the type and severity of the penalties. Banks are subject to the "Interagency Guidelines Establishing Standards for Safeguarding Customer Information," and credit unions are subject to the "Guidelines for Safeguarding Member Information." In this section, we will refer to them collectively as the *Interagency Guidelines*.

The ***Interagency Guidelines*** require every covered institution to implement a comprehensive written information security program that includes administrative, technical, and physical safeguards appropriate to the size and complexity of the bank or credit union and the nature and scope of its activities. To be in compliance, the information security program must include policies and processes that require institutions to perform the steps illustrated in Figure 13-3.

FIGURE 13-3   Policies and Processes Required for Compliance

It is up to each institution to develop a program that meets these objectives. The ISO 27002:2013 standard provides an excellent framework to develop a GLBA-compliant information security program.

In Practice

Regulatory Language Definitions

To understand the scope and mandate of the information security regulations, we need to start with the terminology. The following definitions apply to all versions of the Interagency Guidelines. Note that with the exception of credit unions, the user of services is referred to as a *customer* (in the case of credit unions, they are referred to as *members*).

- ■ *Consumer information* means any record about an individual, whether in paper, electronic, or other form, that is a consumer report or is derived from a consumer report and that is maintained or otherwise possessed by or on behalf of the institution for a business purpose. The term does not include any record that does not personally identify an individual.

- ■ *Customer or member information* means any record containing NPPI, about a customer or member, whether in paper, electronic, or other form, that is maintained by or on behalf of the financial institution.

- ■ *Customer or member information system* means any method used to access, collect, store, use, transmit, protect, or dispose of customer or member information.

- ■ *Service provider* means any person or entity that maintains, processes, or otherwise is permitted access to customer information through its provision of services directly to the financial institution.

- ■ *Administrative safeguards* are defined as governance, risk management, oversight, policies, standards, processes, programs, monitoring, and training designed and implemented with the intent of establishing and maintaining a secure environment.

- ■ *Technical safeguards* are defined as controls that are implemented or enforced by technological means.

- ■ *Physical safeguards* are defined as controls designed to protect systems and physical facilities from natural threats and/or man-made intrusions.

Involve the Board of Directors

The Interagency Guidelines require that the Board of Directors or an appropriate committee of the Board approve the bank's written information security program. The Board is also tasked with overseeing the development, implementation, and maintenance of the information security program, including assigning specific responsibility for its implementation and reviewing reports from management.

As corporate officials, directors have a fiduciary and legal responsibility. For example, financial institutions that do not comply with the GLBA are subject to civil penalties of $100,000 *per violation.* Officers and directors of that institution can be held personally liable as well, with penalties of $10,000 *per violation.*

Board members are generally chosen for their experience, business acumen, and standing in the community. It can be assumed that they understand business goals, processes, and inherent risks. Even experienced professionals, however, do not always have an in-depth natural understanding of information security issues. Institutions are expected to provide their Boards with educational opportunities to become and remain proficient in the area. Recognizing that this is a specialized body of knowledge, the Interagency Guidelines include the provision for delegation and distribution of responsibilities.

Examples of delegation include the following:

- Delegating Board oversight to a subcommittee whose members include directors and representatives of the financial institution, such as a Chief Information Security Officer (CISO) or Chief Risk Officer (CRO)

- Assigning information security management program oversight and management to a CISO or CRO

- Assigning implementation and maintenance of administrative controls to the Information Security Officer

- Assigning implementation and maintenance of technical controls to the Director of Information Technology

- Assigning implementation and maintenance of physical controls to the facilities manager

- Assigning design and delivery of information security training and awareness programs to the training department

- Assigning verification of controls to the internal audit department

- Assigning risk evaluation to the risk management committee

- Assigning the evaluation of technology initiatives to the technology steering committee

- Creating a multidisciplinary information security advisory committee that includes the representatives of all the aforementioned roles and departments

Information security crosses many boundaries and involves multiple domains. Experience has shown us that institutions that have adopted a cross-functional multidisciplinary approach, as shown in Figure 13-4, have a stronger and more successful information security program.

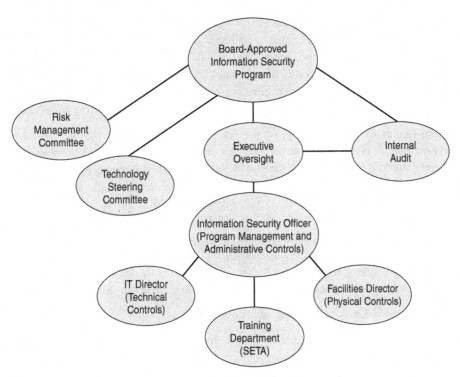

FIGURE 13-4   A Cross-functional Multidisciplinary Approach

In Practice

GLBA Section III-A: Involve the Board of Directors

The Board of Directors or an appropriate committee of the Board of each bank or credit union shall:

- Approve the written information security program.

- Oversee the development, implementation, and maintenance of the information security program, including assigning specific responsibility for its implementation and reviewing reports from management.

Assess Risk

Financial institutions are expected to take a risk-based approach to information security. The process begins with identifying threats. ***Threats*** are defined as potential dangers that have the capacity to cause harm. It is incumbent upon each institution to continually engage in a ***threat assessment***, which is the identification of the types of threats and attacks that may affect the institution's condition and operations or may cause data disclosures that could result in substantial harm or inconvenience to customers. A threat assessment must take into consideration a number of factors, including the size and type of the institution, services offered, geographic location, experience of personnel, infrastructure design, operating systems, vulnerability of applications, and cultural attitudes and norms. At a minimum, financial institutions must address the threats of unauthorized access, unauthorized data modification, system infiltration, malware, destruction of data or systems, and denial of service (DoS).

The systematic rating of threats based on level of impact and likelihood sans controls is used to determine the *inherent risk*. A *risk assessment* is used to evaluate the corresponding safeguards to calculate *residual risk*, which is defined as the level of risk after controls have been implemented. The Federal Financial Institutions Examination Council (FFIEC) recommends using the NIST risk management framework and methodology as described in Special Publication 800-53 to calculate residual risk. Multiple categories of risk are defined by the FDIC as relevant for financial institutions, including strategic, reputational, operational, transactional, and compliance:

- *Strategic risk* is the risk arising from adverse business decisions, or the failure to implement appropriate business decisions in a manner that is consistent with the institution's strategic goals.

- *Reputational risk* is the risk arising from negative public opinion.

- *Operational risk* is the risk of loss resulting from inadequate or failed internal processes, people, and systems or from external events.

- *Transactional risk* is the risk arising from problems with service or product delivery.

- *Compliance risk* is the risk arising from violations of laws, rules, or regulations, or from non-compliance with internal policies or procedures or with the institution's business standards.

Risk assessments and corresponding risk management decisions must be documented and reported to the Board of Directors or designee. The reports are used by both independent auditors and regulators to evaluate the sufficiency of the institution's risk management program.

In Practice

GLBA Section III-B: Assess Risk

Each bank or credit union shall:

- Identify reasonably foreseeable internal and external threats that could result in unauthorized disclosure, misuse, alteration, or destruction of customer information or customer information systems.

- Assess the likelihood and potential damage of these threats, taking into consideration the sensitivity of customer information.

- Assess the sufficiency of policies, procedures, customer information systems, and other arrangements in place to control risks.

Manage and Control Risk

The Interagency Guidelines require that financial institutions design their information security programs to control the identified risks, commensurate with the sensitivity of the information as well as the complexity and scope of their activities. The agencies recommend using the ISO standards as the framework for financial institution information security programs. Table 13-2 maps the GLBA information security objectives and the ISO security domains.

TABLE 13-2   GLBA Requirement ISO 27002:2013 Cross-Reference

GLBA Requirement	Corresponding ISO 27002:2013 Domain
II. Standards for Safeguarding Customer Information	
A. Information Security Program Requirements	Information Security Policies Compliance Management
III. Development and Implementation of Information Security Program	
A. Involve the Board of Directors	Organization of Information Security
B. Assess Risk	Refer to ISO 27005: Risk Management
C1. Manage and Control Risk	Asset Management Human Resources Security Physical and Environmental Security Communications Security Operations Security Access Control Information Systems Acquisition, Development, and Maintenance Information Security Incident Management Business Continuity
C2. Train Staff	Human Resources Security
C3. Test Key Controls	Communications Security Operations Security Information Systems Acquisition, Development, and Maintenance Information Security Incident Management Business Continuity
C4. Properly Dispose of Information	Asset Management
D. Oversee Service Provider Arrangements	Communications Security Operations Security
E. Adjust the Program	Information Security Policies Compliance Management
F. Report to the Board	Organization of Information Security
Supplement A to Appendix B to Part 364 Interagency Guidance on Response Programs for Unauthorized Access to Customer Information and Customer Notice	Information Security Incident Management

Federal Financial Institutions Examination Council (FFIEC) Information Technology Examination Handbook (IT Handbook)

A must-read supporting resource is *Federal Financial Institutions Examination Council (FFIEC) Information Technology Examination Handbook* (IT Handbook). The FFIEC is an interagency body empowered to prescribe uniform principles, standards, and report forms for the federal examination of financial institutions by the Board of Governors of the Federal Reserve System (FRB), the FDIC, the NCUA, the OCC and the Consumer Financial Protection Bureau (CFPB), and to make recommendations to promote uniformity in the supervision of financial institutions. The IT InfoBase spans a number of topics, including Information Security, IT Audit, Business Continuity Planning, Development and Acquisition, Management, Operations, and Outsourcing Technology Services.

The FFIEC InfoBase is the de facto guide for a financial institution that wants to ensure it has a GLBA-compliant information security program that meets regulatory expectations. Resources include explanatory text, guidance, recommended examination procedures and work papers, presentations, and resource pointers. The InfoBase can be accessed from the FFIEC home page (www.ffiec.gov).

FFIEC Cybersecurity Assessment Tool

The FFIEC developed the Cybersecurity Assessment Tool to help financial institutions identify their risks and assess their cybersecurity maturity. The Cybersecurity Assessment Tool is aligned with the principles of the FFIEC Information Technology Examination Handbook (IT Handbook) and the NIST Cybersecurity Framework.

The FFIEC Cybersecurity Assessment Tool can be accessed at https://www.ffiec.gov/cyberassessmenttool.htm.

The FFIEC Cybersecurity Assessment Tool addresses two main topics:

- **The Inherent Risk Profile:** Categorizes the institution's inherent risk before implementing controls.

- **The Cybersecurity Maturity:** Contains domains, assessment factors, components, and individual declarative statements across five maturity levels to identify specific controls and practices that are in place.

To complete the cybersecurity assessment, the executive team first assesses the organization's inherent risk profile based on the five categories shown in Figure 13-5.

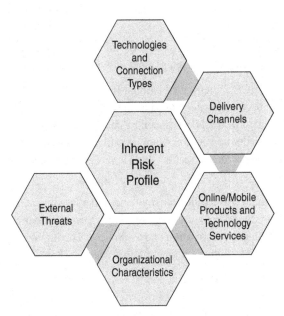

FIGURE 13-5 Inherent Risk Profile

The organization's executives evaluate the overall cybersecurity maturity level for the domains shown in Figure 13-6.

FIGURE 13-6 Evaluating the Overall Cybersecurity Maturity

Training

The Interagency Guidelines require institutions to implement an ongoing information security awareness program, to invest in training, and to educate executive management and directors.

The National Initiative for Cybersecurity Education (NICE), led by the National Institute of Standards and Technology (NIST), establishes a taxonomy and common lexicon that describes cybersecurity work and workers. The NICE Framework is documented in the NIST Special Publication 800-181. It is intended to be applied in the public, private, and academic sectors. Many organizations, including financial services institutions, use the NICE Framework to categorize the skills and training necessary for their cybersecurity workforce.

The goal of education is to explain why, and the anticipated outcome is insight and understanding. The goal of training is to explain how, and the anticipated outcome is knowledge and skill. Last, the goal of awareness is to explain what, and the anticipated outcome is information and awareness. The impact of education is long term, the impact of training is immediate, and the impact of awareness is short term.

At a minimum, financial institutions are expected to deliver and document annual enterprisewide training. The training can be instructor-led or online. Recommended topics include an overview of state and federal regulatory requirements, an explanation of user-focused threats, such as malware and social engineering, and a discussion of best practices and information resources acceptable use. It is commonplace for institutions to coordinate the distribution and signing of the acceptable use agreement with the annual training.

A popular concept that allows you to provide performance-based learning and assessment is the concept of cyber ranges. Cyber ranges are interactive, virtual representations of your organization's network, systems, and applications in order to provide a safe, legal environment to gain hands-on cyber skills and a secure environment for product development and security posture testing. You can use physical hardware or a combination of actual and virtual components.

In Practice

GLBA Section IIIC-2: Training

Train staff to implement the bank's information security program.

Note: Many organizations are leveraging the National Initiative for Cybersecurity Education (NICE) framework to develop security training for their employees.

Testing

Safeguards are meaningful only if they perform as anticipated. The regulatory agencies expect institutions to regularly test key controls and safeguards at a frequency that takes into account the rapid evolution of threats. High-risk systems should be subject to independent testing at least once a year. Independent testing means that the in-house or outsourced personnel who perform and report on the testing have no relationship to the design, installation, maintenance, and operation of the targeted system, or the policies and procedures that guide its operation. They should also be protected from undue influence or retaliatory repercussions.

The tests and methods utilized should be sufficient to validate the effectiveness of the security process in identifying and appropriately controlling security risks. The three most commonly used testing methodologies are audit, assessment, and assurance:

- An *audit* is an evidence-based examination that compares current practices against a specific internal (for example, policy) or external (for example, regulations or audit standard such as Control Objectives for Information and Related Technology [COBIT]) criteria.

- An *assessment* is a focused privileged inspection to determine condition, locate weakness or vulnerabilities, and identify corrective actions.

- An *assurance* test measures how well the control or safeguard works generally by subjecting the system or device to an actual attack, misuse, or an accident. Assurance tests can be *black box*, meaning with no prior knowledge of the system or process being tested, or *white box*, meaning with knowledge of the system or process being tested.

Because testing may uncover nonpublic customer information, appropriate safeguards to protect the information must be in place. Contracts with third parties that provide testing services should require that the third parties implement appropriate measures to meet the objectives of the Interagency Guidelines and that any exposure of NPPI be reported immediately.

In Practice

GLBA Section IIIC-3: Testing

Regularly test the key controls, systems, and procedures of the information security program. The frequency and nature of such tests should be determined by the bank's risk assessment. Tests should be conducted or reviewed by independent third parties or staff independent of those that develop or maintain the security programs.

Oversee Service Provider Arrangements

A *third-party service provider relationship* is broadly defined by the regulatory agencies to include all entities that have entered into a business relationship with a financial institution. This includes parties that perform functions on behalf of the institution, provide access to products and services, or perform marketing, monitoring, or auditing functions.

The Interagency Guidelines require financial institutions to ensure that service providers have implemented security controls in accordance with GLBA requirements. In June 2008, the Financial Institution Letter FIL-44-2008 "Guidance for Managing Third-Party Risk" made clear that an "institution can outsource a task, but it cannot outsource the responsibility." It is up to the institution to ensure that the controls and safeguards designed, managed, and maintained by third parties are equivalent to or exceed internal policies and standards.

Recommended service provider oversight procedures include the following:

- Conducting a risk assessment to ensure that the relationship is consistent with the overall business strategy and to ensure that management has the knowledge and expertise to provide adequate oversight

- Using appropriate due diligence in service provider research and selection

- Implementing contractual assurances regarding security responsibilities, controls, and reporting

- Requiring nondisclosure agreements (NDAs) regarding the institution's systems and data

- Providing a third-party review of the service provider's security though appropriate audits and tests

- Coordinating incident response policies and contractual notification requirements

- Reviewing at least annually significant third-party arrangements and performance

The **Bank Service Company Act (BSCA)**, 12 USC 1861-1867, gives federal financial regulators statutory authority to regulate and examine the services a technology service provider (TSP) performs for FDIC-insured financial institutions. According to the *FFIEC Outsourcing Technology Services Handbook*, TSP relationships should be subject to the same risk management, security, privacy, and other internal controls and policies that would be expected if the financial institution were conducting the activities directly. To maintain an accurate database of TSPs, BSCA requires insured financial institutions to notify their appropriate federal banking agency in writing of contracts or relationships with third parties that provide certain services to the institution. Selected TSPs are examined on a 24-, 36-, or 48-month cycle. Distribution of the exam results is restricted to financial institutions that have signed a contract with the TSP. Ironically, this means that the findings are not available during the initial due-diligence phase.

In Practice

GLBA Section III-D: Oversee Service Provider Relationships

Each bank shall:

- Exercise appropriate due diligence in selecting its service providers.

- Require its service providers by contract to implement appropriate measures designed to meet the objectives of these guidelines.

- Where indicated by the bank's risk assessment, monitor its service providers to confirm that they have satisfied their obligations as required by paragraph D.2. As part of this monitoring, a bank should review audits, summaries of test results, or other equivalent evaluations of its service providers.

Adjust the Program

A static information security program provides a false sense of security. Threats are ever increasing. Organizations are subject to change. Monitoring the effectiveness of the security program and personnel is essential to maintaining a secure environment, protecting customer information, and complying with regulatory objectives. Evaluation results should be carefully analyzed and, as appropriate, adjustments to the information security program implemented. At a minimum, the information security policy should be reviewed annually. Modifications to policy must be communicated to the Board of Directors. It is the responsibility of the Board of Directors to annually reauthorize the information security policy and, by extension, the information security program.

In Practice

GLBA Section III-E: Adjust the Program

Each bank shall monitor, evaluate, and adjust, as appropriate, the information security program in light of any relevant changes in technology, the sensitivity of its customer information, internal or external threats to information, and the bank's own changing business arrangements, such as mergers and acquisitions, alliances and joint ventures, outsourcing arrangements, and changes to customer information systems.

Report to the Board

Throughout the year, the Board of Directors or designated committee should receive information security program updates and be immediately apprised of any major issue. Additionally, the Interagency Guidelines require each institution to provide an annual Information Security and GLBA Compliance report to the Board of Directors or designated committee. The report should describe the overall status of the information security program and the bank's compliance with the Interagency Guidelines. The report should detail the following:

- Regulatory examination results and post-examination follow-up.

- Security incidents that occurred in the previous 12 months, including a synopsis of response and impact.

- Major IT and security initiatives completed in the previous 12 months, in progress and scheduled.

- Information security program–related governance activities, including a synopsis of roles, responsibilities, and significant decisions.

- Independent audit and testing conducted in the previous 12 months. The description should include type of test, date of test, tester, test objective, test results, recommendations, follow-up, and, if applicable, remediation plan.

- Risk assessments conducted in the previous 12 months. The description should include methodology, focus areas, results, follow-up, and, if applicable, remediation plan.

- Service provider oversight activities. The description should include due diligence, contract updates, monitoring, and, if applicable, identified issues and remediation plan.

- Employee training conducted in the previous 12 months. The description should include the type of training, conduct, participation, and evaluation.

- Updates to and testing of the incident disaster recovery, public health emergency, and business continuity plan.

- Updates to and testing of the incident response plan and procedures.

- Recommended changes to the information security program or policy that require Board approval or authorization.

The final section of the report should be management's opinion of the institution's compliance with information security–related state and federal regulations and guidance. Conversely, if in management's opinion the institution does not comply with applicable regulations or guidance, the issues should be fully documented and a remediation plan presented.

New York's Department of Financial Services Cybersecurity Regulation (23 NYCRR Part 500)

The New York Department of Financial Services (DFS) created a regulation that took effect on March 1, 2017, and that is designed to promote the protection of customer information as well as the information technology systems of regulated entities. This regulation requires any individual or organization operating under or required to operate under a license, charter, certificate, permit, accreditation, or similar authorization under the banking law, insurance law, or the financial services law that do business in the state of New York to assess their cybersecurity risk profile and design a solid program to address such cybersecurity risks. The NY DFS Cybersecurity Regulation can be accessed at www.dfs.ny.gov/legal/regulations/adoptions/dfsrf500txt.pdf; the key parts are as follows:

- Section 500.00 is an introduction to the rule, and Section 500.01 defines the terms used throughout the rule.

- Section 500.02 states that "each Covered Entity shall maintain a cybersecurity program designed to protect the confidentiality, integrity and availability of the Covered Entity's Information Systems."

- Section 500.03 dictates that "each Covered Entity shall implement and maintain a written policy or policies, approved by a Senior Officer or the Covered Entity's board of directors (or an appropriate committee thereof) or equivalent governing body, setting forth the Covered Entity's policies and procedures for the protection of its Information Systems and Nonpublic Information stored on those Information Systems."

- The NY DFS Cybersecurity Regulation states in Section 500.04 that "each Covered Entity shall designate a qualified individual responsible for overseeing and implementing the Covered Entity's cybersecurity program and enforcing its cybersecurity policy (for purposes of this Part, "Chief Information Security Officer" or "CISO"). The CISO may be employed by the Covered Entity, one of its Affiliates or a Third-Party Service Provider."

- Section 500.05 requires the covered entity to perform security penetration testing and vulnerability assessments on an ongoing basis. The cybersecurity program needs to include monitoring and testing, developed in accordance with the Covered Entity's Risk Assessment, designed to assess the effectiveness of the Covered Entity's cybersecurity program. The regulation dictates that "the monitoring and testing shall include continuous monitoring or periodic Penetration Testing and vulnerability assessments." The organization must conduct an annual security penetration test and a biannual vulnerability assessment.

- Section 500.06 specifies that each covered entity shall securely maintain an audit trail of supported systems.

- Section 500.07 specifies that "each Covered Entity shall limit user access privileges to Information Systems that provide access to Nonpublic Information and shall periodically review such access privileges."

- Additionally, Section 500.08 states that the institution's application security "procedures, guidelines and standards shall be periodically reviewed, assessed and updated as necessary by the CISO (or a qualified designee) of the Covered Entity." As such, when Covered Entities are acquiring or merging with a new company, Covered Entities will need to do a factual analysis of how these regulatory requirements apply to that particular acquisition. Some important considerations include, but are not limited to, what business the acquired company engages in, the target company's risk for cybersecurity, including its availability of PII, the safety and soundness of the Covered Entity, and the integration of data systems. The Department emphasizes that Covered Entities need to have a serious due diligence process, and cybersecurity should be a priority when considering any new acquisitions.

- Section 500.09 states that the "Risk Assessment shall be updated as reasonably necessary to address changes to the Covered Entity's Information Systems, Nonpublic Information or business operations."

- Similar to GLBA, the NY DFS Cybersecurity Regulation specifies (in Section 500.10) that each covered entity needs to provide cybersecurity personnel "with cybersecurity updates and training sufficient to address relevant cybersecurity risks; and verify that key cybersecurity personnel take steps to maintain current knowledge of changing cybersecurity threats and countermeasures." Section 500.11 addresses third-party service provider security policies.

- Section 500.12 specifies that each covered entity shall use multifactor authentication.

- Section 500.13 strictly specifies that "each Covered Entity shall include policies and procedures for the secure disposal on a periodic basis of any Nonpublic Information identified in section 500.01(g)(2)-(3) of this Part that is no longer necessary for business operations or for other legitimate business purposes of the Covered Entity, except where such information is otherwise required to be retained by law or regulation, or where targeted disposal is not reasonably feasible due to the manner in which the information is maintained."

- Section 500.14 covers training and monitoring.

- Section 500.15 mandates encryption of nonpublic information.

- Section 500.16 mandates that each Covered Entity "shall establish a written incident response plan designed to promptly respond to, and recover from, any Cybersecurity Event materially affecting the confidentiality, integrity or availability of the Covered Entity's Information Systems or the continuing functionality of any aspect of the Covered Entity's business or operations."

- Section 500.17 requires each Covered Entity to annually submit to the Superintendent a written statement covering the prior calendar year by February 15, certifying that the Covered Entity is in compliance with the requirements stated in the regulation. In addition, it dictates that the Covered Entity needs to maintain all records, schedules, and data supporting the certificate for a period of five years. The Superintendent also needs to be notified within 72 hours from the determination of the occurrence of a Cybersecurity Event impacting the Covered Entity.

An important element to point out about the NY DFS Cybersecurity Regulation is that it overlaps with the guidance and requirements for entities that are already in compliance with the GLBA or have met the FFIEC standards outlined in their IT Handbook. Most financial organizations that are considered covered entities under the NY DFS Cybersecurity Regulation will have already addressed some requirements outlined in GLBA or FFIEC IT Handbook. However, it is important to know that while there is overlap in the requirements, there are also some substantial differences needing to be addressed to comply with the NY DFS Cybersecurity Regulation. Understanding these differences will help you leverage existing investments in security and develop a plan of action to address any gaps.

What Is a Regulatory Examination?

The regulatory agencies are responsible for oversight and supervision of financial institutions. Included in this charge is ensuring that the financial institutions soundly manage risk; comply with laws and regulations, including GLBA, the NY DFS Cybersecurity Regulation, and others; and, as appropriate, take corrective action. Representatives of the regulatory agencies examine their respective banks and credit unions. Depending on size, scope, and previous examination findings, exams are conducted every 12 to 18 months. Included in the exam is an evaluation of policies, processes, personnel, controls, and outcomes.

Examination Process

GLBA security is included in the Information Technology Examination. Institutions are given 30- to 90-days' notice that an examination is scheduled. An Information Technology Officer's questionnaire is sent to the institution with the expectation that the institution will complete and return the questionnaire and supporting documentation (including Board reports, policies, risk assessments, test results, and training materials) prior to the examination date. The length of the exam and number of on-site examiners depends on the complexity of the environment, previous findings, and examiner availability. The examination begins with an entrance meeting with management. The agenda of the entrance meeting includes explaining the scope of the examination, the role of each examiner, and how the team will conduct the exam. During the exam, the examiners will request information, observe, and ask questions. At the end of the exam, an exit meeting is held to discuss findings and potential solutions. Post-examination, the regulatory agency will issue a draft report for management's review for accuracy. Taking into consideration management's response, the agency will issue a written report to the Board of Directors, which includes the examination ratings, any issues that have been identified, recommendations, and, if required, supervisory action.

The NY DFS Cybersecurity Regulation mandates that "each Covered Entity shall maintain for examination by the Department all records, schedules and data supporting this certificate for a period of five years." It also specifies that each Covered Entity is to annually submit to the Superintendent, by February 15, a written statement covering the prior calendar year, certifying that the Covered Entity is in compliance with the requirements stated in the regulation. In addition, it dictates that the Covered Entity needs to maintain all records, schedules, and data supporting the certificate for a period of five years. The Superintendent also needs to be notified within 72 hours from the determination of the occurrence of a Cybersecurity Event impacting the Covered Entity.

Examination Ratings

The *Uniform Rating System for Information Technology (URSIT)* is used to uniformly assess financial institutions. The rating is based on a scale of 1 to 5, in ascending order of supervisory concern, with 1 representing the best rating and least degree of concern, and 5 representing the worst rating and highest degree of concern. URSIT is part of the FFIEC.

Per URSIT standards:

- Financial institutions that are rated as a "1" exhibit strong performance in every respect. Weaknesses in IT are minor in nature and are easily corrected during the normal course of business. Risk management processes provide a comprehensive program to identify and monitor risk relative to the size, complexity, and risk profile of the entity.

- Financial institutions rated as a "2" exhibit safe and sound performance but may demonstrate modest weaknesses in operating performance, monitoring, management processes, or system development. Generally, senior management corrects weaknesses in the normal course of business. Risk management processes adequately identify and monitor risk relative to the size, complexity, and risk profile of the entity. As a result, supervisory action is informal and limited.

- Financial institutions and service providers rated composite "3" exhibit some degree of supervisory concern because of a combination of weaknesses that may range from moderate to severe. If weaknesses persist, further deterioration in the condition and performance of the institution or service provider is likely. Risk management processes may not effectively identify risks and may not be appropriate for the size, complexity, or risk profile of the entity. Formal or informal supervisory action may be necessary to secure corrective action.

- Financial institutions and service providers rated composite "4" operate in an unsafe and unsound environment that may impair the future viability of the entity. Operating weaknesses are indicative of serious managerial deficiencies. Risk management processes inadequately identify and monitor risk, and practices are not appropriate given the size, complexity, and risk profile of the entity. Close supervisory attention is necessary and, in most cases, formal enforcement action is warranted.

- Financial institutions and service providers rated composite "5" exhibit critically deficient operating performance and are in need of immediate remedial action. Operational problems and serious weaknesses may exist throughout the organization. Risk management processes are severely deficient and provide management little or no perception of risk relative to the size, complexity, and risk profile of the entity. Ongoing supervisory attention is necessary.

Supplemental to the rating, if violations of any law or regulations are identified, the agency must provide detailed information, including legal numerical citations and name, a brief description of the law or regulation (or portion of it) that is in violation, a description of what led to the violation, and corrective action taken or promised by management.

Personal and Corporate Identity Theft

Personal and corporate identity theft is one of the fastest growing crimes worldwide. ***Personal identity theft*** occurs when a criminal fraudulently uses a name, address, SSN, bank account or credit card account number, or other identifying information without consent to commit a crime.

Corporate identity theft occurs when criminals attempt to impersonate authorized employees, generally for the purpose of accessing corporate bank accounts to steal money. This type of attack is known as a *corporate account takeover.* Using specially crafted malware, criminals capture a business's online banking credentials or compromise the workstation used for online banking. The criminals then access online accounts and create fraudulent ACH or wire transfers. The transfers are directed "money mules" who are waiting to withdraw the funds and send the money overseas. Once the funds are offshore, it is very difficult for law enforcement to recover them.

What Is Required by the Interagency Guidelines Supplement A?

Supplement A, "Interagency Guidance on Response Programs for Unauthorized Access to Customer Information and Customer Notice," describes response programs, including customer notification procedures, that a financial institution should develop and implement to address unauthorized access to or use of customer information that could result in substantial harm or inconvenience to a customer. The guidance enumerates a number of security measures that each financial institution must consider and adopt, if appropriate, to control risks stemming from reasonably foreseeable internal and external threats to the institution's customer information. The guidance stresses that every financial institution must develop and implement a risk-based response program to address incidents of unauthorized access to customer information. The response program should be a key part of an institution's cyber-security program. Supplement A emphasizes that an institution's response program should contain procedures for the following:

- Assessing the nature and scope of an incident, and identifying what customer information systems and types of customer information have been accessed or misused.

- Notifying its primary federal regulator as soon as possible when the institution becomes aware of an incident involving unauthorized access to or use of *sensitive* customer information.

- Being consistent with the agencies' Suspicious Activity Report (SAR) regulations, notifying appropriate law enforcement authorities in addition to filing a timely SAR in situations involving federal criminal violations requiring immediate attention, such as when a reportable violation is ongoing.

- Taking appropriate steps to contain and control the incident to prevent further unauthorized access to or use of customer information—for example, by monitoring, freezing, or closing affected accounts—while preserving records and other evidence.

- Requiring its service providers by contract to implement appropriate measures designed to protect against unauthorized access to or use of customer information that could result in substantial harm or inconvenience to any customers.

- Notifying customers when warranted.

The guidance emphasizes notification requirements. When a financial institution becomes aware of an incident of unauthorized access to sensitive customer information, the institution is required to conduct a reasonable investigation to promptly determine the likelihood that the information has been or will be misused. If the institution determines that misuse of its information about a customer has occurred or is reasonably possible, it must notify its regulatory agency and affected customers as soon as possible. Customer notice may be delayed if an appropriate law enforcement agency determines that notification will interfere with a criminal investigation and provides the institution with a written request for the delay. In this case, the institution should notify its customers as soon as notification will no longer interfere with the investigation. When customer notification is warranted, an institution may not forgo notifying its customers of an incident because the institution believes that it may be potentially embarrassed or inconvenienced by doing so.

Compliance with the Supplement A, "Interagency Guidance on Response Programs for Unauthorized Access to Customer Information and Customer Notice," is included in the FFIEC Information Technology Examination.

Identity Theft Data Clearinghouse

Although the FTC does not have criminal jurisdiction, it supports the identity theft criminal investigation and prosecution through its *Identity Theft Data Clearinghouse*. The Clearinghouse is the nation's official repository for identity theft complaints and a part of the FTC's Consumer Sentinel complaint database. In addition to housing more than a million ID theft complaints, Sentinel offers participating law enforcement agencies a variety of tools to facilitate the investigation and prosecution of identity theft. These include information to help agencies coordinate effective joint action, sample indictments, tools to refresh investigative data through programmed data searches, and access to "hot address" databases.

What Is Required by the Supplement to the Authentication in an Internet Banking Environment Guidance?

In response to the alarming rate of successful corporate account takeover attacks, the financial losses being sustained by both financial institutions and customers, and the impact on public confidence in the online banking system, in October 2011, the regulatory agencies issued updated guidance related to Internet banking safeguards. The FFIEC issued a supplement to the Authentication in an Internet Banking Environment Guidance, which stressed the need for performing risk assessments, implementing effective strategies for mitigating identified risks, and raising customer awareness of potential risks. In a departure from other guidance, the supplement was specific in its requirements and opinion of various authentication mechanisms.

Requirements include the following:

- Financial institutions are required to review and update their existing *risk assessments* as new information becomes available, prior to implementing new electronic financial services, or at least every 12 months.

- Financial institutions are required to implement a layered security model. *Layered security* is characterized by the use of different controls at different points in a transaction process so that a weakness in one control is generally compensated for by the strength of a different control.

- Financial institutions are required to offer *multifactor authentication* to their commercial cash management (ACH and wire transfer) customers. Because the frequency and dollar amounts of these transactions are generally higher than consumer transactions, they pose a comparatively increased level of risk to the institution and its customer.

- Financial institutions are required to implement authentication and transactional *fraud monitoring*.

- Financial institutions are required to educate their retail and commercial account holders about the risks associated with online banking. Commercial customers must be notified that their funds are not covered under Regulation E and that they may incur a loss. It is strongly recommended that the awareness programs include risk reduction and mitigation recommendations.

Compliance with the Supplement to the Authentication in an Internet Banking Environment Guidance has been added to the Information Technology Examination. Anecdotal evidence suggests that the guidance has had an impact because losses associated with corporate account takeover are declining.

FYI: Corporate Account Takeover Fraud Advisory

The United States Secret Service, the Federal Bureau of Investigation, the Internet Crime Complaint Center (IC3), and the Financial Services Information Sharing and Analysis Center (FSISAC) jointly issued a Fraud Advisory for Business: Corporate Account Takeover, with the intent of warning business about this type of crime. The advisory noted that cybercriminals are targeting nonprofits, small and medium-sized businesses, municipalities, and school districts across the country. Using malicious software (malware), cybercriminals attempt to capture a business's online banking credentials, take over web sessions, or even remotely control workstations. If the criminal gains access to online bank account login credentials or can take over an online banking session, it is possible for him to initiate and authorize ACH or wire funds transfers. Generally, the criminal will create numerous smaller transactions and send them to domestic "money mules," who are waiting to withdraw the funds and send the money overseas. Once the funds are offshore, it is very difficult for law enforcement to recover them. To make matters worse, financial institutions are not required to reimburse for fraud-related losses associated with commercial accountholder computers or networks. Nor are these losses covered by FDIC insurance.

The information contained in the advisory is intended to provide basic guidance and resources for businesses to learn about the evolving threats and to establish security processes specific to their needs. The advisory and related resources are available at the NACHA Corporate Account Takeover Resource Center website at www.nacha.org/Corporate_Account_Takeover_Resource_Center. Security journalist Brian Krebs has been reporting on the impact of corporate account takeovers on small business for years! For current and archived reports, visit his blog at http://krebsonsecurity.com/category/smallbizvictims.

Summary

Federal law defines a financial institution as "any institution the business of which is significantly engaged in financial activities...." This broad definition includes banks, credit unions, investment firms, and businesses such as automobile dealers, check-cashing businesses, consumer reporting agencies, credit card companies, educational institutions that provide financial aid, financial planners, insurance companies, mortgage brokers and lenders, and retail stores that issue credit cards.

Congress enacted legislation requiring all financial institutions that do business in the United States to protect the privacy and security of customer nonpublic personal information (NPPI). The Gramm-Leach-Bliley Act (GLBA) required that appropriate privacy and security standards be developed and enforced, and assigned this task to various federal agencies. The agencies that regulate banks and credit unions collaborated and in 2001 published the Interagency Guidelines Establishing Standards for Safeguarding Customer Information and the Guidelines for Safeguarding Member Information, respectively. The Federal Trade Commission (FTC) was charged with developing standards for nonregulated businesses that provide financial services, and in 2003 published the Standards for Safeguarding Customer Information, also known as the Safeguards Act. Due to the type of business the regulations apply to, the requirements of the Safeguards Act are not as stringent as the Interagency Guidelines. The FTC does not conduct compliance examinations. The basis for investigation and enforcement actions are consumer complaints.

The Interagency Guidelines Establishing Standards for Safeguarding Customer Information and the Guidelines for Safeguarding Member Information, collectively referred to as the Interagency Guidelines, define cybersecurity program objectives and requirements for banks and credit unions. It is up to each covered entity to implement a comprehensive written cybersecurity program that includes administrative, technical, and physical safeguards appropriate to the size and complexity of the institution and the nature and scope of its activities. To be in compliance, the cybersecurity program must include policies and processes that require institutions to do the following:

- Involve the Board of Directors

- Assess risk

- Manage and control risk

- Oversee service provider arrangements

- Adjust the program

- Report to the Board

It is up to each institution to develop a program that meets these objectives. The NIST Cybersecurity Framework and the ISO 27002:2013 standard provide a good foundation for a regulatory-compliant cybersecurity program.

Financial institutions are expected to take a risk-based approach to cybersecurity. The process begins with identifying threats. *Threats* are defined as potential dangers that have the capacity to cause harm. It is incumbent upon each institution to continually engage in a threat assessment. A *threat assessment* is the identification of the types of threats and attacks that may affect the institution's condition and operations or may cause data disclosures that could result in substantial harm or inconvenience to customers. At a minimum, financial institutions must address the threats of unauthorized access, unauthorized data modification, system infiltration, malware, destruction of data or systems, and DoS. The systematic rating of threats based on level of impact and likelihood sans controls is used to determine the inherent risk. A risk assessment is used to evaluate the corresponding safeguards in order to calculate residual risk. Residual risk is defined as the level of risk after controls and safeguards have been implemented. The Federal Financial Institutions Examination Council (FFIEC) recommends using the NIST risk management framework and methodology as described in Special Publication 800-53 to calculate residual risk. Multiple categories of risk are defined by the FDIC as relevant for financial institutions, including strategic, reputational, operational, transactional, and compliance.

Controls and safeguards can be circumvented by users. Although these actions may be deliberate or accidental, they are often intentionally malicious. To mitigate the risk of circumvention, it is critical that users understand the threat environment, learn best practices, and agree to acceptable use of information and information systems. To this end, institutions are expected to have a security awareness program and to provide annual enterprisewide training.

Controls and safeguards are useful only if they perform as expected. Scheduled testing should be conducted by personnel that are independent of the targeted system. The tests and methods utilized should be sufficient to validate the effectiveness of the controls and safeguards. The three most common testing methodologies are audit, assessment, and assurance.

The Interagency Guidelines require financial institutions to ensure that service providers have implemented security controls in accordance with GLBA requirements. Financial Institution Letter FIL-44-2008, "Third-Party Risk Guidance for Managing Third-Party Risk," clearly states that an institution can outsource a task, but it cannot outsource the responsibility. It is up to the institution to ensure that the controls and safeguards designed, managed, and maintained by third parties comply with the Interagency Guidelines and are equivalent to or exceed internal policies and standards.

The financial institutions' Board of Directors is ultimately responsible for oversight of the cybersecurity program and for compliance with all applicable state and federal regulations. Throughout the year, board members should receive cybersecurity program updates and be immediately apprised of all major security issues. Decisions that may significantly affect the risk profile of the institution must be authorized by the Board. The Interagency Guidelines require each institution to provide a comprehensive annual Cybersecurity and GLBA Compliance report to the Board of Directors or designated committee.

In response to the problem of personal and corporate identity threat, in 2005 the regulatory agencies issued Supplement A, "Interagency Guidance on Response Programs for Unauthorized Access to Customer Information and Customer Notice," and in 2011, "Supplement to the Authentication in an

Internet Banking Environment Guidance." Both supplements focus on threats related to unauthorized access to or use of customer information as well as corresponding controls, including education, incident response programs, and notification procedures.

To ensure compliance with GLBA Interagency Guidelines and supplemental guidance, financial institutions are subject to regulatory examinations. Depending on size, scope, and previous examination findings, exams are conducted every 12 to 18 months. Included in the exam is an evaluation of policies, processes, personnel, controls, and outcomes. The outcome of the examination is a rating based on a scale of 1 to 5, in ascending order of supervisory concern (1 representing the best rating and least degree of concern, and 5 representing the worst rating and highest degree of concern), supervisory comments, and recommendations. Financial institutions that are found not in compliance with regulatory requirements and do not remediate examination findings within an agreed-upon time frame can be subject to closure.

Test Your Skills

MULTIPLE CHOICE QUESTIONS

1. Which of the following statements best defines the type of organizations that are subject to GLBA regulations?

    A. GLBA applies only to banks and credit unions.

    B. GLBA applies only to check cashing businesses.

    C. GLBA applies to any business engaged in financial services.

    D. GLBA applies only to institutions licensed to offer depository services.

2. The Financial Modernization Act of 1999 _____.

    A. prevented the merger of banks, stock brokerage companies, and insurance companies

    B. mandated use of computers in all branch offices

    C. allowed the merger of banks, stock brokerage companies, and insurance companies

    D. introduced the new cybersecurity framework

3. Which of the following agencies is responsible for enforcing GLBA?

    A. The U.S. Department of Commerce

    B. NIST

    C. Federal Trade Commission (FTC)

    D. None of the above

4. Which of the following is *not* considered NPPI?

   A. SSN

   B. The physical address of a company or a bank

   C. Checking account number

   D. PIN or password associated with a financial account or payment card

5. The Interagency Guidelines Establishing Standards for Safeguarding Customer Information was jointly developed by the _____.

   A. Federal Deposit Insurance Corporation (FDIC)

   B. Office of the Comptroller of the Currency (OCC), Federal Reserve System (FRS), and FDIC

   C. Securities and Exchange Commission (SEC) and FDIC

   D. National Credit Union Administration (NCUA) and FDIC

6. Which of the following is not a requirement of the Safeguards Act?

   A. Designate the employee or employees to coordinate the safeguards.

   B. Design a safeguards program, and detail the plans to monitor it.

   C. Select appropriate service providers and require them (by contract) to implement the safeguards.

   D. Enforce the adoption and improvement of the NIST Cybersecurity Framework.

7. Which of the following statements is false about the FTC Safeguards Act?

   A. The FTC does not conduct regulatory compliance audits.

   B. Enforcement is complaint-driven.

   C. Consumers can file a complaint with the FTC.

   D. Consumers can only file a complaint with the respective financial institution.

8. What is the Federal Register?

   A. A series of legal safeguards

   B. A series of physical safeguards

   C. The official daily publication for rules, proposed rules, and notices of federal agencies

   D. A series of technical safeguards

9. The Interagency Guidelines require every covered institution to implement which of the following?

   A. A cybersecurity framework for business partners

   B. A comprehensive written information security program that includes administrative, technical, and physical safeguards appropriate to the size and complexity of the organization

   C. A comprehensive written information security program that includes administrative, technical, and physical safeguards appropriate to the size and complexity of the business partners

   D. A comprehensive written information security program excluding administrative, technical, and physical safeguards

10. Financial institutions are expected to take an _____ approach to cybersecurity.

   A. threat-based

   B. risk-based

   C. audit-based

   D. management-based

11. Which of the following terms describes a potential danger that has the capacity to cause harm?

   A. Risk

   B. Threat

   C. Variable

   D. Vulnerability

12. Which of the following statements best describes a threat assessment?

   A. A threat assessment identifies the types of threats that may affect the institution or customers.

   B. A threat assessment is a systematic rating of threats based on level of impact and likelihood.

   C. A threat assessment is an audit report.

   D. A threat assessment is a determination of inherent risk.

13. Which of the following risk types is defined as a level of risk after controls and safeguards have been implemented?

    A. Ongoing risk

    B. Residual risk

    C. Acceptable risk

    D. Inherent risk

14. Which of the following risk-management frameworks is recommended by the FFIEC?

    A. FAIR Institute

    B. COBIT

    C. NIST

    D. FDIC

15. Which of the following statements is true?

    A. Strategic risk is the risk of loss resulting from inadequate or failed internal processes, people, and systems or from external events.

    B. Reputational risk is the risk of loss resulting from inadequate or failed internal processes, people, and systems or from external events.

    C. Transactional risk is the risk of loss resulting from inadequate or failed internal processes, people, and systems or from external events.

    D. Operational risk is the risk of loss resulting from inadequate or failed internal processes, people, and systems or from external events.

16. The risk arising from problems with service or product delivery is known as

_____.

    A. strategic risk

    B. reputational risk

    C. transactional risk

    D. operational risk

17. Which of the following defines strategic risk?

    A. The risk arising from negative public opinion

    B. The risk arising from negative government regulations

    C. The risk arising from adverse business decisions, or the failure to implement appropriate business decisions in a manner that is consistent with the institution's strategic goals

    D. The risk arising from noncompliant business partners

18. A security awareness and training program is considered which type of control?

    A. Administrative control

    B. Physical control

    C. Technical control

    D. Contractual control

19. Which of the following statements best describes a cyber range?

    A. An enterprisewide security penetration testing program including continuous monitoring and vulnerability management.

    B. Interactive, virtual representations of your organization's network, systems, and applications in order to provide a safe, legal environment to gain hands-on cyber skills and a secure environment for product development and security posture testing.

    C. An enterprisewide security penetration testing program excluding continuous monitoring and vulnerability management.

    D. Independent testing is testing performed by certified professionals.

20. Which of the following test methodologies is a privileged inspection to determine condition, locate weakness or vulnerabilities, and identify corrective actions?

    A. Audit

    B. Assessment

    C. White box

    D. Black box

21. Which of the following is true about "black box" testing?

    A. The individual conducting the testing had prior knowledge of the system and underlying source code of an application.

    B. The individual conducting the testing only had prior knowledge and access to the underlying source code of an application running on the system.

    C. The individual conducting the testing didn't have prior knowledge of the system and underlying source code of an application.

    D. The individual conducting the testing is also the developer of the application running on the system.

22. Per the Interagency Guidance, which of the following entities is responsible for oversight of a financial institution's Cybersecurity Program?

    A. Chief Technology Officer (CTO)

    B. Chief Information Security Officer (CISO)

C. Board of Directors

D. Regulatory Agencies

23. Which of the following is true about the Uniform Rating System for Information Technology (URSIT)?

A. URSIT is a rating based on a scale of 1 to 5, in ascending order of supervisory concern, with 1 representing the best rating and least degree of concern, and 5 representing the worst rating and highest degree of concern.

B. URSIT is a rating based on a scale of 1 to 10, in ascending order of supervisory concern, with 10 representing the best rating and least degree of concern, and 1 representing the worst rating and highest degree of concern.

C. URSIT is a rating based on a scale of 1 to 5, in ascending order of supervisory concern, with 5 representing the best rating and least degree of concern, and 1 representing the worst rating and highest degree of concern.

D. None of the above.

24. Which of the following statements is true about the New York Department of Financial Services (DFS) Cybersecurity Regulation?

A. All financial institutions in New York, New Jersey, and New England are subject to a three-year examination schedule.

B. All financial institutions in New York and New Jersey are subject to a three-year examination schedule.

C. Requires financial services companies that do business in the state of New York to assess their cybersecurity risk profile and design a solid program to address such cybersecurity risks.

D. Requires financial services companies to have a CISO in New York, and the company cannot hire an affiliate or a third-party service provider.

25. Which of the following statements is not true about the NY DFS Cybersecurity Regulation?

A. The organization must conduct an annual security penetration test and a biannual vulnerability assessment.

B. The organization must conduct a security penetration test every two years and an annual vulnerability assessment.

C. The cybersecurity procedures, guidelines and standards shall be periodically reviewed, assessed, and updated as necessary by the CISO (or a qualified designee) of the covered entity.

D. The financial institution needs to provide cybersecurity personnel with cybersecurity updates and training sufficient to address relevant cybersecurity risks, and verify that key cybersecurity personnel take steps to maintain current knowledge of changing cybersecurity threats and countermeasures.

26. Which of the following is not an example of multifactor authentication?

    A. Password and smart token

    B. Password and username

    C. Password and SMS (text) message

    D. Password and out-of-band via a mobile device app

27. Which of the following is not true about controls and safeguards?

    A. Controls and safeguards are useful only if they perform as expected.

    B. Controls and safeguards can be circumvented by users.

    C. The tests and methods utilized should be sufficient to validate the effectiveness of the controls and safeguards.

    D. Controls and safeguards cannot be circumvented by users.

28. Which of the following statements is true?

    A. When a financial institution chooses to outsource a banking function, it must conduct a due-diligence investigation.

    B. When a financial institution chooses to outsource a banking function, it must report the relationship to its regulatory agency.

    C. When a financial institution chooses to outsource a banking function, it must require the service provider to have appropriate controls and safeguards.

    D. All of the above.

29. Which of the following is not a requirement by the Supplement to the Authentication in an Internet Banking Environment Guidance?

    A. Financial institutions are required to educate their retail and commercial account holders about the risks associated with online banking.

    B. Financial institutions are required to educate their retail and commercial account holders about the risks associated with a cyber range.

    C. Financial institutions are required to implement a layered security model. Layered security is characterized by the use of different controls at different points in a transaction process so that a weakness in one control is generally compensated for by the strength of a different control.

    D. Financial institutions are required to implement authentication and transactional fraud monitoring.

30. The FTC does not have criminal jurisdiction; it supports the identity theft criminal investigation and prosecution through which of the following?

   A. FTC Consumer Protection Partners

   B. FTC Identity Theft Data Clearinghouse

   C. NIST Identity Theft Data Clearinghouse

   D. NIST Cybersecurity Framework

EXERCISES

EXERCISE 13.1: Identifying Regulatory Relationships

1. Access the official websites of the Federal Reserve Board (FRB), the Federal Deposit Insurance Corporation (FDIC), the National Credit Union Administration (NCUA), and the Office of the Comptroller of the Currency (OCC) and write a brief synopsis of the mission of each agency.

2. For each agency, identify at least one financial institution (within a 50-mile radius of your location) that it regulates.

3. In matters of cybersecurity, should it matter to consumers who regulates the financial institution they use? Why or why not?

EXERCISE 13.2: Researching the FTC

1. Visit the official FTC website and write a brief synopsis of its mission.

2. Prepare a summary of FTC cybersecurity resources for business.

3. Prepare a summary of an FTC GLBA-related enforcement action.

EXERCISE 13.3: Understanding the Federal Register

1. Locate a Federal Register copy of the Interagency Guidelines Establishing Standards for Safeguarding Customer Information.

2. Highlight the actual regulations.

3. Prepare a brief explaining the other sections of the document.

EXERCISE 13.4: Assessing GLBA Training

1. Go online and find publicly available GLBA-related cybersecurity training.

2. Go through the training and make a list of the key points.

3. Did you find the training effective? Why or why not?

EXERCISE 13.5: Researching Identity Theft

1. Document the steps consumers should take if they have been or suspect they have been the victims of identity theft.

2. Document how a consumer reports identity theft to your local or state police.

3. Document how a consumer files an identity theft complaint with the FTC.

PROJECTS

PROJECT 13.1: Educational Institutions and GLBA

Educational institutions that collect, process, store, and/or transmit nonpublic personal student information, including financial records and SSNs, are subject to GLBA regulations.

1. Locate documents published by your school that relate to compliance with GLBA. If you are not a student, choose a local educational institution. GLBA compliance documentation is generally published on an institution's website.

2. Evaluate the documentation for clarity (for example, is it written in plain language? is it easy to understand and relate to?) and content (does it address the objectives of the Safeguards Act?). Make suggestions for improvement.

3. Prepare a training session for new faculty and administration that describes the school's GLBA compliance policy and standards. Include an explanation of why it is important to safeguard NPPI.

PROJECT 13.2: Exploring the FFIEC Cybersecurity Assessment Tool

The FFIEC developed the Cybersecurity Assessment Tool to help financial institutions identify their risks and assess their cybersecurity maturity. The Cybersecurity Assessment Tool is aligned with the principles of the FFIEC Information Technology Examination Handbook (IT Handbook) and the NIST Cybersecurity Framework.

1. Access and review the FFIEC Cybersecurity Assessment Tool at https://www.ffiec.gov/cyberassessmenttool.htm.

2. Explain how a financial institution must demonstrate its cybersecurity maturity.

3. Explain and provide five examples of how the FFIEC Cybersecurity Assessment Tool maps to the NIST Cybersecurity Framework.

PROJECT 13.3: **Assessing Risk Management**

According to the FFIEC Cybersecurity InfoBase Handbook (Appendix A), the initial step in a regulatory Information Technology Examination is to interview management and review examination information to identify changes to the technology infrastructure, new products and services, or organizational structure.

1. Explain how changes in network topology, system configuration, or business processes might increase the institution's cybersecurity-related risk. Provide examples.

2. Explain how new products or services delivered to either internal or external users might increase the institution's cybersecurity-related risk. Provide examples.

3. Explain how loss or addition of key personnel, key management changes, or internal reorganizations might increase the institution's cybersecurity-related risk. Provide examples.

Case Study

The Equifax Breach

The Equifax breach was one of the most catastrophic cybersecurity breaches in recent history. This is because if you are a United States citizen and have a credit report, there's a good chance that you're one of the 143 million American consumers whose sensitive personal information was exposed. Equifax is one of the three major credit reporting agencies in the United States.

1. The breach lasted from mid-May through July 2017.

2. Threat actors exploited a vulnerability in Apache Struts (CVE-2017-5638) disclosed and fixed several months prior to the attack.

3. Threat actors accessed people's names, social security numbers, birth dates, addresses and, in some instances, driver's license numbers. The Federal Trade Commission (FTC) confirmed that the threat actors also stole credit card numbers for about 209,000 people and dispute documents with personal identifying information for about 182,000 people. Nonpublic information of individuals in the UK and Canada was also compromised.

4. Equifax created a website to guide their customers and help them assess if they have been impacted at https://www.equifaxsecurity2017.com.

5. What guidance and requirements from the regulations described in this chapter could've prevented this breach?

References

Regulations Cited

"12 U.S.C. Chapter 18: Bank Service Companies, Section 1867 Regulation and Examination of Bank Service Companies," accessed 06/2018, https://www.gpo.gov/fdsys/pkg/USCODE-2010-title12/html/USCODE-2010-title12-chap18-sec1867.htm.

"Standards for Safeguarding Customer Information; Final Rule - 16 CFR Part 314" accessed 06/2018, https://www.ftc.gov/policy/federal-register-notices/standards-safeguarding-customer-information-final-rule-16-cfr-part.

"Appendix B to Part 364: Interagency Guidelines Establishing Information Security Standards," accessed 06/2018, https://www.fdic.gov/regulations/laws/rules/2000-8660.html.

"Financial Institution Letter (FIL-49-99), Bank Service Company Act," accessed 06/2018, https://www.fdic.gov/news/news/financial/1999/fil9949.html.

"Financial Institution Letter (FIL-44-2008), Third-Party Risk Guidance for Managing Third-Party Risk," accessed 06/2018, https://www.fdic.gov/news/news/financial/2008/fil08044.html.

"Supplemental Guidance on Internet Banking Authentication, June 28, 2011," official website of the FFIEC, accessed 06/2018, https://www.ffiec.gov/press/pr062811.htm.

Other References

"Start with Security: A Guide for Business," The Federal Trade Commission, accessed 06/2018, https://www.ftc.gov/startwithsecurity.

Financial Services Information Sharing and Analysis Center (FS-ISAC), accessed 06/2018, https://www.fsisac.com.

"FFIEC Cybersecurity Assessment General Observations," accessed 06/2018, https://www.ffiec.gov/press/PDF/FFIEC_Cybersecurity_Assessment_Observations.pdf.

FFIEC IT Booklets and Handouts, accessed 06/2018, https://ithandbook.ffiec.gov/it-booklets.aspx.

FFIEC Cybersecurity Assessment Tool Frequently Asked Questions, accessed 06/2018, https://www.ffiec.gov/pdf/cybersecurity/FFIEC_CAT%20FAQs.pdf.

"Consumer Information—Identity Theft," official website of the Federal Trade Commission, accessed 06/2018, www.consumer.ftc.gov/features/feature-0014-identity-theft.

"FFIEC Information Technology Examination Handbook: Information Security," September 2016, Federal Financial Institutions Examination Council, accessed 06/2018, https://ithandbook.ffiec.gov/ITBooklets/FFIEC_ITBooklet_InformationSecurity.pdf.

"The NIST Cybersecurity Framework and the FTC", Federal Trade Commission video, accessed 06/2018, https://www.ftc.gov/news-events/blogs/business-blog/2016/08/nist-cybersecurity-framework-ftc.

"Fraud Advisory for Business: Corporate Account Takeover," U.S. Secret Service, FBI, IC3, and FS-ISAC, accessed 06/2018, https://www.nacha.org/content/current-fraud-threats-resource-center.

"Reporting Identity Theft," official website of the Federal Trade Commission, accessed 06/2018, https://www.identitytheft.gov.

Gross, Grant, "Banks Crack Down on Cyber-based Account Takeovers," IDG News Service, January 9, 2013, accessed 06/2018, www.networkworld.com/news/2013/010913-banks-crack-down-on-cyber-based-265685.html.

"Identity Theft Impacts," State of California Department of Justice, Office of the Attorney General, accessed 06/2018, https://oag.ca.gov/idtheft.

FTC Complaint Assistant, accessed 06/2018, https://www.ftccomplaintassistant.gov.

"Equifax Twice Missed Finding Apache Struts Vulnerability Allowing Breach to Happen," *SC Magazine*, accessed 06/2018, https://www.scmagazine.com/equifax-twice-missed-finding-apache-struts-vulnerability-allowing-breach-to-happen/article/697693.

"The Equifax Data Breach: What to Do," the Federal Trade Commission, accessed 06/2018, https://www.consumer.ftc.gov/blog/2017/09/equifax-data-breach-what-do.

"Equifax Says Hackers Stole More Than Previously Reported," CNN, accessed 06/2018, http://money.cnn.com/2018/03/01/technology/equifax-impact-more-customers/index.html.

Chapter | **14**

Regulatory Compliance for the Health-Care Sector

Chapter Objectives

After reading this chapter and completing the exercises, you will be able to do the following:

- Explain health-care–related information cybersecurity regulatory compliance requirements.
- Understand the components of a HIPAA/HITECH-compliant cybersecurity program.
- Prepare for a regulatory audit.
- Know how to respond to an ePHI security incident.
- Write HIPAA-related policies and procedures.
- Understand the HIPAA compliance enforcement process.

The genesis of health-care security–related legislation is the Health Insurance Portability and Account-ability Act of 1996 (HIPAA, Public Law 104-191). The original intent of the HIPAA regulation was to simplify and standardize health-care administrative processes. Administrative simplification called for the transition from paper records and transactions to electronic records and transactions. The Department of Health and Human Services (HHS) was instructed to develop and publish standards to protect an individual's electronic health information while permitting appropriate access and use of that information by health-care providers and other entities. Figure 14-1 shows the history of the HIPAA and HITECH Act.

As shown in Figure 14-1, followed by the initial release of HIPAA, the Standards for Privacy of Indi-vidually Identifiable Health Information, known as the HIPAA Privacy Rule, was published in 2002. The Privacy Rule set limits and conditions on the use and disclosure of patient information without patient authorization, and gave patients control over their health information, including the right to examine and obtain a copy of their health records, and to request corrections. The Privacy Rule applies to all formats of protected health information (PHI; for example, paper, electronic, oral).

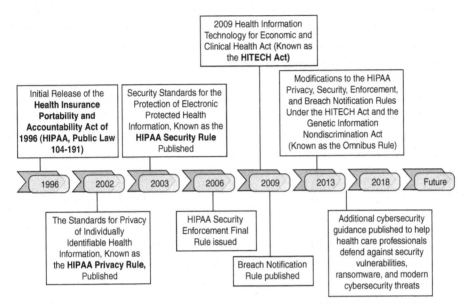

FIGURE 14-1   The History of the HIPAA and HITECH Act

On February 20, 2003, the Security Standards for the Protection of Electronic Protected Health Information, known as the HIPAA Security Rule, was published. The Security Rule required technical and nontechnical safeguards to protect electronic health information. The corresponding HIPAA Security Enforcement Final Rule was issued on February 16, 2006. Since then, the following legislation has modified and expanded the scope and requirements of the Security Rule:

- 2009 Health Information Technology for Economic and Clinical Health Act (known as the HITECH Act)

- 2009 Breach Notification Rule

- 2013 Modifications to the HIPAA Privacy, Security, Enforcement, and Breach Notification Rules under the HITECH Act and the Genetic Information Nondiscrimination Act; Other Modifications to the HIPAA Rules (known as the Omnibus Rule)

Since then the U.S. Department of Health & Human Services (HHS) has published additional cybersecurity guidance to help health-care professionals defend against security vulnerabilities, ransomware, and modern cybersecurity threats: see https://www.hhs.gov/hipaa/for-professionals/security/guidance/cybersecurity/index.html.

In this chapter, we examine the components of the original HIPAA Security Rule, the HITECH Act, and the Omnibus Rule. We discuss the policies, procedures, and practices that entities need to implement to be considered HIPAA compliant. We conclude the chapter with a look at incident response and breach notification requirements.

FYI: ISO/IEC 27002:2013 and NIST Guidance

Section 18 of ISO 27002:2013 is dedicated to the Compliance Management domain, which focuses on compliance with local, national, and international criminal and civil laws, regulatory or contractual obligations, intellectual property rights (IPR), and copyrights.

Corresponding NIST guidance is provided in the following documents:

- **SP 800-122:** "Guide to Protecting the Confidentiality of Personally Identifiable Information (PII)"

- **SP 800-66:** "An Introductory Resource Guide for Implementing the Health Insurance Portability and Accountability Act (HIPAA) Security"

- **SP 800-111:** "Guide to Storage Encryption Technologies for End User Devices"*

- **SP 800-52:** "Guidelines for Selection and Use of Transport Layer Security (TLS) Implementation"*

- **SP 800-77:** "Guide to IPSec VPNs"*

- **SP 800-113:** "Guide to SSL VPNs"*

* Although a number of other NIST publications are applicable, the Department of Health and Human Services specifically refers to the NIST publications for guidance related to data encryption at rest and in motion.

The HIPAA Security Rule

The HIPAA Security Rule focused on safeguarding *electronic protected health information (ePHI)*, which is defined as individually identifiable health information (IIHI) that is stored, processed, or transmitted electronically. The HIPAA Security Rule applies to covered entities and business associates. *Covered entities (CEs)* include health-care providers, health plans, health-care clearinghouses, and certain business associates.

- A *health-care provider* is defined as a person or organization that provides patient or medical services, such as doctors, clinics, hospitals, out-patient services and counseling, nursing homes, hospices, pharmacies, medical diagnostic and imaging services, and durable medical equipment providers.

- A *health plan* is defined as an entity that provides payment for medical services, such as health insurance companies, HMOs, government health plans, or government programs that pay for health care, such as Medicare, Medicaid, military, and veterans' programs.

- A *health-care clearinghouse* is defined as an entity that processes nonstandard health information it receives from another entity into a standard format.

- *Business associates* were initially defined as persons or organizations that perform certain functions or activities that involve the use or disclosure of PHI on behalf of, or provide services to, a CE. Business associate services include legal, actuarial, accounting, consulting, data aggregation, management, administrative, accreditation, and financial. Subsequent legislation expanded the definition of a business associate to a person or entity that creates, receives, maintains, transmits, accesses, or has the potential to access PHI to perform certain functions or activities on behalf of a CE.

What Is the Objective of the HIPAA Security Rule?

The HIPAA Security Rule established national standards to protect patient records that are created, received, used, or maintained digitally by a CE. The Security Rule requires appropriate administrative, physical, and technical safeguards to ensure the confidentiality, integrity, and availability (CIA) of ePHI, as shown in Figure 14-2.

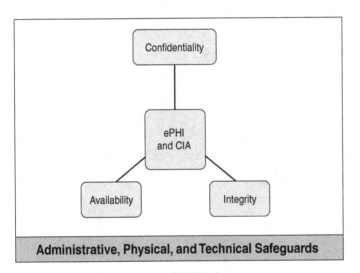

FIGURE 14-2   ePHI and the CIA Triad

In Chapter 3, "Cybersecurity Framework," we discussed the CIA triad and defined its elements as follows:

- *Confidentiality* is the protection of information from unauthorized people, resources, and processes.

- *Integrity* is the protection of information or processes from intentional or accidental unauthorized modification.

- *Availability* is the assurance that systems and information are accessible by authorized users when needed.

The framers of the regulations were realists. They understood that these regulations were going to apply to organizations of various sizes and types throughout the country. They were careful not to mandate specific actions. In fact, many in the health-care sector have criticized the DHHS for being too vague and not providing enough guidance. The rule says that a CE may use any security measures that allow it to reasonably and appropriately implement the standards and implementation specification, taking into account the following:

- The size, complexity, and capabilities of the CE

- The CE's technical infrastructure, hardware, and software capabilities

- The costs of security measures

- The probability of potential risks

The standards were meant to be scalable, meaning that they can be applied to a single-physician practice or to a hospital system with thousands of employees. The standards are technology-neutral and vendor-nonspecific. CEs are expected to choose the appropriate technology and controls for their unique environment.

How Is the HIPAA Security Rule Organized?

Figure 14-3 shows the Security Rule categories.

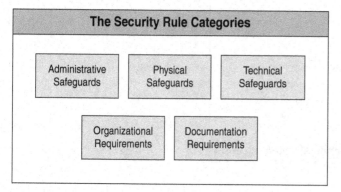

FIGURE 14-3   The HIPAA Security Rule Categories

Within the five categories shown in Figure 14-3 are standards and implementation specifications. In this context, a standard defines what a CE must do; implementation specifications describe how it must be done.

- *Administrative safeguards* are the documented policies and procedures for managing day-to-day operations, conduct, and access of workforce members to ePHI, as well as the selection, development, and use of security controls.

- *Physical safeguards* are the controls used to protect facilities, equipment, and media from unauthorized access, theft, or destruction.

- *Technical safeguards* focus on using technical security measures to protect ePHI data in motion, at rest, and in use.

- *Organizational requirements* include standards for business associate contracts and other arrangements.

- *Documentation requirements* address retention, availability, and update requirements related to supporting documentation, including policies, procedures, training, and audits.

Implementation Specifications

Many of the standards contain implementation specifications. An implementation specification is a more detailed description of the method or approach CEs can use to meet a particular standard. Implementation specifications are either *required* or *addressable*. Where there are no implementation specifications identified for a particular standard, compliance with the standard itself is required.

- A *required* implementation specification is similar to a standard, in that a CE must comply with it.

- For *addressable* implementation specifications, CEs must perform an assessment to determine whether the implementation specification is a reasonable and appropriate safeguard for implementation in the CE's environment.

"Addressable" does not mean optional, nor does it mean the specification can be ignored. For each of the addressable implementation specifications, a CE must do one of the following:

- Implement the specification if reasonable and appropriate.

- If the entity determines that implementing the specification is not reasonable and appropriate, the entity must document the rationale supporting the decision and either implement an equivalent measure that accomplishes the same purpose or be prepared to prove that the standard can be met without implementing the specification.

What Are the Administrative Safeguards?

The Security Rule defines administrative safeguards as the "administrative actions, policies, and procedures used to manage the selection, development, implementation, and maintenance of security measures to protect electronic protected health information and to manage the conduct of the CE's workforce in relation to the protection of that information." The Administrative Safeguards section incorporates nine standards focusing on internal organization, policies, procedures, and maintenance of security measures that protect patient health information.

The Security Management Process §164.308(a)(1)

The first standard is the foundation of HIPAA compliance. The standard requires a formal security management process, which includes risk management (inclusive of risk analysis), a sanction policy, and ongoing oversight.

Risk management is defined as the implementation of security measures to reduce risk to reasonable and appropriate levels to ensure the CIA of ePHI, protect against any reasonably anticipated threats or hazards to the security or integrity of ePHI, and protect against any reasonably anticipated uses or disclosures of ePHI that are not permitted or required under the HIPAA Security Rule. The determination of "reasonable and appropriate" is left to the discretion of the CE. Factors to be considered are the size of the entity, the level of risk, the cost of mitigating controls, and the complexity of implementation and maintenance. Per DHHS guidance, the risk management process includes the following activities:

- Analysis
- Management

Analysis

Figure 14-4 shows the elements of the risk analysis activities.

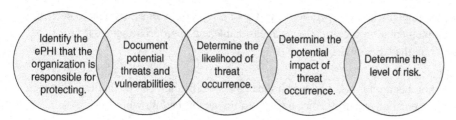

FIGURE 14-4   Risk Analysis Activities

Management

Figure 14-5 shows the elements of the risk analysis activities.

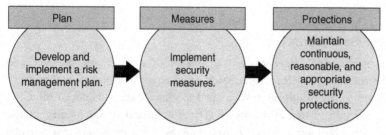

FIGURE 14-5   Risk Management Activities

The Security Rule does not dictate a specific risk assessment methodology. However, DHHS implementation and training materials refer to using NIST SP 800-30: Risk Management Guide for Information Technology Systems as a guide.

CEs must implement sanction policies for security violations in regard to ePHI. Specially, CEs must have a written policy that clearly states the ramifications for not complying with the Security Rules as determined by the organization.

Implied in this requirement is a formal process to recognize and report security violations. The policy needs to apply to all employees, contractors, and vendors. Sanctions might range from a reprimand to termination. Again, this is left to the discretion of the organization. It is also implied that all employees have not only been made aware of the sanction policy but have been trained and understand what is expected of them in regard to security behavior.

An integral component of risk management is continuous monitoring, review, and evaluation. The expectation here is that the CE has a mechanism in place to review information system activity and that these reports are reviewed regularly. System activity includes network, application, personnel, and administrative activities. Before a review can be implemented, three basic questions must be addressed:

1. *What system activity is going to be monitored?* The short answer: audit logs, access reports, and security incident–tracking reports are the most common methods of tracking system activity.

2. *How is this going to be accomplished?* Generally, using built-in or third-party monitoring/audit tools for operating systems, applications, and devices, as well as incident reporting logs.

3. *Who is going to be responsible for the overall process and results?* This is usually assigned to the security officer. Realistically, the security officer may not have the technical skills to interpret the reports, in which case it needs to be a combination of information technology (IT) staff (either internal or outsourced) and the security officer.

Assigned Security Responsibility §164.308(a)(2)

The second standard in the Administrative Safeguards section is Assigned Security Responsibility. There are no separate implementation specifications for this standard. The Security Rule specifically states that the CE must designate an individual as the security officer. The security officer is responsible for overseeing the development of policies and procedures, management and supervision of the use of security measures to protect data, and oversight of personnel access to data. A formal job description should be developed that accurately reflects the assigned security duties and responsibilities. This role should be communicated to the entire organization, including contractors and vendors.

It is important to select a person who can assess effective security and who can serve as a point of contact for security policy, implementation, and monitoring. It should be pointed out that responsibility for compliance does not rest solely with the security officer. Management is still accountable for the actions of the CE. The entire organization is expected to engage in compliance-related activities. The goal is to create a culture of security and compliance.

Workforce Security §164.308(a)(3)

The third standard is Workforce Security. This standard focuses on the relationship between people and ePHI. The purpose of this standard is to ensure that there are appropriate policies, procedures, and safeguards in place in regard to access to ePHI by the entire workforce. The term *workforce* is purposely used instead of *personnel*. **Personnel** are generally those on an organization's payroll. **Workforce** includes anyone who does work at or for the organization. In addition to employees and principals, this includes vendors, business partners, and contractors such as maintenance workers. There are three addressable implementation specifications for this standard: implementing procedures for workforce authorization and supervision, establishing a workforce clearance procedure, and establishing workforce termination procedures.

In Chapter 3, we defined **authorization** as the process of granting users and systems a predetermined level of access to information resources. In this case, the specification refers to determining who should have access to ePHI and the level of access. Implied in this specification is that the organization has defined roles and responsibilities for all job functions. Larger CEs would be expected to document workforce access, including type of permission, under what circumstances, and for what purposes. A small medical practice may specify that all internal staff need access to ePHI as a normal part of their job.

CEs need to address whether all members of the workforce with authorized access to ePHI receive appropriate clearances. The goal of this specification is that organizations establish criteria and procedures for hiring and assigning tasks—in other words, ensuring that workers have the necessary knowledge, skills, and abilities to fulfill particular roles and that these requirements are a part of the hiring process. As a part of this process, CEs need to determine the type of screening required for the position. This can range from verification of employment and educational references to criminal and credit checks. It was not the intent of Congress to mandate background checks, but rather to require reasonable and appropriate screening prior to access to ePHI.

When an employee's role or a contractor's role in the organization changes or their employment ends, the organization must ensure that their access to ePHI is terminated. Compliance with this specification includes having a standard set of procedures that should be followed to recover access control devices (ID badges, keys, tokens), recover equipment (laptops, PDAs, pagers), and deactivate local and remote network and ePHI access accounts.

Information Access Management §164.308(a)(4)

The fourth standard in the Administrative Safeguards section is Information Access Management. The goal of the Information Access Management standard is to require that CEs have formal policies and procedures for granting access to ePHI. You may be thinking, haven't we already done this? Let's review what the previous standard requires of CEs—to determine what roles, jobs, or positions should have permission to access ePHI, to establish hiring practices for those who may be granted access to ePHI, and to have a termination process to ensure access is disabled when a workforce member is terminated or no longer requires access. This standard addresses the process of authorizing and establishing access to ePHI. There are one required and two addressable implementation specifications in this section: isolating health-care clearinghouse functions (required but only applies in limited circumstances), implementing policies and procedures to authorize access, and implementing policies and procedures to establish access.

After an organization has decided what roles need access and who will be filling the roles, the next step is to decide how access will be granted to ePHI. In this standard, we are approaching the question from a policy perspective. Later on we will revisit this question from a technology perspective. The first decision is at what level or levels will access be granted. Options include hardware level, operating system level, application level, and transaction level. Many organizations will choose a hybrid approach. The second decision is the defined basis for granting access. Options here include *identity-based access* (by name), *role-based access* (by job or function), and *group-based access* (by membership). Larger organizations may gravitate toward role-based access because the job may be very well defined. Smaller entities will tend to use identity-based or group-based access because one person may be tasked with multiple roles.

Assuming the organization has made its decisions on access authorization, the next step is to develop policies and procedures to establish, document, review, modify, and, if necessary, terminate a user's access rights to a workstation, transaction, program, or process. What is expected is that each user's rights can be clearly identified. To do so, every user must have a unique identification. Assigned user roles and group membership must be documented. As discussed in Chapter 6, "Human Resources Security," throughout the workforce life cycle, there needs to be a defined user-provisioning process to communicate changes in status, role, or responsibility.

Security Awareness and Training §164.308(a)(5)

Users are the first line of defense against attack, intrusion, and error. To be effective, they must be trained and then reminded of the imminent dangers. The Security and Awareness Training standard requires that the organization implement a security awareness and training program on specific topics. Implied in this standard is that the organization provides training on the overall security program, policies, and procedures. The type of training provided is up to the organization. The goal is to provide training that is appropriate for the audience. The training program should be documented, and there should be a mechanism for evaluating the effectiveness of the training. In designing and implementing a training program, the entity needs to address the items shown in Figure 14-6.

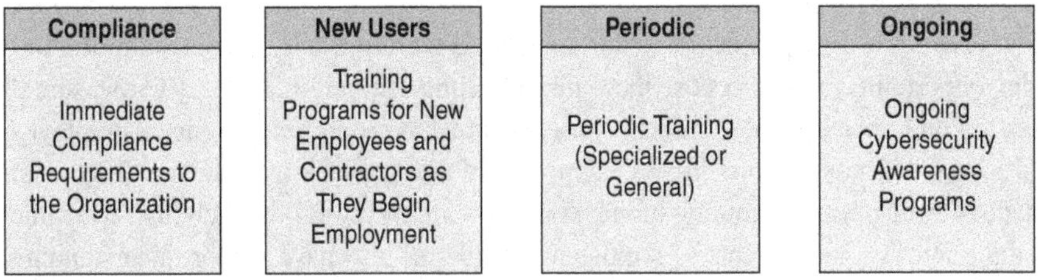

Compliance	New Users	Periodic	Ongoing
Immediate Compliance Requirements to the Organization	Training Programs for New Employees and Contractors as They Begin Employment	Periodic Training (Specialized or General)	Ongoing Cybersecurity Awareness Programs

FIGURE 14-6   Designing and Implementing a Training Program

There are four addressable implementation specifications for this standard. These specifications are illustrated in Figure 14-7.

FIGURE 14-7   Security Awareness and Training Specifications

A security awareness program is designed to remind users of potential threats and their part in mitigating the risk to the organization. According to NIST, the purpose of awareness presentations is simply to focus attention on security. Awareness presentations are intended to allow individuals to recognize IT security concerns and respond accordingly. Security awareness should be an ongoing campaign. Suggested delivery methods include posters, screen savers, trinkets, booklets, videos, email, and flyers. The campaign should be extended to anyone who interacts with the CEs' ePHI. This includes employees, contractors, and business partners. Security awareness programs are an essential component of maintaining a secure environment. Even the most security conscious federal agency has posters prominently displayed as you walk through a locked door reminding you to check that no one else entered with you and to verify that the door clicked shut behind you!

The implementation specification includes three training topics: password management, login procedures, and malware. These are important topics because the associated threats can be mitigated by user behavior. Users need to understand the importance of safeguarding their authentication credentials (passwords, tokens, or other codes) and the immediacy of reporting a suspected password compromise. Users should also be taught to recognize anomalies related to authentication, including an unusually slow login process, credentials that work intermittently, and being locked out unexpectedly, and to report anomalies even if they seem minor. As we've discussed in earlier chapters, malware (short for *malicious software*) is one of the most significant threats faced by all Internet-connected organizations. Users need to be trained in how to disrupt the malware delivery channel, how to respond to suspicious system behavior, and how to report suspicious incidents.

Phishing has been a way into an organization's sensitive data in the past, and it shows no signs of slowing down. Threat actors can fool users into clicking a malicious link or attachment and successfully compromise their system. This is why phishing simulation campaigns are an increasingly popular way for organizations to see how vulnerable their people are to this social engineering attack. In some corporations they use this as a training opportunity, and others use these fake phishing campaigns as a way to measure if their security awareness training is successful. This is because any phishing weakness among an employee of a health-care provider or any organization is likely a symptom of a larger lack of understanding about cybersecurity best practices. Anti-phishing training alone won't provide the cure. It's likely that the same individuals that clicked the links or attachments of a phishing email will also have a poor understanding about password security, secure mobile device practices, and other cybersecurity best practices.

Security Incident Procedures §164.308(a)(6)

In Chapter 11, "Cybersecurity Incident Response," we defined a security incident as any adverse event whereby some aspect of an information system or information itself is threatened: loss of data confidentiality, disruption of data integrity, disruption, or denial of service. This standard addresses both reporting of and responding to cybersecurity incidents. Implied in the standard is that the information users and custodians have had the appropriate training as well as the recognition that outside expertise may be required. There is one implementation specification, and it is required.

Security incident reporting is the foundation of a successful response and recovery process. A security incident reporting program has three components: training users to recognize suspicious incidents, implementing an easy-to-use reporting system, and having staff follow through with investigations and report back their findings to the user. Covered entities are required to have documented procedures in place to support a security incident reporting program.

Incident response procedures address by whom, how, and within what time frame an incident report should be responded to. Procedures should include an escalation path based on the criticality and severity of the incident. This should include when to contact law enforcement and forensics experts as well as when it is appropriate to contact patients regarding a security breach. All incidents should be documented. This information should then be incorporated into the ongoing risk management process.

Contingency Plans §164.308(a)(7)

The Contingency Plans standard would have been more aptly named the Business Continuity Plan standard. In Chapter 12, "Business Continuity Management," we discussed the components of business continuity management, including emergency preparedness, response, operational contingency, and disaster recovery. This standard is closely tied to those components. The objective of the Contingency Plans standard is to establish (and implement as needed) policies and procedures for responding to an emergency situation that damages systems that contain ePHI or the ability to deliver patient services. What is not stated but implied in the standard is the need for a business continuity team that is responsible for management of the plan. There are three required and two addressable implementation specifications for this standard: Conducting an application and data criticality analysis, establishing and implementing a data backup plan, and establishing and implementing a disaster recovery plan are required. Establishing an emergency mode operation plan and testing and revising procedures are addressable.

The data and criticality analysis specification requires CEs to identify their software applications (data applications that store, maintain, or transmit ePHI) and determine how important each is to patient care or business needs, in order to prioritize for data backup, disaster recovery, and/or emergency operation plans. For example, access to electronic medical records would be critical to providing care. On the other hand, claims processing, while important to the financial health of the entity, does not in the short term affect patient care. In Chapter 12, we referred to this process as a *business impact analysis*.

The data backup specification requires that CEs establish and implement procedures to create and maintain retrievable exact copies of ePHI. This means that all ePHI needs to be backed up on a scheduled basis. The implementation mechanism is left up to the organization. However, the procedures to back up (and restore) the data must be documented, and the responsibility to run and verify the backup must be assigned. In addition to verification that the backup job ran successfully, test restores should be conducted regularly. Testing both verifies the media and provides a training opportunity in a low-stress situation. There are few situations more nerve-wracking than that of learning how to restore data in a crisis situation.

Backup media should not remain onsite. It should be securely transported offsite. The location where it is stored needs to be secured in accordance with the organization's security policy.

There are different backup types or levels in the industry. Unfortunately, these terms are not used the same way by everyone. Figure 14-8 shows the elements of the risk analysis activities.

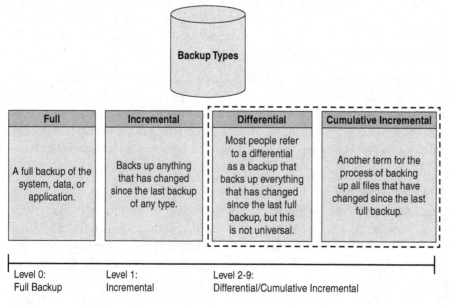

Full	Incremental	Differential	Cumulative Incremental
A full backup of the system, data, or application.	Backs up anything that has changed since the last backup of any type.	Most people refer to a differential as a backup that backs up everything that has changed since the last full backup, but this is not universal.	Another term for the process of backing up all files that have changed since the last full backup.

Level 0:
Full Backup

Level 1:
Incremental

Level 2-9:
Differential/Cumulative Incremental

FIGURE 14-8 Backup Types and Levels

The disaster recovery specification specifically requires that CEs be able to restore any data that has been lost. The initial interpretation is the ability simply to restore data. In actuality, the process is much more complex. Organizations must consider worst-case scenarios. For example, consider the following questions:

- What if the building was not accessible?
- What if equipment was destroyed?
- What if the communications infrastructure was unavailable?
- What if trained personnel were unavailable?

A disaster recovery plan should be developed that addresses the recovery of critical infrastructure, including information systems and communications (phone, data, and Internet) as well as restoration of data.

The emergency mode operation specification requires that ePHI (and by extension, the network) be protected from harm during adverse circumstances, such as a disaster or emergency situation.

The testing and revision procedures specification requires that organizations implement procedures for periodic testing and revision of contingency plans. As discussed in Chapter 12, plans and procedures are purely theoretical until they are tested. The objective of a testing program is to ensure that plans and procedures are accurate, relevant, and operable under adverse conditions. As important as demonstrating success is uncovering inadequacies.

Evaluation §184.308(a)(8)

The Evaluation standard focuses on developing criteria and metrics for reviewing all standards and implementation specifications for compliance. This standard serves as the sole implementation specification and is required. All CEs need to evaluate their compliance status. This is an ongoing process and should occur both on a scheduled basis (an annual review is recommended but not required) and whenever change drivers warrant reassessment. The evaluation can be conducted internally if the organization has staff appropriately trained for the task. Optionally, third parties can be hired to conduct the assessment and report their findings. Prior to contracting with a third party, the vendor should be required to document credentials and experience with HIPAA compliance. The evaluation should review all five categories of requirements—administrative, physical, technical, organizational, and documentation requirements. The desired outcome of the evaluation is acknowledgment of compliance activities and recommendations for improvement.

There is not a formal certification or accreditation process for HIPAA compliance. There is no organization or person who can put an official stamp of approval on the compliance program. The process is one of self-certification. It is left to the organization to determine if its security program and compliance activities are acceptable. If challenged, the organization will need to provide thorough documentation to support its decisions.

Business Associate Contracts and Other Arrangements §164.308(b)(1)

The last standard in the Administrative Safeguards section is Business Associate Contracts and Other Arrangements. The organizational requirements related to this standard are discussed in more detail in §164.314 of the rule, titled "Organizational Policies and Procedures and Documentation." Business associate compliance requirements are further defined in the HITECH Act and the Omnibus Rule, both of which are discussed later in this chapter.

CEs share ePHI for a variety of reasons. The standard states that a CE may permit a business associate to create, receive, maintain, or transmit ePHI on a CE's behalf only if the CE obtains satisfactory assurances that the business associate will appropriately safeguard the information. Services provided by business associates include the following:

- Claim processing or billing
- Transcription
- Data analysis
- Quality assurance
- Practice management
- Application support

- Hardware maintenance
- Administrative services

The required implementation specification requires CEs to document the satisfactory assurances required through a written contract or other arrangement with the business associate that meets the applicable requirements. Implied in this standard is that the CE will establish criteria and procedures for measuring contract performance. Procedures may range from clear lines of communication to onsite security reviews. Of particular importance is a process for reporting security incidents relative to the relationship. If the criteria aren't being met, then a process needs to be in place for terminating the contract. Conditions that would warrant termination should be included in the business associate agreement as well as in performance contracts.

In Practice

HIPAA Administrative Standards Synopsis

All the standards and implementation specifications found in the Administrative Safeguards section refer to administrative functions, such as policy and procedures that must be in place for management and execution of security measures.

Standard	Implementation Specification
Security Management Process	Risk Analysis Risk Management Sanction Policy Information System Activity Review
Assigned Security Responsibility	Assigned Security Responsibility
Workforce Security	Authorization and/or Supervision Workforce Clearance Procedure Termination Procedures
Information Access Management	Isolating Health Care Clearinghouse Functions Access Authorization Access Establishment and Modification
Security Awareness and Training	Security Reminders Protection from Malicious Software Login Monitoring Password Management
Security Incident Procedures	Response and Reporting
Contingency Plan	Data Backup Plan Disaster Recovery Plan Emergency Mode Operation Plans Testing and Revision Procedures Application and Data Criticality Analysis
Evaluation	Evaluation
Business Associate Contracts and Other Arrangements	Written Contract or Other Arrangement

What Are the Physical Safeguards?

The Security Rule defines physical safeguards as the "physical measures, policies, and procedures to protect a CE's electronic information systems and related buildings and equipment, from natural and environmental hazards, and unauthorized intrusion." Physical safeguards are required at all locations that store, process, access, or transmit ePHI. This requirement extends to the telecommuting or mobile workforce.

Facility Access Controls §164.310(a)(1)

The first physical safeguard standard is Facility Access Controls. *Facility* is defined as the physical premises and the interior and exterior of a building. Facility access controls are policies and procedures to limit physical access to ePHI information systems and the facility or facilities in which they are housed, while ensuring that properly authorized access is allowed. There are four addressable implementation specifications for this standard: creating a facility security plan, implementing access control and validation procedures, keeping maintenance records, and establishing contingency operations. All four implementation specifications are addressable.

The facility security plan specification requires that the safeguards used by the entity to secure the premises and equipment from unauthorized access, tampering, and theft be documented. The most basic control that comes to mind are door locks. Implied in this specification is the need to conduct a risk analysis to identify vulnerable areas. The risk analysis would focus on the building perimeter, interior, and computer room/data centers. Areas that would be examined include entry points such as doors, windows, loading docks, vents, roof, basement, fences, and gates. Based on the outcome of the risk assessment, the facility security plan may include controls such as surveillance monitoring, environmental equipment monitoring, environmental controls (air conditioning, smoke detection, and fire suppression), and entrance/exit controls (locks, security guards, access badges).

Access control and validation procedures specification focuses on the procedures used to ensure facility access to authorized personnel and visitors and exclude unauthorized persons. Facility access controls are generally based on their role or function. These functional or role-based access control and validation procedures should be closely aligned with the facility security plan.

The maintenance records implementation specification requires that CEs document such facility security repairs and modifications, such as changing locks, routine maintenance checks, and installing new security devices. Organizations that lease space should require the owner to provide such documentation.

The establishing contingency operations implementation specification is an extension of the contingency plan requirement in the Administrative Safeguards section. An entity needs to establish procedures to ensure authorized physical access in case of emergency. Generally, these procedures are manual overrides of automated systems. The access control system for a computer room may have been designed to use a swipe card or biometric identification. If the facility were to lose power, these controls would be useless. Assuming that entry into the computer room is required, a contingency or alternate plan would be necessary.

Workstation Use §164.310(b)

The Workstation Use standard addresses the policies and procedures for how workstations should be used and protected. This is generally accomplished by establishing categories of devices (such as wired workstation, wireless workstation, mobile device, and smartphone) and subcategories (such as location) and then determining the appropriate use and applicable safeguard. This standard serves as the sole implementation specification.

Workstation Security §164.310(c)

The Workstation Security standard addresses how workstations are to be physically protected from unauthorized users. Physical safeguards and other security measures should be implemented to minimize the possibility of access to ePHI through workstations. If possible, workstations should be located in restricted areas. In situations where that is not possible, such as exam rooms, workstations should be physically secured (locked) and password-protected with an automatic screen saver. Also, USB ports should be disabled. Shoulder surfing is of particular concern here. Shoulder surfing in its most basic form is when a passerby can view information on another person's computer screen by looking at the monitor or capturing an image using a camera or phone. Workstations located in semi-public areas such as reception desks need to be positioned away from the viewing public. If that is not possible, they should be encased in privacy screens. This standard serves as the sole implementation specification.

Device and Media Controls §164.310(d)(1)

The Device and Media Controls standard requires CEs to implement policies and procedures that govern the receipt and removal of hardware and electronic media that contain ePHI, into and out of a facility, and the movement of these items within the facility. Electronic media is defined as "memory devices in computers (hard drives) and any removable/transportable digital memory medium, such as magnetic tape or disk, optical disk, or digital memory card…"

This standard covers the proper handling of electronic media, including the following:

- Receipt
- Removal
- Backup (addressable)
- Storage
- Media reuse (required)
- Disposal (required)
- Accountability (addressable)

There are two required implementation procedures for this standard:

- Maintaining accountability for hardware and electronic media.
- Developing data backup and storage procedures is required.

Implementing reuse policies and procedures and implementing disposal policies and procedures are addressable.

The objective of the maintaining accountability for hardware and electronic media implementation specification is to be able to account at all times for the whereabouts of ePHI. Implied is that all systems and media that house ePHI have been identified and inventoried. The goal is to ensure that ePHI is not inadvertently released or shared with any unauthorized party. This is easy to understand if you envision a paper medical record (chart). Before the record is allowed to leave the premises, it must be verified that the request came from an authorized party. The removal of the chart is logged and a record kept of the removal. The logs are reviewed periodically to ensure that the chart has been returned. This specification requires the same type of procedures for information stored in electronic form.

The developing data backup and storage procedures specification requires that before moving or relocating any equipment that contains ePHI, a backup copy of the data be created. The objective is to ensure that in case of damage or loss, an exact, retrievable copy of the information is available. Concurrent with this action is the implied requirement that the backup media will be stored in a secure location separate from the original media. This specification protects the availability of ePHI and is similar to the data backup plan implementation specification for the Contingency Plans standard of the Administrative Safeguards, which requires CEs to implement procedures to create and maintain retrievable exact copies of ePHI.

The implementing disposal policies and procedures specification requires that there be a process that ensures that end-of-life electronic media that contains ePHI be rendered unusable and/or inaccessible prior to disposal. As discussed in Chapter 7, "Physical and Environmental Security," options for disposal include disk wiping, degaussing, and physical destruction.

Instead of disposing of electronic media, entities may want to reuse it. The implementing reuse policies and procedures specifications require that there be a process to sanitize the media before reuse or reassignment. Often overlooked are hard drives in workstations or printers that are being recycled either within or outside of the organization. Don't assume that because a policy states that ePHI isn't stored on a local workstation that the drive doesn't need to be cleaned. ePHI is found in the most unexpected places, including hidden, temporary, cached, and Internet files, as well as in metadata.

In Practice

HIPAA Physical Standards Synopsis

The Security Rule's physical safeguards are the physical measures, policies, and procedures to protect electronic information systems, buildings, and equipment.

Standard	Implementation Specification
Facility Access Control	Facility Security Plan Access Control and Validation Procedures Maintenance Records Contingency Operations
Workstation Use	Workstation Use
Workstation Security	Workstation Security
Device and Media Control	Data Backup and Storage Accountability Media Reuse Media Disposal

What Are the Technical Safeguards?

The Security Rule defines technical safeguards as "the technology and the policy and procedures for its use that protect electronic protected health information and control access to it." The Security Rule is vendor-neutral and does not require specific technology solutions. A CE must determine which security measures and specific technologies are reasonable and appropriate for implementation in its organization. The basis of this decision making should be a risk analysis.

Technical safeguards include access controls, audit controls, integrity controls, authentication controls, and transmission security. Organizations can choose from a wide range of technology solutions to meet the implementation specifications. 45 CFR §164.306(b), the Security Standards: General Rules, Flexibility of Approach, clearly states that entities may take into account the cost of various measures in relation to the size, complexity, and capabilities of the organization. However, it is not permissible for entities to use cost as the sole justification for not implementing a standard.

Access Control §164.312(a)(1)

The intent of the Access Control standard is to restrict access to ePHI to only those users and processes that have been specifically authorized. Implied in this standard are the fundamental security concepts of *default deny*, *least privilege*, and *need-to-know*. The Access Control standard has two required and two addressable implementation specifications: Requiring unique user identification and establishing emergency access procedures are required. Implementing automatic logoff procedures and encrypting/decrypting information at rest are addressable.

The required unique user identification implementation specification mandates that each user and process be assigned a unique identifier. This can be a name and/or number. The naming convention is at the discretion of the organization. The objective of this specification is accountability. A unique identifier ensures that system activity and access to ePHI can be traced to a specific user or process.

The objective of establishing emergency access procedures is to ensure continuity of operations should normal access procedures be disabled or become unavailable due to system problems. Generally, this would be an administrator or super user account that has been assigned override privileges and cannot be locked out.

The objective of the implementing automatic logoff procedures specification is to terminate a session after a predetermined time of inactivity. The assumption here is that users might leave their workstations unattended, during which time any information their accounts have permission to access is vulnerable to unauthorized viewing. Although the implementation standard incorporates the term "logoff," other mechanisms are acceptable. Examples of other controls include password-protected screen savers, workstation lock function, and disconnection of a session. Based on the risk analysis, it is up to the organization to determine both the predetermined time of inactivity as well as the method of termination.

The addressable specification to encrypting and decrypting data at rest is intended to add an additional layer of protection over and above assigned access permissions. NIST defines *data at rest* as data that resides in databases, file systems, flash drives, memory, and/or any other structured storage method. Figure 14-9 explains the difference between encrypting data at rest and data in motion.

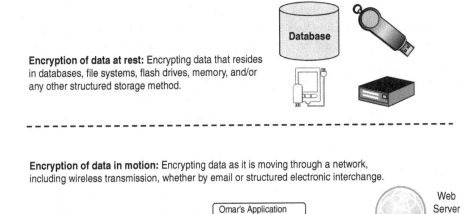

Encryption of data at rest: Encrypting data that resides in databases, file systems, flash drives, memory, and/or any other structured storage method.

Encryption of data in motion: Encrypting data as it is moving through a network, including wireless transmission, whether by email or structured electronic interchange.

FIGURE 14-9 Encrypting Data at Rest vs. Data in Motion

Encryption can be resource-intensive and costly. The decision to encrypt data at rest should be based on the level of risk as determined by a thorough risk analysis. Regardless, there is no question that mobile devices and media should always be encrypted because the potential for loss, theft, or unauthorized access is high. Both the HITECH Act and the Omnibus Rule refer to unencrypted data as "unsecure data" and require that a breach or potential breach of unsecure data be disclosed.

Audit Controls §164.312(b)

The Audit Controls standard requires implementation of hardware, software, and/or procedural mechanisms that record and examine activity in information systems that contain ePHI. This standard is closely tied to the administrative standards requiring information system review and security management. This standard serves as the sole implementation specification.

Organizations must have the means available to monitor system activity to determine if a security violation has occurred. Audit controls can be automatic, manual, or a combination of both. For example, system logs may run continuously in the background, whereas audit of a specific user activity may need to be manually initiated as the need arises. Most operating systems and applications have at least a minimum level of auditing as part of the feature set. The market is replete with third-party options. The Security Rule does not identify data that must be gathered by the audit controls or how often the audit reports should be reviewed. It is the responsibility of the entity to determine reasonable and appropriate audit controls for information systems that contain or use ePHI.

Integrity Controls §164.312(c)(1)

Earlier in this chapter, we defined *integrity* as the protection of information or processes from intentional or accidental unauthorized modification. In a health-care setting, this is of particular importance because modification could jeopardize patient care. The Integrity Controls standard requires organizations to implement technical controls that protect ePHI from improper alteration or destruction. There is one addressable implementation specification: mechanisms to authenticate ePHI. The specification speaks to electronic mechanisms that corroborate that ePHI has not been altered or destroyed in an unauthorized manner. The most common tools used for verification are file integrity checkers, message digests, and digital signatures.

Person or Entity Authentication §164.312(d)

Authentication is defined as the process of identifying an individual, usually based on a username and password. Authentication is different from *authorization*, which is the process of giving individuals access based on their identity. Authentication merely ensures that the individual is who he or she claims to be, but says nothing about the individual's access rights. The Person or Entity Authentication standard requires verification that a person or process seeking access to ePHI is the one claimed. An entity can be a process or a service. This standard serves as the sole implementation specification.

The earlier Access Control standard required identification for accountability. The Authentication standard requires identification for verification. As we discussed in Chapter 9, "Access Control Management," the process of authentication requires the subject to supply identification credentials.

The credentials are referred to as *factors*. There are three categories of factors: knowledge (something the user knows), possession (something a user has), and inherence (something the user is). Single-factor authentication is when only one factor is presented. The most common method of single-factor authentication is the password. Multifactor authentication is when two or more factors are presented. Multilayer authentication is when two or more of the same type of factors are presented. It is up to the CE to decide the appropriate approach. In all cases, users should receive training on how to protect their authentication credentials.

Transmission Security §164.312(e)(1)

The Transmission Security standard states that CEs must implement technical security measures to guard against unauthorized access to ePHI that is being transmitted over an electronic communications network. Implied in this standard is that organizations identify scenarios that may result in modification of the ePHI by unauthorized sources during transmission. Based on the assumption that the facility is secure, the focus is on external transmission. There are two addressable implementation specifications: implementing integrity controls and implementing encryption. Just as in the previous integrity control, the objective of the implementing integrity control specification is to protect ePHI from intentional or accidental unauthorized modification. Looking at integrity in this context, the focus is on protecting ePHI in motion. NIST defines **data in motion** as data that is moving through a network, including wireless transmission, whether by email or structured electronic interchange. The second implementation standard requires that CEs consider the reasonableness of encrypting ePHI in motion. Conventional wisdom dictates that all ePHI transmitted over a public network be encrypted. Security measures are used in tandem to protect the integrity and confidentiality of data in transit. Examples include virtual private networks (VPNs), secure email products, and application layer protocols such as SSL, SSH, and SFTP.

In Practice

HIPAA Technical Standards Synopsis

The Security Rule technical safeguards are the technology and related policies and procedures that protect ePHI and control access to it.

Standard	Implementation Specification
Access Control	Unique User Identification Emergency Access Procedures Automatic Logoff Encryption and Decryption
Audit Controls	Audit Controls
Integrity	Mechanism to Authenticate ePHI
Person or Entity Authentication	Person or Entity Authentication
Transmission Security	Integrity Controls Encryption

What Are the Organizational Requirements?

The next two standards are categorized as organizational requirements and deal specifically with contracts and other arrangements. The standard provides the specific criteria for written contracts or other arrangements between CEs and business associates. The intent of this standard was to contractually obligate business associates to protect ePHI. The 2013 Omnibus Rule extended HIPAA/ HITECH compliance requirements to business associates.

Business Associates Contracts §164.314(a)(1)

Per the Department of Health and Human Services, a "business associate" is a person or entity, other than a member of the workforce of a CE, who performs functions or activities on behalf of, or provides certain services to, a CE that involve access by the business associate to PHI. A business associate also is a subcontractor that creates, receives, maintains, or transmits PHI on behalf of another business associate.

The HIPAA Rules generally require that covered entities enter into contracts with their business associates to ensure that the business associates will appropriately safeguard PHI. Contracts between a covered entity and its business associates must include the following criteria:

- Establish the permitted and required uses and disclosures of PHI by the business associate.

- Provide that the business associate will not use or further disclose the information other than as permitted or required by the contract or as required by law.

- Require the business associate to implement appropriate safeguards to prevent unauthorized use or disclosure of the information, including implementing requirements of the HIPAA Security Rule with regard to ePHI.

- Require the business associate to report to the CE any use or disclosure of the information not provided for by its contract, including incidents that constitute breaches of unsecured PHI.

- Require the business associate to disclose PHI as specified in its contract to satisfy a CE's obligation with respect to individuals' requests for copies of their PHI, as well as make available PHI for amendments (and incorporate any amendments, if required) and accountings.

- To the extent the business associate is to carry out a CE's obligation under the Privacy Rule, require the business associate to comply with the requirements applicable to the obligation.

- Require the business associate to make available to DHHS its internal practices, books, and records relating to the use and disclosure of PHI received from, or created or received by the business associate on behalf of, the CE for purposes of DHHS determining the CE's compliance with the HIPAA Privacy Rule.

- At termination of the contract, if feasible, require the business associate to return or destroy all PHI received from, or created or received by the business associate on behalf of, the covered CE.

- Require the business associate to ensure that any subcontractors it may engage on its behalf that will have access to PHI agree to the same restrictions and conditions that apply to the business associate with respect to such information.

- Authorize termination of the contract by the CE if the business associate violates a material term of the contract. Contracts between business associates and business associates that are subcontractors are subject to these same requirements.

A CE will be considered out of compliance if the entity knew of a pattern of activity or practice of a business associate that constituted a material breach or violation of the business associate's obligations, unless the CE took reasonable steps to cure the breach or end the violation. If such steps are unsuccessful, the CE must terminate the contract or arrangement, if feasible. If not feasible, the problem must be reported to the DHSS Secretary.

The other arrangements implementation specification is an exception and provides for alternatives to the contractual obligation requirement when both the CE and the business associate are government agencies. Provisions include a memorandum of understanding (MOU) and recognition of statutory obligations.

In Practice

HIPAA Organizational Requirements Synopsis

The Security Rule organizational requirements relate to business associate obligations to protect ePHI in compliance with HIPAA requirements and to report any violation or security incident to the CE.

Standard	Implementation Specification
Business Associate Contracts or Other Arrangements	Business Associate Contracts Other Arrangements

---

What Are the Policies and Procedures Standards?

The last two standards are categorized as policy and procedure requirements. There are a total of four implementation specifications, all of which are required.

Policies and Procedures §164.316 (a)

CEs are required to implement reasonable and appropriate policies and procedures to comply with the standards, implementation specifications, or other requirements of the Security Rule. This standard serves as the sole implementation specification.

The policies and procedures must be sufficient to address the standards and implementation specifications and must accurately reflect the actual activities and practices of the CE, its staff, its systems, and its business associates. A CE may change its policies and procedures at any time, provided the changes are documented and implemented in accordance with the Documentation standard.

Documentation §164.316(b)(1)

The Documentation standard requires that all policies, procedures, actions, activities, and assessments related to the Security Rule be maintained in written or electronic form. There are three required implementation specifications: time limit, availability, and updates.

CEs are required to retain all documentation related to the Security Rule for a period of six years from the date of creation or the date it was last in effect, whichever is later. This requirement is consistent with similar retention requirements in the Privacy Rule.

Documentation must be easily accessible to all persons responsible for implementing the procedures to which the documentation pertains. This would include security professionals, systems administrators, human resources, contracts, facilities, legal, compliance, and training.

Documentation must be reviewed periodically and updated as needed in response to operational, personnel, facility, or environmental changes affecting the security of ePHI. Particular attention should be paid to version control.

In Practice

Policies, Procedures, and Documentation Requirements Synopsis

The policies, procedures, and documentation requirements relate to the implementation and maintenance of CEs' HIPAA-related security plans, policies, and procedures.

Standard	Implementation Specification
Documentation	Time Limit Availability Updates

The HIPAA Security Rule Mapping to NIST Cybersecurity Framework

The U.S. Department of Health & Human Services created a series of cybersecurity guidance material that can be accessed in their website at https://www.hhs.gov/hipaa/for-professionals/index.html.

They created a crosswalk document that identifies mappings between NIST's Framework for Improving Critical Infrastructure Cybersecurity and the HIPAA Security Rule. The document can be accessed at

https://www.hhs.gov/sites/default/files/nist-csf-to-hipaa-security-rule-crosswalk-02-22-2016-final.pdf

This document maps each administrative, physical, and technical safeguard standard and implementation specification in the HIPAA Security Rule to a relevant NIST Cybersecurity Framework Subcategory. It is worth noting that some HIPAA Security Rule requirements could map to more than one of the NIST Cybersecurity Framework Subcategories.

A CE should be able to assess and implement new and evolving technologies and best practices that it determines would be reasonable and appropriate to ensure the confidentiality, integrity, and availability of the ePHI it creates, receives, maintains, or transmits. The U.S. Department of Health & Human Services created these mappings between the NIST Cybersecurity Framework subcategories and the HIPAA Security Rule as an informative reference only and do not imply or guarantee compliance with any laws or regulations. CEs need to complete their own cybersecurity risk assessment to identify and mitigate vulnerabilities and threats to the ePHI they create, receive, maintain, or transmit.

The HITECH Act and the Omnibus Rule

The Health Information Technology for Economic and Clinical Health Act (known as the HITECH Act) is part of the American Recovery and Reinvestment Act of 2009 (ARRA). The *HITECH Act* amended the Public Health Service Act (PHSA) with a focus on improving health-care quality, safety, and efficiency through the promotion of health information technology. The HITECH Act dedicated over $31 billion in stimulus funds for health-care infrastructure and the adoption of electronic health records (EHR), including funding for the meaningful use incentive programs. The HITECH Act also widened the scope of privacy and security protections available under HIPAA.

The Modifications to the HIPAA Privacy, Security, Enforcement, and Breach Notification Rules under the HITECH Act and the Genetic Information Nondiscrimination Act; Other Modifications to the HIPAA Rules (known as the Omnibus Rule) was published January 25, 2013, with a compliance date of September 23, 2013. The *Omnibus Rule* finalizes the Privacy, Security, and Enforcement Rules that were introduced in HITECH, modifies the Breach Notification Rule, and expands the definition of "business associates."

Prior to HITECH and the Omnibus Rule, the government had little authority to enforce the HIPAA regulations. Complicating matters was the fact that entire industry segments that stored, processed, transmitted, and accessed ePHI were not explicitly covered by the law. The 2013 Final Omnibus Rule made significant changes in coverage, enforcement, and patient protection in the following ways:

- Expanding the definition of "business associates."

- Extending compliance enforcement to business associates and subcontractors of business associates.

- Increasing violation penalties with potential fines, ranging from $25,000 to as much as $1.5 million.

- Including provisions for more aggressive enforcement by the federal government and requiring the DHHS to conduct mandatory audits.

- Granting explicit authority to state Attorneys General to enforce HIPAA Rules and to pursue HIPAA criminal and civil cases against HIPAA CEs, employees of CEs, or their business associates.

- Defining specific thresholds, response timelines, and methods for security breach victim notification.

What Changed for Business Associates?

The original Security Rule defined a "business associate" as a person or organization that performs certain functions or activities that involve the use or disclosure of PHI on behalf of, or provides services to, a CE. The final rule amends the definition of a "business associate" to mean a person or entity that creates, receives, maintains, transmits, or accesses PHI to perform certain functions or activities on behalf of a CE. The accompanying guidance further defines "access" and specifies that if a vendor has access to PHI to perform its duties and responsibilities, regardless of whether the vendor actually exercises this access, the vendor is a business associate.

Subcontractors and Liability

Effective September 2013, subcontractors of business associates that create, receive, maintain, transmit, or access PHI are considered business associates. The addition of subcontractors means that all HIPAA security, privacy, and breach notification requirements that apply to direct contract business associates of a CE also apply to all downstream service providers. CEs are required to obtain "satisfactory assurances" that their ePHI will be protected as required by the rules from their business associates, and business associates are required to get the same from their subcontractors. Business associates are directly liable and subject to civil penalties (discussed in the next section) for failing to safeguard ePHI in accordance with the HIPAA Security Rule.

As reported in the January 23, 2013, Federal Register, the DHHS estimates that in the United States there are one to two million business associates and an unknown number of subcontractors. Expanding the number of businesses subject to HIPAA regulations is so significant that it could alter the American security landscape.

What Has Changed with Enforcement?

The DHHS OCR was tasked with enforcing the original HIPAA privacy and security rule. However, enforcement was limited. Prior to the HITECH Act, OCR was permitted to assess civil penalties of $100 per violation of the Privacy and Security Rules, up to $25,000 for violations of each requirement during a calendar year. A CE could also bar the imposition of a civil money penalty by demonstrating that it did not know that it violated the HIPAA rules. The HITECH Act increased the amounts of the civil penalties that may be assessed and distinguishes between the types of violations. Additionally, a CE can no longer bar the imposition of a civil money penalty for an unknown violation unless it corrects the violation within 30 days of discovery. Table 14-1 lists the violation categories, per-violation fine, and annual maximum penalty as of September 2013.

TABLE 14-1 HIPAA/HITCH Security Rule Violation Penalties

Violation Category	Per Violation	Annual Maximum
Did Not Know	$100–$50,000	$1,500,000
Reasonable Cause	$1,000–$50,000	$1,500,000
Willful Neglect—Corrected	$10,000–$50,000	$1,500,000
Willful Neglect—Not Corrected	$50,000	$1,500,000

The HITECH Act did not change the criminal penalties that may be assessed for violations of the Privacy and Security Rules. Those penalties remain $50,000 and one year in prison for knowing violations, $100,000 and five years in prison for violations committed under false pretenses, and $250,000 and 10 years in prison for offenses committed for commercial or personal gain. Under the HITECH Act, criminal actions may be brought against anyone who wrongly discloses PHI, not just CEs or their employees. Also, the Act gives the DHHS OCR (in addition to the Department of Justice) the authority to bring criminal actions against these individuals.

State Attorneys General

The HITECH Act expanded the enforcement of HIPAA by granting authority to State Attorneys General to bring civil actions and obtain damages on behalf of state residents for violations of HIPAA Privacy and Security Rules. The Act also allowed for prosecution of business associates.

Proactive Enforcement

Prior to HITECH, the DHHS OCR would investigate potential security of privacy violations if they received a complaint. HITECH requires proactive enforcement, including the mandate to perform periodic audits of CE and business associate compliance with the HIPAA Privacy, Security, and Breach Notification Rules.

FYI: DHHS HIPAA Training

The DHHS and the State Attorneys General created several training resources, including video and computer-based training that is free to use and can be accessed at https://www.hhs.gov/hipaa/for-professionals/training/index.html.

The DHHS also created the "Guide to Privacy and Security of Electronic Health Information" that can be accessed at https://www.healthit.gov/sites/default/files/pdf/privacy/privacy-and-security-guide.pdf. Chapter 4 of the guide covers "Understanding Electronic Health Records, the HIPAA Security Rule, and Cybersecurity."

The DHHS also created a quick response checklist for any organizations that have experienced a cyber attack that can be accessed at https://www.hhs.gov/sites/default/files/cyber-attack-checklist-06-2017.pdf?language=en.

What Are the Breach Notification Requirements?

The original Security Rule did not include standards related to incident response and security breaches. The HITECH Act established several notification requirements for CEs and business associates. In 2009, the DHHS issued the Breach Notification Rule. The Omnibus Rule made significant changes to the Breach Notification Rule's definition of "breach" and provided guidance on a number of Breach Notification Rule requirements.

Safe Harbor Provision

For the purposes of breach notification, ePHI is considered to be secure if it meets the following criteria:

- ePHI has been rendered unusable, unreadable, or indecipherable using an NIST-approved encryption method.

- The decryption tools are stored on a device or at a location separate from the data they are used to encrypt or decrypt.

If a CE or business associate secures ePHI, as noted, and an unauthorized use or disclosure is discovered, the breach notice obligations do not apply. This exception is known as the Safe Harbor Provision. The term "secure ePHI" is specific to the Safe Harbor Provision and does not in any way modify an entity's obligation to comply with the HIPAA Security Rule.

Breach Definition

Per DHHS, "impermissible acquisition, access, or use or disclosure of *unsecured* PHI is presumed to be a breach unless the covered entity or business associate demonstrates that there is a low probability that the PHI has been compromised." To demonstrate that there is a low probability that a breach compromised ePHI, a CE or business associate must perform a risk assessment that addresses the following minimum standards:

- The nature and extent of the PHI involved, including the types of identifiers and the likelihood of re-identification.

- The unauthorized person who used the PHI or to whom the disclosure was made, whether the PHI was actually acquired or viewed.

- The extent to which the risk to the PHI has been mitigated.

Breach notification is not required if a CE or business associate concludes through a documented risk assessment that a low probability exists that the PHI has been compromised. Risk assessments are subject to review by federal and state enforcement agencies.

Breach Notification Requirements

The HIPAA Breach Notification Rule, 45 CFR §§164.400-414, requires CEs and their business associates to provide notification following a breach of unsecured protected health information. CEs are required to notify individuals whose *unsecured ePHI* has been breached (unless excepted by a risk assessment). This is true even if the breach occurs through or by a business associate. The notification must be made without unreasonable delay and no later than 60 days after the discovery of the breach. The CE must also provide notice to "prominent media outlets" if the breach affects more than 500 individuals in a state or jurisdiction. The notice must include the following information:

- A description of the breach, including the date of the breach and date of discovery

- The type of PHI involved (such as full name, social security number, date of birth, home address, or account number)

- Steps individuals should take to protect themselves from potential harm resulting from the breach

- Steps the CE is taking to investigate the breach, mitigate losses, and protect against future breaches

- Contact procedures for individuals to ask questions or receive additional information, including a toll-free telephone number, email address, website, or postal address

CEs must notify DHHS of all breaches. Notice to DHHS must be provided immediately for breaches involving more than 500 individuals and annually for all other breaches. DHHS created an online tool (Breach Portal) that allow CEs to quickly notify the DHHS of any cybersecurity breach. The tool can be accessed at the following link, and it is shown in Figure 4-10: https://ocrportal.hhs.gov/ocr/breach/wizard_breach.jsf?faces-redirect=true.

CEs have the burden of demonstrating that they satisfied the specific notice obligations following a breach, or, if notice is not made following an unauthorized use or disclosure, that the unauthorized use or disclosure did not constitute a breach. DHHS has a public online portal that lists all the breach cases being investigated and archived at https://ocrportal.hhs.gov/ocr/breach/breach_report.jsf.

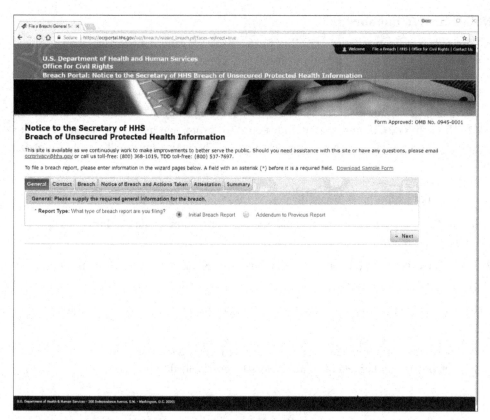

FIGURE 14-10 DHHS Cybersecurity Breach Reporting Tool

Understanding the HIPAA Compliance Enforcement Process

The DHHS Office of Civil Rights (OCR) Authority is responsible for investigating violations and enforcing the Security Rule. The HIPAA Enforcement Rule is codified at 45 CFR Part 160, Subparts C, D, and E. In the original rule, civil penalties were limited to $100 per violation and up to $25,000 per year for each requirement violated. As we discuss later in the chapter, the 2013 Omnibus Rule significantly increased the fines for noncompliance to up to $1,500,000 per violation per year and gave the OCR the power to audit CEs.

The Department of Justice was given the authority to bring criminal action against CEs that wrongly disclose ePHI. Criminal penalties for knowing violations are up to $50,000 and one year in prison, violations committed under false pretenses are up to $100,000 and five years in prison, and offenses committed for commercial or personal gain are up to $250,000 and 10 years in prison.

HIPAA does not require or allow any new government access to medical information, with one exception. The exception is that the Rule does give the U.S. Department of Health and Human Services OCR the authority to investigate complaints that Privacy Rule protections or rights have been violated, and otherwise to ensure that covered entities comply with the Rule.

According to the U.S. Department of Health and Human Services, the OCR may need to look at how a covered entity handled medical records and other personal health information for enforcement purposes only. This is done to ensure the independent review of consumers' concerns over privacy violations. Even so, the Privacy Rule limits disclosures to OCR to information that is "pertinent to ascertaining compliance." OCR will maintain stringent controls to safeguard any individually identifiable health information that it receives. If covered entities could avoid or ignore enforcement requests, consumers would not have a way to ensure an independent review of their concerns about privacy violations under the Rule.

Summary

The intent of the original HIPAA Security Rule and subsequent legislation was to protect patient health information from unauthorized access, disclosure and use, modification, and disruption.

The legislation was groundbreaking, yet many viewed it as another unfunded government mandate. Since adoption, the need to protect ePHI has become self-evident.

The HIPAA Security Rule and subsequent legislation applies to covered entities (CEs). CEs include health-care providers, health plans, health-care clearinghouses, and certain business associates. The Security Rule is organized into five categories: administrative safeguards, physical safeguards, technical safeguards, organizational requirements, and documentation requirements. Within these five categories are standards and implementation specifications. In this context, a standard defines what a CE must do; implementation specifications describe how it must be done. The rule says that a CE may use any security measures that allow it to reasonably and appropriately implement the standards and implementation specification, taking into account the size, complexity, and capabilities of the CE, the cost of the security measures, and the threat environment. The standards were meant to be scalable, meaning that they can be applied to a single-physician practice or to an organization with thousands of employees. The standards are technology-neutral and vendor-nonspecific. CEs are expected to choose the appropriate technology and controls for their unique environments.

There was minimal enforcement power associated with the original regulations. Subsequent legislation (HITECH and the Omnibus Rule) included provisions for aggressive civil and criminal enforcement by the Department of Health and Human Services (DHHS) and the Department of Justice. Authority was granted to State Attorneys General to bring civil actions and obtain damages on behalf of state residents for violations of HIPAA Privacy and Security Rules. Recognizing the right of patients to know when their information was compromised, the Omnibus Rule codifies required incident response and breach notification requirements.

The HIPAA/HITECH/Omnibus requirements mirror cybersecurity best practices. Implementations benefit both providers and patients. Providers are protecting valuable information and information assets. Patients have peace of mind knowing that their trust is being honored.

Test Your Skills

MULTIPLE CHOICE QUESTIONS

1. Which of the following statements best describes the intent of the initial HIPAA legislation adopted in 1996?

   A. The intent of the initial HIPAA legislation was to simplify and standardize the health-care administrative process.

   B. The intent of the initial HIPAA legislation was to lower health-care costs.

C. The intent of the initial HIPAA legislation was to encourage electronic record sharing between health-care providers.

D. The intent of the initial HIPAA legislation was to promote the continued use of paper-based patient records.

2. Which of the following are considered health-care providers by the HIPAA Security Rule?

    A. Clinics

    B. Out-patient services and counseling

    C. Nursing homes

    D. All of the above

3. Which of the following is an entity that provides payment for medical services such as health insurance companies, HMOs, government health plans, or government programs that pay for health care such as Medicare, Medicaid, military, and veterans' programs?

    A. Health-care providers

    B. Health plan

    C. Health-care clearinghouse

    D. All of the above

4. Which of the following statements is *not* true?

    A. HIPAA is technology-neutral.

    B. The HIPAA Security Rule established national standards to protect patient records that are created, received, used, or maintained digitally by a CE.

    C. Business associates were initially defined as persons or organizations that perform certain functions or activities that involve the use or disclosure of PHI on behalf of, or provide services to, a CE.

    D. HIPAA has also been adopted in Brazil and Canada.

5. Which of the following federal agencies is responsible for HIPAA/HITECH administration, oversight, and enforcement?

    A. Department of Health and Human Services

    B. Department of Energy

    C. Department of Commerce

    D. Department of Education

6. Which of the following is *not* a HIPAA/HITECH Security Rule category?

    A. Documentation

    B. Compliance

    C. Physical

    D. Technical

7. Which of the following statements is true?

    A. All implementation specifications are required.

    B. All implementation specifications are optional.

    C. Implementation specifications are either required or addressable.

    D. Addressable specifications are optional.

8. Which of the following statements best defines the documented policies and procedures for managing day-to-day operations, conduct, and access of workforce members to ePHI, as well as the selection, development, and use of security controls?

    A. Physical safeguards.

    B. Compliance safeguards.

    C. Administrative safeguards.

    D. Technical safeguards.

9. In the context of HIPAA/HITECH, which of the following is *not* a factor to be considered in the determination of "reasonable and appropriate" security measures?

    A. Size of the CE

    B. Level of risk

    C. Geographic location of the CE

    D. Complexity of implementation

10. Per DHHS guidance, which of the following activities are included in the risk management process? (Choose two.)

    A. Analysis

    B. Engineering

    C. Management

    D. Postmortem

11. Which of the following statements is true of the role of a HIPAA Security Officer?

    A. The role of a HIPAA Security Officer is optional.

    B. The role of a HIPAA Security Officer can be performed by a committee on a yearly basis.

C. The role of a HIPAA Security Officer should be responsible for technical and nontechnical activities, including network security, security operations center, governance, and external security research.

D. The HIPAA Security Officer is responsible for overseeing the development of policies and procedures, management and supervision of the use of security measures to protect data, and oversight of personnel access to data.

12. Which of the following statements best defines authorization?

A. Authorization is the process of positively identifying a user or system.

B. Authorization is the process of granting users or systems a predetermined level of access to information resources.

C. Authorization is the process of determining who accessed a specific record.

D. Authorization is the process of logging the access and usage of information resources.

13. Which of the following statements is false?

A. Identity-based access is granted by username.

B. Role-based access is granted by job or function.

C. Group-based access is granted by membership.

D. Clinical-based access is granted by patient name.

14. Which of the following is not true about security awareness training?

A. The campaign should be extended to anyone who interacts with the CEs' ePHI.

B. The campaign should not be extended to anyone who interacts with the CEs' ePHI.

C. The campaign can include posters, booklets, and videos.

D. The campaign can include screensavers and email campaigns.

15. Users should be trained to recognize and _____ a potential security incident.

A. report

B. contain

C. recover from

D. eradicate

16. The security incident procedures standard addresses which of the following?

A. Reporting and responding to cybersecurity incidents

B. Only identifying cybersecurity incidents

C. Only responding to cybersecurity incidents

D. Only reporting cybersecurity incidents

17. Which of the following statements is true of a business associate's HIPAA/HITECH compliance requirements?

    A. A business associate's HIPAA/HITECH compliance requirements are the same as a health-care providers'.

    B. A business associate's HIPAA/HITECH compliance requirements are limited to what is in the BA agreement.

    C. A business associate's HIPAA/HITECH compliance requirements are not as stringent as those of a health-care provider.

    D. A business associate's HIPAA/HITECH compliance requirements are exempt if the organization's annual gross revenue is less than $500,000.

18. The Final Omnibus Rule made significant changes in coverage, enforcement, and patient protection in which of the following ways?

    A. Expanding the definition of "business associates."

    B. Extending compliance enforcement to business associates and subcontractors of business associates.

    C. Increasing violation penalties with potential fines, ranging from $25,000 to as much as $1.5 million.

    D. All of the above.

19. Which of the following is *not* an acceptable end-of-life disposal process for media that contains ePHI?

    A. Permanently wipe it

    B. Shred it

    C. Recycle it

    D. Crush it

20. Granting the minimal amount of permissions necessary to do a job reflects the security principle of _____.

    A. need-to-know

    B. default deny

    C. allow some

    D. least privilege

21. Both the HITECH Act and the Omnibus Rule refer to *unsecure data,* which means data _____.

    A. in motion

    B. with weak access controls

    C. that is unencrypted

    D. stored in the cloud

22. Which of the following protocols/mechanisms cannot be used for transmitting ePHI?

    A. SSL

    B. SFTP

    C. Encrypted email

    D. HTTP

23. Which of the following statements is true?

    A. The CE does not have to provide notice to "prominent media outlets" if the breach affects more than 500 individuals in a state or jurisdiction.

    B. The CE must also provide notice to "prominent media outlets" if the breach affects more than 5,000 individuals in a state or jurisdiction.

    C. The CE must also provide notice to "prominent media outlets" if the breach affects more than 500 individuals in a state or jurisdiction.

    D. The CE does not have to provide notice to "prominent media outlets" if the breach affects fewer than 1,500 individuals in a state or jurisdiction.

24. Which of the following changes was *not* introduced by the Omnibus Rule?

    A. The Omnibus Rule expanded the definition of a business associate.

    B. The Omnibus Rule explicitly denied enforcement authority to State Attorneys General.

    C. The Omnibus Rule increased violation penalties.

    D. The Omnibus Rule defined breach notification requirements.

25. A breach notification must include which of the following information?

    A. Steps individuals should take to protect themselves from potential harm resulting from the breach

    B. A description of the breach, including the date of the breach and date of discovery

    C. The type of PHI involved (such as full name, social security number, date of birth, home address, or account number)

    D. All of the above

26. To demonstrate that there is a low probability that a breach compromised ePHI, a CE or business associate must perform a risk assessment that addresses which of the following minimum standards?

    A. Latest version of the operating system running in ePHI servers

    B. The nature and extent of the PHI involved, including the types of identifiers and the likelihood of re-identification

C. A security penetration testing report and corresponding vulnerabilities

D. None of the above

27. The *safe harbor* provision applies to _____.

   A. encrypted data

   B. password management

   C. security penetration testing reports

   D. security penetration testing procedures

28. Which of the following is *not* true?

   A. CEs must notify DHHS of all breaches.

   B. DHHS never publishes the breach cases being investigated and archived to maintain the privacy of the health-care provider.

   C. DHHS created an online tool (Breach Portal) that allows CEs to quickly notify the DHHS of any cybersecurity breach.

   D. DHHS has a public online portal that lists all the breach cases being investigated and archived.

29. A HIPAA standard defines what a covered entity must do; implementation specifications _____.

   A. describe the technology that must be used

   B. describe how it must be done and/or what it must achieve

   C. describe who must do it

   D. describe the tools that must be used

30. Which of the following defines what a breach is?

   A. Impermissible acquisition, access, or use or disclosure of unsecured PHI, unless the covered entity or business associate demonstrates that there is a low probability that the PHI has been compromised.

   B. Impermissible acquisition, access, or use or disclosure of unsecured PHI, even if the covered entity or business associate demonstrates that there is a low probability that the PHI has been compromised.

   C. Impermissible acquisition, access, or use or disclosure of secured PHI, unless the covered entity or business associate demonstrates that there is a low probability that the PHI has been compromised.

   D. Impermissible acquisition, access, or use or disclosure of encrypted PHI, even if the covered entity or business associate demonstrates that there is a low probability that the PHI has been compromised.

EXERCISES

EXERCISE 14.1: Understanding the Difference Between Privacy and Security

1. Explain the difference between the intent of the HIPAA Privacy and HIPAA Security Rules.

2. Which of the security principles—confidentiality, integrity, and/or availability—does the Privacy Rule apply to?

3. Which of the security principles—confidentiality, integrity, and/or availability—does the Security Rule apply to?

EXERCISE 14.2: Understanding Covered Entities

1. In your geographic area, identify a health-care provider organization that is subject to HIPAA Security Rule regulations.

2. In your geographic area, identify a business associate that is subject to HIPAA Security Rule regulations.

3. In your geographic area, identify either a health plan or a health-care clearinghouse that is subject to HIPAA Security Rule regulations.

EXERCISE 14.3: Identifying Key Factors for HIPAA/HITECH Compliance

1. Explain why it is important to maintain an inventory of ePHI.

2. Explain why it is important to conduct HIPAA-related risk assessments.

3. Explain why it is important to obtain senior management support.

EXERCISE 14.4: Developing Security Education Training and Awareness

1. Senior leadership needs to be educated on HIPAA/HITECH requirements. Research and recommend a conference they should attend.

2. A HIPAA security officer needs to stay informed on compliance issues. Research and recommend a peer organization to join, a publication to subscribe to, or an online forum to participate in.

3. The workplace needs to be trained on login monitoring, password management, malware, and incident reporting. Research and recommend an online training program.

EXERCISE 14.5: Creating Documentation Retention and Availability Procedures

1. All HIPAA-related documentation must be retained for a minimum of six years. This includes policies, procedures, contracts, and network documentation. Assuming you will revise the documentation, devise a standard version control procedure.

2. Recommend a way to store the documentation.

3. Recommend a secure, efficient, and cost-effective way to make the documentation available to appropriate personnel.

PROJECTS

PROJECT 14.1: Creating a HIPAA Security Program Manual Outline

You have been tasked with designing a HIPAA security program manual.

1. Write a manual for any one of the following CEs:

    ■ A 100-bed hospital in a metropolitan location.

    ■ A consortium of three nursing homes. The nursing homes share administrative and clinical staff. They are all connected to the same network.

    ■ A multispecialty medical practice consisting of 29 physicians.

2. Write an introduction to the manual explaining what the HIPAA Security Rule is and why compliance is required.

3. Design a table of contents (TOC). The TOC should correspond to the regulations.

4. For each entry in the TOC, assign development of the corresponding policy or procedure to a specific role in the organization (for example, human resources, building maintenance).

PROJECT 14.2: Assessing Business Associates

A business associate is a person or entity that creates, receives, maintains, transmits, accesses, or has the potential to access PHI to perform certain functions or activities on behalf of a CE.

1. How did HITECH and the Omnibus Rule impact business associates?

2. Identify a *business associate* organization either online or locally. Locate any policies or statements that lead you to believe that they recognize their regulatory obligations. What type of due diligence should a CE conduct to ascertain HIPAA/HITECH compliance?

3. Find an example of business associate organizations that were charged by either the FTC or a State Attorney General with a HIPAA/HITECH violation.

PROJECT 14.3: **Developing a HIPAA Training Program**

HIPAA requires that all workforce members receive annual training related to safeguarding ePHI. You have been tasked with developing an instructor-led training module. Your topic is "Disrupting the Malware Distribution Channel."

1. Develop and deliver a training presentation (and post-training quiz) on the topic. The presentation should be at least 10 minutes long. It should be interactive and engage the attendees.

2. Have participants complete the quiz. Based on the results, evaluate the effectiveness of the training.

3. Prepare a security awareness infographic about malware and incident reporting. The purpose of the infographic is to reinforce the training lesson.

Case Study

Indiana Medicaid and the HealthNow Networks Breaches

Indiana's Medicaid unit sent breach notifications to patients after discovering that medical records were exposed beginning in February 2017. According to *Healthcare IT News*, "Indiana's Health Coverage Program said that patient data was left open via a live hyperlink to an IHCP report until DXC Technology, which offers IT services to Indiana Medicaid, found the link on May 10. That report, DXC said, contained patient data including name, Medicaid ID number, name and address of doctors treating patients, patient number, procedure codes, dates of services and the amount Medicaid paid doctors or providers." This breach affected 1.1 million enrolled in the Indiana Medicaid and CHIP programs.

Another recent notable breach was the one of HealthNow Networks. The data of almost a million patients was exposed. According to the *HIPAA Journal*, "the data was discovered by an individual with the Twitter handle Flash Gordon after he conducted a search for unprotected data on the search engine Shodan. The data had been stored in an unprotected root folder on an Amazon Web Service installation owned by a software developer who had previously worked on a database for HealthNow Networks. The project was abandoned long ago, although the data provided to the developer were not secured and could be accessed online. The database contained a range of highly sensitive data, including individuals' names, addresses, email addresses, telephone numbers, dates of birth, Social Security numbers, health insurance information and medical conditions. The data had been collected by the telemarketing firm and individuals had been offered discounted medical equipment in exchange for providing the firm with their data."

1. Based on HIPAA/HITECH/Omnibus Rule regulations, were Indiana Medicaid or HealthNow Networks required to notify patients? Explain your answer.

2. Did Indiana Medicaid or HealthNow Networks make any public statements?

3. Compare how Indiana Medicaid and HealthNow Networks notified patients.

4. Do State Data Breach Notification laws apply to these events?

5. What steps could Indiana Medicaid and HealthNow Networks have taken to prevent or minimize the impact of their data breaches, respectively?

6. Has there been any enforcement action taken or fines levied against Indiana Medicaid or HealthNow Networks?

References

Regulations Cited

Department of Health and Human Services, "45 CFR Parts 160, 162, and 164 Health Insurance Reform: Security Standards; Final Rule," *Federal Register*, vol. 68, no. 34, February 20, 2003.

Department of Health and Human Services, "45 CFR Parts 160 and 164 (19006-19010): Breach Notification Guidance," *Federal Register*, vol. 74, no. 79, April 27, 2009.

"Modifications to the HIPAA Privacy, Security, Enforcement, and Breach Notification Rules 45 CFR Parts 160 and 164 Under the Health Information Technology for Economic and Clinical Health Act and the Genetic Information Nondiscrimination Act; Other Modifications to the HIPAA Rules; Final Rule," *Federal Register*, vol. 78, no. 17, January 25, 2013.

Other References

"Addressing Gaps in Cybersecurity: OCR Releases Crosswalk Between HIPAA Security Rule and NIST Cybersecurity Framework," accessed 06/2018, https://www.hhs.gov/hipaa/for-professionals/security/nist-security-hipaa-crosswalk/index.html.

"HIPAA for Professionals," accessed 06/2018, https://www.hhs.gov/hipaa/for-professionals/index.html.

"HIPAA Security Rule Crosswalk to NIST Cybersecurity Framework," accessed 06/2018, https://www.hhs.gov/sites/default/files/nist-csf-to-hipaa-security-rule-crosswalk-02-22-2016-final.pdf.

"Addressing Encryption of Data at Rest in the HIPAA Security Rule and EHR Incentive Program Stage 2 Core Measures," Healthcare Information and Management Systems Society, December 2012.

Alston & Bird, LLP, "Overview of HIPAA/HITECH Act Omnibus Final Rule Health Care Advisory," January 25, 2013, accessed 06/2018, www.alston.com/advisories/healthcare-hipaa/hitech-act-omnibus-finalrule.

"Certification and HER Incentives, HITECH ACT," accessed 06/2018, https://www.healthit.gov/policy-researchers-implementers/health-it-legislation.

"Guide to Privacy and Security of Health Information," Office of the National Coordinator for Health Information Technology, Version 2.0, accessed on 06/2018, https://www.healthit.gov/sites/default/files/pdf/privacy/privacy-and-security-guide.pdf.

"Fact Sheet: Ransomware and HIPAA", accessed 06/2018, https://www.hhs.gov/sites/default/files/RansomwareFactSheet.pdf.

"HIPAA Omnibus Final Rule Information," accessed 06/2018, https://www.hhs.gov/hipaa/for-professionals/privacy/laws-regulations/combined-regulation-text/omnibus-hipaa-rulemaking/index.html.

"HIPAA Omnibus Rule Summary," accessed 06/2018, http://www.hipaasurvivalguide.com/hipaa-omnibus-rule.php.

"HIPAA Security Rule: Frequently Asked Questions Regarding Encryption of Personal Health Information," American Medical Association, 2010, accessed 06/2018, https://www.nmms.org/sites/default/files/images/2013_9_10_hipaa-phi-encryption.pdf.

"HIPAA Timeline," accessed 06/2018, www.hipaaconsultant.com/hipaa-timeline.

McDermott Will & Emery, LLP. "OCR Issues Final Modifications to the HIPAA Privacy, Security, Breach Notification and Enforcement Rules to Implement the *HITECH* Act," February 20, 2013, accessed 06/2018, www.mwe.com/OCR-Issues-Final-Modifications-to-the-HIPAA-Privacy-Security-Breach-Notification-and-Enforcement-Rules-to-Implement-the-HITECH-Act.

"The HITECH ACT," accessed 06/2018, https://www.hipaasurvivalguide.com/hitech-act-text.php.

"The Privacy Rule," U.S. Department of Health and Human Services, accessed 06/2018, www.hhs.gov/ocr/privacy/hipaa/administrative/privacyrule.

US DHHS Breach Portal, accessed 06/2018, https://ocrportal.hhs.gov/ocr/breach/breach_report.jsf.

"Indiana Medicaid Warns Patients of Health Data Breach," Healthcare IT News, accessed 06/2018, http://www.healthcareitnews.com/news/indiana-medicaid-warns-patients-health-data-breach.

"Nearly 1 Million Patient Records Leaked after Telemarketer Blunder," http://www.healthcareitnews.com/news/nearly-1-million-patient-records-leaked-after-telemarketer-blunder.

"918,000 Patients' Sensitive Information Exposed Online," *HIPAA Journal*, accessed 06/2018, https://www.hipaajournal.com/918000-patients-sensitive-information-exposed-online-8762/.

"A Huge Trove of Patient Data Leaks, Thanks to Telemarketers' Bad Security," ZDNet, accessed 06/2018, http://www.zdnet.com/article/thousands-of-patients-data-leaks-telemarketers-bad-security/.

Chapter 15

PCI Compliance for Merchants

Chapter Objectives

After reading this chapter and completing the exercises, you will be able to do the following:

- Understand the Payment Card Industry Data Security Standard (PCI DSS).
- Recognize merchant responsibilities.
- Explain the 12 top-level requirements.
- Understand the PCI DSS validation process.
- Implement practices related to PCI compliance.

The ever-increasing volume of credit, debit, and gift card transactions makes the payment card channel an attractive target for cybercriminals.

FYI: Consumer Credit, Debit, and ATM Card Liability Limits

According to the Federal Trade Commission, consumers reported losses in excess of $900 million due to fraud per year during the last few years. This is expected to continue to rise. The balance of the loss is borne by the merchant, credit card processor, and the issuing bank.

The Fair Credit Billing Act (FCBA) and the Electronic Fund Transfer Act (EFTA) govern credit card, debit card, and ATM liability if a card is lost or stolen.

Under the FCBA, the maximum liability for unauthorized credit card use is $50. However, if the consumer reports a lost card before the credit card is used, the consumer is not responsible for any unauthorized charges. If a credit card number is stolen, but not the card, the consumer is not liable.

Under the EFTA, debit and ATM card liability depends on how quickly the loss or theft is reported. If the card is reported as lost or stolen before any unauthorized charges are made, the consumer is not responsible for any unauthorized charges. If the card is reported within two days after the consumer learns of the loss or theft, the consumer liability is limited to $50. If the card is reported more than two days but less than 60 days after the consumer learns of the loss or theft, the consumer liability is limited to $500. If the card is reported as lost or stolen more than 60 days after a bank statement is sent, the consumer bears all liability.

To protect cardholders against misuse of their personal information and to minimize payment card channel losses, the major payment card brands—Visa, MasterCard, Discover, JCB International, and American Express—formed the Payment Card Industry Security Standards Council and developed the Payment Card Industry Data Security Standard (PCI DSS). On December 15, 2004, the Council released version 1.0 of the PCI DSS. The latest version at the time of writing was PCI DSS version 3.2 published in April 2016. The standard and collateral documentation can be obtained at https://www.pcisecuritystandards.org.

The PCI DSS must be adopted by any organization that transmits, processes, or stores payment card data, or directly or indirectly affects the security of cardholder data. Any organization that leverages a third-party to manage cardholder data has the full responsibility to ensure that this third party is compliant with the PCI DSS. The payment card brands can levy fines and penalties against organizations that do not comply with the requirements, and/or revoke their authorization to accept payment cards.

In this chapter, we examine the PCI DSS standard. Although designed for a specific constituency, the requirements can serve as a security blueprint for any organization.

Protecting Cardholder Data

Before we proceed with the details about how to protect cardholder data, we must define several key terms that are used within this chapter and defined by the PCI Security Standards Council (PCI SSC) in their Glossary of Terms, Abbreviations, and Acronyms at https://www.pcisecuritystandards.org/documents/pci_glossary_v20.pdf.

- **Acquirer:** Also referred to as "acquiring bank" or "acquiring financial institution." Entity that initiates and maintains relationships with merchants for the acceptance of payment cards.
- **ASV:** Acronym for "Approved Scanning Vendor." An organization approved by the PCI SSC to conduct external vulnerability scanning services.
- **Merchant:** For the purposes of the PCI DSS, a merchant is defined as any entity that accepts payment cards bearing the logos of any of the five members of PCI SSC (American Express, Discover, JCB, MasterCard, or Visa) as payment for goods and/or services. Note that a merchant that accepts payment cards as payment for goods and/or services can also be a service provider, if the services sold result in storing, processing, or transmitting cardholder data on behalf of other merchants or service providers.

- **PAN:** Primary account number (the up-to-19-digit payment card number).

- **Qualified Security Assessor (QSA):** An individual trained and certified to carry out PCI DSS compliance assessments.

- **Service provider:** Business entity that is not a payment brand, directly involved in the processing, storage, or transmission of cardholder data. This also includes companies that provide services that control or could impact the security of cardholder data. Examples include managed service providers that provide managed firewalls, IDS, and other services, as well as hosting providers and other entities. Entities such as telecommunications companies that only provide communication links without access to the application layer of the communication link are excluded.

To counter the potential for staggering losses, the payment card brands contractually require all organizations that store, process, or transmit cardholder data and/or sensitive authentication data to comply with the PCI DSS. PCI DSS requirements apply to all system components where *account data* is stored, processed, or transmitted.

As shown in Table 15-1, *account data* consists of cardholder data plus sensitive authentication data. *System components* are defined as any network component, server, or application that is included in, or connected to, the cardholder data environment. The *cardholder data environment* is defined as the people, processes, and technology that handle cardholder data or sensitive authentication data.

TABLE 15-1 Account Data Elements

Cardholder Data Includes...	Sensitive Authentication Data Includes...
Primary account number (PAN)	Full magnetic stripe data or equivalent data on a chip
Cardholder name	CAV2/CVC2/CVV2/CID
Expiration date	PIN blocks
Service code	

What Is the PAN?

The PAN is the defining factor in the applicability of PCI DSS requirements. PCI DSS requirements apply if the PAN is stored, processed, or transmitted. If the PAN is not stored, processed, or transmitted, PCI DSS requirements do not apply. If cardholder names, service codes, and/or expiration dates are stored, processed, or transmitted with the PAN, or are otherwise present in the cardholder data environment, they too must be protected.

Per the standards, the PAN must be stored in an unreadable (encrypted) format. Sensitive authentication data may never be stored post-authorization, even if encrypted.

The Luhn Algorithm

The Luhn algorithm or Luhn formula is an industry algorithm used to validate different identification numbers including credit card numbers, International Mobile Equipment Identity (IMEI) numbers, National Provider Identifier numbers in the United States, Canadian Social Insurance Numbers, and more. The Luhn algorithm was created by Hans Peter Luhn in 1954. This algorithm is now in the public domain.

Most credit cards and many government identification numbers use the Luhn algorithm to validate valid numbers. The Luhn algorithm is based around the principle of modulo arithmetic and digital roots. It uses modulo-10 mathematics.

FYI: The Elements of a Credit Card

Figure 15-1 shows the following elements located on the front of a credit card:

1. **Embedded microchip:** The microchip contains the same information as the magnetic stripe. Most non-U.S. cards have the microchip instead of the magnetic stripe. Some U.S. cards have both for international acceptance.

2. **Primary account number (PAN).**

3. **Expiration date.**

4. **Cardholder name.**

Figure 15-2 shows the following elements on the back of a credit card:

1. **Magnetic stripe (mag stripe):** The magnetic stripe contains encoded data required to authenticate, authorize, and process transactions.

2. **CAV2/CID/CVC2/CVV2:** All refer to card security codes for the different payment brands.

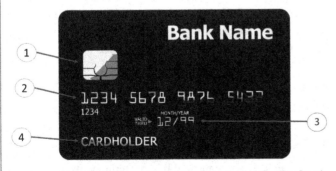

FIGURE 15-1   The Elements of the Front of a Credit Card

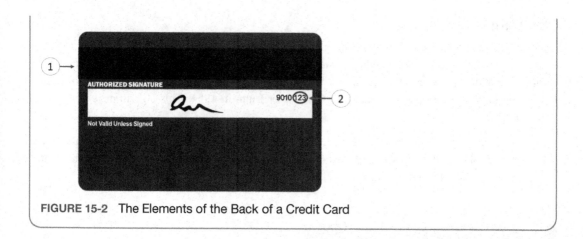

FIGURE 15-2   The Elements of the Back of a Credit Card

Eliminating the collection and storage of unnecessary data, restricting cardholder data to as few locations as possible, and isolating the cardholder data environment from the rest of the corporate network is strongly recommended. Physically or logically segmenting the cardholder data environment reduces the PCI scope, which in turn reduces cost, complexity, and risk. Without segmentation, the entire network must be PCI-compliant. This can be burdensome because the PCI-required controls may not be applicable to other parts of the network.

Utilizing a third party to store, process, and transmit cardholder data or manage system components does not relieve a covered entity of its PCI compliance obligation. Unless the third-party service provider can demonstrate or provide evidence of PCI compliance, the service provider environment is considered to be an extension of the covered entity's cardholder data environment and is in scope.

What Is the PCI DDS Framework?

The PCI DSS framework includes stipulations regarding storage, transmission, and processing of payment card data, six core principles, required technical and operational security controls, testing requirements, and a certification process. Entities are required to validate their compliance. The number of transactions, the type of business, and the type of transactions determine specific validation requirements.

There are multiple points of access to cardholder data and varying technologies. PCI DSS is designed to accommodate the various environments where cardholder data is processed, stored, or transmitted—such as e-commerce, mobile acceptance, or cloud computing. PCI DSS also recognizes that security is a shared responsibility and addresses the obligations of each business partner in the transaction chain.

The PCI DSS consists of six core principles, which are accompanied by 12 requirements. The six core principles are illustrated in Figure 15-3.

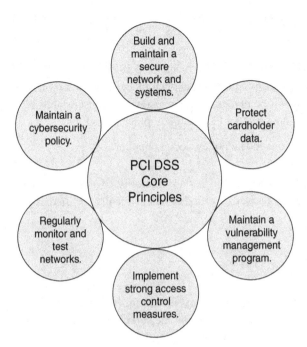

FIGURE 15-3   PCI DSS Six Core Principles

Business-as-Usual Approach

PCI DSS version 3.2 emphasizes that compliance is not a point-in-time determination but rather an ongoing process. *Business as usual* is defined as the inclusion of PCI controls as part of an overall risk-based security strategy that is managed and monitored by the organization. According to the PCI Standards Council, a business-as-usual approach "enables an entity to monitor the effectiveness of their security controls on an ongoing basis, and maintain their PCI DSS compliant environment in between PCI DSS assessments." This means that organizations must monitor required controls to ensure they are operating effectively, respond quickly to control failures, incorporate PCI compliance impact assessments into the change-management process, and conduct periodic reviews to confirm that PCI requirements continue to be in place and that personnel are following secure processes.

Per the PCI Council, the version 3.2 updates are intended to do the following:

- Provide stronger focus on some of the greater risk areas in the threat environment.
- Build greater understanding of the intent of the requirements and how to apply them.
- Improve flexibility for all entities implementing, assessing, and building to the standards.
- Help manage evolving risks/threats.
- Align with changes in industry best practices.

- The Designated Entities Supplemental Validation (DESV) has been incorporated into the PCI DSS standard.

- Several new requirements were identified for service providers in PCI DSS 3.2. These include maintaining a documented description of the cryptographic architecture and reporting on failures of critical security control systems. Additionally, executive management must establish responsibility for protection of cardholder data and the PCI DSS compliance program.

- Eliminate redundant subrequirements and consolidate policy documentation.

This approach mirrors best practices and reflects the reality that the majority of significant card breaches have occurred at organizations that were either self-certified or independently certified as PCI compliant.

What Are the PCI Requirements?

There are 12 top-level PCI requirements related to the six core principles. Within each requirement are subrequirements and controls. The requirements are reflective of cybersecurity best practices. Quite often, the requirement's title is misleading in that it sounds simple, but the subrequirements and associated control expectations are actually quite extensive. The intent of and, in some cases, specific details of the requirements are summarized in the following sections. As you read them, you will notice that they parallel the security practices and principles we have discussed throughout this text.

The PCI DSS consists of 12 requirements. These requirements are listed in Figure 15-4.

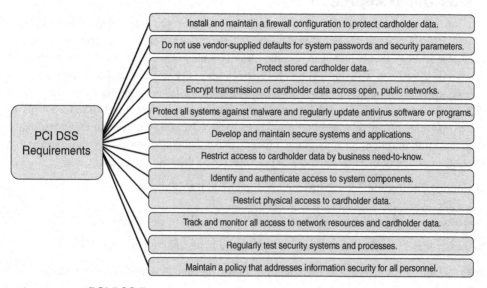

FIGURE 15-4   PCI DSS Requirements

Build and Maintain a Secure Network and Systems

The first core principle—build and maintain a secure network and systems—includes the following two requirements:

1. Install and maintain a firewall configuration to protect cardholder data.

   The basic objective of a firewall is ingress and egress filtering. The firewall does so by examining traffic and allowing or blocking transmissions based on a predefined rule set. The requirement extends beyond the need to have a firewall. It also addresses the following:

   - Identifying and documenting all connections.

   - Designing a firewall architecture that protects cardholder data.

   - Implementing consistent configuration standards.

   - Documenting firewall configuration and rule sets.

   - Having a formal change management process.

   - Requiring rule-set business justification.

   - Scheduling semi-annual firewall rule-set reviews.

   - Implementing firewall security controls, such as antispoofing mechanisms.

   - Maintaining and monitoring firewall protection on mobile or employee-owned devices.

   - Publishing perimeter protection policies and related operational procedures.

2. Do not use vendor-supplied defaults for system passwords and security parameters.

   Although this seems obvious, there may be default accounts, especially service accounts, that aren't evident or are overlooked. Additionally, systems or devices that are installed by third parties may be left at the default for ease of use. This requirement also extends far beyond its title and enters the realm of configuration management. Requirements include the following:

   - Maintaining an inventory of systems and system components.

   - Changing vendor-supplied default passwords on all operating systems, applications, utilities, devices, and keys.

   - Removing or disabling unnecessary default accounts, services, scripts, drivers, and protocols.

   - Developing consistent configuration standards for all system components that are in accordance with industry-accepted system-hardening standards (such as ISO and NIST).

   - Segregating system functions based on security levels.

   - Using secure technologies (for example, SFTP instead of FTP).

   - Encrypting all nonconsole administrative access.

- PCI DSS version 3.2 introduces new requirements for organizations to migrate to modern and strong cryptographic algorithms and protocols. The PCI SSC refers to industry standards and best practices for information on strong cryptography and secure protocols, including the NIST SP 800-52 and SP 800-57 and the OWASP recommendations.

- Publishing configuration management policies and related operational procedures.

Protect Cardholder Data

The second core principle—protect cardholder data—includes the following two requirements:

1. Protect stored card data.

   This is a very broad requirement. As mentioned earlier, the *cardholder data environment* is defined as the people, processes, and technology that handle cardholder data or sensitive authentication data. Sited protection mechanisms include encryption, truncation, masking and hashing, secure disposal, and secure destruction. Requirements include the following:

   - Data retention policies and practices that limit the retention of cardholder data and forbid storing sensitive authentication data post-authorization as well as card-verification code or value.

   - Masking the PAN when displayed.

   - Rendering the PAN unreadable anywhere it is stored.

   - Protecting and managing encryption keys (including generation, storage, access, renewal, and replacement).

   - Publishing data-disposal policies and related operational procedures.

   - Publishing data-handling standards that clearly delineate how cardholder data is to be handled.

   - Training for all personnel that interact with or are responsible for securing cardholder data.

2. Encrypt transmission of cardholder data across open, public networks.

   The objective here is to ensure that data in transit over public networks cannot be compromised and exploited. An open and/or public network is defined as the Internet, wireless technologies including Bluetooth, cellular technologies, radio transmission, and satellite communications. The requirements include the following:

   - Using strong cryptography and security transmission protocols.

   - Forbidding transmission of unprotected PANs by end-user messaging technologies, such as email, chat, instant message, and text.

   - Publishing transmission security policies and related operational procedures.

Maintain a Vulnerability Management Program

The third core principle—maintain a vulnerability management program—includes the following two requirements:

1. Protect all systems against malware and regularly update antivirus software or programs.

   As discussed in previous chapters, malware is a general term used to describe any kind of software or code specifically designed to exploit or disrupt a system or device, or the data it contains, without consent. Malware is one of the most vicious tools in the cybercriminal arsenal. The requirement includes the following:

   - Selecting an antivirus/antimalware solution commensurate with the level of protection required.

   - Selecting an antivirus/antimalware solution that has the capacity to perform periodic scans and generate audit logs.

   - Deploying the antivirus/antimalware solution on all applicable in-scope systems and devices.

   - Ensuring that antivirus/antimalware solutions are kept current.

   - Ensuring that antivirus/antimalware solutions cannot be disabled or modified without management authorization.

   - Publishing antimalware security policies and related operational procedures.

   - Training for all personnel on the implications of malware, disruption of the distribution channel, and incident reporting.

2. Develop and maintain secure systems and architecture.

   This requirement mirrors the best practices guidance in Section 14 of ISO 27002:2013: Information Systems Acquisition, Development, and Maintenance, which focuses on the security requirements of information systems, applications, and code, from conception to destruction. The requirement includes the following:

   - Keeping up-to-date on new vulnerabilities.

   - Assessing the risk of new vulnerabilities.

   - Maintaining a patch management process.

   - Adhering to security principles and best practices throughout the systems development life cycle (SDLC).

   - Maintaining a comprehensive change management process, including back-out and restore procedures.

   - Segregating the production environment from development, staging, and/or testing platforms.

   - Adopting and internally publishing industry-accepted secure coding techniques (for example, OWASP).

   - Implementing code testing procedures.

■ Training developers in secure coding and vulnerability management practices.

■ Publishing secure coding policies and related operational procedures.

FYI: Focus on Malware Controls

Malware has been the tool of choice for some of the most significant data card breaches:

■ January 2018: OnePlus announced that up to 40,000 customers were affected by a security breach that caused the company to shut down credit card payments for its online store.

■ June 2017: The Buckle, Inc. disclosed that its retail locations were hit by malicious software designed to steal customer credit card data.

■ April 2016: Wendy's reported at least 1,025 store locations were hit by a malware-driven credit card breach that began in the fall of 2015.

■ September 2014: Criminals stole over 56 million credit, debit, and gift card data records from Home Depot.

■ November 2013: Criminals used malware to obtain unauthorized access to Target Corp's point-of-sale terminals, resulting in the compromise of 40 million credit and debit cards.

■ January 2012: Criminals used an SQL injection attack to plant malware on the Global Payments, Inc.'s computer network and processing system, resulting in the compromise of 1.5 million credit and debit cards.

■ From 2005–2013, a hacking group from Russia and Ukraine targeted banks and companies, including Nasdaq, 7-11, JetBlue and JC Penney. Threat actors stole 160 million credit and debit card-numbers and breached 800,000 bank accounts.

Implement Strong Access Control Measures

The fourth core principle—implement strong access control measures—includes the following three requirements:

1. Restrict access to cardholder data by business need-to-know.

   This requirement reflects the security best practices of default deny, need-to-know, and least privilege. The objective is to ensure that only authorized users, systems, and processes have access to cardholder data. The requirement includes the following:

   ■ Setting the default cardholder data access permissions to default deny.

   ■ Identifying roles and system processes that need access to cardholder data.

   ■ Determining the minimum level of access needed.

   ■ Assigning permissions based on roles, job classification, or function.

   ■ Reviewing permissions on a scheduled basis.

   ■ Publishing access control policies and related operational procedures.

2. Identify and authenticate access to system components.

There are three primary objectives to this requirement. The first is to ensure that every user, system, and process is uniquely identified so that accountability is possible and to manage the account through its life cycle. The second is to ensure that the strength of authentication credentials is commensurate with the access risk profile. The third is to secure the session from unauthorized access. This section is unique in that it sets specific implementation standards, including password length, password complexity, and session timeout. The requirement includes the following:

- Assigning and requiring the use of unique IDs for each account (user or system) and process that accesses cardholder data and/or is responsible for managing the systems that process, transmit, or store cardholder data.

- Implementing and maintaining a provisioning process that spans the account life cycle from creation through termination. This includes access reviews and removing/disabling inactive user accounts at least every 90 days.

- Allowing single-factor authentication for internal access if passwords meet the following minimum criteria: seven alphanumeric characters, 90-day expiration, and no reuse of the last four passwords. The account lockout mechanism's setting must lock out the user ID after six invalid login attempts and lock the account for a minimum of 30 minutes.

- Requiring two-factor authentication for all remote network access sessions. Authentication mechanisms must be unique to each account.

- Implementing session requirements, including a mandatory maximum 15-minute inactivity timeout that requires the user to reauthenticate, and monitoring remote vendor sessions.

- Restricting access to cardholder databases by type of account.

- Publishing authentication and session security policies and related operational procedures.

- Training users on authentication-related best practices, including how to create and manage passwords.

3. Restrict physical access to cardholder data.

This requirement is focused on restricting physical access to media (paper and electronic), devices, and transmission lines that store, process, or transmit cardholder data. The requirement includes the following:

- Implementing administrative, technical, and physical controls that restrict physical access to systems, devices, network jacks, and telecommunications lines within the scope of the cardholder environment.

- Video monitoring physical access to sensitive areas, correlating with other entries, and maintaining evidence for a minimum of three months. The term *sensitive areas* refers to a data center, server room, or any area that houses systems that store, process, or transmit cardholder data. This excludes public-facing areas where only point-of-sale terminals are present, such as the cashier areas in a retail store.

- Having procedures to identify and account for visitors.

- Physically securing and maintaining control over the distribution and transport of any media that has cardholder data.

- Securely and irretrievably destroying media (that has cardholder data) when it is no longer needed for business or legal reasons.

- Protecting devices that capture card data from tampering, skimming, or substitution.

- Training point-of-sale personnel about tampering techniques and how to report suspicious incidents.

- Publishing physical security policies and related procedures.

FYI: Stealing Card Information Using a Skimmer

According to Brian Krebs, "A greater number of ATM skimming incidents now involve so-called 'insert skimmers,' wafer-thin fraud devices made to fit snugly and invisibly inside a cash machine's card acceptance slot. New evidence suggests that at least some of these insert skimmers—which record card data and store it on a tiny embedded flash drive—are equipped with technology allowing them to transmit stolen card data wirelessly via infrared, the same communications technology that powers a TV remote control."

Skimming is theft of cardholder information by modifying a card swipe device and/or by attaching a card-reading device (AKA a skimmer) to a terminal or ATM. The prized target is debit cardholder data and PINs, which give the criminals the information they need to make counterfeit debit cards and withdraw cash from ATMs.

Skimming can be very lucrative. Before they were caught, a nine-month skimming operation in Oklahoma netted two men $400,000. According to their indictment, defendants Kevin Konstantinov and Elvin Alisuretove installed skimmers at Murphy's gas pumps in the parking lots of Walmart retail stores in Arkansas, Oklahoma, and Texas. They would leave the skimming devices in place for between one and two months. Then they'd collect the skimmers and use the stolen data to create counterfeit cards, visiting multiple ATMs throughout the region and withdrawing large amounts of cash.

Skimming devices are readily available online from dozens of stores for under $50. These devices are usually disguised under the name of "card reader" because they can also serve legitimate purposes. Several of the devices include built-in storage and wireless connectivity, which allow the criminals to transmit the stolen data. According to U.S. Secret Service Special Agent Cynthia Wofford, "Thieves travel to the U.S. for the very purpose of stealing credit and debit card data. The arrests we've made so far have led us to believe they're organized groups."

It is important that merchants learn how to inspect for and recognize skimming devices. "All About Skimmers," an excellent online primer (including pictures), is publicly available on the Krebs on Security site: http://krebsonsecurity.com/all-about-skimmers/.

Regularly Monitor and Test Networks

The fifth core principle—Regularly monitor and test networks—includes the following two requirements:

1. Track and monitor all access to network resources and cardholder data.

    The nucleus of this requirement is the ability to log and analyze card data–related activity, with the dual objective of identifying precursors and indicators of compromise, and the availability of corroborative data if there is a suspicion of compromise. The requirement includes the following:

    - Logging of all access to and activity related to cardholder data, systems, and supporting infrastructure. Logs must identity the user, type of event, date, time, status (success or failure), origin, and affected data or resource.

    - Logging of user, administrator, and system account creation, modifications, and deletions.

    - Ensuring the date and time stamps are accurate and synchronized across all audit logs.

    - Securing audit logs so they cannot be deleted or modified.

    - Limiting access to audit logs to individuals with a need to know.

    - Analyzing audit logs to identify anomalies or suspicious activity.

    - Retaining audit logs for at least one year, with a minimum of three months immediately available for analysis.

    - Publishing audit log and monitoring policies and related operational procedures.

2. Regularly test security systems and processes.

    Applications and configuration vulnerabilities are identified on a daily basis. Ongoing vulnerability scans, penetration testing, and intrusion monitoring are necessary to detect vulnerabilities inherent in legacy systems and/or have been introduced by changes in the cardholder environment. The requirement to test security systems and processes is specific in how often testing must be conducted. This requirement includes the following:

    - Implementing processes to detect and identify authorized and unauthorized wireless access points on a quarterly basis.

    - Running internal and external network vulnerability scans at least quarterly and whenever there is a significant change in the environment. External scans must be performed by a PCI Approved Scanning Vendor (ASV).

    - Resolving all high-risk issues identified by the vulnerability scans. Verifying resolution by rescanning.

    - Performing annual network and application layer external and internal penetration tests using an industry-accepted testing approach and methodology (for example, NIST SP 800-115, OWASP). If issues are identified, they must be corrected and the testing must be redone to verify the correction.

- Using intrusion detection (IDS) or intrusion prevention (IPS) techniques to detect or prevent intrusions into the network.

- Deploying a change detection mechanism to alert personnel to unauthorized modifications of critical system files, configuration files, and content files.

- Publishing security testing policies and related operational procedures.

Maintain a Cybersecurity Policy

The sixth core principle—maintain a cybersecurity policy—includes the final requirement:

1. Maintain a policy that addresses cybersecurity for all personnel.

   Of all the requirements, this may be the most inaptly named. A more appropriate title would be "Maintain a *comprehensive* cybersecurity program *(including whatever we've forgotten to include in the first 11 requirements)*." This requirement includes the following:

   - Establishing, publishing, maintaining, and disseminating a cybersecurity policy. The policy should include but not be limited to the areas noted in the other 11 PCI DSS requirements. The policy should be authorized by executive management or an equivalent body.

   - Annually reviewing, updating, and reauthorizing the cybersecurity policy.

   - Implementing a risk assessment process that is based on an industry-accepted approach and methodology (for example, NIST 800-30, ISO 27005).

   - Assigning responsibility for the cybersecurity program to a designated individual or team.

   - Implementing a formal security awareness program.

   - Educating personnel upon hire and then at least annually.

   - Requiring users to annually acknowledge that they have read and understand security policies and procedures.

   - Performing thorough background checks prior to hiring personnel who may be given access to cardholder data.

   - Maintaining a vendor management program applicable to service providers with whom cardholder data is shared or who could affect the security of cardholder data.

   - Requiring service providers to acknowledge in a written agreement their responsibility in protecting cardholder data.

   - Establishing and practicing incident response capabilities.

   - Establishing and practicing disaster response and recovery capabilities.

   - Establishing and practicing business continuity capabilities.

   - Annually testing incident response, disaster recovery, and business continuity plans and procedures.

The Designated Entities Supplemental Validation (DESV)

The Designated Entities Supplemental Validation (DESV) is a document that Qualified Security Assessors (QSAs) use to validate organizations that must be PCI DSS–compliant. PCI DSS version 3.2 incorporates DESV as an appendix primarily to merge requirements and to strengthen the importance of these requirements in establishing and maintaining ongoing cybersecurity processes. DESV is a list of resources and criteria that is designed to help service providers and merchants address key operational challenges while trying to protect payments and maintain compliance.

DESV includes the following requirements:

- Compliance program oversight

- Proper scoping of an environment

- Guaranteeing that proper mechanisms are used to detect and alert on failures in critical security controls.

Many of the requirements are simply extensions of existing PCI DSS requirements that should be demonstratively tested more regularly, or require more evidence that the control is in place.

In Practice

PCI Topic Summary and Chapter Cross-Reference

Requirement	Topic	Chapter Cross-Reference
Install and maintain a firewall configuration to protect cardholder data.	Perimeter access controls	Ch. 9: "Access Control Management"
Do not use vendor-supplied defaults for system passwords and security parameters.	System inventory	Ch. 5: "Asset Management and Data Loss Prevention"
	System configuration	Ch. 8: "Communications and Operations Security"
Protect stored cardholder data.	Data handling standards	Ch. 5: "Asset Management and Data Loss Prevention"
	Data retention standards	
	User training	Ch. 6: "Human Resources Security"
	Data and system disposal	Ch. 7: "Physical and Environmental Security"
	Key management	Ch. 10: "Information Systems Acquisition, Development, and Maintenance"
Encrypt transmission of cardholder data across open, public networks.	Encryption	Ch. 10: "Information Systems Acquisition, Development, and Maintenance"
	Secure transmission protocols	Ch. 8: "Communications and Operations Security"

Requirement	Topic	Chapter Cross-Reference
Protect all systems against malware and regularly update antivirus software or programs.	Malware protection	Ch. 8: "Communications and Operations Security"
	User training	Ch. 6: "Human Resources Security"
Develop and maintain secure systems and applications.	Standard operating procedures	Ch. 8: "Communications and Operations Security"
	Patch management	
	Change management	
	Systems development life cycle (SDLC)	Ch. 10: "Information Systems Acquisition, Development, and Maintenance"
	Secure coding procedures	
Restrict access to cardholder data by business need-to-know.	Security principles	Ch. 9: "Access Control Management"
	Role-based access control	
	Access reviews	
Identify and authenticate access to system components.	Authentication	Ch. 9: "Access Control Management"
	User provisioning	Ch. 6: "Human Resources Security"
	Session controls	Ch. 9: "Access Control Management"
	User training	Ch. 6: "Human Resources Security"
Restrict physical access to cardholder data.	Physical access controls	Ch. 7: "Physical and Environmental Security"
	Data center monitoring	
	Media security	
	User training	Ch. 6: "Human Resources Security"
Track and monitor all access to network resources and cardholder data.	Audit log collection	Ch. 8: "Communications and Operations Security"
	Audit log analysis	
	Audit log management	
Regularly test security systems and processes.	Vulnerability scanning	Ch. 9: "Access Control Management"
	Penetration testing	
	Detection and alerting	Ch. 8: "Communications and Operations Security"
Maintain a policy that addresses information security for all personnel.	Security policy management	Ch. 4: "Governance and Risk Management"
	Risk assessment	
	Cybersecurity program management	
	Secure awareness program	Ch. 6: "Human Resources Security"
	Background checks	
	Acceptable use agreements	
	Vendor management program	Ch. 8: "Communications and Operations Security"
	Service provider contracts	
	Incident response capabilities	Ch. 11: "Cybersecurity Incident Response"
	Disaster response and recovery capabilities	Ch. 12: "Business Continuity Management"

PCI Compliance

Complying with the PCI standards is a contractual obligation that applies to all entities involved in the payment card channel, including merchants, processors, financial institutions, and service providers, as well as all other entities that store, process, or transmit cardholder data and/or sensitive authentication data. The number of transactions, the type of business, and the type of transactions determine specific compliance requirements.

It is important to emphasize that PCI compliance is not a government regulation or law. The requirement to be PCI-compliant is mandated by the payment card brands in order to accept card payments and/or be a part of the payment system. PCI standards augment but do not supersede legislative or regulatory requirements to protect personally identifiable information (PII) or other data elements.

Who Is Required to Comply with PCI DSS?

Merchants are required to comply with the PCI DSS. Traditionally, a merchant is defined as a seller. It is important to note that the PCI DSS definition is a departure from the traditional definition. For the purposes of the PCI DSS, a merchant is defined as any entity that accepts American Express, Discover, JCB, MasterCard, or Visa payment cards as payment for goods and/or services (including donations). The definition does not use the terms *store*, *seller*, and *retail*; instead, the focus is on the payment side rather than the transaction type. Effectively, any company, organization, or individual that accepts card payments is a merchant. The mechanism for collecting data can be as varied as an iPhone-attached card reader, a parking meter, a point-of-sale checkout, or even an offline system.

Compliance Validation Categories

PCI compliance validation is composed of four levels, which are based on the number of transactions processed per year and whether those transactions are performed from a physical location or over the Internet. Each payment card brand has the option of modifying its requirements and definitions of PCI compliance validation levels. Given the dominance of the Visa brand, the Visa categorization is the one most often applicable. The Visa brand parameters for determining compliance validation levels are as follows. Any entity that has suffered a breach that resulted in an account data compromise may be escalated to a higher level.

- A Level 1 merchant meets one of the following criteria:
  - Processes over six million Visa payment card transactions annually (all channels).
  - A merchant that has been identified by any card association as a Level 1 merchant.
  - Any merchant that Visa, at its sole discretion, determines should meet the Level 1 requirements to minimize risk to the Visa system.

- A Level 2 entity is defined as any merchant—regardless of acceptance channel—processing one million to six million Visa transactions per year.

- A Level 3 merchant is defined as any merchant processing 20,000 to 1,000,000 Visa e-commerce transactions per year.

- A Level 4 merchant is defined as any merchant processing fewer than 20,000 Visa e-commerce transactions per year, and all other merchants—regardless of acceptance channel—processing up to one million Visa transactions per year.

An annual onsite compliance assessment is required for Level 1 merchants. Level 2 and Level 3 merchants may submit a self-assessment questionnaire (SAQ). Compliance validation requirements for Level 4 merchants are set by the merchant bank. Submission of an SAQ is generally recommended but not required. All entities with externally facing IP addresses must engage an ASV to perform quarterly external vulnerability scans.

What Is a Data Security Compliance Assessment?

A *compliance assessment* is an annual onsite evaluation of compliance with the PCI DSS conducted by either a Qualified Security Assessor (QSA) or an Internal Security Assessor (ISA). The assessment methodology includes observation of system settings, processes, and actions, documentation reviews, interviews, and sampling. The culmination of the assessment is a Report on Compliance (ROC).

Assessment Process

The assessment process begins with documenting the PCI DSS cardholder environment and confirming the scope of the assessment. Generally, a QSA/ISA will initially conduct a GAP assessment to identify areas of noncompliance and provide remediation recommendations. Post-remediation, the QSA/ISA conducts the assessment. To complete the process, the following must be submitted to either the acquiring financial institution or payment card brand:

- ROC completed by a QSA or ISA

- Evidence of passing vulnerability scans by an ASV

- Completion of the Attestation of Compliance by the assessed entity and the QSA

- Supporting documentation

FYI: What Are QSAs, ISAs, and ASVs?

The PCI Security Standards Council operates a number of programs to train, test, and certify organizations and individuals to assess and validate adherence to PCI Security Standards. These programs include QSA, ISA, and ASV.

Qualified Security Assessors (QSAs) are organizations that have been qualified by the PCI Security Standards Council to have their employees assess compliance to the PCI DSS standard. Employees of those organizations must be certified by the PCI Security Standards Council to validate an entity's adherence to the PCI DSS.

Approved Scanning Vendors (ASVs) are organizations that validate adherence to certain DSS requirements by performing vulnerability scans of Internet-facing environments of merchants and service providers.

Internal Security Assessors (ISAs) are sponsor companies that have been qualified by the council. The PCI SSC ISA Program consists of internal security audit professionals of sponsor organizations who are qualified through training from the council to improve their organization's understanding of the PCI DSS, facilitate the organization's interactions with QSAs, enhance the quality, reliability, and consistency of the organization's internal PCI DSS self-assessments, and support the consistent and proper application of PCI DSS measures and controls.

Source: PCI Security Standards Council (www.pcisecuritystandards.org/approved_companies_providers/).

Report on Compliance

As defined in the PCI DSS Requirements and Security Assessment Procedures, the ROC standard template includes the following sections:

- Section 1: "Executive Summary"
- Section 2: "Description of Scope of Work and Approach Taken"
- Section 3: "Details about Reviewed Environment"
- Section 4: "Contact Information and Report Date"
- Section 5: "Quarterly Scan Results"
- Section 6: "Findings and Observations"
- Section 7: "Compensating Controls Worksheets" (if applicable)

Sections 1–5 provide a detailed overview of the assessed environment and establish the framework for the assessor's findings. The ROC template includes specific testing procedures for each PCI DSS requirement.

Section 6, "Findings and Observations," contains the assessor's findings for each requirement and testing procedure of the PCI DSS as well as information that supports and justifies each finding. The information provided in "Findings and Observations" summarizes how the testing procedures were performed and the findings achieved. This section includes all 12 PCI DSS requirements.

What Is the PCI DSS Self-Assessment Questionnaire (SAQ)?

The SAQ is a validation tool for merchants that are not required to submit to an onsite data security assessment. Each PCI DSS SAQ includes the following components:

- Questions correlating to the PCI DSS requirements, as appropriate for different environments.

- Attestation of Compliance, which is your declaration of eligibility for completing the applicable SAQ and the subsequent results of a PCI DSS self-assessment.

Per the May 2016 PCI DSS SAQ Instructions and Guidelines, there are eight SAQ categories. The number of questions varies because the questionnaires are designed to be reflective of the specific payment card channel and the anticipated scope of the cardholder environment.

- **SAQ A:** Applicable to merchants who retain only paper reports or receipts with cardholder data, do not store cardholder data in electronic format, and do not process or transmit any cardholder data on their systems or premises. This would never apply to face-to-face merchants.

- **SAQ A-EP:** Applicable only to e-commerce channels who outsource all payment processing to PCI DSS validated third-party providers.

- **SAQ B:** Applicable to merchants who process cardholder data only via imprint machines or standalone, dial-out terminals. This does not apply to e-commerce merchants.

- **SAQ B-IP:** Applicable to merchants using only standalone payment terminals with IP connectivity to the payment processor with no electronic cardholder data storage. This does not apply to e-commerce merchants.

- **SAQ C-VT:** Applicable to merchants who process cardholder data only via isolated virtual terminals on personal computers connected to the Internet. This does not apply to e-commerce merchants.

- **SAQ C:** Applicable to merchants whose payment application systems are connected to the Internet either because the payment application system is on a personal computer that is connected to the Internet (for example, for email or web browsing) or the payment application system is connected to the Internet to transmit cardholder data.

- **SAQ P2PE:** Applicable to merchants who process cardholder data only via payment terminals included in a validated and PCI SSC–listed Point-to-Point Encryption (P2PE) solution. This does not apply to e-commerce merchants.

- **SAQ D:** Applicable to all other merchants not included in descriptions for SAQ types A through C as well as all service providers defined by a payment brand as eligible to complete an SAQ.

Completing the SAQ

To achieve compliance, the response to each question must either be "yes" or an explanation of a compensating control.

Compensating controls are allowed when an organization cannot implement a specification but has sufficiently addressed the intent using an alternate method. If an entity cannot provide affirmative responses, it is still required to submit an SAQ.

To complete the validation process, the entity submits the SAQ and an accompanying Attestation of Compliance stating that it is or is not compliant with the PCI DSS. If the attestation indicates noncompliance, a target date for compliance along with an action plan needs to be provided. The attestation must be signed by an executive officer.

Are There Penalties for Noncompliance?

There are three types of fines that can be applied to all organizations under PCI regulation:

- PCI noncompliance
- Account Data Compromise Recovery (ADCR) for compromised domestic-issued cards
- Data Compromise Recovery Solution (DCRS) for compromised international-issued cards

Noncompliance penalties are discretionary and can vary greatly, depending on the circumstances. They are not openly discussed or publicized.

FYI: Two Major Credit Card Breach Reports in Less than Two Weeks

Nowadays, data breaches happen practically daily. For example, on March 20, 2018, CNN reported that threat actors stole information from more than 5 million credit and debit cards used at Saks Fifth Avenue, Saks Off 5th, and Lord & Taylor stores. The parent company, Hudson Bay, added that the cards were used for in-store purchases, and there is "no indication" online purchases were affected.

A cybersecurity firm called Gemini Advisory was the one that originally identified the breach. According to Gemini Advisory, the same threat actors that compromised Saks Fifth Avenue, Saks Off 5th, and Lord & Taylor stores were also behind data breaches that affected companies including Whole Foods, Chipotle, Omni Hotels & Resorts, and Trump Hotels.

Less than two weeks after this report, Orbitz disclosed a data breach that affected 880,000 credit cards from its consumers. Reports indicated that threat actors put credit and debit card information they obtained from the victims up for sale on the dark web almost immediately after they were exfiltrated.

Fines and Penalties

More financially significant than PCI noncompliance fines, a data compromise could result in ADCR and/or DCRS penalties. Due to the structure of the payment system, if there is a merchant compromise, the payment brands impose the penalties on the bank that issued the account. The banks pass all liability downstream to the entity. The fines may be up to $500,000 per incident. In addition, the entity may be liable for the following:

- All fraud losses perpetrated using the account numbers associated with the compromise (from date of compromise forward)

- Cost of reissuance of cards associated with the compromise (approximately $50 per card)

- Any additional fraud prevention/detection costs incurred by credit card issuers associated with the compromise (that is, additional monitoring of system for fraudulent activity)

- Increased transaction fees

At their discretion, the brands may designate any size compromised merchants as Level 1, which requires an annual onsite compliance assessment. Acquiring banks may choose to terminate the relationship.

Alternately, the payment brands may waive fines in the event of a data compromise if there is no evidence of noncompliance with PCI DSS and brand rules. According to Visa, "to prevent fines, a merchant must maintain full compliance at all times, including at the time of breach as demonstrated during a forensic investigation. Additionally, a merchant must demonstrate that prior to the compromise, the compromised entity had already met the compliance validation requirements, demonstrating full compliance." This is an impossibly high standard to meet. In reality, uniformly when there has been a breach, the brands have declared the merchant to be noncompliant.

> **FYI: Home Depot Pays Banks $25 Million in Data Settlement**
>
> In March 2017, Home Depot agreed to pay $25 million to banks on a settlement in the federal court in Atlanta. The settlement also mandates that Home Depot must tighten its cybersecurity practices and overall security posture. According to Fortune Magazine, in addition to the $25 million settlement, Home Depot has also paid at least $134.5 million in compensation to consortiums made up of Visa, MasterCard, and various banks.

Summary

The Payment Card Industry Data Security Standard, known as PCI DSS, applies to all entities involved in the payment card channel, including merchants, processors, financial institutions, and service providers, as well as all other entities that store, process, or transmit cardholder data and/or sensitive authentication data. The PCI DSS framework includes stipulations regarding storage, transmission, and processing of payment card data, six core principles, 12 categories of required technical and operational security controls, testing requirements, and a validation and certification process. Entities are required to validate their compliance. The number of transactions, the type of business, and the type of transactions determine specific validation requirements.

Compliance with PCI DSS is a payment card channel contractual obligation. It is not a government regulation or law. The requirement to be PCI-compliant is mandated by the payment card brands in order to accept card payments and/or be part of the payment system. PCI standards augment but do not supersede legislative or regulatory requirements to protect PII or other data elements. Overall, the PCI DSS requirements are reflective of cybersecurity best practices.

Test Your Skills

MULTIPLE CHOICE QUESTIONS

1. The majority of payment card fraud is borne by _____.

    A. consumers

    B. banks, merchants, and card processors

    C. Visa and MasterCard

    D. all of the above

2. Which of the following statements best describes an acquirer?

    A. Entity that acquires other banks and merchants

    B. Entity that initiates and maintains relationships with consumers

    C. Entity that initiates and maintains relationships with merchants for the acceptance of payment cards

    D. Entity that protects consumers every time that they acquire services and goods

3. A skimmer can be used to read _____.

    A. the cardholder data

    B. sensitive authentication data

    C. the associated PIN

    D. all of the above

4. According to PCI DDS, which of the following is true of the primary account number (PAN)?

   A. It must never be stored.

   B. It can be stored only in an unreadable (encrypted) format.

   C. It should be indexed.

   D. It can be stored in plain text.

5. Which of the following describes a merchant according to PCI DSS?

   A. Any entity that accepts payment cards bearing the logos of any of the five members of PCI SSC

   B. Any entity that enforces the PCI DSS standard

   C. Any entity that sells training about the PCI DSS standard

   D. Any entity that works with banks and credit card companies to enhance the PCI DSS standard

6. Which of the following tasks is the PCI Security Standards Council *not* responsible for?

   A. Creating a standard framework

   B. Certifying ASVs and QSAs

   C. Providing training and educational materials

   D. Enforcing PCI compliance

7. Which of the following statements is *not* true about the Luhn algorithm?

   A. The Luhn algorithm is an industry algorithm used to validate different identification numbers, including credit card numbers, International Mobile Equipment Identity (IMEI) numbers, National Provider Identifier numbers in the United States, Canadian Social Insurance Numbers, and more.

   B. The Luhn algorithm is now in the public domain.

   C. The Luhn algorithm is now obsolete.

   D. The Luhn algorithm is used by many organizations to validate valid numbers and it uses modulo-10 mathematics.

8. Which of the following statements is not true about the business-as-usual approach?

   A. PCI DSS version 3.2 emphasizes that compliance is not a point-in-time determination but rather an ongoing process.

   B. Business-as-usual is defined as the inclusion of PCI controls as part of an overall risk-based security strategy that is managed and monitored by the organization.

C. Business-as-usual specifies that organizations must monitor required controls to ensure they are operating effectively, respond quickly to control failures, incorporate PCI compliance impact assessments into the change-management process, and conduct periodic reviews to confirm that PCI requirements continue to be in place and that personnel are following secure processes.

D. Business-as-usual specifies that organizations can optionally monitor cybersecurity controls and conduct periodic reviews for management to determine if they have the appropriate workforce to respond to cybersecurity incidents.

9. Per the PCI Council, the version 3.2 updates are intended to do which of the following?

A. Provide stronger focus on some of the greater risk areas in the threat environment.

B. Build greater understanding of the intent of the requirements and how to apply them.

C. Improve flexibility for all entities implementing, assessing, and building to the standards.

D. All of the above.

10. Which of the following statements best describes the PAN?

A. If the PAN is not stored, processed, or transmitted, then PCI DSS requirements do not apply.

B. If the PAN is not stored, processed, or transmitted, then PCI DSS requirements apply only to e-commerce merchants.

C. If the PAN is not stored, processed, or transmitted, then PCI DSS requirements apply only to Level 1 merchants.

D. None of the above.

11. Which of the following statements best describe the cardholder data environment?

A. The people, processes, and technology that handle cardholder data or sensitive authentication data

B. The bank that processes the cardholder information

C. The merchant that processes the cardholder information

D. The retailer that processes the cardholder information

12. The terms CAV2, CID, CVC2, and CVV2 all refer to the _____.

A. authentication data

B. security codes

C. expiration date

D. account number

13. There are 12 categories of PCI standards. To be considered compliant, an entity must comply with or document compensating controls for _____.

  A. all of the requirements

  B. 90% of the requirements

  C. 80% of the requirements

  D. 70% of the requirements

14. Which of the following is *not* considered a basic firewall function?

  A. Ingress filtering

  B. Packet encryption

  C. Egress filtering

  D. Perimeter protection

15. Which of the following is considered a secure transmission technology?

  A. FTP

  B. HTTP

  C. Telnet

  D. SFTP

16. Which of the following statements best describes key management?

  A. Key management refers to the generation, storage, and protection of encryption keys.

  B. Key management refers to the generation, storage, and protection of server room keys.

  C. Key management refers to the generation, storage, and protection of access control list keys.

  D. Key management refers to the generation, storage, and protection of card manufacturing keys.

17. Which of the following methods is an acceptable manner in which a merchant can transmit a PAN?

  A. Using cellular texting

  B. Using an HTTPS/TLS session

  C. Using instant messaging

  D. Using email

18. Which of the following statements is not part of the "protect stored card data" requirement?

   A. Protecting and managing encryption keys (including generation, storage, access, renewal, and replacement)

   B. Publishing data-disposal policies and related operational procedures

   C. Publishing data-handling standards that clearly delineate how cardholder data is to be handled

   D. Selecting an antivirus/antimalware solution commensurate with the level of protection required

19. Which of the following documents lists injection flaws, broken authentication, and cross-site scripting as the top 10 application security vulnerabilities?

   A. ISACA Top Ten

   B. NIST Top Ten

   C. OWASP Top Ten

   D. ISO Top Ten

20. Which of the following security principles is best described as the assigning of the minimum required permissions?

   A. Need-to-know

   B. Default deny

   C. Least privilege

   D. Separation of duties

21. Which of the following is part of the "develop and maintain secure systems and architecture" PCI DSS requirement?

   A. Keeping up-to-date on new vulnerabilities

   B. Assessing the risk of new vulnerabilities

   C. Maintaining a patch management process

   D. All of the above

22. Skimmers can be installed and used to read cardholder data entered at _____.

   A. point-of-sale systems

   B. ATMs

   C. gas pumps

   D. all of the above

23. Which of the following is not part of the "track and monitor all access to network resources and cardholder data" PCI DSS requirement?

    A. Keeping logs up-to-date to identify new security vulnerability patches

    B. Ensuring the date and time stamps are accurate and synchronized across all audit logs

    C. Securing audit logs so they cannot be deleted or modified

    D. Limiting access to audit logs to individuals with a need to know

24. Quarterly external network scans must be performed by a _____.

    A. managed service provider

    B. PCI Approved Scanning Vendor (ASV)

    C. Qualified Security Assessor

    D. independent third party

25. In keeping with the best practices set forth by the PCI standard, how often should cybersecurity policies be reviewed, updated, and authorized?

    A. Once

    B. Semi-annually

    C. Annually

    D. Biannually

26. Which of the following is true of PCI requirements?

    A. PCI standards augment but do not supersede legislative or regulatory requirements to protect personally identifiable information (PII) or other data elements.

    B. PCI standards supersede legislative or regulatory requirements to protect personally identifiable information (PII) or other data elements.

    C. PCI requirements invalidate regulatory requirements.

    D. None of the above.

27. Which of the following is true about Level 1 merchants versus Levels 2–4 merchants?

    A. Level 1 merchants process more than six million payment card transactions annually.

    B. Level 1 merchants must pay a fee greater than $6 million.

    C. Level 1 merchants must have biannual external penetration testing.

    D. Level 1 merchants must complete a self-assessment questionnaire or pay a fine of more than $100,000.

28. PCI DSS version 3.2 incorporates DESV as an appendix primarily to merge requirements and to strengthen the importance of these requirements in establishing and maintaining ongoing cybersecurity processes. DESV is a list of resources and criteria that is designed to help service providers and merchants address key operational challenges while trying to protect payments and maintain compliance. Which of the following is not included in DESV?

   A. Compliance program oversight

   B. Proper scoping of an environment

   C. Guaranteeing that proper mechanisms are used to detect and alert on failures in critical security control

   D. The creation of public security vulnerability disclosure policies

29. Which of the following statements best describes the reason different versions of the SAQ are necessary?

   A. The number of questions varies by payment card channel and scope of environment.

   B. The number of questions varies by geographic location.

   C. The number of questions varies by card brand.

   D. The number of questions varies by dollar value of transactions.

30. Which of the following SAQs do not apply to e-commerce merchants?

   A. SAQ-C

   B. SAQ-B

   C. SAQ C-VT

   D. All of the above

EXERCISES

EXERCISE 15.1: Understanding PCI DSS Obligations

1. Compliance with PCI DSS is a contractual obligation. Explain how this differs from a regulatory obligation.

2. Which takes precedence—a regulatory requirement or a contractual obligation? Explain your answer.

3. Who enforces PCI compliance? How is it enforced?

EXERCISE 15.2: **Understanding Cardholder Liabilities**

1. What should a consumer do if he or she misplaces a debit card? Why?

2. Go online to your bank's website. Does it post instructions on how to report a lost or stolen debit or credit card? If yes, summarize their instructions. If no, call the bank and request the information be sent to you. (If you don't have a bank account, choose a local financial institution.)

3. Explain the difference between the Fair Credit Billing Act (FCBA) and the Electronic Fund Transfer Act (EFTA).

EXERCISE 15.3: **Choosing an Authorized Scanning Vendor**

1. PCI security scans are required for all merchants and service providers with Internet-facing IP addresses. Go online and locate three PCI Council Authorized Scanning Vendors (ASVs) that offer quarterly PCI security scans.

2. Read their service descriptions. What are the similarities and differences?

3. Recommend one of the ASVs. Explain your reasoning.

EXERCISE 15.4: **Understanding PIN and Chip Technologies**

1. Payment cards issued in the United States store sensitive authentication information in the magnetic stripe. What are the issues associated with this configuration?

2. Payment cards issued in Europe store sensitive authentication information in an embedded microchip. What is the advantage of this configuration?

3. Certain U.S. financial institutions will provide a chip-embedded card upon request. Identify at least one card issuer who will do so. Does it charge extra for the card?

EXERCISE 15.5: **Identifying Merchant Compliance Validation Requirements**

Complete the following table:

Merchant Level	Criteria	Validation Requirement
	Processes fewer than 20,000 e-commerce transactions annually	
Level 2		
		Required onsite annual audit

PROJECTS

PROJECT 15.1: Applying Encryption Standards

Encryption is referenced a number of times in the PCI DSS standard. For each of the PCI requirements listed below:

1. Explain the rationale for the requirement.

2. Identify an encryption technology that can be used to satisfy the requirement.

3. Identify a commercial application that can be used to satisfy the requirement.

   - **PCI DSS V3.2. 3.4.1:** If disk encryption is used (rather than file- or column-level database encryption), logical access must be managed separately and independently of native operating system authentication and access control mechanisms (for example, by not using local user account databases or general network login credentials). Decryption keys must not be associated with user accounts.

   - **PCI DSS V3.2. 4.1.1:** Ensure wireless networks transmitting cardholder data or connected to the cardholder data environment are using strong encryption protocols for authentication and transmission and use industry best practices to implement strong encryption for authentication and transmission.

   - **PCI DSS V3.2 6.1:** Establish a process to identify security vulnerabilities, using reputable outside sources for security vulnerability information, and assign a risk ranking (for example, "high," "medium," or "low") to newly discovered security vulnerabilities.

PROJECT 15.2: Completing an SAQ

All major credit card companies have dedicated online portals to explain the way that they keep card member information safe and secure. The following are the links to the security portals for several major credit card companies:

   - American Express: https://merchant-channel.americanexpress.com//merchant/en_US/data-security

   - Discover Card: https://www.discovernetwork.com/en-us/business-resources/fraud-security/pci-rules-regulations/

   - JCB Card: www.global.jcb/en/products/security/pci-dss/

   - MasterCard: https://www.mastercard.us/en-us/merchants/safety-security/security-recommendations/site-data-protection-PCI.html

   - VISA: https://usa.visa.com/support/small-business/security-compliance.html

1. What are the differences and similarities among the information provided by these credit card companies? Describe how they document and address PCI DSS compliance.

2. Explain how they document requirements that apply to both merchants and service providers.

3. Does each company clearly list how anyone can report a security incident?

PROJECT 15.3: Reporting an Incident

Assume you are a Level 2 merchant and your organization suspects a breach of Visa cardholder information.

1. Go to http://usa.visa.com/merchants/risk_management/cisp_if_compromised.html. Document the steps you should take.

2. Does your state have a breach notification law? If so, would you be required to report this type of breach to a state authority? Would you be required to notify customers? What would you need to do if you had customers who lived in a neighboring state?

3. Have there been any major card breaches within the last 12 months that affected residents of your state? Summarize such an event.

Case Study

Payment Card Data Breaches

More than 140 million consumers were impacted by the Equifax breach in 2017. Personal information such as social security numbers, birth dates, addresses, and driver license numbers were exposed. In addition, more than 209,000 credit card numbers were also stolen.

Earlier in 2014, more than 56 million credit and debit card data records were stolen by threat actors from Home Depot. Point-of-sale systems were infected by malware.

Research both events and answer the following questions:

A. Equifax

1. What are the dates of the incident?

2. Who first reported the breach?

3. What information was compromised?

4. How many cardholders were affected?

5. How did Equifax notify cardholders?

6. Is there any indication of how the data was acquired?

7. Is there any evidence that the criminals used the card data?

B. Home Deport

   1. Who first reported the incident?

   2. What are the dates associated with the compromise?

   3. What information was compromised?

   4. How many cardholders were affected?

   5. Is there any indication of how the data was acquired?

   6. Were losses sustained by any organization other than Home Depot?

   7. What type of notification was required?

C. Prior to the breach, both of these organizations were PCI-compliant organizations. Should a card data compromise be a trigger for decertification? Why or why not?

References

"The 17 Biggest Data Breaches of the 21st Century," *CSO Magazine*, accessed 04/2018, https://www.csoonline.com/article/2130877/data-breach/the-biggest-data-breaches-of-the-21st-century.html.

Verizon Data Breach Investigations Reports, accessed 04/2018, http://www.verizonenterprise.com/verizon-insights-lab/dbir/.

"PCI Standards and Cardholder Data Security," Wells Fargo, accessed 04/2018, https://www.wellsfargo.com/biz/merchant/manage/standards.

Krebs, Brian. "All about Skimmers," accessed 04/2018, https://krebsonsecurity.com/all-about-skimmers.

"Genesco, Inc. v. VISA U.S.A., Inc., VISA Inc., and VISA International Service Association," United States District Court for the Middle District of Tennessee, Nashville Division, filed March 7, 2013, Case 3:13-cv-00202.

Credit Freeze FAQs, The Federal Trade Commission, accessed 04/2018, https://www.consumer.ftc. gov/articles/0497-credit-freeze-faqs.

"Merchant PCI DSS Compliance," Visa, accessed 04/2018, http://usa.visa.com/merchants/risk_ management/cisp_merchants.html.

"Payment Card Industry Data Security Standard, Version 3.2," PCI Security Standards Council, LLC, accessed 04/2018, https://www.pcisecuritystandards.org/documents/PCI_DSS_v3-2.pdf.

"Payment Card Industry Data Security Standard, SAQ documents," PCI Security Standards Council LLC, accessed 04/2018, https://www.pcisecuritystandards.org/document_ library?category=saqs#results.

"Payment Card Industry Data Security Standard, Training and Certification," PCI Security Standards Council, LLC, accessed 04/2018, https://www.pcisecuritystandards.org/program_training_and_ qualification/.

"Payment Card Industry Data Security Standard, Glossary of Terms, Abbreviations, and Acronyms," accessed 04/2018, https://www.pcisecuritystandards.org/documents/PCI_DSS_Glossary_v3-2.pdf.

"PCI DSS Quick Reference Guide", PCI SSC, accessed 04/2018, https://www.pcisecuritystandards.org/ documents/PCIDSS_QRGv3_2.pdf.

"Payment Card Industry Data Security Standard and Payment Application Data Security Standard, Version 3.2: Change Highlights," PCI Security Standards Council, LLC, August 2013.

"Credit Card Breach at Buckle Stores," Brian Krebs, accessed 04/2018, https://krebsonsecurity. com/2017/06/credit-card-breach-at-buckle-stores.

"Largest Hacking Fraud Case Launched After Credit Card Info Stolen from J.C. Penney, Visa Licensee," *The Huffington Post*, accessed 04/2018, https://www.huffingtonpost.com/2013/07/25/ credit-card-stolen-visa_n_3653274.html.

"Home Depot to Pay Banks $25 Million in Data Breach Settlement," *Fortune Magazine*, accessed 04/2018, http://fortune.com/2017/03/09/home-depot-data-breach-banks.

"The Costs of Failing a PCI-DSS Audit," Hytrust, accessed 04/2018, https://www.hytrust.com/ wp-content/uploads/2015/08/HyTrust_Cost_of_Failed_Audit.pdf.

OWASP Top 10 Project, accessed 04/2018, https://www.owasp.org/index.php/Category:OWASP_ Top_Ten_Project.

"Payment Card Industry (PCI) Data Security Standard Self-Assessment Questionnaire, Instructions and Guidelines," PCI SSC, accessed 04/2018, https://www.pcisecuritystandards.org/documents/SAQ-InstrGuidelines-v3_2.pdf.

"Saks, Lord & Taylor Breach: Data Stolen on 5 Million Cards," CNN, accessed 04/2018, http://money.cnn.com/2018/04/01/technology/saks-hack-credit-debit-card/index.html.

"Orbitz Says a Possible Data Breach Has Affected 880,000 Credit Cards," The Verge, accessed 04/2018, https://www.theverge.com/2018/3/20/17144482/orbitz-data-breach-credit-cards.

Chapter 16

NIST Cybersecurity Framework

Chapter Objectives

After reading this chapter and completing the exercises, you will be able to do the following:

- Understand the overall goal of the NIST Cybersecurity Framework.
- Identify the Framework's Core, Profile, and Implementation Tiers.
- Explain how the NIST Cybersecurity Framework can be used by any organization as a reference to develop a cybersecurity program.

NIST's Cybersecurity Framework is a collection of industry standards and best practices to help organizations manage cybersecurity risks. This framework is created in collaboration among the United States government, corporations, and individuals. The NIST Cybersecurity Framework is developed with a common taxonomy, and one of the main goals is to address and manage cybersecurity risk in a cost-effective way to protect critical infrastructure. Although designed for a specific constituency, the requirements can serve as a security blueprint for any organization.

FYI: Executive Order 13636, "Improving Critical Infrastructure Cybersecurity"

United States Executive Order 13636, "Improving Critical Infrastructure Cybersecurity," was created in February 2013, and tasked NIST to develop a *voluntary* framework that is centered on existing standards, guidelines, and practices. The main goal is to reduce cybersecurity-related risks to the United States critical infrastructure. Later in 2014, the Cybersecurity Enhancement Act of 2014 reinforced the role of NIST developing such a framework.

Section 7 of Executive Order 13636, "Baseline Framework to Reduce Cyber Risk to Critical Infrastructure," dictates that "the Cybersecurity Framework shall include a set of standards, methodologies, procedures, and processes that align policy, business, and technological approaches to address cyber risks. The Cybersecurity Framework shall incorporate voluntary consensus standards and industry best practices to the fullest extent possible. The Cybersecurity Framework shall be consistent with voluntary international standards when such international standards will advance the objectives of this order, and shall meet the requirements of the National Institute of Standards and Technology Act, as amended (15 U.S.C. 271 et seq.), the National Technology Transfer and Advancement Act of 1995 (Public Law 104-113), and OMB Circular A-119, as revised."

The Executive Order also specifies that the framework "shall provide a prioritized, flexible, repeatable, performance-based, and cost-effective approach, including information security measures and controls, to help owners and operators of critical infrastructure identify, assess, and manage cyber risk." In addition, the framework "shall focus on identifying cross-sector security standards and guidelines applicable to critical infrastructure" and also identify areas for improvement that should be addressed through future collaboration with particular sectors and standards-developing organizations.

Section 10 of the Executive Order includes direction regarding the adoption of the framework among government agencies.

Private sector organizations are often motivated to implement the NIST Cybersecurity Framework to enhance their cybersecurity programs. These organizatiosn often follow the NIST Cybersecurity Framework guidance to lower their cybersecurity-related risks.

In this chapter, we examine the NIST Cybersecurity Framework and discover how it can serve as a security blueprint for any organization attempting to create a security program and analyze its cybersecurity risk.

Introducing the NIST Cybersecurity Framework Components

The NIST Cybersecurity Framework was created through collaboration between industry and government. It consists of standards, guidelines, and practices to promote the protection of critical infrastructure. The prioritized, flexible, repeatable, and cost-effective approach of the framework helps owners and operators of critical infrastructure to manage cybersecurity-related risk.

As mentioned in Chapter 3, "Cybersecurity Framework," one of the goals of NIST's Cybersecurity Framework is to not only help the United States government, but provide guidance to any organization regardless of size, degree of cybersecurity risk, or maturity.

Another thing to highlight is that NIST's Cybersecurity Framework is a living document and will continue to be updated and improved as participants provide feedback on implementation. The latest version of the framework can be obtained at www.nist.gov/cyberframework.

This framework is built from standards, guidelines, and practices to provide a common guidance for organizations to be able to do the following:

- Describe their current cybersecurity posture.

- Describe their target state for cybersecurity.

- Identify and prioritize opportunities for improvement within the context of a continuous and repeatable process.

- Assess progress toward the target state.

- Communicate among internal and external stakeholders about cybersecurity risk.

NIST is very clear that the framework is aimed to complement an existing risk management process and cybersecurity program of your organization. It does not replace such a process or program. You can take advantage of the NIST Cybersecurity Framework to help strengthen your policies and programs by following industry best practices. If your organization does not have an existing cybersecurity program, you can use the NIST Cybersecurity Framework as a reference to develop such a program.

> **Note**
>
> Even though the NIST Cybersecurity Framework was created in the United States, this framework is also used outside of the United States.

NIST's Cybersecurity Framework is divided into three parts, as illustrated in Figure 16-1.

- The Framework Core is "a collection of cybersecurity activities, outcomes, and informative references that are common across critical infrastructure sectors, providing the detailed guidance for developing individual organizational Profiles."

- The Framework Profiles are designed to help the underlying organization align its cybersecurity undertakings with business requirements, risk tolerances, and resources.

- The Framework Tiers are designed to help organizations to view and understand the characteristics of their approach to managing cybersecurity risk.

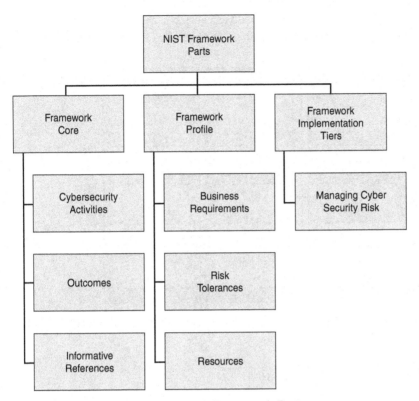

FIGURE 16-1   NIST's Cybersecurity Framework Parts

The Framework Core

The Framework Core is aimed to structure a list of activities to reach certain cybersecurity outcomes and include examples of guidance to achieve such outcomes.

Figure 16-2 lists the functions defined in the NIST Cybersecurity Framework Core.

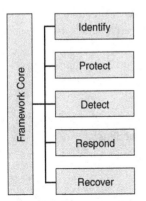

FIGURE 16-2   NIST's Cybersecurity Framework Core Functions

Then the Framework Core is decomposed even further with categories, subcategories, and informative references for each of the framework functions, as illustrated in Figure 16-3.

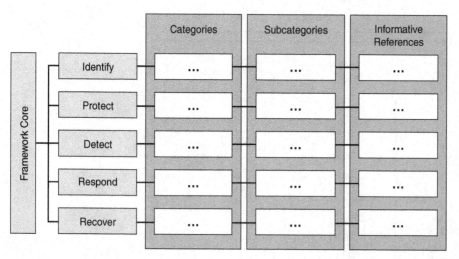

FIGURE 16-3   NIST's Cybersecurity Framework Core Function Categories, Subcategories, and Informative References

The following are the elements illustrated in Figure 16-3:

- Categories group the elements of a function into collections of cybersecurity outcomes, including things like asset management, identity management and access control, security continuous monitoring, response planning, and many more.

- Subcategories are a list of specific outcomes of technical and/or management activities within each category. They can be considered as a set of results to aid in achieving the outcomes of each category.

- Informative references point to industry standards, guidelines, and practices that are beneficial for an organization trying to achieve the outcomes associated with each subcategory. NIST categorizes these informative references as "illustrative and not exhaustive." The informative references are based upon "cross-sector guidance most frequently referenced during the Framework development process." You can even submit a reference for consideration following the instructions outlined at the following site: https://www.nist.gov/cyberframework/reference-submission-page.

The following sections define each of the NIST Cybersecurity Framework functions.

Identify

The Identify function includes the categories and subcategories that define what processes and assets need protection. It is used to develop an understanding in order to analyze and manage cybersecurity risk to systems, assets, data, and capabilities. Figure 16-4 shows the Identify function categories.

FIGURE 16-4   NIST's Cybersecurity Framework Identify Function Categories

In Chapter 5, "Asset Management and Data Loss Prevention," you learned the details about asset management and that assets include personnel, data, devices, systems, and facilities. The NIST Cybersecurity Framework states that assets "enable the organization to achieve business purposes that are identified and managed consistent with their relative importance to business objectives and the organization's risk strategy."

The Business Environment category addresses the need for an organization's mission, objectives, stakeholders, and activities to be comprehended and prioritized. The NIST Cybersecurity Framework specifies that "this information is used to inform cybersecurity roles, responsibilities, and risk management decisions."

The Governance category's purpose is to make sure that the policies, procedures, and processes to manage and monitor the organization's regulatory, legal, risk, environmental, and operational requirements are well comprehended within the organization.

The Risk Assessment category addresses the identification and analysis of cybersecurity risk to the organization's operations, assets, and individuals. The Risk Management Strategy category specifies the establishment of the organization's priorities, constraints, risk tolerances, and assumptions in order to make appropriate operational risk decisions.

The Supply Chain Risk Management category was introduced in NIST Cybersecurity Framework version 1.1, and it specifies that the organization must establish priorities, constraints, risk tolerances, and assumptions in order to make appropriate risk decisions associated with managing supply chain risk. This category was included as a result of the increase of supply chain–based attacks.

FYI: NIST Cybersecurity Framework Spreadsheet

NIST created a spreadsheet that allows you to start reviewing and documenting each of the framework's functions, categories, subcategories, and informative references. The spreadsheet is shown in Figure 16-5 and can be downloaded from https://www.nist.gov/cyberframework.

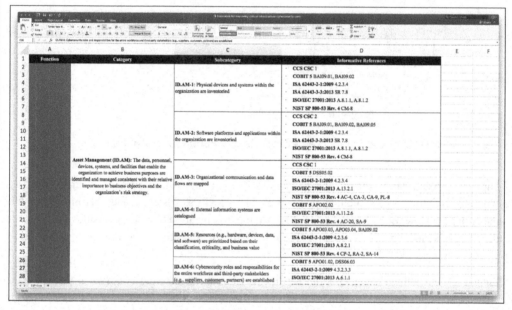

FIGURE 16-5   NIST's Cybersecurity Framework Spreadsheet

Protect

The Protect category of the Identify function demands the development and implementation of relevant safeguards to make sure that critical infrastructure services are protected. Figure 16-6 shows the Protect categories.

The Identity Management, Authentication and Access Control category specifies that physical and logical assets and associated facilities be available only to authorized users, processes, and devices and is "managed consistent with the assessed risk of unauthorized access to authorized activities and transactions."

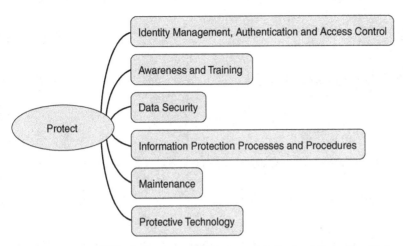

FIGURE 16-6   NIST's Cybersecurity Framework Protect Function Categories

In Chapter 6, "Human Resources Security," you learned the importance of cybersecurity awareness and training. The Awareness and Training category addresses cybersecurity awareness education and demands that your employees be adequately trained to perform their information security–related duties and responsibilities consistent with related policies, procedures, and agreements. The following NIST Special Publications provide guidance on how to develop appropriate cybersecurity awareness training.

- **SP 800-16:** Information Technology Security Training Requirements: A Role- and Performance-Based Model
- **SP 800-50:** Building an Information Technology Security Awareness and Training Program

The Data Security category provides guidance around data management practices in order to protect the confidentiality, integrity, and availability of such data. The Information Protection Processes and Procedures category addresses the need for appropriate policies, processes, and procedures to manage protection of information systems and assets. The Maintenance category provides guidance on how to perform maintenance and repairs of industrial control and information system components. The Protective Technology category provides guidance around the technical implementations used to secure your systems and assets, consistent with the organization's policies, procedures, and agreements.

Detect

The NIST Cybersecurity Framework Detect category specifies the need to develop and implement a good cybersecurity program to be able to detect any cybersecurity events and incidents. Figure 16-7 shows the Detect function categories.

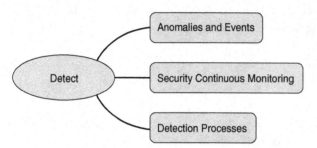

FIGURE 16-7   NIST's Cybersecurity Framework Detect Function Categories

Respond

In Chapter 11, "Cybersecurity Incident Response," you learned the different steps required to have a good incident response process and program within your organization. The guidance in the Detect, Response, and Recover categories are in alignment with the concepts you learned in Chapter 11. Figure 16-8 shows the Respond function categories.

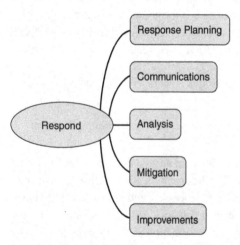

FIGURE 16-8   NIST's Cybersecurity Framework Respond Function Categories

Recover

The Recover category provides guidance on how to recover normal operations after a cybersecurity incident. Figure 16-9 shows the Recover function categories.

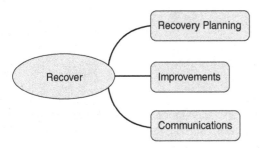

FIGURE 16-9   NIST's Cybersecurity Framework Recover Function Categories

NIST and the cybersecurity community stakeholders are always improving the framework. NIST maintains a roadmap outlining areas for development and future framework features; it can be accessed at https://www.nist.gov/cyberframework/related-efforts-roadmap.

Framework Implementation Tiers ("Tiers")

The NIST Cybersecurity Framework Tiers provide guidance to allow organizations to analyze cybersecurity risk and to enhance their processes to manage such risk. These tiers describe how your risk management practices align with the characteristics defined in the framework. Figure 16-10 lists the four Framework Implementation Tiers.

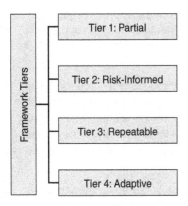

FIGURE 16-10   NIST's Cybersecurity Framework Tiers

Each of the tiers is then further defined in four categories:

- Risk Management Process
- Integrated Risk Management Program
- External Participation
- Cyber Supply Chain Risk Management

NIST Framework Tier Definitions

The following are NIST's definitions for each of the framework's tiers.

Tier 1: Partial

- **Risk Management Process:** Organizational cybersecurity risk management practices are not formalized, and risk is managed in an ad hoc and sometimes reactive manner. Prioritization of cybersecurity activities may not be directly informed by organizational risk objectives, the threat environment, or business/mission requirements.

- **Integrated Risk Management Program:** There is limited awareness of cybersecurity risk at the organizational level. The organization implements cybersecurity risk management on an irregular, case-by-case basis due to varied experience or information gained from outside sources. The organization may not have processes that enable cybersecurity information to be shared within the organization.

- **External Participation:** An organization may not have the processes in place to participate in coordination or collaboration with other entities.

- **Cyber Supply Chain Risk Management:** An organization may not understand the full implications of cyber supply chain risks or have the processes in place to identify, assess, and mitigate its cyber supply chain risks.

Tier 2: Risk-Informed

- **Risk Management Process:** Risk management practices are approved by management but may not be established as organizationwide policy. Prioritization of cybersecurity activities is directly informed by organizational risk objectives, the threat environment, or business/mission requirements.

- **Integrated Risk Management Program:** There is an awareness of cybersecurity risk at the organizational level, but an organizationwide approach to managing cybersecurity risk has not been established. Cybersecurity information is shared within the organization on an informal basis. Consideration of cybersecurity in mission/business objectives may occur at some levels of the organization, but not at all levels. Cyber risk assessment of organizational assets is not typically repeatable or reoccurring.

- **External Participation:** The organization knows its role in the larger ecosystem, but has not formalized its capabilities to interact and share information externally.

- **Cyber Supply Chain Risk Management:** The organization understands the cyber supply chain risks associated with the products and services that either support the business/ mission function of the organization or that are utilized in the organization's products or services. The organization has not formalized its capabilities to manage cyber supply chain risks internally or with its suppliers and partners and performs these activities inconsistently.

Tier 3: Repeatable

- **Risk Management Process:** The organization's risk management practices are formally approved and expressed as policy. Organizational cybersecurity practices are regularly updated based on the application of risk management processes to changes in business/mission requirements and a changing threat and technology landscape.

- **Integrated Risk Management Program:** There is an organizationwide approach to manage cybersecurity risk. Risk-informed policies, processes, and procedures are defined, implemented as intended, and reviewed. Consistent methods are in place to respond effectively to changes in risk. Personnel possess the knowledge and skills to perform their appointed roles and responsibilities. The organization consistently and accurately monitors cybersecurity risk of organizational assets. Senior cybersecurity and noncybersecurity executives communicate regularly regarding cybersecurity risk. Senior executives ensure consideration of cybersecurity through all lines of operation in the organization.

- **External Participation:** The organization understands its dependencies and partners and receives information from these partners that enables collaboration and risk-based management decisions within the organization in response to events.

- **Cyber Supply Chain Risk Management:** An organizationwide approach to managing cyber supply chain risks is enacted via enterprise risk management policies, processes, and procedures. This likely includes a governance structure (for example, Risk Council) that manages cyber supply chain risks in balance with other enterprise risks. Policies, processes, and procedures are implemented consistently, as intended, and continuously monitored and reviewed. Personnel possess the knowledge and skills to perform their appointed cyber supply chain risk management responsibilities. The organization has formal agreements in place to communicate baseline requirements to its suppliers and partners.

Tier 4: Adaptive

- **Risk Management Process:** The organization adapts its cybersecurity practices based on lessons learned and predictive indicators derived from previous and current cybersecurity activities. Through a process of continuous improvement incorporating advanced cybersecurity technologies and practices, the organization actively adapts to a changing cybersecurity landscape and responds to evolving and sophisticated threats in a timely manner.

- **Integrated Risk Management Program:** There is an organizationwide approach to managing cybersecurity risk that uses risk-informed policies, processes, and procedures to address potential cybersecurity events. The relationship between cybersecurity risk and mission/business objectives is clearly understood and considered when making decisions. Senior executives monitor cybersecurity risk in the same context as financial risk and other organizational risks. The organizational budget is based on understanding of current and predicted risk environment and future risk appetites. Business units implement executive vision and analyze system level risks in the context of the organizational risk appetite and tolerances. Cybersecurity risk management is part of the organizational culture and evolves from an awareness of previous activities, information shared by other sources, and continuous awareness of activities on its systems and networks. Cybersecurity risk is clearly articulated and understood across all strata of the enterprise. The organization can quickly and efficiently account for changes to business/mission objectives and threat and technology landscapes in how risk is communicated and approached.

- **External Participation:** The organization manages risk and actively shares information with partners to ensure that accurate, current information is being distributed and consumed to improve cybersecurity before a cybersecurity event occurs.

- **Cyber Supply Chain Risk Management:** The organization can quickly and efficiently account for emerging cyber supply chain risks using real-time or near real-time information and leveraging an institutionalized knowledge of cyber supply chain risk management with its external suppliers and partners as well as internally, in related functional areas and at all levels of the organization. The organization communicates proactively and uses formal (for example, agreements) and informal mechanisms to develop and maintain strong relationships with its suppliers, partners, and individual and organizational buyers.

Who Should Coordinate the Framework Implementation?

NIST defines three levels within an organization that should be engaged to coordinate the framework implementation and a common flow of information. Figure 16-11 illustrates these levels.

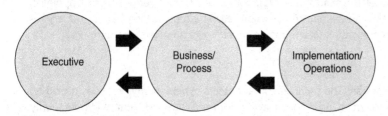

FIGURE 16-11   NIST's Cybersecurity Framework Coordination

As you can see in Figure 16-11, there is a feedback loop between the executive and the business/process levels and another feedback loop between the business/process and the implementation/operations levels.

- **Executive:** Communicates the mission priorities, available resources, and overall risk tolerance to the business/process level.

- **Business/process:** Obtains the executive level inputs into the risk management process, and then collaborates with the implementation/operations level.

- **Implementation/operations:** The stakeholders that are in charge of implementing the framework and communicating the implementation progress to the business/process level.

NIST's Recommended Steps to Establish or Improve a Cybersecurity Program

The following are the steps that NIST's Cybersecurity Framework recommends to establish or improve a cybersecurity program:

STEP 1.   **Prioritize and scope:** First you identify your business objectives and high-level organizational priorities. This must be accomplished first so that you can make strategic decisions regarding cybersecurity implementations and establish the scope of systems and assets that support the selected business line or process. Implementation tiers may be used to set fluctuating risk tolerances.

STEP 2.   **Orient** your strategy and consult predetermined sources to identify threats and vulnerabilities that may be applicable to your systems and assets.

STEP 3.   **Create a current profile** by defining which category or subcategory outcomes from the Framework Core are presently being achieved. NIST's Cybersecurity Framework suggests that you take note of any partially completed outcomes, because this will help you accomplish the steps that follow.

STEP 4.   **Conduct a risk assessment** analyzing your operational environment to identify any risks, and use cyber threat intelligence from internal and external sources to gain a better understanding of the potential impact of any cybersecurity incidents.

STEP 5.   **Create a target profile** for your organization that focuses on the assessment of the framework categories and subcategories, and make sure to describe your organization's cybersecurity goals and outcomes. You can develop your own additional categories and subcategories as appropriate in your environment.

STEP 6.   **Determine, analyze, and prioritize any gaps** in your environment based on the comparison of the Current Profile and the Target Profile. After you do this analysis, create a prioritized action plan to close all those gaps.

STEP 7.   **Implement the action plan** to close the gaps outlined in the previous steps and then monitor your current practices against the Target Profile. NIST's Cybersecurity Framework outlines example informative references regarding the categories and subcategories. You should determine which standards, guidelines, and practices, including those that are sector-specific, work best for your organization and environment.

You can repeat the aforementioned steps as needed to continuously monitor and improve your cybersecurity posture.

Communication with Stakeholders and Supply Chain Relationships

In Chapter 8, "Communications and Operations Security," you learned how communication is paramount for your cybersecurity program. NIST's Cybersecurity Framework provides a common language to communicate requirements with all the stakeholders within or outside your organization that are responsible for the delivery of essential critical infrastructure services. The following are the examples that the NIST Cybersecurity Framework provides:

- An organization may utilize a Target Profile to express cybersecurity risk management requirements to an external service provider (for example, a cloud provider to which it is exporting data).

- An organization may express its cybersecurity state through a Current Profile to report results or to compare with acquisition requirements.

- A critical infrastructure owner/operator, having identified an external partner on whom that infrastructure depends, may use a Target Profile to convey required categories and subcategories.

- A critical infrastructure sector may establish a Target Profile that can be used among its constituents as an initial baseline Profile to build their tailored Target Profiles.

Figure 16-12 illustrates NIST Cybersecurity Framework Cyber Supply Chain Relationship. These include communication with your suppliers, buyers, and non-information technology (IT) or non-operation technology (OT) partners.

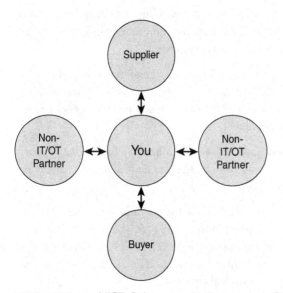

FIGURE 16-12   NIST Cybersecurity Framework Cyber Supply Chain Relationship

Buying decisions can even be influenced by your cybersecurity posture (from your buyers, if applicable) or the posture of your suppliers (when you are purchasing their goods or services). The framework's Target Profiles could be used to make these buying decisions, because these are a prioritized list of organizational cybersecurity requirements. The Profile also can allow you and your organization to make sure that all goods or services you purchase or those that you sell meet cybersecurity outcomes through continuous evaluation and testing methodologies.

NIST's Cybersecurity Framework Reference Tool

NIST created a tool, called the NIST Cybersecurity Framework (CSF) Reference Tool, that allows you to navigate through the framework components and references. This tool can be downloaded from

https://www.nist.gov/cyberframework/csf-reference-tool

The tool can run in Microsoft Windows and Apple Mac OS-X. Figure 16-13 shows the home screen of the CSF tool.

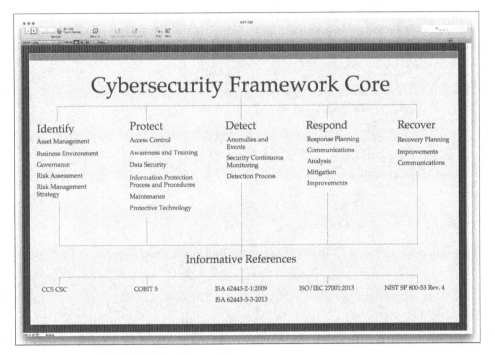

FIGURE 16-13 NIST CSF Tool Home Screen

NIST CSF Reference Tool provides a way for you to browse the Framework Core by

- Functions
- Categories
- Subcategories
- Informative references

Figure 16-14 shows the different views or categories you can explore in the tool.

FIGURE 16-14   NIST CSF Views Pull-Down Menu

Figure 16-15 provides an example of the NIST CSF Reference Tool views (the Cybersecurity Framework Core).

FIGURE 16-15   NIST CSF Cybersecurity Framework Core View

The NIST CSF Reference Tool also allows you to search for specific words and export the current viewed data to different file types, such as tab- or comma-separated text files or XML files, as shown in Figure 16-16.

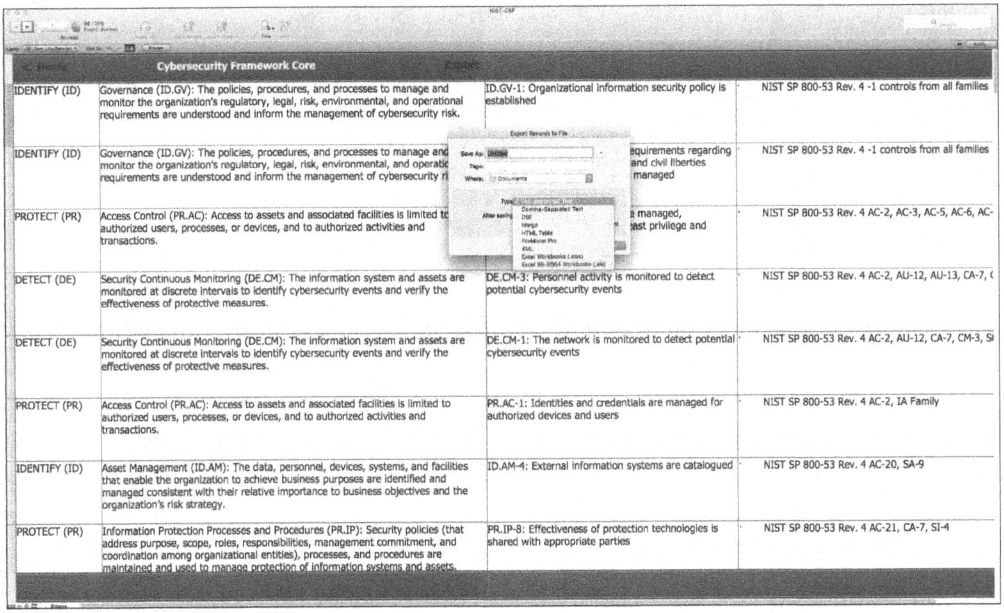

FIGURE 16-16   NIST CSF Export Capability

Adopting the NIST Cybersecurity Framework in Real Life

The NIST Cybersecurity Framework is often used by organizations of many sizes, because it provides guidance that can be very beneficial to establishing your own cybersecurity program and maintaining compliance with certain regulations. For example, in Chapter 14, "Regulatory Compliance for the Health-Care Sector," you learned that the United States Department of Health and Human Services has already aligned and mapped the components of the NIST Cybersecurity Framework with the Health Insurance Portability and Accountability Act (HIPAA) elements. Many organizations need to be compliant with the HIPAA Security Rule and the Payment Card Industry Data Security Standard, as well as their own cybersecurity policy. Many sections of these rules, policies, guidelines, and objectives can be aligned with the various functions, categories, and subcategories of the NIST Cybersecurity Framework Core.

By integrating cybersecurity requirements in this manner, an organization can determine where requirements overlap and, in some cases, may conflict. This allows you to consider alternative methodologies and probably modify your cybersecurity practices to address those requirements.

The NIST Cybersecurity Framework Core subcategory outcomes are meaningful for multiple requirements. For example, priorities can be captured in the structure framework and used as inputs to drive cybersecurity investments, effort, and focus. The work product of cybersecurity requirements management using the NIST Cybersecurity Framework is referred to as a Profile, as we discussed earlier in this chapter. Figure 16-17 provides a good overview of this process.

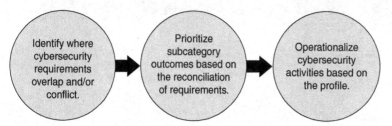

FIGURE 16-17   Operationalizing Cybersecurity Activities Based on the NIST Cybersecurity Framework

The NIST Cybersecurity Framework can also be used to translate among a variety of risk management practices and support your organization as you interact with a wide variety of suppliers (including service providers, product vendors, systems integrators, and other partners). For example, you can even use the framework during market research by asking vendors when responding to a Request for Information (RFI) to include something similar to their Cybersecurity Framework Profile or to express the cybersecurity capabilities of their offerings and organization.

The Implementation Tiers in the NIST Cybersecurity Framework are designed as an overarching measurement of cybersecurity risk management maturity. However, the Implementation Tiers are not prescriptive, as you may find in other maturity models. In addition, following the general guidance in the NIST Cybersecurity Framework allows you to assign cybersecurity responsibility to business units or individuals in an organization. You can specify tasks, responsibilities, and ownership of the cybersecurity program and its associated strategies.

Summary

The NIST Cybersecurity Framework is created in collaboration between the United States government, corporations, and individuals. The NIST Cybersecurity Framework is developed with a common taxonomy, and one of the main goals is to address and manage cybersecurity risk in a cost-effective way to protect critical infrastructure.

The NIST Cybersecurity Framework is aimed to complement an existing risk management process and cybersecurity program of your organization. It does not replace such a process or program. You can take advantage of the framework to help strengthen your policies and programs by following industry best practices. If your organization does not have an existing cybersecurity program, you can use the NIST Cybersecurity Framework as a reference to develop such a program.

In this chapter you learned the different parts of the NIST Cybersecurity Framework. The Framework Core is "a collection of cybersecurity activities, outcomes, and informative references that are common across critical infrastructure sectors, providing the detailed guidance for developing individual organizational Profiles." The Framework Profiles are designed to help the underlying organization align its cybersecurity undertakings with business requirements, risk tolerances, and resources. The Framework Tiers are designed to help organizations to view and understand the characteristics of their approach to managing cybersecurity risk. These tiers describe how your risk management practices align with the characteristics defined in the framework.

You also learned about tools that can be used to navigate through the NIST Cybersecurity Framework components and references. Last, you learned how an organization can align its cybersecurity programs and practices with the NIST Cybersecurity Framework.

Test Your Skills

MULTIPLE CHOICE QUESTIONS

1. The NIST Cybersecurity Framework is built from which of the following?

    A. Laws and regulations

    B. Standards, guidelines, and practices

    C. Checklists developed by cybersecurity professionals

    D. All of the above

2. The NIST Cybersecurity Framework provides a common guidance for organizations to be able to achieve which of the following?

    A. Describe their current cybersecurity posture.

    B. Describe their target state for cybersecurity.

   C. Identify and prioritize opportunities for improvement within the context of a continuous and repeatable process.

   D. All of the above.

3. The NIST Cybersecurity Framework is divided into which of the following parts?

   A. Framework Profile, Implementation Tiers, Outcomes

   B. Framework Profile, Core, Outcomes

   C. Framework Core, Profile, Implementation Tiers

   D. Framework Core, Implementation Tiers, Outcomes

4. The Framework Core is divided into functions. Those functions include which of the following elements?

   A. Implementation Tiers, Categories, Informative References

   B. Implementation Tiers, Identification Elements, Informative References

   C. Categories, Subcategories, Informative References

   D. Standards, Categories, Informative References

5. Categories group the elements of a function into collections of cybersecurity _____.

   A. outcomes

   B. standards

   C. rules

   D. checklists

6. Which of the following is not true about informative references?

   A. Informative references point to industry standards, guidelines, and practices that are beneficial for an organization trying to achieve the outcomes associated with each subcategory.

   B. Informative references are rules that apply only to government institutions trying to achieve the outcomes associated with each subcategory.

   C. NIST mentions that informative references are "illustrative and not exhaustive."

   D. You can submit a reference to be considered to be part of the NIST Cybersecurity Framework informative references.

7. The Risk Assessment category addresses the identification and analysis of cybersecurity risk to the organization's operations, assets, and individuals. The Risk Assessment category is part of which function?

   A. Identify

   B. Detect

C. Protect

D. Respond

8. The Awareness and Training category addresses cybersecurity awareness education so that your employees are adequately trained to perform their information security–related duties and responsibilities consistent with related policies, procedures, and agreements. The Awareness and Training category is part of which function?

A. Identify

B. Detect

C. Protect

D. Respond

9. The Anomalies and Events, Security Continuous Monitoring, and Detection Processes categories are part of which function?

A. Identify

B. Detect

C. Protect

D. Respond

10. Which of the following is true about the NIST Cybersecurity Framework Implementation Tiers?

A. Provide guidance to allow organizations to maintain compliance with FISMA requirements.

B. Provide guidance to allow organizations to analyze cybersecurity risks and to enhance their processes to manage such risk.

C. Provide guidance to allow organizations to maintain compliance with FIPS requirements.

D. Provide guidance to allow organizations to maintain compliance with HIPAA requirements.

11. Who should communicate the mission priorities, available resources, and overall risk tolerance to the business/process level?

A. NIST

B. Executives

C. The United States President

D. The United States Department of Commerce

12. Which of the following is not one of the steps that the NIST's Cybersecurity Framework recommends to establish or improve a cybersecurity program?

   A. Identify your business objectives and high-level organizational priorities.

   B. Use the framework as a checklist for FISMA compliance.

   C. Create a current profile by defining which categories or subcategories are relevant to GDPR compliance.

   D. Create a target profile for your organization.

13. Which of the following is *not* true?

   A. An organization may utilize a Target Profile to express cybersecurity risk management requirements to an external service provider (for example, a cloud provider to which it is exporting data).

   B. An organization may express its cybersecurity state through a Current Profile to report results or to compare with acquisition requirements.

   C. A critical infrastructure owner/operator, having identified an external partner on whom that infrastructure depends, may use a Target Profile to convey required categories and subcategories.

   D. Only critical infrastructure agencies may establish a Target Profile that can be used among their constituents as an initial baseline Profile to build their tailored Target Profiles.

EXERCISES

EXERCISE 16-1: Understanding the NIST Cybersecurity Framework Core

1. Explain how the NIST Cybersecurity Framework Core is aimed to structure a list of activities to reach certain cybersecurity outcomes and include examples of guidance to achieve such outcomes.

2. Explain which parts can be used as guidance to create an incident response program and practice.

3. Explore the informative references in each category. Do you find any that overlap? Did you find any that contradict each other?

EXERCISE 16-2: **Understanding the Implementation Tiers**

1. Describe how an organization's risk management practices can align with the characteristics defined in the framework.

2. What areas of the Implementation Tiers can be used to enhance an organization's risk management process? Explain why.

EXERCISE 16-3: **Using the Framework as Guidance to Manage Cyber Supply Chain Risk Management**

1. Explain how the NIST Cybersecurity Framework can help your organization to establish a baseline requirement to suppliers and partners.

2. Create an example of such a baseline.

PROJECTS

PROJECT 16-1: **NIST's Cybersecurity Framework Spreadsheet**

1. Download NIST's Cybersecurity Framework spreadsheet from https://www.nist.gov/cyberframework.

2. Familiarize yourself with all the different components, categories, subcategories, and informative references of the NIST Cybersecurity Framework.

3. Download NIST's CSF tool from https://www.nist.gov/cyberframework/csf-reference-tool. Familiarize yourself with all the different capabilities of the tool and how it may allow you to start developing your own cybersecurity program.

4. Prepare a report that explains how an enterprise or private sector organization can leverage the framework to help with the following:

   - Identify assets and associated risks.

   - Protect against threat actors.

   - Detect and respond to any cybersecurity events and incidents.

   - Recover after a cybersecurity incident happened.

Case Study

Intel and McAfee Adoption of the NIST Cybersecurity Framework

Intel published and delivered a presentation titled "Cybersecurity Framework: Intel's Implementation Tools and Approach." This presentation can be found at https://www.nist.gov/sites/default/files/documents/cyberframework/cybersecurityframework_6thworkshop_intel_corp.pdf.

Intel's goals in using the NIST Cybersecurity Framework included alignment to their risk tolerance practices. In addition, they used the framework as guidance to communicate risk to their senior executives.

Similarly, McAfee published a blog post titled "We Tried the NIST Framework and It Works" that can be accessed at https://securingtomorrow.mcafee.com/executive-perspectives/tried-nist-framework-works-2.

In their blog post, McAfee explained how they "focused on developing a use case that would create a common language and encourage the use of the Framework as a process and risk management tool rather than a set of static requirements."

Research both implementations and answer the following questions:

1. Why did these companies try to align their cybersecurity programs with the NIST Cybersecurity Framework?

2. What are some of the major benefits?

3. Describe how the efforts at Intel and McAfee are similar and/or different.

4. Research other companies that have also aligned their cybersecurity efforts with the NIST Cybersecurity Framework, and compare the outcomes to those of Intel and McAfee.

References

Executive Order—"Improving Critical Infrastructure Cybersecurity," accessed 04/2018, https://obamawhitehouse.archives.gov/the-press-office/2013/02/12/executive-order-improving-critical-infrastructure-cybersecurity.

Cybersecurity Enhancement Act of 2014, accessed 04/2018, https://www.congress.gov/bill/113th-congress/senate-bill/1353/text.

NIST Cybersecurity Framework, accessed 04/2018, https://www.nist.gov/cyberframework.

NIST Cybersecurity Framework Interactive Framework Resources, accessed 04/2018, https://www.nist.gov/cyberframework/framework-resources-0.

NIST Cybersecurity Framework Roadmap, accessed 04/2018, https://www.nist.gov/cyberframework/related-efforts-roadmap.

"We Tried the NIST Framework and It Works," McAfee, accessed 04/2018, https://securingtomorrow.mcafee.com/executive-perspectives/tried-nist-framework-works-2.

"Cybersecurity Framework: Intel's Implementation Tools and Approach," Intel, accessed 04/2018, https://www.nist.gov/sites/default/files/documents/cyberframework/cybersecurityframework_6thworkshop_intel_corp.pdf.

Applying the NIST Cybersecurity Framework to Elections, accessed 04/2018, https://www.eac.gov/file.aspx?&A=Us%2BFqgpgVZw6CIHjBnD2tHKX0PKbwfShtOKsIx2kbEE%3D.

Appendix A

Cybersecurity Program Resources

National Institute of Standards and Technology (NIST) Cybersecurity Framework

NIST Cybersecurity Framework: https://www.nist.gov/cyberframework

NIST Special Publications

https://csrc.nist.gov/publications/sp

- SP 1800-4: "Mobile Device Security: Cloud and Hybrid Builds"

- SP 1800-2: "Identity and Access Management for Electric Utilities"

- SP 1800-1: "Securing Electronic Health Records on Mobile Devices"

- SP 800-192: "Verification and Test Methods for Access Control Policies/Models"

- SP 800-190: "Application Container Security Guide"

- SP 800-185: "SHA-3 Derived Functions: cSHAKE, KMAC, TupleHash, and ParallelHash"

- SP 800-184: "Guide for Cybersecurity Event Recovery"

- SP 800-183: "Networks of 'Things'"

- SP 800-181: "National Initiative for Cybersecurity Education (NICE) Cybersecurity Workforce Framework"

- SP 800-180: "NIST Definition of Microservices, Application Containers and System Virtual Machines"

- SP 800-175B: "Guideline for Using Cryptographic Standards in the Federal Government: Cryptographic Mechanisms"

- SP 800-167: "Guide to Application Whitelisting"

- SP 800-164: "Guidelines on Hardware-Rooted Security in Mobile Devices"

- SP 800-163: "Vetting the Security of Mobile Applications"

- SP 800-162: "Guide to Attribute Based Access Control (ABAC) Definition and Considerations"

- SP 800-161: "Supply Chain Risk Management Practices for Federal Information Systems and Organizations"

- SP 800-160 Vol. 2: "Systems Security Engineering: Cyber Resiliency Considerations for the Engineering of Trustworthy Secure Systems"

- SP 800-160 Vol. 1: "Systems Security Engineering: Considerations for a Multidisciplinary Approach in the Engineering of Trustworthy Secure Systems"

- SP 800-157: "Guidelines for Derived Personal Identity Verification (PIV) Credentials"

- SP 800-156: "Representation of PIV Chain-of-Trust for Import and Export"

- SP 800-155: "BIOS Integrity Measurement Guidelines"

- SP 800-154: "Guide to Data-Centric System Threat Modeling"

- SP 800-153: "Guidelines for Securing Wireless Local Area Networks (WLANs)"

- SP 800-152: "A Profile for U.S. Federal Cryptographic Key Management Systems (CKMS)"

- SP 800-150: "Guide to Cyber Threat Information Sharing"

- SP 800-147B: "BIOS Protection Guidelines for Servers"

- SP 800-147: "BIOS Protection Guidelines"

- SP 800-146: "Cloud Computing Synopsis and Recommendations"

- SP 800-145: "The NIST Definition of Cloud Computing"

- SP 800-144: "Guidelines on Security and Privacy in Public Cloud Computing"

- SP 800-142: "Practical Combinatorial Testing"

- SP 800-137: "Information Security Continuous Monitoring (ISCM) for Federal Information Systems and Organizations"

- SP 800-135 Rev. 1: "Recommendation for Existing Application-Specific Key Derivation Functions"

- SP 800-133: "Recommendation for Cryptographic Key Generation"
- SP 800-132: "Recommendation for Password-Based Key Derivation: Part 1: Storage Applications"
- SP 800-131A Rev. 1: "Transitions: Recommendation for Transitioning the Use of Cryptographic Algorithms and Key Lengths"
- SP 800-130: "A Framework for Designing Cryptographic Key Management Systems"
- SP 800-128: "Guide for Security-Focused Configuration Management of Information Systems"
- SP 800-127: "Guide to Securing WiMAX Wireless Communications"
- SP 800-126 Rev. 3: "The Technical Specification for the Security Content Automation Protocol (SCAP): SCAP Version 1.3"
- SP 800-125B: "Secure Virtual Network Configuration for Virtual Machine (VM) Protection"
- SP 800-125A: "Security Recommendations for Hypervisor Deployment on Servers"
- SP 800-125: "Guide to Security for Full Virtualization Technologies"
- SP 800-124 Rev. 1: "Guidelines for Managing the Security of Mobile Devices in the Enterprise"
- SP 800-123: "Guide to General Server Security"
- SP 800-122: "Guide to Protecting the Confidentiality of Personally Identifiable Information (PII)"
- SP 800-121 Rev. 2: "Guide to Bluetooth Security"
- SP 800-120: "Recommendation for EAP Methods Used in Wireless Network Access Authentication"
- SP 800-119: "Guidelines for the Secure Deployment of IPv6"
- SP 800-117 Rev. 1: "Guide to Adopting and Using the Security Content Automation Protocol (SCAP) Version 1.2"
- SP 800-117: "Guide to Adopting and Using the Security Content Automation Protocol (SCAP) Version 1.0"
- SP 800-116 Rev. 1: "A Recommendation for the Use of PIV Credentials in Physical Access Control Systems (PACS)"
- SP 800-116: "A Recommendation for the Use of PIV Credentials in Physical Access Control Systems (PACS)"
- SP 800-115: "Technical Guide to Information Security Testing and Assessment"

- SP 800-114 Rev. 1: "User's Guide to Telework and Bring Your Own Device (BYOD) Security"

- SP 800-113: "Guide to SSL VPNs"

- SP 800-111: "Guide to Storage Encryption Technologies for End User Devices"

- SP 800-108: "Recommendation for Key Derivation Using Pseudorandom Functions (Revised)"

- SP 800-107 Rev. 1: "Recommendation for Applications Using Approved Hash Algorithms"

- SP 800-102: "Recommendation for Digital Signature Timeliness"

- SP 800-101 Rev. 1: "Guidelines on Mobile Device Forensics"

- SP 800-100: "Information Security Handbook: A Guide for Managers"

- SP 800-98: "Guidelines for Securing Radio Frequency Identification (RFID) Systems"

- SP 800-97: "Establishing Wireless Robust Security Networks: A Guide to IEEE 802.11i"

- SP 800-96: "PIV Card to Reader Interoperability Guidelines"

- SP 800-95: "Guide to Secure Web Services"

- SP 800-94 Rev. 1: "Guide to Intrusion Detection and Prevention Systems (IDPS)"

- SP 800-92: "Guide to Computer Security Log Management"

- SP 800-88 Rev. 1: "Guidelines for Media Sanitization"

- SP 800-86: "Guide to Integrating Forensic Techniques into Incident Response"

- SP 800-85B-4: "PIV Data Model Test Guidelines"

- SP 800-85A-4: "PIV Card Application and Middleware Interface Test Guidelines (SP 800-73-4 Compliance)"

- SP 800-84: "Guide to Test, Training, and Exercise Programs for IT Plans and Capabilities"

- SP 800-83 Rev. 1: "Guide to Malware Incident Prevention and Handling for Desktops and Laptops"

- SP 800-82 Rev. 2: "Guide to Industrial Control Systems (ICS) Security"

- SP 800-81-2: "Secure Domain Name System (DNS) Deployment Guide"

- SP 800-79-2: "Guidelines for the Authorization of Personal Identity Verification Card Issuers (PCI) and Derived PIV Credential Issuers (DPCI)"

- SP 800-77: "Guide to IPsec VPNs"

- SP 800-76-2: "Biometric Specifications for Personal Identity Verification"

- SP 800-73-4: "Interfaces for Personal Identity Verification"

- SP 800-64 Rev. 2: "Security Considerations in the System Development Life Cycle"

- SP 800-63C: "Digital Identity Guidelines: Federation and Assertions"

- SP 800-63B: "Digital Identity Guidelines: Authentication and Life Cycle Management"

- SP 800-61 Rev. 2: "Computer Security Incident Handling Guide"

- SP 800-53 Rev. 5: "Security and Privacy Controls for Information Systems and Organizations"

- SP 800-53A Rev. 4: "Assessing Security and Privacy Controls in Federal Information Systems and Organizations: Building Effective Assessment Plans"

- SP 800-52: "Guidelines for the Selection, Configuration, and Use of Transport Layer Security (TLS) Implementations"

- SP 800-51 Rev. 1: "Guide to Using Vulnerability Naming Schemes"

- SP 800-50: "Building an Information Technology Security Awareness and Training Program"

- SP 800-48 Rev. 1: "Guide to Securing Legacy IEEE 802.11 Wireless Networks"

- SP 800-47: "Security Guide for Interconnecting Information Technology Systems"

- SP 800-46 Rev. 2: "Guide to Enterprise Telework, Remote Access, and Bring Your Own Device (BYOD) Security"

- SP 800-45 Version 2: "Guidelines on Electronic Mail Security"

- SP 800-44 Version 2: "Guidelines on Securing Public Web Servers"

- SP 800-41 Rev. 1: "Guidelines on Firewalls and Firewall Policy"

- SP 800-40 Rev. 3: "Guide to Enterprise Patch Management Technologies"

- SP 800-37 Rev. 2: "Guide for Applying the Risk Management Framework to Federal Information Systems: a Security Life Cycle Approach"

- SP 800-36: "Guide to Selecting Information Technology Security Products"

- SP 800-35: "Guide to Information Technology Security Services"

- SP 800-34 Rev. 1: "Contingency Planning Guide for Federal Information Systems"

- SP 800-33: "Underlying Technical Models for Information Technology Security"

- SP 800-32: "Introduction to Public Key Technology and the Federal PKI Infrastructure"

- SP 800-30 Rev. 1: "Guide for Conducting Risk Assessments"

- SP 800-25: "Federal Agency Use of Public Key Technology for Digital Signatures and Authentication"

- SP 800-23: "Guidelines to Federal Organizations on Security Assurance and Acquisition/Use of Tested/Evaluated Products"

- SP 800-19: "Mobile Agent Security"

- SP 800-18 Rev. 1: "Guide for Developing Security Plans for Federal Information Systems"

- SP 800-17: "Modes of Operation Validation System (MOVS): Requirements and Procedures"

- SP 800-16 Rev. 1: "A Role-Based Model for Federal Information Technology/Cybersecurity Training"

- SP 800-15: "MISPC Minimum Interoperability Specification for PKI Components, Version 1"

- SP 800-13: "Telecommunications Security Guidelines for Telecommunications Management Network"

- SP 800-12 Rev. 1: "An Introduction to Information Security"

- SP 500-320: "Report of the Workshop on Software Measures and Metrics to Reduce Security Vulnerabilities (SwMM-RSV)"

- SP 500-299: "NIST Cloud Computing Security Reference Architecture"

Federal Financial Institutions Examination Council (FFIEC) IT Handbooks

https://ithandbook.ffiec.gov/it-booklets.aspx

- Audit

- Business Continuity Planning

- Development and Acquisition

- E-Banking

- Information Security

- Management

- Operations

- Outsourcing Technology Services

- Retail Payment Systems

- Supervision of Technology Service Providers

- Wholesale Payment Systems

Department of Health and Human Services HIPAA Security Series

https://www.hhs.gov/hipaa/for-professionals/security/guidance/index.html

- Security 101 for Covered Entities
- Administrative Safeguards
- Physical Safeguards
- Technical Safeguards
- Organizational, Policies and Procedures and Documentation Requirements
- Basics of Risk Analysis and Risk Management
- Security Standards: Implementation for the Small Provider
- HIPAA Security Guidance
- Risk Analysis
- HHS Security Risk Assessment Tool
- NIST HIPAA Security Rule Toolkit Application
- Remote Use
- Mobile Device
- Ransomware
- Federal Information Processing Standards Publication 140-2: Security Requirements for Cryptographic Modules
- NIST HIPAA Security Rule Toolkit Application
- NIST Cybersecurity Framework to HIPAA Security Rule Crosswalk
- FTC HIPAA-related Guidance: "Security Risks to Electronic Health Information from Peer-to-Peer File Sharing Applications"
- FTC HIPAA-related Guidance: "Safeguarding Electronic Protected Health Information on Digital Copiers"
- FTC HIPAA-related Guidance: "Medical Identity Theft"
- OCR Cyber Awareness Newsletters

Payment Security Standards Council Documents Library

https://www.pcisecuritystandards.org/document_library

- PCI DSS v3.2

- Glossary of Terms, Abbreviations, and Acronyms v3.2

- PCI DSS Summary of Changes v3.1 to v3.2

- Prioritized Approach for PCI DSS v3.2

- Prioritized Approach Summary of Changes Version 3.1 to 3.2

- Prioritized Approach Tool

- PCI DSS Quick Reference Guide v3.2

- Small Merchant Reference Guide Order Form

- PCI Quick Reference Order Form

- ROC Reporting Template v3.2

- PCI DSS AOC - Merchants v3.2

- PCI DSS AOC - Service Providers v3.2

- AOC Extra Form for Service Providers

- Supplemental Report on Compliance—Designated Entities v3.2

- Supplemental AOC for Onsite Assessments—Designated Entities v3.2

- Frequently Asked Questions (FAQs) for use with PCI DSS ROC Reporting Template v3.x

- FAQs for Designated Entities Supplemental Validation

SANS Information Security Policy Templates

https://www.sans.org/security-resources/policies

- Acceptable Encryption Policy

- Acceptable Use Policy

- Clean Desk Policy

- Data Breach Response Policy
- Disaster Recovery Plan Policy
- Digital Signature Acceptance Policy
- Email Policy
- Ethics Policy
- Pandemic Response Planning Policy
- Password Construction Guidelines
- Password Protection Policy
- Security Response Plan Policy
- End User Encryption Key Protection Policy
- Acquisition Assessment Policy
- Bluetooth Baseline Requirements Policy
- Remote Access Policy
- Remote Access Tools Policy
- Router and Switch Security Policy
- Wireless Communication Policy
- Wireless Communication Standard
- Database Credentials Policy
- Technology Equipment Disposal Policy
- Information Logging Standard
- Lab Security Policy
- Server Security Policy
- Software Installation Policy
- Workstation Security (For HIPAA) Policy
- Web Application Security Policy

Information Security Professional Development and Certification Organizations

- International Information Systems Security Certification Consortium (ISC2): https://isc2.org

- Information Systems Audit and Control Association (ISACA): https://isaca.org

- Information Systems Security Association, Inc. (ISSA): https://issa.org

- SANS Institute: https://sans.org

- Disaster Recovery Institute (DRI): https://drii.org

- CompTIA: https://www.comptia.org

- The Forum of Incident Response and Security Teams (FIRST): https://first.org

- The Institute of Internal Auditors: https://theiia.org

- EC-Council: https://www.eccouncil.org/

Appendix B

Answers to the Multiple Choice Questions

Seek guidance from your course instructor to complete the chapter exercises and projects.

Chapter 1

1. D
2. A
3. B
4. A
5. A
6. D
7. C
8. D
9. B
10. D
11. C
12. A
13. C
14. A
15. C
16. D
17. C
18. A
19. D
20. D
21. C
22. B
23. D
24. D
25. C

Chapter 2

1. B
2. C
3. D
4. C
5. C
6. A
7. C
8. D
9. B
10. D
11. B
12. B
13. C
14. D
15. B
16. A
17. A
18. C
19. D
20. D

21. A
22. A
23. C
24. B
25. D
26. C
27. A
28. B
29. C
30. C

Chapter 3

1. C
2. C and D
3. A
4. A
5. A
6. B
7. A and C
8. C
9. C
10. D
11. B
12. C
13. B
14. D
15. C
16. D
17. C

18. D
19. C
20. B
21. B
22. D
23. A
24. B
25. C
26. C
27. C
28. A
29. B
30. D
31. A, C, and D

Chapter 4

1. D
2. C
3. A
4. D
5. D
6. A
7. B
8. B
9. C
10. A
11. D
12. A
13. B

14. C
15. D
16. B
17. B
18. C
19. B
20. D
21. B
22. A
23. D
24. A
25. C
26. B
27. C
28. D
29. C
30. E

Chapter 5

1. B
2. C
3. A
4. D
5. A
6. D
7. D
8. B
9. D
10. D

11. B

12. C

13. B

14. C

15. C

16. D

17. A

18. A

19. C

20. D

21. A

22. C

23. C

24. D

25. B

26. D

27. B

28. D

29. A

30. B

8. D

9. B

10. B

11. C

12. A

13. B

14. B

15. C

16. A

17. D

18. B

19. C

20. B

21. A

22. D

23. C

24. B

25. D

26. A

27. A

28. C

29. A

30. B

5. A

6. A

7. C

8. C

9. A

10. B

11. C

12. D

13. A

14. A

15. C

16. A

17. D

18. C

19. B

20. D

Chapter 6

1. D

2. C

3. C

4. A

5. B

6. D

7. A

Chapter 7

1. D

2. C

3. A

4. D

Chapter 8

1. C

2. B

3. A

4. B

5. A

6. A

7. D

8. A

9. A

10. B

11. D

12. B

13. C

14. B

15. D

16. A

17. A

18. A

19. B

20. A

21. B

22. D

23. B

24. A

25. B

26. D

27. A

28. B

29. D

30. A

Chapter 9

1. D

2. D

3. B

4. A

5. C

6. C

7. C

8. A

9. A

10. B

11. C

12. B

13. B

14. D

15. B

16. C

17. A

18. A

19. C

20. C

Chapter 10

1. B

2. D

3. A

4. B

5. B

6. D

7. A

8. C

9. B

10. A

11. C

12. D

13. B

14. A

15. B

16. C

17. B

18. C

19. D

20. C

21. A

22. B

23. B

24. A

25. D

26. C

27. D

28. A

29. D

30. A

Chapter 11

1. B

2. B

3. B

4. A

5. D

6. C

7. B

8. C, D, and E

9. D

10. B

11. C

12. B

13. D

14. D

15. C

16. B

17. D

18. C

19. A

20. C

21. A

22. C

23. A

Chapter 12

1. B

2. C

3. B

4. B

5. D

6. D

7. C

8. A

9. B

10. D

11. C

12. C

13. C

14. B

15. A

16. A

17. D

Chapter 13

1. C

2. C

3. C

4. B

5. B

6. D

7. D

8. C

9. B

10. B

11. B

12. A

13. B

14. C

15. D

16. C

17. C

18. A

19. B

20. B

21. C

22. C

23. A

24. C

25. B

26. B

27. D

28. D

29. B

30. B

Chapter 14

1. A

2. D

3. B

4. D

5. A

6. B

7. C

8. C

9. C

10. A and C

11. D

12. B

13. D

14. B

15. A

16. A

17. A

18. D

19. C

20. D

21. C

22. D

23. C

24. B

25. D

26. B

27. A

28. B

29. B

30. A

6. B

7. C

8. D

9. D

10. A

11. A

12. B

13. A

14. B

15. D

16. A

17. B

18. D

19. C

20. C

21. D

22. D

23. A

24. B

25. C

26. A

27. A

28. D

29. A

30. D

Chapter 16

1. B

2. D

3. C

4. C

5. A

6. B

7. A

8. C

9. B

10. B

11. B

12. B

13. D

Chapter 15

1. B

2. C

3. D

4. B

5. A

Index

classification. *See* information classification

clear desks and screens, 216

clearance, government, 186

client nodes, 353

Clinton, William, 9, 18, 46, 463

cloud computing, 165, 210, 259

CloudLock, 165

CMM (capability maturity model), 115

CNC (command and control) systems, 81–82

COBIT (Control Objectives for Information and Related Technologies), 118, 477

Code of Practice (ISO). *See* 27000 series standards (ISO/IEC)

cognitive passwords, 299–300

Cognitive Threat Analytics (CTA), 297

cold sites, 442

collaboration services, 266

Collector entity (syslog), 271

command and control (CnC) systems, 81–82, 251–252, 440–441

commercial off-the-shelf software. *See* COTS (commercial off-the-shelf software)

Commodity Futures Trading Commission (CFTC), 466

Common Vulnerability Scoring System (CVSS), 76–77, 387–390

Common Weakness Enumeration (CWE), 346

communications security. *See also* operations security

  change control, 243–247

  collaboration services, 266

  disaster response plans, 441

  email, 261–267

  NIST Cybersecurity Framework, 237

  overview, 24–25, 236–237

  recovery, 446

  SOPs (standard operating procedures), 238–243

  stakeholder communication, 595–596

  supply chain communication, 595–596

  threat intelligence and information sharing, 278–280

Communications Security domain (ISO 27002 standard), 90, 237

compliance management. *See* financial institutions, regulatory compliance for; health-care sector, regulatory compliance for

Compliance Management domain (ISO 27002 standard), 92, 504

Compliance Officers, 113

compliance risk, 472

components, policy

  administrative notations, 59

  definition section, 60–61

  enforcement clause, 58

  exceptions, 57–58

  exemption process, 57–58

  goals and objectives, 55–56

  introduction, 52–54

  policy heading, 54–55

  sample policy, 56–57

  table of, 51

  terms and definitions, 60–61

  version control, 51–52

CompTIA, 617

Computer Emergency Response Team. *See* CERT (Computer Emergency Response Team)

Confidential (C) information

  handling standards, 157

  national security information, 153

  private sector, 154

confidentiality

  confidentiality agreements, 191

  cryptography and, 350

  defined, 74–77

  FIPS-199 (Federal Information Processing Standard 199), 150

  legislation, 75

consolidated policies, 49–51

Constitution, as policy, 6

consumer information, 469

containment, eradication, and recovery phase (incident response), 382–383

containment, fire, 219

content filtering, 315

G

N